World Economic and Financial Surveys

WORLD ECONOMIC OUTLOOK
September 2005

Building Institutions

International Monetary Fund

©2005 International Monetary Fund

Production: IMF Graphics Section
Cover and Design: Luisa Menjivar-Macdonald
Figures: Theodore F. Peters, Jr.
Typesetting: Choon Lee

World economic outlook (International Monetary Fund)
World economic outlook: a survey by the staff of the International
Monetary Fund.—1980– —Washington, D.C.: The Fund, 1980–

    v.; 28 cm.—(1981–84: Occasional paper/International Monetary
Fund ISSN 0251-6365)
    Annual.
    Has occasional updates, 1984–
    ISSN 0258-7440 = World economic and financial surveys
    ISSN 0256-6877 = World economic outlook (Washington)
    1. Economic history—1971– —Periodicals.   I. International
Monetary Fund.   II. Series: Occasional paper (International
Monetary Fund)

HC10.W7979   84-640155

                          338.5'443'09048—dc19
                                    AACR 2 MARC-S

Library of Congress   8507

    Published biannually.
ISBN 1-58906-454-2

Price: US$49.00
(US$46.00 to full-time faculty members and
students at universities and colleges)

Please send orders to:
International Monetary Fund, Publication Services
700 19th Street, N.W., Washington, D.C. 20431, U.S.A.
Tel.: (202) 623-7430   Telefax: (202) 623-7201
E-mail: publications@imf.org
Internet: http://www.imf.org

recycled paper

CONTENTS

Tables

Figures

ASSUMPTIONS AND CONVENTIONS

A number of assumptions have been adopted for the projections presented in the *World Economic Outlook*. It has been assumed that real effective exchange rates will remain constant at their average levels during July 8–August 5, 2005, except for the currencies participating in the European exchange rate mechanism II (ERM II), which are assumed to remain constant in nominal terms relative to the euro; that established policies of national authorities will be maintained (for specific assumptions about fiscal and monetary policies in industrial countries, see Box A1); that the average price of oil will be $54.23 a barrel in 2005 and $61.75 a barrel in 2006, and remain unchanged in real terms over the medium term; that the six-month London interbank offered rate (LIBOR) on U.S. dollar deposits will average 3.6 percent in 2005 and 4.5 percent in 2006; that the three-month euro deposits rate will average 2.1 percent in 2005 and 2.4 percent in 2006; and that the six-month Japanese yen deposit rate will yield an average of 0.1 percent in 2005 and of 0.2 percent in 2006. These are, of course, working hypotheses rather than forecasts, and the uncertainties surrounding them add to the margin of error that would in any event be involved in the projections. The estimates and projections are based on statistical information available through early September 2005.

The following conventions have been used throughout the *World Economic Outlook:*

. . .   to indicate that data are not available or not applicable;

—   to indicate that the figure is zero or negligible;

–   between years or months (for example, 2003–04 or January–June) to indicate the years or months covered, including the beginning and ending years or months;

/   between years or months (for example, 2003/04) to indicate a fiscal or financial year.

"Billion" means a thousand million; "trillion" means a thousand billion.

"Basis points" refer to hundredths of 1 percentage point (for example, 25 basis points are equivalent to ¼ of 1 percent point).

In figures and tables, shaded areas indicate IMF staff projections.

Minor discrepancies between sums of constituent figures and totals shown are due to rounding.

As used in this report, the term "country" does not in all cases refer to a territorial entity that is a state as understood by international law and practice. As used here, the term also covers some territorial entities that are not states but for which statistical data are maintained on a separate and independent basis.

FURTHER INFORMATION AND DATA

This report on the *World Economic Outlook* is available in full on the IMF's Internet site, www.imf.org. Accompanying it on the website is a larger compilation of data from the WEO database than in the report itself, consisting of files containing the series most frequently requested by readers. These files may be downloaded for use in a variety of software packages.

Inquiries about the content of the *World Economic Outlook* and the WEO database should be sent by mail, electronic mail, or telefax (telephone inquiries cannot be accepted) to:

World Economic Studies Division
Research Department
International Monetary Fund
700 19th Street, N.W.
Washington, D.C. 20431, U.S.A.
E-mail: weo@imf.org   Telefax: (202) 623-6343

PREFACE

The analysis and projections contained in the *World Economic Outlook* are integral elements of the IMF's surveillance of economic developments and policies in its member countries, of developments in international financial markets, and of the global economic system. The survey of prospects and policies is the product of a comprehensive interdepartmental review of world economic developments, which draws primarily on information the IMF staff gathers through its consultations with member countries. These consultations are carried out in particular by the IMF's area departments together with the Policy Development and Review Department, the International Capital Markets Department, the Monetary and Financial Systems Department, and the Fiscal Affairs Department.

The analysis in this report has been coordinated in the Research Department under the general direction of Raghuram Rajan, Economic Counsellor and Director of Research. The project has been directed by David Robinson, Deputy Director of the Research Department, together with Tim Callen, Division Chief, Research Department.

Primary contributors to this report also include Nicoletta Batini, Roberto Cardarelli, Thomas Helbling, Kalpana Kochhar, Kenneth Kuttner, Subir Lall, Douglas Laxton, Gian Maria Milesi-Ferretti, Sam Ouliaris, S. Hossein Samiei, Martin Sommer, Nikola Spatafora, Marco Terrones, and Toh Kuan. Paul Atang, Nathalie Carcenac, Stephanie Denis, Angela Espiritu, Manuela Goretti, and Yutong Li provided research assistance. Laurent Meister, Mahnaz Hemmati, Casper Meyer, and Ercument Tulun managed the database and the computer systems. Sylvia Brescia, Celia Burns, and Seetha Milton were responsible for word processing. Other contributors include Tamim Bayoumi, Arvind Subramanian, Robin Brooks, Ralph Bryant, Marcos Chamon, To-Nhu Dao, Marc de Fleurieu, Maria González, Simon Johnson, Alejandro Justiniano, Kornélia Krajnyák, Chris Lane, Andrei Levchenko, Davide Lombardo, Akito Matsumoto, Enrique Mendoza, Paul Nicholson, Christopher Otrok, Alessandro Prati, Catriona Purfield, Francesca Recanatini, James Robinson, Kenichi Ueda, and Susanna Mursula. Marina Primorac of the External Relations Department edited the manuscript and coordinated the production of the publication.

The analysis has benefited from comments and suggestions by staff from other IMF departments, as well as by Executive Directors following their discussion of the report on August 31 and September 2, 2005. However, both projections and policy considerations are those of the IMF staff and should not be attributed to Executive Directors or to their national authorities.

FOREWORD

The *World Economic Outlook* is a cooperative effort. A few core staff members put it together, but in doing so they rely heavily on staff around the IMF. I thank David Robinson, Tim Callen, members of the World Economic Studies Division, and all the IMF staff from other divisions and departments who worked together to bring this *World Economic Outlook* to you.

The world economy has proved tremendously resilient over the last few years. Disease, natural disasters, and soaring oil prices have only caused minor blips in an overall picture of healthy growth. Despite the ravages wrought by Hurricane Katrina on the U.S. Gulf Coast, and the spillover effects on the rest of the world, global growth forecasts for 2005 are unchanged since the April *World Economic Outlook*, while the growth projections for 2006 have been revised downward only slightly. This robust overall outlook, however, hides a number of serious imbalances. Let me start with a framework, overly simplistic no doubt, which draws on the findings in Chapter II to think about how we got here.

The current situation, I believe, has its roots primarily in a series of past crises, in particular, the emerging market crises in Asia and Latin America, the Japanese banking crisis in the 1990s, and the information technology boom and bust in a number of industrial countries around the turn of the millennium. Excessive investment was at the heart of all these crises, and the natural reaction was a sharp falloff in investment and only very cautious recovery since then. The policy response to this muted investment, and the outcomes, have differed across countries. In some industrial countries, notably the United States, accommodative fiscal and monetary policies have spurred credit-fueled consumption growth. By contrast, in a number of emerging markets, historically lax policy has become far less accommodative. Primary surpluses have emerged for the first time in some countries. Monetary policy has been tight. Most countries have brought down inflation, in some cases aided by adopting inflation targets (see Chapter IV—as an aside, countries need not develop the entire apparatus for inflation targeting in advance; what is important is they have the commitment to drive change after the launch).

With corporations in emerging markets cautious about investing and governments prudent about expenditure, growth has primarily been export led. The positive gap between savings and investment has led a number of emerging market countries to run current account surpluses for the first time.

We should celebrate the implicit policy coordination that has enabled us to weather these crises, which might otherwise have been much more serious. Industrial country governments used their greater monetary and fiscal room for maneuver to adopt the expansionary policies that helped emerging markets—whose governments needed to display austerity—grow their way out of difficulty.

Some see this state of affairs, with rich countries consuming more and being supplied and financed by emerging markets, as a new world order. I see it as a temporary and effective response to crises, which now needs to be reversed. The world economy thus needs to make two kinds of transitions. First, consumption has to give way smoothly to more investment, as past excess capacity is worked off and as policy accommodation in industrial countries is withdrawn. Second, the locus of domestic demand has to shift from countries running deficits to countries running surpluses so as to reduce the current account imbalances that have built up.

There are reasons to worry whether these transitions will take place smoothly. First, with spiraling asset prices fueled by global liquidity, goods prices kept quiescent by excess capacity and global trade, and interest rates held down by muted investment, domestic and external imbalances have been easily financed. Traditional signals such as inflation, interest rates, and exchange rates have not started flashing. Instead, bottlenecks are developing elsewhere, as in oil supplies. It may well be that easy finance has given economies a longer leash, and traditional signals have become overly anchored. The concern then is that when they change, as change they must, they will do so abruptly, with attendant consequences to growth. Alternatively, other signals such as oil prices will step in to do the job.

Second, while domestic demand is picking up, far more is needed in emerging markets and oil producers. But a low-quality government-led, or finance-fueled, investment binge is not the answer—we have already experienced the consequences of those in the past. Instead, structural reforms to product, labor, and financial markets are needed, so that high-quality private sector investment can emerge. It is here that the good may have been the enemy of the perfect. Strong exports and decent government policies have led a number of countries to generate growth without the necessary deep-rooted reforms that would have created strong, sustainable domestic demand. These countries are overly dependent on demand elsewhere, which in turn is fueled by unsustainable processes. This worry about whether transitions will take place smoothly is what leads me to believe that, despite a central scenario of robust growth, the risks are weighted to the downside.

Clearly, for world growth to be sustained, domestic demand in countries running current account deficits (notably but not exclusively the United States), stimulated by policy accommodation and easy financing conditions, will have to be cooled at a measured pace. Domestic demand will have to be strengthened in surplus countries, not through unsustainable expansionary policies but through structural reforms. The precise actions vary from country to country (see Appendix 1.2) but, taken together, they can give financial markets the confidence that a resolution of the imbalances is in the cards, which will make markets willing to continue financing a smooth transition. A welcome by-product of shared responsibility is that it will help each country's policymakers guide the domestic debate away from the finger-pointing and the protectionist solutions that otherwise come naturally and which would be the surest way to precipitate the unhappy outcomes that we all seek to avoid.

Let me turn to the poorest countries. It is good that industrial countries are contemplating more, and better, financial assistance to poor countries. But it is important not to pin all our development hopes on one instrument: aid. If there is anything that more than 50 years of modern development economics has taught us, it is humility about how little we really know. In the 1960s, everyone would have picked India over South Korea as the likely growth star. In the period after the 1980s, few would have given Mauritius or Botswana a chance of attaining east Asian rates of growth.

Though no one has the "magic bullet" for growth, there are some things that do seem important. These include sensible macroeconomic management, with fiscal discipline, moderate inflation, and a reasonably competitive exchange rate; laws and structural policies that create an environment conducive to private sector activity with low transaction costs; and opening up the economy to international trade. In addition, an educated population that sees opportunities in growth and competition is undoubtedly an asset.

Chapter III offers additional reasons why some of these environmental factors may be important. While it has become commonplace to say that institutions are important for economic growth, the predominant view among economists has been that a country's institutions are largely predetermined by its historical past—for example, by the nature of its colonizers. Chapter III provides refreshing evidence that institutions do indeed change, sometimes quite rapidly. And these institutional transitions are associated with substantial increases in private sector investment and economic growth. For example, institutional transitions in Benin and Zambia were associated with an increase in growth rates of 4 percentage points or more. The chapter finds that institutional transitions are more likely to take place in countries that have high education, are located near other countries with good institutions, and are more open to trade. This means that, in addition to providing aid, the outside world should encourage policies that create these institution-friendly environments in poor countries. Rich countries can help, for example, by reducing the impediments they place in the way of poor country exports and coaxing these countries to lower their own trade barriers.

From the perspective of both reducing global imbalances and fostering development, one much-needed area of collective action is the Doha Round. World Trade Organization members have not yet reached even so-called first approximations of an agreement. As a result, the preparation of the Hong Kong SAR Ministerial meeting in December becomes more difficult. Countries need to pay more than just lip service to liberal trading arrangements. In particular, large nations must take the lead in fulfilling their responsibilities to the world community by reaching a bold agreement to which the rest of the world can subscribe.

Raghuram Rajan
Economic Counsellor and Director, Research Department

The expansion remains broadly on track, with global growth forecasts for 2005 and 2006 largely unchanged from the last *World Economic Outlook* (Table 1.1 and Figure 1.1), although risks are still slanted to the downside. Following a temporary slowdown in mid-2004, global GDP growth picked up through the first quarter of 2005, with robust services sector output more than offsetting slowing global growth in manufacturing and, latterly, trade. In the second quarter, however, in part reflecting the impact of higher oil prices, signs of a renewed "soft patch" emerged, with leading indicators turning downward and business confidence weakening in most major countries (Figure 1.2). While global manufacturing and trade are now strengthening, and leading indicators have picked up, the continuing rise in crude oil and refined product prices—latterly exacerbated by the catastrophic effects of Hurricane Katrina—is an increasingly important offset.

Within this broad picture, the regional differences highlighted in the April 2005 *World Economic Outlook* have become more marked:

- *Global current account imbalances—a key medium-term risk to the outlook—have increased yet again.* The U.S. current account deficit is now projected to rise to over 6 percent of GDP in 2005, 0.3 percent of GDP higher than projected in April, driven by higher oil prices and continued relatively strong domestic demand. On the surplus side, the key counterparts are Japan; China; the Middle East oil exporters, which as a result of soaring oil prices are now running a larger surplus in U.S. dollar terms than emerging Asia; the Commonwealth of Independent States; and some small industrial countries. Even so, capital inflows to the United States have remained strong, aided by robust private and official flows.

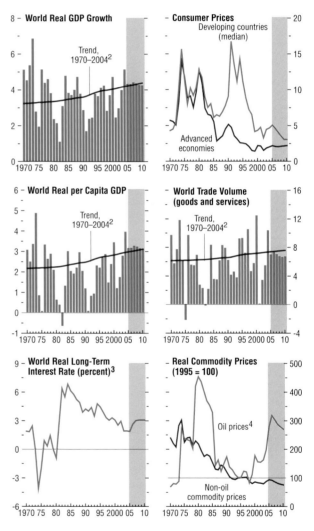

Figure 1.1. Global Indicators[1]
(Annual percent change unless otherwise noted)

Global growth is projected to be slightly above trend in 2005–06, while inflation remains moderate.

[1]Shaded areas indicate IMF staff projections. Aggregates are computed on the basis of purchasing-power-parity (PPP) weights unless otherwise noted.
[2]Average growth rates for individual countries, aggregated using PPP weights; the aggregates shift over time in favor of faster-growing countries, giving the line an upward trend.
[3]GDP-weighted average of the 10-year (or nearest maturity) government bond yields less inflation rates for the United States, Japan, Germany, France, Italy, the United Kingdom, and Canada. Excluding Italy prior to 1972.
[4]Simple average of spot prices of U.K. Brent, Dubai Fateh, and West Texas Intermediate crude oil.

Table 1.1. Overview of the *World Economic Outlook* Projections
(Annual percent change unless otherwise noted)

	2003	2004	Current Projections 2005	Current Projections 2006	Difference from April 2005 Projections 2005	Difference from April 2005 Projections 2006
World output	**4.0**	**5.1**	**4.3**	**4.3**	**—**	**−0.1**
Advanced economies	1.9	3.3	2.5	2.7	−0.1	−0.3
United States	2.7	4.2	3.5	3.3	−0.2	−0.3
Euro area	0.7	2.0	1.2	1.8	−0.4	−0.5
Germany	0.2	1.6	0.8	1.2	—	−0.7
France	0.9	2.0	1.5	1.8	−0.5	−0.4
Italy	0.3	1.2	—	1.4	−1.2	−0.6
Spain	2.9	3.1	3.2	3.0	0.5	0.1
Japan	1.4	2.7	2.0	2.0	1.2	—
United Kingdom	2.5	3.2	1.9	2.2	−0.7	−0.4
Canada	2.0	2.9	2.9	3.2	0.1	0.2
Other advanced economies	2.5	4.4	3.2	3.9	−0.2	—
Newly industrialized Asian economies	3.1	5.6	4.0	4.7	—	−0.1
Other emerging market and developing countries	6.5	7.3	6.4	6.1	0.1	0.1
Africa	4.6	5.3	4.5	5.9	−0.4	0.5
Sub-Sahara	4.1	5.4	4.8	5.9	−0.4	0.4
Central and eastern Europe	4.6	6.5	4.3	4.6	−0.2	0.1
Commonwealth of Independent States	7.9	8.4	6.0	5.7	−0.5	−0.2
Russia	7.3	7.2	5.5	5.3	−0.5	−0.3
Excluding Russia	9.2	11.0	7.1	6.8	−0.6	−0.2
Developing Asia	8.1	8.2	7.8	7.2	0.3	—
China	9.5	9.5	9.0	8.2	0.5	0.2
India	7.4	7.3	7.1	6.3	0.5	−0.1
ASEAN-4	5.4	5.8	4.9	5.4	−0.5	−0.4
Middle East	6.5	5.5	5.4	5.0	0.3	0.1
Western Hemisphere	2.2	5.6	4.1	3.8	—	0.1
Brazil	0.5	4.9	3.3	3.5	−0.4	—
Mexico	1.4	4.4	3.0	3.5	−0.8	0.3
Memorandum						
European Union	1.3	2.5	1.6	2.1	−0.4	−0.4
World growth based on market exchange rates	2.6	4.0	3.1	3.2	—	−0.2
World trade volume (goods and services)	**5.4**	**10.3**	**7.0**	**7.4**	**−0.5**	**−0.2**
Imports						
Advanced economies	4.1	8.8	5.4	5.8	−1.1	−0.5
Other emerging market and developing countries	11.1	16.4	13.5	11.9	1.5	0.9
Exports						
Advanced economies	3.1	8.3	5.0	6.3	−0.9	−0.5
Other emerging market and developing countries	10.8	14.5	10.4	10.3	0.4	0.6
Commodity prices (U.S. dollars)						
Oil[1]	15.8	30.7	43.6	13.9	20.5	19.8
Nonfuel (average based on world commodity export weights)	6.9	18.5	8.6	−2.1	4.7	3.0
Consumer prices						
Advanced economies	1.8	2.0	2.2	2.0	0.2	0.2
Other emerging market and developing countries	6.0	5.8	5.9	5.7	0.4	1.1
London interbank offered rate (percent)[2]						
On U.S. dollar deposits	1.2	1.8	3.6	4.5	0.3	0.4
On euro deposits	2.3	2.1	2.1	2.4	−0.2	−0.5
On Japanese yen deposits	0.1	0.1	0.1	0.2	−0.1	−0.2

Note: Real effective exchange rates are assumed to remain constant at the levels prevailing during July 8–August 5, 2005. See Statistical Appendix for details and groups and methodologies.

[1]Simple average of spot prices of U.K. Brent, Dubai, and West Texas Intermediate crude oil. The average price of oil in U.S. dollars a barrel was $37.76 in 2004; the assumed price is $54.23 in 2005, and $61.75 in 2006.

[2]Six-month rate for the United States and Japan. Three-month rate for the euro area.

- *Associated with this, growth divergences across regions remain wide.* The expansion has continued to be led by the United States and China, where the growth momentum has remained robust. Growth projections for 2005 in most other regions have been marked downward—with the important exceptions of Japan and India—with the renewed weakness in the euro area of particular concern. Monetary policy stances are becoming correspondingly more differentiated: the Federal Reserve and the Bank of Canada have raised policy rates, the European Central Bank and the Bank of Japan have remained on hold, and the Bank of England and the Swedish Riksbank have reduced interest rates in recent months.

- *Despite the further rise in the U.S. current account deficit, the U.S. dollar appreciated modestly in trade-weighted terms during the first eight months of 2005* (Figure 1.3). Movements in industrial country currencies varied widely, with the Canadian dollar appreciating further and the yen and euro depreciating, the latter seemingly reflecting increasingly unfavorable short-term interest rate differentials and growing political uncertainties in Europe following the rejection of the European Union's constitution in France and the Netherlands. In emerging markets, bilateral exchange rate movements against the U.S. dollar were diverse, but—except in the ASEAN-4—trade-weighted exchange rates have generally appreciated, particularly in Latin America. Following the Chinese exchange reform on July 21, 2005—including a 2.1 percent revaluation, the adoption of a reference basket of currencies, and a 0.3 percent daily fluctuation range against the U.S. dollar—the renminbi has remained broadly unchanged against the U.S. dollar; movements in other regional currencies—bar the Indonesian rupiah, which came under significant pressure in late August—have generally been modest.

Oil prices have continued their ascent, hitting a new nominal high of some $65 a barrel in late August, before falling back somewhat thereafter (Appendix 1.1, "Recent Developments in

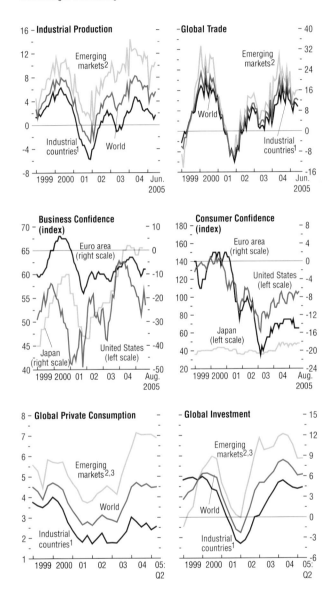

Figure 1.2. Current and Forward-Looking Indicators
(Percent change from a year ago unless otherwise noted)

Global industrial production and trade growth slowed during 2004, but show tentative signs of stabilizing.

Sources: Business confidence for the United States, the Institute for Supply Management; for the euro area, the European Commission; and for Japan, Bank of Japan. Consumer confidence for the United States, the Conference Board; for the euro area, the European Commission; and for Japan, Cabinet Office. All others, Haver Analytics.
[1] Australia, Canada, Denmark, euro area, Japan, New Zealand, Norway, Sweden, Switzerland, the United Kingdom, and the United States.
[2] Argentina, Brazil, Bulgaria, Chile, China, Colombia, Czech Republic, Estonia, Hong Kong SAR, Hungary, India, Indonesia, Israel, Korea, Latvia, Lithuania, Malaysia, Mexico, Pakistan, Peru, the Philippines, Poland, Romania, Russia, Singapore, Slovak Republic, Slovenia, South Africa, Taiwan Province of China, Thailand, Turkey, Ukraine, and Venezuela.
[3] Data for China, India, Pakistan, and Russia are interpolated.

Figure 1.3. Global Exchange Rate Developments

After depreciating steadily since early 2002, the U.S. dollar has appreciated so far in 2005, offset primarily by a depreciation of the euro, pound sterling, and yen.

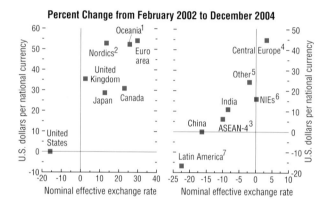

Percent Change from February 2002 to December 2004

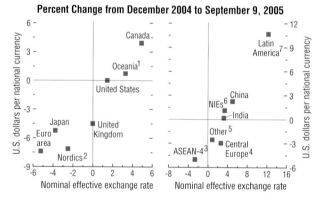

Percent Change from December 2004 to September 9, 2005

Sources: Bloomberg Financial Markets, LP; and IMF staff calculations.
[1] Australia and New Zealand.
[2] Denmark, Norway, and Sweden.
[3] Indonesia, Malaysia, the Philippines, and Thailand.
[4] Czech Republic, Hungary, and Poland.
[5] Russia, South Africa, and Turkey.
[6] Hong Kong SAR, Korea, Singapore, and Taiwan Province of China.
[7] Argentina, Brazil, Chile, Colombia, Mexico, Peru, and Venezuela.

Commodity Markets").[1] Despite the recent OPEC quota increase, markets remain concerned that the current very low spare production capacity will be insufficient to meet demand growth next winter, while short-term supply uncertainties have persisted, most recently as the result of the extensive damage to oil production and refining facilities in the Gulf Coast of the United States caused by Hurricane Katrina. While the impact of Hurricane Katrina on crude oil prices has been contained by releases from strategic reserves, as well as an offer by Saudi Arabia to boost crude production by 0.5 million barrels a day, shortages in refining capacity have added to pressures on refined product prices, particularly in the United States. More generally, while strong demand continues to play a key role in oil market developments, recent price pressures also appear to reflect growing concerns about future tightness in oil markets; consistent with this, long-run futures prices have moved increasingly closely with short-run spot prices, suggesting greater uncertainty about the stability of long-run market fundamentals.[2] Nonfuel commodity prices, which in aggregate remained stable during much of 2004, have since picked up in response to both strong demand—especially for metals—and supply disruptions, including bad weather. After weakening sharply in the second half of 2004, semiconductor revenues picked up in early 2005, particularly in the United States; correspondingly, industry analysts revised upwards their sales forecasts for 2005. However, the underlying strength of the upturn is still uncertain, and revenues have been declining recently.

Global headline inflation has picked up slightly in response to higher oil prices, but remains at moderate levels (Figure 1.4). Among the major industrial countries, core inflation

[1]The oil price used in the *World Economic Outlook* is the simple average of the spot prices of West Texas Intermediate, U.K. Brent, and Dubai crudes.
[2]See "Will the Oil Market Continue to Be Tight?" *World Economic Outlook*, April 2005, for a detailed discussion of factors affecting long-run oil demand and supply.

appears generally contained, inflationary expectations well-anchored, and wage increases moderate, although the impact of higher oil prices—and, in the United States, rising unit labor costs—will need to be carefully watched. Inflationary pressures have risen somewhat more in emerging markets, with forecasts for 2005 revised upward in most regions. With inflationary expectations in these countries generally less well anchored, the impact of oil price or other shocks is inevitably more pronounced; in addition, overheating pressures in some countries with large external surpluses are playing an increasing role.

Financial market conditions remain benign (Figure 1.5).[3] Long-run interest rates, while volatile, continue to be unusually low around the world; global equity markets have remained resilient, supported by strong corporate profits and increasingly solid balance sheets; and, apart from some rise in high yield spreads, credit spreads remain moderate. Emerging market financing conditions are very favorable (Figure 1.6), in part reflecting improved economic fundamentals and the increased presence of long-term investors, but also the continued search for yield; while net private capital inflows are projected to decline in 2005, this primarily reflects recycling of surpluses in oil producers (Table 1.2). Financial institutions' balance sheets appear relatively solid, although with long-run interest rates low and yield curves flattening, market participants have sought to boost returns through increasingly complex and leveraged strategies. Some of those trades resulted in material losses by a number of hedge funds when General Motors and Ford were downgraded, although the impact was relatively contained and the ensuing turbulence did not spill over into other markets.

The low level of long-run interest rates across the globe remains, in the words of Federal Reserve Chairman Greenspan, a conundrum.

[3]See the September 2005 *Global Financial Stability Report* for a detailed discussion.

Figure 1.4. Global Inflation
(Annualized percent change of three-month moving average over previous three-month average)

Headline inflation has risen with higher oil prices, along with some increase in core inflation in emerging markets.

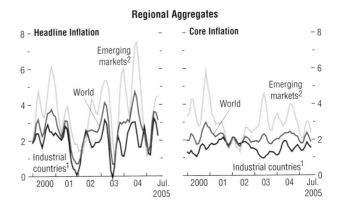

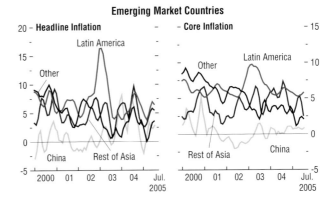

Sources: Haver Analytics; and IMF staff calculations.
[1]Canada, Denmark, euro area, Japan, Norway, Sweden, the United Kingdom, and the United States.
[2]Brazil, Chile, China, India, Indonesia, Hungary, Korea, Mexico, Poland, South Africa, and Taiwan Province of China.

Figure 1.5. Developments in Mature Financial Markets

Long-term interest rates have fallen back across the globe, accompanied by flattening yield curves.

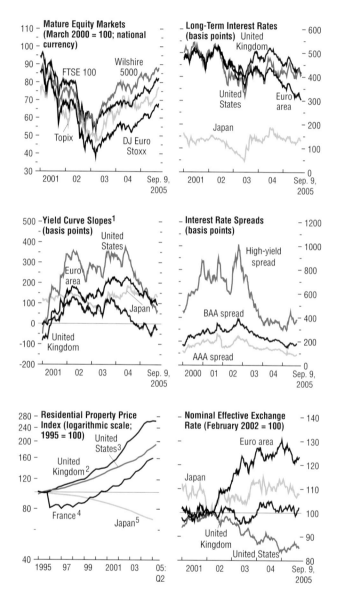

Sources: Bloomberg Financial Markets, LP; Office of Federal Housing Enterprise Oversight; Japan Real Estate Institute; Halifax; National Institute for Statistics and Economic Studies; and IMF staff calculations.

[1] Ten-year government bond minus three-month treasury bill rate.
[2] Halifax housing index as measured by the value of all houses.
[3] House price index as measured by the value of single-family homes in the United States as a whole, in various regions of the country, and in the individual states and the District of Columbia.
[4] Housing price index: all homes.
[5] Urban land price index: average of nationwide residential areas.

While this partly reflects low and well-anchored inflationary expectations, real interest rates remain well below historical averages, a situation difficult to reconcile with economic fundamentals, including rising public debt. Given that low interest rates are a global phenomenon, the causes seem likely to be global in nature. While financial market factors are clearly contributing,[4] trends in actual and desired global saving and investment likely also play an important role (Chapter II, "Global Imbalances: A Saving and Investment Perspective"). One widely cited view (see Bernanke, 2005) is that the rise in saving in emerging markets has led to a global "savings glut," driving down global interest rates and—through its effects on asset prices—contributing to the steady fall in household saving in industrial countries. However, as can be seen from Figure 1.7, other factors have also been important. Beyond the deterioration in the fiscal positions in industrial countries, which has substantially reduced global savings since 2000, the rising surplus in the corporate sector in industrial countries is particularly striking. As a share of GDP, corporate profits in industrial countries are historically high, while private nonresidential investment is unusually low, suggesting that post-bubble corporate caution, excess capacity, or other structural and balance sheet constraints are—to varying extents—still at play. Similar trends can also be observed in many emerging markets, particularly in emerging Asia (except China, where corporate saving and investment have both risen sharply).

Correspondingly, corporate sector behavior—and in particular the disposition of record net surpluses—will be key for the global outlook in coming years. One scenario—broadly consistent with the World Economic Outlook baseline forecast—is that as balance sheet restructuring nears completion, and with corporate liquidity at unprecedented levels, both corporate invest-

---

[4] See the September 2005 *Global Financial Stability Report* for a discussion, including the increasing demand for duration by pension funds.

ment and wages will rise, accompanied by a corresponding increase in short- and long-term interest rates. While higher interest rates would adversely affect demand—particularly in countries where strong asset prices have been supporting consumption—this should be consistent with continued solid global growth. However, less benign scenarios are also possible. For example, with investment in some countries still constrained by structural and other impediments, the adjustment process may be asymmetric, possibly adding to global imbalances. Equally, strong corporate cash flow may be obscuring the inflationary and supply-side impact of recent shocks, notably higher oil prices and, in some countries, the adverse effect of exchange rate appreciation on margins. If that is the case, further adjustment may be needed as corporate profitability returns to more normal levels.

Against this background, global GDP growth is projected to average 4.3 percent in 2005 and 2006. Within this, global growth is expected to slow slightly through early 2006, picking up modestly thereafter (Figure 1.8) with the adverse impact of higher oil prices offset by still-accommodative macroeconomic policies (with only moderate tightening expected in major countries in 2006—Figure 1.9); benign financial market conditions, especially low long-run interest rates; and—as discussed above—increasingly solid corporate balance sheets. Looking across the key countries and regions:

- In *industrial countries*, GDP growth in the United States has eased moderately, but is projected to remain the highest in the G-7, underpinned by solid productivity growth; despite the appalling cost in life and property from Hurricane Katrina, the direct impact on GDP growth—as is generally the case for natural disasters—appears likely to be moderate (see below). The indirect effects—particularly as a result of higher gasoline prices—may be more of a concern; with household savings at record lows, this increases the risk of a sharp slowing in private consumption growth especially if the housing market, which is becoming increasingly richly valued, were to weaken. In

Figure 1.6. Emerging Market Financial Conditions

Emerging market financing conditions remain benign, with spreads at very low levels.

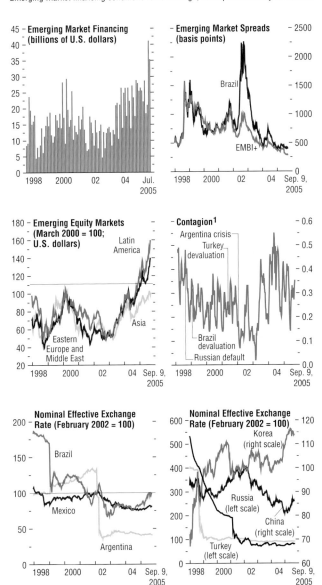

Sources: Bloomberg Financial Markets, LP; Capital Data; and IMF staff calculations.
[1]Average of 30-day rolling cross-correlation of emerging debt market spreads.

Table 1.2. Emerging Market and Developing Countries: Net Capital Flows[1]
(Billions of U.S. dollars)

	1994–96	1997	1998	1999	2000	2001	2002	2003	2004	2005	2006
Total											
Private capital flows, net[2]	156.4	191.7	76.2	86.0	74.3	66.2	68.2	158.2	232.0	132.9	53.8
Private direct investment, net	98.5	146.2	158.6	173.2	167.0	178.6	142.7	153.4	189.1	209.2	206.1
Private portfolio flows, net	65.0	60.8	42.6	69.5	21.0	−83.6	−87.6	−7.3	64.0	−28.6	−19.0
Other private capital flows, net	−7.0	−15.3	−125.0	−156.7	−113.7	−28.8	13.0	12.1	−21.1	−47.7	−133.3
Official flows, net	15.2	28.4	56.0	18.3	−52.1	−0.6	10.6	−61.7	−81.0	−137.1	−139.3
Change in reserves[3]	−97.3	−105.2	−34.8	−93.4	−113.2	−115.9	−185.7	−364.6	−517.4	−510.5	−506.8
Memorandum											
Current account[4]	−88.7	−82.6	−51.6	38.9	127.2	91.5	143.8	229.1	319.4	490.2	570.9
Africa											
Private capital flows, net[2]	2.0	7.9	7.9	10.1	−1.0	7.4	3.4	10.7	14.2	22.7	18.3
Private direct investment, net	2.3	7.7	6.6	9.4	8.0	22.3	14.7	14.6	13.9	19.5	17.8
Private portfolio flows, net	3.6	7.4	4.3	9.1	−1.8	−7.6	−0.9	0.1	6.3	5.5	6.3
Other private capital flows, net	−3.8	−7.3	−3.0	−8.4	−7.3	−7.2	−10.4	−4.1	−6.0	−2.2	−5.8
Official flows, net	2.8	−4.4	2.6	1.8	0.2	−1.9	1.8	2.8	—	−8.7	1.7
Change in reserves[3]	−4.7	−11.3	1.7	−2.8	−12.7	−12.4	−8.1	−19.4	−35.5	−38.6	−61.0
Central and eastern Europe											
Private capital flows, net[2]	12.3	20.2	27.3	36.7	39.0	11.8	55.8	48.1	58.0	72.3	58.6
Private direct investment, net	9.3	11.6	19.2	22.6	23.9	23.9	25.2	14.9	23.8	32.5	30.3
Private portfolio flows, net	4.0	5.4	−1.3	5.7	3.1	0.5	1.7	7.5	28.3	24.1	22.0
Other private capital flows, net	−1.0	3.2	9.4	8.4	12.0	−12.7	28.8	25.8	5.9	15.7	6.3
Official flows, net	0.4	−3.3	0.3	−2.6	1.6	5.6	−7.6	−5.4	−5.7	−5.7	−2.8
Change in reserves[3]	−14.2	−10.7	−9.5	−11.3	−2.8	7.4	−11.6	−11.7	−14.8	−17.0	−2.3
Commonwealth of Independent States[5]											
Private capital flows, net[2]	−0.8	19.9	6.4	−6.4	−12.9	−1.9	−9.5	16.5	9.4	−10.3	0.4
Private direct investment, net	3.2	5.9	5.3	4.2	2.4	4.6	4.0	5.3	13.4	8.6	8.5
Private portfolio flows, net	−7.7	17.6	7.7	−3.1	−6.1	−9.2	−8.2	−4.8	4.1	−16.2	−1.1
Other private capital flows, net	3.7	−3.6	−6.7	−7.5	−9.2	2.7	−5.3	16.0	−8.1	−2.6	−7.0
Official flows, net	9.2	8.7	10.0	0.1	−4.3	−4.5	−1.7	−5.1	−4.6	−5.2	−2.9
Change in reserves[3]	−3.2	−4.3	7.5	−2.7	−17.2	−11.3	−11.7	−33.8	−54.8	−80.7	−112.2
Emerging Asia[6]											
Private capital flows, net[2,7]	92.7	36.6	−49.9	11.8	7.5	14.7	21.0	62.0	132.9	84.6	34.1
Private direct investment, net	50.6	55.7	56.6	67.1	59.8	48.6	47.5	67.1	81.6	84.2	83.8
Private portfolio flows, net	25.3	6.8	8.7	55.8	20.1	−54.7	−60.2	4.9	25.8	−3.3	−1.4
Other private capital flows, net[7]	16.8	−26.0	−115.2	−111.1	−72.4	20.7	33.7	−10.0	25.4	3.8	−48.2
Official flows, net	−3.3	22.7	15.4	−0.3	−11.7	−11.3	5.2	−16.6	5.8	13.1	16.2
Change in reserves[3]	−48.7	−36.0	−52.9	−87.5	−52.5	−90.9	−149.9	−227.8	−342.7	−291.6	−234.9

the euro area, the tentative recovery in domestic demand in the second half of 2004 has slowed considerably. While incoming data are broadly consistent with a strengthening of activity in the second half of 2005, GDP growth forecasts for 2005 have been marked down, particularly for Italy; risks remain to the downside, given continued weak final domestic demand and the euro area's lack of domestic resilience to external shocks. In contrast, Japan's economy is regaining momentum, with GDP growth rising sharply in the first quarter of 2005 and recent data pointing to continued, if more sedate, expansion there-

after. GDP growth is now expected to average about 2 percent in both 2005 and 2006, with downside risks coming primarily from external factors.

- While growth prospects for *emerging market and developing countries* in aggregate have remained broadly unchanged, this disguises substantial changes in regional and individual forecasts, reflecting the impact of oil and other commodity price changes, exposure to global manufacturing and trade, as well as country-specific factors. In *emerging Asia*, GDP growth in China has continued to exceed expectations; with substantial liquidity remaining in

Table 1.2 *(concluded)*

	1994–96	1997	1998	1999	2000	2001	2002	2003	2004	2005	2006
Middle East[8]											
Private capital flows, net[2]	4.2	7.4	13.7	−4.7	1.2	7.2	−2.8	2.4	7.5	−51.7	−66.2
Private direct investment, net	4.0	7.6	9.6	4.1	3.4	7.7	7.4	15.3	9.7	18.4	18.9
Private portfolio flows, net	−1.3	−6.8	−2.3	0.7	3.3	−3.5	−5.1	−5.9	9.7	−40.3	−48.7
Other private capital flows, net	1.5	6.6	6.5	−9.4	−5.4	2.9	−5.2	−7.0	−11.9	−29.8	−36.4
Official flows, net	4.7	−0.8	10.4	13.7	−30.7	−15.5	−7.6	−44.7	−71.1	−121.5	−141.8
Change in reserves[3]	−9.6	−16.5	8.8	−1.0	−29.5	−11.6	−3.3	−34.4	−45.9	−54.5	−76.5
Western Hemisphere											
Private capital flows, net[2]	46.1	99.7	70.8	38.5	40.5	27.0	0.4	18.5	9.9	15.2	8.5
Private direct investment, net	29.2	57.6	61.3	65.8	69.4	71.3	43.9	36.1	46.6	46.1	46.7
Private portfolio flows, net	41.1	30.3	25.6	1.3	2.4	−9.1	−14.9	−9.0	−10.3	1.7	4.0
Other private capital flows, net	−24.2	11.7	−16.1	−28.6	−31.3	−35.3	−28.7	−8.5	−26.4	−32.5	−42.2
Official flows, net	1.4	5.5	17.2	5.6	−7.2	27.0	20.6	7.3	−5.4	−9.1	−9.7
Change in reserves[3]	−16.9	−26.5	9.6	11.9	1.5	2.9	−1.0	−37.5	−23.7	−28.1	−19.8
Memorandum											
Fuel exporters											
Private capital flows, net[2]	−13.6	27.4	17.2	−22.3	−36.6	−9.7	−20.1	11.9	3.9	−76.6	−91.5
Nonfuel exporters											
Private capital flows, net[2]	170.0	164.3	59.1	108.3	110.9	75.8	88.3	146.4	228.1	209.5	145.3

[1]Net capital flows comprise net direct investment, net portfolio investment, and other long- and short-term net investment flows, including official and private borrowing. In this table, Hong Kong SAR, Israel, Korea, Singapore, and Taiwan Province of China are included.
[2]Because of data limitations, "other private capital flows, net" may include some official flows.
[3]A minus sign indicates an increase.
[4]The sum of the current account balance, net private capital flows, net official flows, and the change in reserves equals, with the opposite sign, the sum of the capital account and errors and omissions. For regional current account balances, see Table 25 of the Statistical Appendix.
[5]Historical data have been revised, reflecting cumulative data revisions for Russia and the resolution of a number of data interpretation issues.
[6]Consists of developing Asia and the newly industrialized Asian economies.
[7]Excluding the effects of the recapitalization of two large commercial banks in China with foreign reserves of the Bank of China (US$45 billion), net private capital flows to emerging Asia in 2003 were US$107 billion while other private capital flows net to the region amounted to US$35 billion.
[8]Includes Israel.

the banking system, risks of a rebound in credit and investment growth remain a concern. Growth in India has also remained robust with the continued expansion in services, including information technology, and accelerating industrial production. Elsewhere in the region, after a slow first quarter, GDP growth is projected to pick up in line with global manufacturing, although much will depend on the expected rebound in the information technology (IT) sector, as well as oil prices. After a strong rebound in 2004, GDP growth in *Latin America* has slowed, particularly in Brazil, where domestic demand fell back in early 2005 in response to monetary tightening to contain inflation, and political uncertainties in some countries are an increasing risk. Strong export growth and improved macroeconomic policy performance should help sustain the regional expansion going for-

ward, while the widespread prefinancing of forthcoming debt repayments will help reduce the risk of financial market volatility in response to current political uncertainties and forthcoming elections. Rising oil production and prices have continued to support GDP growth in the *Middle East*, accompanied by dramatic improvements in external current account and fiscal positions. Despite strong domestic demand, inflation—outside Iran—has so far remained contained, but fiscal and structural policies will need to be carefully managed to ensure that higher oil revenues can be effectively absorbed. In Turkey, while GDP growth has slowed to a more sustainable pace, the current account deficit has widened further, underscoring the need for firm implementation of the authorities' economic program. Elsewhere, GDP growth in Russia has slowed since mid-2004, reflecting rising

Figure 1.7. Savings Glut or Investment Drought?[1]
(Percent of world GDP)

The rise in emerging market savings in recent years has been offset by falling industrial country savings, particularly by governments. Net corporate savings in industrial countries are unusually strong, owing to both buoyant profits and low investment.

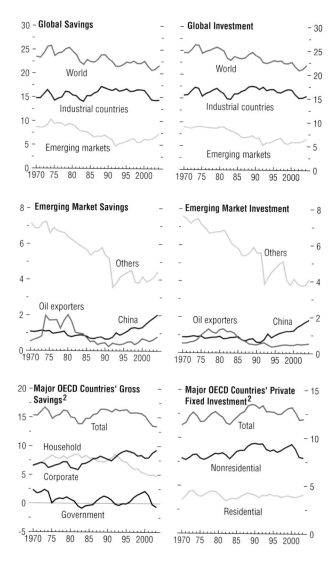

Sources: OECD Analytical Database; OECD, *Economic Outlook;* and IMF staff calculations.
[1]Group composite ratios are sums of individual country data after conversion to U.S. dollars at the average market exchange rates over the sum of total GDP in U.S. dollars for the group.
[2]Excludes Denmark, Greece, Iceland, Ireland, Luxembourg, New Zealand, Norway, Portugal, and Switzerland from the WEO industrial country group because their data are not available.

capacity constraints and the adverse effect of the Yukos affair; growth in emerging Europe has also eased, with the key risks including high current account deficits—notably in Hungary—and strong credit growth.

- In the *poorest countries,* GDP growth in sub-Saharan Africa is forecast to moderate to 4.8 percent in 2005—0.4 percentage point lower than expected last April—partly reflecting a sharp slowdown in Nigeria as oil production nears capacity. Growth in oil-importing countries, while slowing, has so far held up surprisingly well, with the adverse impact of higher oil prices so far offset by stronger non-oil commodity prices, as well as the benefits of improved macroeconomic stability and ongoing structural reforms. Looking forward, the IMF staff projects GDP growth to rebound to 5.9 percent in 2006, led by surging growth in oil producers as new capacity comes on stream. However, with oil prices now increasing more rapidly than nonfuel commodities, downside risks for net oil importers have increased (Figure 1.10), and, as always, much will depend on the strength of policies, improved political stability, and favorable weather conditions.[5]

Looking forward, short-term risks remain slanted to the downside. Beyond geopolitical risks—underscored once again by the tragic events in London in July—there are three broad concerns:

- *High and volatile oil prices remain a significant global risk.* Since end-2004, spot oil prices have risen by over $20 a barrel; with the market very tight and long-run futures prices increasingly poorly grounded, a substantial further jump in oil prices cannot be ruled out (indeed, options markets suggest a 15 percent chance that West Texas crude could rise above $80 a barrel—see Appendix 1.1). To date, the impact of higher oil prices on global growth has been surprisingly moderate, in part reflecting the fact that

---

[5]In part reflecting these factors, fall *World Economic Outlooks* between 1990 and 2003 overestimated GDP growth in sub-Saharan Africa in the coming year by an average of 1.5 percentage points.

higher oil prices have owed much to strong global demand as well as relatively well-anchored inflationary expectations; however, it may also have reflected less benign factors, including the possibility that consumers have treated a significant portion of the oil shock as temporary, and—in some cases—a lack of pass-through to domestic prices.[6] With recent oil price increases owing less to demand pressures, further price increases could have a less benign impact, especially if they had a signifi-cant effect on consumer confidence and there-fore spending. In addition, the impact on inflationary expectations could become much more marked, raising the risk of a sharp rise in interest rates, and adverse supply-side effects would be a much greater concern. The effect on countries and regions where domestic demand is already weak—notably the euro area—as well as on many oil-importing emerg-ing market and developing countries could also be serious.[7]

- *Protectionist sentiment is rising, driven by global imbalances and growing fears of emerging market competition.* In the United States, a bill to impose across-the-board tariffs on China in the absence of an early revaluation in the ren-minbi gathered widespread Congressional sup-port earlier this year; in the euro area, the recent withdrawal of the Services Directive was due in part to fears of "social dumping" from eastern Europe. The removal of quotas on tex-tiles and clothing—despite being perhaps the most advertised move in trade history—has also triggered protectionist sentiments, includ-ing renewed restraints on exports from China, in many countries.

- *Financial market conditions could tighten signifi-cantly,* which is of particular concern if—as described above—the result of a jump in

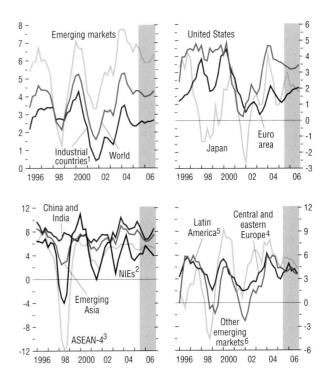

Figure 1.8. Global Outlook
(Real GDP; percent change from four quarters earlier)

Global growth is expected to slow moderately through early 2006, picking up somewhat thereafter.

Sources: Haver Analytics; and IMF staff estimates.
[1]Australia, Canada, Denmark, euro area, Japan, New Zealand, Norway, Sweden, Switzerland, the United Kingdom, and the United States.
[2]Hong Kong SAR, Korea, Singapore, and Taiwan Province of China.
[3]Indonesia, Malaysia, the Philippines, and Thailand.
[4]Czech Republic, Estonia, Hungary, Latvia, and Poland.
[5]Argentina, Brazil, Chile, Colombia, Mexico, Peru, and Venezuela.
[6]Israel, Russia, South Africa, and Turkey.

---

[6]A permanent 10 percent increase in crude oil prices is estimated to reduce global GDP by 0.1–0.15 percentage point over a year, assuming it is demand driven and there is only a limited impact on inflationary expectations (see Appendix 1.1, pp. 64–65, for a more detailed discussion).
[7]See IMF (2005b).

Figure 1.9. Fiscal and Monetary Policies in the Major Advanced Countries

Fiscal and monetary policies are expected to tighten modestly in 2006 in most G-7 countries.

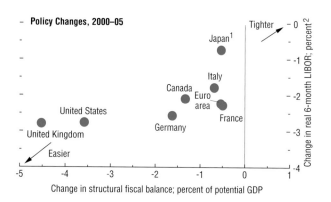

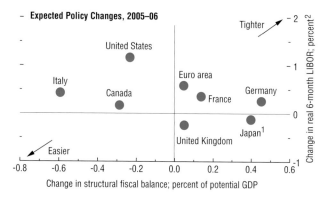

Source: IMF staff estimates.
[1]For Japan, excludes bank support.
[2]Three-month rate for euro area, France, and Germany.

inflationary expectations, rather than a more gradual adjustment in savings and investment behavior. In such circumstances, the possibility of a simultaneous weakening of housing markets would be a particular concern; there could also be a significant impact on some emerging markets. As discussed in the IMF's September 2005 *Global Financial Stability Report*, risks related to increasingly complex arbitrage and leveraged investment strategies underscore the need for vigilance by supervisors and regulators.

Notwithstanding these risks, the short-term outlook remains generally solid, with the global economy having proved remarkably resilient to the shocks of the last several years. While this in part reflects fundamentals—including considerably improved monetary frameworks (Chapter IV, "Does Inflation Targeting Work in Emerging Markets?"), greater economic flexibility, improved financial system resilience, and reduced vulnerabilities in emerging markets—it also owes much to more transitory factors, not least the unusually low interest rates and the continued willingness of investors to finance large global imbalances. But looking forward, while there are clear positive factors—including the ongoing effects of the IT revolution—the longer-run foundations of the expansion seem considerably shakier. In particular, the recovery continues to depend unduly on developments in the United States and China—both of which face major adjustment challenges—and, as discussed below, limited progress has been made in addressing the major medium-term risks to the expansion.

Indeed, in some ways, recent developments have exacerbated the adjustment challenges ahead. While benign financial conditions have in many cases been used well—especially by emerging markets to restructure and prefinance debt—richly valued housing markets around the world could prove an uncomfortable legacy, especially since it takes longer for households to restore their balance sheets in a low-inflation environment. In addition, the rise in oil prices—with oil-producing countries becoming an increasingly large counterpart to the U.S. current account deficit—will further complicate the resolution of global imbalances. Given the size of the increase in oil revenues relative to their economies, and the uncertainties as to how permanent they will prove, it will inevitably take a considerable time for them to adjust. In the short run, this may prove to be a factor sustaining current imbalances—especially if oil producers invest their surpluses in U.S. dollar–denominated assets—but with U.S. external liabilities rising further, this could come at the cost of a more serious problem in the longer term.

Turning to policies, short-run monetary requirements have become increasingly divergent, reflecting differing cyclical situations. In the United States, the present measured pace of tightening appears appropriate, although signs of rising labor market pressures will need to be carefully monitored; further tightening will also likely be needed in China, especially if signs of a rebound in investment growth strengthen, and will be aided by the greater scope for exchange rate flexibility as a result of recent reforms. In contrast, monetary policy has remained on hold in the euro area, and if incoming data confirm that inflationary pressures remain contained and the expected recovery fails to materialize, an interest rate cut should be considered; in Japan, the current accommodative stance remains appropriate and the quantitative easing policy should remain in place until deflation is unambiguously defeated. In cases where house price inflation remains robust, a combination of moral suasion and, if necessary, prudential measures could help limit potential risks; over the longer term, regulatory features—including those that potentially constrain supply—that may exacerbate price pressures also need to be addressed.

As indicated above, the key challenge remains to use the expansion to address underlying economic vulnerabilities and boost long-run growth:

- *The rising level of global imbalances, and their changing distribution, remains a central medium-term risk.* To date the adverse effects have been relatively limited, in part because—despite very large capital losses on U.S. dollar–denominated assets since the U.S. dollar

Figure 1.10. Trade Gains and Losses from Commodity Price Movements Relative to 2002[1]
(Percent of 2002 GDP)

Rising nonfuel commodity prices have only partly offset the losses from higher oil prices for many of the poorest countries.

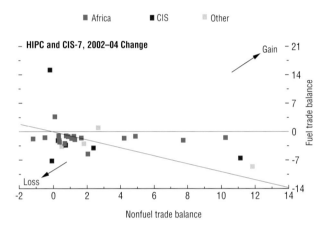

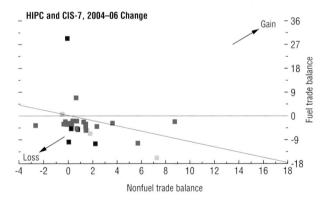

Source: IMF staff estimates.
[1]The figure shows the impact of the projected rise in commodity prices between 2002–04 and 2004–06 relative to 2002 prices on nonfuel trade balance (horizontal axis) and fuel trade balance (vertical axis).

began to depreciate in early 2002—foreigners have continued to increase their holdings without demanding any interest rate premium.[8] While this benign situation could persist for some time, it will not continue forever; and finding out just when it might end is an experiment best not undertaken. As discussed in detail in Appendix 1.2, "How Will Global Imbalances Adjust?" a sharp decline in the demand for U.S. assets, combined with rising protectionist pressures, could well lead to a global recession; in contrast, concerted action to reduce imbalances could help forestall the risks of a disorderly adjustment, limit the size of external exposures and the attending risks, and sustain global growth during the adjustment process. Since the last *World Economic Outlook* was published in April, there has been some progress in implementing the policy strategy to address global imbalances. Notably, the fiscal outlook in the United States has improved, aided by a rebound in revenues (although emergency spending associated with Hurricane Katrina will add to the deficit in the short run); there have also been important further steps toward greater exchange rate flexibility in Asia, notably in China and Malaysia. However, there remains a considerable way to go. The projected fiscal adjustment in the United States over the medium run remains unambitious, and in Asia the scope for flexibility in the new exchange rates should be fully utilized; moreover, progress since April with financial reform in Asia, or further structural reforms to boost domestic demand and growth in Japan and the euro area, has been limited. Oil-exporting countries will also need to play their part, including by taking advantage of higher revenues to boost expenditures in areas where social returns are high (subject to cyclical considerations) and to accelerate growth-enhancing structural reforms;[9] over the medium term, real

exchange rate appreciation may also be necessary. Even so, as noted above, adjustment in oil-exporting countries will take time, underscoring the need for other countries to make progress now.

- *Unsustainable medium-term fiscal positions remain a key risk.* Among the major industrial countries, fiscal deficits are expected to decline only modestly over the medium term (outside Canada, which remains in surplus), with rising public debt ratios in Japan, Italy, and Germany of particular concern (Table 1.3). In most countries, despite past reforms, fiscal pressures from aging populations remain a serious concern, especially for health care. Encouragingly, emerging market countries have improved their fiscal positions noticeably in recent years, although, in many, public debt is still well above sustainable levels (Box 1.1, "Is Public Debt in Emerging Markets Still Too High?").

- *More ambitious efforts are required to address constraints to long-run growth.* Despite some welcome progress, most countries and regions face significant structural challenges, including product and labor market reforms in the euro area and Japan; financial and corporate reform in much of emerging Asia; improving the investment climate in Latin America, the Commonwealth of Independent States, and the Middle East; and strengthening banking supervision in central and eastern Europe.

- *From a multilateral perspective, a successful outcome to the Doha Round remains critical to support global growth over the medium term.* To date, progress has been disappointing, and time is running out to reach agreement on an ambitious trade liberalization at the upcoming World Trade Organization (WTO) Ministerial meeting in Hong Kong SAR in December. Key issues that remain to be determined include modalities for eliminating export subsidies and tariff cuts on agricultural goods; nonagricultural tariffs, including the extent of cuts by

[8]See "Globalization and External Imbalances," Chapter III, *World Economic Outlook,* April 2005 for a detailed discussion.
[9]See "How Should Middle Eastern and Central Asian Oil Exporters Use Their Oil Revenues?" Box 1.6 in the April 2005 *World Economic Outlook* for a detailed discussion.

Table 1.3. Major Advanced Economies: General Government Fiscal Balances and Debt[1]
(Percent of GDP)

	1989–98	1999	2000	2001	2002	2003	2004	2005	2006	2010
Major advanced economies										
Actual balance	−3.5	−1.2	−0.2	−1.8	−4.1	−4.6	−4.1	−4.0	−4.1	−2.8
Output gap[2]	0.4	1.3	2.2	0.6	−0.8	−1.5	−0.8	−0.9	−0.8	—
Structural balance[2]	−3.5	−1.5	−1.4	−2.0	−3.7	−3.9	−3.7	−3.6	−3.6	−2.8
United States										
Actual balance	−3.4	0.6	1.3	−0.7	−4.0	−4.6	−4.0	−3.7	−3.9	−2.3
Output gap[2]	0.5	3.3	3.5	0.9	−0.9	−1.5	−0.8	−0.6	−0.6	—
Structural balance[2]	−3.4	−0.3	0.3	−0.8	−3.5	−3.8	−3.5	−3.2	−3.5	−2.3
Net debt	54.1	44.6	39.3	38.3	41.0	43.8	44.9	46.0	47.6	47.4
Gross debt	69.5	62.8	57.1	56.6	58.7	60.6	60.7	60.9	61.7	58.8
Euro area										
Actual balance	...	−1.3	−0.9	−1.8	−2.5	−2.8	−2.7	−3.0	−3.1	−2.0
Output gap[2]	...	0.3	1.8	1.4	0.2	−1.1	−1.0	−1.6	−1.6	—
Structural balance[2]	...	−1.6	−1.8	−2.4	−2.6	−2.5	−2.2	−2.3	−2.3	−1.9
Net debt	...	60.7	58.3	58.3	58.3	59.9	60.4	61.6	62.6	62.0
Gross debt	...	72.5	70.0	68.9	68.8	70.1	70.6	72.3	73.1	71.9
Germany[3]										
Actual balance	−2.4	−1.5	1.3	−2.8	−3.7	−4.0	−3.7	−3.9	−3.7	−3.2
Output gap[2]	1.3	0.1	1.7	1.5	0.2	−1.3	−1.0	−1.6	−1.7	—
Structural balance[2,4]	−2.7	−1.5	−1.7	−3.1	−3.5	−3.4	−3.2	−3.3	−2.9	−3.1
Net debt	37.3	53.5	51.5	52.1	54.3	57.7	59.9	63.1	65.6	70.7
Gross debt	48.8	59.6	58.7	57.9	59.6	62.8	64.5	67.7	70.1	74.7
France										
Actual balance	−3.7	−2.5	−1.5	−1.5	−3.1	−4.2	−3.7	−3.5	−3.9	−1.2
Output gap[2]	−1.0	−0.6	1.2	1.0	—	−1.4	−1.4	−2.0	−2.1	—
Structural balance[2,4]	−2.9	−2.2	−2.1	−2.1	−3.1	−3.4	−2.6	−2.6	−2.4	−1.2
Net debt	37.2	48.6	47.0	48.2	48.5	53.0	55.2	56.8	58.5	56.2
Gross debt	46.4	58.3	56.6	56.1	58.1	62.7	64.8	66.4	68.2	65.8
Italy										
Actual balance	−8.4	−1.7	−0.8	−3.2	−2.7	−3.2	−3.2	−4.3	−5.1	−4.4
Output gap[2]	−0.4	0.4	1.5	1.2	−0.2	−1.3	−1.3	−2.5	−2.3	—
Structural balance[2,4]	−8.3	−2.0	−2.7	−3.9	−3.5	−2.8	−2.9	−3.4	−4.0	−4.3
Net debt	106.6	109.2	105.6	105.5	103.1	103.1	103.0	105.5	107.1	111.7
Gross debt	112.7	115.5	111.3	110.9	108.3	106.8	106.6	109.3	110.9	115.6
Japan										
Actual balance	−1.9	−7.2	−7.5	−6.1	−7.9	−7.8	−7.2	−6.7	−6.2	−5.2
Excluding social security	−4.1	−8.3	−8.0	−6.2	−7.7	−7.9	−6.9	−6.3	−5.8	−4.8
Output gap[2]	0.9	−1.6	−0.3	−1.3	−2.5	−2.3	−0.9	−0.4	—	—
Structural balance[2,4]	−2.2	−6.6	−7.3	−5.5	−6.8	−6.9	−6.8	−6.6	−6.2	−5.2
Excluding social security	−4.3	−7.9	−7.9	−5.9	−7.1	−7.4	−6.8	−6.2	−5.8	−4.8
Net debt	23.3	53.8	59.3	64.5	71.5	76.0	82.1	88.3	93.3	106.7
Gross debt	85.6	131.1	139.3	148.8	158.4	164.7	169.2	174.4	177.8	182.1
United Kingdom										
Actual balance	−3.7	1.1	3.9	0.8	−1.5	−3.2	−3.0	−3.2	−3.4	−2.0
Output gap[2]	−0.2	−0.1	1.1	0.7	−0.1	−0.4	0.3	−0.3	−0.4	—
Structural balance[2,4]	−3.6	1.0	1.3	0.3	−1.7	−3.1	−3.0	−3.2	−3.2	−2.0
Net debt	38.1	40.0	34.2	32.7	32.7	34.5	36.4	37.9	40.2	43.9
Gross debt	43.7	44.6	41.6	38.4	37.9	39.3	41.1	42.5	44.8	48.5
Canada										
Actual balance	−5.1	1.6	2.9	0.7	−0.1	—	0.7	0.5	0.3	0.5
Output gap[2]	−0.3	0.6	1.9	0.3	0.3	−0.5	−0.4	−0.4	−0.1	—
Structural balance[2,4]	−4.8	1.3	2.0	0.4	−0.2	0.3	0.9	0.7	0.4	0.5
Net debt	78.9	75.4	65.3	60.2	57.9	51.4	46.8	43.9	41.3	32.1
Gross debt	110.5	111.6	101.5	100.3	97.4	91.9	87.9	83.0	78.4	62.6

Note: The methodology and specific assumptions for each country are discussed in Box A1 in the Statistical Appendix.

[1]Debt data refer to end of year. Debt data are not always comparable across countries. For example, the Canadian data include the unfunded component of government employee pension liabilities, which amounted to nearly 18 percent of GDP in 2001.

[2]Percent of potential GDP.

[3]Data before 1990 refer to west Germany. Beginning in 1995, the debt and debt-service obligations of the Treuhandanstalt (and of various other agencies) were taken over by the general government. This debt is equivalent to 8 percent of GDP, and the associated debt service, to ½ to 1 percent of GDP.

[4]Excludes one-off receipts from the sale of mobile telephone licenses (the equivalent of 2.5 percent of GDP in 2000 for Germany, 0.1 percent of GDP in 2001 and 2002 for France, 1.2 percent of GDP in 2000 for Italy, and 2.4 percent of GDP in 2000 for the United Kingdom). Also excludes one-off receipts from sizable asset transactions, in particular 0.5 percent of GDP for France in 2005.

Box 1.1. Is Public Debt in Emerging Markets Still Too High?

The September 2003 *World Economic Outlook* noted with concern the rising trend in public debt in emerging market economies. At that time, public debt was viewed as being too high in many emerging market economies—25–50 percent of GDP was seen as an appropriate level in that *World Economic Outlook*—and the steady increase in public debt since the mid-1990s had taken debt above the levels in industrial countries. This box provides an update of the situation.

Over the past two years, emerging market economies have made encouraging progress in reducing the vulnerabilities they face from high public debt levels. By the end of 2005, public debt ratios in emerging markets will likely have fallen by some 8 percentage points of GDP since 2002, to an average of about 60 percent of GDP (top panel in the figure).[1] In contrast, the average debt ratio in industrial countries is projected to have increased by almost 3 percentage points of GDP over the same period.[2]

Public debt ratios have fallen in most emerging market countries. In a 25-country sample, public debt ratios are projected to increase between 2002–05 in just 6 countries and to fall in the remaining 19. Public debt ratios have fallen most significantly in Latin America (an average decline of 13 percent of GDP, to about 52¼ percent of GDP by end-2005),[3] followed by the Middle East and Africa region (by 11 percent of GDP, to about 77¼ percent of GDP), and Asia

Note: The main authors of this box are María González and Davide Lombardo.

[1]This analysis is based on a sample of 25 emerging market countries, taken from an update of the databases used for Chapter III of the September 2003 *World Economic Outlook*. Only countries with continuous data from 1992 are used.

[2]The worsening appears to be led both by a slowdown in economic activity and a weakening of the fiscal stance in industrial countries. Between 1995–2002 and 2003–05, average growth in the industrial countries declined from nearly 3.1 to 2.3 percent, while their average primary surplus fell from about 2¼ percent of GDP to about 1 percent of GDP.

[3]The average decline in Latin America excluding Argentina is projected at about 6 percent of GDP.

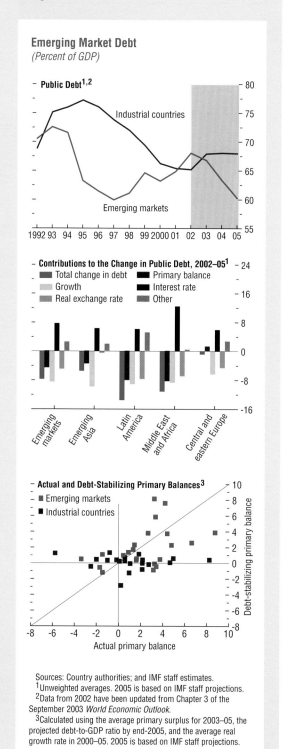

Emerging Market Debt
(Percent of GDP)

Sources: Country authorities; and IMF staff estimates.
[1]Unweighted averages. 2005 is based on IMF staff projections.
[2]Data from 2002 have been updated from Chapter 3 of the September 2003 *World Economic Outlook.*
[3]Calculated using the average primary surplus for 2003–05, the projected debt-to-GDP ratio by end-2005, and the average real growth rate in 2000–05. 2005 is based on IMF staff projections.

(by 5 percent of GDP, to 58 percent of GDP). Only in the central and eastern European countries have public debt ratios increased (about 1 percent of GDP, to 53½ percent of GDP).

The structure of public debt has also improved. The share of foreign-currency-denominated debt in total public debt declined from about 55 percent at end-2002 to just under half by end-2005 (IMF staff estimate). This is the result of both real exchange rate appreciations in many countries during this period and improved public sector debt management. Countries have benefited from favorable global financial market conditions in recent years, which have seen spreads on emerging market debt decline to historic lows. The average implicit interest rate (calculated as the ratio of the interest bill over the total debt stock of the previous period) has fallen for emerging market economies by about 2 percentage points, most notably in the Middle East and Africa region.

What accounts for the 8 percent of GDP decline in emerging market public debt ratios between 2002 and 2005? Real GDP growth rates have been particularly strong by historical standards, contributing 8½ percent of GDP to the reduction of the average public debt stock (middle panel in the figure). At the same time, real exchange rate appreciations have contributed nearly 5 percent of GDP, and primary fiscal surpluses (reflecting a mix of adjustment and favorable cyclical effects), a further 5 percent of GDP. Countervailing factors have been the automatic debt increase resulting from positive real interest rates, increasing the average debt ratio by 7.8 percent of GDP, and residual factors (including the recognition of off-balance-sheet liabilities and the use of part of the fiscal surpluses to build up liquidity cushions rather than to reduce gross debt) accounting for an increase of some 2.6 percent of GDP. In some specific cases (as in Argentina and Ecuador), public debt ratios have been reduced through debt-restructuring operations.

While the regional trends have been broadly similar, some differences stand out. In the central and eastern European countries, primary fiscal deficits have added to the debt ratio. The effect of appreciating real exchange rates has been particularly strong in those regions (such as Latin America and Middle East and Africa) with relatively high shares of foreign-currency-denominated debt and in countries (such as Uruguay) that had experienced large exchange rate depreciations that have since been partially reversed.

Looking forward, emerging market economies should entrench and—in some cases—intensify their recent fiscal consolidation efforts. An average public debt ratio of 60 percent of GDP is still too high, and debt-related vulnerabilities need to be reduced further. Despite the recent progress, the average primary balance over 2002–05 for many countries has fallen short of what would have been needed to reduce or even stabilize the debt-to-GDP ratio under average historical values for real GDP growth and interest rates—arguably better proxies for their respective medium-term values than more recent observations—which underscores the need for further adjustment (see bottom panel in the figure).[4] Moreover, the recent decline in public debt has taken place in the face of an unusually favorable combination of circumstances—real exchange rate appreciation, historically-high growth rates, buoyant commodity prices, and an increase in financial market risk appetite. It will be key for emerging market countries to continue to take advantage of the current favorable circumstances, and to stay the course if and when growth slows down.

[4]The estimates suggest that the primary balance in those emerging market countries that remain below their debt-stabilizing level would need to increase on average by about 4½ percent of GDP to become sustainable according to this metric. (See Chapter III of the September 2003 *World Economic Outlook* for details on the concept of the debt-stabilizing primary balance.) For this exercise, the real interest rate on emerging market debt has been estimated as the U.S. long-term real interest rate plus the respective average EMBI spread for the 2000–05 period, with the exception of Ecuador (2005 spreads) and Argentina (average EMBI spread following the settlement of the debt exchange). For industrial countries, the real interest rate has been proxied by the inflation-adjusted yield on benchmark 10-year government bonds.

middle-income countries; and services, where progress has lagged substantially. In addition, as emphasized in past issues of the *World Economic Outlook*, the continuing risks and pressures in oil markets underscore the need to reduce obstacles to investment, including in refining; strengthen energy conservation; and improve transparency.

The improvement in growth prospects in many of the world's poorest countries has been an especially welcome development over the past few years. Beyond the continued robust expansions in China and India, which account for over half of the world's poor, the GDP growth rate in the Heavily Indebted Poor Countries (HIPC)—while still far too slow—has also risen to an average 5 percent in 2001–05, despite the adverse effects of the global slowdown and—in many cases—commodity prices during this period (Figure 1.10). As encouraging, there is renewed commitment in the international community to provide additional resources, reflected in the G-8 agreement at Gleneagles in July (which, along with other donor commitments, should raise official development assistance by $50 billion, and aid to Africa by $25 billion, by 2010); the European Union's undertaking to increase aid to the UN target of 0.7 percent of GNP by 2015; and proposals to cancel concessional multilateral debt of the heavily indebted poor countries.

The priorities now are twofold. First, the international community must follow through expeditiously on its commitments, and accompany this with an ambitious trade liberalization—particularly for agricultural products—under the Doha Round. Second, developing countries must move rapidly to put in place the policies needed for sustainable growth and poverty reduction. In this connection, a central challenge is to build sound, accountable, and transparent institutions, the theme of this edition of the *World Economic Outlook*. As discussed in Chapter III, "Building Institutions," a country's institutions—typically the product of its entire political, economic, and cultural history—can be quite persistent, but are not immutable. Over

the past 30 years, many emerging and developing countries have made progress in improving their institutions, and this has generally been followed by stronger growth and higher investment. While there is no single road to success—and indeed efforts at "institutional engineering" may well prove counterproductive—the chapter identifies a variety of conditions under which good institutions appear most likely to flourish. Perhaps the most important of these—consistent with the view that good institutions are most likely to grow in an environment where rent-seeking is limited—is greater openness to the outside world, reinforcing the arguments for developing countries themselves to undertake ambitious liberalization under the Doha Round.

United States and Canada: Strong U.S. Growth, but Rising Housing Market Risks

In the United States, GDP growth remained strong in the first half of 2005, underpinned, as in 2004, by strong income growth and steady improvements in labor market conditions, supportive financial market conditions, and rising house prices. Incoming data—including manufacturing and services sector activity surveys, employment data, and retail sales—generally suggest the momentum of the expansion remains solid. However, the near-term outlook has been overshadowed by the devastating loss of life and property caused by Hurricane Katrina, which is almost certain to be the most expensive natural disaster in recent years. The immediate direct output effects of the disruption in production are likely to be modest, given the affected area's relatively small economic size, and will be increasingly offset by the stimulus from reconstruction involving significant government spending. However, given the area's importance in hydrocarbon production—with the initial refinery capacity shut down in the aftermath of Hurricane Katrina accounting for some 13 percent of national capacity—and as a national transportation hub, there could be larger indirect effects on consumption and fixed investment through temporarily higher

Table 1.4. Advanced Economies: Real GDP, Consumer Prices, and Unemployment
(Annual percent change and percent of labor force)

	Real GDP				Consumer Prices				Unemployment			
	2003	2004	2005	2006	2003	2004	2005	2006	2003	2004	2005	2006
Advanced economies	**1.9**	**3.3**	**2.5**	**2.7**	**1.8**	**2.0**	**2.2**	**2.0**	**6.6**	**6.3**	**6.1**	**5.9**
United States	2.7	4.2	3.5	3.3	2.3	2.7	3.1	2.8	6.0	5.5	5.2	5.2
Euro area[1]	0.7	2.0	1.2	1.8	2.1	2.1	2.1	1.8	8.7	8.9	8.7	8.4
Germany	−0.2	1.6	0.8	1.2	1.0	1.8	1.7	1.7	9.6	9.2	9.5	9.3
France	0.9	2.0	1.5	1.8	2.2	2.3	1.9	1.8	9.5	9.7	9.8	9.6
Italy	0.3	1.2	—	1.4	2.8	2.3	2.1	2.0	8.7	8.5	8.1	7.8
Spain	2.9	3.1	3.2	3.0	3.1	3.1	3.2	3.0	11.5	11.0	9.1	8.0
Netherlands[2]	−0.1	1.7	0.7	2.0	2.2	1.4	1.4	−2.6	3.7	4.6	5.0	4.5
Belgium	1.3	2.7	1.2	2.0	1.5	1.9	2.3	1.9	7.9	7.8	7.9	8.0
Austria	1.4	2.4	1.9	2.2	1.3	2.0	2.0	1.8	4.3	4.8	5.0	4.7
Finland	2.4	3.6	1.8	3.2	1.3	0.1	1.0	1.5	9.0	8.8	8.0	7.8
Greece	4.7	4.2	3.2	2.9	3.4	3.1	3.5	3.3	9.7	10.5	10.5	10.5
Portugal	−1.1	1.0	0.5	1.2	3.3	2.5	2.3	2.5	6.3	6.7	7.4	7.7
Ireland	4.4	4.5	5.0	4.9	4.0	2.3	2.3	2.5	4.7	4.5	4.2	4.0
Luxembourg	2.4	4.4	3.1	3.2	2.0	2.2	2.4	2.7	3.8	4.4	4.8	5.2
Japan	1.4	2.7	2.0	2.0	−0.2	—	−0.4	−0.1	5.3	4.7	4.3	4.1
United Kingdom[1]	2.5	3.2	1.9	2.2	1.4	1.3	2.0	1.9	5.0	4.8	4.7	4.8
Canada	2.0	2.9	2.9	3.2	2.7	1.8	2.2	2.5	7.6	7.2	6.8	6.7
Korea	3.1	4.6	3.8	5.0	3.5	3.6	2.8	2.9	3.6	3.5	3.6	3.3
Australia	3.3	3.2	2.2	3.2	2.8	2.3	2.6	2.7	6.0	5.5	5.1	5.1
Taiwan Province of China	3.3	5.7	3.4	4.3	−0.3	1.6	2.0	1.8	5.0	4.4	4.3	4.2
Sweden	1.5	3.6	2.6	2.8	2.3	1.1	0.8	1.8	4.9	5.5	5.2	4.9
Switzerland	−0.4	1.7	0.8	1.8	0.6	0.8	1.3	1.4	3.4	3.5	3.7	3.7
Hong Kong SAR	3.2	8.1	6.3	4.5	−2.6	−0.4	1.0	1.3	7.9	6.8	5.7	4.6
Denmark	0.7	2.4	2.2	2.1	2.1	1.2	1.7	1.8	5.8	6.0	5.6	5.5
Norway	0.4	2.9	3.1	3.3	2.5	0.4	1.4	2.1	4.5	4.5	4.2	4.0
Israel	1.7	4.4	4.2	3.9	0.7	−0.4	1.2	2.3	10.7	10.3	9.1	8.7
Singapore	1.4	8.4	3.9	4.5	0.5	1.7	0.7	1.7	4.7	4.0	3.6	3.4
New Zealand[3]	3.4	4.8	2.5	2.5	1.8	2.3	2.7	2.7	4.7	3.9	4.0	4.2
Cyprus	1.9	3.7	3.8	4.0	4.1	2.3	2.5	2.5	3.5	3.6	3.2	3.0
Iceland	4.2	5.2	5.8	4.9	2.1	3.2	3.4	3.5	3.4	3.1	2.3	1.7
Memorandum												
Major advanced economies	1.8	3.2	2.5	2.6	1.7	2.0	2.1	2.1	6.7	6.4	6.1	6.0
Newly industrialized Asian economies	3.1	5.6	4.0	4.7	1.5	2.4	2.2	2.3	4.4	4.1	4.0	3.7

[1]Based on Eurostat's harmonized index of consumer prices.

[2]In 2006, as a statistical effect, the introduction of a new health care system will lower Harmonized Index of Consumer Price (HICP) inflation by 4 percentage points (but only in that year) as private health expenditures drop out of the consumption basket; otherwise inflation would be positive.

[3]Consumer prices excluding interest rate components.

input prices, particularly for gasoline and other refined oil products.

Against this background, GDP growth is projected to be somewhat weaker than previously expected in the latter part of 2005, with private consumption affected by higher gasoline prices and population displacement. In 2006, growth is expected to return to trend, driven primarily by a pickup in fixed investment, reflecting firms' healthy balance sheets, strong profitability, and capital stocks that are below trend in some sectors (Table 1.4). With U.S. growth continuing to outstrip that of other large advanced economies in 2005–06 and, with higher oil prices, the current account deficit is projected to widen to over 6 percent of GDP in 2005 (Table 1.5). Looking forward, assuming no further real depreciation of the U.S. dollar and a moderate fiscal consolidation, the current account deficit would remain at this level through the rest of the decade, accompanied by a further substantial rise in U.S. external liabilities (Appendix 1.2). Within this, the steady deterioration of the investment income account—still surprisingly in surplus

**Table 1.5. Selected Economies:
Current Account Positions**
(Percent of GDP)

	2003	2004	2005	2006
Advanced economies	**−0.8**	**−1.0**	**−1.3**	**−1.4**
United States	−4.7	−5.7	−6.1	−6.1
Euro area[1]	0.3	0.5	0.2	0.2
Germany	2.1	3.8	4.3	4.4
France	0.4	−0.4	−1.3	−1.5
Italy	−1.3	−0.9	−1.7	−1.4
Spain	−3.6	−5.3	−6.2	−6.9
Netherlands	2.8	3.3	4.9	5.3
Belgium	4.5	3.4	4.2	4.0
Austria	−0.5	0.6	—	−0.3
Finland	4.0	4.0	3.4	4.4
Greece	−5.6	−3.9	−3.9	−4.0
Portugal	−5.4	−7.5	−8.4	−7.7
Ireland	—	−0.8	−1.4	−1.8
Luxembourg	9.4	6.9	8.4	9.1
Japan	3.2	3.7	3.3	3.0
United Kingdom	−1.5	−2.0	−1.9	−1.8
Canada	1.5	2.2	1.5	1.7
Korea	2.0	4.1	2.0	1.5
Australia	−5.9	−6.4	−5.7	−5.0
Taiwan Province of China	10.2	6.1	4.3	4.6
Sweden	7.6	8.2	7.4	6.7
Switzerland	13.2	12.0	10.8	11.3
Hong Kong SAR	10.3	9.8	10.3	10.2
Denmark	3.3	2.5	1.9	2.2
Norway	12.8	13.5	18.3	21.4
Israel	0.7	1.3	1.7	1.3
Singapore	29.2	26.1	25.7	22.7
New Zealand	−4.2	−6.4	−7.4	−7.7
Cyprus	−3.4	−5.8	−4.0	−3.2
Iceland	−5.1	−8.5	−12.0	−11.4
Memorandum				
Major advanced economies	−1.5	−1.7	−2.1	−2.2
Euro area[2]	0.3	0.6	0.4	0.3
Newly industrialized Asian economies	7.4	7.2	5.5	5.0

[1]Calculated as the sum of the balances of individual euro area countries.
[2]Corrected for reporting discrepancies in intra-area transactions.

(Box 1.2, "Why Is the U.S. International Income Account Still in the Black, and Will This Last?") will be an increasing headwind, with rising debt and higher interest rates likely to reduce the U.S. net income balance by about 1 percent of GDP in coming years.

Near-term risks to growth are mixed, albeit tilted to the downside. While business and consumer confidence remain healthy, the continuing rise in prices for oil and downstream petroleum products could have a larger negative impact on growth in the near term. Moreover, while productivity growth remains solid, a further slowdown could adversely affect capital inflows and add to cost pressures, increasing the risk of a jump in long-run interest rates. More generally, the very low level of household savings—closely linked to developments in the housing market—remains a significant concern. Since the late 1990s, house prices in the United States have risen rapidly, although with considerable variation across states. IMF staff estimates suggest that at least 18 states, accounting for more than 40 percent of U.S. GDP, are currently experiencing housing booms (Figure 1.11), and, by some measures, the implications for the national level are such that—for the first time since 1970—the national housing market is booming as well.[10] Rising prices have supported the increase in home mortgage borrowing from about 3 percent of GDP in 2000 to close to 8 percent of GDP in early 2005, with about one-third in the form of net equity extraction, which, in turn, has been underlying the household sectors' financing gap—the excess of household spending on residential investment and consumer durables over gross household savings. Moreover, a rising share of new mortgages is being financed in a riskier fashion, including through negative amortization and floating rate instruments.

While house price booms do not necessarily end in busts, recent house price increases have raised concerns that the market could be increasingly susceptible to a correction.[11] While high housing prices partly reflect underlying

[10]Booms are defined as the peak-to-peak increases or, alternatively, as the cumulative eight-quarter pre-peak increases in inflation-adjusted housing prices that exceed a threshold. The thresholds are based on the top quartiles of all increases in a sample of house prices in 14 industrial countries during 1970–2002 (see Chapter II, *World Economic Outlook,* April 2003, and Helbling and Terrones, 2003, for details). To assess current housing market conditions, house prices in 2005:Q2 were assumed to have reached a peak.

[11]See also Chapter I in IMF (2005c).

fundamentals—including increased incomes, wealth, and demographics—they also reflect the present very low level of interest rates, which is unlikely to be sustained. Moreover, the ratio of house prices to rents—equivalent to a price-earnings ratio for housing—has reached new highs. On the positive side, supervisory agencies recently issued guidance to promote sound risk management practices for home equity lending, and sound financial sector balance sheets and the broader distribution of real estate–related risks through asset securitization and other financial innovations have reduced financial market risks. However, the impact on the real economy could be more severe, with even a slow-down in house price inflation—prompted for example by higher interest rates (with variable-rate products constituting about one-third of new mortgages in 2004–05 compared with about one-fifth on average)—having the potential to significantly slow private consumption growth in the future.

While headline inflation has fluctuated around 3 percent in the first half of 2005, reflecting higher prices for oil and other raw materials, core inflation—as measured by the personal consumption expenditure deflator—has remained restrained, running at about 1.7 percent in the first half of the year. But with growth exceeding potential, and policy interest rates still below most estimates of neutral levels, the Federal Reserve has continued to raise policy rates steadily: looking forward, further measured withdrawal of monetary stimulus seems likely to be appropriate. However, as usual, much will depend on the incoming data, with the steady increase in unit labor costs, as well as higher oil prices, needing to be particularly carefully watched.

Against the background of a low national sav-ings rate, a large current account deficit, and impending demographic pressures, fiscal consoli-dation remains a macroeconomic policy priority. Owing to strong revenue growth, the FY2004 unified budget deficit fell to 3.6 percent of GDP—over 1 percent of GDP lower than anticipated—and was expected to decrease

Figure 1.11. United States: House Prices and Household Demand

Rapid house price increases have supported growth in household expenditure and surging housing market transactions. Some 15–18 states are estimated to be experiencing a housing boom. Low interest rates have contributed to maintaining affordability, although leverage and riskier financing have also been on the rise.

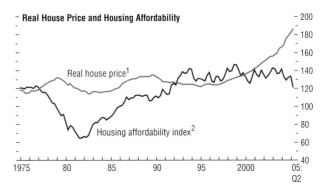

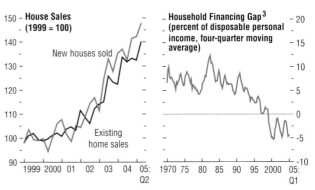

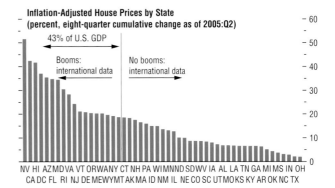

Sources: Haver Analytics; and IMF staff calculations.
[1]Office of Federal Housing Enterprise Oversight house price index adjusted by the total CPI (1982–84 = 100).
[2]Index = 100 when median family income qualifies for an 80 percent mortgage on a median-priced existing single-family home. A rising index indicates more buyers can afford to enter the market.
[3]Net acquisition of financial assets by households minus net increase in their financial liabilities (equals gross household savings minus household capital expenditure).

Box 1.2. Why Is the U.S. International Income Account Still in the Black, and Will This Last?

The increase in the U.S. current account deficit in recent years has taken place mostly as a result of a widening of the goods and services trade balance. Somewhat surprisingly, the other main component of the current account—the income balance, which comprises returns on foreign assets and liabilities of U.S. residents—has remained in surplus. Indeed, net income flows have boosted the current account balance by about ¼ percent of GDP since 2000 even as the U.S. net foreign debt ratio has risen by about one-third, from some 15 percent of GDP to over 20 percent of GDP (see the figure).[1] Two questions follow from these developments. What explains the continuing surpluses on the income account, given large and growing U.S. net foreign liabilities? And is this remarkable performance likely to continue? To answer these questions, the income flows from debt holdings and foreign direct investment (FDI) are examined separately.

On the debt side, the fall in U.S. interest rates—reflecting accommodative monetary policies and low premiums on longer debt maturities—has largely offset the impact of the rise in U.S. net foreign debt liabilities. The latter accounts for almost all of the market rise in U.S. net foreign liabilities in recent years. The net positions for other types of holdings—foreign direct investment, portfolio equities, and "other" assets, mainly comprising bank loans—have remained broadly balanced.

Regarding FDI, there has been a consistent surplus of about 1 percent of GDP on associated incomes over the past 20 years even though holdings of *foreign direct investment* assets and liabilities are approximately balanced. This reflects yields on U.S. assets abroad that are much higher than those on foreign investment

in the United States.[2] With no significant differences in returns on other types of international assets and liabilities, this surplus explains why the income account has remained in surplus over recent years despite the fact that the United States is a significant net debtor.[3]

Various explanations have been proposed for why rates of return on U.S. direct investment abroad remain almost twice as large as those on equivalent foreign inflows. The rate of return on U.S. investment abroad is similar to that achieved by domestic companies in the United States and other countries. Accordingly, the main issue seems to be the low rate of return on foreign investment in the United States, a somewhat surprising result given the widespread view that the United States is an attractive location for foreign ventures.

Structural factors play a role.[4] Foreign affiliates are slightly more concentrated in industries with low returns, tend to be less profitable when their market share is small, and have higher leverage, and new ventures have lower rates of return, presumably reflecting the initial costs of entering the U.S. market. Indeed, the maturation of earlier FDI may help explain the narrowing differentials in returns over recent years. In addition, yields on U.S. investment abroad may reflect a risk premium, given that about one-third of these investments are in emerging markets.

Note: The main authors of this box are Tamim Bayoumi, Kornélia Krajnyák, and Alejandro Justiniano.

[1]Chapters 3 and 4 of IMF (2005c) discuss the deterioration of the U.S. trade balance and U.S. international investment position, respectively.

[2]Although the yields gap has narrowed over time, the impact on income flows has been offset by an increase in gross FDI assets and liabilities as a ratio to GDP.

[3]For completeness, a small surplus has been maintained over recent years on the income account for equity portfolio investment, reflecting both slightly higher rates of return and gross stock of assets compared to liabilities. Net flows on "other" investments have remained close to balanced.

[4]See Mataloni (2000), Grubert (1997), and references therein. For example, the rate of return on assets of FDI firms tended to be substantially lower than the industry average in motor vehicle production, rubber and plastic products, and electronic equipment over 1988–97.

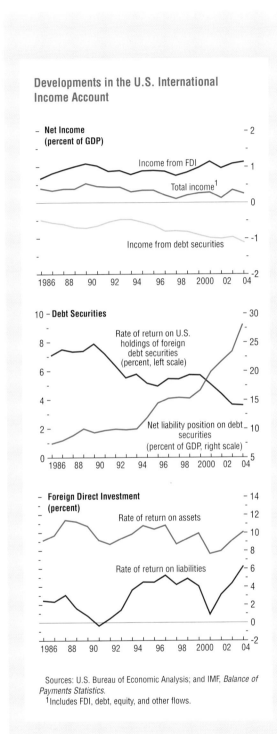

Developments in the U.S. International Income Account

Sources: U.S. Bureau of Economic Analysis; and IMF, *Balance of Payments Statistics.*
[1] Includes FDI, debt, equity, and other flows.

The size of the difference in rates of return, however, has led researchers to ask whether mechanisms that transfer profits to the foreign host company also play a role in reducing observed yields on foreign affiliates in the United States. For example, foreign firms could buy U.S. subsidiaries to acquire new products or processes, whose profits may then be booked abroad. Indeed, royalties (and dividends) are less important in foreign affiliates' incomes than in those of domestically owned U.S. companies. In addition, transfer pricing of components may be used to move profits out of the United States for tax purposes. Rates of return tend to be lower for subsidiaries whose host companies are in low-tax jurisdictions and those that import and export larger amounts of components with their hosts. In addition, on a firm-by-firm basis, foreign subsidiaries in the United States have an unusual concentration of taxable profits around zero. However, these characteristics also tend to be true of firms with minority foreign stakes (25–50 percent) as opposed to fully foreign-owned firms—and thus may only explain a limited amount of the differential in yields.

Looking ahead, the support to the U.S. current account from income flows is likely to erode rapidly—indeed, the IMF staff projects that the U.S. international income position will move into deficit later this year. Rising global interest rates will raise the deficit on income flows from debt instruments, a trend reinforced by continuing increases in the net foreign liabilities from large U.S. current account deficits. With about equal contributions from interest rate and debt increases, this could reduce the net income balance of the United States by about 1 percent of GDP in coming years, putting downward pressure on the current account and exchange rate.

further to 2.7 percent of GDP in FY2005 prior to the emergency spending associated with Hurricane Katrina, which, according to budget

requests to date, may amount to some 0.5 percent of GDP. That said, the strong revenue rebound may partly reflect the unwinding of factors that depressed tax collections in the aftermath of the collapse of the equity bubble, and future fiscal receipts will probably grow more in line with corporate profits and income growth. And looking forward, the U.S. Administration's plan to reduce the unified budget deficit to below 2 percent of GDP by FY2009 remains both relatively unambitious, and—since it depends on unprecedented compression of discretionary nondefense spending, while not providing funding for operations in Iraq and Afghanistan beyond FY2006 or the reform of the Alternative Minimum Tax—subject to considerable risk.

Given the relatively favorable outlook, a bolder adjustment effort is warranted, with the aim of achieving broad budget balance—excluding social security—by 2010. Such an adjustment would require consideration of revenue measures, given the already very stringent spending discipline assumed in the U.S. Administration's proposals. Options include broadening the income tax base by curbing deductions, a national consumption tax, or an energy tax. The consolidation efforts would be supported by a legislated budget rule, with pay-as-you-go provisions for all expenditures, including tax expenditures. Recent steps to address the solvency of the Social Security system, including a proposal for slowing benefits growth, are welcome, and only relatively modest additional steps would be required to eliminate the system's underfunding, if implemented in a timely manner. However, Medicare outlays are on an explosive path, and urgent steps are needed to address the system's underfunding and to increase the efficiency of the U.S. health care system.

In Canada, real GDP growth has rebounded, driven primarily by strong consumption, which has been underpinned by robust employment gains—with unemployment reaching a 30-year low—strong wage increases, and rising house prices. Consumer price pressures have remained contained; core inflation remains below 2 percent. Nevertheless, with labor market conditions tightening and unit labor costs increasing, price

developments need to be monitored carefully, and the Bank of Canada has appropriately resumed withdrawing monetary stimulus. Fiscal policy is expected to remain on a steady course, with the general government continuing to run a surplus of about ½ percent of GDP, and the net public debt ratio is projected to decline steadily in the coming years. If this prudence is sustained in the face of political demands for higher government spending, the country will be in a favorable position when the fiscal pressures arising from population aging begin to emerge. However, to ensure long-term fiscal sustainability with an aging population, prudent fiscal policies will need to be accompanied by reforms aimed at increasing the efficiency of health care systems and structural policies to boost productivity growth and economic flexibility.

Western Europe: The Recovery Continues to Struggle

The tentative expansion in the euro area has faltered once again. After showing signs of revival in the second half of 2004, final domestic demand has since slowed considerably; while GDP growth averaged about 1¼ percent in the first half of 2005, this primarily reflected a stronger contribution from net exports. On the political front, the rejection of the European Union (EU) constitution by France and the Netherlands, as well as the subsequent and acrimonious failure to agree on the EU budget, have so far had a limited effect on confidence, with the financial market impact limited to a small widening of spreads for high debt countries, and a moderate depreciation of the euro.

Looking forward, the outlook is highly uncertain. While confidence indicators remain subdued, incoming data—notably for exports and, more tentatively, manufacturing—have generally strengthened. Moreover, corporate balance sheets have continued to improve, with profitability continuing to rise, aided by prudent wage setting; employment has been more resilient than during past cycles (although unemployment remains high); long-run interest rates are at historic lows; and solid global growth and recent euro depreciation should also be supportive. Against this background, the expansion is expected to gradually regain momentum in the second half of the year, with euro area GDP growth projected to average 1.2 percent in 2005, rising to 1.8 percent in 2006 (0.4 and 0.5 percentage point lower than projected last April). That said, the consistent overestimation of the strength of the expansion in the euro area in recent years, as well as the fact that corporations as yet show little sign of investing their now substantial profits, underscore the risks of a more extended period of weakness. Notably, the lack of internal dynamism makes the euro area particularly susceptible to external shocks, including higher oil prices, a renewed sharp appreciation of the euro, or a rebound in global interest rates. A number of country-specific risks also remain, including richly valued housing markets (Spain and Ireland) and high household debt-to-income ratios and a high concentration of bank lending in Portugal.

Economic performance across the euro area remains very diverse. Among the major countries, domestic demand in Spain and—except in the second quarter of 2005—France has been relatively strong, while net exports have subtracted from growth. In contrast, domestic demand in Germany, and to a lesser extent Italy, has been considerably weaker, although German GDP has increasingly been boosted by strong net exports (see Box 1.3, "What Explains Divergent External Sector Performance in the Euro Area?"). In fact, these developments are not especially unusual (Figure 1.12), and reflect a variety of factors, including differences in underlying productivity growth and in fiscal stances, as well as country-specific and other shocks. But they are also indicative of less benign factors, including rigidities in product and labor markets across the zone. Differences in competitiveness can take a considerable time to reverse, and—partly associated with that—inflation differentials can

Figure 1.12. Euro Area: Growth Divergences Since EMU
(Cumulative difference from euro area average in percent, 1999–2004)

The level and composition of growth have differed widely across euro area countries over the past five years. This has partly resulted from differences in inflation rates across the area, reflected in both real interest rates and unit labor costs.

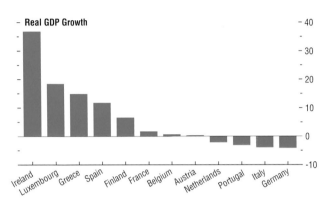

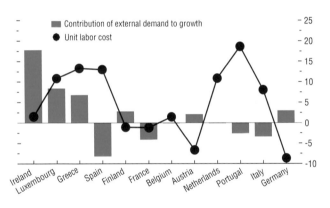

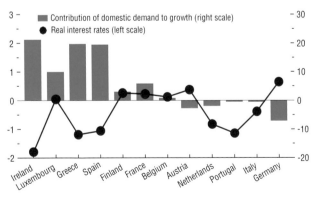

Sources: OECD, *Economic Outlook;* and IMF staff calculations.

Box 1.3. What Explains Divergent External Sector Performance in the Euro Area?

Against the generally weak economic performance in the euro area in recent years, there have been striking divergences in the external sector contribution to growth among the three largest countries. In Germany, net exports have contributed strongly to growth, in fact exceeding the cumulative increase in GDP over 2001–04. In Italy, however, net exports have contributed negatively to real growth since 2002, whereas in France, the contribution of the external sector switched from being marginally positive in 2001–02 to appreciably negative in 2003–04.

These differences in the contribution of external demand to growth mask significant variations between countries in import and export growth dynamics, on the one hand, and in goods and services growth on the other (see the figure). To understand what has been driving this variation, IMF staff conducted an econometric exercise to identify the main determinants of imports and exports for each of the three major euro area countries.[1]

For imports, it is the relative import content of domestic and foreign demand that accounts for most of the difference in import growth between the three countries. In particular, the vigor of export growth explains most of the recent evolution of imports in Germany, likely reflecting an increase in the share of intermediary imports in the production of exported manufactured capital goods. Conversely, the resilience of Italian imports owes much to the stability of domestic consumption.

Nonetheless, most of the divergences in external sector performances originate from export growth dynamics. Uneven demand developments in the key trading partners of the major euro area countries are partly responsible. Since 2001, France has faced consistently lower effective foreign demand growth than Germany and

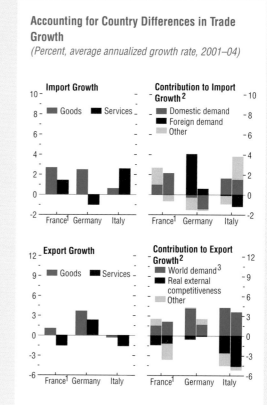

Accounting for Country Differences in Trade Growth
(Percent, average annualized growth rate, 2001–04)

Sources: IMF, *International Financial Statistics;* and IMF staff calculations.
[1]For France, "goods" refer to the manufacturing sector and "services" to the rest of the economy.
[2]The first stacked bar for each country refers to goods, and the second one to services.
[3]Calculated as a weighted average of trade partners' GDP.

Italy, reflecting weak domestic demand in the latter two economies. In addition, exporters in France and Italy are less geared toward fast-growing areas—such as emerging Asia and the United States—than their German counterparts. However, in the case of Italy, the strength of effective global demand has been insufficient to prevent a collapse of sales abroad. Tellingly, between 2001 and 2004 import demand in Italy's trade partners increased, on average, by 4 percent a year in real terms, whereas the volume of Italian exports has actually fallen.

Another source of disparity in export performances is the sectoral composition of

Note: The main authors of this box are Celine Allard and Silvia Sgherri.
[1]Based on quarterly data from the 1980s, except for Germany, where the sample period starts only after reunification.

exports. Whereas Germany has traditionally specialized in the more dynamic sector of manufactured capital goods, France and Italy have been somewhat hampered by their concentration on consumer goods, which are more vulnerable to competitive pressures from emerging markets.

The most important factor explaining recent differences in export performance among euro area countries, however, is the divergence in price and cost competitiveness. In this respect, even if the euro area countries share the same currency, in real terms, their price position vis-à-vis trading partners has evolved very differently. Owing to wage moderation, tax cuts, and cost retrenchment, relatively low inflation has contributed to a limited appreciation of the real effective exchange rate in Germany, whereas higher average inflation has caused a slightly stronger appreciation in France. At the same time, Italy has experienced a steady deterioration in competitiveness—owing to plunging labor productivity and rising production costs—that has hobbled its export performance.

Because divergences in relative prices and costs have been blurred by different productivity developments, the external competitiveness channel has not been able, recently, to smooth cyclical differences across the major euro area countries. Conceptually, in the absence of independent monetary and exchange rate policies, countries facing weak cyclical positions are likely

to experience lower inflation and enjoy an improvement in competitiveness relative to the other members of the union. However, this link is found to be quite tenuous. Member states with comparatively large positive output gaps in the late 1990s have managed to contain unit labor cost pressures, whereas those with comparatively lower cyclical pressures have registered large losses in competitiveness in the past few years. The most striking case is Italy. Here, the weakness of domestic demand has been coupled with a negative contribution of exports, which have been hampered by unit labor costs that have risen faster than those of the country's main European competitors. Thus, the stagnation of the Italian economy has not prevented a further deterioration in external sector performance.

In addition to productivity developments, another factor that appears to have dampened the effectiveness of the competitiveness adjustment mechanism among euro area countries is the behavior of exporters' margins. If margins are maintained in the face of a deterioration in competitiveness owing to unfavorable developments in productivity, export performance will suffer, with additional negative effects on growth. In Italy, for example, exporters appear to have responded to the appreciation of the euro by passing on to export prices a higher-than-average percentage of the increase in unit labor costs, to preserve profitability.

be very persistent.[12] This complicates national policymaking, including by exacerbating pressures in housing markets, particularly when the scope for offsetting policy action is limited. These rigidities also make area-wide monetary policy management more costly; if area-wide product and labor market competitiveness were brought to U.S. levels, the sacrifice ratio (the output cost of reducing inflation by

1 percentage point) would be reduced by one-third.[13]

Given the continued weakness of domestic demand, inflationary pressures in the euro area are easing. While headline inflation remains above 2 percent, in part reflecting the impact of higher oil prices, core inflation has slowed significantly, unit labor costs are essentially flat, and inflationary expectations remain reasonably well

---

[12]See, for instance, Ortega (2003) and European Central Bank (2005).
[13]See "Unemployment and Labor Market Institutions: Why Reforms Pay Off," Chapter IV the April 2003 *World Economic Outlook*.

anchored. Against this background, headline inflation is expected to fall back to an average 1.8 percent in 2006, broadly in line with the European Central Bank (ECB) target of close to but less than 2 percent. Past underestimation of inflation—in part due to unexpected increases in administered prices—and oil price risks provide some reason for caution, but overall excessive monetary tightness appears a greater risk than excessive monetary ease. If inflationary pressures remain restrained, and the expected recovery fails to materialize—or if the euro appreciates significantly—an interest rate cut should be considered.

On the fiscal side, the euro area deficit is projected to rise to 3 percent of GDP in 2005, with five countries—France, Germany, Greece, Italy, and Portugal—expected to exceed the 3 percent of GDP limit, in some cases by significant margins. With fiscal pressures from aging set to accelerate very shortly, most countries should ideally achieve a broadly balanced fiscal position by the end of the decade—requiring an average improvement in structural balances of about ½ percentage point of GDP annually—accompanied by further progress in pension and health reforms. The IMF staff's assessment of present budgetary policies, particularly in the largest countries, suggests they fall far short of meeting this requirement, with most showing little improvement or a deterioration in 2005–06; in particular, in Italy, significant—and as yet unidentified—adjustment will be required to reduce the general government deficit to the authorities' target of 3.8 percent of GDP in 2006. This will pose a key test of the revised Stability and Growth Pact procedures, and it will be important that the additional flexibility they allow is not used as an excuse to postpone adjustment altogether. Both the realism and public understanding of national Stability Plans could be improved if they were reviewed by independent fiscal councils and debated in parliaments.

In the United Kingdom, GDP growth has proved weaker than expected. Private consumption growth slowed sharply in the first half of 2005, in part reflecting higher interest rates,

oil price increases, and the cooling—if still elevated—housing market; while export growth—which weakened sharply in the first quarter—is showing signs of recovery, business confidence has weakened. Correspondingly, GDP growth is now projected at 1.9 percent in 2005, 0.7 percentage point lower than expected in April, before recovering to 2.2 percent in 2006, with higher oil prices and weaker euro area growth key downside risks. While CPI inflation has risen above 2 percent, reflecting in part rising oil prices, core inflation remains moderate and private sector wage growth has eased. Against this background, the Bank of England appropriately reduced interest rates by 25 basis points in August; looking forward, future moves will depend on incoming data, especially with respect to domestic demand. With IMF staff projections suggesting no improvement in the fiscal deficit in 2005 or 2006, fiscal consolidation remains necessary to ensure that the golden rule is met over the next cycle.

Following strong recoveries in 2004, performance in the Nordic countries has become more divergent. In Norway, high oil prices have supported strong GDP growth, prompting the Norges Bank to begin the tightening cycle; growth in Denmark is expected to remain broadly unchanged from 2004 at 2.2 percent, notwithstanding a temporary weakening of domestic demand in early 2005. The outlook in Sweden weakened markedly in the first quarter, accompanied by slowing demand growth in key European trading partners. While substantial fiscal stimulus in the pipeline will help support activity, the Riksbank cut interest rates by 50 basis points in late June. In Switzerland, the expansion has also weakened, reflecting the general slowdown in global manufacturing and weak euro area domestic demand; with inflation risks low, the Swiss National Bank has appropriately maintained a very accommodative monetary stance. Early elimination of the structural federal deficit and decisive reforms of pension and health systems remain key to addressing looming pressures from aging, along with competition-enhancing measures to boost low potential growth.

With Europe's per capita GDP having stagnated at about 70 percent of the level in the United States for the past 30 years, raising potential growth remains a central challenge. In this connection, a key issue in many countries is to raise labor utilization: apart from the direct economic and social benefits, this could also substantially improve the solvency of national pension systems. Since the mid-1990s, progress has clearly been made (Figure 1.13), and more recent reforms, such as Agenda 2010 in Germany, should lead to further improvements. But with many countries unlikely to achieve the Lisbon target of an employment rate of 70 percent by 2010, there is much further to go. Priorities vary across countries, but include minimum wages and greater flexibility in wage bargaining (France, Germany, and Italy); lowering tax wedges (Germany, Greece, Italy, the Netherlands, Spain); reforming employment protection (France, Greece, Italy, Portugal, Spain); reducing incentives for early retirement (Austria, Belgium, France, Germany, Greece); and reforms to social safety nets including— depending on the country—welfare, unemployment, or invalidity programs (Belgium, Germany, Greece, the Netherlands, Norway, and Spain). A further challenge will be to ensure sufficient demand for the rising supply of older—and lower-productivity—workers in the labor force, which could, inter alia, require reforms to systems of seniority pay.

Looking forward, a key question is how to accelerate the reform momentum. At the central level, priorities remain the completion of the internal market—a potentially important support for labor market reforms, although the recent rejection of the Services Directive was a setback—and further financial market integration. However, as stressed in the revised Lisbon Strategy, the key to further progress increasingly resides at the national level; with signs of growing reform fatigue, this will be a challenging task. In this context, in cases where structural reforms are expected to yield significant long-term fiscal benefits, short-term trade-offs with fiscal adjustment should not be ruled out. National

Figure 1.13. Europe: Why Has per Capita GDP Stagnated Relative to the United States?

Since 1970, strong European productivity growth has been offset by falling working hours and lower labor utilization. While these trends have partly reversed since 1995, low labor utilization remains a key concern, especially in continental Europe.

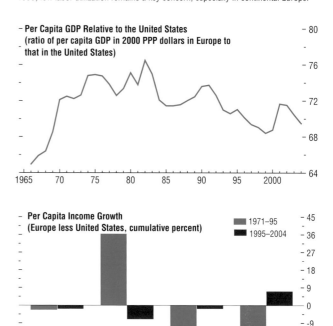

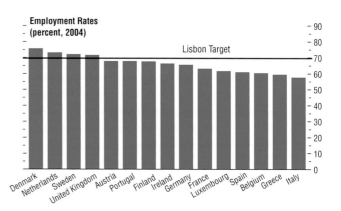

Sources: OECD, *Economic Outlook;* Eurostat; and IMF staff calculations.
[1] Includes differences in age structure of the population.

governments will need to make the case for reform more clearly, including—as the Kok (2004) report stresses—bringing out clearly the costs of failing to act; preparation of National Action Plans under the revised Lisbon Agenda, and their debate in parliament, will be an important step in that process.

Japan: A Strong Rebound, but Reforms Need to Continue

The Japanese economy expanded strongly in the first half of 2005, driven by a recovery in private final domestic demand. Robust private consumption was underpinned by a strengthening labor market—full-time employment is expanding for the first time in seven years and wage growth has turned positive—while business investment grew strongly as corporate profitability remained high. Net exports, however, contributed little to growth, marking a turnaround from earlier in the cycle when exports—particularly to China and the rest of emerging Asia—were the main growth engine.

Recent indicators suggest that the positive growth momentum seen in the first half of the year will continue. The recovery in wages and employment is continuing to support private consumption, the June Tankan survey showed business confidence increasing and firms revising upward their investment plans, and progress was made in reducing inventories in the second quarter. Export growth is also expected to rebound as the global economic environment remains supportive and the IT sector adjustment runs its course. Consequently, real GDP is now projected to expand by 2 percent in both 2005 and 2006. While domestic demand is recovering, there are downside risks to the outlook, particularly given the continued rise in oil prices and the possibility of renewed upward pressures on the yen in an environment of large global current account imbalances.

Considerable progress has been made in addressing weaknesses in the bank and corporate sectors in recent years, and this progress has put the economy in a better position to sustain an expansion. In particular, the Financial Services Agency has increased its regulatory pressure on banks, and in turn this has forced banks to deal more forcefully with their problem borrowers. As a consequence of these actions, and the cyclical recovery in the economy, nonperforming loans have fallen by more than one-half among the major banks (somewhat less for the regional banks), corporate debt levels have declined, excess capacity in the corporate sector has fallen, and the return on assets in the bank and corporate sectors has increased (Figure 1.14). Further, the coverage of deposit insurance was successfully scaled back at end-March 2005, evidence of solid public confidence in banking system stability.

This reform momentum in the bank and corporate sectors needs to be maintained. To this end, the government has announced a program to create a more efficient and flexible financial system ("The Program for Further Financial Reform"). Some of the key issues that will need to be addressed in the period ahead are as follows.

- The profitability of Japanese banks—which is low by international standards—needs to be increased and the banks' capital bases strengthened so they can better support growth. One component of raising profitability will be to increase interest margins, including by improving credit assessment processes and ensuring that loans, particularly to higher risk borrowers, are appropriately priced (see Bank of Japan, 2001, 2004).[14] This process will be aided by planned steps to improve risk management and tighten regulation using the Basel II Accord of the Basel Committee on Banking Supervision as the overarching framework. Recent large bank mergers have been

---

[14]Noninterest income of Japanese banks is also low compared with that of their U.S. counterparts (see Chapter II of the September 2005 *Global Financial Stability Report*).

undertaken with a view to raising profitability. The envisioned privatization of Japan Post will also help bank profitability if it eliminates the competitive advantages that this government-owned entity with huge bank and insurance businesses currently enjoys.

- The corporate sector needs to earn a higher rate of return on its assets, with reform particularly needed in the domestically oriented sectors of the economy. While the manufacturing sector has made significant strides in boosting profitability since the recession in 2001, much less progress has been made in the construction, retail, and wholesale sectors. Moreover, despite the considerable progress in deleveraging, corporate debt remains elevated in some sectors and further adjustment seems desirable.

As highlighted in the recent report by the expert committee of the Council on Economic and Fiscal Policy ("Japan's 21st Century Vision"), structural reforms are needed to raise productivity, allow the Japanese economy to reap the full benefits of globalization, and cope with ongoing population aging. Among the most important are steps to increase product market competition; improve flexibility in the labor market; encourage foreign direct investment, which remains very low by international standards; and reduce agricultural trade protection.

Mild deflation continues, with the core CPI declining by 0.2 percent (year-on-year) in July, and the GDP deflator falling by 0.9 percent (year-on-year) in the second quarter of the year. Land prices (residential and commercial) are also still declining, although at a slowing rate (and are actually now rising in central Tokyo). Until deflation is decisively beaten, it is important that the Bank of Japan maintain its very accommodative monetary policy stance. A premature end to the existing quantitative easing framework would endanger the progress that has been made in tackling deflation in recent years. Consideration needs to be given to how to guide expectations when inflation returns, and the announcement of an explicit medium-term inflation objective could be a useful

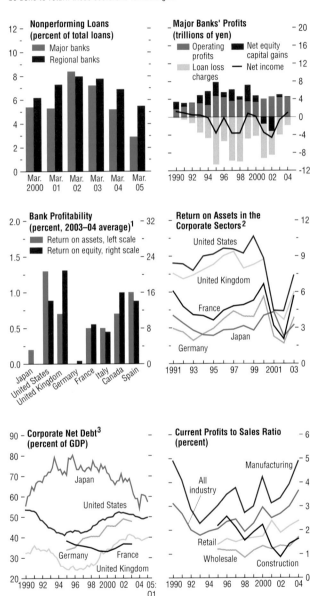

Figure 1.14. Japan: Indicators of Bank and Corporate Sector Financial Health

Considerable progress has been made in strengthening the bank and corporate sectors in Japan. International comparisons, however, suggest that more needs to be done to return these sectors to full strength.

Sources: National authorities; Financial Services Agency; Fitch Research; European Central Bank; Haver Analytics; CEIC Data Company Limited; and IMF staff calculations.
[1] 2002–03 average for Germany, France, and Italy because 2004 data were not yet available.
[2] Percent, mean-weighted by market capitalization.
[3] Defined as financial liabilities less financial assets of the nonfinancial corporate sector.

Table 1.6. Selected Asian Economies: Real GDP, Consumer Prices, and Current Account Balance
(Annual percent change unless otherwise noted)

	Real GDP				Consumer Prices[1]				Current Account Balance[2]			
	2003	2004	2005	2006	2003	2004	2005	2006	2003	2004	2005	2006
Emerging Asia[3]	**7.5**	**7.9**	**7.3**	**6.9**	**2.4**	**4.0**	**3.9**	**4.4**	**4.3**	**4.1**	**3.7**	**3.4**
China	9.5	9.5	9.0	8.2	1.2	3.9	3.0	3.8	3.2	4.2	6.1	5.6
South Asia[4]	**7.1**	**7.1**	**7.0**	**6.3**	**3.9**	**4.3**	**4.7**	**5.6**	**1.3**	**−0.2**	**−1.9**	**−2.1**
India	7.4	7.3	7.1	6.3	3.8	3.8	3.9	5.1	1.2	−0.1	−1.8	−2.0
Pakistan	5.7	7.1	7.4	6.5	2.9	7.4	9.9	9.8	3.4	0.2	−1.7	−2.3
Bangladesh	5.8	5.8	5.7	6.0	5.4	6.1	6.2	5.8	0.2	−0.4	−1.5	−1.8
ASEAN-4	**5.4**	**5.8**	**4.9**	**5.4**	**4.1**	**4.5**	**6.4**	**5.1**	**5.5**	**4.4**	**2.2**	**2.4**
Indonesia	4.9	5.1	5.8	5.8	6.8	6.1	8.2	6.5	3.4	1.2	−0.4	0.7
Thailand	6.9	6.1	3.5	5.0	1.8	2.7	4.2	2.7	5.6	4.5	−2.5	−2.5
Philippines	4.5	6.0	4.7	4.8	3.5	6.0	8.2	7.5	1.8	2.7	2.1	1.9
Malaysia	5.4	7.1	5.5	6.0	1.1	1.4	3.0	2.5	12.9	12.6	13.5	12.4
Newly industrialized Asian economies	**3.1**	**5.6**	**4.0**	**4.7**	**1.5**	**2.4**	**2.2**	**2.3**	**7.4**	**7.2**	**5.5**	**5.0**
Korea	3.1	4.6	3.8	5.0	3.5	3.6	2.8	2.9	2.0	4.1	2.0	1.5
Taiwan Province of China	3.3	5.7	3.4	4.3	−0.3	1.6	2.0	1.8	10.2	6.1	4.3	4.6
Hong Kong SAR	3.2	8.1	6.3	4.5	−2.6	−0.4	1.0	1.3	10.3	9.8	10.3	10.2
Singapore	1.4	8.4	3.9	4.5	0.5	1.7	0.7	1.7	29.2	26.1	25.7	22.7

[1]In accordance with standard practice in the *World Economic Outlook,* movements in consumer prices are indicated as annual averages rather than as December/December changes, as is the practice in some countries.
[2]Percent of GDP.
[3]Consists of developing Asia, the newly industrialized Asian economies, and Mongolia.
[4]The country composition of this regional group is set out in Table F in the Statistical Appendix.

element of a post-deflation monetary policy framework.

Sustained fiscal consolidation is needed to reverse the ongoing rise in public debt and to make room for the pressures that population aging will place on the budget. Against this background, a further reduction in the budget deficit is envisaged during 2005–06, and the government has announced the goal of achieving primary budget balance (excluding social security) by the early 2010s, which would require a fiscal adjustment of about ½ percent of GDP a year. While welcome, this target may not, however, be sufficient to stabilize public debt over the medium term, and more ambitious fiscal consolidation—on the order of ¾ percentage point of GDP a year—is likely to be needed.[15] Such fiscal consolidation will be more easily maintained in an environment of sustained solid growth, again emphasizing the importance of continued structural reforms. Further, the gov-

ernment has announced few details of how it intends to achieve its fiscal objectives, and the early publication of a more concrete deficit reduction strategy would enhance the credibility of fiscal policy.

Emerging Asia and the Pacific: Balanced, Twin-Engined Growth Needed

In 2004, GDP growth in emerging Asia's economies rose to 7.9 percent, driven by vigorous exports and a marked pickup in domestic demand in late 2003 and early 2004, underpinned by supportive macroeconomic policies and financial market conditions (Table 1.6). However, from mid-2004, regional divergences increased markedly: while growth in China and India remained relatively robust, the expansion in much of the rest of the region slowed, reflecting the impact of higher oil prices and the IT sector correction. With conditions in the IT sec-

[15]See IMF (2005a)

tor starting to improve, and recent data suggesting that industrial production and trade in the region are picking up, the expansion is expected to strengthen during the year, with regional GDP growth projected to average over 7 percent in 2005 and close to that in 2006. Regional inflation picked up in 2004, but—with some exceptions—remains well contained.

Within this broad picture, consistent with the assessment for the globe as a whole, risks are increasingly slanted to the downside. Persistently high oil prices will adversely affect activity, especially since a number of countries—including India, Indonesia, Malaysia, and Thailand—have yet to pass through the full effect of past increases to domestic prices, in some cases at substantial fiscal cost. More generally, much depends on the strength of the pickup in the IT sector as well as developments in the United States and, increasingly, China (Figure 1.15). Elsewhere in the region—with the exception of India, and to some extent Indonesia and Thailand—there are only modest signs of autonomous domestic demand-led growth. Consequently, the region has a particularly large stake in an orderly reduction of global imbalances and the avoidance of a pickup in protectionist pressures. Country-specific risks are also a concern, including in Indonesia, where excess liquidity and the rising budgetary cost of oil subsidies led to significant financial market pressures in late August, and in the Philippines, where, after several months of improving fundamentals, the recent political turmoil has raised concerns about the prospects for economic reforms and led to downward revisions to the ratings outlook.

On the external side, the regional current account surplus is projected to decline only modestly from 4.1 percent of GDP to 3.7 percent of GDP in 2005. This aggregate figure disguises sharply different trends across the region, with a marked increase in the current account surplus in China to over 6 percent of GDP offset by reductions—to varying degrees—elsewhere in the region (except in Hong Kong SAR and Malaysia). In China, this has reflected continued

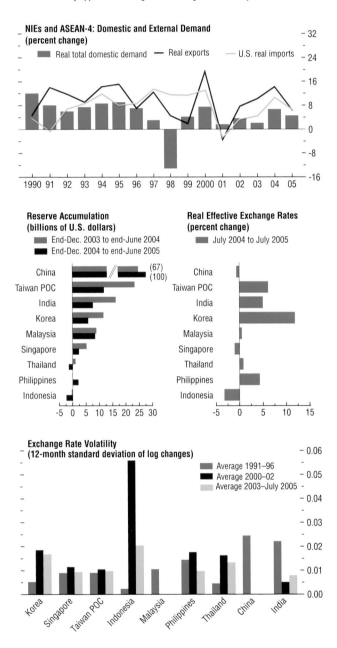

Figure 1.15. Emerging Asia: Growth, Reserves, and Exchange Rate Flexibility

With little autonomous domestic demand in Asia, the outlook is closely linked to export growth. A shift toward domestic demand will need to be accompanied by nominal currency appreciation and greater exchange rate flexibility.

Sources: CEIC Data Company Limited; IMF, *International Financial Statistics;* and IMF staff calculations.

rapid growth in manufacturing exports—aided by the ending of textile quotas—along with a sharp slowdown in import growth, seemingly related to slowing demand for imported capital goods as well as import substitution in some sectors. Elsewhere, weaker current account positions reflect a variety of factors, including higher oil prices, slower growth in IT exports, and exchange rate appreciation (Korea, Taiwan Province of China); and country-specific factors, including the adverse effect of the tsunami (Thailand). There have been similar shifts in the composition of reserve accumulation in the region. Although the monthly average pace of reserve accumulation in emerging Asia thus far in 2005 remains broadly unchanged from 2003 and 2004, China now accounts for nearly two-thirds of the regional average, compared with less than one-third in the previous two years.

Looking forward, the key challenge facing the region remains to achieve appropriately balanced, twin-engined, growth consistent with an orderly reduction in external surpluses over the medium term. In China, where investment is very strong, this will require a gradual shift in the composition of demand toward private consumption, which—at 40 percent of GDP—is at a historic low. In most other countries, as discussed in more detail in Chapter II, the continued very low level of private investment is the greater concern, underscoring the need to complete the unfinished reform agenda in financial and corporate sector restructuring, including improvements in governance. A shift in the composition of growth toward domestic demand will need to be accompanied by a corresponding appreciation of regional exchange rates over the medium term (Appendix 1.2). While the inflationary impact of strong external surpluses has been contained through extensive sterilization, such a strategy will become increasingly difficult over time, and exposes regional central banks to growing capital losses on their reserves. Against this background, a gradual move to greater exchange rate flexibility remains critical. In this connection, the recent exchange rate reforms in China—and the shift to a managed float in

Malaysia—are important steps in the right direction, both for the countries concerned and for the region, and the scope for greater exchange rate flexibility afforded by the reforms should be taken full advantage of in the period ahead.

Turning to individual countries, the expansion in China has continued to exceed expectations, with GDP growth now forecast at 9 percent in 2005, easing to 8¼ percent in 2006. Investment growth has moderated somewhat from the levels of early 2004, reflecting a variety of administrative and monetary tightening measures, but remains above 20 percent; moreover, the contribution from net exports has risen sharply, as described above. With large external surpluses continuing to add to considerable excess liquidity in the banking system, open market operations need to be strengthened to reduce excess liquidity, and further monetary tightening will be needed if signs of a rebound in investment growth intensify. The currency reform in July—comprising an initial 2 percent revaluation of the renminbi, a shift to setting the central rate with reference to a currency basket, and an allowable daily fluctuation rate of 0.3 percentage point against the U.S. dollar—is an important step toward greater flexibility, which, if fully utilized, should facilitate the conduct of monetary policy in the period ahead. On the fiscal side, the projected reduction in the budget deficit in 2005, along with continued gradual fiscal consolidation thereafter, will help address large off-budget fiscal liabilities and make room for future demands on public funds arising from population aging, bank restructuring, and public enterprise reform without jeopardizing debt sustainability. More generally, further reform of the banking system and public enterprises and the development of domestic capital markets remain critical to maintaining macroeconomic stability and ensuring that China's large savings are efficiently utilized to support medium-term growth. Measures to address rural-urban disparities, including through improving conditions for interregional labor mobility, are also needed.

Economic activity in India is expected to moderate from the strong pace of the past two years to about 7 percent in 2005. Strong domestic demand arising from the industrial recovery, and higher oil prices, have led to a sharp widening of the trade balance, but buoyant service exports and remittances are expected to help limit the impact on the current account deficit. After rising sharply in mid-2004, inflation has fallen to the mid-single digits thanks in part to the incomplete pass-through of oil prices as well as monetary tightening; however, underlying inflationary pressures and rapid nonfood credit growth bear close monitoring. While progress has been made in reducing the general government deficit, aided by lower interest rates and reduced subsidies, it remains close to 8 percent of GDP (and off-budget costs of oil price subsidies have risen). Consequently, further fiscal consolidation remains a priority, including tax base broadening and full pass-through of oil price increases, as well as improvements in states' finances; the uniform state-level value-added tax (VAT) introduced in April 2005 may prove crucial in this regard. It is now critical to build a political consensus to significantly accelerate the pace of structural reforms, to ensure that India can achieve growth of 7–8 percent, absorb its growing labor force, and realize the demographic "dividend" (Box 1.4, "Is India Becoming an Engine for Global Growth?"). Much greater progress is needed in building infrastructure—including especially in the energy sector, where India is forecast to experience rapid demand growth in the next two decades; in increasing labor market flexibility and dismantling regulatory impediments in product markets; and in pension reforms.

Growth in Pakistan and Bangladesh is expected to remain strong in 2005, underpinned by robust agricultural and manufacturing growth, and supportive macroeconomic policies. An important challenge in Pakistan is to deal decisively with the overheating of the economy, with the authorities needing to stand ready to take additional monetary policy tightening measures. Fiscal policy needs to be managed tightly to reduce the burden on monetary policy to contain demand pressures. The strong growth in

exports of cotton manufactures in early 2005 suggests that Pakistan's investments in the textile sector in anticipation of the expiry of quotas are paying off. In contrast, Bangladesh—the first country to benefit from assistance under the Trade Integration Mechanism—is expected to be negatively affected by the quota expiry although recent measures by the European Union and the United States to curtail garment imports from China may moderate the impact, underscoring the need for flexible exchange rate management. In both countries, priority needs to be given to energy sector reforms, and in Bangladesh, tax, trade, and investment regime reforms are also needed to achieve sustained high growth.

Following a slowdown from mid-2004, GDP growth in the NIEs and ASEAN-4 countries is generally projected to pick up in the second half of 2005 and in 2006. With policy rates still at or close to zero in real terms, and inflationary pressures edging upward, monetary policy tightening in most countries has continued, with the important exception of Korea, where low interest rates have helped to lift consumption by reducing household debt burdens. With the exception of Malaysia, where the ringgit has appreciated marginally since the introduction of the managed float, most ASEAN-4 currencies have come under downward pressure, particularly in Indonesia as noted above. Following the Bank of Indonesia's announcement of an increase in interest rates and reserve requirements in late August, financial markets have stabilized but remain fragile; the government also announced that domestic fuel prices would be raised after October, although with no set timetable or specificity on the extent of the increase. Looking forward, the key macroeconomic priorities remain continued fiscal consolidation—particularly in the Philippines, where large external financing requirements and high public debt remain significant vulnerabilities—along with structural measures to support medium-term growth and boost still-low private investment (Chapter II). Beyond the unfinished agenda of corporate and financial

Box 1.4. Is India Becoming an Engine for Global Growth?

India's recent growth performance places it among the world's fastest growing economies. India experienced 7.7 percent annual growth in 2003–04, higher than growth in all other Asian economies except China, and well above its own trend growth rate since the early 1990s of about 6 percent. As a result, India's share of world output, at PPP-adjusted exchange rates, has increased from about 4.3 percent in 1990 to 5.8 percent in 2004.

One question arising from India's recent robust growth is whether it has become an engine for global growth. Given its sheer size, the pickup in growth in India has had an impact on world growth, albeit substantially smaller than that of China. Over the past two years, India has accounted for just under one-fifth of Asian growth and almost 10 percent of world growth, compared with 53 percent and 28 percent, respectively, for China. However, spillovers from Indian growth remain limited. For example, IMF staff estimates that the acceleration in Indian import growth during 2003–04 had only a marginal spillover to regional growth, adding 0.1–0.4 percentage point to growth in selected Asian countries.

India's limited role to date as a growth engine reflects the fact that it remains a relatively closed economy. While its recent growth performance is comparable to take-offs experienced by other Asian economies in the last quarter-century, it has been far less dependent on global and regional trade (see the figure). Although India has received much attention for its success as an outsourcing destination and is attracting large financial inflows,[1] trade linkages remain weak. India still only accounts for 2½ percent of the global trade in goods and services, which is small when compared with the shares of China and the newly industrialized Asian economies (10½ percent and 9.3 percent, respectively). India's participation in regional and global production chains is also in its infancy. For exam-

Note: The main author of this box is Catriona Purfield.
[1]In 2004, India accounted for one-fourth of the portfolio flows to emerging Asia.

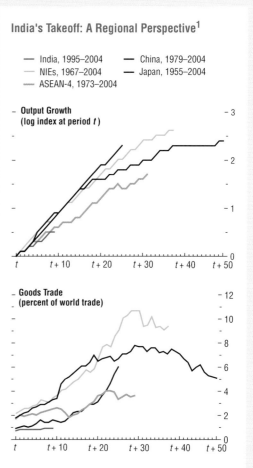

India's Takeoff: A Regional Perspective[1]

— India, 1995–2004   — China, 1979–2004
— NIEs, 1967–2004   — Japan, 1955–2004
— ASEAN-4, 1973–2004

Source: IMF staff estimates.
[1]Take-off is defined as the point when a country experienced real growth of at least 10 percent in the three-year moving average of the value of exports.

ple, the share of intraregional trade in the total trade of nonindustrial Asia rose from 27½ percent in 1986–90 to 38 percent in 1998–2002, but India's contribution to this trade remains small, at less than 1 percent.

Various factors have hindered India's integration. Despite substantial tariff reductions in recent years, India remains a relatively protected economy, with tariffs averaging 22 percent (18 percent in trade-weighted terms)—above the average emerging Asia and global tariff rates of 9½ percent and 11½ percent, respectively—and significant nontrade barriers remain. Moreover, a range of structural impediments—including restrictive labor laws and onerous red tape—have retarded the growth of manufacturing, which has been the main driver of export-oriented growth in Asia. Reflecting this, the contribution of industry to GDP and employment, at 27 percent and 34 percent respectively, remains well below that of Asia as a whole. Foreign direct investment (FDI) has been hindered by a difficult business climate as well as by caps on FDI in certain sectors (Jain-Chandra, 2005). And the growing inadequacy of India's infrastructure constitutes a major obstacle to private investment and export potential. Fay and Yepes (2003) estimate that infrastructure investment would need to rise to 7–8 percent of GDP a year, an increase of 3 percent of GDP, if India is to maintain its current trend growth. But progress in addressing this bottleneck has been constrained by persistent large fiscal deficits, which, although declining in recent years, remain in the 8 percent of GDP range.

Despite these constraints, India's recent growth spurt has been accompanied by a marked opening to the global economy, albeit from a relatively closed starting point. In 2003–04, India's imports (including services) rose by 33 percent a year, 4 times as fast as in 1990–2002, buoyed by strong investment and consumer demand. Exports grew by 34 percent a year, up from 8 percent in 1990–2002, as India's steel and petrochemical industries have benefited from the global commodity boom and India expanded into engineering goods, pharmaceuticals, and business services. Asia has been a major beneficiary of India's growing openness, although, as already noted, the impact on regional growth has been small. By end-2004, Asia's share in Indian goods imports had risen to 28 percent, up 4 percentage points since 2000. India's exports to Asia accounted for one-third of its total goods exports in 2004, up from less than one-fourth in 2000, driven by the increase in trade with China. Between 2003–04, the growth in exports to China accounted for 15 percent of India's total export growth.

With the authorities actively seeking to strengthen global linkages, India should begin playing a bigger role in the world economy. The IMF staff projects that over the period 2004/05–2009/10, Indian exports will more than double, while imports will nearly triple. The government's objectives are even more ambitious. In this context, tariffs have been reduced significantly, and the government aims to reach ASEAN levels in the next several years by reducing the simple average tariff rate by almost 11 percentage points. Regional trade agreements are being negotiated with South Asia, Mercosur, ASEAN, and China, among others. Controls on inward FDI and external commercial borrowing by domestic firms are being eased and the emergence of world-class Indian corporates is being encouraged by the lifting of controls on outward investment. India has made a start in creating fiscal space for greater public investment, and is seeking to attract greater private participation in infrastructure.

A dynamic and open Indian economy would have an important impact on the world economy. If India continues to embrace globalization and reform, Indian imports could increasingly operate as a driver of global growth as it is one of a handful of economies forecast to have a growing working-age population over the next 40 years. Some 75–110 million will enter the labor force in the next decade, which should—provided these entrants are employed—fuel an increase in savings and investment given the higher propensity for workers to save. Faster growth, rising incomes, and the accompanying urbanization and industrialization of India will, however, exert further pressure on the already tight global energy market. As the seventh-largest importer of crude oil in the world, India is one of the world's more energy-intensive economies, importing over 70 percent of its oil needs. However, with vehicle ownership forecast to quadruple by 2030, oil demand and its dependence on imported crude is likely to rise. Such estimates may be conservative, however, as car ownership could be expected to rise much faster if growth continues to accelerate from trend levels. India's emergence alongside China will thus present important economic opportunities, as well as challenges for the global economy.

sector reforms, key issues include upgrading infrastructure including in the power sector (Indonesia, the Philippines, and Thailand), reducing skill shortages (Malaysia), and further trade liberalization and rationalization of the regulatory environment (Indonesia, Korea, and Thailand).

After several years of steady strong growth in Australia and New Zealand, the pace of activity is forecast to moderate in both countries. The slowing in Australia reflects a welcome cooling of the housing market and the impact of the appreciated exchange rate. Similar trends are at work in New Zealand, although weak growth in exports is likely to play a greater role in the slow-down. Capacity utilization and unemployment rates remain at or near record levels in both economies, but inflation remains under control, owing to timely tightening of monetary policy in both countries. The external current account deficits have widened markedly in both coun-tries, reflecting the appreciation of their curren-cies, with the deterioration being sharper in New Zealand owing to the strength of domestic demand; but a rebalancing of growth from external sources is expected in coming years, given the strength of global commodity demand, especially for the commodities exported by Australia. Medium-term prospects in both Australia and New Zealand are strong, owing to a consistent track record of fiscal prudence and structural reforms aimed at maintaining compet-itive product markets and flexible labor markets. Fiscal policy has been focused on generating operating surpluses and reducing debt, as the authorities continue to prepare for long-term spending pressures from population aging and rising health care costs. As for structural reforms, the Australian government has intro-duced tax and welfare reforms to improve work incentives. In addition, it has announced plans for significant reform of the industrial relations system aimed at moving toward a single national system, reducing the coverage of unfair dismissal laws, changing the determination of minimum wages, and increasing flexibility in working conditions.

Latin America: Will This Be a More Resilient Expansion?

In Latin America, growth has moderated to a more sustainable pace after a sharp rebound in 2004 (Table 1.7). Strong commodity and raw material exports and—in most large economies—broad terms-of-trade gains continue to support the growth momentum, although manufacturing exports have weakened somewhat in tandem with the slowdown in global manufacturing. After some uptick in the second half of 2004, inflation in the region has generally stabilized, but remains volatile with continued heightened commodity price variability. Looking forward, the expansion is projected to continue at a solid pace, with growth remaining above the 1990s average through 2005–06, underpinned by both external and domestic demand growth.

There are downside risks to the near-term outlook, including in particular a weakening of global nonfuel commodities markets, from a slowing of industrial country growth—particularly in the United States if the impact of Hurricane Katrina is greater than currently expected—or from a sharper rise in interest rates in industrial countries. Moreover, if spreads on emerging market debt were to widen, this would adversely affect budget and external posi-tions in many countries and, given high levels of public debt and financial dollarization, increase vulnerabilities. Further increases in oil prices could add to these vulnerabilities in net oil importers, although they would further benefit oil-exporting countries in the region. Rising political uncertainties, as a result of both country-specific events and the crowded regional election schedule over the next year, are also a source of risk, underscoring the need for contin-ued sound policy implementation and cautious debt management.

Nevertheless, prospects are that the current expansion will be more resilient than earlier ones (Figure 1.16). In particular, the availability of external financing is less likely to become a con-straint for sustained, low-inflation growth, as growth has been driven to an important extent by strong and geographically more diversified

Table 1.7. Selected Western Hemisphere Countries: Real GDP, Consumer Prices, and Current Account Balance

(Annual percent change unless otherwise noted)

	Real GDP				Consumer Prices[1]				Current Account Balance[2]			
	2003	2004	2005	2006	2003	2004	2005	2006	2003	2004	2005	2006
Western Hemisphere	**2.2**	**5.6**	**4.1**	**3.8**	**10.6**	**6.5**	**6.3**	**5.4**	**0.4**	**0.9**	**0.9**	**0.6**
Mercosur[3]	**2.7**	**6.0**	**4.4**	**3.8**	**13.4**	**5.7**	**7.0**	**5.8**	**1.4**	**1.9**	**1.4**	**0.4**
Argentina	8.8	9.0	7.5	4.2	13.4	4.4	9.5	10.4	5.8	2.0	1.3	0.1
Brazil	0.5	4.9	3.3	3.5	14.8	6.6	6.8	4.6	0.8	1.9	1.7	0.7
Chile	3.7	6.1	5.9	5.8	2.8	1.1	2.9	3.3	−1.5	1.5	0.3	−0.7
Uruguay	2.2	12.3	6.0	4.0	19.4	9.2	5.2	6.5	−0.3	−0.8	−2.8	−5.3
Andean region	**1.6**	**7.5**	**5.1**	**4.1**	**10.5**	**8.4**	**6.5**	**6.7**	**3.4**	**4.2**	**5.4**	**5.9**
Colombia	4.1	4.1	4.0	4.0	7.1	5.9	5.2	4.8	−1.5	−1.0	−1.8	−1.5
Ecuador	2.7	6.9	2.7	2.8	7.9	2.7	2.0	2.0	−1.8	—	0.2	2.4
Peru	4.0	4.8	5.5	4.5	2.3	3.7	1.8	2.6	−1.8	—	0.3	0.3
Venezuela	−7.7	17.9	7.8	4.5	31.1	21.7	16.6	18.0	13.6	12.7	15.9	14.9
Mexico, Central America, and Caribbean	**1.7**	**4.0**	**3.1**	**3.6**	**6.0**	**7.1**	**4.9**	**4.2**	**−1.7**	**−1.3**	**−1.4**	**−1.1**
Mexico	1.4	4.4	3.0	3.5	4.5	4.7	4.3	3.6	−1.4	−1.1	−1.1	−0.8
Central America[3]	3.5	3.6	3.2	3.2	5.8	7.8	7.7	5.7	−5.0	−4.9	−5.1	−4.4
The Caribbean[3]	1.6	2.1	3.6	4.8	18.6	27.2	5.9	6.6	−0.4	1.3	−0.5	−0.9

[1]In accordance with standard practice in the *World Economic Outlook*, movements in consumer prices are indicated as annual averages rather than as December/December changes, as is the practice in some countries. The December/December changes in the CPI for 2003, 2004, 2005, and 2006 are, respectively, for Brazil (9.3, 7.6, 5.1, and 4.5); for Mexico (4.0, 5.2, 3.9, and 3.4); for Peru (2.5, 3.5, 1.8, and 2.5), and for Uruguay (10.2, 7.6, 6.5, and 5.5).

[2]Percent of GDP.

[3]The country composition of this regional group is set out in Table F in the Statistical Appendix.

exports and by terms-of-trade gains. Some countries are now running small current account surpluses—with the regional surplus expected to average more than ½ percent of GDP in 2005–06. In contrast, capital inflows provided much of the impetus in earlier recovery episodes, and growth was largely driven by domestic demand, with current account deficits widening and real exchange rates appreciating in the process. Another factor has been the reduction in the exposure to some short-term risks relative to earlier periods, as many governments have used the current benign international financial conditions to prefinance forthcoming debt service obligations, while current account and external reserves positions are much stronger. Improved macroeconomic policy frameworks have also helped the expansion's resilience. The strengthening of fiscal positions—in contrast to the procyclical policies that led to larger deficits in earlier periods—has been an important step forward, reinforced by the greater focus on achieving and sustaining low inflation—including

through the adoption of inflation-targeting frameworks in Brazil, Chile, Colombia, Mexico, and Peru (see Chapter IV, "Does Inflation Targeting Work in Emerging Markets?").

The improved resilience bodes well for the future but, going forward, it will also be important to build on the foundations for higher sustained growth, not only for reasons of insurance—the strong global commodity prices and demand that have partly underpinned strong export growth may not last—but also to close the gap with the growth performance in other dynamic emerging market regions. This will require addressing the fundamental causes of low saving and investment ratios, which continue to lag those in other regions. While the efforts at reducing macroeconomic vulnerabilities will help, complementary structural policy reforms still have some way to go. Specifically, further progress is needed in fostering trade openness and foreign direct investment, in strengthening the rule of law and the enforcement of contracts, and in improving regulatory

Figure 1.16. Latin America: An Anatomy of Recent Expansions

The resilience of the expansions in Latin America has improved compared with earlier ones, helped by strong and more diversified export growth, less reliance on capital inflows, and strong current account and reserve positions.

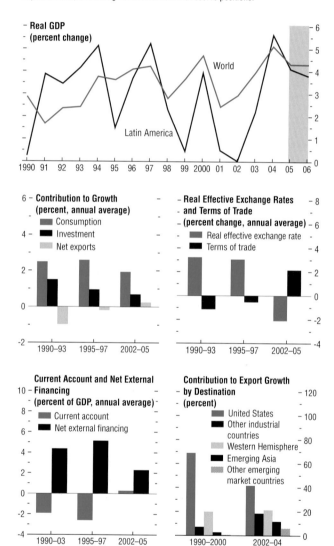

Sources: IMF, *Direction of Trade Statistics;* and IMF staff calculations.

frameworks governing the business environ-ment, including by strengthening competition policy.

Turning to individual countries, economic growth in Argentina has lost some of last year's strong rebound momentum, but remains robust. With growing wage pressures and some mone-tary accommodation on account of unsterilized foreign exchange interventions, inflation has accelerated, with annual rates rising from 6 per-cent at end-2004 to above 9 percent in July. While the policy interest rates were raised, fur-ther tightening is required, not least in view of the procyclical fiscal easing targeted in the 2005 budget. To sustain solid growth over the medium term, prudent fiscal policies, structural reforms—including the phased elimination of distortionary taxes, the strengthening of the institutional framework of intergovernmental fis-cal relations, and improved incentives for private sector participation in the provision of public services—and a resolution of the remaining arrears to private creditors will be required. In Uruguay, growth is projected to slow from over 12 percent in 2004 to 6 percent this year, partly reflecting a closing output gap, moderating growth in trading partners, and terms-of-trade losses. Financial indicators have improved, but significant vulnerabilities related to the high public debt and dollarization remain. Reforms to ensure sustained rapid growth and sufficiently large primary budget surpluses to put debt on a firm downward path will be the key policy challenges.

In Brazil, growth slowed from mid-2004, as domestic demand moderated in response to the tightening of the monetary policy stance, but rebounded in the second quarter of 2005, led by recovery in private consumption and investment. Growth for the year as a whole is now projected at 3.3 percent (compared with 3.7 percent in the April 2005 *World Economic Outlook*), owing prima-rily to a weaker-than-expected first quarter. Recent activity indicators point to some upside potential to the growth outlook, but higher oil prices and the possible fallout from the political uncertainties add to the downside risks. After rising from 6.5 percent at end-December 2004 to over 8 percent in May, inflation declined to 6 percent in August. Inflation expectations for end-2005 are now close to the end-2005 mid-point target of 5.1 percent, and further declines in core inflation would allow for a gradual easing of the monetary stance. Fiscal performance remains favorable, with the primary surplus running above target through July, and maintaining a tight fiscal stance will be key to reducing public debt ratios further. In view of the need to accommodate essential social and infrastructure spending while maintaining large budget surpluses, reforms are needed to reduce budgetary rigidities and increase the quality and efficiency of spending. Economic activity in Chile continues to expand at a robust pace, driven by favorable export developments and a pickup in investment. Inflation has remained around the midpoint of the official target range, although core inflation has begun to rise, and the central bank has appropriately continued to tighten monetary policy. The government continues to adhere to the structural budget balance rule, and with strong growth and high copper prices, the central government surplus is projected to rise to close to 3 percent of GDP this year.

In the Andean region, economic activity in Venezuela expanded strongly in 2005, underpinned by an expansionary fiscal policy. Inflation remains high but has declined, reflecting continued price controls and some tightening of monetary policy. Favorable oil market conditions provide an opportunity for lasting improvements on the recent erratic growth performance through decisive measures to strengthen the fiscal position, liberalize the economy, and improve the investment climate. In Colombia, growth held steady in early 2005 with strong export growth, while inflation continued to decline. The fiscal situation is improving and ensuring public debt sustainability remains a key medium-term policy challenge. Structural fiscal reforms are needed to support the authorities' budget targets, including reducing the extent of distortionary taxes, simplifying the value-added

tax, and strengthening the revenue-sharing mechanism between the central and regional governments. In Peru, growth remains buoyant, driven by high commodity prices and strong exports, a rebound in agricultural output, and a recovery in fixed investment. Progress in reducing the budget deficit has helped to lower public debt, but the legal and institutional frameworks for fiscal management need to be strengthened further, including at the subnational level. In Ecuador, growth in early 2005 remained solid on the back of higher oil exports—owing to volume and price increases—despite the political crisis, although downside risks to the outlook have increased. High oil prices are masking fiscal vulnerabilities, and measures to modify the fiscal policy framework and the social security system have weakened investor confidence despite declines in public debt. In Bolivia, macroeconomic developments remain favorable, although the uncertain political situation and the highly dollarized financial system present important risks.

In Mexico, growth slowed more than expected in the first half of 2005, reflecting the soft patch in U.S. industrial production and a corresponding slump in automobile-related exports and weak agricultural production. It is expected, however, to rebound in the second half of the year—supported by the recovery in the U.S. manufacturing sector, and steady domestic demand—and annual growth in 2005 is projected at 3 percent. A year of steady and substantial monetary policy tightening—short-term rates rose approximately 500 basis points from early 2004 to April 2005—helped bring core inflation down to 3.4 percent at midyear. The Bank of Mexico started to ease its policy stance in late August, but any relaxation is likely to be gradual, as the bank remains concerned that inflation and inflation expectations are still above its 3 percent target. On the fiscal side, oil revenues are likely to again exceed budget projections, and the priority should be on using these additional revenues to reduce the public debt, although there is also some scope for increasing capital expenditure. Further structural reforms

Table 1.8. Emerging Europe: Real GDP, Consumer Prices, and Current Account Balance
(Annual percent change unless otherwise noted)

	Real GDP				Consumer Prices[1]				Current Account Balance[2]			
	2003	2004	2005	2006	2003	2004	2005	2006	2003	2004	2005	2006
Emerging Europe	**4.6**	**6.6**	**4.3**	**4.6**	**9.5**	**6.7**	**4.9**	**4.4**	**−4.3**	**−4.9**	**−4.8**	**−4.9**
Turkey	5.8	8.9	5.0	5.0	25.2	10.3	8.4	6.9	−3.3	−5.1	−5.6	−5.3
Excluding Turkey	4.1	5.6	4.1	4.4	3.7	5.2	3.5	3.3	−4.8	−4.8	−4.4	−4.8
Baltics	**8.4**	**7.5**	**7.1**	**6.5**	**0.6**	**3.1**	**4.0**	**3.3**	**−8.5**	**−10.0**	**−9.5**	**−8.8**
Estonia	6.7	7.8	7.0	6.0	1.3	3.0	3.9	2.8	−12.1	−12.7	−10.9	−9.9
Latvia	7.5	8.5	7.8	6.8	2.9	6.3	6.3	5.1	−8.2	−12.3	−10.5	−9.4
Lithuania	9.7	6.7	6.8	6.5	−1.2	1.2	2.7	2.5	−7.0	−7.1	−8.1	−7.9
Central Europe	**3.5**	**5.0**	**3.5**	**4.0**	**2.2**	**4.2**	**2.5**	**2.7**	**−4.0**	**−3.8**	**−3.3**	**−3.8**
Czech Republic	3.2	4.4	4.1	3.9	0.1	2.8	2.0	2.5	−6.1	−5.2	−3.5	−3.2
Hungary	2.9	4.2	3.4	3.6	4.7	6.8	4.0	3.6	−8.8	−8.8	−8.5	−8.0
Poland	3.8	5.4	3.0	4.0	0.8	3.5	2.2	2.5	−2.2	−1.5	−1.0	−2.5
Slovak Republic	4.5	5.5	5.0	5.4	8.5	7.5	2.7	2.7	−0.9	−3.5	−6.3	−6.4
Slovenia	2.5	4.6	3.9	4.0	5.6	3.6	2.6	2.5	−0.4	−0.9	−1.6	−0.8
Southern and south- **eastern Europe**	**4.5**	**6.6**	**4.7**	**4.8**	**9.2**	**8.2**	**6.4**	**5.1**	**−6.6**	**−6.8**	**−7.0**	**−6.7**
Bulgaria	4.3	5.6	5.5	5.5	2.3	6.1	4.4	3.5	−9.2	−7.5	−9.0	−8.5
Croatia	4.3	3.8	3.4	3.9	1.8	2.1	3.0	2.5	−6.0	−4.8	−4.8	−4.1
Cyprus	1.9	3.7	3.8	4.0	4.1	2.3	2.5	2.5	−3.4	−5.8	−4.0	−3.2
Malta	−1.9	1.0	1.5	1.8	1.9	2.7	2.4	1.9	−5.8	−10.4	−10.5	−8.6
Romania	5.2	8.3	5.0	5.0	15.3	11.9	8.8	6.9	−6.8	−7.5	−7.9	−7.8

[1]In accordance with standard practice in the *World Economic Outlook*, movements in consumer prices are indicated as annual averages rather than as December/December changes, as is the practice in some countries.
[2]Percent of GDP.

are needed to boost medium-term growth, including in the energy and telecommunications sectors, labor market reforms to increase productivity and employment in the formal sector, and the strengthening of the judicial and regulatory systems to improve the business climate.

In Central America, growth has begun to ease, reflecting partly lower demand from the United States, but also weaker investor confidence on account of increased political uncertainty in a number of countries. The expected ratification of the Central American Free Trade Agreement (CAFTA) has already provided some impetus to investment, and with the agreement now ratified in the United States and three other countries, governments in the region should strive to use it as an opportunity to boost growth and standards of living—especially those of lower-income households—including through structural reforms aimed at lowering barriers to trade. In the Caribbean, growth is projected to strengthen in 2005, as tourism activity is expected to recover from the losses caused by last year's hurricanes.

The key policy challenge in most countries is to strengthen budgets and ensure public debt sustainability.

Emerging Europe: Is Rapid Credit Growth a Cause for Concern?

Growth in emerging Europe remains robust, although the pace of expansion has eased since the middle of last year (Table 1.8). Exports have been affected by weaker growth in western Europe and the appreciation of regional currencies during 2004, while domestic demand has slowed as the surge in activity in the run-up to EU accession has abated. Indeed, with confidence remaining weak in the euro area and oil prices continuing to rise, the risks to the outlook are slanted to the downside. Nevertheless, concerns remain about possible overheating in some countries. Although inflation remains well contained—headline CPI inflation increased last year due to a number of EU accession–related tax adjustments, but is now returning to lower rates—credit growth is exceptionally strong, property prices have surged, and external imbalances are large.

A key question is whether strong credit growth, which is particularly apparent in the Baltic countries, Bulgaria, Hungary, and Romania, is part of the ongoing process of "financial deepening"—credit-to-GDP ratios still remain relatively low—or whether some countries are now experiencing a credit boom, a situation where credit is expanding at an unsustainable pace (Figure 1.17). The experience in emerging markets shows that credit booms can be very costly—they are typically followed by sharp economic downturns and financial crises.[16] A particular concern at present is that credit is largely being financed by bank borrowing from abroad, encouraged by low international interest rates and relatively stable exchange rates. This stands in contrast to earlier years when credit expansion was financed mostly from domestic deposit accumulation. With foreign currency lending (mostly in euros) representing a large share of outstanding credit, households and small and medium-sized enterprises—which have borrowed heavily in recent years, but are unlikely to have suitable exchange rate hedges—are particularly vulnerable to movements in exchange rates. Banks themselves are also exposed in the event of default on the loans, although the relatively strong prudential indicators do suggest that banking systems in general are well shielded from adverse shocks.

Against this background, measures are needed to reduce the risks that are associated with strong credit growth.[17] A number of steps have been taken in this direction—and credit growth

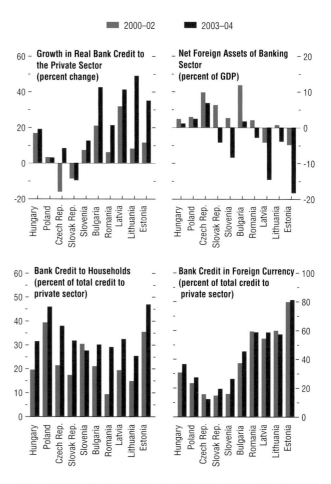

Figure 1.17. Emerging Europe: Is Strong Credit Growth a Cause for Concern?

Credit is growing strongly in many emerging European countries. Much of the credit is directed at the household sector and is in foreign currency.

Sources: National authorities; IMF, *International Financial Statistics;* and IMF staff calculations.

[16]In emerging markets, real GDP typically falls about 5 percent below trend after the collapse of a credit boom. Further, three-fourths of credit booms are associated with a banking crisis and almost seven-eighths with a currency crisis (see the April 2004 *World Economic Outlook*).

[17]See Hilbers and others (2005) and Duenwald, Gueorguiev, and Schaechter (2005) for a discussion of recent credit trends in central and eastern European countries and possible policy responses.

has slowed modestly in some countries—but further efforts will be needed to upgrade monitoring and supervisory practices, ensure that tax distortions that affect housing markets are minimized, and better inform borrowers about the risks they face, and how exchange and interest rate movements could affect their debt-servicing costs. More generally, fiscal consolidation is needed to manage demand pressures, contribute to a reduction in the large current account deficits, and pave the way for adoption of the euro.

Turning to individual countries, the expansion in Poland has slowed since mid-2004, and growth this year is projected at 3 percent (down from 5.4 percent in 2004). Consumption has weakened in the face of slower wage growth and still-high unemployment, and the inventory accumulation that boosted growth prior to tax and regulatory changes accompanying EU accession has dissipated. Export growth, while still robust, has also weakened as the zloty appreciated last year and growth in western Europe slowed, although the current account deficit is small. Inflation remains well contained: the central bank responded quickly to signs of rising price pressures in mid-2004, and inflation has since declined, allowing interest rates to be reduced in recent months. Fiscal policy implementation, however, has been disappointing, with the general government deficit remaining high. The government will need to deliver an ambitious fiscal consolidation plan based on a reduction in social transfer spending and an overhaul of the tax system.

In Hungary, the economy slowed in late 2004 and early 2005 as consumption was adversely affected by the weak labor market and a decline in consumer sentiment, but has strengthened more recently. The trade deficit has narrowed, but with the investment income balance deteriorating, the overall current account deficit remains large. Despite some pickup in foreign direct investment (FDI) inflows, this deficit requires significant debt financing, which increases the economy's vulnerability to swings in investor sentiment. Reducing the fiscal

deficit in a sustained way remains a key policy priority. This will require expenditure reforms in the pension, health, and education sectors. Increased labor market flexibility and wide-ranging tax reforms—based on lower rates and a broader base—are also needed to boost growth potential. In Slovenia, growth is expected to slow modestly in 2005 as export growth and domestic demand weaken. The economy appears well poised to adopt the euro, although challenges remain, particularly to consolidate the progress that has been made in reducing inflation.

In the Czech Republic, growth is expected to be about 4 percent in 2005–06. Expanding production capacity has boosted net exports, although investment is projected to slow. The stronger currency, intensifying retail competition, and productivity improvements are keeping inflationary pressures subdued, enabling the central bank to ease monetary policy this year. A key challenge is to maintain the recent progress that has been made in reducing the fiscal deficit; this will require the strict control of expenditures, including through the reform of entitlements and measures to slow the long-term growth of age-related spending. Growth remains robust in the Slovak Republic and, although the current account deficit has widened sharply, this mostly reflects imports of investment goods associated with foreign direct investment. Looking forward, macroeconomic policies need to focus on consolidating the recent gains made in reducing inflation.

Strong growth—driven by domestic demand—continues in the Baltic countries. Rapid credit growth has boosted consumption, while low real interest rates and a sharp rise in EU grants are providing a stimulus to investment. Against this background, inflationary pressures have picked up, particularly in Latvia (although partly owing to one-off factors), and current account deficits remain very large. The key policy challenges are to lower potential vulnerabilities from the large external deficits and to contain inflation. Fiscal policy will need to take the lead in achieving these objectives, although further steps are also needed to slow credit growth, including by reducing incentives in the tax system that encourage mortgage borrowing.

Growth in Bulgaria and Romania remains strong, although recent heavy floods pose a downside risk. Domestic demand is growing strongly, supported by rising wage incomes and rapid credit growth. Large current account deficits continue to present a risk to the outlook in both countries, but financing is strong (largely comprising FDI and EU transfers), while in Romania inflation remains close to 10 percent and needs to be reduced further. Against this background, it is important that the authorities maintain a tight fiscal policy stance, take further steps to slow the pace of credit growth, and push ahead with structural reforms that improve the investment climate, encourage FDI inflows, and raise productivity. In Romania, monetary policy needs to focus increasingly on reducing inflation, and the recent shift to an inflation targeting regime should help in this regard (see Chapter IV).

Growth is expected to slow in the Balkan countries this year, largely owing to weaker domestic demand. In Croatia, inflation remains well contained and fiscal consolidation has helped reduce the current account deficit. In Bosnia and Herzegovina and Serbia and Montenegro, the large current account deficits are a significant vulnerability, while inflation has risen sharply in Serbia and Montenegro. To address these vulnerabilities, fiscal policy needs to be tightened, the rapid expansion of credit slowed, and structural reforms implemented to boost export competitiveness.

In Turkey, economic activity is slowing to a more sustainable pace, with growth of 5 percent projected this year (compared with 8.9 percent in 2004). However, after slowing significantly in the second half of 2004, domestic demand has started to strengthen, helped by lower interest rates and a pickup in credit. Inflation is on track to reach this year's target of 8 percent. Although capital inflows have remained buoyant and a large part of this year's external financing

requirement has already been met, abrupt shifts in market sentiment pose a risk to the financing of the large current account deficit. Against this background, the government's continued commitment to implementing its reform program is very important. Policies should focus on reducing the external deficit and maintaining market confidence, in particular by ensuring that the primary surplus target of 6.5 percent of GNP is comfortably achieved.

Commonwealth of Independent States: Favorable Short-Term Outlook Masks Medium-Term Investment Risks

After a remarkable acceleration in 2003–04, real GDP growth in the Commonwealth of Independent States (CIS) has slowed noticeably in 2005. This has especially been the case in Russia, where policy uncertainty, the Yukos affair, and sharply higher marginal tax rates in the oil sector—to almost 90 percent at prices above $25 a barrel—have been key factors behind sluggish investment and sharply lower output growth in the oil sector, and in Ukraine, where political uncertainty has adversely affected activity and investment. However, consumption growth has generally remained buoyant, reflecting strong spillovers from favorable commodity market developments, strong wage growth, and rapid money supply and credit expansion. This has led to growing pressures on prices, especially in Russia and Ukraine, and regional inflation has picked up after a long period of sustained disinflation. Foreign currency reserves have generally continued to rise, as terms-of-trade-related increases in the current account surpluses of major energy- and metals-exporting countries have more than offset increases in capital outflows owing to heightened political and policy uncertainty.

Looking forward, regional growth is expected to remain robust at 6 percent in 2005 and 5.7 percent in 2006, with consumption remaining the main driving force, as fiscal easing is expected in a number of countries (Table 1.9). Despite this, the region's current account

Table 1.9. Commonwealth of Independent States: Real GDP, Consumer Prices, and Current Account Balance
(Annual percent change unless otherwise noted)

	Real GDP				Consumer Prices[1]				Current Account Balance[2]			
	2003	2004	2005	2006	2003	2004	2005	2006	2003	2004	2005	2006
Commonwealth of Independent States	**7.9**	**8.4**	**6.0**	**5.7**	**12.0**	**10.3**	**12.6**	**10.5**	**6.3**	**8.3**	**10.6**	**10.3**
Russia	7.3	7.2	5.5	5.3	13.7	10.9	12.8	10.7	8.2	10.3	13.2	13.0
Ukraine	9.6	12.1	5.5	5.4	5.2	9.0	14.2	12.1	5.8	10.5	5.0	0.2
Kazakhstan	9.3	9.4	8.8	7.7	6.4	6.9	7.4	7.1	−0.9	1.3	3.9	2.8
Belarus	7.0	11.0	7.1	4.0	28.4	18.1	12.1	12.5	−2.4	−4.6	−3.7	−3.4
Turkmenistan	17.1	17.2	9.6	6.5	5.6	5.9	13.5	5.0	2.7	1.2	3.2	2.2
CIS-7	**7.4**	**8.3**	**8.9**	**10.7**	**8.6**	**7.5**	**10.8**	**8.9**	**−6.8**	**−9.9**	**−5.6**	**2.1**
Armenia	13.9	10.1	8.0	6.0	4.7	6.9	2.2	3.9	−6.8	−4.7	−5.1	−5.4
Azerbaijan	11.5	10.2	18.7	26.6	2.2	6.7	12.7	8.3	−27.8	−30.4	−12.8	9.0
Georgia	11.1	6.2	7.5	4.5	4.8	5.7	9.0	7.0	−7.2	−7.6	−11.8	−7.2
Kyrgyz Republic	7.0	7.1	4.0	5.5	3.1	4.1	5.0	4.0	−3.0	−2.8	−4.9	−4.8
Moldova	6.6	7.3	6.0	5.0	11.7	12.5	13.3	11.9	−6.6	−4.4	−4.6	−3.2
Tajikistan	10.2	10.6	8.0	7.0	16.4	7.1	7.2	5.0	−1.3	−4.0	−4.9	−4.3
Uzbekistan	1.5	7.1	3.5	2.5	14.8	8.8	14.1	13.0	8.9	0.8	4.5	3.9
Memorandum												
Net energy exporters[3]	7.6	7.6	6.0	5.9	12.8	10.4	12.4	10.3	7.0	8.9	11.9	12.0
Net energy importers[4]	9.2	11.4	5.9	5.2	8.8	10.1	13.0	11.4	2.2	4.9	1.5	−1.2

[1]In accordance with standard practice in the *World Economic Outlook*, movements in consumer prices are indicated as annual averages rather than as December/December changes, as is the practice in some countries.
[2]Percent of GDP.
[3]Includes Azerbaijan, Kazakhstan, Russia, Turkmenistan, and Uzbekistan.
[4]Includes Armenia, Belarus, Georgia, Kyrgyz Republic, Moldova, Tajikistan, and Ukraine.

surplus is projected to rise further to about 10½ percent of GDP in 2005–06 on account of the higher oil prices. Near-term risks to growth are likely to be on the upside, given the outlook for oil and other commodities, although there are also downside risks, including a slowdown in growth in China, risks to investor confidence from market-unfriendly government interventions, and prudential risks associated with continued rapid credit growth.

Inflation is forecast to increase by over 2 percentage points to 12.6 percent in 2005, reflecting rapid consumption growth, production that is close to capacity in some sectors, and continued substantial net foreign exchange inflows in the context of monetary regimes that generally seek to limit real exchange rate appreciation with partly sterilized interventions. There are some upside risks to inflation with widespread pressures for further increases in government spending, partly owing to the opportunities provided by rising budget surpluses in oil-exporting countries, especially in Kazakhstan and Russia—

at the regional level, the surplus is projected to increase by 2½ percentage points to about 4½ percent of GDP in 2005. In these circumstances, the appropriate policy mix would include a combination of tighter monetary policy and greater exchange rate appreciation to keep inflation in check, which, depending on absorptive capacity and progress with structural reforms, could provide some room to increase high-priority expenditure and implement tax reforms. At the same time, the rapid credit growth over the past few years calls for the close monitoring of prudential risks in the banking sector and further strengthening of regulatory frameworks.

In contrast to favorable short-term prospects, there are some significant downside risks to growth in the medium term. In particular, investment outlays as a share of GDP have, on average, remained at about 21 percent of GDP in the CIS countries despite a very favorable growth performance, some 5 percentage points below the average in the transition economies of emerging

Europe (Figure 1.18).[18] Initially, when growth rebounded after the 1998 crises in the region, capacity constraints were less of a concern but, as the rising pressures on wages and prices indicate, the relatively weak investment growth increasingly appears to constrain growth— especially outside the commodity-producing sectors, which have received the bulk of investment outlays—and is an impediment to much-needed economic diversification in view of long-term commodity market risks. A more hospitable business climate is an essential precondition for more investment, but related structural reforms in the region—including in the area of enterprise reform—continue to lag those in other transition economies in emerging Europe. This underscores the need for greater resolve in advancing reforms to develop fully the institutions and structures to support property rights and competition, with rule-based government interventions guided by transparent objectives.

Turning to individual countries, economic growth in Russia slowed further to about 5½ percent in the first half of 2005, reflecting not only sluggish growth in mining and resource extraction—partly owing to the adverse effects of the Yukos affair on capacity expansion in the oil sector—but also in manufacturing, which has been hurt by capacity constraints, rising input costs, and ruble appreciation. On the demand side, buoyant private consumption growth was the main driving force, supported by strong growth in real incomes, while investment was subdued for reasons noted above. Looking forward, growth is projected to remain at about 5½ percent in 2005–06, supported primarily by continued buoyant consumption growth on the back of higher government spending. With sharply higher oil prices, the budget surplus will nevertheless increase in 2005. Inflation is projected to remain some 4–5 percent above the 8 percent target—underscoring the need for monetary policy to focus on decisive disinflation,

[18]Azerbaijan, where large foreign direct investment in the oil sector supported an investment ratio of more than 35 percent, is a notable exception.

Figure 1.18. Commonwealth of Independent States: Investment, Growth, and Structural Reforms

Investment ratios in the CIS countries remain below those in emerging European countries despite a very favorable growth performance, partly reflecting lagging structural reforms. Given large output declines early in the transition, low investment ratios are only beginning to constrain growth, as output levels recover.

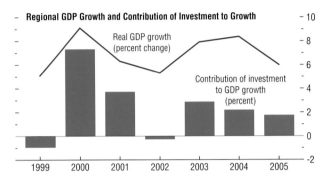

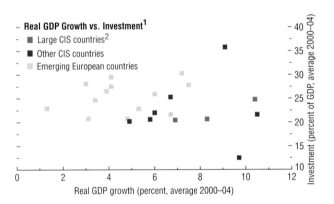

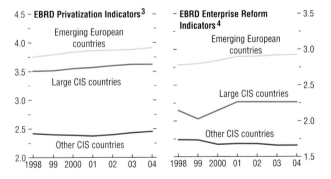

Sources: EBRD; and IMF staff calculations.
[1]Excluding Uzbekistan and Turkmenistan owing to lack of investment data.
[2]Russia, Ukraine, and Kazakhstan.
[3]Average of small- and large-scale privatization index.
[4]Average of enterprise reform and competition policy index.

supported by greater upward exchange rate flexibility and fiscal discipline. The weakness of the investment climate, including that due to pervasive discretionary government interference, remains a major deterrent to private sector confidence and investment, including in the oil sector. The increase in oil revenue provides an important opportunity to accelerate the structural reform agenda, which—apart from some progress in banking sector reform, where the establishment of deposit insurance has led to some welcome consolidation in the sector—is at a standstill.

After soaring to over 12 percent in 2004, GDP growth in Ukraine has slowed noticeably, primarily on account of decelerating export demand, but also due to sluggish investment growth owing to the protracted reprivatization debate. Looking forward, growth is projected at about 5½ percent in 2005–06, supported by buoyant consumption following sharp hikes in public pensions and wages, but the uncertain investment climate and a possible fall in metal prices constitute considerable downside risks. With monetary policy defending the nominal de facto peg of the hryvnia against the dollar and fiscal policy ratcheting up public wages and pensions, inflation has been steadily increasing, reaching about 14½ percent in June. Reducing inflation to single-digit rates is a key policy priority. On the fiscal side, the budget deficit may exceed the target of 2½ percent of GDP in 2005 and will continue to deteriorate without adjustment, partly reflecting backward indexation of wages and benefits. To ensure sustainability, public sector wage schedules and entitlement programs must be adjusted in a forward-looking manner, which would also contribute to disinflation efforts. In Kazakhstan, GDP growth is projected to moderate to 8.8 percent in 2005, as the pace of new oil production capacity coming onstream decelerates somewhat. Economic diversification remains a policy priority, requiring improvements in the investment climate, as discussed above, and reforms aimed at increasing trade openness, including through the acceleration of WTO accession discussions.

The low-income CIS-7 economies continue to register robust growth, driven by strong activity in the larger countries in the region and, to varying degrees, by favorable commodity market conditions. Looking forward, growth is projected to remain solid, in part supported by foreign direct investment, improved conditions for agricultural production, and new capacity in resource extraction coming onstream, especially in the case of Azerbaijan and Uzbekistan (both oil). However, with much higher oil prices and, unlike in 2003–04, less scope for offset from increases in other commodity prices, external current account deficits of net energy importers have widened, which is a concern in view of high levels of external debt. In the circumstances, maintaining appropriately tight fiscal policies and ensuring adequate pass-through of higher energy prices to consumers and producers remain key to ensuring viable external positions.

Africa: How Can the Benefits of a Rising Working-Age Population Be Maximized?

Growth in sub-Saharan Africa is expected to slow to 4.8 percent this year, following the 5.4 percent expansion in 2004 (Table 1.10). The economies in the region continue to be underpinned by the strength of global demand, improved domestic macroeconomic policies—which have delivered the lowest inflation in 30 years—progress with structural reforms and fewer armed conflicts. Further, the recent appreciation of the dollar against the euro, if sustained, should boost non-oil exports of the CFA franc zone countries. Growth in 2004, however, was also boosted by temporary factors, not all of which are being repeated this year. In the oil-exporting countries, there were large increases in output in Angola, Chad, and Equatorial Guinea as new oil production came onstream (this largely offset the slowdown in Nigeria, which is expected to continue in 2005—see below). In oil-importing countries, agricultural production in Ethiopia rebounded strongly after a severe drought.

Table 1.10. Selected African Countries: Real GDP, Consumer Prices, and Current Account Balance
(Annual percent change unless otherwise noted)

	Real GDP				Consumer Prices[1]				Current Account Balance[2]			
	2003	2004	2005	2006	2003	2004	2005	2006	2003	2004	2005	2006
Africa	**4.6**	**5.3**	**4.5**	**5.9**	**10.4**	**7.8**	**8.2**	**7.0**	**−0.5**	**0.1**	**1.6**	**3.5**
Maghreb	**6.2**	**5.0**	**3.7**	**5.6**	**2.2**	**2.9**	**2.9**	**3.3**	**7.1**	**7.1**	**9.9**	**12.4**
Algeria	6.9	5.2	4.8	5.3	2.6	3.6	3.5	4.3	13.0	13.1	19.1	23.6
Morocco	5.5	4.2	1.0	5.9	1.2	1.5	2.0	2.0	3.6	2.2	−1.6	−2.8
Tunisia	5.6	5.8	5.0	5.9	2.8	3.6	2.9	2.5	−2.9	−2.0	−2.6	−2.5
Sub-Sahara	**4.1**	**5.4**	**4.8**	**5.9**	**13.0**	**9.3**	**9.8**	**8.2**	**−3.0**	**−2.1**	**−1.0**	**0.8**
Horn of Africa[3]	**1.0**	**8.8**	**7.7**	**9.9**	**10.6**	**8.4**	**7.2**	**6.5**	**−6.1**	**−6.1**	**−5.8**	**−2.5**
Ethiopia	−4.2	11.5	7.3	5.0	15.1	8.6	6.8	6.0	−2.7	−6.2	−5.7	−8.2
Sudan	4.6	6.9	8.0	13.6	7.7	8.4	7.5	7.0	−7.8	−6.2	−6.0	−0.8
Great Lakes[3]	**4.3**	**5.7**	**5.8**	**6.2**	**8.3**	**6.7**	**11.7**	**5.5**	**−2.3**	**−3.9**	**−5.2**	**−6.6**
Congo, Dem. Rep. of	5.7	6.8	6.6	7.0	12.8	3.9	23.2	8.0	−1.5	−5.5	−5.1	−7.9
Kenya	2.8	4.3	4.7	4.9	9.8	11.6	11.0	5.1	−0.2	−3.2	−5.6	−6.2
Tanzania	7.1	6.7	6.9	7.2	4.5	4.3	4.1	4.0	−2.4	−5.5	−5.1	−6.6
Uganda	4.5	5.8	5.9	6.6	5.7	5.0	8.2	4.5	−6.3	−1.7	−3.2	−5.5
Southern Africa[3]	**2.5**	**4.8**	**5.2**	**9.5**	**56.4**	**43.8**	**28.5**	**27.5**	**−3.4**	**−0.2**	**0.5**	**4.6**
Angola	3.4	11.1	14.7	27.6	98.3	43.6	22.0	10.5	−5.2	4.4	8.8	15.9
Zimbabwe	−10.4	−4.2	−7.1	−4.8	365.0	350.0	190.4	253.1	−2.8	−6.9	−5.8	−1.5
West and Central Africa[3]	**7.3**	**6.5**	**3.9**	**5.3**	**9.4**	**8.0**	**9.9**	**5.5**	**−4.1**	**−0.3**	**3.4**	**6.3**
Ghana	5.2	5.8	5.8	5.8	26.7	12.6	14.3	8.7	1.7	−2.7	−4.0	−4.5
Nigeria	10.7	6.0	3.9	4.9	14.0	15.0	15.9	7.3	−2.7	4.6	9.5	13.4
CFA franc zone[3]	**5.5**	**7.6**	**3.3**	**4.6**	**1.4**	**0.2**	**2.8**	**2.6**	**−5.8**	**−3.6**	**−1.0**	**0.3**
Cameroon	4.1	3.5	2.8	4.3	0.6	0.3	1.5	1.8	−2.1	−0.9	−0.7	−0.2
Côte d'Ivoire	−1.6	1.6	1.0	2.0	3.3	1.5	3.0	3.0	0.9	−1.4	2.1	2.6
South Africa	**2.8**	**3.7**	**4.3**	**3.9**	**5.8**	**1.4**	**3.9**	**5.3**	**−1.5**	**−3.2**	**−3.7**	**−3.5**
Memorandum												
Oil importers	3.4	4.6	4.3	5.2	9.9	7.1	7.8	7.4	−1.8	−2.8	−3.7	−3.5
Oil exporters[4]	8.4	7.5	5.1	7.8	12.0	10.0	9.3	5.9	2.9	7.3	12.8	17.3

[1]In accordance with standard practice in the *World Economic Outlook,* movements in consumer prices are indicated as annual averages rather than as December/December changes, as is the practice in some countries.
[2]Percent of GDP.
[3]The country composition of this regional group is set out in Table F in the Statistical Appendix.
[4]Includes Chad and Mauritania in this table.

Oil-exporting countries in the region are benefiting from the continuing increase in oil prices, but with non-oil commodity prices not rising as strongly as in 2004, other countries are facing a much more challenging environment. This is particularly the case for cotton exporters—including Benin, Burkina Faso, Mali, and Togo—given the continued slide in world cotton prices (see Box 1.5, "Pressures Mount for African Cotton Producers"). Countries with large textile sectors (including Kenya, Lesotho, Madagascar, Mauritius, and Swaziland) are being affected by the elimination of world textile trade quotas, although the extent of the impact at this early stage is still uncertain. Elsewhere, output is

expected to decline further in Zimbabwe in 2005, bringing the cumulative decline since the late 1990s to about 34 percent, while poor harvests have affected several countries in eastern and southern Africa and resulted in food production shortfalls.

Looking ahead to 2006, growth is expected to accelerate to 5.9 percent, which, if achieved, would be the strongest expansion in sub-Saharan Africa since the early 1970s. Underlying growth is again expected to be robust, although country-specific developments are largely responsible for the pickup relative to this year. In particular, the coming onstream of new oil production facilities in Angola and Mauritania is expected to

Box 1.5. Pressures Mount for African Cotton Producers

Cotton production is key to macroeconomic stability and rural cash incomes in a number of low-income countries, particularly in west Africa. Although two-thirds of global cotton is produced by China, the United States, India, and Pakistan, many smaller producers are highly dependent on cotton. In some countries, up to one-third of the population works in the cotton sector and cotton accounts for up to two-thirds of exports (see the table). A combination of the long-term trend decline in cotton prices, large cotton producer subsidies in developed countries, and an unfinished domestic reform agenda have brought into question the future of cotton as a major cash crop export in many of these countries.

Real cotton prices—as for most primary commodity prices—exhibit a long-term downward trend as well as large short-term volatility (see the figure). Recent price movements have brought real prices near to a 40-year low and pose a challenge for macroeconomic performance in cotton dependent exporters. Most vulnerable in this respect are low-income African countries, where cotton dependence is particularly high and the scope for diversification is low owing to small holder production. CFA franc zone cotton producers have, in addition, been squeezed by currency appreciation against the dollar, which has lowered local currency receipts.

Global cotton trade is distorted by various market and trade interventions in some cotton-producing countries that depress prices and reduce incomes of other cotton producers, mostly in developing countries. The subsidy equivalent of these interventions is estimated to

Note: The main author of this box is Chris Lane.

have amounted to $4.9 billion in the 2003 season, equivalent to 18 percent of the value of world production. Against this background, four cotton-dependent African countries (Benin, Burkina Faso, Chad, and Mali) launched a Cotton Initiative in May 2003 in the context of the current round of multilateral trade negotiations (the Doha Development Agenda). They requested (1) the elimination of all forms of cotton export subsidies and other trade-distorting domestic support; (2) that compensation be paid until all subsidies are removed; and (3) that least-developed countries receive bound duty-free and quota-free market access for cotton and its by-products.

In August 2004, the World Trade Organization (WTO) Council agreed to address the trade aspects of the cotton sector "ambitiously, expeditiously, and specifically" in all three pillars of the agricultural negotiations—market access, export competition, and domestic support. Indeed, tentative agreement has been reached to eliminate all agricultural export subsidies, albeit with no specific deadline yet agreed, and to reduce other forms of trade-distorting support. The development aspects of cotton in the Doha Development Agenda are to be tackled separately, including through the exchange of information in a Subcommittee on Cotton. Both the United States and the European Union have put in place assistance packages for developing country cotton producers ranging from temporary balance of payments and budget support to technical assistance and scientific support.

Cotton producers have also been buoyed by a recent WTO ruling that concluded that support to cotton producers in the United States violated WTO rules. In 2004, Brazil charged that U.S. cotton subsidies caused harm to their inter-

Indicators of Cotton Dependence in Selected Countries, 2004
(Percent)

	Benin	Burkina Faso	Mali	Togo
Exports of cotton/total exports goods and services	35	61	28	14
Cotton exports/GDP	4.4	6.0	5.2	6.5

Source: IMF staff estimates.

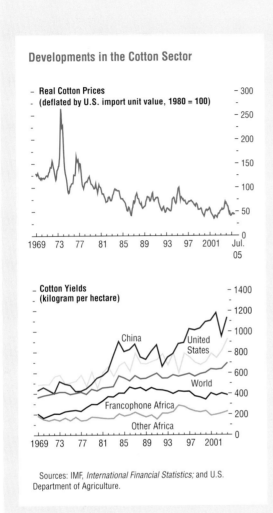

Developments in the Cotton Sector

Real Cotton Prices
(deflated by U.S. import unit value, 1980 = 100)

Cotton Yields
(kilogram per hectare)

China
United States
World
Francophone Africa
Other Africa

Sources: IMF, *International Financial Statistics;* and U.S. Department of Agriculture.

supply elasticities (Baffes, 2005, surveys the literature). A central estimate by the Food and Agricultural Policy Research Institute is that global agricultural subsidy removal would raise cotton prices by 12 percent over the period until 2012, equivalent to over $200 million a year for African producers. Additional gains would depend on gaining market share from industrial countries in competition with other developing country producers.

African producers have recognized, including at a May 2005 conference organized by the IMF, that the medium-term future of their cotton sectors depends on a number of factors besides the expeditious removal of trade-distorting subsidies and donor support. In particular, a key role falls on domestic policy reforms that would increase the competitiveness of cotton producers through liberalization and privatization, thus creating the incentives to cut costs, raise efficiency including through adoption of higher yielding seeds, and become more responsive to price signals.

The need for domestic policy reform is most pressing in Africa, where cotton yields have stagnated over the past decade against improvements elsewhere. In francophone west and central Africa, which accounts for two-thirds of African cotton production, the government retains an influential role in the cotton sector. Yields in Africa have been held back by the poor quality of marginal land and low levels of investment. The rapid adoption of genetically modified cotton that reduces pests and pesticide costs, and which now accounts for 35 percent of world production, has put Africa at a significant competitive disadvantage. Elbehri and Macdonald (2004) estimate that the adoption of genetically modified cotton in west and central Africa could boost production by about 12 percent and raise world export share from 10 percent to 13 percent.

With the challenges evident, African producers are putting reforms into place. For example, Burkina Faso has begun trials of genetically modified cotton, and Mali is committed to privatizing its state purchasing monopoly and has

ests. The WTO ruled in favor of Brazil, and this decision was upheld on appeal in March 2005. As a consequence, the U.S. Administration announced legislation in July 2005 that would eliminate export subsidies under the "Step-2" program as well as export credit subsidies that fell foul of WTO limits.

How much would the removal of cotton subsidies benefit African producers? Several studies have indicated that subsidy removal would raise world prices and shift production from subsidized to nonsubsidized regions. The projected increase in world prices, however, is highly divergent based on the choice of base year, methodology, assumptions on price, and demand and

Box 1.5 *(concluded)*

also linked domestic prices more closely to world prices to curb losses. Less progress has been made on liberalizing regional cotton trade, which is now broadly recognized as an essential complement to the broader trade agenda of the Doha Round and development partner assistance. While there remains some support for regional price stabilization funds, the size and persistence of cotton price changes make such projects unlikely to offer substantive insurance to producers. Actions to improve hedging mechanisms, presently dominated by contracts in U.S. cotton, could likely serve producers more effectively.

substantially boost growth in these countries in 2006, while oil production is also expected to increase in Nigeria.

At this juncture, the risks to these projections are tilted to the downside. While the recent commitment by the G-8 to boost aid and debt relief to the region could increase confidence, investment, and growth, an extended period of high oil prices—particularly if combined with a sharper-than-expected decline in non-oil commodity prices—would adversely affect many countries in the region (as it did in 1999–2000). Further, with global imbalances widening, a renewed decline of the dollar against the euro cannot be ruled out, which would adversely affect the CFA franc zone countries. More generally, past *World Economic Outlooks* have systematically overestimated growth in sub-Saharan Africa, largely because of the susceptibility of the region to natural disasters, climatic change that affects the agricultural sector, political instability, and other unanticipated shocks.

Looking forward, despite the favorable short-term outlook, most African countries still face enormous challenges in achieving the strong growth rates that are needed to substantially reduce poverty. Demographic trends, however, should help over the medium term. The share of the working-age population in sub-Saharan Africa is starting to rise, and it is projected to increase substantially over the next 40–50 years (Figure 1.19), despite the HIV/AIDs pandemic, which has taken a terrible toll on human life in the region.[19] This could help strengthen growth prospects if these additional workers are absorbed into the labor force. Given the higher saving propensity of workers, this could raise saving, which in turn would help finance additional investment, and boost output. Estimates in the September 2004 *World Economic Outlook* suggested that this "demographic dividend" could boost per capita growth in the region by about 0.3 percentage point a year. Of course, demographic change will also bring challenges, including that a larger population will put pressures on the environment.

To reap the full benefits of this projected rise in the share of the working-age population, further reforms will be necessary to strengthen the investment environment and foster private sector-led growth. A premium needs to be placed on building the economic and political institutions that are critical for developing a vibrant private sector–based economy, and there are examples within Africa where countries have achieved decisive improvements in their institutional structures (see Chapter III). As discussed in Chapter III, trade openness, education, transparency, and external anchors all play important roles in helping countries develop strong and effective institutions. Important initiatives are being undertaken in these areas across sub-Saharan Africa, but more needs to be done. Transparency remains too limited despite the important steps that are being undertaken through the Extractive Industries Transparency

[19]See United Nations (2004). For a discussion of the economic impact of HIV/AIDS in Africa, see Haacker (2004).

Initiative (EITI); progress under the African Peer Review Mechanism—a regional initiative launched through the New Partnership for Africa's Development to peer-review economic and political governance—has so far been slow and should be accelerated; and trade regimes need further liberalization. An emphasis also needs to be placed on developing the infrastructure to support private sector activity—on a broad range of measures, infrastructure development in Africa lags far behind other developing countries—as well as on increasing investment, including in human capital, and on making labor markets more flexible.

The global community needs to support Africa's reform efforts. A successful outcome of the Doha Round, particularly the liberalization of trade in agricultural goods, would bring substantial benefits for many African countries. The renewed commitment of the international community to provide additional resources to Africa, reflected in the G-8 agreement at Gleneagles, Scotland, in July is particularly welcome, although further improvements in governance, accountability, and transparency—as discussed above—are crucial if the full benefits are to be realized.

Turning to individual countries, the outlook for South Africa remains favorable, with growth expected to accelerate to 4.3 percent in 2005, although a deterioration in the external outlook—which would hurt the prices of commodity exports—and elevated house prices present downside risks. Inflation remains relatively well contained, although the pickup in unit labor costs, higher oil prices, the weakening of the rand this year, and rapid credit growth present upside risks. Fiscal policy implementation has remained sound, and the general government deficit is expected to remain below 2 percent of GDP this year. This prudent fiscal management has created the scope for moderate and targeted increases in social and infrastructure spending over the next few years. Despite some recent growth in formal sector employment, unemployment remains very high, and reforms are needed to boost the demand for labor.

Figure 1.19. Sub-Saharan Africa: Maximizing the Benefits of the Demographic Dividend

Sub-Saharan Africa will see a significant increase in its working-age population. To absorb these people productively into the labor force, increased investment in infrastructure, equipment, and education will be needed.

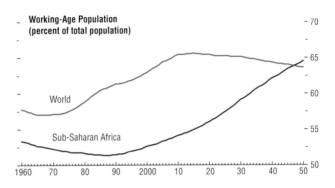

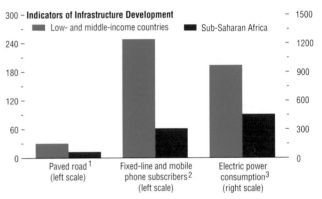

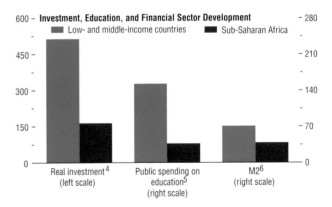

Sources: World Bank, *World Development Indicators;* United Nations; and IMF staff calculations.
[1] Calculated as percent of total roads.
[2] Calculated as subscribers per 1,000 people.
[3] Calculated as kwh per capita.
[4] Calculated as real investment in 1995 U.S. dollars per person aged 15–64.
[5] Calculated as current U.S. dollar per person aged 0–14.
[6] Calculated as percent of GDP.

In Nigeria, real GDP growth is expected to slow further in 2005, before rebounding in 2006. These trends are importantly driven by the oil and gas sector—existing capacity constraints mean that oil output will increase only slightly this year, but new production is expected to come onstream in 2006, boosting output. Growth in the non-oil sector remains robust, although there are increasing signs of overheating. Inflation has picked up again—partly owing to higher food prices—and monetary growth has accelerated sharply. The central bank needs to take steps to rein in monetary growth and bring inflation back down. Regarding fiscal policy, the 2005 budget incorporates a large overall surplus—underpinned by a sharp increase in revenues from the oil and gas sector—but contains a significant increase in spending. While additional spending should contribute to the government's development objectives, it needs to be carefully managed to ensure it does not put further upward pressure on inflation or crowd out private investment. Looking forward, a strengthening of public sector expenditure management is essential to ensure that oil revenues are used efficiently and that the benefits from the recent agreement by the Paris Club creditors on a concessional debt treatment for Nigeria are maximized. The government has continued to move forward with its structural reform program, including partially liberalizing pricing in the petroleum sector and improving governance and transparency. Nevertheless, subsidies on domestic petroleum products are large, the pace of the privatization program has disappointed, and the financial health of the banking system has deteriorated.

In the Maghreb region, growth is expected to slow slightly in Algeria this year. While higher oil prices should underpin stronger activity in the hydrocarbons sector, fiscal consolidation and tighter monetary policy—which has curtailed credit growth—are expected to slow growth in the non-oil economy. Inflation has been well contained, and the external position has strengthened significantly with the rise in oil prices. Regarding fiscal policy, it is important

that the government remain committed to the broad parameters of the expenditure restraint set out in the 2005 budget, although additional oil revenues will permit some increase in well-targeted spending to support economic reforms. The authorities are continuing to make progress in liberalizing external trade and the energy and telecommunications sectors but, with unemployment still very high, further structural reforms—particularly in the banking and public enterprise sector—are needed to raise growth potential in the non-oil sector. In Morocco, growth is expected to slow owing to unfavorable weather conditions that have affected agricultural output and to a weak performance in the textile sector, reflecting in part the elimination of world textile trade quotas. Growth in Tunisia is projected to remain strong, with the slowdown in the textile sector being less pronounced so far. Given the degree of both Morocco and Tunisia's integration with the European Union, weak European demand is a potential risk to growth in the region.

Middle East: Managing Booming Oil Exports

With the sharply higher oil prices, the Middle East region has seen accelerating oil export revenues that—in real U.S. dollars—outstrip those of the 1970s and early 1980s (Figure 1.20). Reflecting the terms-of-trade gains, and with crude oil production in the region increasing to a 20-year high, oil-exporting countries—which account for more than 95 percent of the region's output—have enjoyed a robust growth performance, and external current account and fiscal balances have improved dramatically. Despite strong domestic demand, inflation has generally remained subdued—except, as discussed below, in the Islamic Republic of Iran—owing both to considerable flexibility and openness in product markets and, in the context of pegged exchange rates, to low global inflation. Looking forward, prospects remain favorable, given the oil market outlook, and regional GDP growth is projected at 5.4 percent in 2005

(Table 1.11). With continued prudent financial policies and oil production close to capacity, growth is expected to moderate slightly to 5 percent in 2006. The regional current account surplus is projected to rise further to about 21 percent of GDP in 2005—close to $200 billion—and to 23½ percent of GDP in 2006.

With a significant proportion of the oil revenue increase expected to be permanent, managing these revenues will be a central challenge, both domestically and—as discussed previously—for global imbalances. On the one hand, the revenue provides the opportunity to address some of the long-standing economic problems in the region, including the financing of reforms that would generate employment for the rapidly growing working-age population, the key medium-term policy challenge in most countries. On the other hand, the oil revenues are generally large compared with output, and spending can be increased only gradually, depending on macroeconomic conditions and a country's absorptive capacity. In this regard, it will be critical to avoid two mistakes of the 1970s and early 1980s. First, due priority should be given to expenditure that will have a lasting impact on growth, productivity, and standards of living. Otherwise, the supply-side response will be small, and growth will fluctuate with oil market conditions, with a tendency for boom-bust cycles and high macroeconomic volatility. Second, expenditure should only be increased by amounts that can be sustained. Otherwise, changing oil market conditions can trigger large adjustment needs that are very difficult to implement. Developments to date suggest that policymakers in the region have learned from past mistakes. Based on current policy projections, spending multipliers—the fraction of additional oil revenue spent by governments—are now lower than during the boom of the 1970s, especially in the GCC countries.

At the current juncture, the appropriate set of policies varies across countries, but will include the following elements. First, given high unemployment and generally very low inflation, there is scope for higher government expenditure

Figure 1.20. Middle East: Oil Shocks and Macroeconomic Management

With soaring oil export proceeds, prudent macroeconomic policies are key to avoiding the boom-bust cycle associated with the first and second oil shocks (1973 and 1979).

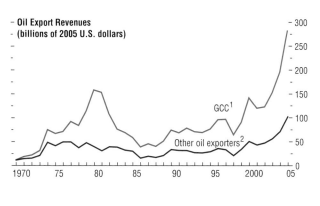

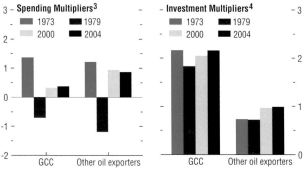

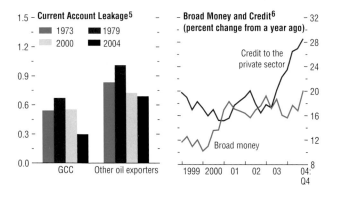

Sources: IMF, *International Financial Statistics;* and IMF staff calculations.
[1]The Cooperation Council of the Arab States of the Gulf (GCC) includes Bahrain, Kuwait, Oman, Qatar, Saudi Arabia, and United Arab Emirates.
[2]Consists of Egypt, I.R. of Iran, Libya, Syrian Arab Republic, and Yemen.
[3]Government spending growth over a five-year period (starting in the year indicated) as a fraction of growth in oil export revenue over the same period.
[4]Investment growth over a five-year period (starting in the year indicated) as a fraction of growth in government spending over the same period.
[5]Defined as one minus the ratio of cumulative current account balance over a five-year period (starting in the year indicated) to cumulative oil export revenue over the same period.
[6]Oil-exporting countries only.

Table 1.11. Selected Middle Eastern Countries: Real GDP, Consumer Prices, and Current Account Balance
(Annual percent change unless otherwise noted)

	Real GDP				Consumer Prices[1]				Current Account Balance[2]			
	2003	2004	2005	2006	2003	2004	2005	2006	2003	2004	2005	2006
Middle East	**6.5**	**5.5**	**5.4**	**5.0**	**7.1**	**8.4**	**10.0**	**9.7**	**8.0**	**12.4**	**21.1**	**23.5**
Oil exporters[3]	**6.9**	**5.5**	**5.6**	**5.2**	**8.8**	**9.1**	**11.1**	**10.9**	**9.6**	**15.0**	**24.9**	**27.4**
Iran, I.R. of	6.7	5.6	5.7	5.4	15.6	15.6	18.5	18.5	0.6	2.5	8.7	8.0
Saudi Arabia	7.7	5.2	6.0	4.7	0.6	0.3	1.0	1.0	13.1	20.5	32.4	37.3
Kuwait	9.7	7.2	3.2	3.2	1.0	1.8	1.8	1.8	17.5	29.2	44.8	50.2
Mashreq	**3.2**	**4.3**	**4.3**	**4.6**	**3.3**	**6.9**	**8.3**	**7.2**	**1.4**	**0.3**	**−0.7**	**−1.6**
Egypt	3.1	4.1	4.8	5.0	3.2	8.1	8.8	8.0	2.4	4.4	4.6	3.4
Syrian Arab Republic	2.6	3.4	3.5	4.0	5.0	4.6	10.0	5.0	6.0	1.9	0.2	−1.1
Jordan	4.1	7.7	5.0	2.5	1.6	3.4	3.7	8.4	11.3	−0.4	−12.3	−13.5
Lebanon	5.0	6.0	—	3.0	1.3	3.0	2.0	2.0	−12.5	−16.0	−16.9	−16.5
Memorandum												
Israel	1.7	4.4	4.2	3.9	0.7	−0.4	1.2	2.3	0.7	1.3	1.7	1.3

[1]In accordance with standard practice in the *World Economic Outlook,* movements in consumer prices are indicated as annual averages rather than as December/December changes, as is the practice in some countries.
[2]Percent of GDP.
[3]Includes I.R. of Iran, Iraq, Kuwait, Libya, Oman, Qatar, Saudi Arabia, Syrian Arab Republic, and Yemen.

without risks of overheating. If high public debt ratios are a concern, higher oil revenue should be used to reduce them to sustainable levels. Second, other capacity-enhancing reforms will be key to ensuring that higher expenditure will have lasting supply-side effects, including reforms that contribute to increasing trade openness and private sector participation and investment in major sectors. Third, while appropriately gradual expenditure increase will help to avoid undue pressure on real exchange rates, it will be important to allow for some of the inevitable real appreciation associated with higher oil revenue to take place. Finally, policymakers need to be mindful of financial sector implications. With oil export proceeds being partly invested in the domestic banking system, broad money and credit growth has begun to accelerate. This, together with buoyant investor confidence and an apparent increase in investor home bias, has underpinned large increases in equity and property prices, raising some concerns about increasing prudential risks in the financial sector. Supervisors need to monitor such risks carefully.

Turning to individual countries, growth in the Islamic Republic of Iran is expected at 5.7 percent in 2005, primarily reflecting robust domestic demand and a rebound in agricultural production after a weather-related slump in 2004. With strong domestic demand and expansionary monetary policy, inflation has remained above 15 percent. Since the scope of monetary control is limited by inadequate instruments, fiscal policy tightening is required to reduce inflation, supported by greater exchange rate flexibility. With elections completed, policymakers should take advantage of the current favorable economic conditions and push ahead with structural reforms, especially those aimed at increasing labor market flexibility and improving the business climate for private investment.

In Saudi Arabia, real GDP growth is expected to accelerate to 6 percent in 2005 before moderating to 4.7 percent in 2006. Driven by higher oil revenue, budget surpluses have soared, allowing for a substantial reduction in public debt, which is projected to decrease to below 50 percent of GDP by end-2005. Private non-oil sector growth is expected to benefit from ongoing reforms lifting restrictions to private sector participation in postal and railways services, electricity generation, water desalination, and non-oil mining. Divestment of government assets in these sectors would further enhance the scope for private sector development in the economy.

In Iraq, the economic reconstruction continues, although the volatile security situation and the slow progress in expanding oil production remain obstacles. After surging to over 30 percent in 2004, consumer price inflation has begun to moderate, but with unstable supply conditions, inflation volatility remains high. Looking forward, the new government faces daunting medium-term challenges, including advancing the reconstruction of the country's infrastructure, reducing macroeconomic instability, and developing the institutions that can support a market-based economy.

In Egypt, the expansion gained momentum in the second half of 2004, and growth is expected to remain robust at about 5 percent throughout 2005–06. Buoyant export growth, partly owing to the pound's depreciation during 2001–04, remains the key driving force. Additional support comes from a moderate rebound in domestic demand, owing to the favorable confidence effects of the government's new resolve in moving ahead with structural reforms. Inflation has begun to decrease from the high levels reached in 2004. Looking forward, a new policy framework with a clearly defined nominal anchor is needed to guide the conduct of monetary policy in the context of greater exchange rate flexibility. Net public debt has stabilized at about 65 percent of GDP, but with government borrowing remaining at about 7 percent of GDP, decisive multiyear fiscal adjustment is required to put public debt on a declining path and make room for more private investment.

Elsewhere in the Mashreq, growth in Jordan is expected to moderate to 5 percent in 2005, from 7.7 percent last year, reflecting the adverse impact on domestic demand of higher oil prices. In view of the latter, and given a substantial reduction in external budgetary grants, the current account deficit is projected to widen to 12.3 percent of GDP in 2005. To maintain medium-term macroeconomic stability, fiscal policy needs to be tightened decisively, including through a

reduction in budgetary subsidies on petroleum products. In Lebanon, the recent political turmoil had a large adverse impact on economic activity, with output contracting in the first half of the year. Activity should recover with restored political stability, and growth is projected to resume next year. Expenditure restraint has kept the fiscal situation in check, but with very high levels of public debt and financial vulnerabilities, substantial fiscal consolidation is required for lasting improvements.

After rebounding in 2004, growth in Israel remained strong in the first half of this year. Growth in 2005 is now projected at 4.2 percent, underpinned by solid high-technology exports and private consumption. Core inflation and inflation expectations have remained within the Bank of Israel's target range of 1–3 percent, and monetary policy has appropriately been held steady. Given the vulnerabilities associated with the high level of public sector debt—at over 100 percent of GDP—strict adherence to the medium-term budget deficit target of 3 percent of GDP remains essential, and the credibility of the current fiscal policy framework should be enhanced with a medium-term spending plan.

Appendix 1.1. Recent Developments in Commodity Markets

The authors of this appendix are To-Nhu Dao, Paul Nicholson, Sam Ouliaris, and Hossein Samiei.

The overall index of primary commodity prices increased by 29 percent in U.S. dollar terms (35 percent in SDR terms) during January–August 2005 (Figure 1.21).[20] Energy prices, which rose by 41 percent, remained the main driver of the index, reflecting strong growth in crude oil consumption and expectations of tight crude oil and product markets going forward. As a result, both spot and futures prices of oil and petroleum products have become extremely sensitive to short-term developments—as clearly demon-

---

[20]Unless otherwise stated, percentage changes and summary statistics refer to the January 2005–August 2005 period.

Figure 1.21. Oil Prices, Futures, and Production

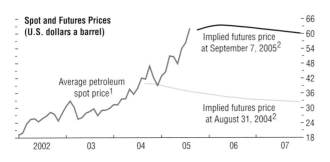

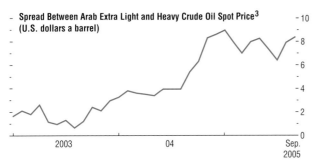

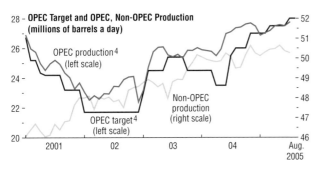

Sources: International Energy Agency; Bloomberg Financial Markets, LP; IMF, *International Financial Statistics;* and IMF staff calculations.

[1]Average petroleum spot price of West Texas Intermediate, U.K. Brent, and Dubai Fateh crude.

[2]Five-day weighted average of NYMEX Light Sweet Crude, IPE Dated Brent, and implied Dubai Fateh.

[3]Saudi Arabian crude oil deliverable in Asia. Arab Extra Light (Berri) has an API gravity of 37 and a sulphur content of 1.15. Arab Heavy (Safaniya) has an API gravity of 27 and a sulphur content of 2.8.

[4]Excluding Iraq.

strated by the initial impact of Hurricane Katrina on crude oil and petroleum product prices.

In contrast to the energy component, the non-fuel commodity price index rose by only 5 percent in U.S. dollar terms (9 percent in SDR terms) over the same period, led by metal and food prices. Metals prices rose by 9 percent largely because of robust demand arising from the current global economic expansion. Food prices rose by 4 percent owing to strong growth in China's demand for soybeans. Reduced harvests in South America and lower North American grain output forecasts placed upward pressure on prices of agricultural products.

Crude Oil

Crude oil prices continued their rise during 2005 even though the growth in crude oil consumption has been broadly in line with expectations. While shortfalls in non-OPEC supply have contributed to the rise, it appears that crude oil prices are being increasingly driven by expectations of future tightness in the market. These expectations are based on forecasts of continued robust global economic growth, low spare capacity among OPEC producers, and fears that the recent slowdown in non-OPEC production may be somewhat permanent. With limited upstream (i.e., crude oil production) and downstream (i.e., refinery) spare capacity, short-term disruptions to product or crude oil production, which prior to 2003 had temporary effects on oil prices, have become powerful catalysts for higher prices. Interestingly, even long-dated futures prices are now more responsive to daily market news, prompting some analysts to argue that speculative activity is having an excessive influence on crude oil futures prices.

The sensitivity of prices to short-term developments was strikingly demonstrated by the damage recently caused by Hurricane Katrina to the oil and gas infrastructure in the Gulf of Mexico, which is responsible for 20 percent of daily U.S. crude oil domestic production and nearly 50 percent of its total refinery capacity. Crude oil, gasoline, and natural gas prices spiked as the hurricane hit the continental shores of the United States on August 31, but eased somewhat following decisions by the U.S. Administration and the International Energy Agency (IEA) to release oil from their strategic reserves (the latter to bolster global crude oil supplies by 2 mbd[21] for 30 days), and an offer by Saudi Arabia to increase its crude oil production by 500 thousand barrels a day. While the impact of Hurricane Katrina on crude prices is likely to be temporary—indeed the actions taken by the IEA and others may even trigger some weakening in crude oil prices in the period ahead—product prices are likely to remain high and volatile for sometime yet because of delays in restoring refinery production.

The steady rise in crude oil prices over the past year has occurred despite OPEC's systematic efforts to ease fears about potential supply shortages. OPEC's accommodative stance, by maintaining actual production and official quotas at record levels for most of 2005, has allowed OECD commercial crude oil stocks to rise to near six-year highs (Figure 1.22). This stance reflects a growing concern that the seasonal surge in crude oil consumption during the Northern Hemisphere winter will require a large draw on commercial inventories. Oil futures have moved into a near-term contango position since December 2004 on these concerns, with the delivery price increasing steadily through to the first quarter of 2006. Interestingly, futures prices remained in contango even after Hurricane Katrina hit the Gulf of Mexico, suggesting that traders remain more concerned about seasonal tightness than about the initial effects of Hurricane Katrina on crude oil production.

Price Developments

The average petroleum spot price[22] (APSP) rose by 44 percent during January–August 2005.

---

[21]Mbd refers to millions of barrels a day, while kbd denotes thousands of barrels a day.

[22]The IMF average petroleum spot price (APSP) is an equally weighted average of the WTI, Brent, and Dubai crude oil prices. Unless otherwise noted, all subsequent references to the oil price are to the APSP.

Figure 1.22. Commercial Oil Inventories, World Refinery Capacity, and Option Prices

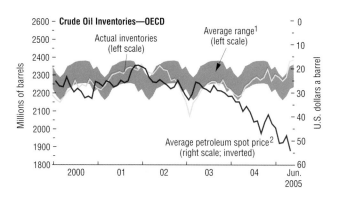

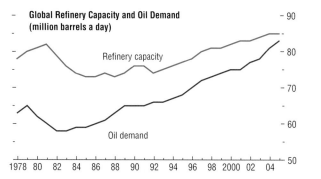

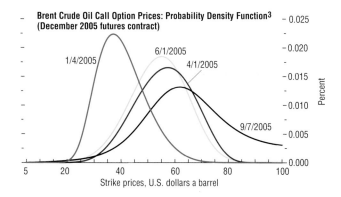

Sources: International Energy Agency; Bloomberg Financial, LP; and IMF staff calculations.
[1]Average of each calendar month during 1992–2004, plus a 40 percent confidence interval based on past deviations.
[2]Average petroleum spot price of West Texas Intermediate, U.K. Brent, and Dubai Fateh crude.
[3]Call options are European-style options for an option to buy (call) International Petroleum Exchange Brent Contract for December 2005 delivery.

After exceeding $50 a barrel for most trading days in March–April 2005, the APSP eased during May on seasonal weakness in oil consumption. However, the APSP began a steady rise soon after, and eventually breached the $65 mark at beginning of September—with the nominal West Texas Intermediate (WTI) spot price closing at $69.81 (see Figure 1.21). As of August 31, the APSP was 72 percent above the average for 2004 and three times the 20-year average of $21.73. Moreover, price differentials between light and heavy grades of crude oil remain high because of shortage of light crude oil, limited refinery capacity to distill heavier grades of crude oil, and the fact that OPEC's marginal production is mostly of the heavy type. Hurricane Katrina increased these differentials further by reducing the production of light crude oil in the Gulf of Mexico, and forcing the shutdown of U.S. refineries. Lastly, crude oil price volatility over the first eight months of 2005 (as measured by the variance of daily crude oil prices) was 2.8 times that of the same period in 2004 (Figure 1.22).

High refinery utilization rates in 2005 have also made petroleum product prices very sensitive to unexpected refinery outages—as demonstrated by the 28 percent rise in U.S. wholesale (front month) gasoline futures in the immediate aftermath of Hurricane Katrina. Despite announcements by the U.S. Administration and the IEA to release oil from their strategic reserves, higher crude oil supplies are unlikely to result in greater supply of petroleum products in the near term, owing to refinery closures. Indeed, wholesale gasoline futures prices eased significantly on September 2, largely on news of an increase in gasoline shipments to the United States from Europe and the reopening of a major pipeline between the Gulf coast and the East Coast.

Consumption

Though consumption growth has eased relative to 2004 levels and is broadly in line with expectations, it remains high, suggesting that the higher crude oil prices have so far not had a significant impact on consumption. Owing to

Table 1.12. Global Oil Demand by Region
(Millions of barrels a day)

	Demand 2005	Annual Change	
		(mbd)	(percent)
North America	25.65	0.29	1.1
Europe	16.34	0.05	0.3
OECD Pacific	8.67	0.14	1.6
China	6.75	0.32	5.0
Other Asia	8.79	0.27	3.2
Former Soviet Union	3.77	0.03	0.8
Middle East	5.88	0.29	5.2
Africa	2.89	0.09	3.2
Latin America	4.97	0.11	2.3
World	83.72	1.60	1.9

Source: International Energy Agency, *Oil Market Report*, August 2005.

some apparent weakness in demand in the United States and China during the first quarter of 2005, the increase in global consumption in the first half of 2005, at 1.6 percent year-on-year (or 1.3 mbd), was lower than the increase of 4.0 percent (3.2 mbd) during the same period in 2004. However, this increase remains high compared with OPEC-10's (excluding Iraq) spare capacity, which stood at 1.4 mbd (annual basis) at end-July 2005.

The IEA increased its forecast for 2005 consumption growth from 1.4 mbd (at the end of 2004) to 1.8 mbd (in March) before lowering it to 1.6 mbd in July, citing apparent weakness in the United States' and China's demand for oil (Table 1.12). While the IEA's projection has so far been corroborated by actual consumption data, it is somewhat lower than that made by other analysts (for example, the U.S. Department of Energy). Looking ahead, China's crude oil consumption, despite some weakening, remains potentially strong, while consumption in non-OECD countries—especially the Middle East and emerging markets other than China—is growing relatively rapidly. In the case of the Middle East, the higher consumption growth reflects in part the windfall gains of higher oil prices in 2003–04 and a limited increase in domestic prices.

Production

OPEC's efforts to accommodate rising consumption of crude oil have coincided with lower-than-expected average growth in non-OPEC output, which (excluding processing gains and natural gas liquids) declined to 0.2 mbd (year-on-year) in the first half of 2005. This slowdown has raised concerns about the projected strength in non-OPEC crude oil production growth for the second half of 2005. Russian production, in particular, has been weaker than expected in the first half of 2005, and production for 2005 is projected to decline in Mexico, the North Sea, and Canada. Given low investment in infrastructure and aging oil fields, many analysts expect the growth in non-OPEC production for 2005 to weaken further. For example, the IEA recently revised non-OPEC production growth down from 1.1 mbd in January to 0.7 mbd in August 2005. Some analysts caution that this trend has a longer-run implication, providing corroborative evidence that non-OPEC oil fields are peaking and that current production, in the absence of new reserve discovery and substantial investments, will soon move into permanent decline.

Given slower production growth in non-OPEC countries, the need for OPEC production—the so-called "call on OPEC"—is rising. In response, OPEC has increased its members' quotas by 4.5 mbd since mid-2004, well above the growth in consumption over the same period, with the most recent increase of 0.5 mbd effective July 2005.

While overall OPEC production remains above official quotas, some OPEC members have found it difficult to meet their quota allotments, thereby increasing supply uncertainty. According to the IEA, Venezuelan crude oil output fell unexpectedly in the first half of 2005 by 2.4 percent (year-on-year), while Indonesian production fell 2.6 percent (year-on-year) because of declining wells that have not been replaced. Moreover, Iraqi output continues to decline because of an aging infrastructure and frequent attacks by insurgents—Iraqi crude oil production in the first half of 2005 was 11 percent lower than a year earlier.

Despite these uncertainties, OPEC has committed to meeting the year's crude oil demand in full, allowing commercial inventories to rise in the second quarter in anticipation of increased consumption later in the year. This policy—which suggests that the organization anticipates facing binding constraints if it were to satisfy residual demand fully in the fourth quarter—is the most telling sign of OPEC's efforts to stabilize the market. As a result, by June 2005 total OECD commercial inventories increased 5.7 percent on a year-on-year basis, and are currently equivalent to 53 days of forward consumption. Moreover, prior to the release of crude oil to offset production losses from Hurricane Katrina, the U.S. strategic petroleum reserve (SPR) reached its stated capacity of about 700 million barrels. Comfortable commercial inventory levels, in the absence of unforeseen problems with production, should soften the impact of the upcoming Northern Hemisphere winter on prices.

Short-Term Prospects and Risks

Owing to strong apparent demand and limited supply, particularly of light sweet crude, many analysts have raised their oil price projections for 2005–06. *World Economic Outlook* projections for the APSP, which are based on futures markets, have been revised to $54.23 for 2005 and $61.75 for 2006, compared with $46.50 for 2005 and $43.75 for 2006 in the April 2005 *World Economic Outlook*. These higher price forecasts reflect a growing consensus that recent levels of consumption are likely to be more persistent and will continue to tax available spare capacity, thereby amplifying the price effects of any exogenous supply shocks. Though the impact of Hurricane Katrina on crude prices may not be long lasting, it has clearly increased short-term risks. Moreover, terrorism and insurgent attacks in the Middle East remain a real concern. Based on option prices, the probability that the price of West Texas Intermediate will rise above $80 by December is now 20 percent, compared with zero percent in early 2005.

While upside risks to prices remain, a major unknown is when crude oil consumption will respond meaningfully (and by how much) to higher prices. During the oil price hikes of the 1970s and 1980s, oil consumption responded with a significant lag, and only after the higher prices created a tangible impact on importers' current accounts and consumers' share of expenditure on oil products. With lower oil intensity, even higher prices may be necessary before there is a significant impact on the world economy and a subsequent unwinding of crude oil prices.

Longer-Term Prospects, Futures Prices, and the Role of Speculation

In contrast to previous episodes of large crude oil price increases, long-dated futures prices have increased significantly during the past two years. Specifically, the correlation between six-year-out futures and spot prices has been about 0.9 since 2003, compared with almost zero during 2000–02, when spot prices also drifted upward. More generally, econometric evidence suggests that since 2003 variations in spot prices now explain a larger portion of movements in long-dated futures prices.

The volatility of long-dated futures prices has also significantly increased in recent years. Before 2003, long-dated futures showed almost no volatility: the variance of (the rate of change in) prices during 2000–02 was only 0.05, compared with 0.15 during January 2003–June 2005. Futures markets for crude oil have also become much deeper: the volume of 6-year futures contracts is 330 percent greater than the 1997–2005 average. In contrast, near-term contracts are only 150 percent higher.

The large increase in total contracts and volatility in prices have led some analysts to suggest that the ability of speculators to influence prices in these markets has increased. Some analysts go even further and suggest the presence of a speculative bubble in oil prices—especially in futures prices. They interpret the oil price increase in the broader context of an increase in asset prices, including long-term bonds and real estate.

While the day-to-day movements in long-dated futures prices are hard to explain, the persistent increase of the past two years can be largely attributed to actual and perceived changes in fundamentals, in particular: (1) the perception that demand has permanently shifted upward owing to strong growth in emerging countries (especially China and India); (2) a growing awareness that supply from non-OPEC sources might peak in the next 5–10 years, and decline permanently thereafter; and, in view of current rates of oil consumption growth, (3) limited upstream investment in countries where oil reserves are plentiful, with obvious implications for future productive capacity relative to growing demand. While smaller oil companies and some oil exporters have boosted investment, oil majors and national oil companies have generally been slow to respond to higher oil prices according to the IEA. Investment by major international oil companies appears to have been constrained by (1) downsizing in these companies in the 1990s; (2) an apparent desire to distribute higher profits to shareholders; and (3) impediments to foreign investment in oil-exporting countries, some of which are largely closed to foreign investment (such as Saudi Arabia, Mexico, and Kuwait), while some others are introducing regulations discouraging foreign investment (such as Russia and Venezuela). These impediments often reflect the divergence between the interests of international oil companies and host governments. Investment by national oil companies, furthermore, appears inadequate given the current momentum in demand. These companies generally remain cautious in increasing upstream investment significantly, given their experience with the capacity overhang of the 1980s and competing budgetary demands for oil revenues— particularly after many years of low oil prices.

These structural factors could, to some degree, also explain the increased upward bias in long-term futures prices. Long-term futures prices have responded asymmetrically to spot prices in the past two years, rising more or less proportionally when spot prices rise (from peak to trough), but falling back by about one-third

Table 1.13. Causality Tests: Spot Price, Long-Term Futures Prices, and Net Long Position[1]

	Short-Run Component[2]		Long-Run Component[3]	
	2/11/1997–12/26/2000	10/21/2003–6/28/2005	2/11/1997–12/26/2000	10/21/2003–6/28/2005
Dependent Variable: Spot Price				
Explanatory variables				
Long-term futures price	×	×	×	•
Net long position	×	×	×	×
Dependent Variable: Long-Term Futures Price				
Explanatory variables				
Spot	×	•	•	•
Net long position	×	×	×	•
Dependent Variable: Net Long Position				
Explanatory variables				
Spot	•	•	•	•
Long-term futures price	×	×	×	×

Source: IMF staff calculations.

[1]A dot (or ×) indicates the presence (or absence) of a causal link from the explanatory variable to the dependent variable. The statistical analysis is based on approximate ideal band pass filters of the time series variables (see Corbae and Ouliaris, 2005). Causality is tested using weekly data and Granger causality tests involving two lags.

[2]The "short-run component" isolates the short-run impulses in the time series.

[3]The "long-run component" isolates the long-run trend in the time series.

when they decline. This ratcheting effect suggests that the short-term price declines in the oil market are not expected to last, and that future demand-supply conditions will remain fundamentally tight.

Nonetheless, the extent to which futures markets increasingly respond to day-to-day events, such as temporary supply disruptions, is puzzling. Recent large upward swings in futures prices have often occurred at times when no new information about fundamentals has become available. For example, the large increases in prices in June–July 2005 appear to reflect diminishing pressure from short-sellers, as opposed to any fundamental movements in demand or supply.

The short-term behavior of prices together with higher volatility and increased trading activity in the futures markets suggest that speculative activity might be playing a greater role in driving spot and futures prices. To formally assess this issue, Granger causality tests based on a tri-variate vector autoregression (VAR) involving spot prices, long-term futures prices, and noncommercial net long positions—the latter being a proxy for speculative activity, in the absence of better measures—were con-

ducted. The tests were also carried out on the short- and long-run components of the data separately to determine whether speculative activity only matters over subcomponents of the data.

The statistical results, which are based on weekly data spanning 1997–2005, suggest that speculative activity does *not* precede movements in spot prices for either the short- or long-run components of the spot price (Table 1.13). There is evidence, however, of a modest impact on the long-run component of long-dated futures prices. Irrespective of the component of the data considered, the causality tests imply that speculative activity *follows* movements in spot prices, thereby raising doubt about speculative activity being a key driver of spot prices. In particular, the results suggest that noncommercial net long positions increase after spot prices increase, suggesting that speculators generally assume that a rising trend in spot prices will continue. Lastly, spot prices appear to influence both the short- and long-run movements of long-dated futures prices. This is especially true for the recent period, with the most likely explanation being lower and limited spare capacity among OPEC members in recent years, which has made the market far more responsive to geopolitical events.

Given these results, it can be argued that market fundamentals (rather than speculative activity) remain the main driver of both spot and futures prices—although speculative activity has some modest impact on futures prices. In addition, events that move spot prices on a day-to-day basis (news of supply disruptions, for example) are affecting long-dated futures prices to a greater extent than in the 1990s. This may suggest that uncertainties about prospects for long-term supply and demand has increased volatility in the futures market and caused some loss of direction.

Are Higher Oil Prices Affecting Global Activity?

Crude oil prices remain a key input in the determination of global economic prospects. A rise in crude oil prices affects the global economy through a variety of channels.[23]

- An initial fall in global aggregate demand owing to a transfer of income from oil consumers to oil producers, which tend to have a lower propensity to consume than oil consumers on average.
- A supply-side effect reflecting higher production costs and lower profit margins. However, with falling oil intensity over the past three decades, especially in industrial countries, this effect has become weaker.
- A rise in inflation resulting from higher production costs, depending on the response of monetary policy and the extent to which consumers and producers can offset the declines in incomes and profits, respectively.
- A potential impact on activity through lower consumer and investor confidence and reduced willingness to commit to longer-term capital projects.
- A lasting impact on energy demand and supply over time, depending on the duration and extent of the price increases.

In contrast with the experience of the 1970s, however, the significant increase in oil prices since 2003 appears so far to have had a limited impact on the global economy. Indeed, projected global growth for 2005 remains healthy at 4.3 percent—a marginal decline of 0.8 percent compared with the 5.1 percent growth estimated for 2004. MULTIMOD simulations based on historical estimates of the parameters, for example, would suggest a fall in activity over 2 percent of GDP owing to the rise in prices. This estimate is based on the simple rule implied by the IMF (2000) study, which associates a persistent US$5 exogenous increase in oil prices to 0.3 percent reduction in world activity.[24] Elasticities obtained from other studies (for example, Jones, Leiby, and Paik, 2004) would suggest an even larger impact on the global economy—closer to 4 percent.

Two questions naturally arise: (1) why has the current increase in oil prices had such a benign effect on the global economy compared with the oil price shocks of the 1970s? and (2) what is the likely impact of higher prices in the period ahead as they become increasingly driven by expectations?

The limited impact of higher crude oil prices reflects, first and foremost, the fact that, in contrast to the 1970s, crude oil prices have risen largely because of a significant (and somewhat unexpected) increase in consumption, rather than an exogenous supply shock. As a result, most of the increase in prices (especially prior to 2005) has acted as an "automatic stabilizer," operating to slow robust global growth rather than raise costs for the same level of global output. Second, there has been a substantial decline in oil intensity since the early 1980s. Global oil intensity is now about 38 percent lower compared with the late 1970s, implying that any increase in crude oil prices will necessarily have a lower first-round negative effect on global growth. Third, higher oil prices have yet

---

[23]IMF (2000) contains a comprehensive analysis of the impact of higher crude oil prices on the global economy.

[24]It goes without saying that this, and other similar simple rules, obviously do not apply in all circumstances. The impact of a US$5 increase in prices, for example, also depends on initial conditions, relating to, for example, the level of oil prices and the output gap.

to manifest themselves in core inflation, mitigating the need for higher interest rates (and lower output) to ward off second-round core inflation effects. Improved monetary policy credibility in industrial countries and a subdued global inflation environment (in part reflecting low labor costs in China and other major Asian exporters) appear to have anchored inflationary expectations.

Taking into account these offsetting factors, the impact of an oil price shock is less than earlier rules of thumb imply. For example, revised MULTIMOD simulations assuming the oil prices are increased by a demand shock and inflationary expectations remain well anchored suggest that a persistent 10 percent increase in oil prices is associated with a 0.1–0.15 percent reduction in global GDP. These simulations would imply that the cumulative effect of the oil price rise since 2003 on global activity may have been in the 1 to 1½ percent range.

A number of other factors may also have further mitigated the impact. First, given the continuing growth in crude oil consumption—and, in some countries, declining household savings—it may be that oil consumers are treating part of the price increase as temporary in nature despite higher long-dated futures prices. Second, in a number of countries, the pass-through of higher oil prices to domestic prices has been limited, financed by explicit or implicit budgetary subsidies. Both factors may have further reduced the impact of higher oil prices on inflation and activity.

Looking forward, however, the impact of higher oil prices may not continue to be so benign. If the increase in oil prices is permanent—as futures markets suggest—budgetary subsidies and consumer behavior will ultimately need to adjust. More generally, with limited excess capacity among OPEC producers, the market remains vulnerable to shocks. As such, further increases in oil prices cannot be ruled out (as options markets suggest). These increases—especially if driven by concerns about the availability of supply- rather than demand-side shocks, as seems to be increasingly

the case in 2005—are likely to have more marked effects on inflationary expectations, requiring a more active monetary policy response. There may also be adverse effects on consumer confidence, which has been relatively resilient to date. Indeed, IMF staff estimates suggest that higher interest rates combined with adverse impacts on consumer/investor confidence (in line with past experience) could double the impact of the revised rule of thumb given above.

Nonenergy Commodity Prices

Average nonenergy prices rose by 5 percent in U.S. dollar terms (and 9 percent in SDR terms) during January–August 2005, with metals and food prices being the main drivers of the nonenergy index (Table 1.14; Figure 1.23). While most metals markets reacted to further reductions in inventory positions and specific labor issues of mining companies, strong Chinese demand for soybeans pushed the food index higher. Looking forward, the upward momentum in nonenergy commodity prices is expected to ease for the remainder of 2005 as supply responds strongly to 2004 prices. On average, the nonenergy commodity price index for 2005 is projected to register an overall gain of 9 percent.

Turning to specific commodity markets, metals prices have increased by 9 percent since January and are expected to plateau, reflecting an easing in the overall tightness of the metals sector. Robust demand for construction and manufacturing products in both the United States and China increased metals prices during 2004, and continue to do so in 2005. Robust steel demand has resulted in a significant increase in iron ore—steel producers signed new contracts to purchase iron ore at prices 71.5 percent higher than last year. Copper prices rose by 20 percent to an all-time high, as inventory levels of copper fell to historical lows and recent strikes by mining workers threatened world supplies. Uranium prices increased by 44 percent in 2005—following a

Table 1.14. Nonenergy Commodity Prices
(Percent change from January to August 2005)

	U.S. Dollar Terms	Contribution[1]	SDR Terms
Food	3.7	42.9	8.0
Beverages	0.2	6.6	4.4
Agricultural raw materials	−1.1	20.7	3.1
Metals	8.6	29.8	13.1
Overall Nonenergy	4.6	100.0	9.0

Sources: IMF, Primary Commodity Price Database, and IMF staff estimates.

[1]Contributions to change in overall nonenergy price index in U.S. dollar terms, in percent. Contributions to change in SDR terms are similar.

Figure 1.23. Nonenergy Commodities

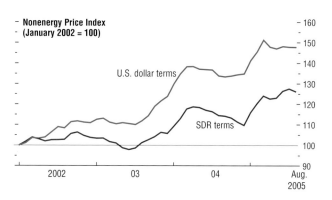

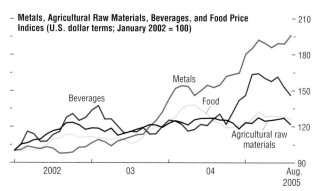

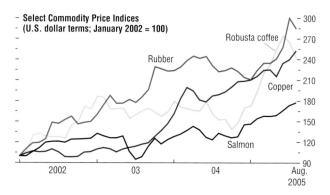

Source: IMF staff calculations.

60 percent increase in 2004—because the extra demand arising from newly constructed (and planned) nuclear reactors exceeds existing global mine capacity. In contrast, aluminum prices increased only slightly, reflecting the impact of a significant growth in exports from China. Looking forward, mine activity is expected to increase for almost all metals, most likely allowing inventories to recover in 2006, and prices to ease.

Overall beverage prices have remained unchanged since January as the strength of Robusta coffee prices has been offset by price reductions for other products. Severe drought conditions in Vietnam (the largest producer of Robusta coffee) have pushed Robusta prices up by 40 percent since January. In contrast, sizable tea harvests in Asia have allowed prices to ease by 10 percent. Looking forward, a better-than-expected harvest in Brazil should ease coffee prices, though Robusta prices could stay relatively high owing to crop damage caused by the drought in Vietnam.

Food prices, which went up by 4 percent during January–August 2005, are expected to ease later in the year as relatively large global harvests of many food items are expected this year. While unfavorable weather conditions in several growing regions (e.g., North and South America) have raised concerns about the summer and fall harvests of coarse grains and soybeans, China is expected to absorb much of the record harvest of soybeans for 2005. Chinese demand, coupled with the poor weather conditions in key growing areas, has pushed soybean prices up 18 percent since January. Salmon prices rose by 21 percent during a period of robust demand and limited supply. In contrast, banana prices declined by 43 percent over the same period as supplies outpaced consumption in European markets, where consumers switched to local fruits owing to hotter than normal weather conditions.

Agricultural raw material prices fell by 1 percent for the first eight months of 2005 as the supply of raw materials outpaced global demand. Timber prices have experienced a pronounced turnaround during 2005. Softwood prices have declined by about 14 percent since January, after increasing by about 15 percent in 2004. Increased harvests have helped to ease timber prices. The strong weight of timber in the index has obscured strength in cotton and rubber prices. Cotton prices have risen 5 percent owing to strong Chinese demand. Rubber prices have strengthened 35 percent since January because higher oil prices raised synthetic rubber prices and temporary supply disruptions of natural rubber restricted substitution. Looking forward, increased demand for raw materials is expected because of strong global economic growth. This should help to keep agricultural raw materials prices from contracting further in 2005, especially for timber.

Hurricane Katrina, which devastated ports and cities in the U.S. southern region (a large hub for grain exports and warehouses for other commodities), appears to have had only a temporary impact on specific nonfuel commodity markets. The temporary closure of ports and transportation blockage in the Mississippi River slowed down U.S. exports of soybeans, wheat, and corn. Hurricane Katrina also damaged cotton crops from Mississippi to Georgia. The current status of stockpiles of a significant amount of coffee and base metals, including nearly half of the world's inventories of zinc, remains unknown. Lumber prices have risen on expectations of significant construction activities to rebuild affected areas.

Semiconductor Markets

Following a record increase of 28 percent in 2004, sales revenue grew at a substantially lower rate during January–July 2005 compared with the same period in 2004. Most of the decline reflects weak average semiconductor prices (Figure 1.24). By July, the average (seasonally adjusted) selling price for semiconductors had fallen by 9 percent, though specific sectors posted larger price falls. For example, dynamic random access memory (DRAM) prices have fallen 37 percent on average since January. Looking forward, semiconductor prices are expected to rebound in the second half of the year owing to seasonal back-to-school purchases and holiday-season demand, with the rebound muted somewhat by the release of inventories. Sales revenue growth for 2005 is now projected at 6 percent compared with a zero percent growth forecast at end-2004.

Purchases of semiconductor production equipment appear to be contracting. The global book-to-bill ratio (an indicator of future relative to current investment) is hovering around 0.9, compared with the 2004 average of about 1.0. Lower capital investment in 2005 reflects in part an overhang in capacity arising from the large investment projects in 2004, which resulted in a significant fall in capacity utilization from 0.95 in 2004:Q2 to 0.88 in 2005:Q2. This spare capacity has resulted from the strong growth in production facilities of 9.5 percent over the past year, outstripping by a wide margin the growth in production of about 2 percent. Utilization rates in leading-edge production facilities, however, remain high, suggesting that overall prices of leading-edge products will not soften further.

Consumer demand for new electronics has been affected by a combination of high energy prices, rising interest rates, and falling confidence. However, falling prices for maturing consumer products should support sales going forward. While the most recent hike in energy prices has dampened business optimism somewhat, business purchases should eventually provide a strong market for the latest computing technology.

Appendix 1.2. How Will Global Imbalances Adjust?

The authors of this appendix are Doug Laxton and Gian Maria Milesi-Ferretti, with support from Susanna Mursula. The simulations using the Global Economy Model have greatly benefited from earlier work by Dirk Muir and Paolo Pesenti.

Background

Global imbalances have been widening in the past few years. Since 1996, the U.S. current account balance has deteriorated substantially, mirrored by improvements in the current account balance of emerging Asia, oil-producing developing countries (especially in recent years), and, to a lesser extent, small industrial countries such as Switzerland, Norway, and Sweden (Figure 1.25). The euro area's current account has remained close to balance, with divergent developments between surplus countries (Germany, the Benelux countries, and Finland) and deficit countries (such as Greece, Portugal, and Spain).

The deterioration of the U.S. current account was matched by a substantial appreciation of the U.S. dollar, which rose by some 35 percent in real effective terms between mid-1995 and early 2002, matched by real effective depreciations in the euro area and emerging Asia (Figure 1.26). Since early 2002, the U.S. dollar has depreciated by some 12 percent, matched primarily by appreciations of the euro and of the currencies of other main industrial countries; currencies in emerging market trading partners have remained broadly unchanged. Correspondingly, the depreciation of the U.S. dollar to date has offset less than one-half of the earlier appreciation, and has been significantly more muted than was the case during the adjustment episode of the mid-1980s.

As global current account imbalances have grown, the dispersion in net foreign asset posi-

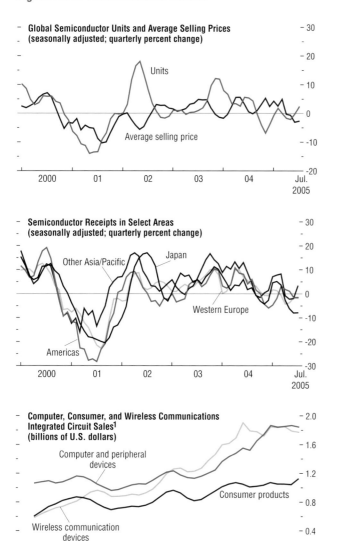

Figure 1.24. Semiconductor Market

Global Semiconductor Units and Average Selling Prices (seasonally adjusted; quarterly percent change)

Units

Average selling price

2000   01   02   03   04   Jul. 2005

Semiconductor Receipts in Select Areas (seasonally adjusted; quarterly percent change)

Other Asia/Pacific   Japan

Western Europe

Americas

2000   01   02   03   04   Jul. 2005

Computer, Consumer, and Wireless Communications Integrated Circuit Sales[1] (billions of U.S. dollars)

Computer and peripheral devices

Consumer products

Wireless communication devices

2002   03   04   Jul. 2005

Sources: World Semiconductor Trade Statistics; and IMF staff calculations.
[1]Sectors are defined by the final use of integrated circuits (ICs) in product categories. Definition excludes dual/multipurpose chips. Three-month moving averages.

tions (the difference between a country's claims on the rest of the world, and the rest of the world's claims on it) has correspondingly increased (Figure 1.27).[25] The U.S. net foreign asset position steadily deteriorated between 1996 and 2002, while Japan, some small industrial countries, emerging Asia, and oil exporters have built up significant creditor positions. Since 2002, despite widening current account deficits, United States' net liabilities have actually declined as a share of GDP. This is mainly due to valuation effects: the depreciation of the dollar and strong stock market performance outside the United States have resulted in substantial capital gains by the United States on its net external position (which includes assets mostly denominated in foreign currencies and liabilities denominated in U.S. dollars).[26]

Current World Economic Outlook projections, based on the assumption of constant real exchange rates, suggest little improvement in global imbalances. The U.S. current account deficit is projected to remain at about 6 percent of GDP into the medium term, with some improvement in the U.S. fiscal position offset by low private savings and rising interest payments, matched by continued large surpluses in Japan, emerging Asia, and oil-exporting countries. Hence the United States' net external position would continue to deteriorate, reaching a record 50 percent of GDP by 2010, matched by rising net creditor positions in the rest of the world.

Long-Run Sustainability Implications

Examining the stylized facts presented in the previous section, two key questions arise. What caused the widening in external imbalances? And what are the implications for long-run sustainability? We discuss these issues in turn.

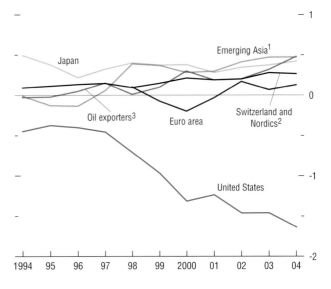

Figure 1.25. Current Account Balances
(Percent of world GDP)

Source: IMF staff calculations.
[1]China, Hong Kong SAR, Korea, Malaysia, Singapore, Taiwan Province of China, and Thailand.
[2]Norway, Sweden, and Switzerland.
[3]Algeria, Bahrain, Egypt, I.R. of Iran, Jordan, Kuwait, Libya, Russia, Saudi Arabia, Syrian Arab Republic, United Arab Emirates, and Yemen.

---

[25]The net foreign asset data are from the comprehensive database developed by Lane and Milesi-Ferretti (2005), with data for 2004 based on preliminary calculations by the authors.

[26]These capital gains are not incorporated in the current account.

Figure 1.26. Real Effective Exchange Rates

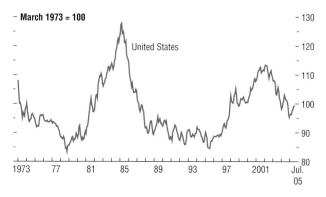

Sources: U.S. Federal Reserve Board; and IMF staff calculations.
[1]China, Hong Kong SAR, India, Indonesia, Korea, Malaysia, the Philippines, Singapore, Taiwan Province of China, and Thailand.

Beginning with the causes of imbalances, there is considerable consensus that the dollar appreciation and buildup of U.S. current account deficits during the second half of the 1990s were associated with high productivity growth and a shift in preference toward U.S. assets, possibly as a consequence of overoptimistic expectations about future asset returns, the Asian crisis, and sluggish economic performance in Europe and Japan.[27] However, even following the sizable correction in stock market valuations after 2000 and the slowdown in economic activity in the United States, the U.S. current account deficit did not adjust. A number of factors have been at play.

- Fiscal and monetary policies in the United States became sharply expansionary—both absolutely and relative to other countries— thus sustaining domestic demand. In addition, booming house prices, fueled by low interest rates, have contributed to a reduction in household saving.

- Investment in a number of key countries, such as Germany and Japan, has remained depressed, and—with the exception of China—investment in emerging Asian countries continues to be weak, relative to historical standards.

- National saving rates in China and oil-exporting countries have risen sharply.

Views on the relative importance of these factors vary. Some authors have emphasized the role of U.S. fiscal imbalances and foreign-exchange intervention by Asian central banks (Roubini and Setser, 2005), while others have downplayed the role of fiscal policy and highlighted the importance of a "global saving glut" (particularly in emerging markets) reducing world interest rates (Bernanke, 2005).

Looking forward, as already described, the global imbalances are clearly unsustainable in

---

[27]On the impact of U.S. productivity shocks and related expectations, see Erceg, Guerrieri, and Gust (2002) and Hunt (2002). Hunt and Rebucci (2003) explore the combined implications of a U.S. productivity shock and a shift in preference toward U.S. assets.

the long term: if the U.S. external current account balance excluding investment income remained at its current level of over 5 percent of GDP, there would be an unbounded accumulation of external liabilities.[28] To date, however, the United States has experienced little difficulty in financing imbalances, reflecting partly increased financial globalization—which has boosted the allocation of wealth to foreign financial instruments—and partly substantial purchases of U.S. bonds by monetary authorities, particularly in Asia.

Views again differ, however, as to how long this situation can persist. On the one hand, the "new Bretton Woods hypothesis"—advanced by Dooley, Folkerts-Landau, and Garber (2003, 2004)—posits that the constellation of external imbalances partly reflects the deliberate actions (e.g., de facto pegs) of "periphery" countries—particularly China—seeking export-led growth as a development strategy, which they believe can continue for a significant period. Another "benign" view of imbalances stresses the role of globalization, with the weakening in the correlation between national saving and domestic investment reflecting the better functioning and increasing integration of global capital markets. Finally, the rise in U.S. indebtedness has been described as reflecting optimal private sector behavior, and hence not a source of concern, in line with the Lawson doctrine. More specifically, U.S. imbalances are viewed as the natural consequence of a large increase in the stock of U.S. wealth and weak investment opportunities in other countries, rather than the consequence of large U.S. fiscal deficits and private sector over-borrowing (Backus and Lambert, 2005; Cooper, 2005).

On the other hand, a number of authors (see, for example, Obstfeld and Rogoff, 2004, 2005; Roubini and Setser, 2005; and Blanchard,

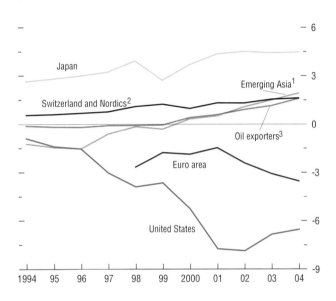

Figure 1.27. Net Foreign Assets
(Percent of world GDP)

Source: Lane and Milesi-Ferretti (2005).
[1] China, Hong Kong SAR, Korea, Malaysia, Singapore, Taiwan Province of China, and Thailand.
[2] Norway, Sweden, and Switzerland.
[3] Algeria, Bahrain, Egypt, I.R. of Iran, Jordan, Kuwait, Libya, Russia, Saudi Arabia, Syrian Arab Republic, United Arab Emirates, and Yemen.

[28]To stabilize its external liabilities as a percentage of GDP, a debtor country must run a surplus on its external current account excluding net investment income (assuming, as is generally the case, that the interest rate it pays on its external liabilities exceeds its long-run growth rate).

Giavazzi, and Sa, 2005) emphasize that the current pattern of global imbalances will have to be unwound through a substantial real depreciation of the dollar. While financial globalization makes it easier to finance external imbalances, these authors note that, given the small size of the U.S. traded goods sector relative to the size of the U.S. economy, the trade deficit expressed as a share of traded goods production is very large. As a consequence, the relative price of non-traded goods in the United States has to fall substantially to ensure that the consumption of traded goods by U.S. residents declines, making room for an adjustment in the trade balance.[29] While the models are of course less specific on the timing of this adjustment, they underscore that the longer current account deficits are sustained, the bigger the stock of U.S. external liabilities, and the larger the ultimate adjustment in real exchange rates that will be required.

Model-Based Adjustment Scenarios

In this section we present a baseline scenario for global current account rebalancing and then consider potential risks and possible policy initiatives that would help mitigate these risks. The scenarios are based on a four-region version of the Global Economy Model (GEM), comprising the United States, the euro area and Japan, emerging Asian economies, and the rest of the world. In the model, described in more detail in Faruqee and others (2005) and the April 2005 *World Economic Outlook*, each region produces both tradable and nontradable goods, with bilateral trade flows taking place between the blocs. Both goods markets and labor markets are char-

acterized by the presence of imperfect competition and nominal rigidities, and consumers are non-Ricardian—that is, they treat a portion of government debt as net wealth—so that changes in macroeconomic policies can have significant short- and long-term effects.

Turning to policies, monetary policy in the United States, the Japan–euro area bloc, and the rest of the world is characterized by an interest rate feedback rule that gradually moves inflation toward a constant desired rate.[30] In contrast, in emerging Asia the exchange rate is assumed to be pegged to the U.S. dollar (although the implications of a shift to a more flexible exchange rate regime, accompanied by a monetary policy rule similar to the other regions, are also considered). Fiscal policy plays a more passive role, stabilizing the debt-to-GDP ratio in the medium term.

The desired level of net foreign assets (or foreign liabilities) in each region over the medium term plays a key role in determining the equilibrium level of current account balances—and therefore exchange rates. In the long run, the United States is assumed to be the only debtor region, with the remaining regions holding positive net foreign assets.[31]

Before turning to the scenarios, it is important to underscore three additional points.
• The model provides *simulations*, not *forecasts*, with key parameter assumptions in GEM broadly in line with those in similar large-scale macroeconomic models. One important assumption for these scenarios is the value chosen for the elasticity of substitution between traded goods produced in different countries, which leads to higher price elastici-

---

[29]Estimates presented by Obstfeld and Rogoff (2004, 2005) suggest that the real effective depreciation of the dollar needed to eliminate the U.S. current account deficit is about 30 percent, with a corresponding large appreciation in Asia and the euro area (although they do not allow for supply-side effects, which would tend to reduce the extent of the depreciation). Using a different model, which emphasizes shocks to asset markets, Blanchard, Giavazzi, and Sa (2005) also come to the conclusion that a substantial—if gradual—dollar depreciation is likely to occur over the medium term, which would bring the U.S. trade balance to sustainable levels.

[30]Japan is assumed to have exited from deflation and the zero interest rate constraint on monetary policy is thus assumed to be no longer binding.

[31]Ghironi, Iscan, and Rebucci (2005) describe how differences in agents' discount factors across countries lead to nonzero net foreign asset positions in the long run.

ties of demand for both exports and imports than is normally found in standard export and import equations. Consequently, estimates of the exchange rate adjustments that need to accompany global rebalancing in the scenarios may be regarded as conservative.

- No model incorporates every aspect of the real world, and GEM is no exception. In particular, the financial market sector is quite limited—there are no portfolio effects (notably valuation effects on gross external positions and differences in rates of return between external assets and liabilities), no room for sterilized intervention, and limited scope for the financial sector to amplify the effect of real shocks. Finally, the model does not explicitly incorporate oil prices and consequently cannot be used to address the potential role of oil exporters in the adjustment process.[32]
- The model does not match historical data perfectly. Therefore, caution should be exercised in interpreting the short-run movements in certain variables during the first periods of the simulations, which may simply reflect the adjustment of these variables to the path suggested by the model.

Adjustment Without Policies

Because, as described above, the global imbalances are unsustainable over the long run, the issue is not *whether* but *how* they adjust. This section looks at how the global economy might adjust in the absence of policy changes, barring modest fiscal adjustments, to ensure that public debt stabilizes in the long run. We consider two scenarios: a relatively benign baseline, in which non-U.S. residents are willing to continue increasing their holdings of U.S. assets for a considerable period without demanding a large risk premium; and a more disorderly adjustment, in which there is a sudden loss in demand for U.S. assets combined with a surge in protectionist pressures across the globe.

Benign Baseline Scenario

In the benign scenario, as noted above, it is assumed for the sake of illustration that policies remain broadly unchanged relative to their 2004 levels[33] (in practice, since GEM does not allow for sterilized intervention, the exchange rate in emerging Asia adjusts more rapidly in this scenario than might otherwise be the case). In the United States, the budget deficit remains at its 2004 level of 4 percent of GDP, and in other regions there is a modest tightening of fiscal policies to ensure that public debt is broadly sustainable over the longer term.[34] Consequently, current account adjustment is primarily driven by changes in private sector behavior, which must in turn be consistent with the desired level of net foreign assets (or liabilities) in each region. In this scenario the initial constellation of current account imbalances is generated by low private (and public) saving in the United States, together with strong foreign demand for U.S. assets.[35] As the various shocks that drive the current constellation of imbalances unwind, the world economy gradually adjusts toward its long-run equilibrium. The scenario results are displayed in Figures 1.28–1.30, together with bands that provide a measure of uncertainty surrounding the model results. Adjustment across the various regions takes place broadly as follows.

- In the *United States*, the gradual reduction in private consumption necessary to raise savings

---

[32]Chapter II discusses in more detail the implications of saving and investment behavior in oil-exporting countries for global imbalances.

[33]As described in the main text, some measures have in fact been taken since that time.

[34]A constant deficit of 4 percent of GDP in the United States does imply some fiscal consolidation, because the increase in the stock of debt from its current level raises the interest burden, so that the underlying primary balance must strengthen.

[35]The baseline scenario also allows for persistent differentials in productivity growth (higher growth in emerging Asia and lower growth in the Japan–euro area bloc) and an increase in appetite for imports from emerging Asia. However, these factors have a more modest impact on the dynamics of current accounts than do the assumptions about saving behavior.

Figure 1.28. United States: Baseline Scenario
(Percent of GDP unless otherwise noted)

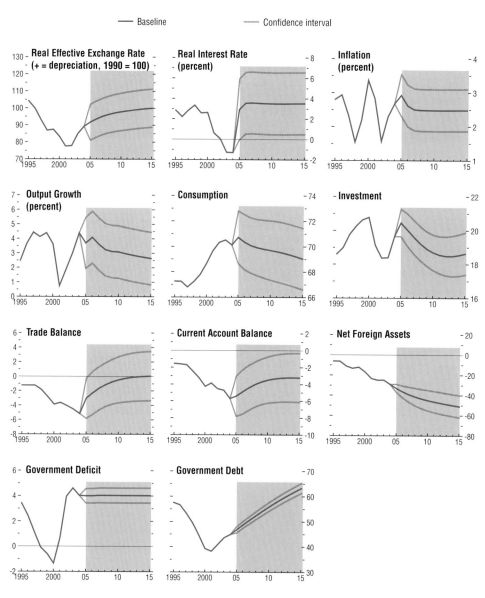

Source: IMF staff estimates.

is accompanied by higher real interest rates—which also reduce private investment through 2010—and a further real effective depreciation of the U.S. dollar of about 15 percent over the long term.[36] This results in some slowdown in GDP growth, and a steady reduction in the current account deficit to about 3½ percent of GDP by 2010 (Figure 1.28), and to 3 percent of GDP over the long run, with U.S. net foreign liabilities eventually stabilizing at about 70 percent of GDP.[37]

- The main counterpart of U.S. adjustment is in *emerging Asia*, where the current account surplus gradually declines to about 2 percent of GDP, consistent with maintaining a substantial net creditor position over the longer term, with a sharp rise in private consumption more than offsetting some decline in investment over the longer term (Figure 1.29).[38] This is accompanied by a gradual real exchange rate appreciation of about 15 percent, which—if exchange rates do not adjust—is achieved through a persistent positive inflation differential vis-à-vis trading partners. Productivity growth declines over the medium term as the level of productivity catches up to the levels in more advanced economies.

- The impact on *Japan and the euro area* is relatively limited, with the current account surplus projected to decline by about 0.5 percent of GDP over the next 10 years, accompanied by a 5 percent real effective appreciation (Figure

1.30). Productivity growth is assumed to remain below trend over the medium term and to eventually recover gradually, generating a similar trend in private investment.

- In the *rest of the world*, the adjustment process in the current account is similar to the one in emerging Asia, given the strong trade linkages with the United States (mainly Canada and Mexico), but real exchange rate changes are muted because there is a smaller underlying change in its preferences for holding U.S. assets.

In summary, this adjustment scenario is characterized by a sizable—if relatively gradual—private sector–led adjustment, accompanied by somewhat lower U.S. and global growth, and noticeable but orderly exchange rate adjustments in a number of regions. All in all, the scenario looks fairly benign, but it depends critically on the willingness of foreigners to accommodate a further substantial buildup in U.S. foreign liabilities, in the face of further foreign exchange losses—as noted above, not included in the model—without demanding a large risk premium.[39]

A More Abrupt Adjustment

The second scenario looks at the impact of a much more abrupt and disorderly adjustment, assuming a combination of a temporary rise in protectionist pressures,[40] accompanied by a sudden decline in demand for U.S. assets—including an abandonment of pegs in emerging

[36]A lower elasticity of substitution between traded goods produced in different countries would imply a larger dollar depreciation. On the other hand, the valuation effects of exchange rate changes (not fully captured in the model) would mitigate somewhat the size of the needed adjustment, by inflicting capital losses on holders of dollar assets and thus improving the U.S. net external position.

[37]The model is calibrated to match the U.S. current account during the historical period but it underpredicts the U.S. trade deficit, because it assumes that the U.S. income balance is negative, in proportion to the outstanding stock of U.S. net external liabilities. Consequently, the change in the trade balance between its actual level in 2004 and the predicted one in 2005 is magnified.

[38]As mentioned earlier, the model does not match historical data perfectly—in particular, it predicts higher-than-realized investment and inflation in emerging Asia. The first periods of the simulations thus reflect an increase of these variables to the path suggested by the model.

[39]The baseline assumes that real interest rates in the United States are about 50 basis points higher than in the rest of the world. A larger risk premium on U.S. dollar liabilities would increase the trade surplus required to stabilize the net external position, and would therefore act as a brake on the accumulation of external liabilities by the United States (as exemplified in the next scenario).

[40]In GEM, this is modeled as a substantial—if temporary—increase in margins in product markets in all regions, which is particularly large for the traded goods sector.

Figure 1.29. Emerging Asia: Baseline Scenario
(Percent of GDP unless otherwise noted)

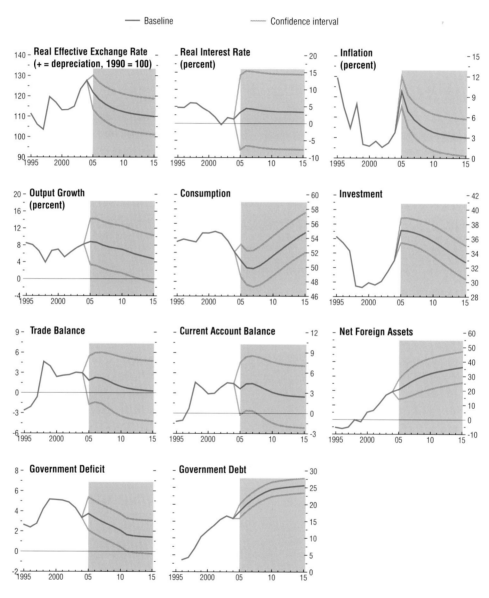

Source: IMF staff estimates.

Figure 1.30. Japan and Euro Area: Baseline Scenario
(Percent of GDP unless otherwise noted)

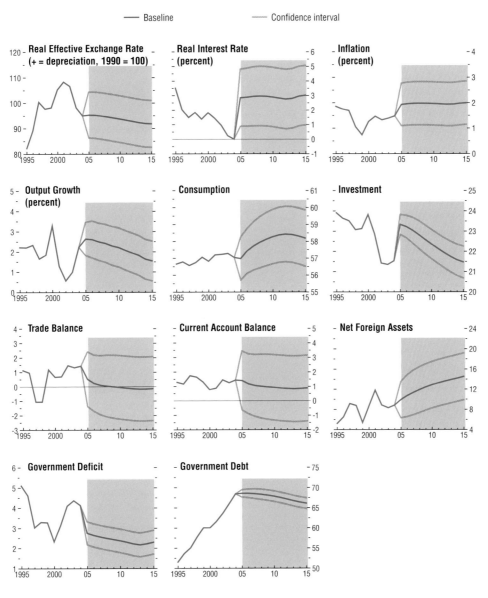

Source: IMF staff estimates.

Asia. The decline in demand for U.S. assets is assumed to be stronger in emerging Asia than in other regions, and to be reflected in a general decline in the desire to hold foreign assets.

Scenario results are presented in Figure 1.31, with the blue line reporting the "benign" baseline and the red line the abrupt adjustment outcomes. The consequence of these shocks is a sharp contraction in U.S. economic activity, relative to the baseline. The shift in portfolio preferences away from U.S. assets forces a large real depreciation of the dollar and a sharp correction in the U.S. trade balance. Together with the increase in protectionism, this leads to rising inflationary pressures, requiring a significant short-term monetary tightening, which amplifies the contractionary effect on GDP growth.

The economies of emerging Asia experience a sharp real appreciation, a deterioration in the trade and current account balances, and a slowdown in economic activity. The appreciation, together with a monetary policy tightening (as the focus of monetary policy shifts from the exchange rate peg to an inflation target), helps contain inflationary pressures relative to the baseline. In the euro area and Japan, growth slows sharply, the current account deteriorates, and the real exchange rate appreciates on impact, helping to contain the jump in prices arising from protectionism.[41] Finally, in the remaining countries, the pattern of adjustment is qualitatively similar to the one in the euro area and Japan.

In summary, this scenario highlights the danger that sudden shifts in market sentiment, along with rising protectionist pressures, could entail for global growth. Given the very large short-term exchange rate adjustments that take place in this scenario, there is also significantly greater risk of financial market disruption—not explicitly considered in GEM—with further negative implications for global stability and growth.

How Can Policies Help?

How can policies help reduce the risks of a disorderly adjustment taking place, and limit the impact on global growth? To address this key policy question, we present three illustrative scenarios, which highlight the implications of increased exchange rate flexibility in emerging Asia, faster fiscal consolidation in the United States, and growth-enhancing structural reforms in the euro area and Japan (see Box 1.6, "Policies to Reduce Global Imbalances").

Greater Exchange Rate Flexibility in Emerging Asia

As has already been described in the benign baseline scenario, exchange rates in emerging Asia will need to appreciate over the medium term. Consequently, the key questions are how this is achieved—whether through a nominal appreciation or through higher inflation—and when it takes place. To emphasize the implications of an increase in exchange rate flexibility in emerging Asia, not driven by disruptive events as in the previous scenario, we consider a scenario where the move toward increased exchange rate flexibility in the region is accompanied by a decline in the rate of accumulation of foreign exchange reserves, leading to a reduced stock of net foreign assets relative to the baseline. The decline in holdings of foreign assets by emerging Asia is spread across all other regions, but is stronger vis-à-vis the United States.

The results are presented in Figure 1.32 (red line), together with those of the baseline (blue line). The shift in exchange rate and reserves policy in emerging Asia is accompanied by a more rapid—but still gradual—real effective appreciation relative to the baseline, which helps stymie inflationary pressures.[42] The downward adjustment in the current account is mirrored by

---

[41]If the portfolio shock entailed higher demand by emerging Asia for euro area or Japanese assets, rather than a generalized decline in demand for foreign assets, there would be a larger initial appreciation of the euro and the yen and a smaller appreciation in emerging Asia.

[42]Over the medium term, the real effective appreciation in this scenario is actually lower than in the baseline, because the net foreign asset position is smaller and hence the equilibrium trade deficit is smaller.

Figure 1.31. Disruptive Adjustment

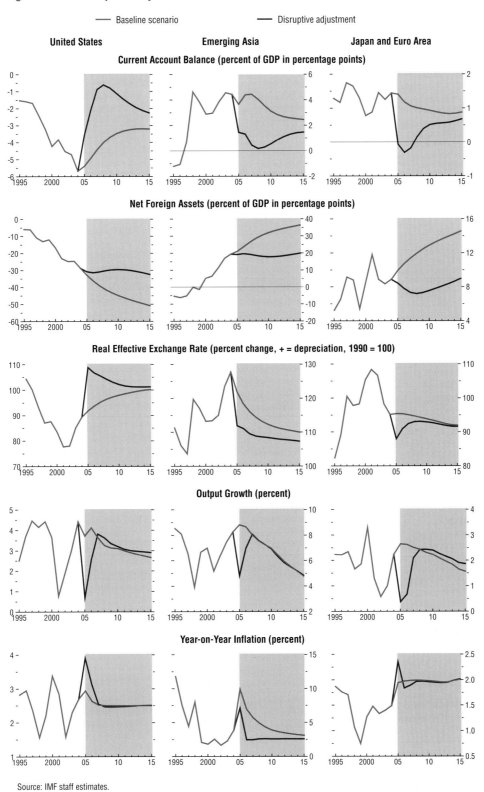

Source: IMF staff estimates.

Figure 1.32. Greater Exchange Rate Flexibility in Emerging Asia

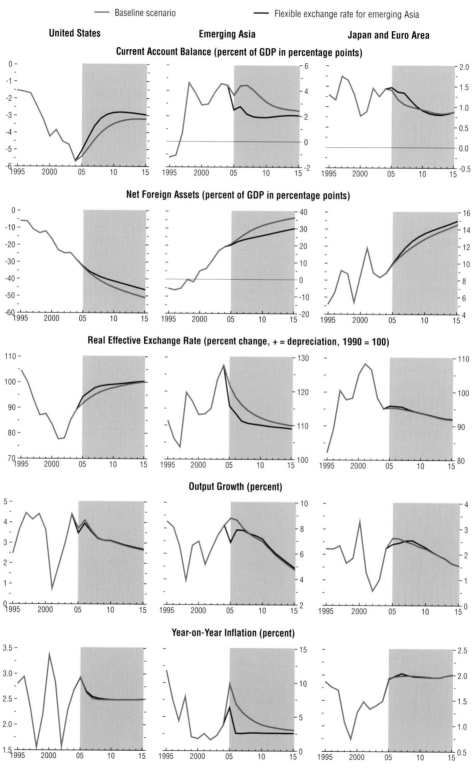

Source: IMF staff estimates.

Box 1.6. Policies to Reduce Global Imbalances

This box sets out, in broad terms, policies in each country/region that would contribute to an orderly adjustment in global imbalances.

In the *United States*, the priority is to increase national savings, with the main policy instrument available to achieve this being fiscal consolidation. The projections underlying the fiscal adjustment scenario assume that the federal budget excluding Social Security is balanced by 2013, and that reform of entitlement programs ensures their long-term fiscal sustainability. Achieving this objective would require the following.

- Full implementation of the adjustment plans in current U.S. Administration projections (as contained in the 2006 Mid-Session Review), including tight limits on discretionary spending. This would be facilitated by the introduction of a legislated fiscal rule requiring the costs of proposals to increase the deficit to be offset elsewhere in the budget.
- Revenue-enhancing measures, preferably through base broadening. These could include eliminating tax exemptions (for example, the deductibility of state and local taxes, interest on state and local bonds, mortgage relief, and employer contributions for medical insurance premiums); raising energy taxes; or the introduction of a federal VAT or sales tax.

In *emerging Asia*, the priorities are to allow greater exchange rate flexibility, consistent with the required medium-term appreciation of regional currencies, along with measures to strengthen domestic demand.

- In China, the authorities should take full advantage of the additional exchange rate flexibility afforded by the recent exchange rate reform. This, in turn, would facilitate greater upward exchange rate flexibility in other countries in the region, as appropriate.
- On the demand side, priorities differ across countries. In China, where investment is already high, reforms to strengthen the social

safety net would allow households to reduce precautionary savings; improved household access to credit—subject to strict prudential requirements—would also contribute. Elsewhere, the issue is primarily relatively low investment. While that may partly reflect the lingering impact of the crisis, which should gradually ebb over time, policies need to focus on supporting that process by addressing weaknesses in the investment climate, including by completing outstanding financial sector reforms, reducing entry requirements, promoting a level playing field, and clarifying the framework for labor relations.

In *euro area countries*, the key contribution to help ensure an orderly reduction in global imbalances is through measures to boost growth and domestic demand. In this connection, progress in structural reform has been achieved in a number of areas—for example, pension reform in France and Italy and the "Hartz-IV" reforms in Germany. However, significant scope remains for packages of measures designed not only to raise employment and productivity, but also to strengthen competition in product markets, and thereby reduce markups and increase real wages, such as the following.[1]

- *Increasing product market competition.* At the euro area level, the priority is to implement the Services Directive, which could substantially increase cross-border provision of services. In individual countries, priorities include increasing competition in the network, telecommunications, and transport industries (France, Italy); deregulation in the retail sector (France, Italy); and reducing barriers to entry in services, particularly professional services (Germany).
- *Increasing labor market competition and flexibility.* Priorities vary widely across countries, but for the largest countries they include reforming minimum wages (France) and allowing greater flexibility in wage bargaining (Germany and Italy); lowering tax wedges (Germany and

Note: The main author of this box is Gian Maria Milesi-Ferretti.

[1]See, for example, Estevão (2005).

Box 1.6 *(concluded)*

Italy); and reforming employment protection (all countries) and social safety nets (France and Germany).

In *Japan*, priorities for reforms to raise competition and growth include the following.

- *Further improving flexibility and participation in labor markets.* Key measures would include clarifying the conditions for dismissing workers, and implementing more family-friendly policies to encourage women to enter (or reenter) the labor force.
- Enhancing competition in product markets. Regulation could be relaxed further in sheltered sectors (e.g., retail sector, network industries). The Fair Trade Commission could further stiffen penalties for anticompetitive behavior. There is also scope for allowing more private sector involvement in health and education at a national level (in line with "Special Zones" initiatives).
- *Reforming the agricultural sector.* This sector can particularly benefit from reform, in light of its current high protection and low efficiency. Reducing import barriers and moving toward direct payments to farmers would bolster productivity and enhance growth prospects.
- Continuing to strengthen the financial and corporate sector, including by pressing ahead with implementation of the authorities' Program for Further Financial Reform and the privatization of Japan Post.

In the *oil-producing countries*, the challenge is to achieve an orderly increase in domestic demand in response to higher oil revenues, while avoiding wasteful expenditures—a key problem in the 1970s. Within this, the appropriate policies vary significantly across countries, depending on cyclical conditions—which in some cases limit the room for immediate budgetary expansion—as well as the medium-term fiscal outlook.[2] However, there are three common elements:

- *Boosting expenditures in areas where social returns are high*, including—depending on the country—education and health; infrastructure; schemes to boost private sector employment; and strengthened social protection schemes;
- *Taking advantage of a stronger external position to address structural constraints to growth*, for instance, by improving the investment climate and, in some countries, reducing restrictiveness of trade regimes; and
- *Allowing gradual real exchange rate appreciation as appropriate*, consistent with higher domestic absorption over the medium term.

[2]See "Oil Market Developments and Issues" (IMF, 2005b) and Box 1.6 in the April 2005 *World Economic Outlook*, "How Should Middle Eastern and Central Asian Oil Exporters Use Their Oil Revenues?" for a more detailed discussion.

an improvement in both the United States and the euro area–Japan region. As a reflection of these developments, over the medium term net foreign assets in emerging Asia and net liabilities in the United States will be smaller than in the baseline. While there is a temporary slowdown in GDP growth in emerging Asia, related to the weaker contribution to growth coming from net exports, consumption is higher relative to the

baseline.[43] As noted above, the model simulations probably underestimate the impact of a more flexible exchange rate policy since—because GEM does not allow for sterilization—a portion of the effect is effectively included in the baseline.

This scenario can also provide insights on the possible consequences of the opposite policy choice by emerging Asia—namely, sustained

[43]The slowdown in growth is accentuated by the tightening of monetary policy in response to high inflation in the baseline. Allowing for sterilization in the baseline would imply a more modest difference in the monetary policy stance, and hence in growth, between the two scenarios.

sterilization. While GEM does not allow for this policy choice, the effect of delayed adjustment through sterilization can be approximated by assuming that emerging Asia raises its desired level of net foreign assets (the opposite of what is postulated in Figure 1.32). Symmetrically to the scenario presented above, this policy choice would induce an initial exchange rate *depreciation* relative to the baseline, which may help growth in the region over the short run, but at the cost of higher inflation, lower consumption, and larger external imbalances.

In sum, with the move toward a more flexible exchange rate, the nominal and real exchange rates appreciate, facilitating external adjustment, stimulating domestic consumption, and containing inflationary pressures relative to the baseline. From a domestic perspective, increased exchange rate flexibility would thus help emerging Asia cope with rapid external adjustment needs without jeopardizing macroeconomic stability.

Rapid Fiscal Consolidation in the United States

We consider next a scenario featuring a substantial reduction in the U.S. budget deficit over the medium term (some of which is already under way). This is assumed to take place through a cut in government consumption of ¾ percent of GDP and a gradual but ultimately sizable increase in taxation, leading to a broadly balanced budget by 2010.[44] The fiscal consolidation, which is assumed to become fully credible after two years, results in a sizable reduction in the debt-to-GDP ratio over the medium term.[45]

It is also assumed that the U.S. fiscal consolidation is accompanied by an increase in exchange rate flexibility in emerging Asia, along the lines described above.

Results are presented in Figure 1.33 as deviations from the scenario of Figure 1.32 featuring flexible exchange rates in emerging Asia. The tightening of U.S. fiscal policy leads to a notable improvement in the current account—by about 2 percent over 10 years—and a reduction in U.S. net foreign liabilities by over 10 percent over the same horizon, accompanied by a modest depreciation of the U.S. dollar.[46] This comes at the cost of an initial slowdown in U.S. growth, although over time the reduction in U.S. government debt leads to a reduction in long-term interest rates, boosting private investment and eventually raising long-run output above that in the baseline scenario.[47]

In the rest of the world, the impact on growth is broadly similar—though somewhat smaller in magnitude—to that in the United States, with a short-run decline in growth and a subsequent recovery bringing output above its baseline level in the long run, helped by lower real interest rates. All regions also experience a deterioration in the current account—most pronounced in emerging Asia—and a slight appreciation of their currencies.

Overall, these simulations indicate that fiscal consolidation in the United States would have a noticeable effect on the current account balance, and—over time—on U.S. net external liabilities, thereby reducing external risks. The adjustment entails short-term output costs, in

---

[44]Over the long term, the deficit rises again on account of demographic pressures, and is eventually stabilized at 3 percent.

[45]A fiscal consolidation that was fully credible from the outset would induce a more moderate output contraction by ensuring a more rapid decline in interest rates. For technical details and examples of credible and noncredible deficit reductions, see Bayoumi and Laxton (1994).

[46]See Kumhof, Laxton, and Muir (2005) for a more comprehensive assessment of medium- and long-term effects of fiscal consolidation on output and external imbalances in the United States using a four-country version of the IMF's Global Fiscal Model (GFM). Botman and others (2005) discuss structure and properties of a two-country version of the model.

[47]It should be acknowledged that the projected impact of fiscal policy on the current account is at the high end of existing estimates in the literature. For example, Erceg, Guerrieri, and Gust (2005) find a smaller response of the current account to fiscal policy, primarily because they assume that the fiscal adjustment is temporary, with no long-run change in public debt, and because half of the consumers are assumed to have an infinite planning horizon. In this event, of course, the adverse impact of fiscal consolidation on growth will also be lower.

Figure 1.33. Incremental Effects of Fiscal Consolidation in the United States
(Deviation from baseline; x-axis in calendar years)

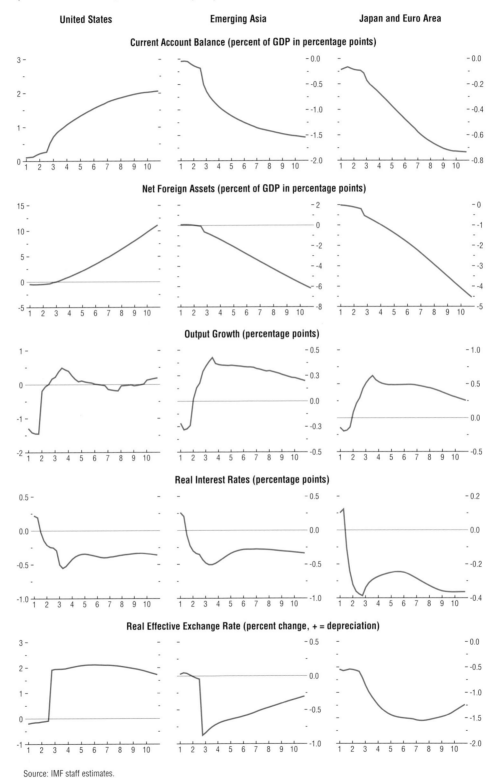

Source: IMF staff estimates.

both the United States and—to a lesser degree—the rest of the world. However, over time the positive effects of sustained lower real interest rates would imply an increase in global output of about 0.2 percentage points.[48]

Structural Reform in the Euro Area and Japan

Finally, we look at the implications of stronger growth in the euro area and Japan through structural policies aimed at improving competition, raising capital accumulation, and reducing distortions in labor and product markets. To study such a scenario we follow Bayoumi, Laxton, and Pesenti (2004) and assume that price markups in both the tradable and nontradable sectors in Europe and Japan decline gradually to U.S. levels over a 10-year period.[49] Labor market reform is introduced gradually, and takes the form of an increase in labor market competition. Consumers and investors initially treat labor and product market reforms as temporary—credibility builds over time, and the reforms become fully credible after three years.[50] The prospect of a comprehensive structural reform package in these countries is also assumed to gradually reduce precautionary saving, thus entailing some reduction in the long-run creditor position of the region (and a corresponding increase in foreign assets in the other regions).

The results presented in Figure 1.34 show the additional effects of these reforms relative to a baseline where U.S. fiscal policy is tighter and emerging Asia moves to a flexible exchange rate. The boost to competitiveness results in a significant investment-driven increase in GDP growth in Europe and Japan, which starts materializing after two years. This in turn results in a deterioration in the external current account; and—after an initial appreciation—a long-term depreciation of the real effective exchange rate.[51] Higher growth in Europe and Japan leads to a general improvement in current account balances and some appreciation of real effective exchange rates elsewhere; there are also modest positive spillover effects to growth on the rest of the world, with global growth rising by about ¼ percentage point over the medium term.[52] To the extent that brighter productivity prospects are reflected in asset prices, spillover effects may be magnified by financial market linkages that are not included in the model.

In sum, structural reforms in the euro area and Japan would help spur global growth, while also contributing to reducing external imbalances—albeit to a lesser extent than the U.S. fiscal consolidation presented earlier. It should be noted that the adjustment path will depend critically on the effects of these reforms on confidence—and thereby precautionary savings. If structural reforms led to greater uncertainty in the short run, the positive impact on growth—and the rise in the current account deficit—would likely be delayed. In contrast, if the reform package was fully credible, the prospect of higher and more certain growth in these countries could encourage consumer spending, boosting the impact of higher productivity growth on the global rebalancing of external positions.

Benefits of Joint Action

The current constellation of global imbalances arises from a combination of shocks and economic trends across several countries and

---

[48]A more modest response of investment to lower interest rates would imply a smaller impact on growth than the model suggests.

[49]Several studies have highlighted the benefits of product market reforms aimed at spurring competition—including through facilitating market entry or market access—for output and productivity growth. See, for example, Nicoletti and Scarpetta (2003) and Salgado (2002).

[50]Given that the initial markups in the euro area and Japan are calibrated on their level in 1995, the effects of competition-enhancing policies adopted since then may already be in the pipeline.

[51]The increase in productivity is particularly strong in the nontraded goods sector, generating a reverse Balassa-Samuelson effect.

[52]Batini, N'Diaye, and Rebucci (2005) examine the implications of an increase in productivity growth in Japan in a five-region version of GEM and find similar results.

Figure 1.34. Incremental Effects of Competition-Friendly Policies in Europe and Japan
(Deviation from baseline, x-axis in calendar years)

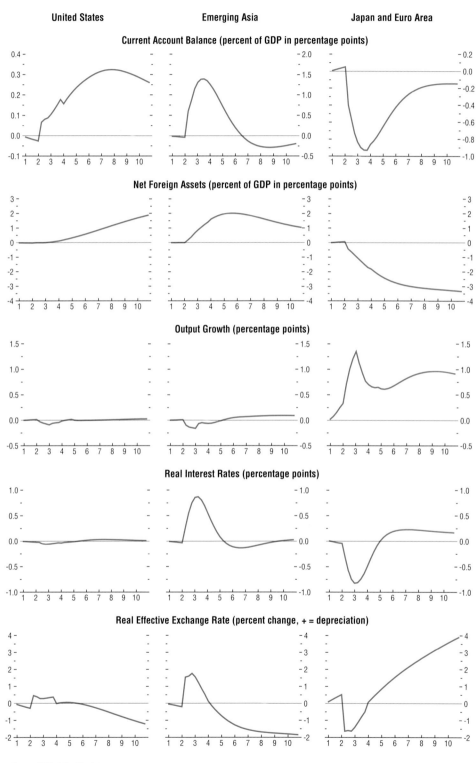

Source: IMF staff estimates.

regions. Current account adjustment foremost requires changes in private sector behavior, which will in time inevitably take place: the role of policy measures is to facilitate these changes and minimize the attendant risks. The variety of factors driving current patterns of international borrowing and lending—including a number that are not explicitly captured by the model[53]—also implies that policy actions by a country taken individually may have a relatively modest impact, but in combination with actions by other countries can add up to significant adjustment.

The scenarios just described illustrate these points. They show that while a relatively benign private sector–driven unwinding of external imbalances is possible, the rising stock of U.S. external liabilities would involve significant risk, exemplified by the low-probability but high-cost abrupt adjustment scenario. The three adjustment scenarios illustrate the benefits and costs of three public policy actions that would facilitate this adjustment while simultaneously being in each country's own national interest. Other such actions—including measures to boost private investment in some parts of Asia, or measures to facilitate the absorption of oil revenues in oil-producing countries—are discussed in more detail in Chapter II. While each such measure would bring about desirable changes, benefits would be magnified and risks minimized by joint action on the part of all major actors in the global economy, this being a clear instance in which coordinated policies would be a public good.

More specifically, combined policy action along the lines described in the various scenarios would have the following desirable consequences.

- Global imbalances in general, and the ultimate buildup in U.S. net foreign liabilities in particular, would be significantly reduced (Figure 1.35). Correspondingly, the risk of an

[53]As already mentioned, the model does not explicitly allow for sterilized intervention, nor does it include low investment in emerging Asia (excluding China), oil price developments, or booming asset prices (discussed in Chapter II).

Figure 1.35. Scenarios for Global Adjustments
(Percent of GDP)

Combined policy action—with the effects of individual measures on the baseline shown cumulatively in the figure—could significantly reduce global imbalances.

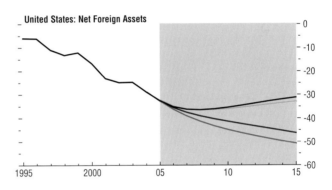

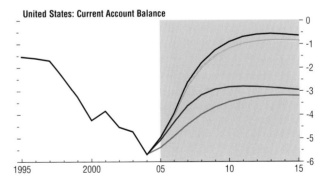

Source: IMF staff estimates.

abrupt adjustment in imbalances would be considerably limited.

- Global growth would be better balanced than in the baseline scenario, and significantly higher over the medium term, reflecting both lower global interest rates and stronger productivity growth in the euro area and in Japan.

- Last, but not least, each individual region would be better off. Emerging Asia's consumption would increase, as residents benefit from more favorable terms of trade; consumption and growth in the euro area and Japan would be stimulated by higher productivity; the United States would face lower risks of a decline in appetite for U.S. assets, and the recovery in private and public saving would contribute to lower interest rates relative to the baseline; and the rest of the world would also benefit from more appreciated real exchange rates and lower world interest rates.

While the combined adjustment scenario is clearly superior to the baseline from an overall perspective, two final points should be noted.

- First, there is a possibility that global growth could be weaker than expected, especially if structural adjustment in the euro area and Japan were to have a negative effect on confidence. This is perhaps of somewhat lesser concern in the current environment of relatively strong global growth, and—as the analysis above suggests—such risks would be reduced the more credible the underlying policy measures in all regions are seen to be.

- Second, the unwinding of imbalances will, even in a relatively favorable scenario, require significant exchange rate adjustment—in this connection, as already noted, the simulations may be conservative.[54] Policymakers and private sector decision makers will need to ensure that national economies and financial and nonfinancial corporations are resilient in the face of potential changes.

References

Backus, David, and Fréderic Lambert, 2005, "Current Account Fact and Fiction" (unpublished; New York: New York University).

Baffes, John, 2005, "The 'Cotton Problem,'" *World Bank Research Observer*, Vol. 20 (Spring), pp. 109–44.

Bank of Japan, 2001, "Developments in Profits and Balance Sheets of Japanese Banks in Fiscal 2000 and Banks' Management Tasks," *Bank of Japan Quarterly Bulletin*, Vol. 9 (November).

———, 2004, *Overview of Japanese Banks: Observations from Financial Statements for Fiscal 2003* (July).

Batini, Nicoletta, Papa N'Diaye, and Alessandro Rebucci, 2005, "The Domestic and Global Impact of Japan's Policies for Growth," in "Japan: 2005 Article IV Consultation—Staff Report; Staff Supplement; and Public Information Notice on the Executive Board Discussion," IMF Country Report No. 05/273 (Washington: International Monetary Fund).

Bayoumi, Tamim, and Douglas Laxton, 1994, "Government Deficits, Debt, and the Business Cycle," in *Deficit Reduction—What Pain, What Gain?* ed. by William B.P. Robson and William M. Scarth (Toronto: C.D. Howe Institute).

———, and Paolo Pesenti, 2004, "Benefits and Spillovers of Greater Competition in Europe: A Macroeconomic Assessment," NBER Working Paper No. 10416 (Cambridge, Massachusetts: National Bureau of Economic Research).

Bernanke, Ben, 2005, "The Global Saving Glut and the U.S. Current Account Deficit," Sandridge Lecture, Virginia Association of Economics, Richmond, Virginia, March 10.

Blanchard, Olivier, 1990, "Suggestions for a New Set of Fiscal Indicators," OECD Working Paper, Department of Economics and Statistics (Paris: OECD, April).

———, Francesco Giavazzi, and Filipa Sa, 2005, "The U.S. Current Account and the Dollar," NBER Working Paper No. 11137 (Cambridge, Massachusetts: National Bureau of Economic Research).

Botman, Denis, Dirk Muir, Douglas Laxton, and Andrei Romanov, 2005, "A New-Open-Economy-Macro Model for Fiscal Policy Evaluation"

---

[54]In contrast to what is sometimes suggested, both demand *and* prices (the exchange rate) must change if current account adjustment is to be achieved while maintaining full employment.

(unpublished; Washington: International Monetary Fund).

Cooper, Richard, 2005, "The Sustainability of the U.S. External Deficit," *CESifo Forum*, Vol. 6 (Spring), pp. 3–7.

Council on Economic and Fiscal Policy, 2005, "Japan's 21st Century Vision" (Tokyo).

Corbae, Philip Dean, and Sam Ouliaris, 2005, "Extracting Cycles from Nonstationary Data," in *Econometric Theory and Practice: Frontiers of Analysis and Applied Research*, ed. by P. Dean Corbae, Steven N. Durlauf, and Bruce E. Hansen (Cambridge, United Kingdom: Cambridge University Press, forthcoming).

Dooley, Michael, David Folkerts-Landau, and Peter Garber, 2003, "An Essay on The Revived Bretton Woods System," NBER Working Paper No. 9971 (Cambridge, Massachusetts: National Bureau of Economic Research).

———, 2004, "The U.S. Current Account Deficit and Economic Development: Collateral for a Total Return Swap," NBER Working Paper No. 10727 (Cambridge, Massachusetts: National Bureau of Economic Research).

Duenwald, Christoph, Nikolay Gueorguiev, and Andrea Schaechter, 2005, "Too Much of a Good Thing? Credit Booms in Transition Economies: The Cases of Bulgaria, Romania, and Ukraine," IMF Working Paper 05/128 (Washington: International Monetary Fund).

Elbehri, Aziz, and Steve Macdonald, 2004, "Estimating the Impact of Transgenic Cotton Bt Cotton on West and Central Africa: A General Equilibrium Approach," *World Development*, Vol. 32 (December), pp 2049–64.

Erceg, Christopher, Luca Guerrieri, and Christopher Gust, 2002, "Productivity Growth and the Trade Balance in the 1990s: The Role of Evolving Perceptions" (unpublished; Washington: Board of Governors of the Federal Reserve System).

———, 2005, "Expansionary Fiscal Shocks and the Trade Deficit," International Finance Discussion Paper 825, Board of Governors of the Federal Reserve System.

Estevão, Marcelo, 2005, "Product Market Regulation and the Benefits of Wage Moderation," IMF Working Paper (Washington: International Monetary Fund, forthcoming).

European Central Bank, 2005, "Monetary Policy and Inflation Differentials in a Heterogeneous Currency Area," *ECB Monthly Bulletin* (May), pp. 61–77.

Faruqee, Hamid, and others, 2005, "Current Accounts and Global Rebalancing in a Multi-Country Simulation Model," NBER Working Paper No. 11583 (Cambridge, Massachusetts: National Bureau of Economic Research).

Fay, Marianne, and Tito Yepes, 2003, "Investing in Infrastructure: What Is Needed from 2000 to 2010?" World Bank Policy Research Working Paper No. 3102 (Washington: World Bank).

Ghironi, Fabio, Talan B. Iscan, and Alessandro Rebucci, 2005, "Net Foreign Asset Positions and Consumption Dynamics in the International Economy," IMF Working Paper 05/82 (Washington: International Monetary Fund).

Grubert, Harry, 1997, "Another Look at the Low Taxable Income of Foreign-Controlled Companies in the United States," Office of Tax Analysis Paper No. 74 (Washington: U.S. Treasury Department). Available via the Internet: *http://www.treas.gov/ota/ota74.pdf*.

Haacker, Markus, ed., 2004, *The Macroeconomics of HIV/AIDS* (Washington: International Monetary Fund),

Helbling, Thomas, and Marco Terrones, 2003, "Asset Price Booms and Busts—Stylized Facts from the Last Three Decades of the 20th Century," presented at the European Central Bank workshop, "Asset Prices and Monetary Policy," Frankfurt, December 11–12.

Hilbers, Paul, and others, 2005, "Assessing and Managing Rapid Credit Growth and the Role of Supervisory and Prudential Policies," IMF Working Paper 05/151 (Washington: International Monetary Fund).

Hunt, Benjamin, 2002, "U.S. Productivity Growth, Investor Sentiment and the Current Account Deficit—Multilateral Implications," in "United States: Selected Issues," IMF Country Report No. 02/165 (Washington: International Monetary Fund).

———, and Alessandro Rebucci, 2003, "The U.S. Dollar and The Trade Deficit: What Accounts for the 1990s?" IMF Working Paper 03/194 (Washington: International Monetary Fund).

International Monetary Fund, 2000, "The Impact of Higher Oil Prices on the Global Economy" (Washington). Available via the Internet: http://www.imf.org/external/pubs/ft/oil/2000/oilrep.pdf.

———, 2005a, "Japan—2005 Article IV Consultation; Staff Supplement; and Public Information Notice on the Executive Board Discussion," IMF Country Report No. 05/273 (Washington).

————, 2005b, "Oil Market Developments and Issues" (Washington, March 1). Available via the Internet: http://www.imf.org/external/np/pp/eng/2005/030105.htm.

————, 2005c, "United States: Selected Issues," IMF Country Report No. 05/258 (Washington).

Jain-Chandra, Sonali, 2005, "Foreign Direct Investment in India: How Can It Be Increased?" in "India—Selected Issues," IMF Country Report No. 05/87 (Washington: International Monetary Fund).

Jones, Donald W., Paul N. Leiby, and Inja K. Paik, 2004, "Oil Price Shocks and the Macroeconomy: What Has Been Learned Since 1996," *Energy Journal*, Vol. 25, No. 2, pp. 1–32

Kok, Wim, ed., 2004, "Facing the Challenge: Report from the High Level Group on the Lisbon Strategy, chaired by Wim Kok (Luxembourg: European Council).

Kumhof, Michael, Douglas Laxton, and Dirk Muir, 2005, "The Consequences of U.S. Fiscal Consolidation for the Current Account" (unpublished; Washington: International Monetary Fund).

Lane, Philip, and Gian Maria Milesi-Ferretti, 2005, "The External Wealth of Nations Mark II: Revised and Extended Estimates of External Assets and Liabilities" (unpublished; Washington: International Monetary Fund).

Mataloni, Raymond J. Jr., 2000, "An Examination of Low Rates of Return of Foreign-Owned U.S. Companies," *Survey of Current Business* (March), pp. 55–73.

Nicoletti, Giuseppe, and Stefano Scarpetta, 2003, "Regulation, Productivity, and Growth: OECD Evidence," *Economic Policy*, Vol. 36 (April), pp. 9–72.

Obstfeld, Maurice, and Kenneth Rogoff, 2004, "The Unsustainable U.S. Current Account Position Revisited," NBER Working Paper No. 10869 (Cambridge, Massachusetts: National Bureau of Economic Research).

————, 2005, "Global Current Account Imbalances and Exchange Rate Adjustments," *Brookings Papers on Economic Activity* (forthcoming).

Ortega, Eva, 2003, "Persistent Inflation Differentials in Europe," Banco de España Working Paper, WP 0305 (Madrid : Banco de España).

Roubini, Nouriel, and Brad Setser, 2005, "Will the Bretton Woods 2 Regime Unravel Soon? The Risk of a Hard Landing in 2005–2006," paper presented at the symposium of the Federal Reserve Bank of San Francisco and the University of California Berkeley, "Revived Bretton Woods System: A New Paradigm for Asian Development?" San Francisco, February 4.

Salgado, Ranil, 2002, "Impact of Structural Reforms on Productivity Growth in Industrial Countries," IMF Working Paper 02/10 (Washington: International Monetary Fund).

United Nations, 2004, *World Population Prospects: The 2004 Revision* (New York).

CHAPTER II

GLOBAL IMBALANCES: A SAVING AND INVESTMENT PERSPECTIVE

Global saving and investment rates have fallen and current account imbalances have widened to unprecedented levels, yet real long-term interest rates remain low in most countries. How did the global economy arrive at this position? Some have argued that the catalyst is the substantial changes that have taken place in Asia, where saving has risen but investment has collapsed since the late 1990s. According to this view, the swing in the saving-investment gap—from deficit to large surplus—in emerging Asia has resulted in an excess global supply of saving (a global saving "glut") that has been channeled to the United States to finance its large current account imbalance (Bernanke, 2005). At the same time, this would explain the low level of long-term real interest rates, which is needed to equilibrate desired saving and planned investment on a global basis. Others have argued that the sharp drop in national saving in the United States—reflecting the deterioration in the fiscal position and the increase in housing wealth—and the recent rebound in investment are at the root of current account imbalances (see, for example, Roubini and Setser, 2005). Thus, according to these observers, current global imbalances are mainly the result of policy decisions—both fiscal and monetary—in the United States. By itself, however, this would not explain the low level of real interest rates, as a higher demand for net saving from the United States would lead (everything else equal) to higher, not lower, global interest rates.

This chapter examines the main factors that have driven the recent evolution of saving and investment across the globe, to shed light on both existing global imbalances and low real interest rates. The analysis covers 46 countries (21 industrial and 25 emerging market economies; 5 of which are oil producing) that account for over 90 percent of world GDP.[1] Specifically, the chapter addresses the following questions.

- What factors account for recent movements in saving and investment in industrial, emerging market, and oil-producing countries? Are these changes due to country-specific developments, or do they reflect broader global and regional trends?
- Looking forward, what policies can help change existing saving-investment gaps, and lead to a reduction in global imbalances?

An important theme running through the chapter is that the current constellation of current account imbalances and low real interest rates is the result of important changes in saving and investment patterns across the world. In particular, the chapter finds that unusually low investment rates across the globe are a contributing factor to low real long-term interest rates. In addition, the chapter also finds that the current pattern of external imbalances largely reflects a series of diverse and unrelated regional developments. As a result, the unwinding of these imbalances will require economic responses across a large number of countries.

The main authors of this chapter are Marco Terrones and Roberto Cardarelli, with support from Enrique Mendoza and Chris Otrok. Stephanie Denis provided research assistance.

[1]An important preliminary consideration is that any analysis of saving and investment is affected by concerns about the quality of the data (Schmidt-Hebbel and Servén, 1999). Saving, for instance, is usually calculated as the difference between income and consumption. Reflecting this, the measures of saving normally do not adjust for changes in net worth due to asset price movements, including house prices. Similarly, there is growing consensus that the measures of investment should include expenditure on research and development and education, as well as households' spending on durable goods.

Figure 2.1. Global Saving, Investment, and Current Accounts
(Percent of world GDP)

Global saving and investment have been trending downward since the early 1970s. They reached historic lows in 2002, and have recovered modestly since then.

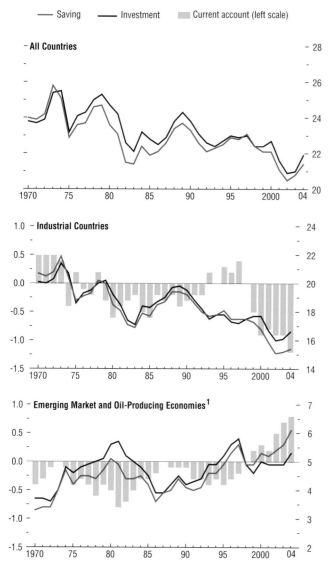

Sources: OECD Analytical Database; World Bank, *World Development Indicators;* and IMF staff calculations.
[1]Includes Norway.

Global Saving and Investment: The Current State of Play

The world economy is experiencing changes in both saving and investment behavior that are having implications for the configuration of current account imbalances and the level of real interest rates. Global saving and investment (as a percent of GDP) fell sharply in the decade following the first oil price shock in the early 1970s, but were then relatively stable until the late 1990s.[2] More recently, however, they again declined, hitting historic lows in 2002 before modestly recovering over the past two years (Figure 2.1). These global trends mainly reflect developments in the industrial countries, where both saving and investment have been trending downward since the 1970s. In contrast, saving in the emerging market and oil-producing economies has risen over this period, while investment, after increasing substantially up to the time of the Asian financial crisis, has since fallen and remains below the levels of the mid-1990s. As a result of these trends, the industrial country share of global saving and investment has dropped from about 85 percent in 1970 to 70 percent at present.

Focusing in more detail on developments since 1997—the period when substantial global current account imbalances have emerged—about two-thirds of the fall in saving rates in the industrial countries has been due to a reduction in private saving, with falling household saving only partly offset by higher corporate saving.[3]

---

[2]In this chapter, saving and investment ratios are calculated as U.S. dollar saving and investment divided by U.S. dollar GDP at current exchange rates. Global saving and investment should in principle be equal because of the requirement that current account balances sum to zero across the globe. In practice, however, this is not the case because of statistical problems that give rise to the so-called global current account discrepancy. In addition, in this study, the sample does not cover the whole world.

[3]A full offset between corporate and household saving could be expected as households are the ultimate owners of corporations. However, the extent to which households "pierce the corporate veil" has not been fully assessed. Poterba (1987) finds that changes in corporate saving are only partly offset (between 25 to 50 percent) by changes in household saving in the United States.

Indeed, corporate saving has now overtaken household saving as the main source of private sector saving in industrial countries.[4] In contrast, after dipping in the immediate aftermath of the Asian financial crisis, the saving rate in emerging market and oil-producing economies has resumed its secular increase, reaching a record-high level in 2004. A substantial part of this increase reflects higher public saving.

These aggregate developments, however, mask considerable variation between the countries and regions. The recent deterioration in saving rates in industrial countries has been particularly marked in the United States, Japan, and, to a lesser extent, the euro area countries (Figure 2.2). In Japan and the euro area, this has continued the decline in saving that began in the early 1990s, driven by a large drop in public saving in the former and lower private (household) saving in the latter (Figure 2.3). In the United States, saving has declined sharply since the late 1990s—accelerating the secular downward trend—driven initially by a drop in private saving and since 2000 by the swing in the budget from surplus to substantial deficit. Furthermore, in both Japan and the United States, corporate saving has risen substantially, offsetting lower household saving. In the other industrial countries, saving has been flat in recent years, after rebounding from the drop in the early 1990s.

Saving rates in emerging market and oil-producing countries have caught up with and largely overtaken those of industrial countries (when measured against their own GDP; see Figure 2.4). Particularly remarkable has been the very sharp increase in saving in China, especially since 2000 (see Box 2.1). Elsewhere in Asia, saving rates remain high, although they have declined since the early 1990s. In other emerging market countries, saving has risen

[4]This trend has become more accentuated since 2000 as corporations in several industrial countries have sought to strengthen their balance sheets. In contrast with the past, however, the financial sector has contributed substantially to the recent increase in corporate saving (JPMorgan Chase & Co., 2005).

Figure 2.2. Saving and Investment in the Industrial Countries

(Percent of each subregion's GDP)

The recent sharp drop in saving in the United States and the decline in investment in Japan and the euro area countries have contributed to recent global current account imbalances.

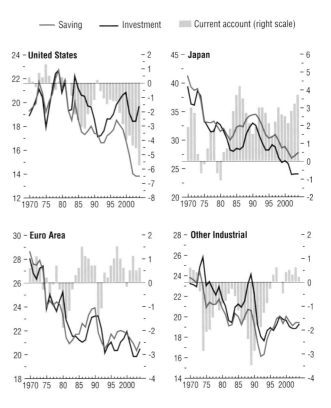

Sources: OECD Analytical Database; World Bank, *World Development Indicators;* and IMF staff calculations.

93

Figure 2.3. Saving Trends Across Regions

(Percent of each subregion's GDP)

Despite the increase in corporate saving, private saving in most industrial country regions has fallen over the past decade. Public saving in most industrial country regions has declined recently, but it has risen in China and oil-producing countries.

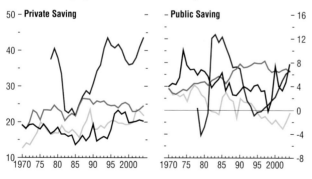

Sources: OECD Analytical Database; World Bank, *World Development Indicators;* and IMF staff calculations.
[1] Includes Norway.
[2] Data unavailable in 2004 for all regions except the United States.

sharply in recent years, driven by higher public saving in Latin America. Lastly, saving in oil-producing countries has also increased considerably, owing to the impact of higher oil prices on public saving.

Investment rates have fallen across virtually all industrial country regions, although this has been most noticeable in Japan and the euro area countries, where they reached historic lows in 2002 (see Figure 2.2). Given that investment in these regions started out higher than elsewhere, this has underpinned a convergence of investment rates across industrial country regions to about 20 percent of GDP in 2004 (although not a convergence in growth rates). Investment rates in the United States are broadly unchanged from their levels in 1997, although they remain below the peak in 2000. Of course, the decline in the nominal investment ratios over time partly reflects the fact that capital goods have become relatively less expensive—mainly owing to the extensive process of information technology (IT) capital deepening and productivity growth in the capital good–producing sectors.[5] In volume terms, the fall in average investment rates in industrial countries has been more modest.

Investment rates differ substantially across emerging market economies (see Figure 2.4). Investment in China has surged since 2000, and stood at 45 percent of GDP in 2004. With the exception of China and a handful of other countries, however, investment rates have fallen in emerging market economies since the Asian financial crisis. Indeed, investment rates in east Asia have declined by more than 10 percentage points of GDP since their peak in the mid-1990s and have not rebounded

[5]The shift toward IT capital has also increased the average depreciation rate, an effect that works in the direction of increasing the amount of gross capital formation consistent with a constant, desired, level of net investment. Indeed, several authors, including Tevlin and Whelan (2003), attribute the U.S. investment boom in the late 1990s mainly to the rise in capital depreciation.

Table 2.1. Average Correlations of Saving and Investment Ratios

	1970–2004	1970–96	1997–2004
	Saving		
Across all regions	0.15	0.18	0.22
Between industrial regions	0.58	0.68	0.48
Between emerging market regions	0.03	0.04	0.27
Between industrial and emerging market regions	−0.16	−0.19	−0.08
	Investment		
Across all regions	0.27	0.22	0.36
Between industrial regions	0.68	0.69	0.53
Between emerging market regions	0.12	0.11	0.30
Between industrial and emerging market regions	. . .	−0.14	0.24

Source: IMF staff estimates.

despite a sharp increase in public investment. Investment in oil-producing countries has also remained low despite the recent strength of oil prices.

As is evident from Figures 2.2–2.4, saving and investment in the large industrial countries have followed broadly similar trends in recent years. There appears to be much more divergence in behavior, however, among emerging market countries. The correlations reported in Table 2.1 confirm this. Saving and investment ratios are strongly correlated in industrial country regions, although this correlation has declined in recent years, while there is a lower—but rising—correlation across emerging market countries. There is little correlation between saving in industrial and emerging market countries, although the degree of co-movement of investment rates across all regions has increased over the past seven years, possibly reflecting the global nature of the IT-related productivity shock. The correlation between saving and investment rates within each region has been significantly positive on average over the period considered, although the strength of this association, originally documented by Feldstein and Horioka (1980), has fallen over time (from an average of 0.6 in 1970–96 to 0.4 during 1997–2004).

Figure 2.4. Saving and Investment in the Emerging Market and Oil-Producing Economies

(Percent of each subregion's GDP)

The sharp drop in investment in east Asia and increase in saving in the oil-producing countries are two other important developments behind the recent global current account imbalances.

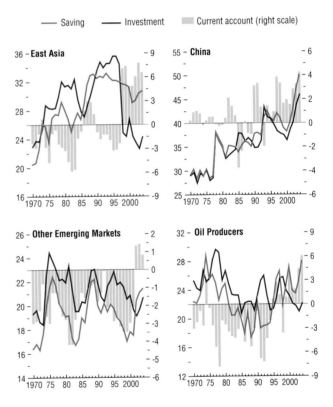

Sources: OECD Analytical Database; World Bank, *World Development Indicators;* and IMF staff calculations.

Box 2.1. Saving and Investment in China

After averaging some 40 percent of GDP during the 1990s, China's gross domestic saving rate has increased sharply to close to 50 percent of GDP over the past five years (see the figure). This has been accompanied by a smaller—but still substantial—rise in gross capital formation to about 45 percent of GDP, along with a widening external current account surplus. The present levels of saving and investment are very high, both in terms of China's own historical experience, and by comparison with experience in other advanced or developing countries.[1]

Analysis of both saving and investment in China is hampered by a variety of data limitations, and the sectoral breakdown presented in the figure should be taken only as being broadly indicative of underlying trends. With that caveat, several interesting points stand out.

- Corporate saving has risen sharply since 2000. Profitability has increased substantially in both the state-owned enterprise and—even more—the non-state-owned enterprise sectors, driven by a combination of strong economic growth; low interest rates; falling unit labor costs; reductions in employee benefits (see below); and—in resource sectors—rising commodity prices. More generally, the high level of corporate saving may also partly reflect the still-underdeveloped financial sector in China—including domestic bond and equity markets—as well as the limited access of non-state-owned enterprises to financial markets (forcing them to finance investment primarily through retained earnings).

- In contrast to recent experiences in many other countries—see the main text—the rise

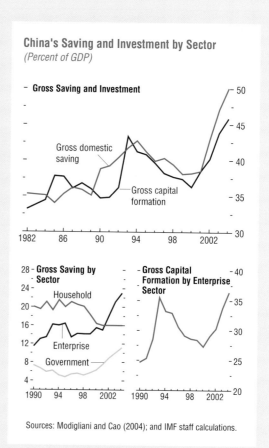

China's Saving and Investment by Sector
(Percent of GDP)

Sources: Modigliani and Cao (2004); and IMF staff calculations.

in corporate saving has been accompanied by a surge in investment, in both state- and non-state-owned firms.[2] Sectorally, this has been concentrated in infrastructure; in manufacturing, especially aluminum, steel, autos, and cement; and in real estate. While China has clear infrastructural needs, particularly in the underdeveloped western and central provinces, and demand growth in many of these sectors has been strong, this has raised concerns about potential overcapacity, and—if

Note: The main authors of this box are Marcos Chamon and Akito Matsumoto.

[1] Such comparisons need to be treated with caution given the possibility that GDP is underestimated in China (Barnett and Brooks, 2005).

[2] Including majority state-owned shareholding firms, state-controlled firms still accounted for almost 60 percent of urban fixed asset investment in 2004 (Barnett and Brooks, 2005).

investment is not efficient—a potential further buildup of nonperforming loans. Such concerns are underlined by recent research. Manufacturing investment in China is strongly correlated with corporate liquidity, suggesting that expansion considerations, not profitability, may be driving investment (Barnett and Brooks, 2005). Moreover, state-owned enterprise profits do not seem to be a factor in determining lending by state-owned banks (Podpiera, 2005), and interprovincial bank flows appear to favor provinces with a high share of state-owned enterprises in their output at the expense of high-growth provinces (Boyreau-Debray and Wei, 2005), although less than was previously the case (Aitken, 2005).

- Household saving has remained broadly constant in recent years—following some decline in the late 1990s—but, at close to 25 percent of disposable income, remains very high (despite low real interest rates on bank deposits, the dominant vehicle for household savings). This high level of household saving appears in part to reflect demographic developments, including the gradual aging of the population. Losses or uncertainty in the future provision of housing, health, education, and pension benefits—which were traditionally provided by state-owned enterprises—may also result in high levels of precautionary saving. Households' limited access to credit for the purchase of durable goods and housing likely further contributes to their saving motives.[3]
- Government saving has also increased markedly, driven by higher revenues. This increase has been used partly to strengthen the fiscal position, but mainly to finance a substantial increase in investment, particularly by local governments.

Looking forward, with the investment share very high, a key medium-term challenge is to

increase the efficiency of investment, accompanied by a welfare-enhancing shift in the composition of domestic demand from investment toward consumption. To some extent, this will occur naturally. For example, strong corporate profits will—with some lag—feed through into wages; slowing growth in commodity prices will gradually lower profit rates in the resource sector; and—over the longer term—population aging will gradually reduce the household saving rate. But economic policies also have an important role to play.

- First, on the macroeconomic side, recent administrative measures to slow investment need to be accompanied by a tightening of monetary policy—both by reducing excess liquidity and by further raising lending rates—which would be facilitated by the scope for greater exchange rate flexibility afforded by recent reforms.
- Second, continued efforts to improve governance of state-owned enterprises and make their behavior more market oriented (and accountable to their owners) will be key. One immediate step could be to require profitable state-owned enterprises to pay dividends, which would reduce corporate incentives for excessive investment. It would also provide the government with resources to help fund existing pension and social liabilities, thereby reducing incentives for precautionary saving by households (see Box 3.5 in the September 2004 *World Economic Outlook*).
- Third, financial sector reforms—both to strengthen the banking sector and to further develop bond and equity markets—are critical to improve the intermediation of China's large pool of saving and to direct it to the most productive investments (Prasad and Rajan, 2005). This would provide alternative vehicles for saving and additional sources of financing for firms and households, and would have the added benefit of promoting banking reforms by exposing state banks to domestic competition.

[3]These effects are quantified in Chamon and Prasad (2005).

Consistent with the decline in the cross-country correlation between saving and investment, external current account imbalances (relative to domestic GDP) have, on average, increased, and the dispersion across industrial—and, to a lesser extent, emerging market—countries has widened (see Chapter III of the April 2005 *World Economic Outlook)*. In particular, external imbalances between some major economic areas—notably the United States, Asia, and oil producers—are at record levels. Interestingly, the current constellation of external imbalances is very different from that in the mid-1980s—the last period of large global imbalances. At that time, the external deficit of the United States peaked at slightly above 3 percent of GDP in 1987, and was largely matched by surpluses in a relatively small number of countries (particularly Japan and the euro area countries). In contrast, current account imbalances are now dispersed across a much wider group of countries and involve many emerging market and oil-producing economies. Between 1997 and 2004, about two-thirds of the increase in the U.S. current account deficit has been balanced by higher external surpluses in emerging market and oil-producing countries, with the rest matched by larger surpluses in industrial countries (mainly Japan).

The transformation of emerging markets from net importers to net exporters of capital in recent years is difficult to reconcile with the predictions of economic theory (Lucas, 1990), or with the historical pattern of international capital flows, particularly in the period before World War I when capital flowed from the core countries of western Europe to the new settlements. While some have argued that these developments are the result of policy decisions in emerging markets—mainly reflecting the desire to accumulate foreign exchange reserves that could be used as a buffer in the event of turbulence in financial markets (Bernanke, 2005)—they could also reflect the lack of profitable investment opportunities in emerging market economies vis-à-vis industrial countries (see Box 2.2).

What Drives Saving, Investment, and the Current Account?

What are the main factors that have been driving recent saving and investment behavior across the globe? This section uses two approaches—econometric analysis and a dynamic factor model—to investigate this issue.

Econometric Results

Building on a burgeoning literature on the determinants of saving and investment, separate dynamic panel models for saving and investment were estimated using data for 46 industrial, emerging market, and oil-producing countries (and separately for the industrial and emerging market subsamples) over 1972–2004.[6] The key results of this analysis—which are shown in Table 2.2 and described in more detail in Appendix 2.1—are described below.[7]

For saving, the estimated equations fit the data well and indicate the following.

- *Higher output growth boosts saving.* A sustained 1 percentage point increase in per capita output growth in industrial countries would over time lead to an almost 1 percent of GDP increase in the national saving rate.[8] For emerging market economies, the estimated impact is smaller, at ½ percent of GDP.

---

[6]See, for instance, Masson, Bayoumi, and Samiei (1995); Edwards (1995); Haque, Pesaran, and Sharma (1999); and Loayza, Schmidt-Hebbel, and Servén (2000), among others.

[7]These equations have been estimated using Generalized Method of Moments, which controls for the potential endogeneity of the explanatory variables (see, for instance, Arellano and Bond, 1991). Indeed, the Hansen tests for all reported regressions suggest that the lagged values of the variables are valid instruments.

[8]This can be calculated from Table 2.2, column 2, as the ratio of the coefficient on per capita output growth (0.28) over one minus the coefficient of lagged saving (0.7); that is, $0.28/(1 - 0.7) \approx 1$.

Table 2.2. Global Saving and Investment: Panel Regression[1]

	Saving (percent of GDP)			Investment (percent of GDP)		
	All	Industrial countries	Emerging market economies	All	Industrial countries	Emerging market economies
Lag-dependent variable						
Percent of GDP saving	**0.62**	**0.70**	**0.71**	. . .	. . .	. . .
Investment	. . .	. . .	. . .	**0.76**	**0.80**	**0.80**
Main determinants						
Real per capita GDP growth	**0.17**	**0.28**	**0.13**	**0.26**	**0.33**	**0.23**
Real interest rate[2]	0.01	–0.07	0.01	. . .	**–0.08**	. . .
Credit (percent of GDP)	**–3.47**	**–1.53**	**–2.51**	**–1.36**	**0.81**	**–1.64**
Change in credit (annual percent of GDP)	**–2.17**	**–0.94**	**–7.39**	**0.08**	**0.02**	**0.12**
Elderly dependency ratio	**–0.44**	**–0.43**	**–0.66**	**–0.09**	**–0.04**	*–0.19*
Public saving (percent of GDP)	**0.27**	**0.15**	**0.24**	. . .	. . .	. . .
Terms-of-trade growth	**0.08**	**0.06**	**0.08**	. . .	. . .	. . .

Source: IMF staff calculations.
Note: Bold-faced values are statistically significant at the 5 percent level. Values in italics are statistically significant at the 10 percent level.
[1]The estimated effects reported in the text are the long-term effects calculated as the ratio of the estimated coefficients over one minus the coefficient of the lagged-dependent variable.
[2]In the investment equation, this is the cost of capital.

- *Fiscal consolidation is associated with increased saving,* as higher public saving is only partially offset by adjustments in private saving behavior (i.e., Ricardian equivalence does not hold, consistent with the findings of other studies). A 1 percent of GDP increase in public saving in industrial countries would lead over time to a ½ percent of GDP increase in national saving.[9] In emerging markets, the impact is larger, raising national saving by 0.85 percent of GDP, reflecting in part the less developed financial markets in these countries that make it more difficult for households to smooth consumption over time.

- *Increases in private sector credit are associated with a reduction in saving.* This may reflect the fact that households face borrowing constraints that are normally relaxed by the process of deregulation and innovation in financial markets. Private credit is also likely capturing wealth effects associated with the sharp increase in asset prices, particularly house prices, which are believed to have driven the

reduction in household saving in a number of industrial countries over the last decade, but especially in the United States (see Faulkner-MacDonagh and Mühleisen, 2004). The regression results suggest that a 10 percent of GDP increase in credit in industrial countries would lead over time to a reduction of ½ percent of GDP in the saving rate. The impact is again larger in emerging markets, at 0.9 percent of GDP, possibly because of the lower levels of financial intermediation and higher dependency on bank credit in these economies.

- *As populations age, this puts downward pressure on saving.* Given that people tend to dissave during their retirement years, an increase in the elderly dependency ratio—the ratio of those aged over 65 to the working age population—should reduce saving (see Box 2.3). This is confirmed by the regression results, which suggest that an increase in the elderly dependency ratio of 1 percentage point in the industrial countries would over time reduce saving by about 1½ percent of GDP. Because of the

[9]De Mello, Kongsrud, and Price (2004) find that the Ricardian offset for 21 OECD countries ranges from ⅓ to ½. Using a different approach, Gale and Orszag (2004) find a similar result for the United States.

Box 2.2. Return on Investment in Industrial and Developing Countries

In recent years, international capital has flowed from the developing world to a number of industrial countries, particularly the United States. This is hard to reconcile with standard economic theory, which holds that—given restrictions on mobility of labor—industrial countries with abundant capital should export capital to developing countries, where capital is scarce but labor plentiful, and the return on capital is expected to be higher. This puzzle was addressed specifically by Lucas (1990). This box provides some estimates of the realized return on capital in developing and industrial countries to see if they shed light on why capital is flowing the "wrong way."[1]

A first look at returns seems to deepen the puzzle. The table uses national accounts data to compare the realized return on aggregate capital over the past decade in emerging markets with that in the G-7 countries. The focus is on emerging markets as a subset of developing countries since these countries receive gross capital inflows and are thus integrated into international capital markets. The return on aggregate capital is defined as the value added paid to capital owners divided by the aggregate capital stock.[2] Across emerging markets this measure averages 13.3 percent over the past decade, compared with 7.8 percent in the G-7. If returns are higher, why would capital be flowing from emerging markets to industrial countries? Of course, higher risk may deter investors from investing in emerging markets. However, it may also be the case that true average returns to

investors are much lower than what national accounts–based measures suggest. For one thing, they may reflect predominantly small and medium-sized firms that are difficult to invest in. Moreover, in emerging markets they may disproportionately reflect state-owned companies, for which claims on capital may not be traded. Finally, the quality of the underlying national accounts data may in some cases be poor.

An alternative measure of the return on capital is the internal rate of return on invested capital (calculated by Fama and French, 1999, for publicly traded, nonfinancial companies in the United States). The internal rate of return is the discount rate that sets the net present value of cash flows into and out of the corporate sector equal to zero. It captures the return to an investor who buys firms at market value, receives or covers their subsequent cash flow, and then sells them at market value.[3] Compared with simply looking at the performance of equity markets over a certain horizon, this measure is more comprehensive since it provides a return on all invested capital, including debt and equity. Compared with the return on aggregate capital, this measure has the advantage that it is based on publicly traded companies, so that domestic and foreign investors can buy and sell the shares of these companies.

To calculate the internal rate of return across countries, IMF staff used Worldscope, an international database that covers balance sheet and other information from annual reports of

Note: The main authors of this box are Robin Brooks and Kenichi Ueda.

[1]Klingen, Weder, and Zettelmeyer (2004) investigate a similar question for sovereign debt. They find that returns on sovereign debt in emerging markets barely exceed returns on U.S. treasury bonds.

[2]Profit income in the system of national accounts is the value added paid to capital owners. The capital stock for each country is estimated by cumulating fixed capital formation over time, using the perpetual inventory method with 1951 as the initial year. The initial capital stock is assumed, but recent estimates for the capital stock are robust to changes in initial stocks.

[3]The present value is calculated at the initial year, 1994. The actual cash flows are used for 1994 to 2003, and the value of future cash flows is approximated by the market capitalization in 2003. More formally, the internal rate of return is the discount rate, r, that solves the following equation for each country:

$$V_{1994} = \sum_{t=1(1994)}^{T(2003)} \frac{X_t - I_t}{(1+r)^t} + \sum_{t=1(1994)}^{T(2003)} \frac{FS_t - FB_t}{(1+r)^t} + \frac{V_{2003}}{(1+r)^T},$$

where V denotes the sum of the market value of firms; X, the sum of cash earnings; I, the sum of gross investment; FS, the sum of the market value of firms that exit from the sample; and FB, the sum of market value of firms that enter the sample.

Estimated Rates of Return on Invested Capital, 1994–2003
(Percent, unless otherwise indicated)

	Return on Capital	Coverage	Size[1]	Internal Rate of Return
Latin America[2]	12.9	56.0	37.7	−4.7
Emerging Asia[3]	14.7	79.6	97.2	−4.6
Other emerging markets[4]	11.3	70.2	42.5	−4.7
Average	*13.3*	*70.5*	*64.1*	*−4.7*
G-7, of which:	7.8	78.8	83.2	2.4
United Kingdom	7.7	79.0	149.1	2.6
United States	9.9	79.8	126.8	8.6

Source: IMF staff calculations.
[1]Percent of GDP.
[2]Argentina, Brazil, Chile, Colombia, Mexico, and Peru.
[3]China*, Hong Kong SAR, India, Indonesia*, Korea, Malaysia*, the Philippines, Singapore*, Taiwan Province of China*, and Thailand. Asterisk indicates countries where data on return of capital are not available.
[4]Czech Republic*, Hungary*, Israel, Morocco*, Pakistan*, Poland*, Russia*, and South Africa. Asterisk indicates countries for which data on return of capital are not available.

publicly traded firms. These data are subject to several caveats. As the table illustrates, coverage of publicly traded firms in emerging markets is not as good as in the G-7 countries. On average over the 1994–2003 period, Worldscope covers 71 percent of listed firms in emerging markets, according to the *S&P Global Stock Markets Factbook,* while it covers 79 percent in the G-7. In addition, the stock market is substantially smaller in relation to economic activity in emerging markets than in the G-7. On average over this period, market capitalization in percent of GDP is 64 percent in emerging markets, compared with 83 percent in the G-7. In other words, the proxy for the return on capital in emerging markets needs to be interpreted with caution, both because the stock market captures a smaller share of productive capital in these economies and because coverage is less comprehensive.

The table provides the internal rate of return for the nonfinancial corporate sector for the past decade, measured in local currency and deflated using the price index for investment goods. The internal rate of return is −4.7 percent across emerging markets over the period, while it is 2.4 percent on average in the G-7.[4] On this

measure, the return on capital for publicly traded firms in the nonfinancial corporate sector was lower in emerging markets than in the G-7 during 1994–2003.

Of course, the short time horizon may bias the results against emerging markets, where returns on investment may only be realized over a longer horizon.[5] The short time horizon also carries the added risk that cyclical and crisis effects may dominate the results; indeed, returns have recovered strongly in emerging markets over the past few years. Nevertheless, the return on capital—as measured by the internal rate of return—for publicly traded firms in emerging markets has been below that in the G-7 for the 1994–2003 period. This is especially striking because the return on capital is measured in local currency. It therefore does not incorporate currency risk, which for many emerging markets is substantial. As a result, attainable rates of return for domestic and foreign investors may help explain the current direction of international capital flows. Still, further research is needed to understand why the return from investing in publicly traded firms in emerging market countries has been lower than in industrial countries, and whether this result holds over different time periods.

[4]This result is consistent with other measures of corporate performance, such as the return on assets or an alternate internal rate of return based on acquiring costs of assets calculated by Fama and French (1999).

[5]To put this in perspective, Fama and French (1999) calculate the internal rate of return in the United States for a period of 47 years.

Box 2.3. Impact of Demographic Change on Saving, Investment, and Current Account Balances

The world is in the midst of major demographic transitions in which declining fertility rates and increasing life expectancy are significantly altering the age structure of national populations. The timing and speed of demographic changes, however, are highly asymmetric across countries. Advanced economies began their transition several decades earlier than developing countries; hence the age composition of populations differs greatly between developed and developing countries (see the figure). Ongoing demographic changes will have significant albeit uncertain impacts on saving, investment, and current account balances in the years ahead (Bryant, 2004).

How do demographic changes affect saving, investment, and the current account?

Demographic impacts on saving stem from individuals smoothing consumption over their lifetimes while the age distribution of their income follows a hump-shaped profile. This "life-cycle" behavior entails dissaving when individuals are young, little saving early in adult life, high saving at the middle and end of the working life, and then low or negative saving after retirement. Changes in the age composition of the population therefore affect aggregate personal saving. In particular, a demographic transition initially increases household saving as it reduces the number of young dependents and increases the number of working adults, but eventually it reduces saving as a larger portion of the population retires and reaches old age.

There remain, however, some uncertainties about saving behavior in the later stages of the life cycle. Studies based on macroeconomic data generally support the predictions of life-cycle approaches (for example, an increase in the elderly dependency ratio—which shows the population aged 65 and older as a share of the working-age (age 15–64) population—reduces saving). Studies based on microeconomic data,

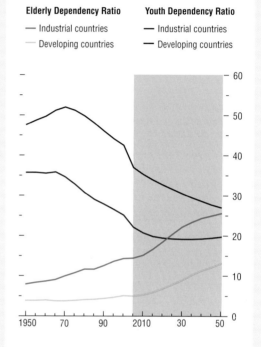

Population Structure, 1950–2050
(Percent of total population)

Elderly Dependency Ratio
— Industrial countries
— Developing countries

Youth Dependency Ratio
— Industrial countries
— Developing countries

Source: United Nations, *World Population Prospects: The 2000 Revision.*

however, have cast some doubt on the extent to which the elderly dissave (Poterba, 2004). This may be because simplified applications of the life-cycle approach do not adequately take into account the desire of the elderly to leave bequests, or their uncertainties about their lifespan after retirement and the financial support they will need. Some empirical studies based on household survey data do not adequately incorporate the public-pension portion of elderly incomes, and this is why they may appear at odds with life-cycle behavior (Miles, 1999).

With regard to investment, empirical studies generally find that investment is positively related to the share of the young in the population (Higgins, 1998). Countries with higher youth dependency rates—which show the population aged 0–14 as a share of the working-age

Note: The main authors of this box are Ralph C. Bryant and Marc de Fleurieu.

population—face a relatively higher demand for investment related to the development of human capital (schools) and to a growing labor force (infrastructure). As a population ages, however, the labor force grows more slowly and the level and composition of investment shift with the needs of a more elderly population (medical facilities).

The net effect on the saving-investment balance tends therefore to vary during the different stages of a demographic transition.[1] Countries with a relatively young population should experience current account deficits, as investment demand outstrips domestic saving. As children age, fertility rates decline, and life expectancy rises, the ratio of active workers to the total population increases, which in turn tends to cause saving to rise faster than investment. Hence, as economies go through the middle stages of a demographic transition, they should experience current account surpluses. Eventually, as the aging of the population continues, the net impact on the saving-investment balance becomes ambiguous, reflecting uncertainty about the relative effects of rising elderly ratios on saving and investment. Although higher elderly dependency is often associated with an excess of investment over saving, and hence a current-account deficit, this partial correlation has lower statistical reliability and may not be a robust guide to the effects of rising elderly dependency ratios on current account balances (Higgins, 1998; Bosworth and Keys, 2004).

Demographics and capital flows

According to UN projections, elderly dependency ratios in the advanced countries will nearly double by 2050. At the same time, working-age populations will rise significantly in many developing countries. How will these population trends affect capital flows in the future? For developing countries, an IMF study (see the September 2004 *World Economic Outlook*) found that demographic forces are likely to lead to improved current account positions over time as more of the population move through their higher saving years. In industrial countries, demographic trends will probably reduce current account surpluses in Japan and Europe during the course of the next 50 years. In the United States, the demographic transition is less steep and demographic forces by themselves may have smaller effects on the current account balance.

Understanding how demographic change will affect saving, investment, and net capital flows is far from complete. There are uncertainties not only about the demographic projections themselves, but also about the reactions of private saving and investment as the demographic transitions unfold. Households—in both advanced and developing countries—will probably respond according to the broad predictions of the life-cycle model; but aggregate saving, investment, and net capital flows will also be significantly influenced by other factors, including international differences in policies and business-cycle conditions.

What can the role of labor migrations be?

A remaining issue to consider is the possible role of labor mobility in the demographic adjustment process. Most macroeconomic models assume that labor does not move across countries. This omission could lead model predictions to overstate the role of capital flows in the adjustment process because movements of labor from regions with rising working-age populations to those with rising elderly dependency ratios are a possible alternative to capital flows.[2]

---

[1]Empirical work suggests that, on average, about half of the demographic effects on national saving are matched by changes in domestic investment, with the remainder altering the saving-investment balance (Higgins, 1998; and Helliwell, 2004).

[2]Also, the assumption of perfect capital mobility and perfect foresight ignores the presence of capital account restrictions and political risk in developing countries. As a result, model predictions of the magnitude of demographically induced capital flows to and from developing countries could be overstated.

Box 2.3 *(concluded)*

More research is needed to clarify the net benefits of migration for both recipient and sending countries. Permanent immigration tends to have a neutral effect on a recipient country's public saving—immigrants are as likely to claim pension and healthcare benefits as national citizens (Fehr, Jokisch, and Kotlikoff, 2004). The effects on private saving could be significant, though dampened by the extent to which migrants send remittances to their home country. For sending countries, per-

manent emigration is a net loss apart from remittances.

Government policies inhibit the flow of people across borders. In fact, immigration policies are a more significant determinant of migration than the willingness of individuals to migrate. Large movements of people across borders in the coming decades are thus unlikely—under current policies—to significantly mediate the macroeconomic effects of asymmetric demographic transitions.

different population characteristics in emerging countries, the elderly dependency ratio is not found to be a significant explanator of saving behavior in those countries.

- *Saving is positively related to improvements in the terms of trade*, which are normally expected to be transitory (the "Harberger-Metzler" effect). The results suggest that a 1 percentage point increase in terms-of-trade growth would imply an increase of ¼ percent of GDP in the saving rate.

- *Saving behavior does not appear to be affected by rate of return considerations.* While saving and real interest rates are generally expected to be positively related—with the strength of this relationship likely to depend on the size of households' net asset position (see Deaton, 1992)—the regression results did not show a statistically significant impact (at the 5 percent level). This finding is consistent with previous empirical work.

In turn, the estimated investment equation suggests the following.

- *Stronger output growth leads to higher investment rates.* This could reflect demand shocks, responses to changes in productivity, or the presence of financial market imperfections.[10] The results suggest that a sustained 1 percent-

age point increase in per capita output growth in the industrial countries would over time lead to a 1.6 percent of GDP increase in the investment rate. In emerging markets, the impact is smaller, at 1.1 percent of GDP.

- *Increased availability of credit is associated with higher investment*, given that firms, in part, depend on external finance. The regression results, however, suggest that the effects of an increase in credit on investment, although statistically significant, are modest.

- *An increase in the cost of capital is associated with lower investment.* Here, the cost of capital is measured as the product of the real interest rate and the relative price of capital (investment deflator over GDP deflator). In the industrial countries, a 1 percent increase in the cost of capital would, over time, lead to a 0.4 percent of GDP reduction in the investment rate.[11]

What do these equations tell us about the factors that could explain recent movements in saving and investment? At the outset, the ability of both regressions to capture recent developments varies considerably across countries, reflecting both the panel nature of the regressions and the heterogeneity in regional saving and investment behavior (as documented in the previous section). The results suggest that

[10]See Blanchard and Fischer (1989). Indeed, both past and future output growth and real interest rates are expected to influence investment (see, for example, Romer, 1996).
[11]See Pelgrin, Schich, and de Serres (2002) for a related result.

two factors are particularly important in explaining the decline in saving in industrial countries over 1997–2004 (Figure 2.5). First is the increase in credit to the private sector, which is likely approximating for wealth effects from the sharp increase in house prices in many countries (but not Japan). Second is the fall in public saving, which is particularly important in the United States—where according to the regression estimates it accounted for over one-third of the 4½ percentage point decline in national saving since 1997—and Japan. Another factor that has played an important role in Japan and the euro area—but not in industrial countries as a group—is the rise in the elderly dependency ratio.

Turning to emerging markets, the results also suggest that two factors have been key drivers of the recent increase in saving. First, there has been a sharp increase in public sector saving, particularly in China and the oil-producing countries (which has more than offset the weakening in public saving in east Asia). Second, stronger output growth has boosted saving in all emerging market regions (again, this appears particularly important in China, where it likely contributed to the sharp increase in corporate saving—see Box 2.1). In contrast, rising oil prices have had a modestly negative effect, with the boost to saving in oil-producing countries offset by the adverse effect elsewhere (particularly in parts of Asia).

The investment equation is less successful than the saving equation in tracking recent developments. This result is similar to other recent studies, which have found that traditional econometric models of investment have difficulty explaining recent trends.[12] The equation overpredicts investment in both the industrial and emerging market regions, in some cases by

[12]According to Tevlin and Whelan (2003), there are three main reasons that account for this failure: (1) the falling price of computer equipment played a key role in the investment behavior of the 1990s; (2) capital depreciation rates rose significantly during the 1990s; and (3) depreciation is not homogenous across the diverse types of capital.

Figure 2.5. Explaining Saving and Investment Rate Movements Between 1997 and 2004
(Change in percent of GDP unless otherwise noted)

While the recent evolution of saving is largely explained by the economic fundamentals included in the regression analysis, the evolution of investment is not.

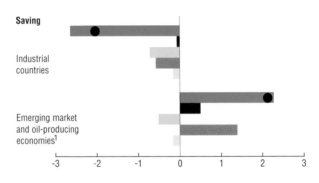

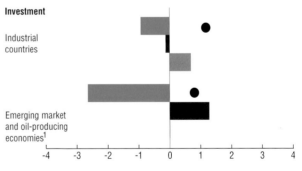

Source: IMF staff calculations.
[1]Includes Norway.

large margins. For instance, while the equation predicts that investment should have increased in industrial countries—largely as a result of the decline in the cost of capital—investment in several key industrial countries, including Japan and the Large Euro countries (see footnote 15), fell. Similarly, the equation fails to explain the drop in investment in emerging markets, particularly in the east Asian countries. The equation suggests that the investment accelerator—whereby investment rates and output growth move in the same direction—has not worked as strongly as expected in recent years in these countries, most likely because corporates have focused on reducing debt and strengthening balance sheets, rather than on investing in capital (see Box 2.4 for a discussion of investment in Asian emerging markets).[13] One conclusion of this analysis is that investment appears to be below the levels that would usually be associated with this stage of the economic cycle, and this may be an important factor in explaining both the current low level of real long-term interest rates and the shift of emerging market economies from net importers to net exporters of capital.

A Model of Saving, Investment, and the Current Account

The econometric analysis provides some important insights into what may be driving recent saving and investment behavior, but it also has drawbacks. Most important, each variable is considered separately in the analysis, rather than as part of an integrated economic system. As was highlighted in the previous subsection, saving and investment—and indeed many of their potential determinants, including output and interest rates—are highly correlated, particularly across industrial countries but also increasingly in emerging markets. This suggests that it is very important to be able to capture the interactions between variables and across countries within an integrated and consistent framework. One approach is to use a multiregion macroeconomic model—such as the IMF's Global Economic Model (GEM)—that explicitly captures such interactions (see Appendix 1.2). An alternative that is used here is to estimate a dynamic factor model to examine the extent to which "global" economic conditions have been driving saving, investment, and current account balances across regions.[14]

The dynamic factor model that was estimated considers five variables—real GDP growth, short-term real interest rates, saving rates, investment rates, and current account balances—and decomposes them into the following four estimated (unobserved) components (see Appendix 2.1 for more details on the model):[15]

- A world factor that captures the common shocks affecting all regions and all variables of the model. This will reflect major global

---

[13]There is also evidence that the current low corporate investment in the euro area reflects the high leverage levels of these corporations (Jaeger, 2003).

[14]Several important features of the model are worth stressing. First, while bivariate correlations capture the degree of contemporaneous co-movement of the saving and investment ratio for any pair of regions, the global factors estimated in the model capture all intertemporal (e.g., including leads and lags) cross-country correlations among the variables considered. Second, by estimating the global and country-/region-specific factors *simultaneously*, the model correctly identifies the relative importance of global and region-specific developments. Third, the global factors estimated in this model are independent of the choice of any particular weighting scheme, contrary to those obtained as cross-country averages of variables, as in Glick and Rogoff (1995) and Dees and others (2005).

[15]For this exercise, the countries in the sample were divided into 12 regions. These are the United States, Japan, Anglo-Saxon (Australia, Canada, New Zealand, and the United Kingdom), Large Euro (Italy, France, and Germany), Small Euro (Austria, Belgium, Finland, Greece, Ireland, the Netherlands, Portugal, and Spain), Other Industrial (Denmark, Sweden, and Switzerland), East Asia 1 (Indonesia, Korea, Malaysia, the Philippines, and Thailand), East Asia 2 (Hong Kong SAR, Singapore, and Taiwan Province of China), China, Latin America (Argentina, Brazil, Chile, Colombia, and Peru), Other Emerging Markets (Egypt, India, Israel, Morocco, Pakistan, South Africa, and Turkey), and Oil-Producing Countries (I.R. of Iran, Mexico, Norway, Saudi Arabia, and Venezuela). Before the model was estimated, all time series were linearly detrended to avoid the possibility of nonstationarity.

Box 2.4. Is Investment in Emerging Asia Too Low?

Investment in emerging Asia fell during the regional financial crises in the late 1990s, and has since remained at these lower levels (except in China). For Hong Kong SAR, Singapore, and Taiwan Province of China, the decline has taken investment rates to levels not seen in over three decades, while investment in Indonesia, Korea, Malaysia, and Thailand, after reaching historical peaks in the early to mid-1990s, has returned to levels comparable to those in the mid-1980s.

Corporate investment in emerging Asia has fallen particularly sharply—the investment to capital ratio fell by one-half between 1993–96 and 1997–2003—although an increase in public investment has offset part of this decline. The drop in corporate investment in the region reflects a sharp decline in the Tobin's q—as the market value of the corporations fell sharply relative to the replacement cost of capital—and the efforts of corporations to strengthen their balance sheets and streamline their operations as the financial and economic environment deteriorated. In particular, leverage and liquidity have improved significantly since 1997, as shown in the first figure, even if they have not yet reached their pre-1997 levels.[1]

These developments raise two related questions: Is investment in emerging Asia now too low? What are the prospects for a rebound in investment?

While these are clearly difficult questions to answer, one way of addressing the first is to compare the investment and capital-output ratios in each country with estimates of their long-run equilibrium (steady-state) levels. To the extent that these countries are still in a transition period (that is, their capital-output ratio is below its long-run level), investment rates should be above their long-run level. Such calculations are shown in the second

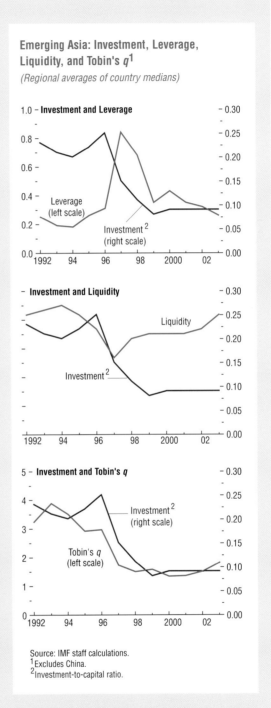

Emerging Asia: Investment, Leverage, Liquidity, and Tobin's q[1]

(Regional averages of country medians)

Source: IMF staff calculations.
[1]Excludes China.
[2]Investment-to-capital ratio.

Note: The main authors of this box are Roberto Cardarelli and Marco Terrones.

[1]A description of the database is provided in Appendix 2.1.

figure. In making these calculations, a depreciation rate of 5 percent is used in estimating the capital stock (the average depreciation rate for

Box 2.4 *(concluded)*

Emerging Asia: Capital/Output and Investment/Output Relative to Steady-State Level

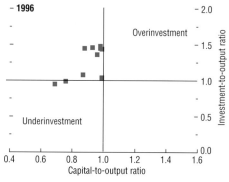

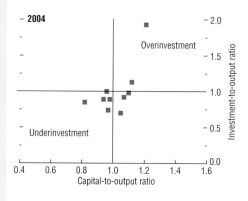

Source: IMF staff estimates.

emerging markets in 2004 was about 5 percent,[2] although in the future this may be too low an estimate given that depreciation rates have been increasing over the past decade owing to the compositional shift in the aggregate capital stock toward short-lived assets such as computers and software).[3] A further critical issue is the choice of the steady-state levels of the capital

stock and investment. Here, they are estimated from a standard neoclassical growth model, using conservative estimates of capital ratios and potential output growth, although alternatives were also tried and yielded broadly similar results.[4]

In 1996—the year prior to the regional financial crisis—almost all countries were investing relatively more than in the steady state as they increased their capital stock toward its long-run level. This does not preclude the possibility that these countries could have been overinvesting during this period as they moved too quickly toward the long-run level (Sachs and Radelet, 1998). Indeed, for some countries, such as Malaysia, the investment rate in 1996 appears to be consistent with an excessive speed of convergence, as reflected in a capital ratio that in 2004 is higher than its estimated long-term level. For these countries, the fall in investment is a response to the excess capacity built over the past decade. In 2004, however, some countries were investing relatively less than in the steady state despite the fact that their capital stock was below its long-run level (and, therefore, were in the "underinvestment" quadrant). This appears to be the case, in particular, for Indonesia, the Philippines, and Thailand. On the other hand, there is some evidence of overinvestment in China.

Of course such evidence is tentative, and even if investment rates are too low in some countries at present it is difficult to know when they may rebound. On a positive note, Tobin's *q* appears to be starting to recover, which, given the close relationship with investment in the region and the improved balance sheet position of corporations, suggests that the investment outlook may be turning more positive.

[2]Based on consumption of fixed capital from the National Accounts, deflated by the investment deflator.
[3]A depreciation rate of 7 percent yielded a broadly similar outcome to that shown in the second figure (see Appendix 2.1).

[4]For example, broadly similar results were achieved when steady-state values of capital and investment ratios were set as the averages for industrial countries over an eight-year period (for example, for 2004, the average of ratios in industrial countries over 1996–2004). For a description of the methodology, see Appendix 2.1.

However, the low level of investment may also reflect structural changes in these economies, such as the shift toward less capital and more skill- and knowledge-intensive type of exports, particularly information technology–related products and services (Lee, McKibbin, and Park, 2004) and the start of a demographic transition toward an older population structure (see Box 2.3). Both factors suggest that emerging Asian countries could face a slower pace of

capital accumulation in the future than they have in the past.[5]

[5]Anecdotal evidence suggests that another potential "structural" explanation for the lower investment rate in many emerging Asian countries involves the relocation of production facilities from these countries to China. Unfortunately, lack of data on bilateral foreign direct investment flows that distinguish between greenfield investment and mergers and acquisitions prevents any quantitative estimate of the phenomenon.

economic events, such as oil price increases or global technological progress.

- A factor common to each of the five variables in the model. For instance, the saving factor captures the common shocks affecting saving rates across all regions (reflecting, for example, the ongoing process of financial innovation) but not other variables.
- A region-specific factor that reflects common shocks affecting the five variables within each region. For instance, the process of European integration may affect all economic variables in the European countries, but not in other regions.

- An idiosyncratic term capturing region-specific shocks to each individual variable in each region.

The results from the dynamic factor model indicate that a high proportion of the variations in saving and investment rates in industrial countries are explained by global factors (defined as the sum of the world factor and the variable-specific factors—see Table 2.3). Indeed, much of the recent cyclical evolution in saving and investment in these countries— with the important exception of Japan—can be explained by the global factor, suggesting that industrial countries have been subject to

Table 2.3. Variance Decomposition

	Output (y)	Short-Term Interest Rate (r)	Current Account (CA)	Saving Rate (S)	Investment Rate (I)
Average for all countries					
Global	37	51	36	39	34
World	18	8	7	24	21
Aggregate	19	43	28	15	14
Region plus idiosyncratic	63	48	63	60	65
Average for industrial countries					
Global	57	80	32	71	59
World	27	10	7	45	35
Aggregate	30	70	25	26	23
Region plus idiosyncratic	43	20	43	28	41
Average for emerging market and oil-producing countries					
Global	17	23	39	7	10
World	8	7	8	3	6
Aggregate	9	16	32	4	4
Region plus idiosyncratic	83	77	83	92	89

Source: IMF staff calculations.

Figure 2.6. Saving: Global Factor[1]
(Percent of GDP)

The global factor plays an important role in explaining fluctuations of saving rates in industrial countries, but fails to account for the recent decline in saving in Japan and large euro area countries. Saving rates in emerging markets have been largely unexplained by the global factor.

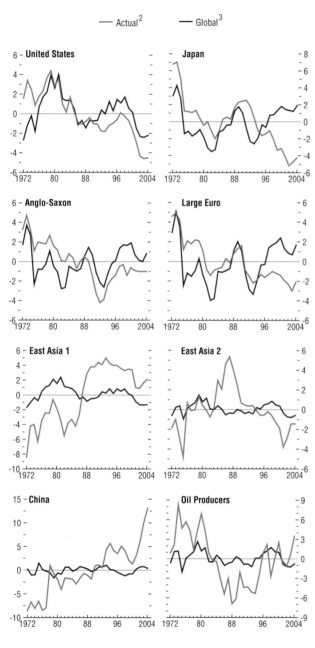

Source: IMF staff calculations.
[1]See footnote 15 in main text for definition of country groupings.
[2]Actual time series have been rescaled by subtracting the average of the period.
[3]The global factor is the sum of the world and saving factors. For each region, the world and saving factors are multiplied by their factor loadings in the saving equation.

similar shocks in the variables affecting saving and investment (Figures 2.6 and 2.7).[16] Subsequent causality tests suggest that it is the high degree of co-movement in productivity and asset prices across industrial countries that is driving this observed co-movement of saving and investment.[17] These results are similar to those from the econometric analysis, suggesting that common developments in credit/asset prices and output growth/productivity are the most important factors driving the evolution in saving and investment across most industrial countries.

In emerging market countries, on the other hand, the global factor has been much less important in explaining movements in saving and investment. Rather, these regions have been more likely to experience region-specific saving and investment cycles, a reflection of the large differences in economic structures, institutions, and policies between the two groups of countries.[18] For example, the rapid acceleration of saving in China and oil-producing countries in recent years is described by the model as a

[16]Figures 2.6, 2.7, and 2.8 plot the global factors together with actual (not detrended) time series. However, it is worth stressing that, because the model is estimated based on detrended data, the common factors are not able to explain trend developments in the observable variables and, in particular, the trend decline of saving and investment ratios in Japan and Large Euro countries, as well as the trend increase in these ratios in China.

[17]This is done through a series of bivariate Granger causality tests. In particular, movements in the global saving factor appear to be related to changes in real house prices in the United States, while the global investment factor appears to be related to total factor productivity growth in industrial countries. These results are consistent with the existence of a strong co-movement in housing prices across industrial countries, as discussed in "The Global House Boom," in Chapter 2 of the September 2004 *World Economic Outlook,* and with other studies showing the relevance of productivity dynamics in explaining the co-movement of investment across G-7 countries (Gregory and Head, 1999; and Kose, Otrok, and Whiteman, 2004).

[18]This result is in line with that of Kose, Otrok, and Whiteman (2003), who find that output and investment dynamics are much more idiosyncratic in developing countries than in developed ones.

highly idiosyncratic event. The same is true for the sharp drop in investment in east Asia after the 1997 regional financial crisis, a finding that is consistent with the results from the panel regression.

The results from the dynamic factor model reveal a high degree of synchronization between the current account balances in industrial and emerging market economies (as would be expected given that the movements of regional saving-investment gaps are subject to the global constraint that saving should be equal to investment).[19] On average, the global current account factor explains about one-third of the variation in current account balances for both industrial and emerging market economies. This result, however, is largely driven by relatively high shares for a small group of regions (the United States, Japan, the Large Euro area, and the East Asia 2 countries).

Interestingly, the global current account factor captures the global imbalances episode in the mid-1980s better than it does the current one (Figure 2.8). This is likely because—as noted in the previous section—the imbalances in the mid-1980s were largely concentrated in a relatively small number of countries (in particular, the United States, Japan, the Large Euro area, and the East Asia 2 countries). In contrast, the imbalances are now distributed across a larger number of countries, and appear to be more a result of region-specific (idiosyncratic) events rather than any single global event (although clearly the recent increase in oil prices has added to the size of the imbalances over the past two years). This clearly has important implications for how existing imbalances can be resolved, with actions needed across a broad group of countries.

[19]As the regions considered in this study account for a large share of world GDP, their current account balances cannot all move independently of each other. The dynamic factor model accommodates this constraint, as the sign of the impact of the global factors on the current account balances differs across regions (it is positive for three regions and negative for the other nine).

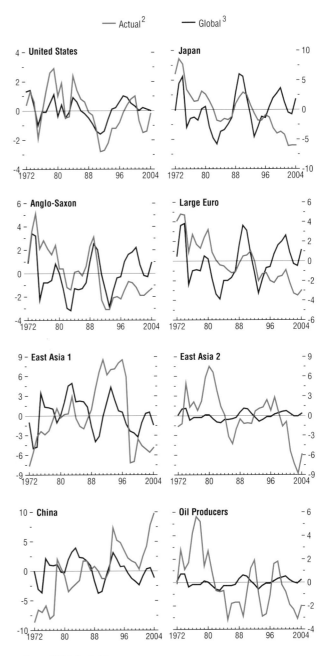

Figure 2.7. Investment: Global Factor[1]
(Percent of GDP)

While the fluctuations of investment rates in industrial countries are relatively synchronized, in the emerging market economies they are more the result of idiosyncratic shocks.

— Actual[2]   — Global[3]

Source: IMF staff calculations.
[1]See footnote 15 in main text for definition of country groupings.
[2]Actual time series have been rescaled by subtracting the average of the period.
[3]The global factor is the sum of the world and investment factors. For each region, the world and investment factors are multiplied by their factor loadings in the investment equation.

Figure 2.8. Current Account: Global Factor[1]
(Percent of GDP)

The global current account factor captures well the current account imbalances in the mid-1980s. More recently, it fails to account for the recent developments in the United States, East Asia 1 countries, China, and oil-producing countries.

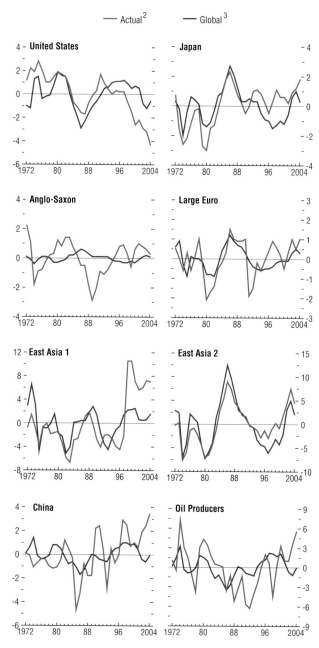

Source: IMF staff calculations.
[1]See footnote 15 in main text for definition of country groupings.
[2]Actual time series have been rescaled by subtracting the average of the period.
[3]The global factor is the sum of the world and current account factors. For each region, the world and current account factors are multiplied by their factor loadings in the current account equation.

How Can Existing Global Current Account Imbalances Be Reduced?

The results from the previous section indicate that saving, investment, and current account balances have been affected both by factors that are common across many countries, such as rising asset prices/credit—which appear particularly important in industrial countries—and by factors that are specific to particular regions and countries.

What do these findings suggest about how existing global current account imbalances could be resolved? To address this question, a factor-augmented vector autoregressive (FAVAR) model was estimated that combines the estimated factors from the dynamic factor model with other variables of interest in selected countries (see, for instance, Bernanke, Boivin, and Eliasz, 2005). This approach has the advantage of yielding a parsimonious model that is able to capture global linkages and spillovers.

The particular simulations considered are an increase in U.S. national savings; an increase in investment in Asia and oil-producing countries; stronger real output growth in Japan and the Large Euro countries; and an increase in real interest rates in the United States. The results of the analysis are as follows.[20]

- *An increase in U.S. national saving rates would have a significant positive effect on the U.S. current account deficit* (Figure 2.9). A permanent (over the three-year horizon considered by the forecasts) 1 percent of GDP increase in the U.S. gross national saving rate would reduce the U.S. current account deficit by about

[20]The FAVAR model used to forecast the current account imbalances comprises the world factor, the global current account factor, the regional current account balance, and the variable of interest (e.g., the U.S. saving rate). The results are presented as differences between the forecast of the current account balance obtained imposing a specific time path on the variable of interest (conditional forecasts) and the forecast obtained from the unrestricted VAR (unconditional forecasts).

½ percent of GDP after three years.[21] Higher saving in the United States—and the associated reduction in domestic demand—would also reduce the current account surpluses in the Large Euro countries and Japan, by ¼ and ¾ percentage point of GDP by 2007, respectively. In the East Asia 2 countries, the projected decline in the current account surplus would be much larger—close to 3 percentage points of GDP by 2007—owing to the much higher exposure of these countries to trade with the United States (see Table 2.4).

- *An investment recovery in Asia (excluding China) and oil-producing countries would offer a significant contribution to the resolution of current account imbalances.* An increase in the investment ratio in the East Asian 1 countries (Indonesia, Korea, Malaysia, the Philippines, Thailand)—as firms in this region complete their process of deleveraging and begin to increase their capital stock—would have an important impact on current account imbalances.[22] For example, a 5 percent of GDP permanently higher investment rate in these countries—which would reverse about one-half of the decline that has occurred since the peak in 1996—would reduce the U.S.

[21]Model-based analyses of the effect of U.S. fiscal policy on the current account deficit yield similar results. For example, Kumhof, Laxton, and Muir (2005) find that a permanent 1 percentage point of GDP increase in the U.S. government saving ratio—increasing the U.S. national saving rate by ¾ percentage point—improves the U.S. current account by almost ½ percent of GDP on average during the first five years. Moreover, current account changes as a ratio to GDP are similar across other regions of the world. If the duration of the fiscal consolidation effort is restricted to five years, the current account improvement is smaller—about ¼ percentage point of GDP—similar to that reported in Erceg, Guerrieri, and Gust (2005).

[22]It should be noted that these results are based on a model estimated over the past three decades, a period during most of which several emerging markets, particularly the fast-growing economies of southeast Asia and China, were much smaller and less important for world trade. Hence, an analysis based on past data likely underestimates the role played by adjustments in this group of countries today.

Figure 2.9. How Would the Current Account React to an Increase in the U.S. Saving Ratio?[1]
(Percent of GDP)

A 1-percent-of-GDP increase in the U.S. national saving rate would have a significant positive effect on the U.S. current account deficit, while negatively affecting the current account balances of Japan and the Large Euro and East Asia 2 countries.

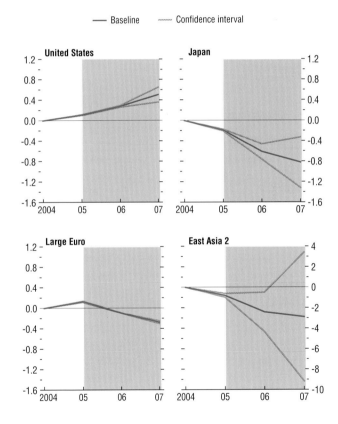

Source: IMF staff estimates.
[1]See footnote 15 in main text for definition of country groupings.

Table 2.4. Average Trade by Region, 1970–2004
(Percent of regional GDP)

	United States	Japan	Anglo-Saxon	Other Industrial	Large Euro	Small Euro
United States	. . .	2.0	4.0	0.3	1.5	0.7
Japan	4.8	. . .	1.9	0.3	1.2	0.6
Anglo-Saxon	14.3	2.5	. . .	1.8	6.1	4.2
Other Industrial	3.9	1.6	5.5	. . .	17.4	7.4
Large Euro	3.0	1.0	3.3	2.8	. . .	7.0
Small Euro	3.3	1.1	5.4	2.9	18.3	. . .
East Asia 1	11.2	12.9	3.9	0.8	3.6	2.0
East Asia 2	36.7	27.9	15.9	4.1	14.2	5.8
China	3.3	4.5	1.3	0.3	1.9	0.8
Other Emerging Markets	2.7	1.0	1.8	0.8	4.0	1.7
Latin America	4.3	1.2	1.0	0.5	2.7	1.4
Oil Producers	13.9	3.4	3.5	2.2	5.4	2.9

	East Asia 1	East Asia 2	China	Other Emerging Markets	Latin America	Oil Producers
United States	1.0	0.5	0.5	0.5	0.5	1.8
Japan	2.7	0.9	1.1	0.5	0.4	1.5
Anglo-Saxon	1.2	0.9	0.6	1.1	0.4	1.6
Other Industrial	0.7	0.7	0.4	1.1	0.7	3.3
Large Euro	0.6	0.4	0.5	1.3	0.6	1.5
Small Euro	0.8	0.4	0.4	1.1	0.7	1.9
East Asia 1	. . .	5.6	2.1	1.1	0.5	2.0
East Asia 2	30.7	. . .	39.1	4.8	1.2	6.4
China	2.1	4.9	. . .	0.4	0.4	0.4
Other Emerging Markets	0.7	0.5	0.3	. . .	0.3	1.0
Latin America	0.4	0.2	0.4	0.4	. . .	1.4
Oil Producers	1.3	0.6	0.4	1.0	1.1	. . .

Sources: IMF, *Direction of Trade Statistics;* and IMF staff calculations.

current account deficit by about ¾ percent of GDP after three years (Figure 2.10). An equivalent increase in the investment rate in oil-producing countries, as they devote a larger share of their oil revenues to the accumulation of capital, has a broadly similar impact on the U.S. current account deficit.

- *An increase in real GDP growth in Japan and the Large Euro countries would help reduce the U.S. current account deficit.* A ½ percent a year increase in real GDP growth in Japan would reduce the U.S current account deficit by about 0.2 percent of GDP after three years, while worsening the current account in Japan by 0.3 percent of GDP and having almost no effect on the current account of Large Euro countries (Figure 2.11). A ½ percent a year increase in real GDP growth in Large Euro countries would have a broadly similar impact on the U.S. current account deficit.

- *An increase in real short-term interest rates in the United States would have a limited impact on the*

current account. A cumulative 2 percentage point increase over the next three years would have a very modest impact on current account balances in the United States or other countries (about 0.1 percent of GDP by 2007) (Figure 2.12). This is consistent with the high co-movement of interest rates, saving, and investment across industrial countries, meaning that as interest rates rise in the United States they are also likely to increase elsewhere. Correspondingly, saving and investment in other industrial countries will be affected, with little impact on global imbalances. Of course, if higher interest rates have more of an effect in countries that have been experiencing house price booms, the impact on saving and current account balances could be larger.

Overall, these results suggest that an increase in U.S saving, achieved most directly through fiscal consolidation, is likely to have a significant impact on the current account deficit in the

United States and would reduce surpluses in Japan, the Large Euro countries, and Asia. Stronger growth in Japan and Europe and a pickup in investment in emerging market economies would also play a role in addressing current imbalances. On the other hand, an increase in real interest rates in the United States would have a limited impact on its external deficit, given the spillovers on saving and investments ratios in other regions. These results emphasize the importance of adequately addressing cross-country linkages in any analysis of policies to reduce global imbalances.

Conclusions

Global saving and investment are near historic lows, having fallen markedly since the late 1990s. These trends largely reflect developments in industrial countries; in emerging markets, saving has continued to rise, although investment has not recovered since its fall in the aftermath of the Asian financial crisis. The decline in global saving and investment has been due both to factors that have commonly affected a large number of countries—such as increases in credit and asset prices—and to country-/region-specific developments. Most important among these are the decline in public saving in the United States, demographic changes in Japan and Europe, and the slump in investment in Asian economies (excluding China) in the aftermath of the regional financial crisis.

The recent paths of saving and investment have had significant implications for the distribution of current account imbalances across the world. In particular, the U.S. current account deficit has reached unprecedented levels, and large surpluses have emerged in other regions. Contrary to the situation in the mid-1980s—the last period of significant global imbalances—when the imbalances were concentrated among a relatively small group of countries, the current situation involves a much wider set of players, including many emerging market countries. Consequently, the policy response will need to involve many more countries, and coordinating

Figure 2.10. How Would Current Account Imbalances React to Changes in the Investment Rate in Asia?[1]
(Percent of GDP)

A 5-percent-of-GDP increase in the investment rate in East Asia 1 countries would have a relatively significant effect on the U.S. current account deficit.

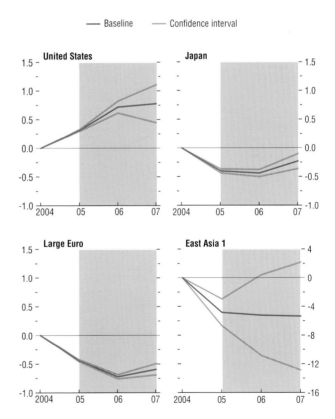

Source: IMF staff estimates.
[1]See footnote 15 in main text for definition of country groupings.

Figure 2.11. How Would the Current Account React to Changes in Japan's GDP Growth?[1]
(Percent of GDP)

A 1/2 percent acceleration in real GDP growth in Japan would help reduce the U.S. current account deficit.

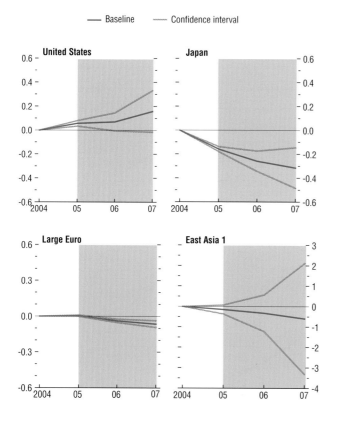

Source: IMF staff estimates.
[1]See footnote 15 in main text for definition of country groupings.

this response will require considerable efforts from international policymakers.

As the current constellation of external imbalances reflects a series of diverse and unrelated regional shocks, a number of economic and policy developments will be required to unwind them. In particular, the results in this chapter indicate that steps to raise saving in the United States, boost growth in Japan and Europe, and increase investment in Asia—including completing ongoing financial and corporate restructuring—and in oil-exporting countries would all move global current account imbalances in the right direction.

Finally, the analysis suggests that unusually low investment rates for this stage of the economic cycle have resulted in an excess supply of saving that may be contributing to the low level of real long-term interest rates. This low investment is largely a result of the still-ongoing efforts by corporates in many countries to strengthen their balance sheets by paying down debt. Consequently, despite strong corporate profit growth, investment has generally remained weak. The evolution of investment is therefore likely to be a critical factor determining long-term interest rates going forward. A return of investment to a more normal cyclical relationship with growth would likely put upward pressure on interest rates.

Appendix 2.1. Sample Composition, Data Sources, Methods, and Results

The main authors of this appendix are Marco Terrones and Roberto Cardarelli. Stephanie Denis provided research assistance.

This appendix provides details on the data sources, samples, and econometric methods and results of the study discussed in the main text.

Sample and Data Sources

- The sample used in this chapter comprises the following 46 industrial and emerging market countries. Industrial countries: Australia,

Austria, Belgium, Canada, Denmark, Finland, France, Germany, Greece, Ireland, Italy, Japan, the Netherlands, New Zealand, Norway, Portugal, Spain, Sweden, Switzerland, the United States, and the United Kingdom. Emerging markets: Argentina, Brazil, Chile, China, Colombia, Egypt, Hong Kong SAR, India, Indonesia, I.R. of Iran, Israel, Korea, Malaysia, Mexico, Morocco, Pakistan, Peru, the Philippines, Saudi Arabia, Singapore, South Africa, Thailand, Taiwan Province of China, Turkey, and Venezuela.[23] The oil-exporting countries subgroup is defined as comprising I.R. of Iran, Mexico, Norway, Saudi Arabia, and Venezuela. The data are annual and cover 1970–2004.

- Data were taken from a variety of sources, including the Organization for Economic Cooperation and Development's (OECD) Analytical Database, the Global Financial Database, the IMF's *International Financial Statistics* and the *World Economic Outlook,* national authorities, the World Development Indicators from the World Bank, and Worldscope.

- The main series used in the chapter are as follows.

  - *Saving and investment rates.* These series were constructed using data from the OECD Analytical Database, World Development Indicators, and the *World Economic Outlook.*

  - *Interest rates.* The short-term interest rate series were mainly obtained from the Global Financial Database and the IMF's *International Financial Statistics.*

  - *Investment deflator.* This deflator was calculated using the OECD Analytical Database and the *World Economic Outlook.*

  - *Private credit (by deposit money banks and other financial institutions) to GDP ratio.* Obtained from the World Bank's Financial Structure Development Database.

[23]I.R. of Iran and Saudi Arabia are not usually included among the emerging market economies.

Figure 2.12. How Would the Current Account React to Changes in the U.S. Real Interest Rate?[1]
(Percent of GDP)

A 200 basis point increase in real interest rates in the United States would have a minor effect on global current account imbalances.

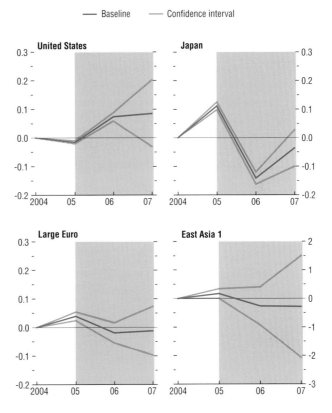

Source: IMF staff estimates.
[1]See footnote 15 in main text for definition of country groupings.

- *Elderly and youth dependence ratios.* These series were obtained from the World Bank's World Development Indicators.
- Corporate data series used in Box 2.3. The corporate data set used in Box 2.3 is based on information from nonfinancial publicly traded firms and reported in the Worldscope database. The data set includes information for nine emerging Asian economies—namely, Hong Kong SAR, India, Indonesia, Korea, Malaysia, the Philippines, Singapore, Taiwan Province of China, and Thailand.[24] The data were then used to construct ratios of investment (investment expenditures over book value of plant, machinery, and equipment), leverage (short-term debt over market value of equity), liquidity (cash flow over book value of machinery, capital, and equipment), and Tobin's *q* (market value of equity plus book value of long-term debt over book value of machinery, capital, and equipment) by country, using median values.

Dynamic Panel Model of Saving and Investment

Building on existing literature on saving and investment, IMF staff estimated a dynamic panel model for these two variables using data for the 46 countries over the 1972–2004 period.

The model postulates that saving, in any given country (*i*) and year (*t*), is explained by the following factors:

$$S_{it} = \gamma S_{i(t-1)} + X_{it}\beta + v_i + \eta_t + u_{it}, \qquad (1)$$
$$(i = 1, \ldots, N; \, t = 2, \ldots, T)$$

where S_{it} is the saving rate for country *i* in period *t*; X_{it} is a matrix comprising information on the explanatory variables for country *i* in period *t*; v_i is a country-specific effect; and η_t is a time-specific effect (which would capture the rest of the world trends). The right-hand-side variables included in the saving regression are of two types.

- Past saving rate, $S_{i(t-1)}$. This term captures the extent to which saving rates are persistent—that is, the extent current saving rates are correlated with past rates.
- Economic determinants of saving, X_{it}. The following determinants were considered, with the expected sign of the relationship between saving and each determinant in parentheses: per capita output growth (+); real interest rate (+); credit to the private sector (–); terms-of-trade growth (+); public sector saving (+); and the elderly and youth dependency ratios (–). For a discussion, see, for instance, Edwards (1995); Higgins (1998); Haque, Pesaran, and Sharma (1999); Loayza, Schmidt-Hebbel, and Servén (2000); and the May 1995 *World Economic Outlook*.

Similarly, the model postulates that investment, in any given country (*i*) and year (*t*), is explained by the following factors:

$$I_{it} = \gamma I_{i(t-1)} + X_{it}\beta + v_i + \eta_t + u_{it}, \qquad (2)$$
$$(i = 1, \ldots, N; \, t = 2, \ldots, T)$$

where I_{it} is the investment rate for country *i* in period *t*, X_{it} is a matrix comprising information on the explanatory variables for country *i* in period *t*, v_i is a country-specific effect, and η_t is a time-specific effect (which would capture the rest of the world trends). The right-hand-side variables included in the investment regression are of two types.

- Past investment rate, $I_{i(t-1)}$. This term captures the extent to which investment rates are persistent. If investment is a highly persistent process, higher investment rates today would be associated with higher investment rates tomorrow.
- Economic determinants of investment, X_{it}. The following determinants were considered, with the expected sign of the relationship between investment and each determinant in parentheses: per capita output growth (+); credit to the private sector (+); the cost of cap-

---

[24]Because investment in China has behaved differently from that in other countries in the region, China was excluded from the analysis.

ital (–)—measured as the ratio of real interest to the relative price of capital;[25] and the elderly and youth dependency ratios (undetermined). For a discussion, see, for instance, Romer (1996); Higgins (1998); Auerbach (2002); and Pelgrin, Schich, and de Serres (2002).

These regression equations were estimated using the Generalized Method of Moments estimator with robust errors (to correct for heterogeneity in the error term).

A Dynamic Factor Model

Dynamic factor models have become increasing popular among economists,[26] as they describe the covariance or co-movement between a group of (observable) time series as the result of the relationship between these variables and a small number of unobservable variables, known as factors. These unobserved factors can be regarded as indexes of common activity—across the entire data set (e.g., global activity) or across subsets of the data (e.g., for a particular region).

To estimate the factors, the dynamic factor model decomposes each observable variable—for example, the saving rate for the United States—into components that are common across all observable variables or common across a subset of variables. In particular, for each of the 12 regions considered in the chapter, the analysis uses five observable variables: real output growth (g), real short-term interest rates (r), ratio of the current account balance to GDP (CA), saving rate (S), and investment rate (I).[27] In the model, there are three types of factors: the common factor (f^W), 5 factors specific to each observed variable (f^i, one per variable) and 12 region-specific factors (f^j, one per region). So there are 60 (5 × 12) "regression" equations to be estimated, and 60 time series to be explained by 18 (1 + 5 + 12)

factors. For example, for the United States the regressions estimated are:

$$y_t^{US} = a_{y,US} + b_{y,US}^W f_t^W + b_{US}^y f_t^y + b_y^{US} f_t^{US} + \varepsilon_{t,US}^y$$

$$r_t^{US} = a_{r,US} + b_{r,US}^W f_t^W + b_{US}^r f_t^r + b_r^{US} f_t^{US} + \varepsilon_{t,US}^r$$

$$CA_t^{US} = a_{CA,US} + b_{CA,US}^W f_t^W + b_{US}^{CA} f_t^{US} + b_{CA}^{US} f_t^{US} + \varepsilon_{t,US}^{CA}$$

$$S_t^{US} = a_{S,US} + b_{S,US}^W f_t^W + b_{US}^S f_t^S + b_S^{US} f_t^{US} + \varepsilon_{t,US}^S$$

$$I_t^{US} = a_{I,US} + b_{I,US}^W f_t^W + b_{US}^I f_t^I + b_I^{US} f_t^{US} + \varepsilon_{t,US}^I.$$

In this system, f^W is the world factor, the component common to all variables in all countries—that is, every variable depends on this common factor and that dependence varies across each variable i and country j through the parameter $b_{i,j}^W$, which is called the factor loading; f^i is the global factor for variable i, capturing co-movement across the world in this variable that is not explained by the world factor; and f^{US} is a U.S.-specific factor, which captures co-movement across all five variables within the United States that is not captured by either type of global factor. Finally, ε is the "unexplained" idiosyncratic error.

The model captures dynamic co-movement by allowing the factors (fs) and idiosyncratic terms (ε) to be (independent) autoregressive processes. That is, each factor depends on lags of itself and an i.i.d. innovation to the variable:

$$f_t = \phi(L)f_t + u_t,$$

where $\phi(L)$ is a lag polynomial and u_t is normally distributed. All the factor loadings (bs), and lag polynomials are independent of each other. Because the factors are unobservable, special methods must be employed to estimate them; in the chapter, the model is estimated using Bayesian techniques as described in Kose, Otrok, and Whiteman (2003).

To measure the contribution of each factor to the variation in the observable variables, the volatility in each aggregate variable has been decomposed into components due to each

---

[25]Because of lack of information on taxes, the measure of cost of capital used in this chapter takes into account neither differences in taxes across countries nor tax changes in a given country.

[26]See, for example, Stock and Watson (2002) and Forni, Lippi, and Reichlin (2004).

[27]Before estimating the dynamic factor model, the observables were detrended.

Table 2.5. Variance Decomposition for Country Regions
(Percent)

Region	Factor	Output (y)	Short-Term Real Interest Rate (r)	Current Account (CA)	Saving Rate (s)	Investment Rate (i)
United States	Global	82.2	53.3	53.8	83.9	44.5
	World	7.0	0.2	3.9	11.1	22.7
	Aggregate	75.2	53.1	49.9	72.8	21.8
	Region and idiosyncratic	17.5	46.5	45.9	11.2	54.8
Japan	Global	25.2	69.9	60.4	29.3	52.6
	World	6.0	24.8	2.9	13.9	21.4
	Aggregate	19.1	45.1	57.6	15.3	31.2
	Region and idiosyncratic	74.7	30.3	39.8	69.9	47.7
Anglo-Saxon	Global	74.8	93.8	4.0	55.3	53.4
	World	20.1	0.5	0.2	54.8	45.5
	Aggregate	54.7	93.3	3.9	0.5	7.9
	Region and idiosyncratic	25.3	5.8	95.9	44.2	45.8
Other Industrial	Global	57.5	85.4	18.5	91.3	69.0
	World	42.6	21.2	18.3	60.3	38.8
	Aggregate	14.9	64.3	0.1	30.9	30.2
	Region and idiosyncratic	42.5	14.6	81.2	8.4	30.5
Large Euro	Global	29.4	90.5	42.5	81.6	63.2
	World	23.2	4.4	9.9	68.5	40.8
	Aggregate	6.2	86.1	32.5	13.0	22.3
	Region and idiosyncratic	70.1	9.0	57.2	18.1	37.0
Small Euro	Global	71.3	86.4	11.5	85.0	69.2
	World	62.5	7.8	8.2	63.7	46.0
	Aggregate	8.7	78.6	3.3	21.4	23.2
	Region and idiosyncratic	28.4	13.4	87.7	14.4	30.9
East Asia 1	Global	2.5	49.1	37.6	9.4	21.2
	World	0.3	16.5	34.0	0.6	17.1
	Aggregate	2.2	32.6	3.6	8.8	4.0
	Region and idiosyncratic	97.4	50.4	62.2	90.4	78.3
East Asia 2	Global	35.7	19.2	97.2	6.5	1.5
	World	0.1	16.0	0.3	2.5	0.9
	Aggregate	35.6	3.3	96.9	4.0	0.6
	Region and idiosyncratic	64.2	80.6	2.5	92.8	97.8
China	Global	29.6	3.4	13.3	3.7	14.3
	World	19.4	0.4	3.7	2.5	6.7
	Aggregate	10.3	2.9	9.6	1.2	7.6
	Region and idiosyncratic	70.4	96.4	86.7	96.1	85.3
Other Emerging Markets	Global	2.3	9.1	36.2	7.2	21.4
	World	2.2	3.5	1.5	6.5	8.9
	Aggregate	0.1	5.6	34.7	0.7	12.5
	Region and idiosyncratic	97.6	90.7	63.5	91.9	78.4
Latin America	Global	7.5	33.3	33.8	3.2	1.3
	World	4.1	4.7	0.3	0.4	0.3
	Aggregate	3.4	28.6	33.4	2.7	1.1
	Region and idiosyncratic	92.3	65.8	66.0	96.6	98.5
Oil Producers	Global	23.6	23.1	18.4	14.2	1.7
	World	23.5	1.8	5.8	7.9	1.2
	Aggregate	0.2	21.3	12.5	6.3	0.5
	Region and idiosyncratic	76.1	76.7	81.8	85.5	97.7
Average	Global	36.8	51.4	35.6	39.2	34.4
	World	17.6	8.5	7.4	24.4	20.9
	Aggregate	19.2	42.9	28.2	14.8	13.6
	Region and idiosyncratic	63.0	48.4	64.2	60.0	65.2

Source: IMF staff calculations.

Table 2.6. Investment and Capital Ratios for Emerging Asia

	Steady State			1996		2004	
	Capital-output ratio	Potential real growth rate	Investment ratio	Investment ratio	Capital ratio	Investment ratio	Capital ratio
Depreciation rate at 5 percent							
China	2.5	5.0	23.8	34.4	2.2	45.6	3.0
Hong Kong SAR	2.7	4.0	23.1	31.3	2.6	22.4	2.9
India	2.5	5.0	23.8	25.4	2.2	23.5	2.4
Indonesia	2.5	5.0	23.8	23.3	1.9	21.0	2.4
Korea	2.8	4.7	25.5	37.5	2.7	28.6	3.1
Malaysia	3.1	5.0	29.5	42.5	3.0	20.5	3.3
Philippines	2.7	4.0	23.3	24.0	2.7	17.0	2.6
Singapore	2.9	4.5	26.3	38.0	2.7	24.0	3.1
Taiwan Province of China	2.5	5.0	23.8	22.5	1.7	20.1	2.0
Thailand	3.0	5.0	28.7	41.1	3.0	25.3	3.0
Depreciation rate at 7 percent							
China	2.1	5.0	24.3	34.4	2.0	45.6	2.7
Hong Kong SAR	2.3	4.0	24.2	31.3	2.2	22.4	2.5
India	2.0	5.0	22.9	25.4	1.8	23.5	2.0
Indonesia	2.0	5.0	22.9	23.3	1.7	21.0	2.0
Korea	2.4	4.7	27.1	37.5	2.4	28.6	2.6
Malaysia	2.7	5.0	30.9	42.5	2.7	20.5	2.8
Philippines	2.2	4.0	23.4	24.0	2.2	17.0	2.1
Singapore	2.5	4.5	27.7	38.0	2.4	24.0	2.6
Taiwan Province of China	2.0	5.0	22.9	22.5	1.5	20.1	1.7
Thailand	2.6	5.0	29.7	41.1	2.6	25.3	2.4

Source: IMF staff estimates.

factor. Table 2.5 reports the median of the posterior distribution of the variance decompositions for each region. For example, the variance of the saving rate for the United States is

$$var(S_t^{US}) = (b_{US}^W)^2 \, var(f_t^W) + (b_{US}^S)^2 \, var(f_t^S)$$
$$+ (b_{US}^S)^2 \, var(f_t^{US}) + var(\varepsilon_{t,US}^S),$$

and, therefore, the variance in U.S. saving rates attributable to the world factor is

$$\frac{(b_{US}^W)^2 \, var(f_t^W)}{var(S_t^{US})}.$$

Steady-State Level of Investment and Capital Output Ratio for Emerging Asia

Steady-state levels of investment rates are estimated based on standard neoclassical growth models, and thus as a function of the steady-state capital-output ratio, the depreciation rate, and the trend growth rate of output:

$$i^* = \frac{k^* \, (g + d)}{(1 + g)},$$

where i^* is the (steady-state) ratio of real gross fixed investment to real output, k^* is the (steady-state) capital-output ratio, g is potential output growth, and d is the depreciation rate. Thus, i^* is a positive function of k^*, g, and d. Capital stock is estimated based on a standard perpetual inventory method

$$K_t = K_{t-1}(1 - d) + I_t.$$

Two depreciation rates are used: 5 percent and 7 percent. With data on gross fixed real investment starting from 1950 (obtained using the Penn World Table Version 6.0), the initial estimate of capital stock is obtained assuming that the country is at steady-state capital-output ratio in 1950. To obtain this ratio, the averages of k, g, and d over 1950–60 are used. However, different periods and parameter values are used to test the sensitivity of the capital stock to the choice of its initial value, and the results show that the guess at the initial capital stock becomes relatively unimportant decades later (Easterly and Levine, 2001; and

Klenow and Rodriguez-Clare, 2001, adopt a similar methodology).

For a given depreciation rate, the steady state capital stock ratio, k^*, for each country is found as the maximum value of the capital-output ratio on average over long (15- and 20-year) subperiods between 1950 and 2004. However, when such capital-output ratio is lower than 2.5 (2) if calculated with a 5 (7) percent depreciation rate, it is set to this level to minimize the dispersion of capital ratios across countries and reduce possible measurement errors. Indeed, the steady-state capital-output ratios are in the range of 2 to 3.5 (see Table 2.6), a reasonable estimate for this group of countries (the average for industrial countries over the 1970–2004 period is slightly below 3). Potential growth rates are obtained from the World Economic Outlook database, but are capped at 5 percent a year when above this value.

References

Aitken, Brian, 2005, "The Historical Dominance of Banks in China's Financial System," IMF Working Paper (Washington: International Monetary Fund, forthcoming).

Arellano, Manuel, and Stephen Bond, 1991, "Some Tests of Specification for Panel Data: Monte Carlo Evidence and an Application to Employment Equations," *Review of Economic Studies*, Vol. 58 (April), pp. 277–97.

Auerbach, Alan J., 2002, "Investment," in *The Concise Encyclopedia of Economics*, ed. by David R. Henderson (Indianapolis: Liberty Fund, Inc.). Available via the Internet: http://www.econlib.org/library/Enc/Investment.html.

Barnett, Steven, and Ray Brooks, 2005, "What's Driving Investment in China," IMF Working Paper (Washington: International Monetary Fund, forthcoming).

Bernanke, Ben, 2005, "The Global Saving Glut and the U.S. Current Account Deficit," remarks at the Sandridge Lecture, Virginia Association of Economics, Richmond, Virginia.

———, Jean Boivin, and Piotr Eliasz, 2005, "Measuring the Effects of Monetary Policy: A Factor-Augmented Vector Autoregressive (FAVAR) Approach," *Quarterly Journal of Economics*, Vol. 120 (January), pp. 387–422.

Blanchard, Olivier, and Stanley Fischer, 1989, *Lectures on Macroeconomics* (Cambridge, Massachusetts: MIT Press).

Bosworth, Barry P., and Benjamin Keys, 2004, "Increased Life Expectancy: A Global Perspective," in *Coping with Methuselah: The Impact of Molecular Biology on Medicine and Society*, ed. by Henry Aaron and William Schwartz (Washington: Brookings Institution Press), pp. 247–83.

Boyreau-Debray, Genevieve, and Shang-Jin Wei, 2005, "Pitfalls of a State-Dominated Financial System: The Case of China," NBER Working Paper No. 11214 (Cambridge, Massachusetts: National Bureau of Economic Research).

Bryant, Ralph, 2004, "Cross-Border Macroeconomic Implications of Demographic Change," in *Global Demographic Change: Economic Impacts and Policy Challenges, Jackson Hole, Wyoming, August 26–28, 2004, a Symposium Sponsored by the Federal Reserve Bank of Kansas City*, ed. by Gordon H. Sellon, Jr. (Kansas City: Federal Reserve Bank of Kansas City).

Chamon, Marcos, and Eswar Prasad, 2005, "Determinants of Household Saving in China," IMF Working Paper (Washington: International Monetary Fund, forthcoming).

Deaton, Angus, 1992, *Understanding Consumption*, Clarendon Lectures on Economics (Oxford: Oxford University Press).

Dees, Stephane, Filippo di Mauro, Hashem Pesaran, and Vanessa Smith, 2005, "Exploring the International Linkages of the Euro Area: A Global VAR Analysis," CESifo Working Paper No. 1425 (Munich: CESifo).

De Mello, Luiz, Per Mathis Kongsrud, and Robert Price, 2004, "Saving Behaviour and the Effectiveness of Fiscal Policy," OECD Economics Department Working Paper No. 397 (Paris: Organization for Economic Cooperation and Development).

Easterly, William, and Ross Levine, 2001, "It's Not Factor Accumulation: Stylized Facts and Growth Models," *World Bank Economic Review*, Vol. 15, No. 2, pp. 177–219.

Edwards, Sebastian, 1995, "Why Are Saving Rates So Different Across Countries? An International Comparative Analysis," NBER Working Paper No. 5097 (Cambridge, Massachusetts: National Bureau of Economic Research).

Erceg, Christopher, Luca Guerrieri, and Christopher Gust, 2005, "Expansionary Fiscal Shocks and the Trade Deficit," International Finance Discussion

Paper No. 825 (Washington: Board of Governors of the Federal Reserve System).

Fama, Eugene, and Kenneth French, 1999, "The Corporate Cost of Capital and the Return on Corporate Investment," *Journal of Finance*, Vol. 54 (December), pp. 1939–67.

Faulkner-MacDonagh, Chris, and Martin Mühleisen, 2004, "Are U.S. Households Living Beyond Their Means?" *Finance and Development*, Vol. 41, No. 1, pp. 36–9.

Fehr, Hans, Sabine Jokisch, and Laurence Kotlikoff, 2004, "The Role of Immigration in Dealing with the Developed World's Demographic Transition," NBER Working Paper No. 10512 (Cambridge, Massachusetts: National Bureau of Economic Research).

Feldstein, Martin, and Charles Horioka, 1980, "Domestic Saving and International Capital Flows," *Economic Journal*, Vol. 90 (June), pp. 314–29.

Forni, Mario, Marco Lippi, and Lucrezia Reichlin, 2004, "Opening the Black Box: Structural Factor Models Versus Structural VARs," CEPR Discussion Paper No. 4133 (London: Centre for Economic Policy Research).

Gale, William, and Peter Orszag, 2004, "Budget Deficits, National Saving, and Interest Rates," *Brookings Papers on Economic Activity: 2,* Brookings Institution, pp. 101–210.

Glick, Reuven, and Kenneth Rogoff, 1995, "Global Versus Country-Specific Productivity Shocks and the Current Account," *Journal of Monetary Economics*, Vol. 35 (February), pp. 159–92.

Gregory, Allan, and Allen Head, 1999, "Common and Country-Specific Fluctuations in Productivity, Investment, and the Current Account," *Journal of Monetary Economics*, Vol. 44 (December), pp. 423–51.

Haque, Nadeem, Hashem Pesaran, and Sunil Sharma, 1999, "Neglected Heterogeneity and Dynamics in Cross-Country Savings Regressions," IMF Working Paper 99/128 (Washington: International Monetary Fund).

Helliwell, John F., 2004, "Demographic Changes and International Factor Mobility," in *Global Demographic Change: Economic Impacts and Policy Challenges, Jackson Hole, Wyoming, August 26–28, 2004, a Symposium Sponsored by the Federal Reserve Bank of Kansas City,* ed. by Gordon H. Sellon, Jr. (Kansas City: Federal Reserve Bank of Kansas City).

Higgins, Matthew, 1998, "Demography, National Savings, and International Capital Flows," *International Economic Review,* Vol. 39 (May), pp. 343–69.

International Monetary Fund, 2004, "People's Republic of China: Article IV Consultation—Staff Report, Staff Statement, and Public Information Notice on the Executive Board Discussion," IMF Country Report No. 04/351 (Washington: International Monetary Fund).

JPMorgan Chase & Co., 2005, "Corporates Are Driving the Global Saving Glut," *Global Issues* (London: JPMorgan Research, June 24).

Jaeger, Albert, 2003, "Corporate Balance Sheet Restructuring and Investment in the Euro Area," IMF Working Paper 03/117 (Washington: International Monetary Fund).

Klenow, Peter, and Andrés Rodriguez-Clare, 1997, "The Neoclassical Revival in Growth Economics: Has It Gone Too Far?" *NBER Macroeconomics Annual 1997* (Cambridge, Massachusetts: MIT Press), pp. 73–102.

Klingen, Christoph, Beatrice Weder, and Jeromin Zettelmeyer, 2004, "How Private Creditors Fared in Emerging Debt Markets, 1970–2000," IMF Working Paper 04/13 (Washington: International Monetary Fund).

Kose, Ayhan, Christopher Otrok, and Charles Whiteman, 2003, "International Business Cycles: World, Region, and Country-Specific Factors," *American Economic Review,* Vol. 93 (September), pp. 1216–39.

———, 2004, "Understanding the Evolution of the World Business Cycle" (unpublished).

Kumhof, Michael, Douglas Laxton, and Dirk Muir, 2005, "Consequences of U.S. Fiscal Consolidation for the Current Account," Chapter IV in "United States: Selected Issues," IMF Country Report No. 05/258 (Washington: International Monetary Fund).

Lee, Jong-Wha, Warwick McKibbin, and Yung Chul Park, 2004, "Transpacific Trade Imbalances: Causes and Cures," Brookings Discussion Papers in International Economics, No. 162 (August).

Loayza, Norman, Klaus Schmidt-Hebbel, and Luis Servén, 2000, "Saving in Developing Countries: An Overview," *World Bank Economic Review,* Vol. 14 (September), pp. 393–414.

Lucas, Robert, 1990, "Why Doesn't Capital Flow from Rich to Poor Countries?" *American Economic Review: Papers and Proceedings,* Vol. 80 (May), pp. 92–96.

Masson, Paul, Tamim Bayoumi, and Hossein Samiei, 1995, "Saving Behavior in Industrial and

Developing Countries," *Staff Studies for the World Economic Outlook* (Washington: International Monetary Fund).

Miles, David, 1999, "Modelling the Impact of Demographic Change Upon the Economy," *Economic Journal,* Vol. 109 (January), pp. 1–36.

Modigliani, Franco, and Shi Larry Cao, 2004, "The Chinese Saving Puzzle and the Life-Cycle Hypothesis," *Journal of Economic Literature,* Vol. 42 (March), pp. 145–70.

Pelgrin, Florian, Sebastian Schich, and Alain de Serres, 2002, "Increases in Business Investment Rates in OECD Countries in the 1990s: How Much Can Be Explained by Fundamentals?" OECD Working Paper No. 327 (Paris: Organization for Economic Cooperation and Development).

Podpiera, Richard, 2005, "Progress in Banking Reform," IMF Working Paper (Washington: International Monetary Fund, forthcoming).

Poterba, James, 1987, "Tax Policy and Corporate Saving," *Brookings Papers on Economic Activity: 2,* Brookings Institution, pp. 455–503.

———, 2004, "The Impact of Population Aging on Financial Markets," NBER Working Paper No. 10851 (Cambridge, Massachusetts: National Bureau of Economic Research).

Prasad, Eswar, and Raghuram Rajan, 2005, "China's Financial-Sector Challenge," op-ed article, *Financial Times* (London), May 10.

Romer, David, 1996, *Advanced Macroeconomics* (New York: McGraw-Hill).

Roubini, Nouriel, and Brad Setser, 2005, "Will the Bretton Woods 2 Regime Unravel Soon? The Risk of a Hard Landing in 2005–2006," paper presented at the symposium of the Federal Reserve Bank of San Francisco and the University of California Berkeley, "Revived Bretton Woods System: A New Paradigm for Asian Development?" San Francisco, February 4.

Sachs, Jeffrey, and Steven Radelet, 1998, "The Onset of the East Asian Financial Crisis," NBER Working Paper No. 6680 (Cambridge, Massachusetts: National Bureau of Economic Research).

Schmidt-Hebbel, Klaus, and Luis Servén, 1999, "Saving Across the World" (Washington: World Bank).

Stock, James, and Mark Watson, 2002, "Macroeconomic Forecasting Using Diffusion Indexes," *Journal of Business and Economic Statistics,* Vol. 20 (April), pp. 147–62.

Tevlin, Stacey, and Karl Whelan, 2003, "Explaining the Investment Boom of the 1990s," *Journal of Money, Credit and Banking,* Vol. 35 (February), pp. 1–22.

With one billion people in developing countries living on less than $1 a day, the alleviation of extreme poverty remains high on the policy agenda of the international community. Despite the progress made in poverty reduction in some regions of the world over the past two decades, reaching the Millennium Development Goal (MDG) of halving poverty by 2015 remains out of reach for most developing countries—with the notable exception of east and south Asia—based on current trends.[1] Sub-Saharan Africa, in particular, faces daunting challenges, with the incidence of poverty having risen in recent decades. Many middle-income countries also need to reduce unemployment and improve the lack of economic opportunity for large sections of their populations, to improve standards of living and foster a stable social environment.

It is widely accepted that sustained high rates of economic growth are the key to further progress. While global growth reached 30-year highs in 2004—with sub-Saharan Africa recording its strongest growth performance in nearly a decade—in most countries growth rates remain well below what is needed to meet the MDGs.[2] With considerable progress having been made toward a stable macroeconomic environment—an essential precondition for sustained growth—the challenge has increasingly become how to improve the quality of domestic institutional frameworks (such as stronger property rights, lower corruption, and better governance). For example, as discussed in the April 2003 *World Economic Outlook*, if insti-

tutions in Africa could be improved to the level in developing Asia, African per capita GDP might be expected to almost double over the long term (Figures 3.1 and 3.2).

If higher growth depends importantly on better institutions, the key question must be how those better institutions can be built. To date, partly reflecting the weakness of the data on institutions, the economic literature on this topic is very limited. This chapter aims to review some of the central issues involved, with the hope that it will stimulate further debate and research on this important issue, focusing on the following questions.

- How have institutions changed in the past 30 years?
- What are the main factors that have driven these institutional changes?
- What has been the role of the external environment—and external institutional mechanisms—in helping strengthen institutions in individual countries?

The chapter is organized as follows. Following a brief theoretical discussion of the factors that might be expected to affect institutional change, the chapter reviews the history of institutional developments, with a particular focus on the experience of the past 30 years, using a newly constructed database of "institutional transitions." This is followed by an econometric analysis of the factors determining institutions and institutional transitions, and a more detailed look at the role of three external factors—external anchors, aid, and transparency. The final section concludes.

The main authors of this chapter are Subir Lall, Nikola Spatafora, and Martin Sommer, with support from Simon Johnson, Arvind Subramanian, Andrei Levchenko, and James Robinson. Angela Espiritu provided research assistance.

[1]See Chen and Ravallion (2004) for poverty estimates and UN Millennium Project (2005), Table 9, for projections.

[2]Sub-Saharan Africa would require a weighted average growth rate per capita of 5 percent a year during 2005–15, while the average growth rate during 1990–2004 has been 0.2 percent (See IMF and World Bank, 2005, pp. 4–7, and the April 2005 *World Economic Outlook*).

Figure 3.1. Institutions and Income per Capita: Impact of Raising Regional Institutional Quality
(Percent change)

Substantial gains in income per capita could materialize if developing economies improved their institutional quality. For example, the April 2003 *World Economic Outlook* estimated that if the institutional quality in sub-Saharan Africa rose to the level of developing Asia, income per capita would, in the long run, increase by about 85 percent.

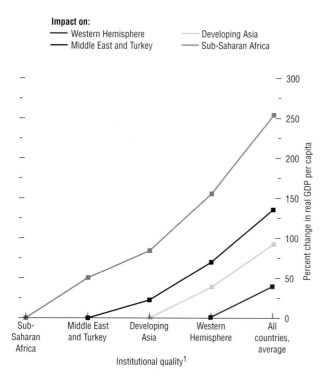

Source: IMF, *World Economic Outlook* (April 2003).
[1] Measured by Kaufmann, Kraay, and Zoido-Lobaton's (1999) aggregate governance indicator. See Appendix 3.1 for details. This figure is not to scale: in particular, the horizontal axis does not accurately capture differences in the quality of institutions. See Figure 3.2 for the actual institutional scores.

The Role of Institutions

In the broadest terms, institutions can be defined as the set of formal rules—and informal conventions—that provide the framework for human interaction and shape the incentives of members of society.[3] From an economic perspective, good institutions ensure two desirable outcomes: that there is relatively equal access to economic opportunity (a "level playing field"), and that those who provide labor and capital are appropriately rewarded and their property rights are protected (see, for example, Acemoglu and Johnson, 2003). At the outset, it is important to note that many different institutional forms—depending, for example, on a country's history or culture—can produce good institutional outcomes (Box 3.1). Correspondingly, the emphasis of this chapter will be very much on institutional outcomes[4] and the circumstances under which these may change.

Economic institutions are, of course, closely related to political institutions. Political institutions shape the incentives of the political executive and determine the distribution of political power, which includes the ability to shape economic institutions and the distribution of resources. In turn, economic institutions, by determining the relative affluence of various groups of society, also help shape political institutions. As groups grow wealthier, they can use their economic power to influence political institutions in their favor. This suggests two broad conclusions.

- Good economic institutions are most likely to flourish in a "rent-free" environment,[5] in which small groups are not able to take advantage of—for example—a monopoly position in

[3]See North (1991).
[4]These outcomes are measured using a number of available indices on broad economic institutions, as described in Appendix 3.1.
[5]Rent-seeking is defined as the pursuit of uncompensated value from other economic agents, in contrast with profit-seeking, where entities seek to create value through mutually beneficial economic activity. See Krueger (1974) for the first coinage of the term and its relationship to trade restrictions.

a particular industry or activity, or privileged access to natural resources.

• Good economic institutions are likely to be accompanied by good political institutions. If political power is broadly shared and subject to checks and balances, there is much less risk that those with political power will take advantage of their position to extract rents themselves.

Since a country's institutions are the result of a complex interaction of economic and political factors, as well as its history and culture, they are likely to be quite persistent. Changing institutions can be a slow and difficult process, requiring both significant domestic political will and more fundamental measures to reduce the opportunity and incentives for particular groups to capture economic rents. Indeed, if the underlying causes of institutional weaknesses are not addressed, reform efforts may well have little effect on institutional outcomes, with changes in one institution simply being offset by changes in another (the so-called "see-saw" effect—see Acemoglu and others, 2003). This does not mean, however, that institutional outcomes are immutable. Indeed, as the chapter will illustrate, over the past 30 years, significant—and sometimes quite rapid—institutional improvements have occurred across a broad range of countries (Figure 3.3). Such changes have been the consequence of specific events (such as the end of colonialism or the collapse of communism), specific policies addressing institutional weaknesses, and also the broader economic and social environment, helping reshape the economic incentives of society. As the next section will show, all these factors have been important in shaping institutional changes in countries.

When Do Institutions Change?

A review of the historical experience provides useful insights into the paths that countries have taken in building their institutions and what the main determinants of institutional change have been. Against this backdrop, a more detailed examination of the past three decades—a period

Figure 3.2. Developing Economies: Recent Developments in Institutional Quality by Region[1]

Over the past decade, institutional quality has, on average, improved in central and eastern Europe and Latin America. Institutional quality in sub-Saharan Africa and the CIS continues to be significantly below the institutional quality in other regions.

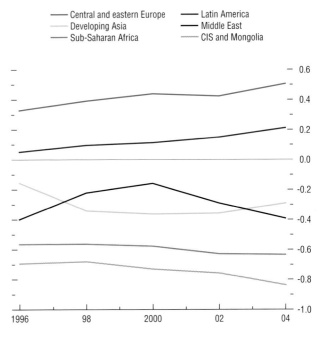

Sources: Kaufmann, Kraay, and Mastruzzi (2005); and IMF staff calculations.
[1]Regional scores were calculated as simple averages. Institutional quality is measured by Kaufmann, Kraay, and Mastruzzi's (2005) aggregate governance index. For more information, see Appendix 3.1. The regional classification of countries is based on the current *World Economic Outlook* regional groupings.

Figure 3.3. Evolution of Economic Institutions[1]

Economic institutions as measured by Gwartney and Lawson's Economic Freedom Index have improved across the world over the past three decades. However, sub-Saharan Africa and many other—mostly low-income—countries continue to have low institutional scores.

IBRD 34140

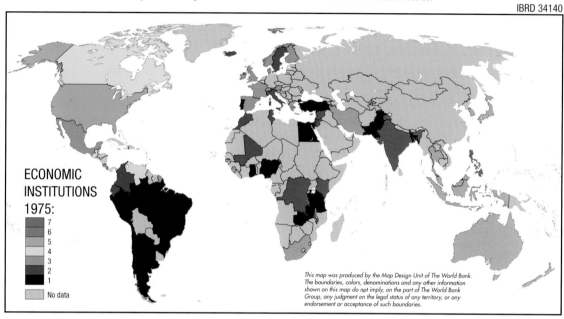

This map was produced by the Map Design Unit of The World Bank. The boundaries, colors, denominations and any other information shown on this map do not imply, on the part of The World Bank Group, any judgment on the legal status of any territory, or any endorsement or acceptance of such boundaries.

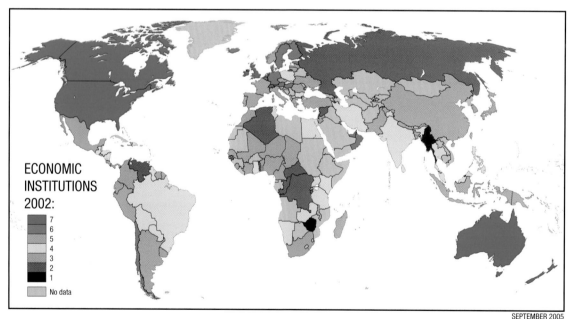

SEPTEMBER 2005

Sources: Gwartney and Lawson (2004); and IMF staff calculations.

[1] The measure of economic institutions is based on Gwartney and Lawson's Economic Freedom Index. Scores for individual countries were rescaled to the range from 1 to 7 with higher scores reflecting better institutional quality. See Appendix 3.1 for further details.

Box 3.1. Developing Institutions to Reflect Local Conditions: The Example of Ownership Transformation in China Versus Central and Eastern Europe

As discussed in the main text of this chapter, institutional reforms are only successful if they durably change incentive structures in the economy. This implies that the reforms need to be well grounded in the local environment and take into consideration the specific constraints that influence the speed of reform and the particular form that the institutions can take. For example, the processes of ownership transformation in China and the central and eastern European countries (CEECs) differed substantially, yet both effectively transformed incentives to create an environment conducive to fast growth. In many CEECs, economies rapidly moved from state to private ownership during the first half of the 1990s using a variety of privatization methods. These transformed firms as well as new private firms went on to become the drivers of growth. By contrast, during the initial phase of China's transition, most new firms were neither private firms nor state-owned enterprises, but collectively owned enterprises with significant ownership and managerial involvement by the local governments. The most important of these collectives were "township-village enterprises"—an indigenous Chinese institutional form.[1] This box discusses how the two different approaches to reform in China and CEECs were consistent with the countries' initial conditions and constraints.

Role of Initial Conditions

Different initial conditions strongly influenced the approach to ownership transformation in China and CEECs. The Chinese economy was largely agricultural through the 1970s,[2] and the agricultural reforms of 1978 generated rapid improvements in productivity and output.[3] Against the backdrop of strong growth, policymakers could take a considered approach with the design of reforms in other sectors.[4] Moreover, a large pool of surplus labor helped boost the growth impact of the Chinese incremental reforms (see the October 2000 *World Economic Outlook*). In contrast, the CEECs faced more complex initial conditions: most output and employment was concentrated in the industrial sector. The collapse of central planning led to output losses and unemployment, creating a difficult political environment for the new democratic governments that came to power across the region. Rapid privatization was often a political mandate, and the only option to avoid a transformation trap.

During its transformation, China was initially seen to maintain little protection of private property rights (see, for example, Qian, 2003). Local government involvement in the township-village enterprises provided an effective substitute for the perceived weaknesses in the protection of private ownership. The township-village enterprise ownership structure may also have helped alleviate some of the consequences of China's underdeveloped financial markets, as local governments assessed

Note: The main author of this box is Martin Sommer.

[1]The share of township-village enterprises in total employment rose from 7 percent in 1978 (identified in the main text as the beginning year of economic transition) to 19 percent in 1995 (*China Statistical Yearbook*, 2004). In 1995, the township-village enterprises contributed about 25 percent of industrial output—an increase from 15 percent in 1985 (*China Statistical Yearbook*, 1996).

[2]According to the *China Statistical Yearbook* (2004), the agricultural sector generated about 70 percent of total employment in 1978.

[3]Because the agricultural sector had been heavily repressed, freeing it up had immediate payoffs (World Bank, 1996). Between 1981 and 1984, agriculture grew on average by 10 percent a year, largely because the shift to family farming improved incentives. Sachs and Woo (1997) point out that agricultural productivity soared after 1978 though productivity growth decelerated sharply in the mid-1980s as the initial growth impulse faded away.

[4]Besides township-village enterprises, other examples of the Chinese experimental approach are the Household Responsibility System of Land Leaseholds and the Special Economic Zones.

Box 3.1 *(concluded)*

the risks of start-up businesses under their control and served as guarantors of loans to individual township-village enterprises (Naughton, 1994).

In many CEECs, economic reforms followed dramatic changes in the political regime. Given the failures of the centrally planned model, the attitude toward the concepts of market economy and private ownership was enthusiastic and, despite initial difficulties, the rule of law has gradually improved owing to new legislation and court reform. The proximity of, and the prospect of membership in, the European Union also encouraged the CEECs to adopt standardized ownership forms (see the October 2000 *World Economic Outlook* for a detailed discussion of transition in the CEECs). Complete private ownership could thus develop from the very onset of reforms.[5]

Role of Different Stakeholders in Society

The Chinese reform of ownership structures created pro-growth incentives while being consistent with the interests of the main stakeholders. Local governments considered township-village enterprises as an opportunity to obtain additional fiscal revenue to augment the provision of public goods such as maintaining order, building roads, and providing water and irrigation systems (Qian, 2003). The central government also benefited by being able to avoid large transfers and redistributions at the local level. Township-village enterprises provided stronger pro-growth momentum than existing state-owned enterprises because local officials had incentives to maximize profits of township-village enterprises (Oi, 1995). Township-village enterprises also faced less restrictive labor market conditions

and did not need to provide extensive social services like housing and pension to their workers.[6] In fact, some township-village enterprises were de facto private enterprises registered as township-village enterprises (Sachs and Woo, 1997). In contrast, in the CEECs, there was an expectation in the aftermath of political changes that a rapid change in the corporate ownership would help correct for the past inefficiencies. Since transition was socially costly, policymakers often used mass privatization and other schemes to share some benefits of transition with the population, using asset transfers to partially compensate for lost incomes and employment.

Evolution of Ownership Forms in China

Clearly, the success of township-village enterprises was conditional on other parts of the reform package—gradual liberalization of prices and production, anonymity of business transactions—which reduced the risk of expropriation—and fiscal federalism (Qian, 2003). However, the growth of township-village enterprises slowed down in the 1990s with further liberalization and opening of the Chinese economy. Concerns about underemployment led to a steady liberalization of the rules governing the formation of township-village enterprises. The township-village enterprises also started moving toward standard ownership forms, facilitated by their spontaneous corporatization into shareholding cooperatives or transformation into privately owned and even joint-venture companies. Sachs and Woo (1997) attribute this process to the economic success of coastal township-village enterprises needing to hire migrant labor while the existing mem-

---

[5]However, the actual process of ownership transformation was often complicated by the lack of capital, weaknesses in the banking system, inefficient courts and legal system—conducive to phenomena such as asset stripping—and other impediments.

[6]Township-village enterprises operated with generally hard budget constraints (local governments, though, provided some subsides and gave preferential tax treatment). Social safety nets generally extended only to the state sector—about 20 percent of the population (World Bank, 1996), although some township-village enterprises provided social insurance.

bers of the township-village enterprises were hesitant to share dividends with the new township-village enterprise workers. The process of ownership transformation was further supported by the practical difficulties faced by outsiders in investing in township-village enterprises. The increased openness of the Chinese economy also created the need for more transparent private-property institutions. Finally, the perceived protection of private ownership strengthened over time and some privately owned companies chose to register as standard corporations rather than as township-village enterprises.

Concluding Remarks

The experience of China and the CEECs provide several general lessons. First, the initial conditions matter and, therefore, reform strategies need to be country specific. Second, successful institutional transitions create pro-growth incentives without making the key stakeholders worse off, and any organic reform needs to be compatible with the interests of stakeholders in society. Finally, the optimal design of specific institutions may change over time: given the local specifics, China benefited from the township-village enterprise as a transitional institution toward full-fledged private ownership.

of significant changes in institutions—using a newly constructed database of institutional transitions, yields valuable clues to the specific factors that have facilitated significant changes in institutions in the recent past.

Some General Trends in Institutional Change from the Beginning of the Nineteenth Century

Over the past two centuries, both political and economic institutions have undergone profound changes, although the pace and character of these changes has varied by country. In general, countries broadly followed either a good or a bad institutional path and rarely managed to change paths in the absence of significant changes in the environment. Those with better institutions strengthened them organically over time and reaped the benefits of substantial growth. Countries of western Europe and the United States and other newly settled lands such as Canada, Australia, and New Zealand exemplified the experience typical of this group. Those with weaker institutions found themselves in a trap where poor institutions and lagging economic performance continued to reinforce each other. This was the pattern in many countries of eastern Europe and Latin America, in China and Russia, and in the colonies of Africa and Asia.

Japan is a rare example of a country initially on a weaker path that managed to put itself on a dramatically better institutional path.

The divergent paths taken by countries can in many instances be explained by the onset and interaction of two revolutionary processes. One was the industrial revolution, defined by the availability of radically new production possibilities based on industrial technology and the application of science. The other was the constitutional revolution, whereby political power was subject to constraints and power holders were made accountable, at least to some subset of the population. The restraint—or even overthrow—of the monarchies in the Netherlands, France, the Hapsburg Empire, and the United Kingdom were prominent examples of the establishment of such constitutionalism in Europe, while the American Revolution set the stage for constitutionalism in an independent United States.

Countries that experienced the constitutional revolution before the industrial revolution embarked on a virtuous circle of investment, economic growth, and further beneficial institutional changes. With political influence already somewhat widespread and the power of the state sufficiently constrained, the industrial revolution created wide access to the opportunities from industrialization. Underpinned by relatively secure property rights, the broadly level playing field allowed entry and competition into profitable activities, with rent-seeking kept within bounds. Where the industrial revolution arrived before the advent of constitutionalism, existing political elites wielding relatively unconstrained power were able to create institutions that restricted entry and maintained weak property rights, organizing the economy to maximize the extraction of rents. This institutional mechanism created its own inertia, driven by the competition among various groups to appropriate these rents.

Economies where sectors that lent themselves easily to rent extraction—such as commodities—were large, and where openness to trade was limited, were relatively slow in establishing constitutionalism. The local political leadership or colonial powers could more easily appropriate rents, with the advent of the industrial revolution merely serving to deepen the already existing institutional structures. In contrast, constitutionalism appears often to have emerged relatively early in nations where relatively "rent-proof" sectors emerged leading to the empowerment of new economic classes, such as merchants who grew powerful with the spread of international trade.

An interesting example relates to China's early adoption of "modern" institutions, including private ownership of land, a high degree of specialization and labor mobility, and well-functioning product and labor markets—underpinned by a meritocratic bureaucracy and a common written language—creating incentives for technological innovation and growth that propelled it to its position as the richest economy in the world and a prominent trading power from the second century B.C. to the fourteenth century A.D. (see Chao, 1986; Lin, 1995; and Needham, 1954–97). However, China's abrupt retreat from international trade in the middle of the fifteenth century and its return to an agrarian base, just as European countries began to expand trade (see, for example,

Maddison, 2003, and Pomeranz, 2000), played an important role in determining the path of institutional change over the next five centuries.

Not all major changes in institutions, however, followed the dynamic triggered by sequencing of constitutionalism and the industrial revolution. The Meiji Restoration of Japan in the 1860s underpinned a rapid modernization of institutions, against the threat of external competition; Turkey modernized its economic institutions in the 1920s for similar reasons. In other cases, apparently large changes in governments and formal institutions had little impact on outcomes—the so-called Iron Law of Oligarchy.[6] For example, the Bolivian Revolution of 1952, the Mexican Revolution of 1910, and the establishment of the Brazilian Republic of 1889 all appear to have changed the underlying institutional outcomes relatively little. This suggests that efforts to change institutions durably and positively are unlikely to succeed unless the fundamental factors that determine economic incentives are durably altered.

Experience of the Past 30 Years

Despite the tendency for institutional persistence, the evidence of the past 30 years suggests that rapid institutional change is possible, helping raise living standards more than was previously thought possible. Several profound changes since the 1950s appear to have significantly improved the potential for institutional improvements. First, the collapse of colonial empires altered an institutional system geared toward the systematic extraction of rents and removed one major beneficiary of that system. Second, rapid technological improvements increased the opportunities for industrialization across a range of sectors and away from rent-intensive sectors. Third, globalization afforded hitherto-unavailable economic opportunities against the backdrop of declining transportation and communication costs. Finally, the fall of

---

[6]See Michels (1911).

Table 3.1. Frequency of Institutional Transitions[1]

		Political Transitions by Region and Decade[2]						
Decades	Africa	Central and Eastern Europe	CIS and Mongolia	Developing Asia	Middle East	Latin America	Newly Industrialized Asian Economies	Total
1960s	0 (0.00)	0 (0.00)	0 (0.00)	0 (0.00)	0 (0.00)	0 (0.00)	0 (0.00)	0 (0.00)
1970s	0 (0.00)	0 (0.00)	0 (0.00)	1 (0.54)	0 (0.00)	3 (1.30)	0 (0.00)	4 (0.38)
1980s	0 (0.00)	1 (0.63)	0 (0.00)	1 (0.52)	0 (0.00)	8 (3.48)	2 (5.00)	12 (0.89)
1990s	18 (3.77)	12 (7.74)	4 (3.08)	2 (1.00)	1 (0.78)	8 (3.48)	0 (0.00)	45 (3.23)
2000s	1 (0.53)	2 (3.33)	1 (1.92)	1 (1.25)	0 (0.00)	0 (0.00)	1 (5.56)	6 (1.11)
All years	19 (1.00)	15 (2.16)	5 (0.87)	5 (0.61)	1 (0.18)	19 (1.89)	3 (1.70)	67 (1.17)

		Economic Transitions by Region and Decade[2]						
Decades	Africa	Central and Eastern Europe	CIS and Mongolia	Developing Asia	Middle East	Latin America	Newly Industrialized Asian Economies	Total
1970s	0 (0.00)	0 (0.00)	0 (0.00)	1 (1.23)	0 (0.00)	1 (0.87)	0 (0.00)	2 (0.45)
1980s	3 (0.97)	0 (0.00)	0 (0.00)	2 (1.48)	3 (4.00)	1 (0.40)	1 (2.50)	10 (1.13)
1990s	10 (3.03)	8 (6.35)	1 (5.00)	3 (2.14)	2 (2.50)	12 (4.80)	1 (2.50)	37 (3.75)
2000s	2 (1.01)	8 (8.33)	2 (11.11)	0 (0.00)	0 (0.00)	4 (2.67)	0 (0.00)	16 (2.59)
All years	15 (1.53)	16 (4.75)	3 (4.41)	6 (1.33)	5 (2.15)	18 (2.35)	2 (1.39)	65 (2.18)

Sources: Marshall and Jaggers (2003); Gwartney and Lawson (2004); and IMF staff calculations.

[1]For each cell, upper number denotes the number of transitions occurring in that region and decade. Numbers in parentheses denote the corresponding annual probability of a transition. See Appendix 3.1 for further details.

[2]In some country cases, transitions cannot be identified owing to limited availability of data.

communism in the late 1980s and early 1990s radically altered the governance structures in many formerly communist nations, taking away another major source of institutional persistence (see Figure 3.3).

To look at recent institutional transitions more concretely, IMF staff conducted an analysis identifying the key episodes in the transition of economic institutions covering developing countries since 1970 (see Appendix 3.1 for the list of transitions by country and Table 3.1 for the summary by region). Institutional transitions were identified using publicly available databases of

institutions augmented by information from country desks where possible.[7] Transitions were defined based on three key criteria:

- Transitions led to at least a minimum level of institutional quality, corresponding approximately to the middle of the range of possible institutional scores (for political transitions, 0 on the Polity score, which ranges from −10 to +10; for economic transitions, 4 points on the Cato Economic Freedom score, which ranges from 1 to 10);

- Transitions involved a significant increase in institutional quality (for political transitions,

[7]The specific transition episodes identified using the Cato Institute Economic Freedom and Polity indices have been augmented by IMF staff estimates when the external databases were incomplete or generated results incongruous with the general consensus.

Figure 3.4. Developing Economies: Impact of Economic Transitions on Output Growth, Private Investment, and Productivity Growth[1]

(Economic transition at time t)

Institutional transitions lead to substantial improvements in GDP growth, private investment, and productivity growth.

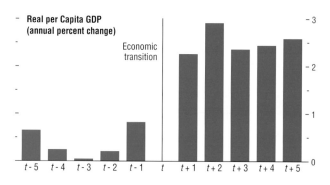

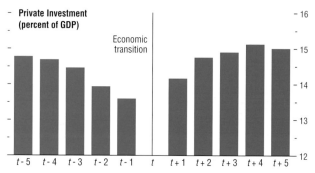

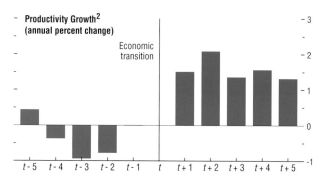

Sources: Gwartney and Lawson (2004); Klenow and Rodriguez-Clare (2004); Penn World Table Version 6.1; World Bank, *World Development Indicators* (2005); and IMF staff calculations.

[1]Only the countries that experienced institutional transition during 1970–2004 are included in the sample. All variables are expressed as three-year moving averages. See Appendix 3.1 for further details.

[2]Total factor productivity growth.

4 points on the Polity Score—that is, two-thirds of the standard deviation; for economic transitions, 1 point on the Cato Economic Freedom score—that is, 1 standard deviation);

- Transitions were durable and not subsequently reversed (in cases of successive positive transitions, only the first was recorded).

Given the element of subjectivity associated with any measure of institutions, the precise timing of an economic transition is inevitably subject to some uncertainty. Nonetheless, the analysis identified a relatively large number of economic transitions (65), although the levels of economic institutions achieved at the end of the identified transitions varied by country. In some cases they approached advanced country levels, but in others they only achieved improvements relative to their own past. However, they do appear, in general, to be associated with a clear structural break in economic performance: the identified economic transitions are associated with a subsequent 2 percentage point increase in GDP growth (Figure 3.4).[8] The volume of private sector investment improved durably but by a relatively modest amount, suggesting that the quality of investment improved substantially with transition, supported by the evidence on trends in total factor productivity in pre- and post-transition periods. These aggregate results are relatively robust to the precise year of transition identified for individual countries.

The analysis of recent transitions suggests that economic transitions were often, but not always, preceded by political transitions (Figures

[8]Of course, growth transitions do not always follow institutional transitions. A study of 43 developing countries with initially weak institutions found that institutions improved after the initial surge in growth rates in those countries that managed to sustain the growth episode (Johnson, Ostry, and Subramanian, 2005). Interestingly, the explanatory factors that helped sustain the growth surges are found to be consistent with those associated with institutional transitions (explained in the section of this chapter on "What Changes Institutions?"), suggesting they may have both a direct initial impact on growth and an indirect one by subsequently improving institutions.

3.5 and 3.6).[9] The former communist economies of central and eastern Europe comprised
nearly one-third of all identified transitions,
given the widespread political transitions that
generally led to substantial improvements in
property rights, allowing greater access to economic opportunity and improving the incentives of the population to invest capital and
labor in productive activities. Economic transitions in the early 1990s were followed by relatively rapid changes in institutions in countries
such as the Czech Republic, Hungary, and
Poland, but somewhat more slowly in the Baltics,
which had been under more direct control during communist times, and where European
Union (EU) accession prospects provided a
powerful additional incentive for economic
transformation. Accession prospects also helped
transform economic institutions in eastern
European economies like Bulgaria and Romania
late in the 1990s, relatively long after political
transition compared with their western neighbors. Most countries of the Commonwealth of
Independent States (CIS) were generally slower
to transition in terms of economic institutions,
even when large changes in political institutions
took place relatively early. Transitions to more
representative political systems across many
countries in Africa after the end of the Cold
War also led to significant changes in economic
institutions in some countries.

In Latin America, too, political transitions
generally preceded economic transitions, but
they often followed major economic crises. In
Argentina, political transition began with the
introduction of a democratic government in late
1983, and economic transition began in the
early 1990s after an outburst of hyperinflation
and a long history of macroeconomic instability.
In Brazil, democratic elections were called in
1985, and the introduction of the *real* plan in
1994 paved the way for deeper reforms in the
late 1990s. In many other smaller countries too,

[9]See Giavazzi and Tabellini (2004) for the relationship
between political and economic liberalizations.

Figure 3.5. Number of Institutional Transitions by Region[1]

(Size of bubble represents the number of transitions over five-year intervals)

Looking at the past three decades, most political and economic transitions took place after 1989. Rapid political transitions were often associated with the end of the Cold War. The economic transitions were more evenly spread across the 1990s and 2000s.

Political Transitions[2]

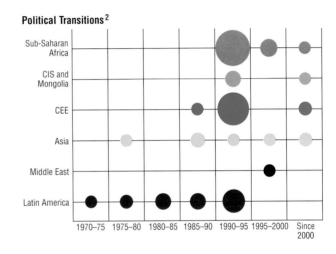

Economic Transitions[2]

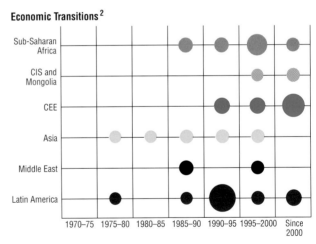

Sources: Gwartney and Lawson (2004); Marshall and Jaggers (2003); and IMF staff calculations.

[1]Only developing economies are included except for Asia, which also includes any transitions in the newly industrialized economies. For a more detailed discussion of the identification of institutional transitions and the list of countries included in each region, see Appendix 3.1.

[2]In some countries, transitions cannot be identified owing to the limited availability of data.

Figure 3.6. Institutional Transitions by Region[1]
(Right scale for economic institutions; left scale for political institutions)

On average, political transitions have accompanied or preceded improvements in economic institutions.

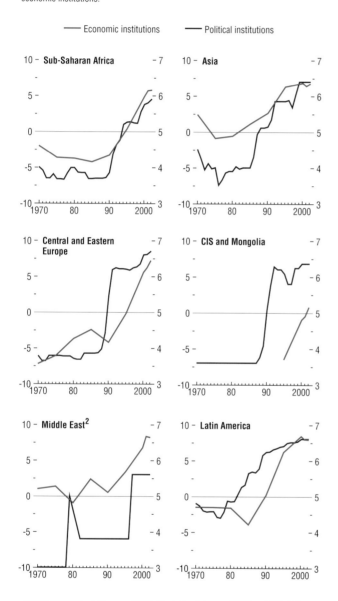

Sources: Gwartney and Lawson (2004); Marshall and Jaggers (2003); and IMF staff calculations.
[1]Scores represent average institutional quality in the countries that recorded a favorable institutional transition. Economic and political transitions are considered separately. Political institutional quality is measured by Marshall and Jaggers' (2003) Polity index. Economic institutional quality is measured by Gwartney and Lawson's (2004) Economic Freedom index. For a more detailed discussion of the identification of institutional transitions and the list of countries included in each region, see Appendix 3.1.
[2]The sample of political transitions in the Middle East consists only of I.R. of Iran.

economic transition began after democratic governments came into office. By contrast, in Chile, the military government that came to power in 1973 initiated changes in economic institutions following years of weak economic policies. In Mexico, the electoral reforms of 1993 broadly coincided with changes in economic institutions related to the signing of the North American Free Trade Agreement (NAFTA), central bank independence, and membership of the OECD.

Many Asian countries did not witness dramatic changes in political institutions ahead of improvements in economic institutions. Economic transitions in Asia were in two broad phases, with the newly industrialized economies (NIEs) (Hong Kong SAR, Korea, Singapore, and Taiwan Province of China) prominent in the first phase of transition in the 1960s, characterized by rapid industrialization and integration with the global economy. The second phase included China in the late 1970s, where agrarian reform that resulted in an improved growth performance was followed by institutional reforms related to the industrial sector (see Box 3.1). This phase also included Indonesia, Malaysia, and Thailand and some smaller countries. Spurred by the visible success of some economies in the region, transformation of economic institutions was subsequently also undertaken in India and several other countries.

While changes in economic institutions were triggered by many different factors, there appear to be a number of underlying similarities in their economic circumstances.

- In many cases, the desire by policymakers to modernize the country through rapid industrialization and exports was a trigger for the subsequent improvement in economic institutions. The early example of east Asia since the 1960s, including Hong Kong SAR, Korea, Singapore, and Taiwan Province of China, captures many of these aspects.
- The transition of economic institutions tends to have a strong regional dimension, as evident from the clustering of transitions in Asia, emerging Europe, and Latin America in distinct time periods (Figure 3.5 and Table 3.1).

• Countries with large natural resource sectors tended to have fewer transitions. Since the performance of exports in these sectors was determined to a large extent by global demand and price conditions, there were relatively few competitive benefits from innovation and investment, making them much more amenable to the expropriation of rents. Furthermore, the dominance of natural resources meant that demand for the better institutions necessary to support growth in other sectors was by definition limited. Chile was a relatively rare counterexample, where economic transition was accompanied by the rapid growth of the mining, agriculture, and fisheries sectors, while in Africa, Botswana and Ghana stand out as natural resource-rich countries that were relatively successful in transforming their institutions.

What Changes Institutions?

Analytical considerations and the recent historical experience suggest that a number of distinct factors are influential in determining the quality of institutions and the transition to improved institutions. These can be broadly grouped into those factors that relate to the availability of economic rents, external factors, and initial conditions. To look at these issues in more detail, IMF staff undertook two econometric exercises. The first exercise examined the determinants of institutional transitions, while the second exercise analyzed what explains levels of institutional quality and their variation among countries.

At the outset, it should be noted that the econometric exercises rely to a considerable extent on relatively new indices, and that—by their nature—data on institutional quality are more subjective than other economic measures. Furthermore, since institutions are closely related to economic performance, endogeneity

of the variables considered may complicate the analysis. To some extent, this has been addressed by using instrumental variables and multiple sources when available, but residual endogeneity issues could remain a concern, particularly for the second exercise. The analysis of institutional transitions is broadly consistent with information available from IMF country desks, further validating the use of available indices. Finally, a comparison of various indices of institutions—although limited by country and time coverage—suggests that the indices are broadly correlated and contain similar qualitative information. Appendix 3.1 contains a detailed description of the data and econometric techniques employed. Overall, the empirical exercises do provide some useful insights into the main factors driving institutions.

Institutional Transitions

From the perspective of what policies can do to improve institutions, it is of interest to analyze those developing countries that have experienced rapid institutional transitions. The IMF staff's exercise identified a large number of significant economic and political transitions, with the year of the beginning of transition reported in Appendix 3.1. For each region and each decade, Table 3.1 summarizes the number of transition episodes, as well as the frequency of transitions in a region.[10]

Are institutional transitions frequent or rare? The exercise identified political transitions in 68 countries, and economic transitions in 65 countries.[11] At a broad level, a country would have had about a 20 percent chance of experiencing an institutional transition in any given decade. To undertake a more in-depth analysis, a probit model was estimated linking the probability of an institutional transition to the country's level of openness, accountability, education, natural resources, developments in

---

[10]Since the identification of transitions is primarily based on applying a filter to aggregate measures of institutional quality, the results presented in Appendix 3.1 may not be fully comprehensive.

[11]Political and economic data are available for 138 and 103 developing countries, respectively.

Table 3.2. Institutional Transitions: Probit Estimates[1]

Variables	Transitions in Economic Freedom[2]
Openness	6.20**
Press freedom	4.47**
Catch-up to neighbors	10.16**
Schooling	7.30**
Aid	−5.97**
Fuel exports	+
Initial income	−11.88**

Sources: Barro and Lee (2000); Freedom House (2005); Gwartney and Lawson (2004); Penn World Table Version 6.1; Wacziarg and Welch (2003); World Bank (2005); IMF (2004a); and IMF staff calculations.
[1]One and two asterisks denote statistical significance at the 10 percent and 5 percent level, respectively. Coefficients indicate the impact of a one-standard-deviation change in the independent variable on the percentage probability of a transition.
[2]Measure of Economic Freedom from Gwartney and Lawson (2004).

Figure 3.7. Openness and Economic Transitions[1]

Economic transitions take place more often in open economies.

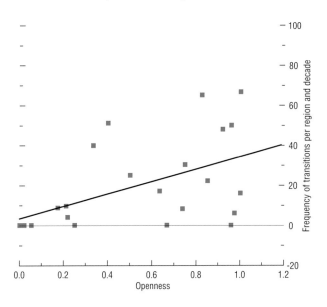

Sources: Gwartney and Lawson (2004); Wacziarg and Welch (2003); and IMF staff calculations.
[1]Frequency of transitions is calculated as the ratio of the number of regional transitions and the regional sample size, converted into percent. In the figure, each point corresponds to the frequency of transitions and the average openness in a region over a decade from 1970–2004.

neighboring countries, foreign aid, and other potential explanatory factors (see Table 3.2). Several conclusions are relatively robust to various specifications (see Appendix 3.1 for details).

- *Trade openness is significantly associated with a greater likelihood of institutional transitions* (Figure 3.7). Indeed, a move from complete autarky to full liberalization is associated with about a 15 percentage point increase in the probability of transition. This is consistent with the hypothesis that greater openness allows for a greater role of export sectors that are rent-proof and require innovation, and creates momentum for positive institutional changes. In addition, increased import penetration reduces the ability of domestic producers to sustain monopolistic rents, which impede institutional improvement.[12]

- *Transitions are also more likely in countries with high levels of press freedom, which is a broad indicator of the accountability of political institutions in a country.* Greater accountability of political insti-

[12]Theoretical and empirical links between openness and institutional development are developed in Rajan and Zingales (2003a, 2003b). Also, as noted in Appendix 3.1, the institutional indices used in the analyses exclude any components associated with trade openness, to ensure that any results on openness are not a statistical artifact.

Table 3.3. Institutional Quality: Panel and Cross-Sectional IV Estimates[1]

| | Panel | Cross-Section | | |
| | | | Governance indicators | |
Variables	Economic freedom[2]	Economic freedom[2]	Aggregate governance index[3]	Corruption subindex[4]
Openness	+	0.34**	0.30**	0.31**
Accountability[5]	+	0.22*	0.42**	0.38**
Initial income	0.98**	0.26**	0.35**	0.43**
Fuel exports	−0.14**	−0.13**	−	−
Aid	−	−	0.14*	0.19**
Regional institutional quality	0.24**	−	−	−
Schooling	−	0.19*	+	+

Sources: Barro and Lee (2000); Freedom House (2005); Gwartney and Lawson (2004); Kaufmann, Kraay, and Mastruzzi (2005); Heritage Foundation (2005); Penn World Table Version 6.1; Wacziarg and Welch (2003); World Bank (2005); IMF (2004a); and IMF staff calculations.
[1]One and two asterisks denote statistical significance at the 10 percent and 5 percent level, respectively. All coefficients are standardized. Country fixed effects and a time trend were included in the panel specification. For more information on the independent variables, data, and methodology, see Appendix 3.1.
[2]Measure of economic freedom from Gwartney and Lawson (2004) for panel, and from Heritage Foundation (2005) for cross-section.
[3]Average of five institutional quality measures from Kaufmann, Kraay, and Mastruzzi (2005); see text for details.
[4]Measure of corruption from Kaufmann, Kraay, and Mastruzzi (2005).
[5]Accountability is measured as Freedom House's (2005) press freedom in the panel and Kaufmann, Kraay, and Mastruzzi's (2005) voice and accountability index in the cross-section.

tutions is associated with policies and institutional reforms that are beneficial for the broader economy, with the political leadership answerable to a broad cross-section of the population, which favorably aligns the incentives of the leadership with that of the whole economy.

- *Countries are also more likely to experience institutional improvements if their neighbors have higher institutional quality.* This is consistent with the view that a strong regional effect is present for institutional transitions—economic transitions are more likely to happen in clusters of countries within a region around the same time. This is reflective of both the direct impact on institutional improvements in countries that are close competitors and the demonstration effects of regional success stories.
- *The probability of economic transitions is also higher for higher levels of education.* This is consistent with the notion that more educated populations are more effective participants in broader decision making.
- *In contrast, aid levels in the probit estimates appear to have a negative impact on the probability of transition to a higher institutional level.* This may, of course, reflect the fact that countries receiving higher aid flows are those that suffer from a broader set of disadvantageous initial condi-

tions, impeding their likelihood of experiencing an institutional transition. A more detailed discussion of the impact of aid is contained in the section of this chapter on "Institutions and the External Environment."

In addition, higher initial per capita income has a negative impact on the probability of transitions, consistent with the observation that countries with a higher per capita income in the sample typically already had a high level of institutions at the beginning of the sample period. Somewhat surprisingly, the impact of fuel exports is not found to be statistically significant in affecting the probability of transition in economic institutions.

Levels of Institutional Quality

To examine further the role of various determinants of institutional quality, the second exercise looked at the determinants of broad institutional quality in a sample of 90 advanced and developing countries over the period 1970–2004, using both cross-sectional and panel regressions (Table 3.3). The main results of this analysis are broadly consistent with, but not identical to, the conclusions of the previous probit regressions. The regressions estimated the relationship between

Figure 3.8. Institutional Quality Relative to the Group of Advanced Countries[1]

(Economic institutions on right scale; others on left scale)

In the countries that experienced institutional transition, institutional improvements (relative to the group of advanced countries) tend to be associated with a high degree of openness, education, and press freedom.

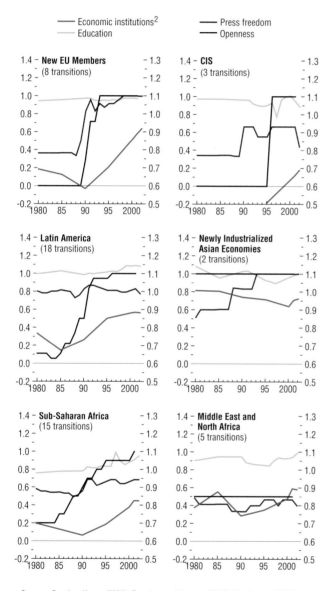

Sources: Freedom House (2005); Gwartney and Lawson (2004); Wacziarg and Welch (2003); World Bank, *World Development Indicators* (2005); and IMF staff calculations.

[1]Only the countries that experienced an economic transition during 1970–2004 are included. In some countries, transitions cannot be identified owing to the limited availability of data. Regional scores were calculated as simple averages of country scores. In this figure, economic freedom, press freedom, and education (primary school enrollment) are expressed as a ratio of the regional score to the average score of advanced countries. Openness is not normalized.

[2]Economic institutional quality is measured by Gwartney and Lawson's (2004) Economic Freedom index. For more information, see Appendix 3.1.

institutional outcomes and several factors, including openness, education, and accountability (see Figure 3.8).[13]

- *Openness is robustly associated with greater institutional quality* (Figure 3.9). The estimates suggest that if a typical developing economy were to increase its openness to the levels prevalent in a typical advanced economy, this would be associated with roughly a one-fourth reduction in the "institutional gap" between the two countries (see also Rodrik, Subramanian, and Trebbi, 2004, and Wei, 2000).

- *Greater accountability of the political executive is associated with higher institutional quality.* This is particularly evident in the cross-section, for which better measures of accountability are available.

- *A higher initial per capita income is also associated with stronger institutions.*[14] This is consistent with the hypothesis that institutional reforms are easier to implement in countries that are more wealthy to begin with (see the April 2003 *World Economic Outlook*). For instance, richer countries can pay higher salaries to civil servants. Certain other explanatory factors are less robust to the choice of specifications.

- *There is some evidence that greater natural-resource dependence is associated with weaker institutions.* Consistent with the probit estimates, the relationship is both statistically and economically significant in the panel regressions. In the cross-section, however, the relationship is not robust across all specifications—in particular, somewhat surprisingly, to governance and corruption measures—which may partly reflect the presence in the sample of several advanced countries.[15]

---

[13]As noted, the IMF staff analysis used a range of institutional measures where available. Owing to space constraints, only one set of regression results is reported but it is broadly representative of the results of the exercise.

[14]Residual endogeneity issues may be of special concern in measuring the impact of initial income.

[15]The lack of available data on economic institutions for some significant oil producers, particularly in central Asia, also makes it more difficult to establish unambiguous relationships.

- *The link between foreign aid and institutional quality is less clear.* The association of aid with broad estimates of economic freedom is not robust in the panel and the cross-sectional regressions. However, the cross-sectional regressions show a positive association between aid and governance indicators, although endogeneity issues are a particular concern here. The varying forms of aid make it particularly difficult to establish a strong link between aggregate aid and the quality of institutions. A more detailed discussion on the impact of aid is contained in the following section.

- *The evidence of the benefit from higher institutional quality in neighboring countries is mixed.* While the association is positive in the panel regressions, consistent with the evidence on transitions, it is difficult to disentangle the impact of regional institutional quality in the cross-sectional analysis, given the lack of a time aspect.

- *The evidence on the link between education and institutions is also mixed.* While education is positively linked with improvements in economic institutions in the cross-sectional analysis (Figure 3.9), the relationship in the panel is broadly insignificant, indicating that education may work through other channels, such as by improving accountability.

The IMF staff exercise also examined the impact of more specific policy levers such as fiscal transparency and central bank independence, but could not find any significant association. While this may in part reflect the lack of longer time series for these measures, it is also consistent with the notion that the broader underlying economic and social factors that shape incentives are what matter more for changing the institutional equilibrium. Specific levers are likely to be effective only when the broader underlying incentives are supportive. Analyses focusing on specific levers and corruption outcomes employing micro-level cross-country data (see Box 3.2) suggest that well-designed levers may have significant impacts when broader conditions are supportive.

Figure 3.9. Openness, Education, Accountability, and Quality of Economic Institutions[1]

(Economic institutions on y-axis; x-axis as stated; 1970–2003)

Trade openness, accountability, and, to a lesser degree, educational attainment are associated with institutional quality, even after controlling for other potential determinants of institutions.

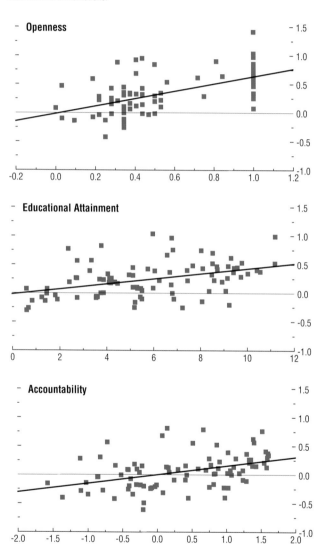

Sources: Barro and Lee (2000); Heritage Foundation (2005); Kaufmann, Kraay, and Mastruzzi (2005); Wacziarg and Welch (2003); and IMF staff calculations.

[1]Institutional quality is measured by Heritage Foundation's Economic Freedom index. The y-axis depicts that portion of the index which is not explained by determinants of institutional quality other than, respectively, openness, educational attainment, and accountability. For more information, see Appendix 3.1.

Box 3.2. The Use of Specific Levers to Reduce Corruption

It is widely accepted that reducing corruption is crucial in helping countries improve their prospects for overall economic development. While empirical studies have shown that factors including colonial heritage, legal traditions, religion, geography, and electoral rules are correlated with levels of corruption, these results provide little guidance in identifying how corruption works or which tools are necessary to address this issue.[1] However, country-specific analyses hold more promise of finding practical policy solutions to the problem of corruption. This box focuses on specific agency-level institutions—such as auditing mechanisms, publicly announced budget and personnel decisions, and merit-based personnel management—and presents new evidence that these are associated with lower corruption in public agencies.[2]

The evidence in this box is based on largely unexplored World Bank Institute (WBI) surveys of public officials in eight Latin American and African countries (Bolivia, Colombia, Guatemala, Guinea, Honduras, Peru, Sierra Leone, and Zambia).[3] These surveys offer three distinct advantages for the study of corruption.

- First, public officials are asked not only to indicate their perceived level of corruption—as is common in cross-country corruption surveys—but also whether specific corruption activities are present in the public agency where they are employed.[4]
- A second advantage of these surveys is that they shed light on different types of corruption corresponding to (1) corruption in public procurement; (2) corruption in budget management; (3) corruption in personnel management; (4) state capture and legal corruption; and (5) administrative corruption. The answers to the questions are used to construct relatively objective indices of corruption and are then combined into a single *overall corruption index*.[5]
- The third advantage of the WBI surveys is that some of the questions assess the presence of specific institutional features that could explain the level of corruption in each public agency.[6] The indicator *audit* is based on several

Note: The main authors of this box are Francesca Recanatini and Alessandro Prati.

[1]See Treisman (2000) for the role of legal traditions in determining corruption; Fisman and Gatti (2002) and Ades and Di Tella (1999) for the role of fiscal decentralization and foreign competition; Persson, Tabellini, and Trebbi (2003) for the role of electoral rules; and Broadman and Recanatini (2002) for the experience of transition countries.

[2]Agency-level institutions such as auditing mechanisms are not the only possible way of reducing corruption. Recent studies have, for example, highlighted the role of public information in reducing financial leakages between central and local governments (Reinikka and Svensson, 2004a, 2004b). Olken (2004) and Kaufmann, Mehrez, and Gurgur (2002) discuss the role of audit, transparency, and voice mechanisms in limiting corruption, and Glaeser and Saks (2004) provide evidence on the role of education.

[3]Over the past five years, the WBI has conducted surveys in about 15 countries to develop a "map" of their institutional strengths and weaknesses. Analysis in this box focuses on a narrower set of eight countries for which comparable data on corruption and

agency-specific institutions are available. The data for the countries analyzed here were collected between 1999 and 2004. Additional information on WBI corruption surveys and data are available via the Internet: http://www.worldbank.org/wbi/governance/capacity-build/d-surveys.html.

[4]Although these corruption evaluations are made by the public officials themselves, Prati, Recanatini, and Tabellini (2005) show that they are significantly positively correlated with the experiences of firms and households that used the services provided by the same public agency. This box focuses on the public officials' surveys because they have more detailed information on the types of corruption, as well as on the institutions that might influence them, than the firms' and households' surveys.

[5]Principal component analysis is used for this aggregation following the approach introduced by Kaufmann, Mehrez, and Gurgur (2002). This approach minimizes respondent bias and measurement error due to individual differences in perceptions.

[6]Using public officials' views on the presence of these institutions has the advantage of providing information on their actual—albeit perceived—role in each public agency as opposed to simply using information on laws and regulations that require them. The latter may, in fact, remain only nominal.

Dependent Variable: Total Corruption—OLS Regression

	Total Corruption
Audit	−0.3580
	(−7.19)***
Merit	−0.1180
	(−2.91)***
Openness	−0.22
	(−3.91)***
Observations	899
R^2	0.89

Note: Country dummies included. Absolute value of t statistics in parentheses. One, two, and three asterisks denote statistical significance at the 10, 5, and 1 percent level, respectively.

questions measuring whether decisions on personnel and budget management, as well as procurement, are subject to regular internal or external audits. The indicator *openness* is based on questions enquiring whether the same set of decisions is publicly announced inside and outside the public agency and whether that agency's financial status is regularly disclosed to the public. The indicator *merit* is based on a set of questions referring to whether decisions on personnel management are based on professional experience, merit, performance, and the level of education.

The data indicate that *overall corruption* varies significantly across public agencies within a country, suggesting that corruption has an important within-country variation that cross-country studies neglect, and that countries face

different governance challenges. Corruption in public procurement is the most severe type of corruption in half the sample, while corruption in budget management dominates the list for another three countries. In the presence of such diverse patterns of corruption across and within countries, the key question becomes whether any general conclusion can be drawn on agency-level institutions that might help these countries curb corruption. The first table shows that, indeed, *audit*, *openness*, and *merit* tend to be associated with lower levels of the overall corruption index. The second table shows that the impact of these agency-level institutions varies across the five types of corruption in a predictable way:[7] audit mechanisms are particularly important in curbing corruption in budget management; merit-based personnel management has its greatest impact on corruption in personnel decisions; and publicly announcing budget and personnel decisions has a particularly strong effect on corruption in budget management.

While these results may be unsurprising, they are intuitively appealing and provide rare

[7]See Prati, Recanatini, and Tabellini (2005) for a detailed discussion of the model specification and the results. The equations for the five corruption-specific indices are estimated with the SUR (Seemingly Unrelated Regression) methodology to take into account the correlation between these indices. Both the OLS and the SUR regressions weight each observation with the number of survey responses on which it is based. The results of the unweighted regressions are very similar.

Comparing Different Types of Corruption: SUR Regression Results

	State Capture and Legal Corruption	Corruption in Personnel	Corruption in Budget Management	Administrative Corruption	Corruption in Public Procurement
Audit	−0.2038	−0.2285	−0.4354	−0.2743	−0.2796
	(4.16)***	(4.26)***	(7.15)***	(4.82)***	(5.02)***
Merit	−0.1037	−0.3550	−0.1463	−0.1601	−0.1117
	(2.59)***	(8.10)***	(2.94)***	(3.44)***	(2.45)***
Openness	−0.1395	−0.1017	−0.3925	−0.2168	−0.2130
	(2.52)**	(1.68)*	(5.71)**	(3.38)***	(3.39)***
No. of observations	909	909	909	909	909

Note: Country dummies included. Absolute value of t statistics in parentheses. One, two, and three asterisks denote statistical significance at the 10, 5, and 1 percent level, respectively.

Box 3.2 *(concluded)*

statistical evidence about policies and institutions that can curb corruption in public agencies. They also suggest that different types of corruption require different policy tools. Nonetheless, there are limits to the policy implications that can be drawn from this evidence and further work is needed to hone policy prescriptions for the reform of public agencies. Specifically, the WBI surveys do not reveal

whether some agencies have better agency-level institutions because these are mandated by law or because their managers apply them in earnest. This distinction is of critical importance for policymakers because in the first case they would only need to introduce appropriate legislation and regulations, while in the second case they need to focus on selecting capable managers and making them accountable.

Institutions and the External Environment

The preceding discussion has highlighted the positive role that external factors can play in institutional development. One key factor—an economy's openness—is significant across many dimensions in supporting positive institutional changes. In addition to domestic policies that reduce barriers to trade, multilateral efforts at liberalizing trade under the current Doha Round could be expected to have a strong positive impact on institutional transformation in countries with weak institutions.

This section looks in more detail at three other factors related to the external environment that have a significant influence on an economy's institutional transformation—namely, external anchors, foreign aid, and improved transparency.

External Anchors

External anchors help foster institutional changes in developing countries by providing domestic policymakers with incentives to undertake substantial changes in economic institutions. The following discussion suggests, however, that external anchors are more effec-

tive when they provide a country with clear and tangible benefits from implementing institutional reforms and when they are supported by a credible commitment mechanism.

Accession to the European Union is the classic example of a successful external anchor. Besides the political benefits of closer integration, prospective EU members saw clear benefits from closer integration in terms of market access for goods and prospects for increased foreign investment, in return for adhering to a formal commitment mechanism and implementing a well-defined set of legislation and reforms implied by the EU *acquis communitaire*.[16] This process helped accession candidates rapidly improve their institutional frameworks toward the level of more advanced economies (Figure 3.10).

To partially overcome the limits of geography and shared market traditions, the European Union introduced the EU Neighborhood Program, which could also facilitate some degree of beneficial institutional changes in more distant countries. The benefits of enhanced EU market access and participation in EU-sponsored programs are meant to provide incentives for market-oriented, governance, and other institutional reforms.[17] If successful, this policy could

[16]The basis for membership eligibility assessments was provided by the Copenhagen Criteria formulated in 1993 (European Union, 1993).

[17]For a detailed description of the EU Neighborhood Program, see European Union (2005). Agreements have been signed with several countries from eastern Europe, the southern Caucasus, and the Mediterranean coast of the Middle East and Africa.

contribute to improved institutional frameworks even in the countries that may not have EU membership ambitions in the medium term.

To a more limited extent, accession to the World Trade Organization (WTO) has also served the role of an external anchor, catalyzing the process of reducing trade barriers and promoting competition. In return for enhanced market access, WTO accession can entail conditionality with beneficial implications for the quality of local institutions. For example, WTO accession supported China's implementation of significant liberalization reforms, including opening up more sectors for private and foreign investment (see Chae and Han, 2001, and Mallon and Whalley, 2004). The WTO appears to have played a smaller role in some other transition economies, reflecting limited WTO rules governing commodities exports, and in some smaller and poorer countries, given the small size of their domestic markets, which has limited their ability to engage more actively in the reciprocal liberalization process.[18]

Regional trade groups such as NAFTA or the Association of Southeast Asian Nations (ASEAN) have had more limited success in improving local institutions as their membership requirements are less stringent. NAFTA helped to lock in some liberalization measures in Mexico, and potentially contributed to improvement in the rule of law (Capital Markets Consultative Group, 2003) and domestic demands for reform—banks, for example, lobbied for an enhanced regulatory framework (Islam and Montenegro, 2002). ASEAN may have played a role in structural and institutional reform in countries such as Cambodia, Lao PDR, and Vietnam (see the April 2003 *World Economic Outlook*).

Can external anchors play a role in other countries and regions? Many countries with weak institutions tend to be geographically (and in terms of trade) concentrated and distant from potential anchors, limiting the emergence of a strong regional anchoring framework

[18]See Mattoo and Subramanian (2004).

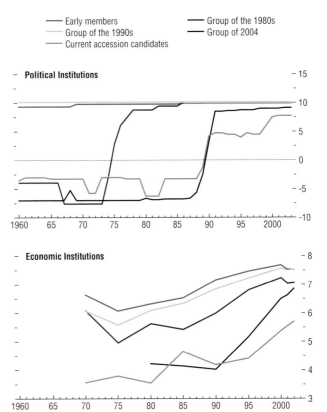

Figure 3.10. Evolution of Institutions in the European Union and in EU Accession Candidates[1]

Institutional frameworks have tended to improve significantly during the process of EU accession: new members and accession candidates have been catching up to the institutional quality of the existing EU members.

— Early members — Group of the 1980s
— Group of the 1990s — Group of 2004
— Current accession candidates

Political Institutions

Economic Institutions

Sources: Gwartney and Lawson (2004); Marshall and Jaggers (2003); and IMF staff calculations.
[1]Regional scores were calculated as simple averages. The composition of the groups is as follows: early members includes Belgium, Denmark, France, Germany, Italy, Ireland, Luxembourg, Netherlands, and the United Kingdom; group of the 1980s includes Greece, Portugal, and Spain; group of the 1990s includes Austria, Finland, and Sweden; group of 2004 includes Czech Republic, Estonia, Hungary, Latvia, Lithuania, Poland, Slovak Republic, and Slovenia (the other two new EU members—Cyprus and Malta—are excluded); finally, the group of current accession candidates includes Bulgaria and Romania (in EU terminology, "acceding countries"), and Croatia and Turkey ("candidate countries"). Political institutional quality is measured by Marshall and Jaggers' (2003) Polity index. Economic institutional quality is measured by Gwartney and Lawson's (2004) Economic Freedom index. For more information, see Appendix 3.1.

that provides incentives and a credible commitment mechanism for countries to undertake deep-seated institutional reforms similar to that of the EU accession countries (see Figure 3.3). Nonetheless, certain policy initiatives hold the prospect of creating potential anchors in the future.

The New Partnership for Africa's Development (NEPAD) constitutes Africa's framework for promoting democracy, stability, economic development—including better governance—and strengthened partnerships with the international community.[19] Through its Peer Review Mechanism, NEPAD could become an important platform for diagnosing institutional weaknesses, formulating policy recommendations, and attracting investment into successfully reforming countries. While NEPAD holds promise as a potentially useful mechanism, the lack of tangible benefits and credible commitment mechanisms creates the risk that any process of institutional development through this mechanism will be slow to gain traction.[20] Strong regional leadership—which has been demonstrated by Algeria, Egypt, Nigeria, Senegal, and South Africa during the process of NEPAD formation—could increase the pace and effectiveness of the peer review process by applying mutual peer pressure.

Looking forward, the role of external anchors in Africa could be made more effective by linking the benefits of trade and investment to a clean bill of institutional health.[21] In this respect, one potential mechanism may be through the creation of a donor country–financed FDI trust fund that makes a commitment to co-finance foreign direct investment projects in return for credible and effective measures to successfully transform institutions. The co-financing would allow risk-sharing with the private sector, generate investment through nondebt flows, and raise investment levels.

Aid and Institutions

There is wide agreement in the international community on the need for substantially increased levels of financial assistance to low-income countries to alleviate poverty and lay the basis for long-run sustained growth.[22] It is also well recognized that governance and "absorptive capacity" more broadly can determine whether financial assistance is well utilized. It is also of interest to ask what aid itself does to institutions.

In principle, aid can affect institutions in a variety of ways.[23] Higher levels of aid can improve the functioning of executive and judicial institutions—including through higher civil service pay—and the quality of economic policies undertaken by countries, especially when accompanied by technical assistance and conditionality targeted toward improving policymaking. More broadly, aid may reduce incentives for rent-seeking by alleviating difficult trade-offs that emerge from resource constraints. Aid, however, can also tax weak institutional capacity through the proliferation of donors and projects.[24] The unpredictability and volatility of aid also increases the stress on budgetary and other sectoral institutions that have to plan expenditures. Furthermore, some types of aid may forestall

---

[19]For a detailed description of NEPAD's objectives, see the April 2003 *World Economic Outlook* and NEPAD (2005).

[20]After four years of its existence, NEPAD has not completed any Peer Reviews. Reports on Ghana and Rwanda, including policy recommendations and action plans, are expected to be published later this year.

[21]The America's Growth and Opportunity Act and the Millennium Development Corporation are recent examples containing such an approach.

[22]See UN Millennium Project (2005) and the Commission for Africa Report (2005).

[23]See Knack (2001) and Bräutigam and Knack (2004) for a detailed elaboration of possible factors to consider.

[24]Birdsall (2004) cites the example of Tanzania, which during the period 2000–02 had to manage 1,300 donor-financed projects, involving an estimated 1,000 donor meetings and 2,400 reports to donors each quarter. The government at one point announced a four-month holiday during which it would not accept donor visits. Knack and Rahman (2004) find that recipients experiencing greater donor fragmentation show greater declines in a measure of bureaucratic quality during the period 1982–2001.

policy reform by postponing the inevitable economic consequences of poor policy choices. Sustained aid also has been found to reduce the contribution of the tradable good sector—a key determinant of institutional quality.[25] Aid may also have deleterious effects on long-run institutional development, by reducing the role of tax collection, potentially creating an incentive at the margin to substitute aid for taxation.[26] While in the short run this may not be a problem, in the long run it may impede accountability and the development of economic institutions.[27]

In practice, the empirical evidence on the net effect of aid on institutions is mixed. Regarding aid's effect on corruption for example, while Alesina and Weder (2002) suggest that an increase in aid is associated with an increase in corruption, Tavares (2003) finds this result to be biased by the fact that less corrupt governments generally tend to receive less aid for a variety of reasons not linked to corruption, and correcting for this bias suggests that an increase in aid in fact reduces corruption. More broadly, Knack (2001) finds a significant negative relationship between aid and governance (comprising bureaucratic quality and rule of law, in addition to corruption) for a broad cross-section of countries, while Bräutigam and Knack (2004) find that in Africa, higher aid levels are associated with larger declines in the quality of governance and in tax revenue as a share of GDP, even when corrected for endogeneity issues and controlling for economic decline and political violence. Svensson (2000) finds that aid is associated with higher corruption in countries that are more fragmented and prone to social conflict. In a study of sub-Saharan African countries, Goldsmith (2001) finds that aid is positively associated with one measure of governance relating to political freedom. All these studies are in the

tradition of cross-country growth regressions and may, consequently, be prone to some of the well-known problems of such regressions (Levine and Renelt, 1992; Durlauf, Johnson, and Temple, 2005; and Rodrik, 2005). Using techniques to avoid some of these problems, Rajan and Subramanian (2005) find that the level of unrequited flows—defined as aid and revenues from oil and natural resources—has a negative impact on institutions in countries with poor institutions (see Box 3.3; individually, the effects of aid and natural resource revenues are quantitatively similar, although not statistically robust).[28] This suggests that countries that receive large unrequited flows and that have weak institutions stand most to gain—in terms of maximizing the benefits of such flows—from strengthening their institutions.

Overall, with existing evidence ambiguous, further research is needed to arrive at more definitive conclusions regarding the impact of aid on institutions. That said, given the levels of financial assistance envisaged under the Millennium Report, low-income countries could witness a dramatic increase in the assistance they receive (Figure 3.11). Under plausible assumptions, aid on average would finance about 60 percent of government expenditure in 37 low-income sub-Saharan African countries, with the ratio exceeding 50 percent in 26 countries and more than 75 percent in half of those. Consequently, policymakers should be mindful of the potential effects in individual cases, and seek to ensure both that aid is provided in ways that minimize any adverse risks to domestic institutions, and that the institutional environment in recipient countries is strengthened to make best use of aid inflows. In this context, well-accepted measures that can minimize such risks and increase aid effectiveness assume

[25]See Arellano and others (2005).

[26]See Azam, Devarajan, and O'Connell (1999); Feyzioglu, Swaroop, and Zhu (1998); and Gupta and others (2004).

[27]On the other hand, Collier (1999) argues that the substitution of aid for taxes can actually be a benefit because it improves the private sector's incentive to work and invest.

[28]The impact of aid can also be expected to depend on the type of aid being considered, as explored in, for example, Gupta and others (2004) and Congressional Budget Office (1997).

Figure 3.11. Aid Dependency Ratios in Sub-Saharan Africa under the Millennium Development Goals[1]

Dependency on aid would increase significantly if the Millennium Development Goals were implemented. The number of countries with ratios of aid to government expenditure exceeding 50 percent would increase from 16 to about 26.

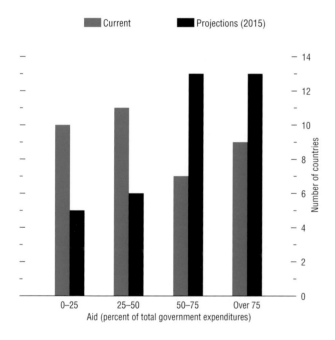

Aid (percent of total government expenditures)

Sources: Moss and Subramanian (2005); World Bank, *World Development Indicators* (2005); and IMF staff estimates.

[1]Current figures refer to 2002 or the latest year for which data are available. Projections are an average over the following six different scenarios for likely aid flows: (1) doubling aid to GDP for all countries; (2) same as (1) except that aid to GDP is tripled for countries in the top two quintiles of the World Bank's CPIA ratings; (3) a 10 percent increase in the ratio of government expenditure to GDP of which 8 percentage points is financed by increased aid; (4) an additional $130 billion in aid distributed equally over all low income countries; (5) an increase in aid per capita of US$70 for all countries; and (6) an increase in government expenditure per capita to $143 for all countries with additional aid financing the increase.

greater importance. Some such measures include the following:

- Safeguards to ensure that long-term accountability of governments to citizens is strengthened despite reduced reliance on taxation;[29]
- Reductions in transaction costs for the recipients of aid through measures such as harmonization of aid delivery and greater use of multilateral channels;[30]
- In the presence of threshold effects, greater selectivity in aid, with priority accorded to countries with strong institutions—envisaged under the U.S. Millennium Challenge Account—and those with a well-formulated strategy to simultaneously improve institutions; and
- For those countries with weak institutions, consideration of alternative modes of aid delivery.[31]

Promoting Transparency

Transparency supports institutional improvements by helping to identify the presence of economic rents in an economy and increasing the penalties for rent extraction. The international community has an important role in promoting transparency in developing countries, for example by recognizing that some unfavorable outcomes such as corruption can be "two-sided." The OECD Convention on Combating Bribery of Foreign Public Officials in International Business Transactions obliges signatory countries—which include all 30 OECD members and 6 nonmembers—to treat the bribery of a foreign public official as a crime on the same

[29]The Commission for Africa proposes, for example, that aid should be conditional on good governance and the government's accountability to citizens.

[30]Recognizing this, the Commission for Africa recommends that aid should be provided in a predictable manner and flexibly over the long term. See also Birdsall (2004).

[31]Easterly (2002) suggests giving aid vouchers directly to people so that they could buy services. Klein and Harford (2005) suggest innovative possibilities for aid delivery, including output-based aid and greater use of the private sector in delivering aid.

Box 3.3. Examining the Impact of Unrequited Transfers on Institutions

The emerging literature has reached ambiguous conclusions on the impact of both aid and natural resource revenues on institutions (see the main text). Since revenues from both aid and natural resources largely accrue to governments but without a corresponding need to tax citizens, it is of interest to ask what similarities there are between these two forms of resources—referred to here as unrequited transfers—in terms of their impact on institutions. To avoid some of the well-known problems of cross-country growth regressions,[1] one technique of estimating the impact of unrequited transfers on institutions is to examine within-country differences in the performance of sectors that are more institution intensive.[2] This method allows for exploiting within-country differential effects (growth differences between institution-intensive industries and non-institution-intensive industries) and a country treatment effect (different aid or resource inflows to a country). It also allows for correcting for country (and industry) effects, which implies that the findings are not as sensitive to particular regression specifications as traditional cross-country regressions.

The estimation strategy runs regressions of the form

$$G_{ij} = K + \zeta_{1 \ldots m} * CI + \zeta_{m+1 \ldots n} * II + \zeta_{n+1} * S_{ij} + \alpha\, (A_j * INS_i) + \varepsilon_{ij},$$

where G_{ij} is the annual average rate of growth of value added of industry i in country j over the 10-year period (1980–90), obtained by normalizing the growth in nominal value added by the GDP deflator; K is a constant; $\zeta_{1 \ldots m}$ are the coefficients of the country fixed effects; CI is country indicators; $\zeta_{m+1 \ldots n}$ are the coefficients of the industry fixed effects; II is industry indicators; ζ_{n+1} is the coefficient of the initial period share of industry i in total value added in country j (which controls for convergence-type effects); S_{ij} is industry i's share of manufacturing in country j in the initial period; A_j is unrequited transfers to country j; and INS_i is the institution intensity of industry i. The coefficient of interest is α, which captures the interaction between unrequited transfers and an industry's institution intensity. If countries that receive more unrequited transfers see a larger negative impact in industrial sectors that are more institution intensive, the coefficient of α should be negative.

A key challenge is to identify institution-intensive sectors. Blanchard and Kremer (1997) develop a measure for the dependence of a sector on the institutional environment—the measure essentially relies on the extent to which transactions needed for production have to be governed by contracts. The greater the number of such transactions, the more the need for institutions that enforce contracts. Following Blanchard and Kremer (1997) and Levchenko (2004), we compute from an input-output matrix (for 1992) of the United States the Herfindahl index of concentration of purchases for sector i, where

$$c_i = \sum_z (\phi_{iz}),$$

where ϕ_{iz} is the share of input z in the production of i. The higher the index, the fewer are the industries the sector buys from, increasing the possibility of regulating transactions through long-term repeated firm-supplier relationships or vertical integration rather than through explicit governance by the courts or regulatory authorities. For example, in the sample, the electric machinery sector (Herfindahl score of 0.07) is more institution intensive than the food products sector (score of 0.25). In countries with lower

Note: The main author of this box is Arvind Subramanian.

[1]See Levine and Renelt (1992); Durlauf, Johnson, and Temple (2005); and Rodrik (2005).

[2]See Rajan and Subramanian (2005), upon which this box draws, and Rajan and Zingales (1998) for the development of this technique. Institution-intensive sectors are defined as those that are most likely to need better institutions in terms of contract enforcement and the protection of property rights.

Box 3.3 *(concluded)*

governance capacity, industries that depend on transactions—that is, score lower on the concentration index—are likely to either have to distort their organization structure or transact less, both of which have adverse effects on growth. One potential concern with this measure is whether, since it is derived from industrial country data, it would apply equally well to developing countries. Another concern is that the index measures the sectoral concentration of purchases—not the concentration in terms of firms—which would be a better measure of "outside" or arm's-length transactions. The empirical analysis seeks to address these concerns by validating the use of this measure of institution intensity. If concentration of outside purchases were a valid measure of institution intensity, then countries that have better institutions should see faster growth in industries that are more institution intensive. This is what the analysis shows, not just for developing countries but also in samples that include industrial countries.

The main conclusions of the analysis are the following.

- First, the level of unrequited transfers has a robust negative relationship with institutions (see the figure).[3] This result holds even after controlling for the possible impact of aid and natural resources in relieving the financial constraint faced by selected sectors (individually, the impacts of aid and natural resource revenues are quantatively similar, but not statistically robust).

- Second, the adverse impact of unrequited transfers is only present in countries with

Impact of Unrequited Transfers on Institutions[1]

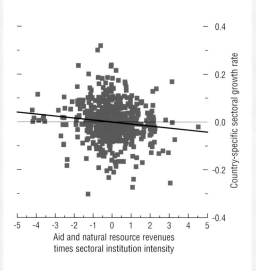

Source: Rajan and Subramanian (2005).

[1]The *x*-axis depicts the ratio of aid and exports of fuel and minerals to GDP in country *j* times institution intensity of industry *i*. The *y*-axis depicts that portion of the annual average growth rate of industry *i* in country *j* which is not explained by determinants other than the above. The regression includes country and industry fixed effects as well as a convergence term.

---

[3]The coefficient on the regression line, which is significant at the 1 percent confidence level, has the following interpretation. Given two countries that are one standard deviation apart in terms of aid and resource rents, and two sectors that are one standard deviation apart in terms of institution intensity, the more institution-intensive sector in the high-rent-receiving country will grow 1 percentage point a year slower than the less institution-intensive sector in the low-rent-receiving country.

weak institutions, and not in countries with stronger institutions. For example, when the sample is divided into countries that were above and below the median value for institutions, the adverse impact of unrequited transfers was significant in the latter and not significant in the former. Moreover, the coefficient for the below-median sample was twice as large as that for the whole sample.

Overall, this analysis reinforces a central message of the main chapter, that in an environment of rapidly increasing aid flows, and in many cases also natural resource revenues, it will be important to consider the potential impact on domestic institutions particularly carefully, and to design delivery mechanisms and accompanying policies in ways that minimize any adverse effects, especially in cases where institutions are already weak.

basis as the bribery of a national public official.[32]

The Extractive Industry Transparency Initiative (EITI), launched by the United Kingdom in 2002, is central to efforts aimed at encouraging governments and companies operating in natural resource–exporting countries to disclose natural resource revenues and payments. EITI is a multi-stakeholder initiative including governments, international organizations, companies, nongovernmental organizations (NGOs), investors, and business and industrial organizations, which agree to EITI Principles aimed at improving transparency in the natural resources sector to improve public accountability. The associated EITI criteria include specific measures to implement the principles, such as a work plan toward independent published audits, with support from international financial institutions when required. Some twenty countries have committed to EITI principles and criteria and eight are already in various stages of implementation, including in some cases the publication of reports on revenues and payments conforming to EITI principles.[33] If widely adopted, this initiative could improve the transparency of revenue data and help reduce corruption and misappropriation related to payments by companies to governments and government-linked entities (see the April 2005 *World Economic Outlook* and the U.K. Department for International Development website).[34] A multi-donor EITI Trust Fund administered by the World Bank provides funding and technical assistance to developing country governments in support of their efforts to take EITI programs forward. More broadly, the IMF and the World Bank are supporting EITI implementation at the country level.

The IMF, the World Bank, and other international agencies also support transparency through, for example, conditionality focused on audits in large government agencies and public companies, and data transparency projects.[35] In Uganda, public expenditure tracking surveys (PETS) helped to increase dramatically the ratio of actual primary education spending to the centrally budgeted allocation (Figure 3.12).[36] The IMF's fiscal transparency code promotes government accountability to its citizens by fostering informed debate about revenues and expenditures. Likewise, its monetary policy and financial policies transparency code can help reduce central bank financing, improve private sector access to credit, and reduce connected lending.[37]

NGOs and trade unions can play a key role in identifying institutional bottlenecks or shaping legislation to support civil society in seeking greater accountability. There are numerous examples of success stories although NGOs, labor unions, and broader civil society are more effective in an environment already characterized by some level of voice and accountability (Figure 3.13).[38]

Conclusions

A country's institutions are shaped by a combination of history, economic structure, political system, and culture. Consequently, institutions tend to be persistent over time. However, as the

---

[32]See description on the Internet: http://www.oecd.org under corruption.

[33]Progress updates are accessible via the Internet at http://www.eitransparency.org/countryupdates.htm.

[34]See the Internet: http://www2.dfid.gov.uk/news/files/extractiveindustries.asp.

[35]In its Country Assistance Strategy for 2004–07, the World Bank anchored its entire project portfolio in Indonesia on anticorruption measures.

[36]Prior to the implementation of PETS, most grant allocations were either redirected by various levels of government or were misappropriated (see Ablo and Reinikka, 1998). Subsequently, leakage of per-student grants to schools fell from almost 90 percent to about 20 percent (Reinikka and Smith, 2004). Uganda has adopted the PETS as its standard tool in several other sectors, and the practice has also spread to other countries, including Zambia and Peru.

[37]For a more detailed discussion of the role of the IMF in supporting institutional changes in developing countries, see the April 2003 *World Economic Outlook*.

[38]For example, a small advisory group initiated a "citizen report card" exercise in Bangalore, India, designed to provide feedback to local providers of public services (Public Affairs Center, 2005). This approach was later replicated in other Indian cities and other countries, such as Albania, the Philippines, Ukraine, and Vietnam.

Figure 3.12. Uganda: Leakage of Schooling Grants[1]
(U.S. dollars per student)

After the implementation of public expenditure tracking surveys and publicity campaign, leakage of primary schooling grants fell from almost 90 percent during 1991–95 to 18 percent in 2001.

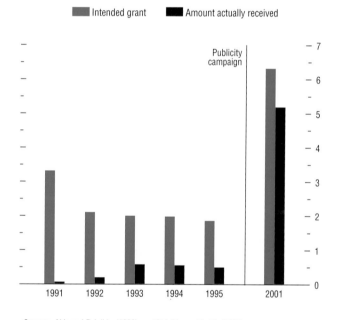

Sources: Ablo and Reinikka (1998); and Reinikka and Smith (2004).
[1]The figures refer to the average capitation grant per student and were converted to U.S. dollars using the average 1991–92 exchange rate.

analysis in this chapter shows, they are not immutable. Over the past 30 years, noticeable institutional improvements have occurred in 65 developing countries, associated—though often with varying lags—with sustained improvements in growth and private investment.

Both theoretical considerations and historical experience suggest that good institutions tend to flourish under two broad circumstances: an economic environment that is not conducive to rent-seeking, and—related to that—the presence of appropriate checks and balances on those wielding political power. Consistent with this, the econometric analysis finds that the transition to good institutions is more likely to occur in countries that are more open, have a greater degree of political accountability, have a higher level of education in the population, and are in the same region as countries with relatively good institutions. Higher aid, on the other hand, could be a hindrance to transitions. Unsurprisingly, many of the factors influencing transitions also appear to support good institutional quality more generally, although given the difficulties associated with identifying the direction of causation in the cross-country analyses, the conclusions are subject to greater uncertainty. Good institutional outcomes appear to be robustly associated with greater economic openness and the degree of accountability of the political executive. Higher initial income is also associated with better institutional quality, and this is also consistent with the observed lower probability of a transition to better institutions—they are likely to be of high quality already. The quality of institutions in neighboring countries, education levels, and the size of the natural resource sector also appear to play a role, but the level of aggregate aid does not appear to be clearly linked to the level of a country's institutions.

Many forms of institutions can deliver good institutional outcomes, and institutional change has to be designed and driven by countries themselves. The analysis in this chapter, however, suggests that external factors can play an important supporting role. Perhaps the strongest and most robust result is that greater openness is associated with better economic institutions, reinforcing the case for developing countries themselves to undertake ambitious trade liberalization under the Doha Round. Beyond that, however, strong regional leadership and well-designed external anchors can play an important role—underscoring the importance of strengthening existing platforms, such as NEPAD—as can greater transparency, particularly in countries with large natural resource sectors. The evidence on the impact of aid flows is ambiguous, but given the projected large increases in the size of inflows in relation to government expenditures in a number of countries in coming years, and the importance of ensuring that aid is effectively used toward the broader goal of poverty reduction, both donors and individual recipient countries need to think through carefully the potential institutional implications on a case-by-case basis, and seek to structure aid delivery—and accompanying policy measures in other areas—in such a way as to minimize any potential adverse effects in each recipient economy.

Appendix 3.1. Sample Composition, Data Sources, and Methods

The main author of this appendix is Angela Espiritu.

This appendix provides further details on the sample composition, the data and their sources, and the empirical strategies used in the analyses underlying the chapter.

The sample consists of 105 countries across all regions, representing both advanced and developing economies. Countries are classified according to the current *World Economic Outlook* (WEO) country groupings. In the main text of Chapter III, developing economies also include emerging market economies. The analyses cover the period 1970–2004. The model regresses country-specific measures of institutional outcomes on a set of regressors including explanatory factors suggested by analytical considerations and a set of exogenous controls. The specific data used in the analyses and their sources are outlined below.

Figure 3.13. Accountability and Improvements in Corruption[1]

Over the past decade, the corruption index has improved more significantly in the countries that are characterized by having high voice and accountability.

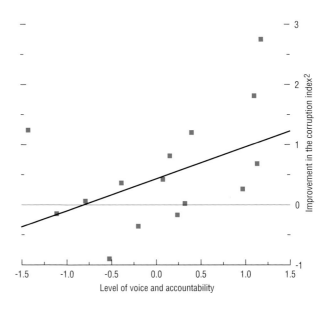

Sources: Kaufmann, Kraay, and Mastruzzi (2005); Transparency International and University of Passau (2004); and IMF staff calculations.
[1] The sample for this figure consists only of the countries where the initial 1995 Transparency International and University of Passau (TI) corruption score is below its mid-range of 5. The level of voice and accountability refers to the average score between 1996 and 2004. For a description of the voice and accountability index, see Appendix 3.1.
[2] The improvement in the TI corruption score refers to the change in the score between 2004 and 1995.

Data and Sources

Measures of Institutional Quality

The measures of institutional quality are as follows.

- Five separate indicators of governance by Kaufmann, Kraay, and Mastruzzi (2005) (KKM):[39] (1) *Corruption*—measures perceptions of corruption, conventionally defined as the exercise of public power for private gain; (2) *Rule of law*—measures the extent to which property rights are protected, and the perceptions on the incidence of crime, the effectiveness of the judiciary, and the enforceability of contracts; (3) *Political stability*—measures perceptions of the likelihood that the government will be overthrown by unconstitutional and/or violent means; (4) *Government effectiveness*—measures the quality of public service, the competence and independence of civil service, and the credibility of the government's policies; and (5) *Regulatory quality*—measures the lack of controls on the goods market, banking system, international trade, and business development. An *aggregate governance index* is also constructed by taking the simple average of the five indicators. Data are available biennially for the period 1996–2004.
- A measure of political risk and a specific indicator of law and order from the International Country Risk Guide Database (ICRG).[40] *Political risk* assesses a country's political stability based on the following components: government stability, socioeconomic conditions, investment profile, internal and external conflict, corruption, military and religion in politics, law and order, ethnic tensions, democratic accountability, and bureaucracy quality. The *law and order* component measures the objectivity of the legal system and the extent to which laws are observed in society. Data are available from 1984 and updated monthly.
- Measures of a country's business environment from the World Bank's *Doing Business Database* (DB).[41] These measures include the cost of starting and closing a business, in terms of time and money, the difficulty of hiring or laying off workers, the requirements and procedures needed to borrow money for business purposes, and the enforceability of contracts. Data are available for 2004.
- The World Bank measures of a country's investment environment from the *Investment Climate Surveys* (IC)[42] database. These measures indicate the over all perception of investors on business constraints, resolution of conflicts, and financial development. Data are available for 2004.
- Measures of *economic freedom* by the Cato Institute and the Heritage Foundation.[43] The Cato Institute index by Gwartney and Lawson (2004) determines a country's degree of economic freedom by looking at five major areas: the size of government, legal structure and security of property rights, access to sound money, freedom to trade internationally, and regulation of credit, labor, and business. Country scores range from 1 (repressed) to 10 (free). Data are available periodically for 1970–2002. The Heritage Foundation (2005) index contains 10 components: trade policy, fiscal burden, government intervention, monetary policy, capital flows and foreign investment, banking and finance, wages and prices, property rights, regulation, and black market. Data are available for 1995–2005.[44]

---

[39]For more details on the KKM indicators, see http://www.worldbank.org/wbi/governance.

[40]For more details on the ICRG indicators, see http://www.countrydata.com.

[41]For more details on the DB indices, see http://rru.worldbank.org/DoingBusiness.

[42]For more details on the IC indices, see http://rru.worldbank.org/investmentclimate.

[43]For more details on the Cato Institute's measure of economic freedom, see http://www.freetheworld.com/download.html. For more information on the Heritage Foundation's measure, see http://www.heritage.org/research/features/index/downloads.cfm.

[44]For the regressions, both indices were recalculated without the trade openness component since a measure of openness, further described below, was used as a regressor.

- Measures of political institutional quality from the Polity IV data set by Marshall and Jaggers (2003).[45] The indices employed are (1) *Polity score*—measures how democratic or autocratic a country is; and (2) *Executive constraint*—measures the extent of constraints on the individuals or groups who hold the executive's decision-making powers. Data are available for 1960–2003.

The Cato Institute's Economic Freedom index was used to measure economic institutions in the majority of analyses because it covers a longer time period and in some cases more countries than the other indices. The Cato index is highly correlated with the alternative measures for those subperiods where both are available. For instance, the correlation coefficients between the Cato index and the Heritage Foundation index, the KKM aggregate governance index, and the KKM corruption measure, are 0.82, 0.84, and 0.78, respectively.

Institutional Catalysts

The institutional catalysts are as follows.

- *Trade openness* comes from Wacziarg and Welch (2003)[46] and is based on average tariff rates, average nontariff barriers, the average parallel market premium for foreign exchange, the existence of an export marketing board, and the existence of a communist party in power. The variable is equal to zero prior to liberalization, and unity from the beginning of liberalization.
- Education measures include both primary and secondary enrollment rates from the World Bank's *World Development Indicators* (WDI), and educational attainment from Barro and Lee (2000).[47] *Primary* or *secondary enrollment rates* refers to the ratio of total primary or secondary enrollment to the population in the corresponding age group. Data are available periodically for 1960–2003. *Educational attainment* is defined as the average years of school of the total population aged 15 and over. Data are available for 1960–2000.
- A measure of accountability of the elites to the broader public from KKM's *voice and accountability* indicator. This index assesses the extent of citizens' participation in the selection of governments, civil liberties, and press freedom. Freedom House's (2005) index measures *press freedom*[48] specifically by looking at the media's legal environment, the political pressures they face, and the extent of society's access to information. Data are available for 1979–2004 for up to 194 countries.
- *External spillovers* are measured by taking the simple and/or weighted average of a country's *regional neighbors'* or *trading partners' institutional quality*. The weights reflect gross domestic product (GDP) when examining regional neighbors, and trade shares when examining trading partners. In the cross-sectional and panel regressions reported in the main text of Chapter III, only the coefficients for the simple average of a country's regional neighbors' institutional quality are shown, while the other measures yield similar results. A *catch-up term* is also derived from these averages by taking the difference of a country's current institutional quality and its neighbors' or trading partners' lagged institutional quality.
- *Natural resource dependence* is measured using an indicator equal to unity if a country's net fuel exports (as reported by WDI) exceed 5 percent of GDP, and equal to zero otherwise.
- *Transparency* from Oxford Analytica[49] offers measures of a country's compliance of international standards and codes, including banking supervision, corporate governance, money laundering, securities regulation, insurance supervision, monetary and fiscal transparency,

---

[45]For more details on the Polity IV Database, see http://www.cidcm.umd.edu/inscr/polity.

[46]For more details on the openness measure, see http://papers.nber.org/papers/w10152.pdf.

[47]For more details on the educational attainment measure, see http://papers.nber.org/papers/w7911.pdf.

[48]For more information on the press freedom index, see http://www.freedomhouse.org/research/pressurvey.htm.

[49]For more information on Oxford Analytica's indicators, see http://www.oxan.com/cr/projects/standardsandcodes.asp.

accounting and auditing, insolvency regimes, and payment systems. Data are available for 2003.

- The *central bank independence* index is drawn from Arnone and others (2005). Data are available for 1991–92 and for 2004.

Controls

- The variables used are (1) the log of *income per capita* from the Penn World Table Version 6.1 (Heston, Summers, and Aten, 2002); (2) *inequality* as measured by the Gini coefficient from WDI; (3) *military expenditure* from the IMF's *Government Finance Statistics* as measured by defense expenditure as a percent of total government expenditures; and (4) *aid* as a percent of GDP from the IMF's *Balance of Payments Statistics Yearbook*.

Sample Composition, Methods, and Other Comments

Cross-Sectional Analysis

The sample consists of 104 countries for the period average of 1970–2004. Results are reported using, as dependent variables, the KKM aggregate index, the KKM corruption measure, and the Heritage Foundation's measure of economic freedom. These results are broadly representative of the results for other measures of institutional quality. Independent variables included openness, schooling, KKM's voice and accountability index, fiscal transparency, central bank independence, net fuel exports, aid, neighbors' institutional quality, and initial income. The model was estimated using two-stage least squares, employing the initial values of the variables as instruments.

Panel Analysis

Reflecting constraints on the availability of the time-series data, the panel regression analyzes institutional outcomes using the Cato Institute's Economic Freedom index. The data set covers a panel of 93 countries over 1970–2004. The data are averaged over five-year periods, with an average of six observations per country. The set of

regressors employed was the same as in the cross section. A fixed-effects linear model was estimated, using the start-period values of the variables as instruments. In this setting, the impact of trade openness is much weaker than in the cross section, as fixed effects absorb much of its explanatory power.

Institutional Transitions

The sample consists of approximately 90 countries over the period 1970–2004. Empirically, for each country the start of a transition, if any, is defined as the first year in which the forward-looking eight-year moving average of the relevant variable is both significantly larger than the backward-looking eight-year moving average and sufficiently high in absolute terms.

Since institutional transitions generally occur over a protracted period, the eight years following the start of a transition are all viewed as part of the same transition episode. Observations following the end of this transition period are dropped. To ensure that the episodes identified are sustained transitions, countries that are identified as having a positive transition but are subsequently followed by a negative transition are excluded. The Polity score by Marshall and Jaggers was used for political transitions, while the Cato Institute's Economic Freedom index was used for economic transitions. For the Polity score, the threshold for change from the backward-looking eight-year moving average to the forward-looking eight-year moving average is 4 points; while the minimum forward-looking moving average score is 0. For the Cato Institute's Economic Freedom index, the threshold for change is 1 point and the minimum level attained is 4 points. The list of transitions identified was reviewed by IMF country desks, and, where appropriate, adjusted. The final list of transitions is presented in Table 3.4.

After identifying the transitions, a dummy variable was set to unity beginning in the year of transition. This variable was then used to run the probit regressions using the same set of regressors as in the cross-sectional and panel specifications, except that, for the neighbors'

Table 3.4. List of Institutional Transitions, 1970–2004[1]

Country	Year of Transition in Economic Institutions	Country	Year of Transition in Economic Institutions
Albania	1993	Lithuania	2000
Argentina	1991	Macedonia, FYR	1994
Bangladesh	1987	Malta	2004
Benin	1992	Mauritius	1985
Bolivia	1985	Mexico	1991
Botswana	1998	Namibia	1995
Brazil	1999	Nicaragua	1994
Bulgaria	1997	Nigeria	2003
Cambodia	1999	Panama	2000
Chile	1976	Paraguay	2004
China	1978	Peru	1993
Costa Rica	1990	Philippines	1994
Croatia	2000	Poland	1990
Czech Republic	1991	Romania	2000
Djibouti	1996	Russia	2000
Dominican Republic	1996	Senegal	1994
Ecuador	2000	Serbia and Montenegro	2001
El Salvador	1994	Sierra Leone	2002
Estonia	1995	Slovak Republic	2000
Georgia	1995	Slovenia	2000
Ghana	1985	South Africa	1996
Guatemala	1994	Sri Lanka	1990
Guinea-Bissau	1994	Syrian Arab Republic	1987
Guyana	1991	Taiwan Province of China	1980
Honduras	2003	Tanzania	1997
Hungary	1995	Togo	1985
Indonesia	1985	Trinidad and Tobago	1993
Iran, I. R. of	1999	Turkey	2001
Jamaica	1993	Uganda	1996
Jordan	1998	Ukraine	2000
Korea	1998	United Arab Emirates	1988
Kuwait	1986	Zambia	1997
Latvia	1999		

Sources: Gwartney and Lawson (2004); and IMF staff calculations.
[1]Some countries experienced significant improvements in political and economic institutions prior to 1970. For example, Korea substantially improved its economic institutions during the 1960s. For more information on the data and methodology used to determine institutional transitions, see Appendix 3.1.

institutional quality, the catch-up term was used instead of just the average. For all regressions in the chapter, both the Cato Institute and Heritage Foundation indices were recalculated without the trade openness component since a measure of openness was used as a regressor.

References

Ablo, Emmanuel, and Ritva Reinikka, 1998, "Do Budgets Really Matter? Evidence from Public Spending on Education and Health in Uganda," World Bank Policy Research Working Paper No. 1926 (Washington: World Bank).

Acemoglu, Daron, and Simon Johnson, 2003, "Unbundling Institutions," NBER Working Paper No. 9934 (Cambridge, Massachusetts: National Bureau of Economic Research).

Acemoglu, Daron, and others, 2003, "Institutional Causes, Macroeconomic Symptoms: Volatility, Crises, and Growth," *Journal of Monetary Economics*, Vol. 50, No. 1, pp. 49–123.

Ades, Alberto, and Rafael Di Tella, 1999, "Rents, Competition, and Corruption," *American Economic Review*, Vol. 89, No. 4, pp. 982–93.

Alesina, Alberto, and Beatrice Weder, 2002, "Do Corrupt Governments Receive Less Foreign Aid?" *American Economic Review*, Vol. 92, No. 4, pp. 1126–37.

Arellano, Cristina, and others, 2005, "The Dynamic Implications of Foreign Aid and Its Variability," IMF Working Paper No. 05/119 (Washington: International Monetary Fund).

Arnone, Marco, and others, 2005, "New Indices of Central Bank Independence," IMF Working Paper (Washington: International Monetary Fund, forthcoming).

Azam, Jean-Paul, Shantayanan Devarajan, and Stephen A. O'Connell, 1999, "Aid Dependence Reconsidered," World Bank Policy Research Working Paper No. 2144 (Washington: World Bank).

Barro, Robert J., and Jong-Wha Lee, 2000, "International Data on Educational Attainment: Updates and Implications," CID Working Paper No. 42 (Cambridge, Massachusetts: Center for International Development).

Birdsall, Nancy, 2004, "Seven Deadly Sins: Reflections on Donor Failings," Center for Global Development Working Paper No. 50 (Washington: Center for Global Development).

Blanchard, Olivier, and Michael Kremer, 1997, "Disorganization," *Quarterly Journal of Economics*, Vol. 112, No. 4, pp. 1091–126.

Bräutigam, Deborah, and Stephen Knack, 2004, "Foreign Aid, Institutions, and Governance in Sub-Saharan Africa," *Economic Development and Cultural Change*, Vol. 52, No. 2, pp. 255–85.

Broadman, Harry G., and Francesca Recanatini, 2002, "Corruption and Policy: Back to the Roots," *Journal of Policy Reform*, Vol. 5, No. 1, pp. 37–49.

Capital Markets Consultative Group, 2003, *Foreign Direct Investment in Emerging Market Countries—Report of the Working Group of the Capital Markets Consultative Group (CMCG)*. Available via the Internet: http://www.imf.org/external/np/cmcg/2003/eng/091803.HTM.

Chae, Wook, and Hongyul Han, 2001, "Impact of China's Accession to the WTO and Policy Implications for Asia-Pacific Developing Economies," Korea Institute for International Economic Policy Working Paper No. 01–02 (March), pp. 1–73.

Chao, Kang, 1986, *Man and Land in Chinese History: An Economic Analysis* (Palo Alto, California: Stanford University Press).

Chen, Shaohua, and Martin Ravallion, 2004, "How Have the World's Poorest Fared Since the Early 1980s?" *World Bank Research Observer*, Vol. 19, No. 2, pp. 141–69.

China Statistical Yearbook, 1996 (Beijing: China Statistical Office).

———, 2004 (Beijing: China Statistical Office).

Collier, Paul, 1999, "Aid 'Dependency': A Critique," *Journal of African Economies*, Vol. 8, No. 4 (Special Issue), pp. 528–45.

Commission for Africa Report, 2005. Available via the Internet: http://www.commissionforafrica.org/english/report/introduction.html.

Congressional Budget Office, 1997, "The Role of Foreign Aid in Development: Costa Rica and Honduras," in *Monthly Budget Review*. Available via the Internet: http://www.cbo.gov/StudiesRpts.cfm.

Durlauf, Steven, Paul Johnson, and Jonathan Temple, 2005, "Growth Econometrics," in *Handbook of Economic Growth*, ed. by P. Aghion and S. Durlauf (Amsterdam: North-Holland, Elsevier, forthcoming). Available via the Internet: http://irving.vassar.edu/faculty/pj/growtheconometrics.pdf.

Easterly, William, 2002, "Inequality Does Cause Underdevelopment: New Evidence," Center for Global Development Working Paper No. 1 (Washington: Center for Global Development).

European Union, 1993, *Copenhagen Criteria*. Available via the Internet: http://europa.eu.int/scadplus/glossary/accession_criteria_copenhague_en.htm.

———, 2005, *European Neighbourhood Policy*. Available via the Internet: http://europa.eu.int/comm/world/enp/public_en.htm.

Feyzioglu, Tarhan, Vinaya Swaroop, and Min Zhu, 1998, "A Panel Data Analysis of the Fungibility of Foreign Aid," *World Bank Economic Review*, Vol. 12, No. 1, pp. 29–58.

Fisman, Raymond, and Roberta Gatti, 2002, "Decentralization and Corruption: Evidence Across Countries," *Journal of Public Economics*, Vol. 83, No. 3, pp. 324–45.

Freedom House, 2005, "Freedom of the Press 2005." Available via the Internet: http://www.freedomhouse.org/research/pressurvey.htm

Giavazzi, Francesco, and Guido Tabellini, 2004, "Economic and Political Liberalizations," NBER Working Paper No. 10657 (Cambridge, Massachusetts: National Bureau of Economic Research).

Glaeser, Edward, and Raven Saks, 2004, "Corruption in America," NBER Working Paper No. 10821 (Cambridge, Massachusetts: National Bureau of Economic Research).

Goldsmith, Arthur A., 2001, "Foreign Aid and Statehood in Africa," *International Organization*, Vol. 55, No. 1, pp. 123–48.

Gupta, Sanjeev, and others, 2004, "Foreign Aid and Revenue Response: Does the Composition of Aid

Matter?" in *Helping Countries Develop: the Role of Fiscal Policy,* ed. by Sanjeev Gupta, Benedict Clements, and Gabriela Inchauste (Washington: International Monetary Fund), pp. 385–406.

Gwartney, James, and Robert Lawson, 2004, *Economic Freedom of the World: 2004 Annual Report* (Vancouver: The Fraser Institute). Available via the Internet: www.freetheworld.com.

Heritage Foundation, 2005, "Index of Economic Freedom." Available via the Internet: http://www.heritage.org/research/features/index.

Heston, Alan, Robert Summers, and Bettina Aten, 2002, "Penn World Table Version 6.1" (October) Center for International Comparisons at the University of Pennsylvania (Philadelphia, Pennsylvania: University of Pennsylvania).

International Monetary Fund, 2004a, *Balance of Payments Statistics Yearbook 2004* (Washington).

———, 2004b, *Government Finance Statistics Yearbook* (Washington).

———, and World Bank, 2005, *Global Monitoring Report 2005* (Washington).

Islam, Roumeen, and Claudio Montenegro, 2002, "What Determines the Quality of Institutions?" World Bank Policy Research Working Paper No. 2764 (Washington: World Bank).

Johnson, Simon, Jonathan D. Ostry, and Arvind Subramanian, 2005, "Can PRGF Policy Levers Improve Institutions and Lead to Sustained Growth?" (Washington: International Monetary Fund, forthcoming).

Kaufmann, Daniel, 2004, "Governance Redux: The Empirical Challenge," in *Global Competitiveness Report 2003–2004* (Geneva: World Economic Forum).

———, Aart Kraay, and Massimo Mastruzzi, 2005, "Governance Matters IV: Governance Indicators for 1996–2004," World Bank Policy Research Working Paper No. 3630 (Washington: World Bank).

Kaufmann, Daniel, Aart Kraay, and Zoido-Lobatón, 1999a, "Aggregating Governance Indicators," World Bank Policy Research Working Paper No. 2195 (Washington: World Bank).

———, 1999b, "Governance Matters," World Bank Policy Research Working Paper No. 2196 (Washington: World Bank).

Kaufmann, Daniel, Gil Mehrez, and Tugrul Gurgur, 2002, "Voice or Public Sector Management? An Empirical Investigation of Determinants of Public Sector Performance Based on a Survey of Public Officials," World Bank Policy Research Working Paper (unpublished; Washington: World Bank).

Klein, Michael, and Tim Harford, 2005, *The Market for Aid* (Washington: International Finance Corporation).

Klenow, Peter J., and Andrés Rodriguez-Clare, 2004, "Externalities and Growth," NBER Working Paper No. 11009 (Cambridge, Massachusetts: National Bureau of Economic Research). Also forthcoming in the *Handbook of Economic Growth*, ed. by P. Aghion and S. Durlauf (Amsterdam: North-Holland, Elsevier).

Knack, Stephen, 2001, "Aid Dependence and the Quality of Governance: Cross-Country Empirical Tests," *Southern Economic Journal,* Vol. 68, No. 2, pp. 310–29.

———, and Aminur Rahman, 2004, "Donor Fragmentation and Bureaucratic Quality in Aid Recipients," World Bank Policy Research Working Paper 3186 (Washington: World Bank).

Krueger, Anne, 1974, "The Political Economy of the Rent-Seeking Society," *American Economic Review,* Vol. 64, No. 3, pp. 291–303.

Levchenko, Andrei, 2004, "Institutional Quality and International Trade," IMF Working Paper 04/231 (Washington: International Monetary Fund).

Levine, Ross, and David Renelt, 1992, "A Sensitivity Analysis of Cross-Country Growth Regressions," *American Economic Review,* Vol. 82, No. 4, pp. 942–63.

Lin, Justin Y., 1995, "The Needham Puzzle: Why the Industrial Revolution Did Not Originate in China," *Economic Development and Cultural Change,* Vol. 43, No. 2, pp. 269–92.

Maddison, Angus, 2003, *The World Economy: Historical Statistics* (Paris: Development Center of the Organization for Economic Cooperation and Development).

Mallon, Glenda, and John Whalley, 2004, "China's Post Accession WTO Stance," NBER Working Paper No. 10649 (Cambridge, Massachusetts: National Bureau of Economic Research).

Marshall, Monty, and Keith Jaggers, 2003, Polity IV data set. Available via the Internet: http://www.cidcm.umd.edu/inscr/polity.

Mattoo, Aaditya, and Arvind Subramanian, 2004, "The WTO and the Poorest Countries: The Stark Reality," *World Trade Review,* Vol. 3, No. 3, pp. 385–407.

Michels, Robert, 1911, *Political Parties: A Sociological Study of the Oligarchical Tendencies of Modern Democracy* (New York: Hearst's International Library).

Moss, Todd, and Arvind Subramanian, 2005, "After the Big Push: the Fiscal Implications of Large Aid Increases" (unpublished; Washington: Center for Global Development).

Naughton, Barry, 1994, "Chinese Institutional Innovation and Privatization from Below," *American Economic*

Review, Papers and Proceedings, Vol. 84 (May), pp. 266–70.

Needham, Joseph, 1954–97, *Science and Civilization in China* (Cambridge, United Kingdom: Cambridge University Press).

New Partnership for Africa's Development (NEPAD), 2005. Available via the Internet: http://www.nepad.org/2005/files/inbrief.php.

North, Douglass C., 1991, "Institutions," *Journal of Economic Perspectives,* Vol. 5, No. 1, pp. 97–112.

Oi, Jean C., 1995, "The Role of the Local State in China's Transitional Economy," *The China Quarterly,* No. 144 (December), pp. 1132–49.

Olken, Benjamin A., 2004, "Monitoring Corruption: Evidence from a Field Experiment in Indonesia" (unpublished; Cambridge, Massachusetts: National Bureau of Economic Research).

Persson, Torsten, Guido Tabellini, and Francesco Trebbi, 2003, "Electoral Rules and Corruption," *Journal of the European Economic Association,* Vol. 1, No. 4, pp. 958–89.

Pomeranz, Ken, 2000, *The Great Divergence: China, Europe, and the Making of the Modern World Economy* (Princeton, New Jersey: Princeton University Press).

Prati, Alessandro, Francesca Recanatini, and Guido Tabellini, 2005, "Why Are Some Public Agencies Less Corrupt Than Others?" IMF Working Paper (Washington: International Monetary Fund, forthcoming).

Public Affairs Center, 2005, "Report Card on Public Services." Available via the Internet: http://www.pacindia.org/rcrc/03Report%20Cards.

Qian, Yingyi, 2003, "How Reform Worked in China," in *In Search of Prosperity—Analytic Narratives on Economic Growth,* ed. by Dani Rodrik (Princeton, New Jersey: Princeton University Press).

Rajan, Raghuram, and Arvind Subramanian, 2005, "Do Unrequited Resources Stymie Institutional Development?" (unpublished; Washington: International Monetary Fund).

Rajan, Raghuram, and Luigi Zingales, 1998, "Financial Dependence and Growth," *American Economic Review,* Vol. 88, No. 3, pp. 559–86.

———, 2003a, "The Great Reversals: The Politics of Financial Development in the Twentieth Century," *Journal of Financial Economics,* Vol. 69, No. 1, pp. 5–50.

———, 2003b, *Saving Capitalism from the Capitalists: Unleashing the Power of Financial Markets to Create Wealth and Spread Opportunity* (New York: Crown Publishing).

Reinikka, Ritva, and Nathaniel Smith, 2004, *Public Expenditure Tracking Surveys in Education* (Paris: UNESCO, International Institute for Education Planning).

Reinikka, Ritva, and Jakob Svensson, 2004a, "The Power of Information: Evidence from a Newspaper Campaign to Reduce Capture," World Bank Policy Research Working Paper No. 3239 (Washington: World Bank).

———, 2004b, "Local Capture: Evidence from a Central Government Transfer Program in Uganda," *Quarterly Journal of Economics,* Vol. 119, No. 2, pp. 679–705.

Rodrik, Dani, 2005, "Why We Learn Nothing from Regressing Economic Growth on Policies" (unpublished; Cambridge, Massachusetts: Harvard University, Kennedy School of Government).

———, Arvind Subramanian, and Francesco Trebbi, 2004, "Institutions Rule: The Primacy of Institutions over Geography and Integration in Economic Development," *Journal of Economic Growth,* Vol. 9, No. 2, pp. 131–65.

Sachs, Jeffrey D., and Wing Thye Woo, 1997, "Understanding China's Economic Performance," NBER Working Paper No. 5935 (Cambridge, Massachusetts: National Bureau of Economic Research).

Svensson, Jakob, 2000, "Foreign Aid and Rent-Seeking," *Journal of International Economics,* Vol. 51, No. 2, pp. 437–61.

Tavares, Jose, 2003, "Does Foreign Aid Corrupt?" *Economics Letters,* Vol. 79, No. 1, pp. 99–106.

Transparency International and The University of Passau, 2004, "2004 Corruption Perceptions Index." Available via the Internet: www.icgg.org/corruption.index.html.

Treisman, Daniel, 2000, "The Causes of Corruption: A Cross-National Study," *Journal of Public Economics,* Vol. 76, No. 3, pp. 399–457.

UN Millennium Project, 2005, *Investing in Development: A Practical Plan to Achieve the Millennium Development Goals* (New York: UNDP).

Wacziarg, Romain, and Karen Horn Welch, 2003, "Trade Liberalization and Growth: New Evidence," NBER Working Paper No. 10152 (Cambridge, Massachusetts: National Bureau of Economic Research).

Wei, Shang-Jin, 2000, "Natural Openness and Good Government," NBER Working Paper No. 7765 (Cambridge, Massachusetts: National Bureau of Economic Research).

World Bank, 1996, *World Development Report* (Washington).

———, 2005, *World Development Indicators* (Washington).

DOES INFLATION TARGETING WORK IN EMERGING MARKETS?

Inflation targeting has become an increasingly popular monetary policy strategy, with some 21 countries (8 industrial and 13 emerging market) now inflation targeters. Other countries are considering following in their footsteps. Yet, while there have been numerous studies of inflation targeting in industrial countries, there has been little analysis of the effects of inflation targeting in emerging market countries.

This chapter makes a first attempt to fill this void. It looks at the experience of the emerging market countries that have adopted inflation targeting since the late 1990s, focusing both on macroeconomic performance and the potential benefits and costs of adopting inflation targeting. A new and detailed survey of 31 central banks was conducted to support the analysis in the chapter. Particular attention is paid to the implications for institutional change and to the feasibility and success of inflation targeting when specific initial conditions, such as central bank independence, are initially absent.

What Is Inflation Targeting and Why Does Inflation Targeting Matter?

It is now widely accepted that the primary role of monetary policy is to maintain price stability.[1] An operating definition of price stability that is now broadly accepted has been offered by Alan Greenspan, Chairman of the Federal Reserve's Open Market Committee: "[P]rice stability obtains when economic agents no longer take account of the prospective change in the general price level in their economic decision making" (Greenspan, Testimony to U.S. Congress, 1996). This is often thought to correspond to an annual rate of inflation in the low single digits.[2]

Inflation targeting is one of the operational frameworks for monetary policy aimed at attaining price stability. In contrast to alternative strategies, notably money or exchange rate targeting, which seek to achieve low and stable inflation through targeting intermediate variables—for example, the growth rate of money aggregates or the level of the exchange rate of an "anchor" currency—inflation targeting involves targeting inflation directly. The literature offers several different definitions of inflation targeting.[3] In practice, however, inflation targeting has two main characteristics that distinguish it from other monetary policy strategies.

- The central bank is mandated, and commits to, a unique numerical target in the form of a level or a range for annual inflation. A single target for inflation emphasizes the fact that price stabilization is the primary focus of the strategy, and the numeric specification provides a guide to what the authorities intend as price stability.

- The inflation forecast over some horizon is the de facto intermediate target of policy. For this reason inflation targeting is sometimes referred to as "inflation forecast targeting" (Svensson, 1998). Since inflation is partially predetermined in the short term because of existing price and wage contracts and/or indexation to past inflation, monetary policy

---

The main authors of this chapter are Nicoletta Batini, Kenneth Kuttner, and Douglas Laxton, with support from Manuela Goretti. Nathalie Carcenac provided research assistance.

[1]See Batini and Yates (2003) and Pianalto (2005).

[2]See Bernanke and others (1999); Mishkin and Schmidt-Hebbel (2001); Brook, Karagedikli, and Scrimgeour (2002); Batini (2004); and Burdekin and Siklos (2004).

[3]See, among others, Leiderman and Svensson (1995); Mishkin (1999); and Bernanke and others (1999).

Table 4.1. Inflation Targeters

	Inflation Targeting Adoption Date[1]	Unique Numeric Target = Inflation	Current Inflation Target (percent)	Forecast Process	Publish Forecast
Emerging market countries					
Israel	1997:Q2	Y	1–3	Y	Y
Czech Republic	1998:Q1	Y	3 (+/–1)	Y	Y
Korea	1998:Q2	Y	2.5–3.5	Y	Y
Poland	1999:Q1	Y	2.5 (+/–1)	Y	Y
Brazil	1999:Q2	Y	4.5 (+/–2.5)	Y	Y
Chile	1999:Q3	Y	2–4	Y	Y
Colombia	1999:Q3	Y	5 (+/–0.5)	Y	Y
South Africa	2000:Q1	Y	3–6	Y	Y
Thailand	2000:Q2	Y	0–3.5	Y	Y
Mexico	2001:Q1	Y	3 (+/–1)	Y	N
Hungary	2001:Q3	Y	3.5 (+/–1)	Y	Y
Peru	2002:Q1	Y	2.5 (+/–1)	Y	Y
Philippines	2002:Q1	Y	5–6	Y	Y
Industrial countries					
New Zealand	1990:Q1	Y	1–3	Y	Y
Canada	1991:Q1	Y	1–3	Y	Y
United Kingdom	1992:Q4	Y	2	Y	Y
Australia	1993:Q1	Y	2–3	Y	Y
Sweden	1993:Q1	Y	2 (+/–1)	Y	Y
Switzerland	2000:Q1	Y	<2	Y	Y
Iceland	2001:Q1	Y	2.5	Y	Y
Norway	2001:Q1	Y	2.5	Y	Y

Source: National authorities.

[1]This date indicates when countries de facto adopted inflation targeting as defined at the beginning of this chapter. Official adoption dates may vary.

can only influence expected future inflation. By altering monetary conditions in response to new information, central banks influence expected inflation and bring it in line over time with the inflation target, which eventually leads actual inflation to the target.

To date, the monetary policy strategy followed by 21 countries has these characteristics, and for the purpose of this chapter these are treated as inflation targeters (Table 4.1).[4] Defining inflation targeting according to these two characteristics makes it clear why, for example, neither the Federal Reserve nor the European Central Bank (ECB) are considered inflation targeters: the former lacks a numerical specification for its price stability objective,[5] while the latter has traditionally given a special status to a "reference

value" for the growth of the euro area M3 broad money aggregate.[6]

Proponents of inflation targeting argue that it yields a number of benefits relative to other operating strategies (see, for example, Truman, 2003). The main benefits are seen as the following.

- *Inflation targeting can help build credibility and anchor inflation expectations more rapidly and durably.* Inflation targeting makes it clear that low inflation is the primary goal of monetary policy and involves greater transparency to compensate for the greater operational freedom that inflation targeting offers. Inflation targets are also intrinsically clearer and more easily observable and understandable than other targets since they typically do not change

[4]According to these criteria, Chile and Israel are not classified as having adopted inflation targeting until the de-emphasis of their exchange rate targets, in 1999 and 1997, respectively.

[5]See Kohn (2003); Gramlich (2003); and Bernanke (2003).

[6]See European Central Bank (1999); Solans (2000); and Issing (2000). However, the ECB has recently de-emphasized the weight attached to this reference value, moving more toward a "pure" inflation-targeting regime. See European Central Bank (2003).

over time and are controllable by monetary means.[7] In this way, inflation targeting can help economic agents better understand and evaluate the performance of the central bank, anchoring inflation expectations faster and more permanently than other strategies, in which the task of the central bank is less clear or less monitorable (see Box 4.1, "A Closer Look at Inflation Targeting Alternatives: Money and Exchange Rate Targets").

- *Inflation targeting grants more flexibility.* Since inflation cannot be controlled instantaneously, the target on inflation is typically interpreted as a medium-term goal. This implies that inflation-targeting central banks pursue the inflation target over a certain horizon, by focusing on keeping inflation expectations at target.[8] Short-term deviations of inflation from target are acceptable and do not necessarily translate into losses in credibility.[9] The scope for greater flexibility could reduce output gap variability (Box 4.1 looks at why some inflation-targeting alternatives may imply higher output costs).

- *Inflation targeting involves a lower economic cost in the face of monetary policy failures.* The output costs of policy failure under some alternative monetary commitments, like exchange rate pegs, can be very large, usually involving massive reserve losses, high inflation, financial and banking crises, and possibly debt defaults.[10] In contrast, the output costs of a failure to meet

the inflation target are limited to temporarily higher-than-target inflation and temporarily slower growth, as interest rates are raised to bring inflation back to target.[11]

Critics, however, have argued that inflation targeting has important disadvantages.

- *Inflation targeting offers too little discretion and so it unnecessarily restrains growth.* Since the success of inflation targeting relies on the establishment of a reputational equilibrium between the central bank and agents in the domestic economy, inflation targeting can work effectively only if the central bank acts consistently and convincingly to attain the inflation target—in other words, for inflation targeting to work well, the central bank must demonstrate its commitment to low and stable inflation through tangible actions. In the initial phases of inflation targeting, demonstrating commitment may require an aggressive response to inflationary pressures, which could temporarily reduce output. More generally, inflation targeting constrains discretion inappropriately: it is too confining in terms of an ex ante commitment to a particular inflation number and a particular horizon over which to return inflation to target.[12] By obliging a country to hit the target so restrictively, inflation targeting can unnecessarily restrain growth.[13]

- *Inflation targeting cannot anchor expectations because it offers too much discretion.* Contrary

---

[7]Money targets, for example, have to be reset yearly and are hard to control because shifts in money demand or in the money multiplier impair the control of money supply and alter the long-run relationship between money and inflation. Likewise, the control of exchange rate targets by the central bank is limited because the level of the exchange rate is ultimately determined by the international demand and supply of the domestic currency vis-à-vis that of the "anchor" currency, and hence shifts in sentiment about the domestic currency can trigger abrupt changes in its relative value that cannot be offset easily by central bank actions. Many central banks have abandoned money and exchange rate targets on these grounds. See Box 4.1.

[8]The horizon over which inflation-targeting central banks attempt to stabilize inflation at target usually varies with the types of shocks that have taken inflation away from target and with the speed of monetary transmission. See Batini and Nelson (2001) for a discussion of optimal horizons under inflation targeting.

[9]Under "full credibility," economic agents under inflation targeting preemptively adjust their plans in the face of incipient inflationary pressures, so that the central bank has to move interest rates even less, and price stabilization comes at even lower output gap variability costs (see, for example, King, 2005).

[10]The experience of Argentina in 2001 is an example of this.

[11]The experience of South Africa in late 2002 is one such case.

[12]The horizon over which inflation-targeting central banks attempt to stabilize inflation at target is not always specified and varies from country to country. See Batini and Nelson (2001) for a discussion of optimal horizons under inflation targeting.

[13]See, among others, Rivlin (2002) and Blanchard (2003).

Box 4.1. A Closer Look at Inflation-Targeting Alternatives: Money and Exchange Rate Targets

Money and exchange rate targets are the main alternative monetary policy strategies to inflation targeting. Both strategies target inflation indirectly, by targeting "intermediate" variables on the assumption that these are both controllable and reliably related to the ultimate objective of policy—inflation. This box discusses strengths and weaknesses of these alternatives, and offers a brief review of the historical experience of countries that have used them.[1]

Money Targets

In the late 1970s and 1980s many central banks built their fight against inflation around money targeting (Goodhart, 1989). Money targeting involves announcing a target every year for the growth of a monetary aggregate[2] on the assumption that controlling the growth of money gives control of inflation.[3] The main benefits of money targets are that data on money are usually available more rapidly than other data—providing early information on the short-term inflation outlook—and that the nominal money supply may be more directly controllable than inflation itself. A tight control of the money stock is also largely incompatible with

debt monetization, and is therefore believed to provide some discipline over fiscal policy. In addition, money targets typically involve little analytical effort, requiring only yearly assumptions on trend real growth, trend money velocity, and the money base multiplier.

On the other hand, money targets have both conceptual and practical shortcomings. Conceptually, under money targets it is more difficult to anchor inflation expectations because money targets introduce a second numerical target to the ultimate target of policy, obscuring the task of the central bank and making it harder to monitor its performance. Money targets are therefore particularly unsuited for countries where the inflation record and central bank credibility are fragile. Money targets are based on the assumptions that the central bank has full control of the nominal money stock—that is, the money multiplier is predictable—and that money velocity is predictable—that is, the long-run relationship between money growth and nominal income growth (and therefore inflation, for given trend real growth) is stable. In practice, money targets were often missed, leading people to question their usefulness as intermediate targets. The only countries that still target money today are developing countries,[4] although even there, neither the money multiplier[5] nor the velocity of money appears stable over time (the two figures show this for a selected group of countries not on IMF programs).

Exchange Rate Targets

There are two main types of exchange rate targets: fixed exchange rates (currency boards, monetary unions, and unilateral dollarization)

Note: The main authors of this box are Nicoletta Batini and Manuela Goretti.

[1]Many of the strengths and weaknesses of intermediate targets relative to inflation targeting are reflected in the experience of the United Kingdom since World War II. See Batini and Nelson (2005).

[2]Most definitions are country specific but money targets usually refer to slightly broader aggregates than base money, that is, aggregates including currency in circulation, sight deposits, and time deposits with unrestricted access.

[3]This assumption finds its origins in a popular identity by Irving Fisher called the "quantity equation" or the "equation of exchanges." The identity states that the value of all economic transactions (or more generally all nominal income generated in an economy) has to be paid with money. It follows that money in circulation times money velocity—that is, the time on average in which a unit of money is spent during a certain period—must equal nominal income. Because of money neutrality, changes in the nominal money stock have no effect on changes in real output in the long run but can thus affect inflation, as long as money velocity is constant.

[4]Of the 22 developing countries that declare themselves money targeters, only 9 periodically disclose their numeric money targets. Five of these nine are on IMF programs. However, numerous countries still monitor money and credit aggregates as part of their overall assessment of economic and financial market conditions.

[5]The instability and unpredictability of the multiplier in developing countries are often a consequence of capital flows (including aid flows), which severely distort growth in the money base.

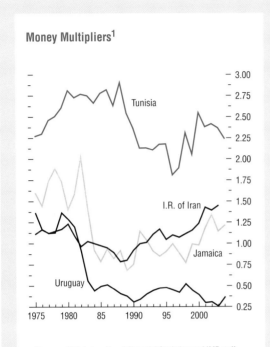

Money Multipliers[1]

Sources: IMF, *International Financial Statistics;* and IMF staff calculations.
[1] Ratio of narrow money (M1) to base money (M0). Actual money targets in I.R. of Iran and Tunisia are broader money aggregates than M1, i.e., M2 and M3 respectively. However, volatility in M1 transmits to these broader aggregates.

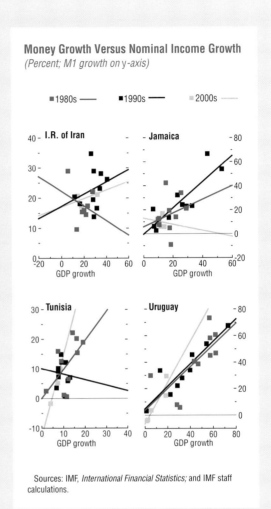

Money Growth Versus Nominal Income Growth
(Percent; M1 growth on y-axis)

■ 1980s —— ■ 1990s —— ■ 2000s ——

Sources: IMF, *International Financial Statistics;* and IMF staff calculations.

and fixed-but-adjustable exchange rates ("pegs," including bilateral or currency basket pegs as well as constant or crawling pegs; pegs can be on a point or a band target).

To various degrees, both types of exchange rate targets involve "adopting" the monetary policy of another country to acquire credibility from a foreign source when this is not available domestically.[6] Fixed-but-adjustable exchange

[6]Monetary unions, like the European Economic and Monetary Union, are a special category of fixed exchange rates where groups of countries abandon their national currencies to embrace a unique and collective new currency. The main benefits of such unions are lower currency transaction costs and the elimination of intra-union exchange rate volatility. Monetary unions, however, imply a partial loss of monetary autonomy—as monetary policy decisions have to be "coordinated" with other members—and a substantial loss in seigniorage for some member countries.

rates are thought to offer most of the credibility gains associated with a fixed exchange rate, but without the inflexibility of more rigid arrangements (see Chapter II of the September 2004 *World Economic Outlook*). Under exchange rate targets, the central bank's sole task is to maintain the value of the domestic money in terms of another country or group of countries. In the absence of effective capital controls, capital flows have to be sterilized and domestic money expansion can only result from money expansion in the "anchor" country, eventually bringing domestic inflation in line with inflation in the "anchor" country. Exchange rate targets also promise to reduce exchange rate volatility.

Box 4.1 *(concluded)*

The main drawbacks of exchange rate targets are three. First, because they imply delegating central bank power to another country, exchange rate targets result in losing much, if not all, monetary autonomy—for example, monetary instruments cannot be used for domestic purposes. Second, exchange rate targets can subject the central bank to speculative attacks and in extreme cases force a parity change that might not have been necessary on fundamental grounds. In addition, because exchange rate targets create a sense of security from currency risk, they can encourage unhedged currency mismatches, implying that successful speculative attacks are often followed by financial and banking crises and debt defaults (Flood and Marion, 1999; Sachs, Tornell, and Velasco, 1996). Third, the burden of achieving the proper real exchange rate falls entirely on the level of domestic prices, and this is particularly costly in terms of output when prices are sticky because then it is output that must adjust first.

Although fixed-but-adjustable pegs have been popular in the past, a consensus appears to have emerged that adjustable pegs can be dangerous arrangements for open economies subject to international capital flows (see, for instance, Fischer, 2001). The fact that they are adjustable makes them more prone to speculative attacks

because, many argue, it signals a less strong commitment than fixed exchange rates. About one-half of the countries with a long-lived—that is, five-year or longer—fixed-but-adjustable exchange rate since 1991 were forced to abandon it following a currency crisis.[7] Most countries that used to have fixed-but-adjustable exchange rates have either given up their national currencies completely by fixing their exchange rates (at present only seven countries—with populations above two million people—have a currency board)[8] or have moved to inflation targeting combined with a floating exchange rate. As discussed in the main text, overall, the recent inflation performance of countries with hard pegs is good, although not as good as that of countries that have moved to inflation targeting. In addition, the costs of policy failure are much higher, as the recent experience in Argentina has demonstrated.

[7]Of the remaining countries with fixed-but-adjustable pegs, about a half are small tourism-dependent economies and highly dependent principalities, all with populations of less than two million.

[8]We consider a "de facto" classification, based on the methodology of Obstfeld and Rogoff (1995). On that basis, the countries that still have a currency board or another currency as legal tender are Bosnia and Herzegovina, Bulgaria, Ecuador, El Salvador, Hong Kong SAR, Lithuania, and Panama.

to those who worry that inflation targeting may be too restraining, some argue that it cannot help build credibility in countries that lack it because it offers excessive discretion over how and when to bring inflation back to target and because targets can be changed as well.[14]

- *Inflation targeting implies high exchange rate volatility.* It is often believed that, because it elevates price stability to the status of the primary goal for the central bank, inflation targeting requires a benign neglect of the

exchange rate. If true, this could have negative repercussions on exchange rate volatility and growth.

- *Inflation targeting cannot work in countries that do not meet a stringent set of "preconditions,"* making the framework unsuitable for the majority of emerging market economies. Preconditions often considered essential include, for example, the technical capability of the central bank in implementing inflation targeting, absence of fiscal dominance, financial market soundness, and an efficient institutional setup

[14]See, for example, Rich (2000, 2001); Genberg (2001); and Kumhof (2002).

to support and motivate the commitment to low inflation.

Inflation Targeting: An Assessment of the Impact

Empirical studies so far have focused primarily on the experience of industrial economies, because these countries, many of which adopted inflation targeting in the early 1990s, have a track record of sufficient length to assess the policy's economic impact.[15] These studies generally suggest that inflation targeting has been associated with performance improvements, although the evidence is typically insufficient to establish statistical significance of these improvements. No study, however, finds that performance has deteriorated under inflation targeting.

The lack of strong evidence from industrial countries may reflect several factors. First, there are only seven or eight inflation targeters to look at, and a limited set of nontargeters to compare them against. Second, the macroeconomic performance of inflation targeters and non-inflation-targeters alike improved during the 1990s for a variety of reasons including, but not limited to, better monetary policy—for example, some aspects of the performance of many non-inflation-targeters along some dimensions were improved by preparations for entry into the European Economic and Monetary Union (EMU). And finally, the fact that most industrial countries entered the 1990s with relatively low and stable inflation makes it more difficult to discern any incremental improvement due to inflation targeting.

In many ways, the experience of emerging markets offers a richer set of data for assessing the effects of inflation targeting than that of the industrial countries. The time span covered is short—ranging from three to seven years—but the sample of inflation targeters and suitable comparison countries is considerably larger. Moreover, because many emerging market inflation targeters experienced relatively high levels of inflation and macroeconomic volatility prior to the adoption of inflation targeting, it should be easier to discern the effects of inflation targeting. Perhaps more crucially, looking at the experience of emerging markets allows a check on how inflation targeting performs during periods of economic turbulence. While the global inflation and financial market environment has generally been benign in recent years, a number of emerging market inflation targeters have been under periods of substantial stress during the course of their inflation-targeting regimes (for example, Brazil and other Latin American inflation targeters in the early 2000s; South Africa in late 2002; and Hungary and Poland in the years since 2000).

For the analysis that follows, we look at 13 emerging market inflation targeters (see Table 4.1).[16] We compare them against the remaining 22 emerging market countries that are in the JPMorgan EMBI Index, plus seven additional countries that are largely classified similarly.[17]

It is useful to begin by reviewing the inflation performance of inflation targeters and non-inflation-targeters over the past 15 years (Figure 4.1). Inflation in both groups was quite high in the early to mid-1990s but, as of 1997, somewhat higher for the non-inflation-targeters, which, as a group, had already begun to disinflate by 1995.[18] Inflation fell in both inflation-targeting and non-

[15]See, for example, Ball and Sheridan (2003); Levin, Natalucci, and Piger (2004); Truman (2003); and Hyvonen (2004), among others.

[16]Apart from the Czech Republic and Israel, all these countries are included in the JPMorgan Emerging Markets Bond Index (EMBI).

[17]These are Botswana, Costa Rica, Ghana, Guatemala, India, Jordan, and Tanzania. We also experiment with excluding these seven countries from the control group.

[18]The hypothesis put forth by Ball and Sheridan (2003) that the countries that chose to adopt inflation targeting were those experiencing a transitory increase in inflation is broadly inconsistent with the data when the country sample is extended to include emerging markets.

Table 4.2. Inflation Outcomes Relative to Target

	Standard Deviation from Target (RMSE) (percentage points)[1]	Frequency of Deviations[2] (percent)		
		Total	Below	Above
All countries	1.8	43.5	24.2	19.3
Stable inflation targets	1.3	32.2	21.7	10.6
Disinflation targets	2.2	59.7	27.7	32.0
Industrial countries	1.3	34.8	22.5	12.3
Emerging market countries	2.3	52.2	25.9	26.2

Source: Roger and Stone (2005).
[1]Inflation outcome relative to target or center of target zone ranges. Equally weighted averages of corresponding statistics for individual countries in relevant groups. Individual country statistics are based on monthly (quarterly for Australia and New Zealand) differences between 12-month inflation rates and centers of target ranges.
[2]Inflation outcomes relative to edges of target ranges.

Figure 4.1. Inflation, 1990–2004[1]
(Percent)

Average inflation has fallen for both inflation targeters and non-inflation-targeters over the past 15 years, but more so for inflation-targeting countries today.

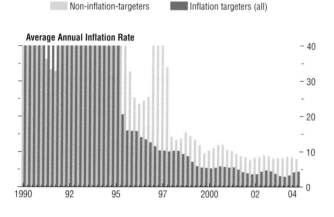

Non-inflation-targeters   Inflation targeters (all)

Average Annual Inflation Rate

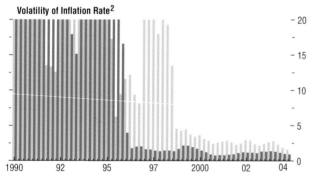

Volatility of Inflation Rate[2]

Sources: IMF, *International Financial Statistics;* and IMF staff calculations.
[1]Regional average for emerging market and selected developing countries; average inflation rates above 40 percent and volatilities above 20 percent are not shown, to enable clearer illustration of smaller average inflation differences in the recent past.
[2]Rolling 1-year standard deviation of inflation.

inflation-targeting countries—but even into 2004, a sizable "wedge" of roughly 3½ percentage points remained. Such a wedge reflects the success of most inflation targeters in keeping actual inflation, on average, close to target, although target misses have occurred, especially for disinflating countries, where target misses have tended to be larger and more frequent than in countries with stable inflation targets (Table 4.2; and Roger and Stone, 2005).

To look at the experience in more detail, we now turn to the economic performance of inflation-targeting countries before and after adopting inflation targeting relative to the performance of non-inflation-targeters. This approach raises the issue of what to use as the "break date" for non-inflation-targeters: while no partitioning of the sample is perfect, we follow Ball and Sheridan (2003) in using the average adoption date for the inflation targeters (1999:Q4) for this purpose (in practice, dates range from 1997:Q2 to 2002:Q1). Other partitions of the sample are also considered and, as reported below, yield very similar results.

As shown in the first panel of Figure 4.2, the level and volatility of inflation prior to the adoption of inflation targeting are, for many countries in the sample, quite high and variable (Figure 4.2). The convergence to low and stable inflation after adoption is striking: in 2004 all countries were clustered in the 1–7 percent range, with a maximum standard deviation of

Table 4.3. Baseline Results

Variables	IT Dummy Variable
CPI inflation	−4.820**
Volatility of CPI inflation	−3.638**
Volatility of real output growth	−0.633
Volatility of output gap	−0.010**

Sources: IMF, *International Financial Statistics;* and IMF staff calculations.

Note: One, two, and three asterisks denote statistical significance at the 10, 5, and 1 percent level, respectively.

2 percent. The non-inflation-targeters also show improvement along both dimensions, and many succeeded in stabilizing inflation at low levels; but as a group, they do display less strong convergence than the inflation targeters, with many continuing to experience relatively high and volatile inflation. For real output growth and volatility, the pattern is less clear: abstracting from one or two outliers, output volatility is generally lower in the "post" period for both groups, with little change in average growth rates.

A more formal statistical analysis, along the lines proposed by Ball and Sheridan (2003), gives very similar results (see Appendix 4.1 for details of this analysis). Underlying the analysis is the assumption that some gauge of macroeconomic performance—call it *X*—depends partly on its own past history, and partly on some underlying mean value of the variable in question. In the case of the inflation rate for inflation targeters, this mean should, of course, correspond to the inflation target; for other countries, this would simply be the "normal" level of inflation to which observed inflation reverts.

The results reaffirm the descriptive statistics and the visual impression from the plots: inflation targeting is associated with a significant 4.8 percentage point reduction in average inflation, and a reduction in its standard deviation of 3.6 percentage points *relative* to other strategies (Table 4.3).[19] The standard deviation of output

[19]This finding is at odds with arguments raised by Kumhof (2002); Genberg (2001); and Rich (2000), among others, that inflation targeting is too soft or too discretionary to actually enable central banks to reduce inflation on a durable basis.

Figure 4.2. Inflation and Growth Performance[1]
(1985–2004; percent; average on x-axis)

Over the past 15 years, there is a stronger convergence to low and stable inflation for inflation targeters than non-inflation-targeters. Growth performance is also more homogeneously better for inflation targeters.

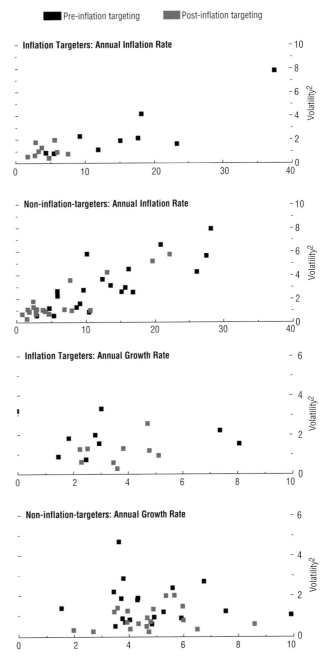

Sources: IMF, *International Financial Statistics;* OECD Analytical Database; and IMF staff calculations.
[1]Period average for emerging market and selected developing countries, with pre-inflation targeting average inflation less than 40 percent.
[2]Rolling one-year standard deviation of inflation.

Table 4.4. Baseline Model Robustness Checks Using Different Classifications

Variables	World Bank Classification by Income		World Bank Classification by Foreign Indebtedness	Emerging Markets	EMBI Classification
	No low-income country	No lower-middle-income country	No severely indebted country		
	IT Dummy Variable				
CPI inflation	−5.025**	−9.406*	−3.820**	−4.972**	−4.653**
Volatility of CPI inflation	−4.138**	−4.209	−1.842	−4.828**	−3.959**
Volatility of real output growth	−0.898	−3.128*	−0.435	−1.235	−0.937
Volatility of output gap	−0.012**	−0.024**	−0.009	−0.014**	−0.012**

Sources: IMF, *International Financial Statistics*; JPMorgan Chase & Co.; national sources; World Bank; and IMF staff calculations.
Note: One, two, and three asterisks denote statistical significance at the 10, 5, and 1 percent level, respectively.

is also slightly lower for the inflation targeters, and the difference from the comparison group of non-inflation-targeters is statistically significant at the 5 percent level. Thus, there is no evidence that inflation targeters meet their inflation objectives at the expense of real output stabilization.[20]

Next, we examined how sensitive the results are to (1) the way the sample was partitioned into "pre" and "post" periods; (2) the exclusion of countries whose inflation was high in the "pre" period; (3) the exclusion of "low-income" countries or of both these and countries that are not "upper-middle-income" according to the World Bank classification by income; (4) the exclusion of the seven non-inflation-targeting countries not included in the JPMorgan EMBI; (5) the exclusion of countries that are severely indebted according to the World Bank classification of country external indebtedness; (6) the exclusion of countries with an exchange rate peg in the "post" period; and finally, (7) different degrees of fiscal discipline among countries.

(Appendix 4.1 describes the controls and the alternative sample partitioning schemes that were used, reporting all the associated results.)

None of these modifications significantly alters the baseline results reported above. As shown in Tables 4.4 and 4.5, inflation targeting continues to be associated with a statistically significant larger reduction in the level and standard deviation of inflation relative to other regimes; and with little or no effect on the volatility of output.[21] The main results of the analysis, therefore, appear to be quite robust, even when the improvement in fiscal performance in the post-inflation-targeting period is accounted for. Interestingly, inflation targeting seems to outperform exchange rate pegs—even when only successful pegs are chosen in comparison.

The result that inflation targeting improves inflation performance more than other regimes is in a sense unsurprising, as the control of inflation is, after all, the central bank's overriding medium-term objective. An interesting question is how performance compares in other dimen-

---

[20]This result suggests that concerns raised by, among others, Friedman (2002); Baltensperger, Fischer, and Jordan (2002); Meyer (2002); Rivlin (2002); and Blanchard (2003), that inflation targeting is too rigid and constrains discretion inappropriately at the expense of the rate or variability of economic growth may be unwarranted, at least for emerging markets.

[21]Inflation targeting advantages relative to other non-inflation-targeting strategies are robust independent of the controls used. However, countries with an initial level of inflation above 40 percent show a relatively smaller reduction in inflation and inflation volatility between the pre- and the post-inflation-targeting-adoption periods. We also find that when severely indebted countries are excluded, inflation targeting still implies statistically significant macroeconomic improvements relative to not having inflation targeting, although the reduction in inflation volatility and output gap volatility is no longer statistically significant.

Table 4.5. Baseline Model Robustness Checks by Date and Control Variables

Variables	Different Dates			Control Variables				
	Starting date: 1990	Actual dates for non-inflation-targeters; starting date = 1985	Time periods 1994–96 vs. 2002–04	Fiscal discipline		Inflation		Exchange rate regime pegs
				Debt/GDP (pre)[1]	Debt/GDP (change)[2,3]	Pre-inflation >40 percent[4]	Pre-inflation >100 percent[5]	
	IT Dummy Variable			IT Dummy/Control Variables				
CPI inflation	−4.818**	−6.519***	−4.520***	−5.254***	−5.910**	−4.411**/10.036**	−4.758**	−5.829**
Volatility of CPI inflation	−3.636**	−4.159***	−2.358**	−3.461**	−4.084**	−3.498**/7.695**	−3.631**	−3.835**
Volatility of real output growth	−0.653	−1.221	−1.030	−0.595	−0.868	−0.649/2.650**	−0.633	−0.751
Volatility of output gap	−0.009**	−0.013**	−0.010*	−0.010**	−0.011**	−0.011**/0.015**	−0.010**	−0.013**

Sources: IMF, *International Financial Statistics*; national sources; and IMF staff calculations.
Note: One, two, and three asterisks denote statistical significance at the 10, 5, and 1 percent level, respectively. Control variables missing when not significant.
[1]Debt in percent of GDP prior to adoption of inflation targeting.
[2]Difference between current and pre-adoption debt in percent of GDP.
[3]The sample does not include Argentina and China because fiscal changes in these countries were many times larger than the average in non-inflation-targeting countries, and were, therefore, biasing the results (showing when included that an improvement in the fiscal stance worsens inflation expectations).
[4]Period average inflation prior to adoption of inflation targeting above 40 percent.
[5]Period average inflation prior to adoption of inflation targeting above 100 percent.

sions that are not directly related to inflation per se, including survey-based inflation expectations, their volatility, nominal exchange rate volatility, foreign reserves volatility, and real interest rate volatility. Finally, inflation-targeting performance was checked with respect to a proxy for the probability of exchange rate crises, using the "exchange market pressure" index based on the seminal work by Girton and Roper (1977) and developed by Eichengreen, Rose, and Wyplosz (1994, 1995).

Using the same statistical framework as before, inflation targeting leads to a reduction in the level and volatility of inflation expectations, along with inflation itself (Table 4.6). This confirms the notion that inflation targeting has an advantage over other regimes at anchoring expectations and building credibility on a more durable basis, even if in emerging markets inflation targets are missed more—and more often— than in industrial countries. In the sample used here, the fiscal position before inflation targeting adoption or the absence of fiscal improvement

after adoption does not seem to affect the ability of inflation targeting to deliver lower or more stable inflation (or inflation expectations) relative to other strategies.[22] Nominal exchange rate volatility is lower, relative to non-inflation-targeters, as is the standard deviation of the real interest rate and the volatility of international reserves.[23] Interestingly, there is evidence at the 5 percent level that inflation targeting is associated with a lower probability of crises, perhaps in part reflecting the greater de jure—if not de facto—flexibility of the exchange rate regime.

The conclusions of this analysis are subject to two important caveats. First, although the success of inflation targeting in emerging markets to date is encouraging, the time elapsed since they adopted inflation targeting is short. This makes it hard to draw definite conclusions about the effects of inflation targeting. Nevertheless, the observed similarities in the behavior of inflation expectations in emerging market and industrial country inflation targeters over a comparable post-inflation-targeting time span bodes

[22]An event study by Celasun, Gelos, and Prati (2004) over time samples predating the adoption of inflation targeting has found that fiscal improvements may have helped lower inflation expectations in some emerging market countries.
[23]Exchange rate volatility in inflation-targeting countries is still lower than in non-inflation-targeting countries even when countries with exchange rate targets are dropped from the non-inflation-targeting control group.

Table 4.6. Baseline Model Robustness Checks: Additional Performance Indicators

Variables	Starting Date 1985	Starting Date 1990	Actual Dates for Non-Inflation-Targeters Starting Date: 1985	Time Periods 1994–96 vs. 2002–04	Fiscal Discipline Debt/GDP (pre)[1]	Fiscal Discipline Debt/GDP (change)[2,3]	Inflation Pre-Inflation >40 percent[4]	Inflation Pre-Inflation >100 percent[5]	Exchange Rate Regime Pegs
	IT Dummy Variable				*IT Dummy/Control Variables*				
5-year π forecast[5]	−2.672**	−2.672**	−3.016**	−2.197	−2.906**	−2.901**	−2.578**	−2.726**	−1.721
Volatility of 5-year π forecast	−2.076**	−2.076**	−1.330**	−1.717**	−1.840*	−1.755**	−1.765**	−2.103**	−1.491**
6–10-year π forecast	−2.185**	−2.185**	−2.558**	−2.184	−2.203*	−2.404*	−2.085**	−2.146*	−1.592*
Volatility of 6–10-year π forecast	−1.737***	−1.737***	−1.232**	−1.596**	−1.350**/ 0.018***	−1.548***	−1.645***	−1.704**	−1.675*
Exchange market pressure index	−0.340**	−0.327*	−0.330	−0.494*	−0.328**	−0.384**	−0.339**	−0.340*	−0.519***/ −0.433*
Exchange rate volatility	−11.090*	−11.107**	−9.303	−3.654	−9.510**	−7.958*	−9.721*	−11.927*	−13.240**
Reserves volatility	−16.333***	−16.384***	−21.945***	−14.770**	−15.458**	−20.886***/ 0.186**	−16.072***	−16.328***	−20.109***
Volatility of real interest rate	−5.025***	−5.025**	−4.695***	−3.020**	−4.985**	−6.186**	−5.129**/ 8.790**	−5.019**	−5.817**

Sources: IMF, *International Financial Statistics;* national sources; and IMF staff calculations.
Note: One, two, and three asterisks denote statistical significance at the 10, 5, and 1 percent level, respectively. Control variables missing when not significant.
[1]Debt in percent of GDP prior to adoption of inflation targeting.
[2]Difference between current and pre-adoption debt in percent of GDP.
[3]The sample does not include Argentina and China because fiscal changes in these countries were many times larger than the average in non-inflation-targeting countries, and were, therefore, biasing the results (showing when included that an improvement in the fiscal stance worsens inflation expectations).
[4]Period average inflation prior to adoption of inflation targeting above 40 percent.
[5]Period average inflation prior to adoption of inflation targeting above 100 percent.
[6]π refers to CPI inflation.

well for what may lie ahead for emerging market inflation targeters (see Box 4.2).

Second, in the absence of a counterfactual, it is difficult to resolve definitively whether inflation targeting is "causal" in generating the observed benefits. In many cases the adoption of inflation targeting coincided with the passage of significant reforms of countries' central banking laws in the early 1990s, which might be interpreted as the manifestation of a shift in preferences toward lower inflation. The fact that these banks *still* felt the need to install a new monetary framework, however, suggests that change of heart is not enough without a framework that allows the central bank to follow through on that intention.

Do "Preconditions" Need to Be Met Before the Adoption of Inflation Targeting?

As noted above, an oft-heard objection to inflation targeting is that it is costly in terms of institutional and technical requirements, making the framework unsuitable for some emerging market economies. The most detailed exposition of this point was made in Eichengreen and others (1999), who argued that technical capabilities and central bank autonomy were severely lacking in most emerging market economies (including several that subsequently adopted inflation targeting).[24] Such countries, the argument goes, would be better off sticking with a "conventional" policy framework, such as an exchange rate peg or money growth

[24]Others who stressed the conceptual relevance of "preconditions" include Agénor (2002); Stone and Zelmer (2000); Carare, Schaechter, and Stone (2002); Khan (2003); and the May 2001 *World Economic Outlook*. More neutral or benign views on the conceptual relevance of "preconditions" can instead be found in Truman (2003); Jonas and Mishkin (2005); Debelle (2001); and Amato and Gerlach (2002).

Box 4.2. Long-Term Inflation Expectations and Credibility

All of the countries that have adopted inflation targeting have had some experience with high inflation, and the move to an inflation targeting regime was seen as an important step to anchor inflation expectations durably once a track record had been established. Indeed, when an inflation targeting regime becomes credible, measures of long-term inflation expectations should become better anchored to the target, and the inflation premium embodied in long-term bond yields should become less sensitive to economic news about near-term inflation developments. So what have been the experiences thus far in inflation-targeting countries, and how do they compare with non-inflation-targeting countries? This box reviews some existing empirical evidence that is based on advanced economies and then extends some of this analysis to a group of emerging market economies.

Recent evidence reported by Levin, Natalucci, and Piger (2004) shows that long-term inflation expectations have become better anchored in inflation-targeting countries that have a well-defined point target for inflation and have established a track record achieving results. Using data on consensus inflation forecasts from Consensus Economics, Levin, Natalucci, and Piger show that long-term inflation expectations (6–10 years in the future) for a group of five inflation-targeting countries (Australia, Canada, New Zealand, Sweden, and the United Kingdom) have become delinked from actual inflation outcomes, while there is evidence that they still respond to actual outcomes in the United States and the euro area.

Similar findings were obtained by Gürkaynak, Sack, and Swanson (2005), who argue there is "excessive" volatility in the forward-yield curve in the United States because the Federal Reserve does not have a numerical objective for inflation to help tie down long-term inflation expectations. In particular, Gürkaynak, Sack, and Swanson show that long-term forward yields in

the United States respond "excessively" to economic news, including surprises in the Federal Reserve's funds rate, which market participants interpret as signals about the Federal Reserve's long-term inflation objectives. To contrast their results with an inflation-targeting country, Gürkaynak, Sack, and Swanson show that such "excess" sensitivity in long-term inflation expectations does not exist in the United Kingdom after the change in their regime in May 1997, which specified a 2.5 percentage point target for inflation and assigned instrument independence to the Bank of England.[1] Indeed, following the changes in the United Kingdom's monetary framework in May 1997, there was a dramatic reduction in long-term inflation expectations (see the figure). The inflation premium on long-term bonds fell in line with the target within a few months and has remained within 1 percentage point of the target ever since. This is in sharp contrast to the period preceding May 1997, when long-term inflation expectations were systematically above both the target range for inflation and actual inflation outcomes.

The experience in the United Kingdom shows how a significant change in fundamentals (central bank instrument independence and a well-defined point target) can have a large and durable effect on anchoring inflation expectations. The experience of other advanced inflation-targeting countries, which had well-defined point targets and central bank independence at the time of announcing their inflation-targeting regimes, shows that long-term inflation expectations were anchored more slowly for the early adopters (Canada, New Zealand, and Sweden) than for the later adopters (Australia, Switzerland, and Norway).

Note: The main authors of this box are Manuela Goretti and Douglas Laxton.

[1]The point target was revised in January 2004 and is now expressed in terms of the Harmonized Index of Consumer Prices (HICP), which has been set at 2.0 percent. The Bank of England reported at the time that this would be consistent with a target of 2.8 percent expressed in terms of the Retail Price Index (RPI), which is the index that is used for indexed bonds.

Box 4.2 *(concluded)*

United Kingdom: Retail Price Index Inflation Expectations 10 Years Ahead[1]
(Percent)

Introduction of new framework, May 1997

Credibility gap

Old target < 2.5

Point target May 97–Dec. 03

New point target Jan. 04

1995   97   99   2001   03   Jun. 2005

Source: Bank of England.
[1]The definition and magnitude of the target changed in January 2004. It is now set at 2.0 percent and is expressed in terms of the year-on-year percent change in the HICP (Harmonized Index of Consumer Price). This is consistent with an estimate of 2.8 percent for the RPI (Retail Price Index), which is the definition used for the indexed bonds.

Standard Deviation of Revisions in Long-Term Inflation Forecasts
(Sample 2003:Q3–2005:Q2)

	Inflation-Targeting	Non-inflation-targeting
All emerging market	0.33	2.19
Eastern Europe	0.38	1.09
Asia	0.27	0.59
Latin America	0.34	4.88

Source: Consensus Economics.

expectations derived from bond markets typically do not exist, we follow Levin, Natalucci, and Piger and turn to data on long-term inflation forecasts (6–10 years ahead) provided by Consensus Economics, which covers 10 inflation-targeting and 9 non-inflation-targeting countries.[2] First, revisions in long-term inflation forecasts (6–10 years) are much smaller in inflation-targeting countries than in non-inflation-targeting countries and this is true if one looks at the sample of countries as a whole or breaks the sample on a regional basis (see the first table). Second, with the exception of Colombia, long-term inflation expectations have fallen within the announced bands for each country since the second quarter of 2002, and they have become more tightly anchored to the midpoints of the target bands or ranges since then.[3] Third, there is no evidence over the past two years that revisions in long-term inflation expectations in the group as a whole have responded to changes in either actual inflation or Levin, Natalucci, and Piger's three-year mov-

There are two potential explanations for this. First, as experience with the regime grows and becomes better understood by the public and bond-market participants, it may take less time to establish a track record and for the inflation target to become a focal point for long-term inflation expectations. Second, it may take less time in cases where a country has already established a reasonable track record in delivering low inflation before it announces an inflation-targeting regime (for example, Switzerland).

What does the evidence say for less advanced countries and how do inflation-targeting countries compare with non-inflation-targeting countries? Since measures of long-term inflation

[2]The inflation-targeting countries covered in the surveys by Consensus Economics are Brazil, Chile, Colombia, Czech Republic, Hungary, Korea, Mexico, Peru, Poland, and Thailand, while the non-inflation-targeting countries are Argentina, China, India, Indonesia, Malaysia, Russia, Turkey, Ukraine, and Venezuela.

[3]Inflation expectations data derived from indexed and conventional bonds suggest that long-term inflation expectations have become more firmly anchored to the target in Colombia than what is suggested by the survey data.

Pooled Regression Estimates of the Effects of Inflation on Revisions in Long-Term Inflation Forecasts
(Sample 2003:Q2–2005:Q2)

	Inflation-Targeting	Non-inflation-targeting
Year-on-year inflation	0.03 (t = 0.89)	0.25 (t = 3.48)
Trend inflation	0.04 (t = 0.55)	0.01 (t = 0.13)

Sources: Consensus Economics, and IMF, *International Financial Statistics.*

Note: Estimation methodology based on Levin, Natalucci, and Piger (2004). Estimates obtained from STATA with robust standard errors.

ing average measure of trend inflation (see the second table). By contrast, for the sample of nine non-inflation-targeting emerging market countries covered by Consensus Economics, the revisions in long-term inflation expectations are significantly and highly correlated with information about recent inflation developments. Indeed, unlike Levin, Natalucci, and Piger's findings for advanced non-inflation-targeting countries, which showed that revisions in long-term inflation expectations depend significantly on a trend measure of inflation, these results suggest that long-term inflation expectations in less-advanced non-inflation-targeting countries are far from being firmly anchored and depend

strongly on revisions in actual headline inflation.[4] While the sample is too short to make claims about individual experiences of these 10 inflation-targeting countries, or to distinguish between point targeters and range targeters, it is interesting that these data for emerging market economies are not inconsistent with the evidence for advanced economies, which suggests that, over time, long-term inflation expectations may become better anchored in inflation-targeting countries than in non-inflation-targeting countries.

[4]The key results are robust when Argentina and Venezuela are removed from the sample of non-inflation-targeting countries. However, in this case revisions in long-term inflation expectations depend significantly on both measures of inflation. In addition, when trend inflation is dropped from the regression for inflation-targeting countries, it remains the case that the parameter estimate is insignificant on actual inflation. As indicated earlier, measures of inflation expectations for Colombia derived from yields on conventional and indexed bonds suggest that long-term inflation expectations have become anchored to the target, while significant differences exist from the estimates derived from the survey data. Eliminating Colombia from the sample of inflation-targeting countries reduces both the magnitude and the significance of the parameters on the inflation variables.

targeting. Such "preconditions" fall into four broad categories.

- *Institutional independence.* The central bank must have full legal autonomy and be free from fiscal and/or political pressure that would create conflicts with the inflation objective.
- *A well-developed technical infrastructure.* Inflation forecasting and modeling capabilities, and the data needed to implement them, must be available at the central bank.
- *Economic structure.* For effective inflation control, prices must be fully deregulated, the economy should not be overly sensitive to

commodity prices and exchange rates, and dollarization should be minimal.
- *A healthy financial system.* To minimize potential conflicts with financial stabilization objectives and guarantee effective monetary policy transmission, the banking system should be sound, and capital markets well developed.

To assess the role of "preconditions" for the adoption of inflation targeting, a special survey was conducted through a questionnaire completed by 21 inflation-targeting central banks, and 10 non-inflation-targeting emerging market central banks.[25] The version of the survey given

[25]These included Botswana, Guatemala, India, Indonesia, Malaysia, Pakistan, Russia, Tanzania, Turkey, and Uruguay.

Table 4.7. Baseline Model Robustness Checks: Preconditions and Current Conditions
(1 = best current practice)

	Inflation Targeters				Non-inflation-targeters Emerging markets	
	Emerging markets		Industrial countries		Pre-adoption of current regime	Current
	Pre-adoption	Current	Pre-adoption	Current		
Technical infrastructure	**0.29**	**0.97**	**0.74**	**0.98**	**0.51**	**0.62**
Data availability	0.63	0.92	0.84	0.94	0.65	0.70
Systematic forecast process	0.10	1.00	1.00	1.00	0.60	0.80
Models capable of conditional forecasts	0.13	1.00	0.38	1.00	0.28	0.35
Financial system health	**0.41**	**0.48**	**0.53**	**0.60**	**0.40**	**0.49**
Bank regulatory capital to risk-weighted assets	0.75	1.00	0.75	1.00	0.71	0.86
Stock market capitalization to GDP	0.16	0.21	0.28	0.44	0.16	0.19
Private bond market capitalization to GDP	0.10	0.07	0.40	0.31	0.29	0.20
Stock market turnover ratio	0.29	0.22	0.28	0.35	0.37	0.45
Currency mismatch	0.92	0.96	1.00	1.00	0.67	0.97
Maturity of bonds	0.23	0.43	0.46	0.52	0.18	0.29
Institutional independence	**0.59**	**0.72**	**0.56**	**0.78**	**0.49**	**0.64**
Fiscal obligation	0.77	1.00	0.75	1.00	0.50	0.70
Operational independence	0.81	0.96	0.63	1.00	0.70	1.00
Central bank legal mandate	0.50	0.62	0.16	0.44	0.40	0.55
Governor's job security	0.85	0.85	1.00	1.00	0.80	0.80
Fiscal balance in percent of GDP	0.48	0.47	0.45	0.78	0.38	0.42
Public debt in percent of GDP	0.47	0.47	0.53	0.54	0.35	0.46
Central bank independence	0.26	0.64	0.44	0.72	0.32	0.55
Economic structure	**0.36**	**0.46**	**0.47**	**0.55**	**0.55**	**0.44**
Exchange rate pass-through	0.23	0.44	0.31	0.50	0.33	0.42
Sensitivity to commodity prices	0.35	0.42	0.44	0.56	0.67	0.55
Extent of dollarization	0.69	0.75	1.00	1.00	0.63	0.60
Trade openness	0.18	0.21	0.13	0.16	0.56	0.19

Sources: Arnone and others (2005); IMF, *Global Financial Stability Report;* IMF, *International Financial Statistics;* national sources; OECD; Ramón-Ballester and Wezel (2004); World Bank, Financial Structure and Economic Development Database; and IMF staff calculations.

to inflation-targeting central banks focused particularly on how policy was formulated, implemented, and communicated—and how various aspects of central banking practice had changed both during and prior to the adoption of inflation targeting.[26] Survey responses were cross-checked with independent primary and secondary sources, and in many cases augmented with "hard" economic data (see Appendix 4.1).

Overall, the evidence indicates that no inflation targeter had all these "preconditions" in

place prior to the adoption of inflation targeting, although—unsurprisingly—industrial economy inflation targeters were generally in better shape than emerging market inflation targeters at least in some dimension (Table 4.7).

- *Institutional independence.* Most of the central banks enjoyed at least de jure instrument independence at the time of inflation-targeting adoption.[27] However, survey responses—corroborated by consulting the relevant central bank laws—indicate that only one-fifth[28] of the

[26]The version for non-inflation-targeters was similar in all respects, but focused on change before and after the current monetary regime.

[27]Instrument independence, which allows the central bank full control over the setting of the policy instrument, is by far the more important criterion of central bank independence. Goal independence, or the ability of the central bank to set macroeconomic objectives unilaterally, is rare, even among industrial country central banks, where these goals are typically determined by the elected government or through consultation between the central bank and the government. See Debelle and Fischer (1994).

[28]This overall picture is borne out by broader measures of central bank independence, notably by indices prepared by Arnone and others (2005), based in turn on the methods of Grilli, Masciandaro, and Tabellini (1991).

emerging market inflation targeters contemporaneously satisfied other key indicators[29] of independence at adoption, and thus can be characterized as having adopted inflation targeting under a very high degree of legal autonomy.[30] Of course, it is possible that even legal provisions designed to shield the central bank from pressures to monetize might be overwhelmed by a dire fiscal imbalance. Data suggest that inflation targeters faced a wide variety of fiscal conditions at the time of inflation targeting adoption. Israel and the Philippines, for example, had high ratios of public debt to GDP and large fiscal deficits, while Chile was in good fiscal shape. The emerging market inflation targeters did, however, tend to have somewhat higher public debt levels than the industrial country inflation targeters.

- *Technical infrastructure.* Central bank survey responses indicate that the majority of industrial country and emerging market inflation targeters started with little or no forecasting capability and no forecasting model at all; and when a small model was available, most central banks report that it was not suitable to make forecasts conditional on different assumptions for the monetary policy instrument.[31] In addition, although industrial country inflation targeters often had some sort of systematic forecast process in place, most emerging market inflation targeters did not. Likewise, data availability at the time of adoption of inflation targeting was not ideal, with emerging market inflation targeters again at a disadvantage on

data availability relative to industrial country inflation targeters.

- *Economic structure.* Results from the survey indicate that none of the inflation targeters enjoyed ideal economic conditions at the time of adoption. Countries were all sensitive to changes in exchange rates and commodity prices when they adopted inflation targeting, and although dollarization was not an issue for industrial inflation targeters, the evidence on dollarization from the survey and data collected in Ramón-Ballester and Wezel (2004) indicates different degrees of dollarization across emerging market inflation targeters—Peru ranking as the most dollarized inflation targeter.[32] Last but not least, the survey indicates that the consumer price index in a number of inflation-targeting countries included at the time of adoption (and in most case still includes) a significant share of administered prices.

- *Healthy financial and banking system.* At adoption, most inflation targeters scored relatively poorly in this area, looking at indicators such as the risk-weighted capital adequacy ratio, measures of financial market depth (ratio of stock market capitalization to GDP, ratio of private bond issuance to GDP, stock market turnover, and the maximum maturity of actively traded nominal bonds, either government or corporate), and the extent of banks' foreign currency open positions.

The fact that none of today's inflation targeters—either individually or on average—had strong "preconditions" suggests that the

[29]These include (1) freedom from any obligation of the central bank to purchase government debt, thus preventing monetization; (2) a high degree of job security for the central bank governor (specifically, a fixed term and provisions that allow him or her to be fired only with cause); (3) whether the central bank operates under an "inflation-focused" mandate in which inflation (price stability) is the sole stated objective; or, if other objectives are specified, the inflation goal takes precedence.

[30]It is also worth noting that legal autonomy was sometimes granted concurrently—or, in one case, after—the adoption of inflation targeting. Many of the central banks in our sample achieved greater independence in the early 1990s (see Jácome, 2001, for a survey of developments in Latin America). Korea and Hungary, on the other hand, became fully independent just as inflation targeting was being adopted, suggesting a recognition of the close connection between the two. The Central Bank of Thailand, which adopted inflation targeting in 2000, continues to operate under a charter from 1942 that says almost nothing on issues of monetary autonomy—although a new central bank law is reportedly under consideration by the Thai parliament.

[31]The exceptions are Canada, Sweden, and the United Kingdom among industrial countries, and Poland and South Africa among emerging markets.

[32]These data are broadly in line with those by Reinhart, Rogoff, and Savastano (2003).

Figure 4.3. Initial Conditions Prior to Adopting Inflation Targeting

(0 = poor; 1 = ideal; for each of the four categories of initial conditions)

Most of the inflation targeters had poor initial conditions prior to the adoption of inflation targeting.

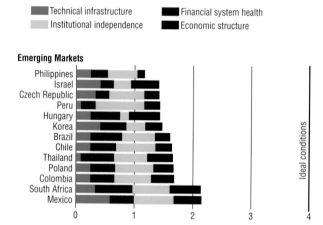

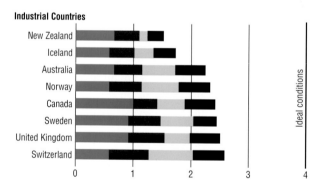

Source: IMF staff calculations.

absence of these "preconditions" is not by itself an impediment to the adoption and success of inflation targeting (Figure 4.3). This is confirmed by more formal econometric tests. Using the "preconditions" listed in Table 4.7 as additional control variables in the regressions of the previous section, we find that no "precondition" enters significantly in the equations explaining the improvement in macroeconomic performance after inflation targeting adoption.

Two other messages emerge from Table 4.7.

- First, in terms of institutional, technical, and economic characteristics, the gap between inflation targeters (at the time of adoption) and potential emerging market inflation-targeting adopters (today) is relatively small, suggesting that these factors should not stand in the way of the successful adoption of inflation targeting in these countries. It is, however, not possible to infer from this analysis whether this is equally true for other countries that may have worse initial conditions than those documented here.

- Second, available evidence and survey responses indicate that the adoption of inflation targeting has been associated with rapid improvements in institutional and technical structures including, for example, developments in data availability and forecasting. Thus, even if meeting institutional and technical standards may not be critical before the adoption of inflation targeting, a proactive approach to making improvements by the central bank and other parts of government after the adoption of inflation targeting may be essential to ensure the conditions needed for the success of inflation targeting after adoption.

Conclusions

Inflation targeting is a relatively new monetary policy framework for emerging market countries. This chapter has made a first effort at assessing the impact of inflation targeting in emerging markets, and while the short time that has elapsed since the adoption of these frameworks certainly means that any assessment must be preliminary, the evidence from the initial years of operation is encouraging. Inflation targeting appears to have been associated with lower inflation, lower inflation expectations, and lower inflation volatility relative to countries that have not adopted it. There have been no visible adverse effects on output, and performance along other dimensions—such as the volatility of interest rates, exchange rates, and international reserves—has also been favorable. All this may explain the appeal of this strategy for emerging markets, where poor past inflation records make it more difficult to build credibility and where keeping to a minimum the output costs of reducing inflation is imperative for social and political reasons. It also may explain why no country has yet abandoned inflation targeting.

Further, while there needs to be a clear agreement between the central bank and the government on the importance of price stability as the overriding objective of monetary policy, it does not appear to be necessary for emerging market countries to meet a stringent set of institutional, technical, and economic "preconditions" for the successful adoption of inflation targeting. Instead, the feasibility and success of inflation targeting appear to depend more on the authorities' commitment and ability to plan and drive institutional change after the introduction of inflation targeting. Consequently, policy advice to countries that are interested in adopting inflation targeting could usefully focus on the institutional and technical goals that central banks should strive for during and after the adoption of inflation targeting to maximize its potential benefits.

Appendix 4.1. Details on Econometric Specifications and on Data from the Survey on Preconditions and Current Conditions

The main authors of this appendix are Nicoletta Batini and Kenneth Kuttner, with support from Manuela Goretti.

This appendix provides details on the baseline and alternative econometric specifications dis-

cussed in the main text measuring the relative macroeconomic performance of inflation targeters versus non-inflation-targeters. The appendix also gives details on data used in the empirical analysis of the main text, including data from the survey.

Econometric Specifications

In line with Ball and Sheridan (2003), macroeconomic performance is considered to depend partly on its own past history, and partly on some underlying mean value of the variable in question. In the case of the inflation rate for inflation targeters, this mean should, of course, correspond to the inflation target; for other countries, this would simply be the "normal" level of inflation to which observed inflation reverts. Mathematically, this process can be expressed as follows:

$$X_{i,t} = \phi[\alpha^T d_{i,t} + \alpha^N (1 - d_{i,t})] + (1 - \phi) X_{i,t-1}, \quad (1)$$

where $X_{i,t}$ is the value of a macroeconomic performance indicator X for country i at time t, α^T is the mean to which X reverts for inflation targeters, α^N is the mean to which X reverts for *non-*inflation-targeters, and $d_{i,t}$ is a variable equal to 1 for inflation targeters and 0 for non-inflation-targeters. The parameter ϕ represents the speed with which X reverts to its group-specific α: a value of ϕ equal to 1 means X reverts completely after one period, while a value of ϕ equal to 0 would imply that X depends only on its past history, with no tendency to revert to any particular value.

The regression used by Ball and Sheridan (2003), and in the results reported in Tables 4.3–4.6, is simply a version of equation (1), rewritten in terms of the change in X, appending an error term e, and assuming there are two periods: "pre" and "post":

$$X_{i,\text{post}} - X_{i,\text{pre}} = \phi\alpha^T d_i + \phi\alpha^N (1 - d_i) - \phi X_{i,\text{pre}} + e_i, \quad (2)$$

or, letting

$$a_0 = \phi\alpha^N, \ a_1 = \phi(\alpha^T - \alpha^N), \text{ and } b = -\phi,$$
$$X_{i,\text{post}} - X_{i,\text{pre}} = a_0 + a_1 d_i + b X_{i,\text{pre}} + e_i. \quad (3)$$

As discussed in the main text, the "pre" period for inflation targeters is defined as 1985 until the quarter prior to the adoption of inflation targeting, while the "post" period runs from inflation targeting adoption through 2004. The break date for non-inflation-targeters is taken to be 1999:Q4, which corresponds to the mean adoption date for emerging market inflation targeters.

In this framework, the relevant parameter for gauging inflation targeting's economic impact is a_1, the coefficient on the inflation targeting dummy variable, and this is what is reported in Tables 4.3–4.6 (a_0 instead captures whether there has been a generalized improvement in macroeconomic performance across countries independently of differences in monetary regimes). Take, for example, the row on CPI inflation in Table 4.3, showing estimates of Equation (3) when X = CPI inflation. There, $a_1 = -4.8$, implying that in countries that have adopted inflation targeting, the reduction in CPI inflation has been on average 4.8 percentage points greater than in countries that have not adopted inflation targeting. Note that if ϕ were known to be zero (i.e., complete mean reversion), the estimated a_1 would be nothing more than the difference in average $X_{post} - X_{pre}$ for inflation targeters versus non-inflation-targeters; the only advantage of the regression method is to be able to control for the initial level of X_{pre}. Furthermore, by focusing on relatively long periods of time, the analysis is largely a comparison of steady states, saying nothing about what happens during the transition to inflation targeting (or any other) policy framework; to do so would obviously require a very careful control of cyclical conditions to distinguish transition effects from the normal trajectory of the business cycle.

The baseline results obtained from estimating Equation (3) on the full sample of 35 emerging market economies of the JPMorgan EMBI Index plus the Czech Republic and Israel (which are inflation targeters, but not part of the index) plus seven countries that are most often classified as emerging markets appear in Table 4.3. Included in the set of X variables are the same gauges of core macroeconomic performance

that appeared in the descriptive tables: CPI inflation, inflation volatility, and the volatility of real GDP growth, and the output gap.

Robustness Checks

One issue that arises in the context of the baseline analysis described above is that the partitioning of the sample into "pre" and "post" periods is somewhat arbitrary—both in determining the starting date for the calculation of the "pre" period averages, and in the assigning of 1999:Q4 as the hypothetical break date for the non-inflation-targeters. In an effort to assess any distortion created by the arbitrariness of the partitioning, the regression Equation (3) was reestimated using two alternative sample partitioning schemes. The first is to start the "pre" period in 1990 rather than 1985, thus largely removing any effects of the Latin American debt crisis from the sample. The second is to change the break date for non-inflation-targeters from 1999:Q4 to the date of the most recent de facto change in monetary policy framework (based on IMF staff calculations and the IMF's *Annual Report on Exchange Arrangements and Exchange Restrictions*). Under these schemes and the baseline partitioning, however, the "pre" and "post" samples vary across countries; therefore, to eliminate any possibility that simple time effects could account for the results, a third alternative partitioning was tried, using a standardized 1994–96 "pre" period, and a standardized 2002–04 "post" period.

A number of additional checks were also performed to ensure that the results are robust to sample selection and to the inclusion of other potentially important factors affecting macroeconomic outcomes. First, to guard against the possibility that a handful of extreme inflation observations might be exerting undue influence on the regression, a control was included for countries whose inflation rate exceeded 40 percent in the "pre" period; a threshold of 100 percent was also tried. Second, Equation (3) was reestimated over a smaller sample, excluding countries defined as "low-income" by the World Bank and also over a sample that excluded the seven countries in our control group not listed in the JPMorgan EMBI. Third, on the full sample a control was included for countries that are severely indebted externally, in line with the World Bank classification of countries' external indebtedness. Fourth, on the full sample a control for countries with an exchange rate peg during the "post" period was used. And finally, again on the full sample, controls were included for the ratio of public debt to GDP in the "pre" period, and the change between "post" and "pre" periods to rule out the possibility that the observed gains in macroeconomic performance are ascribable not to the introduction of inflation targeting but, rather, to improvements in fiscal discipline. Results for these two sets of robustness checks are reported in Tables 4.5 and 4.6.

The significance, sign, and magnitude of additional controls are reported after the slash next to each estimate of the a_1 coefficient (when nothing is reported it means that the control was not significant). Take, for example, the fifth column of Table 4.6, where the significance of a precondition on the debt-to-GDP ratio is examined. Results indicate that the control is only significant for the volatility of 6–10-year inflation expectations, suggesting that having a "bad" debt-to-GDP ratio before the adoption of inflation targeting would entail a 0.018 percentage point smaller reduction in the volatility of inflation expectations usually associated with inflation targeting relative to non-inflation-targeting.

Variable Descriptions and Data Sources

Unless otherwise noted, all data run from 1985:Q1 through 2004:Q4.

- *Inflation rate:* calculated as the annual growth rate of the consumer price index. Quarterly data were obtained from the IMF, *International Financial Statistics,* and from the OECD.
- *Output growth rate:* annual growth rate of real GDP in local currency. Quarterly data were obtained from the IMF, *International Financial Statistics* and *World Economic Outlook*; and from the OECD.

- *Output gap:* calculated as the residual from a regression of the logarithm of real GDP on a constant term, a linear trend, and a quadratic trend.
- *Nominal short-term interest rate:* Three-month money market interest rate or deposit rate. Quarterly data were obtained from the IMF, *International Financial Statistics* and *World Economic Outlook*; and from the OECD.
- *Foreign exchange rate:* local currency per U.S. dollar. Quarterly data were obtained from the IMF, *International Financial Statistics.*
- *International reserves minus gold:* in U.S. dollars. Quarterly data were obtained from the IMF, *International Financial Statistics.*
- *Broad money:* in local currency, broadest definition available. Quarterly data were obtained from the IMF, *International Financial Statistics* and *World Economic Outlook.*
- *Inflation expectations:* survey data obtained from Consensus Economics, Inc. Availability varies by country.

Indicators of Preconditions and Current Conditions

Central Bank Infrastructure

These three survey-based indicators are intended to measure central banks' data resources, modeling and forecasting capabilities. For the regression analysis, an index of central bank infrastructure was created as the simple average of these three measures.

- *Data availability.* Survey questions No. 78 and No. 84 asked whether all essential macroeconomic data were available at the time of inflation targeting adoption. Answers were coded as 1 if all data were available, reliable, and of good quality, and as 0 if any data were missing. A value of 0.25 was assigned if all data were available but most were either highly unreliable because, for example, they were typically subject to large revisions or only available at low frequencies; similarly, if data were all available, but one or few were not reliable or of good quality, a value of 0.75 was assigned.

- *Systematic forecast process.* Survey questions No. 47 through No. 52 asked about the forecasting capabilities in place at the time of adoption. From the responses to these questions, a variable was created and set to 1 if a periodic, systematic forecast process was already in place; the variable was set to 0 if no such process was in place.
- *Models capable of conditional forecasts.* From the same set of questions as for the previous indicator (No. 47 through No. 52), a variable was created and set to 1 if forecasting models capable of generating conditional forecasts were available; the variable was set to 0 if no such models were available.

Health of the Financial System

The following six indicators measure the degree of development and degree of soundness of the banking and financial system. Two are taken from the survey responses, and four are based on nonsurvey data sources. For the regression analysis, an index of banking and financial conditions was created as the simple average of these six measures. In most cases, the health of the United Kingdom's financial system was taken as the benchmark in the construction of components of the index itself, on the grounds that the United Kingdom is widely considered to be financially developed and sound from a financial regulatory point of view.

- *Percentage of banks' risk-weighted assets.* Using data compiled and reported in a previous IMF study,[33] a variable was created and set to 1 for countries in which the banking system, in aggregate, had regulatory capital in excess of 10 percent of risk-weighted assets; the variable was set to 0 for countries not meeting this standard.
- *Stock market capitalization.* Using data from the World Bank, the ratio of stock market capitalization to GDP was calculated for each country in the sample, and scaled to the ratio for the

United Kingdom so that a value of 1 indicates a degree of stock market capitalization comparable to that of the United Kingdom.[34]

- *Depth of private bond market.* Using the same World Bank data, the ratio of privately issued bonds outstanding to GDP was calculated for each country in the sample, and scaled to the ratio for the United Kingdom, so that a value of 1 indicates a degree of private bond market depth comparable to that of the United Kingdom.
- *Stock market turnover.* Using the same World Bank data, the ratio of stock market turnover to GDP was calculated for each country in the sample, and scaled to the ratio for the United Kingdom, so that a value of 1 indicates a transaction volume comparable to that of the United Kingdom.
- *Lack of currency mismatch.* Survey question No. 106 asked central banks to characterize the degree of currency mismatch faced by domestically owned banks. From the responses to this question, a variable equal to 1 was created if the degree of mismatch was described as "none" or "low." The variable was set equal to 0.5 if "some" or "moderate" mismatch was reported, and set to 0 of the degree of reported mismatch was "high."
- *Maturity of bonds.* Survey question No. 114 asked central banks to report the maximum maturity of actively traded bonds. The response to this question was converted to years and divided by 30, so that countries with actively traded 30-year bonds were assigned a value of 1 for this variable.

Institutional Independence

The following six indicators are intended to gauge the degree to which the central bank is able to pursue its monetary policy objectives free from conflict with other, competing objectives. Three are based on the responses to the survey administered to the central banks in our sample

---

[33]IMF (2005).

[34]The underlying data were obtained from the World Bank Financial Structure and Economic Database; available via the Internet: http://www.worldbank.org/research/projects/finstructure/database.htm.

(checked for consistency against other central bank sources), and three are derived from independent data sources. For the regression analysis, an index of institutional autonomy was created as the simple average of these six measures.

- *Absence of fiscal obligation.* Survey questions No. 3 and No. 7 asked central banks whether there was an obligation, either implicit or explicit, to finance government budget deficits. From the responses, a variable was created and set equal to 1 if no such obligation existed, and 0 otherwise.

- *Operational independence.* Survey questions No. 4 and No. 7 asked whether the central bank had full "instrument independence," giving it sole responsibility for setting the monetary policy instrument. A variable was created and set to 1 for those countries reporting full instrument independence, and 0 otherwise.

- *Inflation-focused mandate.* Survey questions No. 14 and No. 18 asked central banks to describe their legal mandate. From these responses, a variable was created and set to 1 if inflation is the only formal objective; to 0.5 if other objectives are specified, but inflation takes precedence; and to 0 if other objectives are specified on an equal footing with inflation.

- *Favorable fiscal balance.* Using primary fiscal balance data from the IMF and the OECD, a variable was created indicating a lack of pressure to finance fiscal deficits. For each country in the sample, the ratio of the primary fiscal balance to GDP was calculated, and averaged over the two years prior to the adoption of inflation targeting. (For non-inflation-targeters, the most recent two years were used.) This ratio was converted to a score ranging from 0 to 1 using a logistic transformation, scaled in such a way that a budget that was in balance or in surplus was assigned a value of 1, and a budget deficit in excess of 3 percent of GDP was assigned a value of 0.[35]

- *Low public debt.* Using data from the OECD and the IMF's Fiscal Affairs Department/World Economic Outlook public debt database, the ratio of public debt to GDP was calculated for the year prior to the adoption of inflation targeting. (For non-inflation-targeters, the most recent available observation was used.) From this, a variable was created equal to the greater of the following two measures: 1 or 1 minus the ratio of debt to GDP. Thus, a country with no public debt would receive a value of 1, and one with a ratio of debt to GDP equal to or greater than 100 would receive a value of 0.

- *Central bank independence.* This variable is the "overall" measure (the average of political and economic) of central bank independence reported by Arnone and others (2005). These data are available for two periods, 1991–92 and 2003, and are scaled so that a value of 1 indicates complete independence while values closer to 0 indicate a diminishing degree of independence.

Economic Structure

The final set of four indicators, which draw on the survey results and independent data sources, are intended to capture a variety of economic conditions that are often thought to affect the likelihood of success of inflation targeting. For the regression analysis, an index of economic conditions was created as the simple average of these four measures.

- *Low exchange rate pass-through.* Survey question No. 96 asked central banks to characterize the degree of exchange rate pass-through. In constructing this variable, the responses were coded as follows: 1 for "low or no pass-through," 0.5 for "moderate pass-through," and 0 for "high pass-through."

- *Low sensitivity to commodity prices.* Survey question No. 97 asked central banks to characterize the degree of sensitivity of inflation to

---

[35]The transformation used is $\exp[2 \times (\text{balance} + 1.5)]/\{1 + \exp[2 \times (\text{balance} + 1.5)]\}$, where "balance" is the fiscal balance, expressed as a percentage of GDP.

commodity price fluctuations. In constructing this variable, the responses were coded as follows: 1 for "not sensitive," 0.5 for "sensitive," and 0 for "very sensitive."

Extent of dollarization. Survey question No. 98 asked central banks to characterize the degree of dollarization in their economies. Using these responses, and data from Ramón-Ballester and Wezel (2004), a variable was constructed whose value was set to 1 for countries with little or no dollarization, to 0.5 for countries with some dollarization, and to 0 for those with a high degree of dollarization.

Extent of trade openness. Using data from the IMF (*International Financial Statistics* and *World Economic Outlook*) and the OECD, the ratio of exports plus imports to GDP was calculated. This ratio was then scaled to that of Singapore (the economy with the largest trade share relative to GDP) and subtracted from 1, resulting in an index that would equal 1 in the hypothetical case of a completely autarkic economy, and equal 0 for an economy with a degree of trade openness comparable to that of Singapore. Inflation targeters' preconditions are calculated using an average of the trade-to-GDP ratio over the two years prior to inflation targeting adoption; for non-inflation-targeters, the score is based on the most recent (2004) data.

References

Agénor, Pierre-Richard, 2002, "Monetary Policy Under Flexible Exchange Rates: An Introduction to Inflation Targeting," in *Inflation Targeting: Design, Performance, Challenges,* ed. by Norman Loayza and Raimundo Soto (Santiago: Central Bank of Chile).

Amato, Jeffrey D., and Stefan Gerlach, 2002, "Inflation Targeting in Emerging Market and Transition Economies: Lessons After a Decade," *European Economic Review,* Vol. 46 (May), pp. 781–90.

Arnone, Marco, and others, 2005, "New Measures of Central Bank Independence," IMF Working Paper (Washington: International Monetary Fund, forthcoming).

Ball, Laurence, and Niamh Sheridan, 2003, "Does Inflation Targeting Matter?" IMF Working Paper 03/129 (Washington: International Monetary Fund).

Also forthcoming in *Inflation Targeting: Theory and Practice,* ed. by Ben S. Bernanke and Michael Woodford (Chicago: University of Chicago Press).

Baltensperger, Ernst, Andreas M. Fischer, and Thomas J. Jordan, 2002, "Abstaining from Inflation Targets: Understanding the Importance of Strong Goal Independence" (unpublished; Berne: Swiss National Bank, October).

Batini, Nicoletta, 2004, "Achieving and Maintaining Price Stability in Nigeria," IMF Working Paper 04/97 (Washington: International Monetary Fund).

———, and Edward Nelson, 2001, "Optimal Horizons for Inflation Targeting," *Journal of Economic Dynamics and Control,* Vol. 25 (June), pp. 891–910.

———, 2005, "The U.K.'s Rocky Road to Stability," Federal Reserve Bank of St. Louis Working Paper No. 2005–020A (St. Louis, Missouri: Federal Reserve Bank of St. Louis).

Batini, Nicoletta, and Anthony Yates, 2003, "Hybrid Inflation and Price-Level Targeting," *Journal of Money, Credit and Banking,* Vol. 35 (June), pp. 283–300.

Bernanke, Ben S., 2003, "A Perspective on Inflation Targeting," remarks at the Annual Washington Policy Conference of the National Association of Business Economists, March 25.

———, and others, 1999, *Inflation Targeting: Lessons From the International Experience* (Princeton, New Jersey: Princeton University Press).

Bernanke, Ben S., and Michael Woodford, 2004, eds., *The Inflation-Targeting Debate,* NBER Studies in Business Cycles, Vol. 32 (Chicago: University of Chicago Press).

Blanchard, Olivier, 2003, "Comment on *Inflation Targeting in Transition Economies: Experience and Prospects,* by Jiri Jonas and Frederic Mishkin," paper prepared for the NBER Conference on Inflation Targeting, Bal Harbour, Florida, January 23–25.

Brook, Anne-Marie, Özer Karagedikli, and Dean Scrimgeour, 2002, "An Optimal Inflation Target for New Zealand: Lessons from the Literature," *Reserve Bank of New Zealand Bulletin,* Vol. 65, No. 3.

Burdekin, Richard C.K., and Pierre L. Siklos, 2004, "Fears of Deflation and Policy Responses Then and Now," in *Deflation: Current and Historical Perspectives,* ed. by Richard C.K. Burdekin and Pierre L. Siklos (Cambridge: Cambridge University Press).

Carare, Alina, Andrea Schaechter, and Mark Stone, 2002, "Establishing Initial Conditions in Support of Inflation Targeting," IMF Working Paper 02/102 (Washington: International Monetary Fund).

Celasun, Oya, R. Gaston Gelos, and Alessandro Prati, 2004, "Obstacles to Disinflation: What Is the Role of Fiscal Expectations?" *Economic Policy: A European Forum* (October), pp. 441–81.

Debelle, Guy, 2001, "The Case for Inflation Targeting in East Asian Countries," in *Future Directions for Monetary Policies in East Asia*, ed. by David Gruen and John Simon (Sydney: Reserve Bank of Australia).

———, and Stanley Fischer, 1994, " How Independent Should a Central Bank Be?" in *Goals, Guidelines, and Constraints Facing Monetary Policymakers*, ed. by Jeffrey C. Fuhrer (Boston: Federal Reserve Bank of Boston).

Eichengreen, Barry, and others, 1999, *Transition Strategies and Nominal Anchors on the Road to Greater Exchange-Rate Flexibility*," Essays in International Finance, No. 213 (Princeton, New Jersey: International Finance Section, Department of Economics, Princeton University).

Eichengreen, Barry, Andrew K. Rose, and Charles Wyplosz, 1994, "Speculative Attacks on Pegged Exchange Rates: An Empirical Exploration with Special Reference to the European Monetary System," in *The New Transatlantic Economy*, ed. by Matthew Canzoneri, Paul Masson, and Vittorio Grilli (Cambridge: Cambridge University Press).

———, 1995, "Exchange Market Mayhem: The Antecedents and Aftermath of Speculative Attacks," *Economic Policy*, Vol. 10 (October), pp. 249–312.

European Central Bank, 1999, *European Central Bank Monthly Bulletin* (January) (Frankfurt).

———, 2003, "Overview of the Background Studies for the Reflections on the ECB's Monetary Policy Strategy" (Frankfurt).

Fischer, Stanley, 2001, "Exchange Rate Regimes: Is the Bipolar View Correct?" in *Finance and Development*, Vol. 38 (June).

Flood, Robert, and Nancy Marion, 1999, "Perspectives on the Recent Currency Crisis Literature," *International Journal of Finance and Economics*, Vol. 4 (January), pp. 1–26.

Friedman, Benjamin, 2002, "The Use and Meaning of Words in Central Banking: Inflation Targeting, Credibility, and Transparency," NBER Working Paper No. 8972 (Cambridge, Massachusetts: National Bureau of Economic Research).

Genberg, Hans, 2001, "Asset Prices, Monetary Policy, and Macroeconomic Stability," *De Economist (Netherlands)*, Vol. 149 (December), pp. 433–53.

Girton, Lance, and Don Roper, 1977, "A Monetary Model of Exchange Market Pressure Applied to Postwar Canadian Experience," *American Economic Review*, Vol. 67 (September), pp. 537–48.

Goodhart, Charles, 1989, "Conduct of Monetary Policy," *Economic Journal*, Vol. 99 (June), pp. 293–346.

Gramlich, Edward M., 2003, "Maintaining Price Stability," remarks by Governor Edward M. Gramlich at the Economic Club of Toronto, Toronto, October 1.

Grilli, Victorio, Donato Masciandaro, and Guido Tabellini, 1991, "Political and Monetary Institutions and Public Financial Policies in the Industrial Countries," *Economic Policy*, Vol. 6 (October), pp. 341–92.

Gürkaynak, Refet, Brian Sack, and Eric Swanson, 2005, "The Sensitivity of Long-Term Interest Rates to Economic News: Evidence and Implications for Macroeconomic Models," *American Economic Review*, Vol. 95 (March), pp. 425–36.

Heise, Michael, 2003, "The Seductive Charm of Inflation Targets," *Financial Times* (July 1).

Hume, David, 1752, "Of Money," reprinted in *Essays: Moral, Political and Literary*, 1758, p. 281.

Hyvonen, Markus, 2004, "Inflation Convergence Across Countries," Research Discussion Paper No. 2004–04 (June) (Sydney, Australia: Economic Research Department, Reserve Bank of Australia).

International Monetary Fund, 2005, "Table 22: Bank Regulatory Capital to Risk-Weighted Assets," *Global Financial Stability Report* (Washington, April).

Issing, Otmar, 2000, "Europe's Challenges After the Establishment of Monetary Union: A Central Banker's View," speech at CESifo Conference on the Issues of Monetary Integration in Europe, Munich, December 1–2.

Jácome, H. Luis Ignacio, 2001, "Legal Central Bank Independence and Inflation in Latin America During the 1990s," IMF Working Paper 01/212 (Washington: International Monetary Fund).

Jonas, Jiri, and Frederick S. Mishkin, 2005, "Inflation Targeting in Transition Countries: Experience and Prospects," in *The Inflation-Targeting Debate*, ed. by Ben S. Bernanke and Michael Woodford, Studies in Business Cycles, No. 32, Part III (Chicago: University of Chicago Press).

Khan, Mohsin, 2003, "Current Issues in the Design and Conduct of Monetary Policy," IMF Working Paper 03/56 (Washington: International Monetary Fund).

King, Mervyn, 2005, "Monetary Policy: Practice Ahead of Theory," Mais Lecture 2005, Cass Business School, City University, London, May 17.

Kohn, Donald, 2003, "Inflation Targeting: Prospects and Problems," panel discussion at the Federal Reserve Bank of St. Louis, St. Louis, Missouri, October 17.

Kumhof, Michael, 2002, "A Critical View of Inflation Targeting: Crises, Limited Sustainability, and Aggregate Shocks," in *Inflation Targeting: Design, Performance, Challenges*, ed. by Norman Loayza and Raimundo Soto (Santiago: Central Bank of Chile).

Leiderman, Leonardo, and Lars E.O. Svensson, eds., 1995, *Inflation Targets* (London: Centre for Economic Policy Research).

Levin, Andrew, Fabio Natalucci, and Jeremy Piger, 2004, "The Macroeconomic Effects of Inflation Targeting," *Federal Reserve Bank of St. Louis Review*, Vol. 86, No. 4, pp. 51–80.

Meyer, Laurence H., 2002, "Inflation Targets and Inflation Targeting," *North American Journal of Economics and Finance*, Vol. 13 (August), pp. 147–62.

Mishkin, Frederick S., 1999, "International Experiences With Different Monetary Policy Regimes," *Journal of Monetary Economics*, Vol. 43 (June), pp. 579–606.

———, and Klaus Schmidt-Hebbel, 2001, "One Decade of Inflation Targeting in the World: What Do We Know and What Do We Need to Know?" Central Bank of Chile Working Papers No. 101 (July).

Obstfeld, Maurice, and Kenneth Rogoff, 1995, "The Mirage of Fixed Exchange Rates," *Journal of Economic Perspectives*, Vol. 9 (Autumn), pp. 73–96.

Pianalto, Sandra, 2005, "The Power of Price Stability" (Cleveland: Federal Reserve Bank of Cleveland, Research Department, May).

Ramón-Ballester, Francisco, and Torsten Wezel, 2004, "International Financial Linkages of Latin American Banks: The Effects of Political Risk and Deposit Dollarization," paper presented at the preparatory workshop for the Second High Level Seminar of the Eurosystem and Latin American Central Banks, Lisbon, October.

Reinhart, Carmen, Kenneth Rogoff, and Miguel Savastano, 2003, "Addicted to Dollars," NBER Working Paper No. 10015 (Cambridge, Massachusetts: National Bureau of Economic Research).

Rich, George, 2000, "Monetary Policy Without Central Bank Money: A Swiss Perspective," *International Finance*, Vol. 3 (November), pp. 439–69.

———, 2001, "Inflation and Money Stock Targets: Is There Really a Difference?" revised version of paper presented at the International Conference on the Conduct of Monetary Policy, Taipei, Taiwan, June 12–13, 1998.

Rivlin, Alice, 2002, "Comment on *U.S. Monetary Policy in the 1990s*," in *American Economic Policy in the 1990s*, ed. by N. Gregory Mankiw, Jeffrey Frankel, and Peter R. Orzag (Cambridge, Massachusetts: MIT Press).

Roger, Scott, and Mark Stone, 2005, "On Target: The International Experience with Achieving Inflation Targets," IMF Working Paper 05/163 (Washington: International Monetary Fund).

Sachs, Jeffrey, Aaron Tornell, and Andrés Velasco, 1996, "The Mexican Peso Crisis: Sudden Death or Death Foretold?" *Journal of International Economics*, Vol. 41 (November), pp. 265–83.

Solans, Eugenio Domingo, 2000, "Monetary Policy Under Inflation Targeting," speech at the Fourth Annual Conference of the Banco Central de Chile, Santiago, December 1.

Stone, Mark R., and Mark Zelmer, 2000, *Adopting Inflation Targeting: Practical Issues for Emerging Market Countries*, IMF Occasional Paper No. 202 (Washington: International Monetary Fund).

Svensson, Lars E.O., 1998, "Inflation Targeting in an Open Economy: Strict or Flexible Inflation Targeting," public lecture held at Victoria University of Wellington, November 1997, *Victoria Economic Commentaries*, Vol. 15, No. 1 (Wellington, New Zealand: Victoria University).

Truman, Edwin M., 2003, *Inflation Targeting in the World Economy* (Washington: Institute for International Economics).

SUMMING UP BY THE ACTING CHAIR

*The following remarks by the Acting Chair were made at the conclusion of the Executive
Board's discussion of the World Economic Outlook on September 2, 2005.*

Executive Directors welcomed the continued strong expansion of the global economy, which has evolved broadly as was expected at the last discussion of the *World Economic Outlook*. Following the strongest performance seen in three decades in 2004, overall economic growth has moderated to a more sustainable pace during 2005, while inflationary pressures remain subdued. Directors observed that, within this overall favorable picture, growth divergences remain wide—with the United States and China still leading global growth, Japan regaining momentum, and the expansion in the euro area remaining subdued—while global imbalances have increased yet again.

Looking forward—and notwithstanding the impact of higher oil prices and global imbalances—Directors expected global economic conditions to remain favorable, with growth underpinned by still-accommodative macroeconomic policies, benign financial market conditions, and increasingly solid corporate balance sheets. Directors cautioned, nonetheless, that the balance of risks to the outlook is slanted to the downside, with projected global growth still unbalanced and significantly dependent on the United States and China. Other key short-term risks identified by Directors include the possibility that financial market conditions could tighten significantly, contributing to a global weakening of richly valued housing markets, and that rising protectionist sentiments in some countries might lead to a tightening of trade barriers and undermine investor confidence.

Directors acknowledged that the limited impact thus far of oil price increases on the global economy is attributable in part to the falling energy intensity of economic activity as well as to well-anchored inflationary expectations. A number of Directors were nevertheless concerned about the impact of high and volatile oil prices going forward, including on oil-importing developing countries. While sharing the view that the growth impact of recent oil price increases has so far been relatively modest, they thought that a substantial further jump in prices could have more serious adverse effects on the global economy, especially in view of the disruption in the wake of Hurricane Katrina to the already strained refinery capacity in the United States. In this regard, several Directors considered it important to increase investment in refinery capacity. Directors welcomed ongoing staff work to gain a deeper understanding of oil market developments, and encouraged further analysis. The importance of strengthened energy conservation and improved oil market data and transparency was also noted.

Directors considered that the rising global imbalances and their changing distribution remain a central risk to the economic outlook over the medium term. In this context, Directors welcomed the staff's analysis of global saving and investment in Chapter II and of global current account adjustment in Appendix 1.2. They agreed with the assessment that unusually low investment rates for this stage of the economic cycle have resulted in an excess supply of saving at the global level, thereby contributing to low real interest rates and the observed distribution of imbalances across major regions. Directors noted that the continued willingness of foreign investors to hold U.S.

dollar assets has so far enabled the large U.S. current account deficit to be financed without difficulty, but emphasized that this situation will not continue indefinitely. They therefore reiterated their call for determined policy efforts to address global imbalances, and to sustain global growth during the adjustment process. In this context, a few Directors also called for improved data on the currency composition of international reserves.

Directors welcomed the progress in implementing the cooperative policy strategy to address global imbalances agreed at the October 2004 IMFC meeting. They noted in particular the improved fiscal position in the United States, the important steps toward greater exchange rate flexibility in China and Malaysia, and the signs of stronger domestic demand in Japan. Nevertheless, they emphasized that considerable further efforts will be required, including more ambitious fiscal adjustment in the United States, the active use of the scope for greater exchange rate flexibility—combined with financial sector reform—in Asia, and further structural reforms in Japan and the euro area. Pointing to the rapidly rising current account surpluses of oil-exporting countries, Directors emphasized that these countries will also need to play their part, such as taking advantage of higher revenues to boost expenditures in areas where social returns are high or allowing some real exchange rate appreciation over the medium term. In addition, Directors suggested that measures to promote a more investor-friendly environment in a number of emerging market economies, including some in Asia, would contribute to reducing imbalances, in view of the current low levels of investment. While recognizing that each of these individual policy actions would help, Directors broadly agreed with the main staff conclusion that the risks of a disruptive adjustment are minimized—and the benefits of adjustment magnified—when actions in support of the cooperative policy strategy are taken together, especially given the growing size of the global imbalances and the larger number of countries involved.

Directors had an interesting exchange of views on the relative importance, timing, and sequencing of the different actions within the agreed strategy of multilateral cooperation. Most Directors believed that fiscal consolidation in the United States remains key to the adjustment, since in their view the steep decline in U.S. national savings is a central cause of the current imbalances. Exchange rate flexibility, particularly in Asia, will be required to facilitate the necessary accompanying changes in exchange rates. Most Directors saw structural reforms for boosting potential growth in Japan and Europe as being an integral part of the strategy, given their potential role in fostering more balanced global growth and in cushioning any negative impact on global growth of a significant fiscal adjustment in the United States—even if their direct impact on imbalances may be smaller, albeit in the right direction.

Directors reiterated their concerns about long-standing vulnerabilities facing the global economy and stressed the need to implement policies to boost long-run growth. They urged policymakers to use the ongoing expansion to address these challenges.

- *First, unsustainable medium-term fiscal positions remain a key risk.* Among the major industrial countries, fiscal deficits are generally expected to decline only modestly over the medium term, and Directors viewed rising public debt in some industrial countries with concern. Encouragingly, emerging market countries have improved fiscal positions, although several Directors thought that public debt still remains too high.

- *Second, more ambitious efforts are required to address constraints to long-run growth.* Directors noted that, despite some welcome progress, most countries and regions face significant structural impediments to stronger growth. Broad-based reforms will therefore be needed, including product and labor market reforms in the euro area; financial and corporate reforms in Japan and much of emerging Asia; strengthened banking supervision in central and eastern Europe; and further improvements in the investment climate in many emerging market economies.

- *Third, successful completion of the Doha Round will be crucial.* Directors agreed that it will be imperative to reach agreement on ambitious trade liberalization at the upcoming WTO Ministerial meeting in Hong Kong SAR in December, including on modalities for eliminating export subsidies and for tariff cuts on agricultural products.

- *Fourth, actions to persevere with efforts to reduce poverty will be key for low-income countries.* Directors welcomed the improvement in growth prospects in many of the world's poorest countries over the last few years. They emphasized that these developing countries must press ahead with the policy reforms needed for sustainable growth and poverty reduction, while the international community must follow through expeditiously on its commitment to provide additional resources and market access.

- *Fifth, there is a role for building sound institutions.* Directors welcomed the staff's analysis of institutions in strengthening developing country prospects. Over the past 30 years, many emerging market and developing countries have made progress in improving their institutions, and this has generally been followed by stronger growth and higher investment. Directors concurred that there is no single road to success, and that institution-building policies should be geared to country-specific circumstances. They took note of the staff's conclusions regarding the variety of conditions under which good institutions appear to flourish. In particular, good institutions are found to be most likely to develop in an environment of openness to the outside world. Several Directors saw a role for Fund technical assistance in institution building in the core areas of the Fund's expertise.

Industrial Countries

Directors welcomed the continued strong expansion of the *U.S.* economy. With household saving at record lows, a sharp slowdown in private consumption growth remains a risk, especially if the housing market weakens. With core inflation well restrained, Directors agreed that further measured withdrawal of monetary stimulus is likely to be appropriate, but emphasized that careful monitoring will be needed of the evolution of unit labor costs that have risen steadily, as well as of possible second-round effects from higher oil prices. The potential risk implicit in households' exposure to the housing market will also merit attention. Directors were encouraged by the improvement in the unified budget deficit, while noting that much of this reflects an exceptional rebound in revenues that is unlikely to continue. Many Directors considered that the relatively favorable outlook and medium-term pressures arising from demographic change call for a more ambitious fiscal adjustment path than currently envisaged. They underscored that this will require consideration of measures to raise revenues—given the already stringent spending discipline assumed in the U.S. Administration's budget proposals—and suggested in this context that consideration should be given to broadening the income tax base, or to taxing consumption more directly through a national consumption tax or an energy tax.

Directors expected the expansion in the *euro area* to regain momentum gradually in the second half of 2005—while noting the risks of a more extended period of weakness, given continuing uncertainty about future structural reforms and oil prices. Against this background, while most Directors viewed the current monetary stance as appropriate, a number thought that an interest rate cut will need to be considered if inflationary pressures remain restrained and the expected pickup in growth fails to materialize. Directors shared the view that, with fiscal pressures from an aging population set to accelerate, most countries should aim for a broadly balanced fiscal position by the end of the decade—requiring an average improvement in structural balances of about ½ percentage point of GDP annually—accompanied by further progress in pension and health reforms. Directors attached particular importance to the need to enhance structural reforms in labor and product markets for improving the growth potential, and highlighted the importance of leadership and determination on the part of national authorities for their effective implementation.

Directors welcomed the rebound in the *Japanese* economy in the first half of 2005. They noted that the expansion is being driven by solid private consumption growth and buoyant business investment. Directors expected the positive growth momentum to continue, although they saw some downside risks—notably, high and volatile oil prices, and the possibility of renewed upward pressures on the yen in an environment of large global current account imbalances. Directors welcomed the considerable progress made in addressing weaknesses in the bank and corporate sectors, which has put the economy in a better position to sustain an expansion. This reform momentum will need to be maintained. Regarding monetary policy, Directors emphasized that the Bank of Japan should maintain its accommodative monetary policy stance until deflation is decisively overcome. Directors agreed that sustained fiscal consolidation will be needed to reverse the ongoing rise in public debt and to accommodate the budgetary pressures arising from population aging.

Emerging Market and Developing Countries

Directors welcomed the continued rapid growth in *emerging Asia*, while noting the marked increase in intraregional divergences. Growth in China and India remains strong. The expansion in much of the rest of the region has slowed, reflecting the impact of higher oil prices and of a correction in the information technology sector. Directors expected the expansion in the region to strengthen during the remainder of 2005. However, downside risks include further increases in oil prices and weak domestic demand. Looking forward, Directors shared the

view that the region has an important stake in fostering an orderly reduction of global imbalances and in promoting open markets. They agreed that the key remaining challenge facing the region is to achieve an appropriate balance between growth in domestic and external demand. In this context, they welcomed the recent exchange rate reforms in China and Malaysia, and urged the authorities to make full use of the increased flexibility. These actions will facilitate domestic macroeconomic management, as well as contribute to the unwinding of global imbalances. Further financial sector reforms and prudent supervision of the banking sector also remain important.

In *Latin America*, Directors expected the expansion to continue at a solid pace, with growth—underpinned by both external and domestic demand—remaining above the average of the last decade through 2005–06. Directors saw some downside risks to the near-term outlook, including from a larger-than-expected increase in interest rates in industrial countries and from political uncertainties in the region. They underscored that managing these risks will call for continued sound policy implementation and cautious debt management. Despite these risks, the current expansion appears to be more resilient than earlier ones, reflecting a combination of improved monetary, fiscal, and external debt management policies, and strong global growth and commodity prices. Directors underscored that it will be important to build on these foundations, and to use the present benign environment in global financial markets for undertaking reforms to address long-standing impediments to faster growth while further strengthening the fiscal and debt positions.

In *emerging Europe*, growth remains firm, although Directors observed that weak confidence in the euro area and rising oil prices pose downside risks. Some Directors were concerned about possible overheating in some countries, given the combination of exceptionally strong credit growth, surging property prices, and large external current account deficits. Directors urged policymakers to adopt measures to reduce the pace of credit growth and the associated risks. In addition, fiscal consolidation will be needed to manage demand pressures and help reduce the large current account deficits—thereby paving the way for the adoption of the euro.

In the *Commonwealth of Independent States*, real GDP growth slowed noticeably in early 2005, primarily reflecting sluggish investment and lower oil sector growth, while inflation picked up after a long period of sustained disinflation. Directors emphasized that a combination of tighter monetary policy and exchange rate appreciation will be needed to keep inflation in check. Depending on each country's absorptive capacity and progress with structural reforms, monetary tightening will provide room for using revenues from oil and commodity exports to increase high-priority expenditures and implement tax reforms. Directors called for greater resolve in advancing reforms to develop fully the institutions and structures to support property rights and competition, with rule-based government interventions guided by transparent objectives.

Directors welcomed the robust economic performance in *sub-Saharan Africa*, which has been underpinned by the strength of global demand, improved domestic macroeconomic policies, progress with structural reforms, and a reduced number of armed conflicts. They emphasized, however, that most African countries still face enormous challenges in achieving the strong growth rates that are needed to reduce poverty substantially and meet the Millennium Development Goals. Directors underscored that further reforms will be necessary to strengthen the investment environment, including building the institutions that will be critical for underpinning a vibrant private sector–based economy. Directors also called on the global community to support Africa's reform efforts. The renewed commitment of the international community to provide additional resources to Africa, reflected

in the G-8 agreement at Gleneagles in July, was particularly welcomed by Directors.

The *Middle East* region continues to enjoy favorable prospects, with buoyant oil export revenue. Despite strong domestic demand, inflation has generally remained subdued. Directors emphasized that, with a significant proportion of higher oil revenue expected to be permanent, managing this revenue will be a central policy challenge. The revenue will provide the opportunity to address some of the long-standing economic problems in the region, including the financing of reforms aimed at generating employment opportunities for the rapidly growing working-age population. Directors underscored, however, that fiscal and structural policies will need to be managed carefully to ensure effective absorption of higher oil revenues.

Directors welcomed the staff's analysis of inflation targeting, which has become an increasingly favored monetary policy strategy in emerging markets. Many Directors considered that inflation targeting can bring important benefits for emerging market countries by lowering inflation and better anchoring inflation expectations, although some other Directors cautioned that—given the relatively short experience with inflation targeting, and the success of some countries with stabilization without adopting an inflation-targeting framework—it is difficult to draw definitive conclusions. Directors also noted the staff's finding that successful adoption of inflation targeting appears to depend less on meeting institutional, technical, and economic preconditions, and more on the authorities' commitment and ability to plan and implement institutional change after the introduction of the regime. While seeing some scope for the necessary conditions to be developed after a country adopts inflation targeting, several Directors nevertheless felt that certain preconditions—especially central bank credibility and independence—remain important for success.

STATISTICAL APPENDIX

The statistical appendix presents historical data, as well as projections. It comprises five sections: Assumptions, What's New, Data and Conventions, Classification of Countries, and Statistical Tables.

The assumptions underlying the estimates and projections for 2005–06 and the medium-term scenario for 2007–10 are summarized in the first section. The second section presents a brief description of changes to the database and statistical tables. The third section provides a general description of the data and of the conventions used for calculating country group composites. The classification of countries in the various groups presented in the *World Economic Outlook* is summarized in the fourth section.

The last, and main, section comprises the statistical tables. Data in these tables have been compiled on the basis of information available through early September 2005. The figures for 2005 and beyond are shown with the same degree of precision as the historical figures solely for convenience; since they are projections, the same degree of accuracy is not to be inferred.

Assumptions

Real effective *exchange rates* for the advanced economies are assumed to remain constant at their average levels during the period July 8–August 5, 2005. For 2005 and 2006, these assumptions imply average U.S. dollar/SDR conversion rates of 1.481 and 1.456, U.S. dollar/euro conversion rate of 1.25 and 1.21, and yen/U.S. dollar conversion rates of 108.9 and 110.8, respectively.

It is assumed that the *price of oil* will average $54.23 a barrel in 2005 and $61.75 a barrel in 2006.

Established *policies* of national authorities are assumed to be maintained. The more specific policy assumptions underlying the projections for selected advanced economies are described in Box A1.

With regard to *interest rates*, it is assumed that the London interbank offered rate (LIBOR) on six-month U.S. dollar deposits will average 3.6 percent in 2005 and 4.5 percent in 2006, that three-month euro deposits will average 2.1 percent in 2005 and 2.4 percent in 2006, and that six-month Japanese yen deposits will average 0.1 percent in 2005 and 0.2 percent in 2006.

With respect to *introduction of the euro*, on December 31, 1998, the Council of the European Union decided that, effective January 1, 1999, the irrevocably fixed conversion rates between the euro and currencies of the member states adopting the euro are as follows.

1 euro =	13.7603	Austrian schillings
=	40.3399	Belgian francs
=	1.95583	Deutsche mark
=	5.94573	Finnish markkaa
=	6.55957	French francs
=	340.750	Greek drachma[1]
=	0.787564	Irish pound
=	1,936.27	Italian lire
=	40.3399	Luxembourg francs
=	2.20371	Netherlands guilders
=	200.482	Portuguese escudos
=	166.386	Spanish pesetas

See Box 5.4 in the October 1998 *World Economic Outlook* for details on how the conversion rates were established.

What's New

In Table 43, the country group composites are calculated as the sum of the U.S dollar values for

---

[1]The conversion rate for Greece was established prior to inclusion in the euro area on January 1, 2001.

Box A1. Economic Policy Assumptions Underlying the Projections for Selected Advanced Economies

The short-term *fiscal policy assumptions* used in the *World Economic Outlook* are based on officially announced budgets, adjusted for differences between the national authorities and the IMF staff regarding macroeconomic assumptions and projected fiscal outturns. The medium-term fiscal projections incorporate policy measures that are judged likely to be implemented. In cases where the IMF staff has insufficient information to assess the authorities' budget intentions and prospects for policy implementation, an unchanged structural primary balance is assumed, unless otherwise indicated. Specific assumptions used in some of the advanced economies follow (see also Tables 12–14 in the Statistical Appendix for data on fiscal and structural balances).[1]

United States. The fiscal projections are based on the Administration's Mid-Session Review of the FY2006 Budget (July 13, 2005) adjusted to take into account: (1) differences in macroeconomic assumptions; (2) IMF staff assumptions about additional defense spending using analysis by the Congressional Budget Office; (3) slower compression in the growth of discretionary spending; and (4) government spending for the clean-up and reconstruction in areas damaged by Hurricane Katrina.

Japan. The medium-term fiscal projections assume that expenditure and revenue of the general government (excluding social security) are adjusted in line with the current government target to achieve a primary fiscal balance by the early 2010s.

Germany. Fiscal projections for 2005–10 are based on IMF staff macroeconomic assumptions and estimates of fiscal adjustment measures and structural reforms.

France. The projections for 2005 are based on the initial budget and the authorities' updated projections of March 2005, adjusted for the IMF staff macroeconomic assumptions and budget execution to date. For 2006–08, the projections are based on the intentions underlying the 2006–08 Stability Program Update, adjusted for the IMF staff macroeconomic assumptions and lower projections of nontax revenue. For 2009–10, the IMF staff assumes unchanged tax policies and real expenditure growth as in the Stability Program Update for 2008.

Italy. The 2005 projections are based on the IMF staff macroeconomic assumptions and its assessment of the authorities' budget. Beyond 2005, projections assume a constant structural primary balance (excluding temporary measures in 2005) and are adjusted for the savings from enacted measures (e.g., the 2004 pension reform, which will have an impact starting from 2008).

United Kingdom. The fiscal projections are based on information provided in the March 2005 Budget. Additionally, the projections incorporate the most recent statistical releases from the Office for National Statistics, including provisional budgetary outturns through 2005:Q1.

Canada. Projections are based on the 2005 budget and updates provided by the authorities. The federal government balance is the desk's estimate of the planning surplus (budgetary balance less contingency and economic reserves).

Australia. The fiscal projections through the fiscal year 2008/09 are based on the 2005–06 Budget Strategy and Outlook. Subsequently, the IMF staff assumes no change in policies.

---

[1]The output gap is actual less potential output, as a percent of potential output. Structural balances are expressed as a percent of potential output. The structural budget balance is the budgetary position that would be observed if the level of actual output coincided with potential output. Changes in the structural budget balance consequently include effects of temporary fiscal measures, the impact of fluctuations in interest rates and debt-service costs, and other noncyclical fluctuations in the budget balance. The computations of structural budget balances are based on IMF staff estimates of potential GDP and revenue and expenditure elasticities (see the October 1993 *World Economic Outlook*, Annex I). Net debt is defined as gross debt less financial assets of the general government, which include assets held by the social security insurance system. Estimates of the output gap and of the structural balance are subject to significant margins of uncertainty.

Austria. Fiscal figures for 2004 are based on the authorities' estimated outturn. Projections for 2005–06 are based on the budgets for 2005 and 2006. Projections for 2007–08 are based on the Austrian Stability Program (2004–08). For 2009–10, projections assume unchanged overall and structural balances from those in 2008.

Belgium. Fiscal projections for 2005 and the subsequent years are based on current government policies and historical expenditure trends, adjusted for the IMF staff macroeconomic assumptions.

Denmark. Projections for 2005 are aligned with the latest official projections and budget, adjusted for the IMF staff macroeconomic projections. For 2006–10, projections are in line with the authorities' medium-term framework— adjusted for the IMF staff macroeconomic projections—targeting an average budget surplus of 1.5–2.5 percent of GDP, supported by a ceiling on real public consumption growth.

Greece. The fiscal projections assume (1) constant ratios of tax and other nontax revenues to GDP; (2) EU transfers falling in the medium term; (3) continuation of the recent trend of an increase in social contributions; (4) continuation of recent trends for wage growth, social spending, and operational spending; (5) a gradual decline in investment spending from peak levels in 2003–04 owing to the 2004 Olympic games; and (6) other spending constant as a ratio to GDP.

Korea. For 2005, it is assumed that the fiscal outcome will be in line with the budget. In the medium term, fiscal policy is assumed to be consistent with achieving a balanced budget excluding social security funds.

Netherlands. The fiscal projections for 2005 and beyond build on the 2005 budget, the latest Stability Program, and other forecasts provided by the authorities, adjusted for the IMF staff's macroeconomic assumptions.

New Zealand. The fiscal projections through the fiscal year 2008/09 are based on the 2005 Budget published in May 2005. For the remainder of the projection period, the IMF staff assumes unchanged policies.

Portugal. Fiscal projections for 2005–09 are based on the authorities' updated Stability Program of June 2005.

Spain. Fiscal projections through 2008 are based on the policies outlined in the national authorities' updated Stability Program of December 2004. These projections have been adjusted for the IMF staff macroeconomic scenario. In subsequent years, the fiscal projections assume no significant changes in these policies.

Sweden. The fiscal projections are based on information provided in the Spring Budget Bill, presented on April 15, 2005.

Switzerland. Estimates for 2004 and projections for 2005–10 are based on IMF staff calculations, which incorporate measures to restore balance in the Federal accounts.

Monetary policy assumptions are based on the established policy framework in each country. In most cases, this implies a nonaccommodative stance over the business cycle: official interest rates will therefore increase when economic indicators suggest that prospective inflation will rise above its acceptable rate or range, and they will decrease when indicators suggest that prospective inflation will not exceed the acceptable rate or range, that prospective output growth is below its potential rate, and that the margin of slack in the economy is significant. On this basis, the LIBOR on six-month U.S. dollar deposits is assumed to average 3.6 percent in 2005 and 4.5 percent in 2006. The projected path for U.S. dollar short-term interest rates reflects the assumption implicit in prevailing forward rates that the U.S. Federal Reserve will continue to withdraw monetary stimulus at a measured pace through 2005. The rate on three-month euro deposits is assumed to average 2.1 percent in 2005 and 2.4 percent in 2006. The interest rate on six-month Japanese yen deposits is assumed to average 0.1 percent in 2005 and 0.2 percent in 2006, with the current monetary policy framework being maintained. Changes in interest rate assumptions compared with the April 2005 *World Economic Outloo*k are summarized in Table 1.1.

the relevant individual countries. This differs from the calculations in the April 2005 and earlier *World Economic Outlooks*, where the composites were weighted by GDP valued at purchasing power parities (PPPs) as a share of total world GDP.

Data and Conventions

Data and projections for 175 countries form the statistical basis for the *World Economic Outlook* (the World Economic Outlook database). The data are maintained jointly by the IMF's Research Department and area departments, with the latter regularly updating country projections based on consistent global assumptions.

Although national statistical agencies are the ultimate providers of historical data and definitions, international organizations are also involved in statistical issues, with the objective of harmonizing methodologies for the national compilation of statistics, including the analytical frameworks, concepts, definitions, classifications, and valuation procedures used in the production of economic statistics. The World Economic Outlook database reflects information from both national source agencies and international organizations.

The comprehensive revision of the standardized *System of National Accounts 1993 (SNA)*, the IMF's *Balance of Payments Manual, Fifth Edition (BPM5)*, the *Monetary and Financial Statistics Manual (MFSM)*, and the *Government Finance Statistics Manual 2001 (GFSM 2001)* represented important improvements in the standards of economic statistics and analysis.[2] The IMF was actively involved in all these projects, particularly the new *Balance of Payments Manual*, which reflects the IMF's special interest in countries'

external positions. Key changes introduced with the new *Manual* were summarized in Box 13 of the May 1994 *World Economic Outlook*. The process of adapting country balance of payments data to the definitions of the new *BPM5* began with the May 1995 *World Economic Outlook*. However, full concordance with the *BPM5* is ultimately dependent on the provision by national statistical compilers of revised country data, and hence the *World Economic Outlook* estimates are still only partially adapted to the *BPM5*.

In line with recent improvements in standards of reporting economic statistics, several countries have phased out their traditional *fixed-base-year* method of calculating real macroeconomic variables levels and growth by switching to a *chain-weighted* method of computing aggregate growth. Recent dramatic changes in the structure of these economies have obliged these countries to revise the way in which they measure real GDP levels and growth. Switching to the chain-weighted method of computing aggregate growth, which uses current price information, allows countries to measure GDP growth more accurately by eliminating upward biases in new data.[3] Currently, real macroeconomic data for Australia, Austria, Canada, Germany, Greece, Ireland, Japan, Luxembourg, the Netherlands, New Zealand, Portugal, Spain, Sweden, the United Kingdom, and the United States are based on chain-weighted methodology. However, data before 1988 (Austria), 1991 (Germany), 1995 (Greece), 1997 (Ireland), 1994 (Japan), 1995 (Luxembourg), 2001 (the Netherlands), 1995 (Portugal), and 2000 (Spain) are based on unrevised national accounts and are subject to revision in the future.

---

[2]Commission of the European Communities, International Monetary Fund, Organization for Economic Cooperation and Development, United Nations, and World Bank, *System of National Accounts 1993* (Brussels/Luxembourg, New York, Paris, and Washington, 1993); International Monetary Fund, *Balance of Payments Manual, Fifth Edition* (Washington, 1993); International Monetary Fund, *Monetary and Financial Statistics Manual* (Washington, 2000); and International Monetary Fund, *Government Finance Statistics Manual* (Washington, 2001).

[3]Charles Steindel, 1995, "Chain-Weighting: The New Approach to Measuring GDP," *Current Issues in Economics and Finance* (Federal Reserve Bank of New York), Vol. 1 (December).

The members of the European Union have adopted a harmonized system for the compilation of national accounts, referred to as ESA 1995. All national accounts data from 1995 onward are presented on the basis of the new system. Revision by national authorities of data prior to 1995 to conform to the new system has progressed, but has in some cases not been completed. In such cases, historical *World Economic Outlook* data have been carefully adjusted to avoid breaks in the series. Users of EU national accounts data prior to 1995 should nevertheless exercise caution until the revision of historical data by national statistical agencies has been fully completed. See Box 1.2, "Revisions in National Accounts Methodologies," in the May 2000 *World Economic Outlook*.

Composite data for country groups in the *World Economic Outlook* are either sums or weighted averages of data for individual countries. Unless otherwise indicated, multiyear averages of growth rates are expressed as compound annual rates of change. Arithmetically weighted averages are used for all data except inflation and money growth for the other emerging market and developing countries group, for which geometric averages are used. The following conventions apply.

- Country group composites for exchange rates, interest rates, and the growth rates of monetary aggregates are weighted by GDP converted to U.S. dollars at market exchange rates (averaged over the preceding three years) as a share of group GDP.
- Composites for other data relating to the domestic economy, whether growth rates or ratios, are weighted by GDP valued at PPPs as a share of total world or group GDP.[4]
- Composites for data relating to the domestic economy for the euro area (12 member coun-

tries throughout the entire period unless otherwise noted) are aggregates of national source data using weights based on 1995 European currency unit (ECU) exchange rates.

- Composite unemployment rates and employment growth are weighted by labor force as a share of group labor force.
- Composites relating to the external economy are sums of individual country data after conversion to U.S. dollars at the average market exchange rates in the years indicated for balance of payments data and at end-of-year market exchange rates for debt denominated in currencies other than U.S. dollars. Composites of changes in foreign trade volumes and prices, however, are arithmetic averages of percentage changes for individual countries weighted by the U.S. dollar value of exports or imports as a share of total world or group exports or imports (in the preceding year).

For central and eastern European countries, external transactions in nonconvertible currencies (through 1990) are converted to U.S. dollars at the implicit U.S. dollar/ruble conversion rates obtained from each country's national currency exchange rate for the U.S. dollar and for the ruble.

Classification of Countries

Summary of the Country Classification

The country classification in the *World Economic Outlook* divides the world into two major groups: advanced economies, and other emerging market and developing countries.[5] Rather than being based on strict criteria, economic or otherwise, this classification has

---

[4]See Box A2 of the April 2004 *World Economic Outlook* for a summary of the revised PPP-based weights and Annex IV of the May 1993 *World Economic Outlook*. See also Anne-Marie Gulde and Marianne Schulze-Ghattas, "Purchasing Power Parity Based Weights for the *World Economic Outlook*," in *Staff Studies for the World Economic Outlook* (International Monetary Fund, December 1993), pp. 106–23.

[5]As used here, the term "country" does not in all cases refer to a territorial entity that is a state as understood by international law and practice. It also covers some territorial entities that are not states, but for which statistical data are maintained on a separate and independent basis.

Table A. Classification by *World Economic Outlook* Groups and Their Shares in Aggregate GDP, Exports of Goods and Services, and Population, 2004[1]

(Percent of total for group or world)

	Number of Countries	GDP		Exports of Goods and Services		Population	
		Advanced economies	World	Advanced economies	World	Advanced economies	World
Advanced economies	**29**	**100.0**	**54.6**	**100.0**	**71.6**	**100.0**	**15.4**
United States		38.2	20.9	14.4	10.3	30.5	4.7
Euro area	12	28.0	15.3	43.7	31.3	32.2	4.9
Germany		7.9	4.3	13.2	9.5	8.6	1.3
France		5.7	3.1	6.7	4.8	6.5	1.0
Italy		5.3	2.9	5.5	3.9	6.0	0.9
Spain		3.2	1.7	3.4	2.4	4.3	0.7
Japan		12.6	6.9	8.0	5.7	13.2	2.0
United Kingdom		5.7	3.1	6.7	4.8	6.2	1.0
Canada		3.5	1.9	4.7	3.4	3.3	0.5
Other advanced economies	13	12.1	6.6	22.5	16.1	14.6	2.2
Memorandum							
Major advanced economies	7	78.8	43.0	59.1	42.3	74.3	11.4
Newly industrialized Asian economies	4	6.4	3.5	13.1	9.4	8.5	1.3
		Other emerging market and developing countries	World	Other emerging market and developing countries	World	Other emerging market and developing countries	World
Other emerging market and developing countries	**146**	**100.0**	**45.4**	**100.0**	**28.2**	**100.0**	**84.6**
Regional groups							
Africa	48	7.2	3.3	7.8	2.2	14.8	12.5
Sub-Sahara	45	5.6	2.5	5.7	1.6	13.5	11.4
Excluding Nigeria and South Africa	43	2.9	1.3	2.7	0.8	9.9	8.4
Central and eastern Europe	15	7.5	3.4	15.0	4.3	3.5	2.9
Commonwealth of Independent States[2]	13	8.3	3.8	9.6	2.7	5.3	4.5
Russia		5.7	2.6	6.4	1.8	2.7	2.3
Developing Asia	23	54.2	24.6	39.2	11.1	61.6	52.1
China		29.0	13.2	20.7	5.9	24.5	20.7
India		13.0	5.9	3.8	1.1	20.1	17.0
Excluding China and India	21	12.2	5.5	14.8	4.2	17.0	14.4
Middle East	14	6.2	2.8	13.7	3.9	4.8	4.0
Western Hemisphere	33	16.5	7.5	14.8	4.2	10.1	8.5
Brazil		5.8	2.6	3.4	1.0	3.4	2.9
Mexico		4.0	1.8	4.2	1.2	2.0	1.7
Analytical groups							
By source of export earnings							
Fuel	18	7.1	3.2	14.2	4.0	7.6	6.4
Nonfuel	128	92.9	42.2	85.8	24.3	92.4	78.2
of which, primary products	23	2.2	1.0	2.4	0.7	5.2	4.4
By external financing source							
Net debtor countries	126	56.4	25.6	52.0	14.8	67.5	57.2
of which, official financing	50	12.9	5.8	9.3	2.6	22.4	19.0
Net debtor countries by debt-servicing experience							
Countries with arrears and/or rescheduling during 1999-2003	56	12.2	5.6	11.4	3.2	23.7	20.1
Other net debtor countries	70	44.2	20.1	40.6	11.5	43.8	37.1
Other groups							
Heavily indebted poor countries	27	1.9	0.9	1.1	0.3	7.6	6.4
Middle East and North Africa	20	8.2	3.7	15.8	4.5	6.8	5.8

[1]The GDP shares are based on the purchasing-power-parity (PPP) valuation of country GDPs. The number of countries comprising each group reflects those for which data are included in the group aggregates.

[2]Mongolia, which is not a member of the Commonwealth of Independent States, is included in this group for reasons of geography and similarities in economic structure.

Table B. Advanced Economies by Subgroup

Major Currency Areas	Euro area		Other Subgroups			
			Newly industrialized Asian economies	Major advanced economies	Other advanced economies	
United States	Austria	Ireland	Hong Kong SAR[1]	Canada	Australia	Korea
Euro area	Belgium	Italy	Korea	France	Cyprus	New Zealand
Japan	Finland	Luxembourg	Singapore	Germany	Denmark	Norway
	France	Netherlands	Taiwan Province	Italy	Hong Kong SAR[1]	Singapore
	Germany	Portugal	of China	Japan	Iceland	Sweden
	Greece	Spain		United Kingdom	Israel	Switzerland
				United States		Taiwan Province of China

[1]On July 1, 1997, Hong Kong was returned to the People's Republic of China and became a Special Administrative Region of China.

evolved over time with the objective of facilitating analysis by providing a reasonably meaningful organization of data. A few countries are presently not included in these groups, either because they are not IMF members and their economies are not monitored by the IMF, or because databases have not yet been fully developed. Because of data limitations, group composites do not reflect the following countries: the Islamic Republic of Afghanistan, Bosnia and Herzegovina, Brunei Darussalam, Eritrea, Liberia, Serbia and Montenegro, Somalia, and Timor-Leste. Cuba and the Democratic People's Republic of Korea are examples of countries that are not IMF members, whereas San Marino, among the advanced economies, and Aruba, among the developing countries, are examples of economies for which databases have not been completed.

Each of the two main country groups is further divided into a number of subgroups. Among the advanced economies, the 7 largest in terms of GDP, collectively referred to as the major advanced countries, are distinguished as a subgroup, and so are the 12 members of the euro area and the 4 newly industrialized Asian economies. The other emerging market and developing countries are classified by region, as well as into a number of analytical groups. Table A provides an overview of these standard groups in the *World Economic Outlook*, showing the number of countries in each group and the average 2004 shares of groups in aggregate PPP-valued

GDP, total exports of goods and services, and population.

General Features and Composition of Groups in the *World Economic Outlook* Classification

Advanced Economies

The 29 advanced economies are listed in Table B. The seven largest in terms of GDP—the United States, Japan, Germany, France, Italy, the United Kingdom, and Canada—constitute the subgroup of *major advanced economies*, often referred to as the Group of Seven (G-7) countries. The euro area (12 countries) and the *newly industrialized Asian economies* are also distinguished as subgroups. Composite data shown in the tables for the euro area cover the current members for all years, even though the membership has increased over time.

In 1991 and subsequent years, data for *Germany* refer to west Germany *and* the eastern Länder (i.e., the former German Democratic Republic). Before 1991, economic data are not available on a unified basis or in a consistent manner. Hence, in tables featuring data expressed as annual percent change, these apply to west Germany in years up to and including 1991, but to unified Germany from 1992 onward. In general, data on national accounts and domestic economic and financial activity through 1990 cover west Germany only, whereas data for the central government and balance of

Table C. European Union

Austria	France	Latvia	Portugal
Belgium	Germany	Lithuania	Slovak Republic
Cyprus	Greece	Luxembourg	Slovenia
Czech Republic	Hungary	Malta	Spain
Denmark	Ireland	Netherlands	Sweden
Estonia	Italy	Poland	United Kingdom
Finland			

payments apply to west Germany through June 1990 and to unified Germany thereafter.

Table C lists the member countries of the European Union, not all of which are classified as advanced economies in the *World Economic Outlook.*

Other Emerging Market and Developing Countries

The group of other emerging market and developing countries (146 countries) includes all countries that are not classified as advanced economies.

The *regional breakdowns* of other emerging market and developing countries—*Africa, central and eastern Europe, Commonwealth of Independent States, developing Asia, Middle East, and Western Hemisphere*—largely conform to the regional breakdowns in the IMF's *International Financial Statistics.* In both classifications, Egypt and the Libyan Arab Jamahiriya are included in the *Middle East* region rather than in Africa. In addition, the *World Economic Outlook* sometimes refers to the regional group of Middle East and North Africa countries, also referred to as the MENA countries, whose composition straddles the Africa and Middle East regions. This group is defined as the Arab League countries plus the Islamic Republic of Iran (see Table D).

Table D. Middle East and North Africa Countries

Algeria	Iraq	Mauritania	Sudan
Bahrain	Jordan	Morocco	Syrian Arab Republic
Djibouti	Kuwait	Oman	Tunisia
Egypt	Lebanon	Qatar	United Arab Emirates
Iran, I.R. of	Libya	Saudi Arabia	Yemen

Table E. Other Emerging Market and Developing Countries by Region and Main Source of Export Earnings

	Fuel	Nonfuel, of Which Primary Products
Africa	Algeria Angola Congo, Rep. of Equatorial Guinea Gabon Nigeria	Botswana Burkina Faso Burundi Chad Congo, Dem. Rep. of Côte d'Ivoire Ghana Guinea Guinea-Bissau Malawi Mauritania Namibia Niger Sierra Leone Uganda Zambia Zimbabwe
Commonwealth of Independent States	Azerbaijan Turkmenistan	Tajikistan Uzbekistan
Developing Asia		Papua New Guinea Solomon Islands
Middle East	Iran, I.R. of Iraq Kuwait Libya Oman Qatar Saudi Arabia Syrian Arab Republic Yemen	
Western Hemisphere	Venezuela	Chile Suriname

Other emerging market and developing countries are also classified according to *analytical criteria.* The analytical criteria reflect countries' composition of export earnings and other income from abroad, exchange rate arrangements, a distinction between net creditor and net debtor countries, and, for the net debtor countries, financial criteria based on external financing source and experience with external debt servicing. The detailed composition of other emerging market and developing countries in the regional and analytical groups is shown in Tables E and F.

Table F. Other Emerging Market and Developing Countries by Region, Net External Position, and Classification as Heavily Indebted Poor Countries

	Net External Position		Heavily Indebted Poor Countries
	Net creditor	Net debtor[1]	
Africa			
Maghreb			
Algeria	*		
Morocco		*	
Tunisia		*	
Sub-Sahara			
South Africa		*	
Horn of Africa			
Djibouti		•	
Ethiopia		•	*
Sudan		*	
Great Lakes			
Burundi		•	
Congo, Dem. Rep. of		•	*
Kenya		•	
Rwanda		•	*
Tanzania		•	*
Uganda		*	*
Southern Africa			
Angola		*	
Botswana	*		
Comoros		•	
Lesotho		*	
Madagascar		•	*
Malawi		•	*
Mauritius		*	
Mozambique, Rep. of		*	*
Namibia	*		
Seychelles		*	
Swaziland		*	
Zambia		•	*
Zimbabwe		*	
West and Central Africa			
Cape Verde		*	
Gambia, The		*	*
Ghana		•	*
Guinea		•	*
Mauritania		*	*
Nigeria		*	
São Tomé and Príncipe		*	*
Sierra Leone		•	*
CFA franc zone			
Benin		•	*
Burkina Faso		•	*
Cameroon		*	*
Central African Republic		•	
Chad		•	*
Congo, Rep. of		•	
Côte d'Ivoire		•	
Equatorial Guinea		*	
Gabon		•	
Guinea-Bissau		•	*
Mali		•	*
Niger		•	*
Senegal		*	*
Togo		•	
Central and eastern Europe			
Albania		*	
Bulgaria	*		
Croatia		*	
Czech Republic		*	
Estonia		*	
Hungary		*	
Latvia		*	
Lithuania		*	
Macedonia, FYR		*	
Malta		*	
Poland		*	
Romania		*	
Slovak Republic		*	
Slovenia	*		
Turkey		*	
Commonwealth of Independent States[2]			
Armenia		*	
Azerbaijan		*	
Belarus			
Georgia		*	
Kazakhstan		*	
Kyrgyz Republic		•	
Moldova		*	
Mongolia		•	
Russia	*		
Tajikistan		*	
Turkmenistan	*		
Ukraine	*		
Uzbekistan		*	
Developing Asia			
Bhutan		•	
Cambodia		•	
China	*		
Fiji		*	
Indonesia		•	
Kiribati	*		
Lao PDR		*	
Malaysia	*		
Myanmar		*	
Papua New Guinea		•	
Philippines		*	
Samoa		*	
Solomon Islands		•	
Thailand		*	
Tonga		*	
Vanuatu			
Vietnam		•	
South Asia			
Bangladesh		•	
India		*	
Maldives		*	
Nepal		•	
Pakistan		•	
Sri Lanka		•	

Table F *(concluded)*

	Net External Position		Heavily Indebted Poor Countries		Net External Position		Heavily Indebted Poor Countries
	Net creditor	Net debtor¹			Net creditor	Net debtor¹	
Middle East				**Mexico, Central America, and Caribbean**			
Bahrain		*		Mexico		*	
Iran, I.R. of	*						
Iraq		*		**Central America**			
Kuwait	*			Costa Rica		*	
Libya	*			El Salvador		•	
Oman	*			Guatemala		*	
Qatar	*						
Saudi Arabia	*			Honduras		•	*
United Arab Emirates	*			Nicaragua		*	*
Yemen	*			Panama		*	
Mashreq				**Caribbean**			
Egypt		*		Antigua and Barbuda		*	
Jordan		*		Bahamas, The		*	
Lebanon		•		Barbados		*	
Syrian Arab Republic		*		Belize		*	
Western Hemisphere				Dominica		*	
Mercosur				Dominican Republic		•	
Argentina		•		Grenada		•	
Bolivia (associate member)		•	*	Guyana		*	*
Brazil		*		Haiti		•	
Chile (associate member)		*		Jamaica		*	
Paraguay		•		Netherlands Antilles		*	
Uruguay		•		St. Kitts and Nevis		*	
Andean region				St. Lucia		•	
Colombia		•		St. Vincent and the Grenadines		*	
Ecuador		*		Suriname		*	
Peru		*		Trinidad and Tobago		*	
Venezuela	*						

¹Dot instead of star indicates that the net debtor's main external finance source is official financing.

²Mongolia, which is not a member of the Commonwealth of Independent States, is included in this group for reasons of geography and similarities in economic structure.

The analytical criterion, by *source of export earnings*, distinguishes between categories: *fuel* (Standard International Trade Classification—SITC 3) and *nonfuel* and then focuses on *nonfuel primary products* (SITC 0, 1, 2, 4, and 68).

The financial criteria focus on *net creditor countries, net debtor countries,* and *heavily indebted poor countries (HIPCs).* Net debtor countries are further differentiated on the basis of two additional financial criteria: by *official external financing* and by *experience with debt servicing.*[6] The HIPC group comprises the countries considered by the IMF and the World Bank for their debt initiative, known as the HIPC Initiative, with the aim of reducing the external debt burdens of all the eligible HIPCs to a "sustainable" level in a reasonably short period of time.[7]

---

[6]During 1999–2003, 56 countries incurred external payments arrears or entered into official or commercial bank debt-rescheduling agreements. This group of countries is referred to as *countries with arrears and/or rescheduling during 1999–2003.*

[7]See David Andrews, Anthony R. Boote, Syed S. Rizavi, and Sukwinder Singh, *Debt Relief for Low-Income Countries: The Enhanced HIPC Initiative,* IMF Pamphlet Series, No. 51 (Washington: International Monetary Fund, November 1999).

List of Tables

Output

Inflation

Financial Policies

Foreign Trade

Current Account Transactions

Table 1. Summary of World Output[1]

(Annual percent change)

	Ten-Year Averages		1997	1998	1999	2000	2001	2002	2003	2004	2005	2006
	1987–96	1997–2006										
World	**3.3**	**3.9**	**4.2**	**2.8**	**3.7**	**4.7**	**2.4**	**3.0**	**4.0**	**5.1**	**4.3**	**4.3**
Advanced economies	**3.0**	**2.7**	**3.5**	**2.6**	**3.5**	**3.9**	**1.2**	**1.5**	**1.9**	**3.3**	**2.5**	**2.7**
United States	2.9	3.3	4.5	4.2	4.4	3.7	0.8	1.6	2.7	4.2	3.5	3.3
Euro area	...	2.0	2.6	2.8	2.7	3.8	1.7	0.9	0.7	2.0	1.2	1.8
Japan	3.2	1.1	1.8	−1.0	−0.1	2.4	0.2	−0.3	1.4	2.7	2.0	2.0
Other advanced economies[2]	3.8	3.3	4.0	1.9	4.7	5.3	1.7	3.2	2.4	3.9	2.8	3.3
Other emerging market and developing countries	**3.8**	**5.3**	**5.2**	**3.0**	**4.0**	**5.8**	**4.1**	**4.8**	**6.5**	**7.3**	**6.4**	**6.1**
Regional groups												
Africa	2.2	4.1	3.4	3.2	2.8	3.3	4.1	3.6	4.6	5.3	4.5	5.9
Central and eastern Europe	0.9	3.7	4.2	2.8	0.5	4.9	0.2	4.4	4.6	6.5	4.3	4.6
Commonwealth of Independent States[3]	...	5.1	1.1	−3.5	5.1	9.1	6.3	5.3	7.9	8.4	6.0	5.7
Developing Asia	7.8	6.7	6.5	4.2	6.2	6.7	5.6	6.6	8.1	8.2	7.8	7.2
Middle East	3.4	4.6	4.7	4.2	2.0	4.9	3.7	4.2	6.5	5.5	5.4	5.0
Western Hemisphere	2.7	2.8	5.2	2.3	0.4	3.9	0.5	—	2.2	5.6	4.1	3.8
Memorandum												
European Union	2.2	2.4	2.9	3.0	2.9	3.9	2.0	1.3	1.3	2.5	1.6	2.1
Analytical groups												
By source of export earnings												
Fuel	2.6	4.6	4.4	3.3	0.9	4.7	3.8	3.6	6.4	7.2	6.0	6.2
Nonfuel	3.9	5.4	5.3	3.0	4.3	5.9	4.1	4.9	6.5	7.3	6.4	6.1
of which, primary products	3.2	3.4	3.7	2.8	1.3	1.8	2.9	2.9	3.3	5.6	4.4	5.1
By external financing source												
Net debtor countries	3.5	4.1	4.6	2.1	2.9	4.6	2.4	3.3	4.9	6.1	5.2	5.2
of which, official financing	4.4	3.5	4.9	−0.5	1.0	3.1	2.2	1.6	5.3	6.1	5.9	5.3
Net debtor countries by debt-servicing experience												
Countries with arrears and/or rescheduling during 1999–2003	3.9	4.0	5.4	−0.4	1.7	3.6	3.0	2.2	5.8	6.6	6.0	5.9
Memorandum												
Median growth rate												
Advanced economies	3.1	3.0	3.8	3.6	3.8	4.1	1.7	1.9	1.9	3.2	2.6	3.0
Other emerging market and developing countries	3.2	4.2	4.7	3.7	3.4	4.1	3.8	3.5	4.5	5.0	4.3	4.5
Output per capita												
Advanced economies	2.3	2.1	2.9	2.0	2.8	3.3	0.6	0.9	1.3	2.7	2.0	2.2
Other emerging market and developing countries	2.1	4.0	3.7	1.6	2.6	4.4	2.7	3.5	5.2	6.0	5.1	4.9
World growth based on market exchange rates	**2.6**	**2.9**	**3.5**	**2.2**	**3.1**	**4.0**	**1.4**	**1.7**	**2.6**	**4.0**	**3.1**	**3.2**
Value of world output in billions of U.S. dollars												
At market exchange rates	23,840	35,281	29,876	29,629	30,727	31,546	31,310	32,517	36,481	40,895	43,886	45,942
At purchasing power parities	28,778	49,104	38,351	39,790	41,827	44,729	46,866	49,015	51,824	55,655	59,560	63,420

[1]Real GDP.

[2]In this table, "other advanced economies" means advanced economies excluding the United States, euro area countries, and Japan.

[3]Mongolia, which is not a member of the Commonwealth of Independent States, is included in this group for reasons of geography and similarities in economic structure.

Table 2. Advanced Economies: Real GDP and Total Domestic Demand
(Annual percent change)

	Ten-Year Averages		1997	1998	1999	2000	2001	2002	2003	2004	2005	2006	Fourth Quarter[1]		
	1987–96	1997–2006											2004	2005	2006
Real GDP															
Advanced economies	**3.0**	**2.7**	**3.5**	**2.6**	**3.5**	**3.9**	**1.2**	**1.5**	**1.9**	**3.3**	**2.5**	**2.7**	. . .	. . .	. . .
United States	2.9	3.3	4.5	4.2	4.4	3.7	0.8	1.6	2.7	4.2	3.5	3.3	3.8	3.3	3.4
Euro area	. . .	2.0	2.6	2.8	2.7	3.8	1.7	0.9	0.7	2.0	1.2	1.8	1.5	1.6	2.0
Germany	2.6	1.3	1.7	2.0	1.9	3.1	1.2	0.1	−0.2	1.6	0.8	1.2	0.5	1.4	1.7
France	1.9	2.2	2.3	3.4	3.2	4.1	2.1	1.3	0.9	2.0	1.5	1.8	2.1	1.2	2.3
Italy	1.9	1.4	2.0	1.8	1.7	3.0	1.8	0.4	0.3	1.2	—	1.4	0.8	0.8	1.4
Spain	2.9	3.7	4.0	4.3	4.2	5.8	3.5	2.7	2.9	3.1	3.2	3.0	2.8	2.5	3.8
Netherlands	2.7	2.1	3.8	4.3	4.0	3.5	1.4	0.1	−0.1	1.7	0.7	2.0	1.7	0.9	2.2
Belgium	2.2	2.2	3.8	2.1	3.2	3.7	0.9	0.9	1.3	2.7	1.2	2.0	2.6	0.9	2.4
Austria	2.5	2.2	1.8	3.6	3.3	3.4	0.8	1.0	1.4	2.4	1.9	2.2	2.5	2.1	2.2
Finland	1.3	3.4	6.2	5.0	3.4	5.0	1.0	2.2	2.4	3.6	1.8	3.2	3.5	3.6	0.8
Greece	1.4	3.8	3.6	3.4	3.4	4.5	4.3	3.8	4.7	4.2	3.2	2.9	4.2	2.7	3.2
Portugal	4.0	1.9	4.0	4.6	3.8	3.4	1.7	0.4	−1.1	1.0	0.5	1.2	0.5	1.2	1.4
Ireland	5.2	7.0	10.8	8.5	10.7	9.2	6.2	6.1	4.4	4.5	5.0	4.9	2.1	5.2	4.9
Luxembourg	5.2	4.9	8.3	6.8	7.3	9.2	2.2	2.3	2.4	4.4	3.1	3.2	. . .	. . .	. . .
Japan	3.2	1.1	1.8	−1.0	−0.1	2.4	0.2	−0.3	1.4	2.7	2.0	2.0	0.9	2.9	1.8
United Kingdom	2.4	2.8	3.2	3.2	3.0	4.0	2.2	2.0	2.5	3.2	1.9	2.2	2.7	2.0	2.3
Canada	2.2	3.5	4.2	4.1	5.5	5.2	1.8	3.1	2.0	2.9	2.9	3.2	3.3	2.9	3.3
Korea	8.4	4.2	4.7	−6.9	9.5	8.5	3.8	7.0	3.1	4.6	3.8	5.0	3.3	3.9	3.9
Australia	3.6	3.5	3.9	5.3	4.3	3.2	2.5	4.0	3.3	3.2	2.2	3.2	1.5	2.7	3.4
Taiwan Province of China	7.6	4.0	6.4	4.3	5.3	5.8	−2.2	3.9	3.3	5.7	3.4	4.3	3.2	4.6	3.5
Sweden	1.5	2.8	2.4	3.6	4.6	4.3	1.0	2.0	1.5	3.6	2.6	2.8	3.2	3.5	2.8
Switzerland	1.4	1.5	1.9	2.8	1.3	3.6	1.0	0.3	−0.4	1.7	0.8	1.8	1.2	1.1	1.9
Hong Kong SAR	5.9	3.7	5.1	−5.0	3.4	10.2	0.5	1.9	3.2	8.1	6.3	4.5	6.8	5.6	5.0
Denmark	1.5	2.0	3.0	2.5	2.6	2.8	1.3	0.5	0.7	2.4	2.2	2.1	3.0	2.4	1.2
Norway	2.9	2.6	5.2	2.6	2.1	2.8	2.7	1.1	0.4	2.9	3.1	3.3	2.6	4.2	2.3
Israel	5.5	3.0	3.6	3.7	2.3	7.7	−0.3	−1.2	1.7	4.4	4.2	3.9	5.6	2.9	4.5
Singapore	9.4	4.3	8.6	−0.8	6.8	9.6	−1.9	3.2	1.4	8.4	3.9	4.5	6.5	2.9	5.6
New Zealand	2.8	3.0	1.9	−0.1	4.4	3.5	2.6	4.7	3.4	4.8	2.5	2.5	3.8	2.9	2.1
Cyprus	5.8	3.7	2.3	5.0	4.8	5.0	4.1	2.1	1.9	3.7	3.8	4.0	. . .	. . .	. . .
Iceland	1.6	4.1	4.7	5.7	4.4	5.7	2.6	−2.1	4.2	5.2	5.8	4.9	. . .	. . .	. . .
Memorandum															
Major advanced economies	2.7	2.5	3.3	2.8	3.1	3.5	1.0	1.1	1.8	3.2	2.5	2.6	2.5	2.6	2.7
Newly industrialized Asian economies	7.9	4.2	5.5	−2.6	7.3	7.9	1.3	5.3	3.1	5.6	4.0	4.7	4.3	4.7	4.3
Real total domestic demand															
Advanced economies	**2.9**	**2.8**	**3.3**	**3.0**	**4.0**	**3.9**	**1.1**	**1.6**	**2.1**	**3.4**	**2.6**	**2.6**	. . .	. . .	. . .
United States	2.7	3.7	4.8	5.3	5.3	4.4	0.9	2.2	3.0	4.7	3.5	3.1	4.5	3.0	3.3
Euro area	. . .	1.9	1.8	3.6	3.5	2.9	1.0	0.4	1.2	2.0	1.4	1.8	1.9	1.3	2.0
Germany	2.6	0.8	0.9	2.3	2.7	2.2	−0.5	−1.9	0.6	0.5	0.1	0.9	0.2	0.1	1.6
France	1.7	2.6	1.1	4.0	3.6	4.3	2.0	1.3	1.8	3.2	2.4	2.0	3.5	1.7	2.4
Italy	1.6	1.7	2.7	3.1	3.2	2.3	1.4	1.2	1.2	1.0	0.4	0.9	1.0	0.5	1.0
Spain	3.3	4.5	3.5	5.6	5.6	6.4	3.7	3.2	3.5	4.7	4.7	4.0	5.0	3.5	4.2
Japan	3.4	0.8	0.7	−1.4	—	1.9	0.8	−1.0	0.7	1.9	2.0	1.9	0.7	2.8	1.8
United Kingdom	2.4	3.2	3.4	4.9	4.1	4.1	2.8	3.2	2.7	3.7	1.6	1.8	3.0	1.1	2.1
Canada	1.8	3.8	5.7	2.4	4.1	4.9	1.3	3.3	4.5	3.7	4.6	3.4	4.9	3.4	3.5
Other advanced economies	5.5	2.8	3.7	−1.6	5.5	5.2	0.6	3.5	1.2	4.0	3.0	3.7	. . .	. . .	. . .
Memorandum															
Major advanced economies	2.6	2.7	3.2	3.5	3.8	3.6	1.0	1.3	2.2	3.4	2.6	2.4	3.0	2.3	2.6
Newly industrialized Asian economies	9.0	2.6	4.2	−8.2	7.8	7.5	—	4.1	−0.1	4.0	3.1	4.5	4.9	5.2	−0.8

[1]From fourth quarter of preceding year.

Table 3. Advanced Economies: Components of Real GDP
(Annual percent change)

	Ten-Year Averages		1997	1998	1999	2000	2001	2002	2003	2004	2005	2006
	1987–96	1997–2006										
Private consumer expenditure												
Advanced economies	**3.0**	**2.7**	**2.8**	**3.0**	**3.9**	**3.8**	**2.2**	**2.1**	**1.9**	**2.8**	**2.5**	**2.3**
United States	2.9	3.7	3.8	5.0	5.1	4.7	2.5	2.7	2.9	3.9	3.4	2.7
Euro area	...	1.9	1.7	2.9	3.3	3.2	1.8	0.9	1.0	1.6	1.2	1.4
Germany	2.9	1.0	0.8	1.5	3.0	2.4	1.9	−0.5	0.1	0.6	−0.3	0.4
France	1.6	2.3	0.2	3.6	3.3	3.5	2.4	2.4	1.6	2.3	1.9	2.1
Italy	1.9	1.7	3.2	3.2	2.6	2.7	0.8	0.4	1.4	1.0	0.7	0.8
Spain	2.8	3.9	3.2	4.4	4.7	5.5	3.2	2.8	2.5	4.3	4.7	4.0
Japan	3.2	0.8	0.8	−0.2	—	0.5	1.1	0.5	0.2	1.5	1.9	1.7
United Kingdom	2.8	3.3	3.6	4.0	4.4	4.6	3.0	3.5	2.6	3.6	1.6	1.8
Canada	2.2	3.5	4.6	2.8	3.8	4.0	2.3	3.7	3.1	3.4	4.0	3.2
Other advanced economies	5.2	3.1	4.0	−1.0	5.9	5.4	2.6	3.7	1.0	3.0	2.9	3.5
Memorandum												
Major advanced economies	2.8	2.7	2.7	3.4	3.6	3.5	2.1	2.0	2.0	2.8	2.4	2.1
Newly industrialized Asian economies	8.2	3.1	4.9	−5.5	8.2	7.4	3.3	4.9	−0.5	1.9	3.1	4.2
Public consumption												
Advanced economies	**2.0**	**2.4**	**1.5**	**1.8**	**2.9**	**2.5**	**2.8**	**3.5**	**2.4**	**2.0**	**1.8**	**2.4**
United States	1.1	2.6	1.8	1.6	3.1	1.7	3.1	4.3	3.0	2.1	2.1	3.2
Euro area	...	1.7	1.4	1.4	1.9	2.3	2.1	2.5	1.5	1.1	1.1	1.8
Germany	1.7	0.5	0.5	1.8	1.2	1.4	0.5	1.4	0.1	−1.6	−0.3	0.3
France	2.1	1.9	2.0	−0.2	1.9	2.2	1.9	2.9	2.1	2.7	1.5	2.1
Italy	1.1	1.4	0.3	0.3	1.4	1.7	3.8	1.9	2.3	0.7	0.8	0.3
Spain	4.3	4.3	2.9	3.7	4.2	4.2	3.9	4.5	3.9	6.4	5.7	4.0
Japan	3.4	2.5	1.1	2.2	4.7	4.9	3.0	2.6	1.2	2.7	1.5	1.2
United Kingdom	1.0	2.5	−0.5	1.1	4.0	3.7	1.7	4.4	4.5	3.1	1.7	1.6
Canada	1.3	2.7	−1.0	3.2	2.1	3.1	3.9	2.6	2.9	2.7	3.4	4.3
Other advanced economies	4.6	2.4	2.8	2.7	1.5	2.0	2.9	3.8	2.1	1.6	2.2	2.7
Memorandum												
Major advanced economies	1.6	2.2	1.2	1.5	3.0	2.4	2.7	3.4	2.4	1.9	1.7	2.3
Newly industrialized Asian economies	6.6	2.6	3.7	2.8	0.3	2.3	3.3	4.2	2.3	1.3	2.5	2.9
Gross fixed capital formation												
Advanced economies	**3.6**	**3.4**	**5.4**	**5.2**	**5.5**	**5.3**	**−0.9**	**−1.9**	**2.0**	**5.3**	**4.4**	**4.1**
United States	3.3	4.9	8.0	9.1	8.2	6.1	−1.7	−3.5	3.3	8.4	7.1	5.3
Euro area	...	2.4	2.8	5.3	6.1	5.1	0.1	−2.3	0.7	1.9	1.5	3.0
Germany	3.0	0.4	1.0	4.0	4.7	3.0	−3.7	−6.1	−0.8	−0.2	−0.8	2.8
France	1.9	3.3	0.1	6.9	7.9	7.5	2.3	−1.7	2.7	2.1	2.9	2.7
Italy	1.6	2.1	2.1	4.0	5.0	6.9	1.9	1.2	−1.8	2.1	−2.1	2.0
Spain	4.2	6.2	5.1	10.1	8.8	8.9	4.5	3.3	5.4	4.4	7.7	4.2
Japan	3.8	−0.1	0.6	−3.8	−1.1	2.0	−1.4	−5.7	0.9	1.7	2.9	3.1
United Kingdom	3.0	4.1	6.7	13.0	2.1	3.5	2.4	3.0	—	4.9	2.9	3.2
Canada	2.0	5.7	15.2	2.4	7.3	4.7	4.0	1.7	5.9	6.6	5.7	4.0
Other advanced economies	7.0	3.1	5.3	−1.4	3.1	6.9	−3.8	3.6	2.0	6.3	4.5	4.6
Memorandum												
Major advanced economies	3.1	3.3	5.2	5.9	5.6	5.0	−0.8	−3.0	2.0	5.3	4.4	4.1
Newly industrialized Asian economies	11.8	1.9	4.1	−10.0	2.7	10.6	−6.5	1.9	1.2	6.7	4.4	5.4

Table 3 *(concluded)*

| | Ten-Year Averages | | 1997 | 1998 | 1999 | 2000 | 2001 | 2002 | 2003 | 2004 | 2005 | 2006 |
	1987–96	1997–2006										
Final domestic demand												
Advanced economies	**3.0**	**2.8**	**3.1**	**3.1**	**4.0**	**3.9**	**1.6**	**1.5**	**2.0**	**3.1**	**2.6**	**2.7**
United States	2.7	3.7	4.3	5.3	5.4	4.5	1.8	1.8	3.0	4.4	3.8	3.3
Euro area	...	2.0	1.9	3.1	3.6	3.4	1.5	0.5	1.1	1.6	1.3	1.8
Germany	2.7	0.8	0.8	2.0	3.0	2.3	0.4	−1.3	−0.1	—	−0.4	0.8
France	1.8	2.4	0.6	3.3	3.8	4.0	2.3	1.7	1.9	2.3	2.0	2.2
Italy	1.7	1.7	2.4	2.8	2.9	3.4	1.6	0.8	0.9	1.1	0.2	0.9
Spain	3.3	4.0	3.5	5.5	5.5	4.7	3.7	3.3	3.5	4.7	1.9	3.5
Japan	3.4	0.8	0.8	−0.9	0.4	1.6	0.7	−0.7	0.6	1.7	2.0	2.0
United Kingdom	2.4	3.2	3.2	4.8	3.9	4.2	2.7	3.6	2.5	3.7	1.8	2.0
Canada	2.0	3.8	5.4	2.8	4.2	4.0	2.9	3.0	3.6	3.9	4.2	3.6
Other advanced economies	5.9	2.9	4.1	−1.4	4.4	5.4	1.1	3.8	1.5	3.5	3.1	3.7
Memorandum												
Major advanced economies	2.6	2.7	2.9	3.5	3.9	3.7	1.6	1.2	2.1	3.1	2.6	2.5
Newly industrialized Asian economies	9.0	2.6	4.3	−6.3	5.3	7.6	0.7	4.0	0.5	2.9	3.4	4.4
Stock building[1]												
Advanced economies	**—**	**—**	**0.3**	**—**	**0.1**	**—**	**−0.5**	**0.1**	**0.1**	**0.3**	**−0.1**	**−0.2**
United States	0.1	—	0.5	—	—	−0.1	−0.9	0.4	0.1	0.4	−0.4	−0.3
Euro area	...	—	−0.1	0.4	−0.1	−0.5	−0.5	−0.1	0.1	0.4	0.1	−0.1
Germany	—	—	0.1	0.4	−0.2	−0.1	−0.9	−0.6	0.6	0.5	0.4	0.1
France	−0.1	0.2	0.5	0.7	−0.2	0.3	−0.3	−0.4	−0.2	0.8	0.4	−0.2
Italy	−0.1	—	0.3	0.3	0.3	−1.1	−0.1	0.4	0.3	−0.1	0.2	—
Spain	—	—	—	0.1	—	0.3	—	—	—	—	—	—
Japan	—	−0.1	−0.1	−0.6	−0.4	0.3	0.1	−0.2	0.2	0.2	—	—
United Kingdom	—	—	0.2	0.1	0.2	−0.1	0.1	−0.3	0.2	0.1	−0.2	−0.2
Canada	0.1	0.1	0.7	−0.3	0.1	0.8	−1.7	0.4	0.9	—	0.2	−0.3
Other advanced economies	—	—	−0.3	−0.6	1.0	−0.1	−0.4	−0.1	−0.2	0.5	—	—
Memorandum												
Major advanced economies	—	—	0.4	—	−0.1	—	−0.6	0.1	0.2	0.3	−0.1	−0.2
Newly industrialized Asian economies	0.1	—	−0.2	−1.9	2.1	−0.1	−0.6	0.1	−0.5	0.9	−0.2	0.1
Foreign balance[1]												
Advanced economies	**—**	**−0.1**	**0.2**	**−0.3**	**−0.5**	**—**	**0.1**	**−0.1**	**−0.2**	**−0.1**	**−0.1**	**0.1**
United States	0.2	−0.6	−0.3	−1.2	−1.0	−0.9	−0.2	−0.7	−0.5	−0.7	−0.2	—
Euro area	...	0.1	0.9	−0.6	−0.7	0.9	0.8	0.5	−0.4	0.1	−0.1	0.1
Germany	0.1	0.6	0.8	−0.4	−0.8	1.0	1.7	1.9	−0.8	1.1	0.7	0.3
France	0.2	−0.3	1.2	−0.5	−0.4	−0.1	0.1	—	−0.9	−1.1	−0.9	−0.2
Italy	0.3	−0.4	−0.6	−1.2	−1.4	0.8	0.3	−0.8	−0.9	0.2	−0.4	0.5
Spain	−0.5	−1.0	0.4	−1.3	−1.4	−0.8	−0.2	−0.7	−1.0	−1.9	−1.7	−1.3
Japan	−0.2	0.3	1.0	0.4	−0.2	0.4	−0.6	0.6	0.6	0.8	—	—
United Kingdom	—	−0.5	−0.2	−1.4	−0.9	−0.1	−0.6	−1.2	−0.2	−0.7	0.3	0.4
Canada	0.2	−0.2	−1.7	1.7	1.4	0.6	0.7	−0.2	−2.4	−0.9	−1.3	0.1
Other advanced economies	−0.3	0.8	0.8	2.5	0.3	0.8	0.9	0.3	1.2	0.8	0.3	0.4
Memorandum												
Major advanced economies	0.1	−0.2	0.1	−0.7	−0.7	−0.2	—	−0.2	−0.4	−0.3	−0.2	0.1
Newly industrialized Asian economies	−1.0	1.7	1.3	6.0	0.3	0.6	1.2	1.2	3.1	2.2	1.1	0.6

[1]Changes expressed as percent of GDP in the preceding period.

Table 4. Advanced Economies: Unemployment, Employment, and Real Per Capita GDP
(Percent)

| | Ten-Year Averages[1] | | 1997 | 1998 | 1999 | 2000 | 2001 | 2002 | 2003 | 2004 | 2005 | 2006 |
	1987–96	1997–2006										
Unemployment rate												
Advanced economies	**6.8**	**6.3**	**6.8**	**6.7**	**6.4**	**5.8**	**5.9**	**6.4**	**6.6**	**6.3**	**6.1**	**5.9**
United States[2]	6.1	5.0	4.9	4.5	4.2	4.0	4.8	5.8	6.0	5.5	5.2	5.2
Euro area	. . .	8.9	10.6	10.0	9.2	8.2	7.9	8.3	8.7	8.9	8.7	8.4
Germany	7.3	8.9	9.7	9.1	8.4	7.8	7.9	8.7	9.6	9.2	9.5	9.3
France	10.4	9.8	11.5	11.1	10.5	9.1	8.4	8.9	9.5	9.7	9.8	9.6
Italy	11.3	9.7	11.7	11.8	11.4	10.6	9.5	9.0	8.7	8.5	8.1	7.8
Spain	20.0	13.0	20.6	18.6	15.6	13.9	10.6	11.5	11.5	11.0	9.1	8.0
Netherlands	6.4	3.8	5.0	3.8	3.2	2.8	2.2	2.8	3.7	4.6	5.0	4.5
Belgium	8.4	8.0	9.2	9.3	8.6	6.9	6.7	7.3	7.9	7.8	7.9	8.0
Austria	3.4	4.3	4.4	4.5	3.9	3.7	3.6	4.1	4.3	4.8	5.0	4.7
Finland	9.7	9.6	12.6	11.4	10.2	9.8	9.1	9.1	9.0	8.8	8.0	7.8
Greece	8.4	10.7	9.8	11.0	12.1	11.4	10.8	10.3	9.7	10.5	10.5	10.5
Portugal	5.8	5.7	6.7	5.0	4.4	3.9	4.0	5.0	6.3	6.7	7.4	7.7
Ireland	14.5	5.3	10.3	7.6	5.6	4.3	3.9	4.4	4.7	4.5	4.2	4.0
Luxembourg	2.0	3.6	3.6	3.1	2.9	2.6	2.6	3.0	3.8	4.4	4.8	5.2
Japan	2.6	4.6	3.4	4.1	4.7	4.7	5.0	5.4	5.3	4.7	4.3	4.1
United Kingdom	8.5	5.5	7.1	6.3	6.0	5.5	5.1	5.2	5.0	4.8	4.7	4.8
Canada	9.5	7.5	9.2	8.4	7.6	6.9	7.2	7.7	7.6	7.2	6.8	6.7
Korea	2.5	4.2	2.6	7.0	6.6	4.4	4.0	3.3	3.6	3.5	3.6	3.3
Australia	8.4	6.4	8.3	7.7	6.9	6.3	6.8	6.4	6.0	5.5	5.1	5.1
Taiwan Province of China	1.7	3.9	2.7	2.7	2.9	3.0	4.6	5.2	5.0	4.4	4.3	4.2
Sweden	4.7	5.3	8.1	6.5	5.6	4.7	4.0	4.0	4.9	5.5	5.2	4.9
Switzerland	2.1	3.0	4.5	3.4	2.4	1.7	1.6	2.3	3.4	3.5	3.7	3.7
Hong Kong SAR	1.9	5.6	2.2	4.7	6.2	5.0	5.1	7.3	7.9	6.8	5.7	4.6
Denmark	9.8	5.8	7.8	6.4	5.5	5.1	4.9	4.9	5.8	6.0	5.6	5.5
Norway	4.9	3.9	4.1	3.2	3.2	3.4	3.5	3.9	4.5	4.5	4.2	4.0
Israel	8.4	9.2	7.7	8.5	8.9	8.7	9.3	10.3	10.7	10.3	9.1	8.7
Singapore	2.6	3.5	1.8	3.2	3.5	3.1	3.3	4.4	4.7	4.0	3.6	3.4
New Zealand	7.5	5.4	6.6	7.4	6.8	6.0	5.3	5.2	4.7	3.9	4.0	4.2
Cyprus	2.6	3.3	3.4	3.4	3.6	3.4	2.9	3.1	3.5	3.6	3.2	3.0
Iceland	2.8	2.4	3.9	2.8	1.9	1.3	1.4	2.5	3.4	3.1	2.3	1.7
Memorandum												
Major advanced economies	6.6	6.2	6.5	6.3	6.1	5.7	5.9	6.6	6.7	6.4	6.1	6.0
Newly industrialized Asian economies	2.3	4.2	2.6	5.4	5.4	4.0	4.2	4.2	4.4	4.1	4.0	3.7
Growth in employment												
Advanced economies	**1.1**	**1.1**	**1.5**	**1.1**	**1.4**	**2.1**	**0.7**	**0.3**	**0.6**	**1.0**	**1.2**	**1.1**
United States	1.5	1.3	2.3	1.5	1.5	2.5	—	−0.3	0.9	1.1	1.6	1.7
Euro area	. . .	1.2	0.8	1.9	1.8	2.2	1.3	0.5	0.2	0.7	1.0	1.1
Germany	0.5	0.5	−0.1	1.2	1.4	1.9	0.4	−0.6	−1.0	0.4	0.2	1.0
France	0.4	1.0	0.4	1.5	2.0	2.7	1.7	0.7	−0.1	−0.1	0.3	0.5
Italy	−0.4	1.0	0.4	1.1	1.3	1.9	2.1	1.5	1.0	0.3	0.4	0.3
Spain	1.7	4.3	3.7	4.2	5.6	5.6	4.1	3.0	4.0	3.9	5.3	3.2
Japan	1.0	−0.2	1.1	−0.7	−0.8	−0.2	−0.5	−1.3	−0.2	0.2	0.6	—
United Kingdom	0.4	1.0	1.8	1.0	1.4	1.2	0.8	0.8	0.9	0.9	0.5	0.2
Canada	1.2	1.9	1.6	2.5	2.7	2.6	1.3	2.4	2.3	1.8	1.2	0.9
Other advanced economies	1.9	1.3	1.3	−0.9	1.6	2.9	1.1	1.6	0.6	1.6	1.8	1.5
Memorandum												
Major advanced economies	0.9	0.9	1.4	1.0	1.1	1.8	0.4	−0.1	0.5	0.7	0.9	1.0
Newly industrialized Asian economies	2.6	1.2	1.8	−2.9	1.5	3.5	1.0	2.0	0.3	1.8	1.7	1.7

Table 4 *(concluded)*

	Ten-Year Averages[1]		1997	1998	1999	2000	2001	2002	2003	2004	2005	2006
	1987–96	1997–2006										
Growth in real per capita GDP												
Advanced economies	**2.3**	**2.1**	**2.9**	**2.0**	**2.8**	**3.3**	**0.6**	**0.9**	**1.3**	**2.7**	**2.0**	**2.2**
United States	1.7	2.2	3.3	3.0	3.3	2.5	−0.3	0.6	1.7	3.2	2.5	2.3
Euro area	. . .	1.7	2.3	2.6	2.5	3.4	1.3	0.5	0.2	1.6	0.9	1.6
Germany	1.9	1.2	1.5	2.0	1.9	3.0	1.1	−0.1	−0.3	1.6	0.3	1.2
France	1.4	1.7	1.9	3.0	2.7	3.5	1.4	0.7	0.3	1.4	1.1	1.3
Italy	1.8	1.2	1.9	1.7	1.6	3.0	1.8	0.5	0.4	0.4	−0.2	1.3
Spain	2.7	3.1	3.8	4.0	3.8	4.6	2.9	2.0	2.3	2.5	2.6	2.5
Japan	2.8	0.9	1.6	−1.3	−0.3	2.2	—	−0.5	1.2	2.6	1.9	1.9
United Kingdom	2.1	2.3	2.9	3.0	2.7	3.7	1.8	1.5	2.0	2.7	1.4	1.7
Canada	0.9	2.5	3.2	3.2	4.7	4.3	0.7	1.9	1.1	2.0	2.0	2.4
Other advanced economies	4.0	2.7	3.4	−0.4	4.4	5.0	0.7	3.0	1.8	3.8	2.6	3.2
Memorandum												
Major advanced economies	2.0	1.9	2.7	2.2	2.5	2.9	0.5	0.6	1.3	2.7	1.9	2.0
Newly industrialized Asian economies	6.8	3.4	4.4	−3.6	6.4	7.0	0.5	4.6	2.5	5.0	3.4	4.2

[1]Compound annual rate of change for employment and per capita GDP; arithmetic average for unemployment rate.
[2]The projections for unemployment have been adjusted to reflect the survey techniques adopted by the U.S. Bureau of Labor Statistics in January 1994.

Table 5. Other Emerging Market and Developing Countries: Real GDP
(Annual percent change)

	Ten-Year Averages		1997	1998	1999	2000	2001	2002	2003	2004	2005	2006
	1987–96	1997–2006										
Other emerging market and developing countries	**3.8**	**5.3**	**5.2**	**3.0**	**4.0**	**5.8**	**4.1**	**4.8**	**6.5**	**7.3**	**6.4**	**6.1**
Regional groups												
Africa	2.2	4.1	3.4	3.2	2.8	3.3	4.1	3.6	4.6	5.3	4.5	5.9
Sub-Sahara	2.2	4.1	4.2	2.4	2.8	3.6	4.1	3.6	4.1	5.4	4.8	5.9
Excluding Nigeria and South Africa	2.3	4.8	5.5	4.3	3.4	2.8	5.2	4.0	3.6	6.5	5.3	7.4
Central and eastern Europe	0.9	3.7	4.2	2.8	0.5	4.9	0.2	4.4	4.6	6.5	4.3	4.6
Commonwealth of Independent States[1]	...	5.1	1.1	−3.5	5.1	9.1	6.3	5.3	7.9	8.4	6.0	5.7
Russia	...	4.7	1.4	−5.3	6.3	10.0	5.1	4.7	7.3	7.2	5.5	5.3
Excluding Russia	...	6.0	0.6	0.8	2.2	6.8	9.1	6.6	9.2	11.0	7.1	6.8
Developing Asia	7.8	6.7	6.5	4.2	6.2	6.7	5.6	6.6	8.1	8.2	7.8	7.2
China	10.0	8.4	8.8	7.8	7.1	8.0	7.5	8.3	9.5	9.5	9.0	8.2
India	5.9	6.0	5.0	5.8	6.7	5.4	3.9	4.7	7.4	7.3	7.1	6.3
Excluding China and India	6.4	3.9	3.8	−4.5	3.8	5.4	3.2	4.8	5.8	6.1	5.4	5.7
Middle East	3.4	4.6	4.7	4.2	2.0	4.9	3.7	4.2	6.5	5.5	5.4	5.0
Western Hemisphere	2.7	2.8	5.2	2.3	0.4	3.9	0.5	—	2.2	5.6	4.1	3.8
Brazil	2.1	2.4	3.3	0.1	0.8	4.4	1.3	1.9	0.5	4.9	3.3	3.5
Mexico	2.5	3.5	6.7	4.9	3.9	6.6	−0.2	0.8	1.4	4.4	3.0	3.5
Analytical groups												
By source of export earnings												
Fuel	2.6	4.6	4.4	3.3	0.9	4.7	3.8	3.6	6.4	7.2	6.0	6.2
Nonfuel	3.9	5.4	5.3	3.0	4.3	5.9	4.1	4.9	6.5	7.3	6.4	6.1
of which, primary products	3.2	3.4	3.7	2.8	1.3	1.8	2.9	2.9	3.3	5.6	4.4	5.1
By external financing source												
Net debtor countries	3.5	4.1	4.6	2.1	2.9	4.6	2.4	3.3	4.9	6.1	5.2	5.2
of which, official financing	4.4	3.5	4.9	−0.5	1.0	3.1	2.2	1.6	5.3	6.1	5.9	5.3
Net debtor countries by debt-servicing experience												
Countries with arrears and/or rescheduling during 1999–2003	3.9	4.0	5.4	−0.4	1.7	3.6	3.0	2.2	5.8	6.6	6.0	5.9
Other groups												
Heavily indebted poor countries	1.8	4.5	4.0	3.6	3.7	2.9	5.1	3.9	4.2	6.4	5.4	5.9
Middle East and north Africa	3.1	4.6	4.1	4.8	2.3	4.5	3.9	4.2	6.3	5.5	5.1	5.6
Memorandum												
Real per capita GDP												
Other emerging market and developing countries	2.1	4.0	3.7	1.6	2.6	4.4	2.7	3.5	5.2	6.0	5.1	4.9
Africa	−0.6	1.8	1.0	0.8	0.4	1.0	1.8	1.4	2.4	3.2	2.4	3.7
Central and eastern Europe	0.2	3.2	3.7	2.3	0.1	4.4	−0.2	3.9	4.2	6.1	3.9	4.2
Commonwealth of Independent States[1]	...	5.3	1.3	−3.3	5.3	9.3	6.6	5.6	8.2	8.6	6.2	6.0
Developing Asia	6.1	5.4	5.0	2.8	4.8	5.4	4.3	5.4	7.0	7.0	6.6	6.1
Middle East	0.8	2.5	2.5	2.1	−0.1	2.8	1.6	2.2	4.4	3.5	3.3	3.0
Western Hemisphere	0.9	1.3	3.6	0.7	−1.1	2.4	−1.0	−1.5	0.7	4.2	2.7	2.4

[1]Mongolia, which is not a member of the Commonwealth of Independent States, is included in this group for reasons of geography and similarities in economic structure.

Table 6. Other Emerging and Developing Countries—by Country: Real GDP[1]

(Annual percent change)

	Average 1987–96	1997	1998	1999	2000	2001	2002	2003	2004	2005	2006
Africa	**2.2**	**3.4**	**3.2**	**2.8**	**3.3**	**4.1**	**3.6**	**4.6**	**5.3**	**4.5**	**5.9**
Algeria	0.8	1.1	5.1	3.2	2.1	2.6	4.7	6.9	5.2	4.8	5.3
Angola	−0.1	7.9	6.8	3.2	3.0	3.1	14.4	3.4	11.1	14.7	27.6
Benin	3.2	5.7	4.0	5.3	4.9	6.2	4.5	3.9	3.1	3.9	4.4
Botswana	7.6	6.7	5.9	5.5	7.6	5.1	5.0	6.6	4.9	3.8	3.5
Burkina Faso	4.7	6.9	8.4	4.1	3.3	6.7	5.2	7.9	4.6	3.5	5.0
Burundi	−0.5	0.4	4.8	−1.0	−0.9	2.1	4.5	−1.2	4.8	5.0	5.0
Cameroon[2]	−2.3	5.1	5.0	4.4	4.2	4.5	4.0	4.1	3.5	2.8	4.3
Cape Verde	5.0	8.5	8.0	11.9	7.3	6.1	5.4	6.2	4.4	6.3	7.7
Central African Republic	−1.7	7.5	3.9	3.6	1.8	0.3	−0.6	−7.6	1.3	2.2	3.5
Chad	3.6	4.2	7.7	−1.7	−0.6	9.9	9.9	11.3	29.7	5.9	7.6
Comoros	0.8	4.2	1.2	1.9	2.4	2.3	2.3	2.1	1.9	2.8	3.3
Congo, Dem. Rep. of	−4.3	−5.4	−1.7	−4.3	−6.9	−2.1	3.5	5.7	6.8	6.6	7.0
Congo, Rep. of	5.0	−0.6	3.7	−3.0	8.2	3.6	5.4	0.3	3.6	9.2	4.9
Côte d'Ivoire	2.8	5.7	4.7	1.5	−3.8	0.1	−1.6	−1.6	1.6	1.0	2.0
Djibouti	−1.5	−0.7	0.1	2.2	0.4	2.0	2.6	3.2	3.0	3.2	3.8
Equatorial Guinea	12.4	151.4	26.0	25.2	27.0	48.1	9.7	21.3	32.8	0.2	6.4
Eritrea	...	7.9	1.8	—	−13.1	9.2	0.7	3.0	1.8	0.8	0.4
Ethiopia	3.1	5.1	−1.4	6.0	5.4	7.7	1.6	−4.2	11.5	7.3	5.0
Gabon	2.5	5.7	3.5	−8.9	−1.9	2.0	—	2.4	1.4	2.2	2.7
Gambia, The	3.3	4.9	6.5	6.4	5.5	5.8	−3.2	6.9	5.1	4.7	4.7
Ghana	4.7	4.2	4.7	4.4	3.7	4.2	4.5	5.2	5.8	5.8	5.8
Guinea	4.2	4.9	4.8	4.7	1.9	4.0	4.2	1.2	2.7	3.0	4.9
Guinea-Bissau	3.5	6.5	−27.2	7.6	7.5	0.2	−7.2	0.6	4.3	2.3	2.6
Kenya	3.1	0.2	3.3	2.4	0.6	4.7	0.3	2.8	4.3	4.7	4.9
Lesotho	6.1	4.8	−3.5	0.5	1.9	3.3	3.7	3.2	3.0	0.8	1.9
Madagascar	1.2	3.7	3.9	4.7	4.7	6.0	−12.7	9.8	5.3	6.3	7.0
Malawi	3.4	6.6	1.1	3.5	0.8	−4.1	2.1	3.9	4.6	2.1	8.2
Mali	3.3	5.3	8.4	3.0	−3.2	12.1	4.3	7.2	2.2	6.4	6.7
Mauritania	3.1	2.8	3.9	7.8	6.7	3.6	2.3	6.4	6.9	5.4	26.9
Mauritius	6.8	5.7	5.9	4.4	8.2	7.1	3.5	3.2	4.3	3.6	3.6
Morocco	3.0	−2.2	7.7	−0.1	1.0	6.3	3.2	5.5	4.2	1.0	5.9
Mozambique, Rep. of	4.9	11.1	12.6	7.5	1.9	13.1	8.2	7.8	7.2	7.7	7.4
Namibia	3.3	4.2	3.3	3.4	3.5	2.4	2.5	3.7	4.2	3.6	3.8
Niger	1.3	2.8	10.4	−0.6	−1.4	7.1	3.0	5.3	0.9	4.2	4.2
Nigeria	3.6	3.2	0.3	1.5	5.4	3.1	1.5	10.7	6.0	3.9	4.9
Rwanda	−3.9	13.8	8.9	7.6	6.0	6.7	9.4	0.9	4.0	4.0	4.3
São Tomé and Príncipe	0.9	1.0	2.5	2.5	3.0	4.0	4.1	4.0	3.8	3.2	4.5
Senegal	2.4	3.3	4.5	6.2	3.0	4.7	1.1	6.5	6.2	5.7	5.0
Seychelles	5.3	12.2	2.5	1.9	4.3	−2.2	1.3	−6.3	−2.0	−2.8	−2.0
Sierra Leone	−4.2	−17.6	−0.8	−8.1	3.8	18.2	27.5	9.3	7.4	7.5	7.1
South Africa	1.7	2.6	0.5	2.4	4.2	2.7	3.6	2.8	3.7	4.3	3.9
Sudan	2.2	10.8	10.1	5.0	9.2	6.5	6.3	4.6	6.9	8.0	13.6
Swaziland	5.6	3.8	2.8	3.5	2.6	1.6	2.9	2.7	2.1	2.0	1.7
Tanzania	3.6	3.5	3.7	3.5	5.1	6.2	7.2	7.1	6.7	6.9	7.2
Togo	2.0	3.5	−2.3	2.4	−0.4	0.6	4.5	4.4	2.9	3.0	3.0
Tunisia	4.3	5.4	4.8	6.1	4.7	4.9	1.7	5.6	5.8	5.0	5.9
Uganda	6.4	5.5	3.6	8.3	5.3	4.8	6.9	4.5	5.8	5.9	6.6
Zambia	−0.3	3.3	−1.9	2.2	3.6	4.9	3.3	5.1	5.0	5.0	5.0
Zimbabwe	3.6	1.4	0.1	−3.6	−7.3	−2.7	−4.4	−10.4	−4.2	−7.1	−4.8

Table 6 *(continued)*

	Average 1987–96	1997	1998	1999	2000	2001	2002	2003	2004	2005	2006
Central and eastern Europe[3]	**0.9**	**4.2**	**2.8**	**0.5**	**4.9**	**0.2**	**4.4**	**4.6**	**6.5**	**4.3**	**4.6**
Albania	−0.8	−10.2	12.7	10.1	7.3	7.2	3.4	6.0	5.9	6.0	6.0
Bosnia and Herzegovina	. . .	29.9	15.9	9.6	5.5	4.3	5.3	4.0	5.7	5.4	5.7
Bulgaria	−4.8	−5.6	4.0	2.3	5.4	4.1	4.9	4.3	5.6	5.5	5.5
Croatia	. . .	6.8	2.5	−0.9	2.9	4.4	5.2	4.3	3.8	3.4	3.9
Czech Republic	. . .	−0.8	−1.0	0.5	3.3	2.6	1.5	3.2	4.4	4.1	3.9
Estonia	. . .	11.1	4.4	0.3	7.9	6.5	7.2	6.7	7.8	7.0	6.0
Hungary	−0.9	4.6	4.9	4.2	5.2	3.8	3.5	2.9	4.2	3.4	3.6
Latvia	. . .	8.3	4.7	3.3	6.9	8.0	6.4	7.5	8.5	7.8	6.8
Lithuania	. . .	7.0	7.3	−1.7	3.9	6.4	6.8	9.7	6.7	6.8	6.5
Macedonia, FYR	. . .	1.4	3.4	4.4	4.5	−4.5	0.9	3.5	2.4	3.8	3.7
Malta	5.9	4.8	3.4	4.1	9.9	−0.4	1.0	−1.9	1.0	1.5	1.8
Serbia and Montenegro	. . .	—	2.5	−18.0	5.0	5.5	3.8	2.7	7.2	4.6	4.8
Poland	1.8	6.8	4.8	4.1	4.0	1.0	1.4	3.8	5.4	3.0	4.0
Romania	−1.8	−6.1	−4.8	−1.2	2.1	5.7	5.1	5.2	8.3	5.0	5.0
Slovak Republic	. . .	4.6	4.2	1.5	2.0	3.8	4.6	4.5	5.5	5.0	5.4
Slovenia	. . .	4.8	3.6	5.6	3.9	2.7	3.3	2.5	4.6	3.9	4.0
Turkey	4.4	7.5	3.0	−4.4	7.4	−7.5	7.9	5.8	8.9	5.0	5.0
Commonwealth of Independent States[3,4]	. . .	**1.1**	**−3.5**	**5.1**	**9.1**	**6.3**	**5.3**	**7.9**	**8.4**	**6.0**	**5.7**
Russia	. . .	1.4	−5.3	6.3	10.0	5.1	4.7	7.3	7.2	5.5	5.3
Excluding Russia	. . .	0.6	0.8	2.2	6.8	9.1	6.6	9.2	11.0	7.1	6.8
Armenia	. . .	3.3	7.3	3.3	6.0	9.6	13.2	13.9	10.1	8.0	6.0
Azerbaijan	. . .	5.8	10.0	7.4	9.2	6.5	8.1	11.5	10.2	18.7	26.6
Belarus	. . .	11.4	8.4	3.4	5.8	4.7	5.0	7.0	11.0	7.1	4.0
Georgia	. . .	10.6	2.9	3.0	1.9	4.7	5.5	11.1	6.2	7.5	4.5
Kazakhstan	. . .	1.6	−1.9	2.7	9.8	13.5	9.8	9.3	9.4	8.8	7.7
Kyrgyz Republic	. . .	9.9	2.1	3.7	5.4	5.3	—	7.0	7.1	4.0	5.5
Moldova	. . .	1.6	−6.5	−3.4	2.1	6.1	7.8	6.6	7.3	6.0	5.0
Mongolia	−0.2	4.0	3.5	3.2	1.1	1.0	4.0	5.6	10.6	5.0	6.0
Tajikistan	. . .	1.8	5.2	3.8	8.3	10.2	9.1	10.2	10.6	8.0	7.0
Turkmenistan	. . .	−11.3	6.7	16.4	18.6	20.4	15.8	17.1	17.2	9.6	6.5
Ukraine	. . .	−3.0	−1.9	−0.2	5.9	9.2	5.2	9.6	12.1	5.5	5.4
Uzbekistan	. . .	2.5	2.1	3.4	3.2	4.1	3.1	1.5	7.1	3.5	2.5

Table 6 *(continued)*

	Average 1987–96	1997	1998	1999	2000	2001	2002	2003	2004	2005	2006
Developing Asia	**7.8**	**6.5**	**4.2**	**6.2**	**6.7**	**5.6**	**6.6**	**8.1**	**8.2**	**7.8**	**7.2**
Afghanistan, I.S. of	. . .	. . .	. . .	. . .	. . .	. . .	28.6	15.7	7.5	13.6	10.9
Bangladesh	4.2	5.3	5.0	5.4	5.6	4.8	4.8	5.8	5.8	5.7	6.0
Bhutan	6.2	7.2	5.8	7.7	9.5	8.6	7.1	6.8	7.9	7.7	13.3
Brunei Darussalam	. . .	2.6	−4.0	2.6	2.8	3.1	2.8	3.8	1.7	3.0	2.2
Cambodia	. . .	5.7	5.0	12.6	8.4	5.5	5.3	7.1	7.7	6.3	6.1
China	10.0	8.8	7.8	7.1	8.0	7.5	8.3	9.5	9.5	9.0	8.2
Fiji	3.5	−2.3	1.2	9.2	−2.8	2.7	4.3	4.8	4.1	1.2	2.5
India	5.9	5.0	5.8	6.7	5.4	3.9	4.7	7.4	7.3	7.1	6.3
Indonesia	7.0	4.5	−13.1	0.8	4.9	3.8	4.4	4.9	5.1	5.8	5.8
Kiribati	2.4	1.9	12.6	9.5	1.6	1.9	−4.2	2.2	−1.4	0.3	0.8
Lao PDR	5.2	6.9	4.0	7.3	5.8	5.8	5.8	5.8	6.4	7.3	7.0
Malaysia	9.1	7.3	−7.4	6.1	8.9	0.3	4.4	5.4	7.1	5.5	6.0
Maldives	7.5	10.4	9.8	7.2	4.8	3.5	6.5	8.4	8.8	1.0	9.0
Myanmar	2.5	5.7	5.8	10.9	13.7	11.3	12.0	13.8	5.0	4.5	3.5
Nepal	5.5	5.3	2.9	4.5	6.1	5.5	−0.6	3.4	3.4	2.5	4.0
Pakistan	4.9	1.8	3.1	4.0	3.0	2.5	4.1	5.7	7.1	7.4	6.5
Papua New Guinea	5.1	−3.9	−3.8	7.6	−1.2	−2.3	−0.8	2.7	2.5	2.8	2.8
Philippines	3.7	5.2	−0.6	3.4	4.4	1.8	4.4	4.5	6.0	4.7	4.8
Samoa	2.5	0.8	2.4	2.6	6.9	6.2	1.8	3.1	3.2	3.2	3.2
Solomon Islands	5.7	−1.4	1.8	−0.5	−14.3	−9.0	−2.4	5.6	5.5	4.4	5.0
Sri Lanka	4.3	6.4	4.7	4.3	6.0	−1.5	4.0	6.0	5.4	5.3	6.0
Thailand	9.5	−1.4	−10.5	4.4	4.8	2.2	5.3	6.9	6.1	3.5	5.0
Timor-Leste, Dem. Rep. of	. . .	. . .	. . .	. . .	15.4	16.6	−6.7	−6.2	1.8	2.5	4.9
Tonga	1.5	−3.0	3.6	2.3	5.6	1.8	2.1	2.9	1.5	2.5	2.8
Vanuatu	3.5	8.4	4.5	−3.2	2.7	−2.7	−4.9	2.4	3.0	2.8	2.6
Vietnam	7.1	8.2	5.8	4.8	6.8	6.9	7.1	7.3	7.7	7.5	7.0
Middle East	**3.4**	**4.7**	**4.2**	**2.0**	**4.9**	**3.7**	**4.2**	**6.5**	**5.5**	**5.4**	**5.0**
Bahrain	4.5	3.1	4.8	4.2	5.3	4.6	5.2	7.2	5.4	7.1	5.2
Egypt	2.8	5.9	7.5	6.1	5.4	3.5	3.2	3.1	4.1	4.8	5.0
Iran, I.R. of	3.1	3.4	2.7	1.9	5.1	3.7	7.5	6.7	5.6	5.7	5.4
Iraq	. . .	. . .	. . .	. . .	. . .	. . .	. . .	. . .	. . .	. . .	. . .
Jordan	3.0	3.3	3.0	3.4	4.3	5.3	5.7	4.1	7.7	5.0	2.5
Kuwait	1.8	2.5	3.7	−1.8	1.9	0.7	−0.5	9.7	7.2	3.2	3.2
Lebanon	−2.5	4.0	2.3	−1.2	1.2	4.2	2.9	5.0	6.0	—	3.0
Libya	−0.3	4.3	−0.4	0.3	1.1	4.5	3.3	9.1	4.4	4.3	4.4
Oman	4.4	6.2	2.7	−0.2	5.5	7.5	2.3	1.9	4.5	3.8	6.2
Qatar	1.4	31.1	11.7	4.5	9.1	4.5	7.3	8.6	9.3	5.5	7.1
Saudi Arabia	3.0	2.5	2.8	−0.7	4.9	0.5	0.1	7.7	5.2	6.0	4.7
Syrian Arab Republic	5.8	5.0	6.8	−3.6	0.6	3.8	4.2	2.6	3.4	3.5	4.0
United Arab Emirates	6.3	6.7	4.3	3.9	5.0	8.0	4.1	11.3	8.5	5.6	4.2
Yemen	. . .	6.4	5.3	3.5	4.4	4.6	3.9	3.1	2.5	3.7	2.0

Table 6 *(concluded)*

	Average 1987–96	1997	1998	1999	2000	2001	2002	2003	2004	2005	2006
Western Hemisphere	**2.7**	**5.2**	**2.3**	**0.4**	**3.9**	**0.5**	**—**	**2.2**	**5.6**	**4.1**	**3.8**
Antigua and Barbuda	3.9	5.6	5.0	4.0	3.5	2.1	2.4	4.9	4.1	2.4	2.6
Argentina	2.6	8.1	3.8	−3.4	−0.8	−4.4	−10.9	8.8	9.0	7.5	4.2
Bahamas, The	2.9	4.9	6.8	4.0	1.9	0.8	1.4	1.9	3.0	3.5	4.0
Barbados	0.7	4.6	6.2	0.5	2.3	−2.6	0.5	2.0	4.4	3.1	3.3
Belize	7.7	3.6	3.7	8.7	13.0	4.6	4.7	9.2	4.6	2.2	2.7
Bolivia	3.9	5.0	5.0	0.4	2.5	1.7	2.4	2.8	3.6	3.9	2.5
Brazil	2.1	3.3	0.1	0.8	4.4	1.3	1.9	0.5	4.9	3.3	3.5
Chile	7.9	6.6	3.2	−0.8	4.5	3.4	2.2	3.7	6.1	5.9	5.8
Colombia	4.2	3.4	0.6	−4.2	2.9	1.5	1.9	4.1	4.1	4.0	4.0
Costa Rica	4.8	5.6	8.4	8.2	1.8	1.0	2.9	6.5	4.2	3.2	2.7
Dominica	3.1	2.4	2.8	1.3	0.3	−3.9	−3.7	0.9	3.7	2.8	2.8
Dominican Republic	3.8	8.3	7.3	8.1	7.8	4.0	4.3	−1.6	2.0	4.5	4.5
Ecuador	2.7	4.1	2.1	−6.3	2.8	5.1	3.4	2.7	6.9	2.7	2.8
El Salvador	4.3	4.2	3.7	3.4	2.2	1.7	2.2	1.8	1.5	2.0	2.0
Grenada	3.5	4.4	7.9	7.3	7.0	−4.4	0.8	5.8	−3.0	0.9	7.0
Guatemala	3.9	4.4	5.0	3.8	3.6	2.3	2.2	2.1	2.7	3.2	3.2
Guyana	3.3	6.2	−1.7	3.0	−1.3	2.3	1.1	−0.7	1.6	−2.6	3.4
Haiti	−1.0	2.7	2.2	2.7	0.9	−1.0	−0.5	0.5	−3.8	1.5	2.5
Honduras	3.6	5.0	2.9	−1.9	5.7	2.6	2.7	3.5	4.6	4.2	4.5
Jamaica	1.7	−1.4	−0.6	1.1	0.8	1.0	1.9	2.0	2.5	0.7	3.7
Mexico	2.5	6.7	4.9	3.9	6.6	−0.2	0.8	1.4	4.4	3.0	3.5
Netherlands Antilles	3.0	0.8	0.9	−2.2	−3.9	2.2	1.2	1.7	−0.1	0.7	1.5
Nicaragua	−0.1	4.0	3.7	7.0	4.1	3.0	0.8	2.3	5.1	3.5	4.0
Panama	2.7	6.5	7.3	3.9	2.7	0.6	2.2	4.3	6.0	3.5	4.0
Paraguay	3.9	3.0	0.6	−1.5	−3.3	2.1	—	3.8	4.0	3.0	3.5
Peru	0.7	6.8	−0.7	0.9	2.9	0.2	4.9	4.0	4.8	5.5	4.5
St. Kitts and Nevis	5.2	7.3	1.0	3.9	6.5	1.7	−0.3	0.6	4.0	3.5	3.6
St. Lucia	4.6	0.6	3.3	3.9	−0.3	−4.1	0.1	2.9	4.0	5.1	5.8
St. Vincent and the Grenadines	4.4	3.1	4.6	4.1	1.8	1.1	3.7	3.9	4.0	4.4	4.2
Suriname	0.6	5.7	1.6	−0.9	−0.1	4.5	3.0	5.3	4.6	4.9	3.3
Trinidad and Tobago	0.3	2.8	7.8	4.4	7.3	4.3	6.8	13.2	6.2	6.3	10.1
Uruguay	3.6	5.0	4.5	−2.8	−1.4	−3.4	−11.0	2.2	12.3	6.0	4.0
Venezuela	2.3	6.4	0.3	−6.0	3.7	3.4	−8.9	−7.7	17.9	7.8	4.5

[1]For many countries, figures for recent years are IMF staff estimates. Data for some countries are for fiscal years.

[2]The percent changes in 2002 are calculated over a period of 18 months, reflecting a change in the fiscal year cycle (from July–June to January–December).

[3]Data for some countries refer to real net material product (NMP) or are estimates based on NMP. For many countries, figures for recent years are IMF staff estimates. The figures should be interpreted only as indicative of broad orders of magnitude because reliable, comparable data are not generally available. In particular, the growth of output of new private enterprises of the informal economy is not fully reflected in the recent figures.

[4]Mongolia, which is not a member of the Commonwealth of Independent States, is included in this group for reasons of geography and similarities in economic structure.

Table 7. Summary of Inflation

(Percent)

| | Ten-Year Averages | | 1997 | 1998 | 1999 | 2000 | 2001 | 2002 | 2003 | 2004 | 2005 | 2006 |
	1987–96	1997–2006										
GDP deflators												
Advanced economies	**3.3**	**1.6**	**1.7**	**1.3**	**0.9**	**1.4**	**1.9**	**1.6**	**1.6**	**1.8**	**1.7**	**1.7**
United States	2.8	2.0	1.7	1.1	1.4	2.2	2.4	1.7	2.0	2.6	2.5	2.1
Euro area	. . .	1.8	1.5	1.6	1.0	1.4	2.7	2.5	2.0	1.9	1.6	1.7
Japan	1.0	−1.0	0.4	−0.2	−1.3	−1.5	−1.3	−1.3	−1.4	−1.2	−1.2	−0.6
Other advanced economies[1]	4.6	1.9	2.6	2.0	1.0	1.9	2.0	1.7	2.0	1.9	1.8	2.3
Consumer prices												
Advanced economies	**3.5**	**1.9**	**2.0**	**1.5**	**1.4**	**2.2**	**2.1**	**1.5**	**1.8**	**2.0**	**2.2**	**2.0**
United States	3.7	2.5	2.3	1.5	2.2	3.4	2.8	1.6	2.3	2.7	3.1	2.8
Euro area[2]	. . .	1.9	1.6	1.1	1.1	2.1	2.3	2.3	2.1	2.1	2.1	1.8
Japan	1.3	−0.1	1.7	0.6	−0.3	−0.9	−0.7	−1.0	−0.2	—	−0.4	−0.1
Other advanced economies	4.5	1.9	2.2	2.3	1.2	1.8	2.1	1.7	1.8	1.8	2.1	2.2
Other emerging market and developing countries	**56.6**	**7.6**	**11.6**	**11.2**	**10.4**	**7.3**	**6.7**	**5.9**	**6.0**	**5.8**	**5.9**	**5.7**
Regional groups												
Africa	28.6	10.2	13.5	9.1	11.5	13.1	12.2	9.6	10.4	7.8	8.2	7.0
Central and eastern Europe	61.3	18.1	51.4	32.7	22.9	22.7	19.4	14.7	9.2	6.5	4.8	4.3
Commonwealth of Independent States[3]	. . .	20.6	18.1	23.7	69.6	24.6	20.3	13.8	12.0	10.3	12.6	10.5
Developing Asia	11.0	3.7	4.9	7.8	2.5	1.9	2.7	2.1	2.6	4.2	4.2	4.7
Middle East	15.3	7.8	8.6	8.4	8.5	5.9	5.4	6.5	7.1	8.4	10.0	9.7
Western Hemisphere	181.9	8.0	11.9	9.0	8.2	7.6	6.1	8.9	10.6	6.5	6.3	5.4
Memorandum												
European Union	9.6	2.2	2.6	2.1	1.7	2.5	2.6	2.2	2.0	2.2	2.1	1.9
Analytical groups												
By source of export earnings												
Fuel	27.0	11.4	15.7	13.1	12.7	10.0	9.6	10.3	11.1	10.3	11.2	10.0
Nonfuel	59.6	7.3	11.2	11.1	10.2	7.1	6.5	5.6	5.6	5.4	5.5	5.4
of which, primary products	62.9	18.4	24.2	12.2	23.5	29.1	26.6	14.6	17.5	12.6	13.7	12.0
By external financing source												
Net debtor countries	65.4	9.0	13.6	15.2	10.6	9.1	8.4	8.3	7.6	6.0	6.2	5.8
of which, official financing	41.7	8.9	8.8	17.9	9.9	6.1	7.2	9.4	7.8	6.9	8.1	6.9
Net debtor countries by debt-servicing experience												
Countries with arrears and/or rescheduling during 1999–2003	50.2	11.9	11.1	20.7	13.3	9.8	11.0	13.6	11.0	9.5	10.4	9.2
Memorandum												
Median inflation rate												
Advanced economies	3.5	2.0	1.8	1.6	1.4	2.7	2.5	2.1	2.1	1.9	2.0	2.0
Other emerging market and developing countries	10.5	4.9	7.2	6.5	4.1	4.3	4.7	3.2	4.4	4.6	5.0	4.5

[1]In this table, "other advanced economies" means advanced economies excluding the United States, euro area countries, and Japan.

[2]Based on Eurostat's harmonized index of consumer prices.

[3]Mongolia, which is not a member of the Commonwealth of Independent States, is included in this group for reasons of geography and similarities in economic structure.

Table 8. Advanced Economies: GDP Deflators and Consumer Prices
(Annual percent change)

	Ten-Year Averages		1997	1998	1999	2000	2001	2002	2003	2004	2005	2006	Fourth Quarter[1]		
	1987–96	1997–2006											2004	2005	2006
GDP deflators															
Advanced economies	**3.3**	**1.6**	**1.7**	**1.3**	**0.9**	**1.4**	**1.9**	**1.6**	**1.6**	**1.8**	**1.7**	**1.7**	...	...	...
United States	2.8	2.0	1.7	1.1	1.4	2.2	2.4	1.7	2.0	2.6	2.5	2.1	2.9	2.4	2.0
Euro area	...	1.8	1.5	1.6	1.0	1.4	2.7	2.5	2.0	1.9	1.6	1.7	1.6	1.6	1.7
Germany	3.7	0.6	0.4	0.6	0.4	−0.6	1.2	1.4	1.1	0.8	0.4	0.7	0.7	0.3	1.1
France	2.3	1.3	1.0	1.1	−0.1	1.5	1.8	2.2	1.4	1.6	1.3	1.7	1.5	1.5	1.8
Italy	5.7	2.4	2.4	2.7	1.6	2.2	2.6	3.1	2.9	2.6	1.9	1.8	2.3	1.3	3.3
Spain	5.6	3.4	2.3	2.4	2.7	2.2	4.2	4.4	4.0	4.1	4.1	3.5	4.5	4.4	3.0
Netherlands	1.6	2.9	2.0	1.7	1.6	3.9	9.7	3.8	2.5	0.9	1.4	1.5	1.0	1.2	1.6
Belgium	2.6	1.7	1.4	1.7	1.4	1.3	1.8	1.8	2.0	2.3	2.0	1.7	2.0	2.7	1.2
Austria	2.9	1.3	—	0.3	0.6	1.8	1.7	1.4	1.4	2.0	1.8	1.8	2.1	1.7	1.5
Finland	3.7	1.4	2.2	3.7	−0.3	3.0	3.2	1.0	−0.3	0.5	0.3	0.6	0.9	−0.1	1.0
Greece	14.4	3.9	6.8	5.2	3.0	3.4	3.5	4.0	3.5	3.4	3.1	3.0	4.1	1.8	2.1
Portugal	8.5	3.3	3.8	3.8	3.1	3.5	4.3	4.4	2.8	2.5	2.5	2.7	2.8	2.4	2.8
Ireland	2.9	4.4	7.7	6.5	4.0	5.5	5.7	5.0	2.0	2.2	2.8	2.6	2.9	3.3	2.0
Luxembourg	2.7	2.4	2.7	2.8	2.6	4.0	1.3	1.2	2.6	1.9	2.3	2.6	...	...	...
Japan	1.0	−1.0	0.4	−0.2	−1.3	−1.5	−1.3	−1.3	−1.4	−1.2	−1.2	−0.6	−0.4	−1.8	0.1
United Kingdom	4.7	2.3	2.9	2.8	2.1	1.2	2.3	3.1	2.9	2.0	2.0	2.1	2.4	1.4	2.3
Canada	2.7	2.0	1.2	−0.4	1.7	4.1	1.1	1.0	3.3	3.1	2.3	2.2	3.5	2.3	2.0
Korea	7.4	2.6	4.6	5.8	−0.1	0.7	3.5	2.8	2.7	2.7	0.4	2.7	2.4	0.4	2.8
Australia	3.4	2.7	1.6	0.5	0.5	4.1	4.0	2.5	3.1	3.6	4.4	2.7	4.1	4.2	2.0
Taiwan Province of China	2.6	−0.2	1.7	2.7	−1.4	−1.7	0.5	−0.9	−2.1	−1.9	−0.5	2.0	−1.6	−0.1	2.2
Sweden	4.8	1.4	1.6	0.8	0.7	1.3	2.3	1.7	2.1	0.8	0.7	2.1	0.9	1.1	2.3
Switzerland	2.5	0.8	−0.1	−0.3	0.7	0.8	0.6	1.7	0.9	0.9	1.3	1.2	1.1	1.2	1.2
Hong Kong SAR	8.0	−2.0	5.7	0.2	−5.9	−6.2	−1.9	−3.6	−5.2	−3.1	−0.6	1.1	−2.1	1.6	0.3
Denmark	3.0	2.0	2.2	1.0	1.8	3.0	2.1	1.6	2.2	1.6	2.1	2.0	0.5	3.1	1.5
Norway	3.2	4.5	2.9	−0.7	6.6	15.9	1.1	−1.6	2.4	5.0	9.0	5.8	7.5	10.4	2.3
Israel	15.3	3.4	9.2	6.5	6.5	1.5	1.9	4.4	—	−0.2	1.7	2.3	1.0	2.3	2.0
Singapore	3.0	0.1	0.4	−2.3	−4.6	4.1	−1.7	−0.4	0.4	3.5	0.7	1.7	6.5	0.9	0.9
New Zealand	3.5	2.2	1.5	1.5	0.7	2.7	4.1	0.4	2.2	3.3	2.9	2.6	4.7	3.0	2.4
Cyprus	4.3	2.9	2.8	2.4	2.3	3.7	3.2	2.2	4.8	2.2	2.5	2.5	...	...	...
Iceland	9.7	3.5	3.1	5.2	2.7	2.8	9.2	5.7	−0.2	2.4	2.8	1.9	...	...	...
Memorandum															
Major advanced economies	2.9	1.4	1.4	1.0	0.8	1.3	1.6	1.4	1.5	1.7	1.6	1.5	2.0	1.3	1.7
Newly industrialized Asian economies	5.8	1.1	3.6	3.7	−1.4	−0.6	1.7	0.8	0.3	0.7	—	2.3	1.0	0.5	2.3
Consumer prices															
Advanced economies	**3.5**	**1.9**	**2.0**	**1.5**	**1.4**	**2.2**	**2.1**	**1.5**	**1.8**	**2.0**	**2.2**	**2.0**	...	...	...
United States	3.7	2.5	2.3	1.5	2.2	3.4	2.8	1.6	2.3	2.7	3.1	2.8	3.4	3.1	2.6
Euro area[2]	...	1.9	1.6	1.1	1.1	2.1	2.3	2.3	2.1	2.1	2.1	1.8	2.4	2.2	1.8
Germany	2.6	1.4	1.5	0.6	0.6	1.4	1.9	1.3	1.0	1.8	1.7	1.7	2.1	1.9	1.6
France	2.6	1.6	1.3	0.7	0.6	1.8	1.8	1.9	2.2	2.3	1.9	1.8	2.3	1.9	1.5
Italy	5.2	2.2	1.9	2.0	1.7	2.6	2.3	2.6	2.8	2.3	2.1	2.0	2.2	2.1	1.9
Spain	5.4	2.8	1.9	1.8	2.2	3.5	2.8	3.6	3.1	3.1	3.2	3.0	3.5	3.2	2.9
Japan	1.3	−0.1	1.7	0.6	−0.3	−0.9	−0.7	−1.0	−0.2	—	−0.4	−0.1	0.6	−0.8	0.2
United Kingdom[2]	4.2	1.5	1.8	1.6	1.4	0.8	1.2	1.3	1.4	1.3	2.0	1.9	1.4	2.0	1.8
Canada	3.1	2.1	1.6	1.0	1.7	2.7	2.5	2.3	2.7	1.8	2.2	2.5	2.3	2.5	2.1
Other advanced economies	5.1	2.1	2.6	3.0	0.9	2.0	2.4	1.7	1.8	2.0	2.0	2.3	...	...	...
Memorandum															
Major advanced economies	3.2	1.8	2.0	1.2	1.4	2.1	1.9	1.3	1.7	2.0	2.1	2.1	2.4	2.1	1.9
Newly industrialized Asian economies	5.3	2.1	3.4	4.6	—	1.2	2.0	1.0	1.5	2.4	2.2	2.3	2.5	2.3	2.3

[1]Annual data are calculated from seasonally adjusted quarterly data.
[2]Based on Eurostat's harmonized index of consumer prices.

Table 9. Advanced Economies: Hourly Earnings, Productivity, and Unit Labor Costs in Manufacturing
(Annual percent change)

	Ten-Year Averages		1997	1998	1999	2000	2001	2002	2003	2004	2005	2006
	1987–96	1997–2006										
Hourly earnings												
Advanced economies	**4.9**	**3.7**	**2.9**	**3.4**	**3.0**	**5.4**	**2.9**	**4.2**	**5.1**	**2.5**	**4.4**	**3.5**
United States	3.4	5.2	2.6	5.8	3.9	9.0	2.4	7.3	8.3	2.2	6.9	4.0
Euro area	. . .	3.3	1.1	2.9	5.2	5.3	4.2	3.4	2.5	2.6	2.8	3.1
Germany	5.8	2.3	1.4	1.3	2.5	3.6	3.5	2.4	2.5	0.7	2.5	3.0
France	4.0	2.5	−0.1	0.6	1.0	3.8	1.2	4.1	4.1	3.4	3.2	3.9
Italy	6.8	2.6	4.2	−1.4	2.3	3.1	3.3	2.3	3.0	3.5	2.9	2.7
Spain	6.6	3.7	4.5	3.3	2.7	2.8	4.0	5.2	5.1	3.2	3.0	3.0
Japan	3.7	0.7	3.1	0.8	−0.7	−0.1	0.9	−1.3	1.0	0.4	1.4	1.3
United Kingdom	6.8	3.8	4.2	4.6	4.0	4.7	4.3	3.5	3.6	3.6	2.6	3.4
Canada	3.8	3.2	2.2	3.9	2.7	2.8	3.1	2.7	3.7	3.9	3.6	3.8
Other advanced economies	9.2	4.7	4.9	3.1	5.5	5.7	5.5	3.1	4.4	4.9	4.6	5.1
Memorandum												
Major advanced economies	4.3	3.6	2.6	3.5	2.7	5.6	2.4	4.4	5.3	2.1	4.6	3.3
Newly industrialized Asian economies	14.0	5.8	5.7	2.5	7.8	6.7	6.7	3.1	6.3	6.5	6.2	6.4
Productivity[1]												
Advanced economies	**3.1**	**3.4**	**4.0**	**2.4**	**3.7**	**5.2**	**0.9**	**4.4**	**4.0**	**4.3**	**2.7**	**2.6**
United States	2.8	4.4	3.6	4.8	3.5	4.6	2.3	7.5	5.2	5.2	4.4	3.0
Euro area	. . .	3.0	3.4	3.6	5.4	6.5	2.2	1.6	1.1	3.0	1.5	2.3
Germany	3.3	3.2	5.3	0.3	2.6	5.3	3.0	1.1	4.3	4.9	2.8	2.8
France	3.9	3.6	5.6	5.5	2.9	6.9	0.9	3.8	0.1	3.9	2.6	4.5
Italy	2.8	0.4	2.7	−0.6	1.5	3.8	−0.8	−2.0	−0.8	−0.3	−0.4	1.1
Spain	2.9	1.5	2.7	1.4	1.4	0.4	−0.1	2.2	4.2	2.6	0.3	0.3
Japan	2.7	2.6	5.0	−3.6	3.3	6.8	−3.0	3.7	5.3	5.3	1.8	1.7
United Kingdom	3.4	3.4	1.5	4.5	4.4	6.3	3.4	1.5	5.1	5.8	0.3	1.4
Canada	2.3	3.1	3.4	4.1	5.5	5.7	−1.4	3.6	1.5	3.1	3.1	3.1
Other advanced economies	4.0	3.5	4.4	1.3	7.1	6.7	−0.4	4.2	3.7	3.2	2.2	3.3
Memorandum												
Major advanced economies	3.0	3.5	3.9	2.5	3.4	5.3	1.1	4.7	4.2	4.7	3.0	2.6
Newly industrialized Asian economies	6.8	5.0	4.8	—	11.1	10.7	−1.3	6.2	5.7	4.6	4.0	5.3
Unit labor costs												
Advanced economies	**1.9**	**0.3**	**−1.0**	**1.1**	**−0.6**	**0.2**	**2.1**	**−0.2**	**1.0**	**−1.7**	**1.6**	**0.9**
United States	0.5	0.8	−0.9	1.0	0.4	4.2	0.2	−0.2	2.9	−2.9	2.4	1.0
Euro area	. . .	0.3	−2.2	−0.7	−0.2	−1.1	2.0	1.8	1.4	−0.4	1.2	0.8
Germany	2.4	−0.9	−3.7	1.0	−0.2	−1.7	0.5	1.3	−1.7	−4.0	−0.3	0.2
France	0.1	−1.1	−5.4	−4.6	−1.8	−2.9	0.2	0.3	4.0	−0.4	0.6	−0.6
Italy	3.9	2.2	1.5	−0.8	0.8	−0.7	4.1	4.3	3.9	3.7	3.3	1.5
Spain	3.6	2.1	1.7	1.9	1.2	2.3	4.1	2.9	0.9	0.6	2.7	2.7
Japan	1.0	−1.8	−1.8	4.6	−3.8	−6.5	4.0	−4.8	−4.1	−4.7	−0.4	−0.4
United Kingdom[2]	3.3	0.4	2.6	0.1	−0.4	−1.5	0.9	2.0	−1.5	−2.0	2.3	2.0
Canada	1.5	0.1	−1.2	−0.1	−2.7	−2.7	4.5	−0.8	2.1	0.8	0.6	0.7
Other advanced economies	5.0	1.0	0.6	2.2	−1.3	−1.1	5.7	−1.1	0.4	1.3	2.1	1.5
Memorandum												
Major advanced economies	1.3	0.1	−1.3	0.9	−0.7	0.3	1.4	−0.3	1.1	−2.4	1.5	0.7
Newly industrialized Asian economies	6.6	0.5	1.2	3.1	−2.7	−3.9	7.5	−3.0	−0.1	1.1	1.7	0.8

[1]Refers to labor productivity, measured as the ratio of hourly compensation to unit labor costs.
[2]Data refer to unit wage cost.

Table 10. Other Emerging Market and Developing Countries: Consumer Prices

(Annual percent change)

	Ten-Year Averages		1997	1998	1999	2000	2001	2002	2003	2004	2005	2006
	1987–96	1997–2006										
Other emerging market and developing countries	**56.6**	**7.6**	**11.6**	**11.2**	**10.4**	**7.3**	**6.7**	**5.9**	**6.0**	**5.8**	**5.9**	**5.7**
Regional groups												
Africa	28.6	10.2	13.5	9.1	11.5	13.1	12.2	9.6	10.4	7.8	8.2	7.0
Sub-Sahara	33.9	12.5	16.4	10.7	14.4	16.8	15.2	11.9	13.0	9.3	9.8	8.2
Excluding Nigeria and South Africa	52.7	17.8	24.3	13.6	23.2	28.1	21.8	13.4	18.2	13.8	12.6	10.2
Central and eastern Europe	61.3	18.1	51.4	32.7	22.9	22.7	19.4	14.7	9.2	6.5	4.8	4.3
Commonwealth of Independent States[1]	...	20.6	18.1	23.7	69.6	24.6	20.3	13.8	12.0	10.3	12.6	10.5
Russia	...	21.9	14.8	27.7	85.7	20.8	21.5	15.8	13.7	10.9	12.8	10.7
Excluding Russia	...	17.5	26.3	15.3	37.0	34.2	17.6	9.3	8.3	9.0	12.1	10.1
Developing Asia	11.0	3.7	4.9	7.8	2.5	1.9	2.7	2.1	2.6	4.2	4.2	4.7
China	11.9	1.3	2.8	−0.8	−1.4	0.4	0.7	−0.8	1.2	3.9	3.0	3.8
India	9.5	5.3	7.2	13.2	4.7	4.0	3.8	4.3	3.8	3.8	3.9	5.1
Excluding China and India	10.8	7.4	6.6	20.8	8.6	2.8	5.9	6.3	4.6	5.5	7.4	6.4
Middle East	15.3	7.8	8.6	8.4	8.5	5.9	5.4	6.5	7.1	8.4	10.0	9.7
Western Hemisphere	181.9	8.0	11.9	9.0	8.2	7.6	6.1	8.9	10.6	6.5	6.3	5.4
Brazil	656.6	7.0	6.9	3.2	4.9	7.1	6.8	8.4	14.8	6.6	6.8	4.6
Mexico	36.7	9.0	20.6	15.9	16.6	9.5	6.4	5.0	4.5	4.7	4.3	3.6
Analytical groups												
By source of export earnings												
Fuel	27.0	11.4	15.7	13.1	12.7	10.0	9.6	10.3	11.1	10.3	11.2	10.0
Nonfuel	59.6	7.3	11.2	11.1	10.2	7.1	6.5	5.6	5.6	5.4	5.5	5.4
of which, primary products	62.9	18.4	24.2	12.2	23.5	29.1	26.6	14.6	17.5	12.6	13.7	12.0
By external financing source												
Net debtor countries	65.4	9.0	13.6	15.2	10.6	9.1	8.4	8.3	7.6	6.0	6.2	5.8
of which, official financing	41.7	8.9	8.8	17.9	9.9	6.1	7.2	9.4	7.8	6.9	8.1	6.9
Net debtor countries by debt-servicing experience												
Countries with arrears and/or rescheduling during 1999–2003	50.2	11.9	11.1	20.7	13.3	9.8	11.0	13.6	11.0	9.5	10.4	9.2
Other groups												
Heavily indebted poor countries	64.8	12.4	19.0	9.9	18.1	24.8	19.1	5.8	8.7	6.6	8.8	5.4
Middle East and north Africa	16.1	6.9	8.7	7.7	7.3	5.0	4.8	5.7	6.1	7.3	8.4	8.3
Memorandum												
Median												
Other emerging market and developing countries	10.5	4.9	7.2	6.5	4.1	4.3	4.7	3.2	4.4	4.6	5.0	4.5
Africa	10.5	5.0	6.4	5.9	4.0	5.1	4.8	3.4	5.6	4.3	5.2	4.9
Central and eastern Europe	50.9	4.6	8.8	8.2	3.3	6.2	5.5	3.1	2.3	3.5	2.7	2.7
Commonwealth of Independent States[1]	...	11.6	17.4	9.4	23.5	18.7	9.8	5.6	5.6	7.1	12.1	7.1
Developing Asia	8.7	4.9	6.2	8.3	4.2	2.5	3.8	3.7	3.8	5.6	5.5	5.0
Middle East	7.1	2.6	3.3	3.0	2.1	1.0	1.6	1.4	1.9	4.6	3.7	3.6
Western Hemisphere	13.4	4.5	7.0	5.1	3.5	4.8	3.6	4.2	4.5	4.4	4.3	4.0

[1]Mongolia, which is not a member of the Commonwealth of Independent States, is included in this group for reasons of geography and similarities in economic structure.

Table 11. Other Emerging Market and Developing Countries—by Country: Consumer Prices[1]

(Annual percent change)

	Average 1987–96	1997	1998	1999	2000	2001	2002	2003	2004	2005	2006
Africa	**28.6**	**13.5**	**9.1**	**11.5**	**13.1**	**12.2**	**9.6**	**10.4**	**7.8**	**8.2**	**7.0**
Algeria	18.2	5.7	5.0	2.6	0.3	4.2	1.4	2.6	3.6	3.5	4.3
Angola	313.3	221.5	107.4	248.2	325.0	152.6	108.9	98.3	43.6	22.0	10.5
Benin	6.4	3.8	5.8	0.3	4.2	4.0	2.4	1.5	0.9	2.5	2.5
Botswana	11.6	8.9	6.5	7.8	8.5	6.6	8.1	9.6	6.6	6.8	7.3
Burkina Faso	3.7	2.4	5.0	−1.1	−0.3	4.7	2.3	2.0	−0.4	4.0	2.0
Burundi	11.3	31.1	12.5	3.4	24.3	9.3	−1.3	10.7	8.0	16.3	7.8
Cameroon[2]	4.4	4.1	3.9	2.9	0.8	2.8	6.3	0.6	0.3	1.5	1.8
Cape Verde	6.7	8.6	4.4	3.9	−2.4	3.8	1.8	1.2	−1.9	0.7	2.3
Central African Republic	2.6	1.6	−1.9	−1.4	3.2	3.8	2.3	4.4	−2.2	2.4	2.3
Chad	4.7	5.6	4.3	−8.4	3.8	12.4	5.2	−1.8	−5.3	3.0	3.0
Comoros	3.1	1.5	1.2	1.1	4.6	5.6	3.5	3.8	4.5	3.0	3.0
Congo, Dem. Rep. of	776.8	199.0	29.1	284.9	550.0	357.3	25.3	12.8	3.9	23.2	8.0
Congo, Rep. of	3.3	13.1	1.8	3.1	0.4	0.8	3.1	1.5	3.6	2.0	2.5
Côte d'Ivoire	6.2	4.2	4.5	0.7	2.5	4.4	3.1	3.3	1.5	3.0	3.0
Djibouti	5.1	2.5	2.2	2.0	2.4	1.8	0.6	2.0	3.1	3.0	2.2
Equatorial Guinea	4.9	3.7	6.0	6.5	4.8	8.8	7.6	7.3	4.2	6.0	5.5
Eritrea	...	3.7	9.5	8.4	19.9	14.6	16.9	22.7	25.1	14.0	12.1
Ethiopia	7.1	−6.4	3.6	4.8	6.2	−5.2	−7.2	15.1	8.6	6.8	6.0
Gabon	3.9	4.1	2.3	−0.7	0.5	2.1	0.2	2.1	0.4	1.0	1.0
Gambia, The	8.8	2.8	1.1	3.8	0.9	4.5	8.6	17.0	14.2	5.0	5.2
Ghana	31.1	27.9	14.6	12.4	25.2	32.9	14.8	26.7	12.6	14.3	8.7
Guinea	8.4	1.9	5.1	4.6	6.8	5.4	3.0	12.9	17.5	26.3	11.8
Guinea-Bissau	55.9	49.1	8.0	−2.1	8.6	3.3	3.3	3.0	3.0	2.0	2.0
Kenya	16.1	11.9	6.7	5.8	10.0	5.8	2.0	9.8	11.6	11.0	5.1
Lesotho	12.4	8.5	7.8	8.6	6.1	6.9	11.7	7.6	5.0	4.3	5.0
Madagascar	19.7	4.5	6.2	8.1	10.7	6.9	16.2	−1.1	14.0	10.4	4.8
Malawi	27.9	9.1	29.8	44.8	29.6	27.2	14.9	9.6	11.6	12.3	9.0
Mali	2.9	−0.7	4.1	−1.2	−0.7	5.2	2.4	−1.3	−3.1	3.8	2.5
Mauritania	6.9	4.5	8.0	4.1	3.3	4.7	3.9	5.5	10.4	13.5	7.2
Mauritius	7.5	6.4	7.0	6.9	5.5	4.8	5.9	5.1	4.3	5.3	5.8
Morocco	4.8	1.0	2.7	0.7	1.9	0.6	2.8	1.2	1.5	2.0	2.0
Mozambique, Rep. of	56.1	6.4	0.6	2.9	12.7	9.1	16.8	13.4	12.6	7.7	7.3
Namibia	11.9	8.8	6.2	8.6	9.3	9.3	11.3	7.2	4.1	5.8	5.0
Niger	3.2	2.9	4.5	−2.3	2.9	4.0	2.7	−1.8	0.4	2.4	2.0
Nigeria	35.9	8.5	10.0	6.6	6.9	18.0	13.7	14.0	15.0	15.9	7.3
Rwanda	15.5	11.7	6.8	−2.4	3.9	3.4	2.0	7.4	12.0	7.0	4.0
São Tomé and Príncipe	37.1	69.0	42.1	16.3	11.0	9.5	9.2	9.6	12.8	15.1	13.4
Senegal	3.1	1.8	1.1	0.8	0.7	3.0	2.3	—	0.5	1.5	1.9
Seychelles	1.7	0.6	2.7	6.3	4.2	1.9	0.2	3.2	3.9	2.3	4.5
Sierra Leone	58.5	14.6	36.0	34.1	−0.9	2.6	−3.7	7.5	14.2	8.5	7.4
South Africa	12.1	8.6	6.9	5.2	5.4	5.7	9.2	5.8	1.4	3.9	5.3
Sudan	84.8	46.7	17.1	16.0	8.0	4.9	8.3	7.7	8.4	7.5	7.0
Swaziland	11.5	7.9	7.5	5.9	7.2	7.5	11.7	7.4	3.5	5.5	5.8
Tanzania	27.6	15.4	13.2	9.0	6.2	5.2	4.6	4.5	4.3	4.1	4.0
Togo	5.3	5.3	1.0	−0.1	1.9	3.9	3.1	−0.9	1.2	1.7	2.0
Tunisia	6.2	3.7	3.1	2.7	3.0	1.9	2.8	2.8	3.6	2.9	2.5
Uganda	54.3	7.7	5.8	0.2	5.8	4.5	−2.0	5.7	5.0	8.2	4.5
Zambia	85.5	24.4	24.5	26.8	26.1	21.7	22.2	21.5	18.0	17.0	11.5
Zimbabwe	20.7	18.8	31.3	58.0	55.6	73.4	133.2	365.0	350.0	190.4	253.1

Table 11 *(continued)*

	Average 1987–96	1997	1998	1999	2000	2001	2002	2003	2004	2005	2006
Central and eastern Europe[3]	**61.3**	**51.4**	**32.7**	**22.9**	**22.7**	**19.4**	**14.7**	**9.2**	**6.5**	**4.8**	**4.3**
Albania	28.4	32.1	20.9	0.4	—	3.1	3.1	2.4	2.9	2.4	3.0
Bosnia and Herzegovina	...	5.6	−0.4	2.9	5.0	3.2	0.3	0.6	0.4	1.0	1.9
Bulgaria	63.2	1,061.2	18.8	2.6	10.4	7.5	5.8	2.3	6.1	4.4	3.5
Croatia	...	3.6	5.7	4.1	6.2	4.9	1.7	1.8	2.1	3.0	2.5
Czech Republic	...	8.5	10.6	2.1	3.9	4.7	1.8	0.1	2.8	2.0	2.5
Estonia	...	11.2	8.2	3.3	4.0	5.8	3.6	1.3	3.0	3.9	2.8
Hungary	21.8	18.3	14.3	10.0	9.8	9.2	5.3	4.7	6.8	4.0	3.6
Latvia	...	8.4	4.6	2.4	2.6	2.5	1.9	2.9	6.3	6.3	5.1
Lithuania	...	8.8	5.1	0.7	1.0	1.3	0.3	−1.2	1.2	2.7	2.5
Macedonia, FYR	...	2.6	−0.1	−2.0	6.2	5.3	2.4	1.2	−0.3	1.2	1.8
Malta	2.4	3.9	3.8	2.2	3.1	2.5	2.7	1.9	2.7	2.4	1.9
Poland	78.2	14.9	11.8	7.3	10.1	5.5	1.9	0.8	3.5	2.2	2.5
Romania	76.8	154.8	59.1	45.8	45.7	34.5	22.5	15.3	11.9	8.8	6.9
Serbia and Montenegro	...	...	29.5	42.1	69.9	91.1	21.2	11.3	9.5	15.4	9.3
Slovak Republic	...	6.1	6.7	10.7	12.0	7.3	3.3	8.5	7.5	2.7	2.7
Slovenia	...	8.4	7.9	6.2	8.9	8.4	7.5	5.6	3.6	2.6	2.5
Turkey	70.9	85.0	83.6	63.5	54.3	53.9	44.8	25.2	10.3	8.4	6.9
Commonwealth of Independent States[3,4]	**...**	**18.1**	**23.7**	**69.6**	**24.6**	**20.3**	**13.8**	**12.0**	**10.3**	**12.6**	**10.5**
Russia	...	14.8	27.7	85.7	20.8	21.5	15.8	13.7	10.9	12.8	10.7
Excluding Russia	...	26.3	15.3	37.0	34.2	17.6	9.3	8.3	9.0	12.1	10.1
Armenia	...	14.0	8.7	0.6	−0.8	3.2	1.1	4.7	6.9	2.2	3.9
Azerbaijan	...	3.7	−0.8	−8.5	1.8	1.5	2.8	2.2	6.7	12.7	8.3
Belarus	...	63.8	73.0	293.7	168.6	61.1	42.6	28.4	18.1	12.1	12.5
Georgia	...	7.0	3.6	19.1	4.0	4.7	5.6	4.8	5.7	9.0	7.0
Kazakhstan	...	17.4	7.3	8.4	13.3	8.4	5.9	6.4	6.9	7.4	7.1
Kyrgyz Republic	...	23.4	−18.6	35.9	18.7	6.9	2.1	3.1	4.1	5.0	4.0
Moldova	...	11.8	7.7	39.3	31.3	9.8	5.3	11.7	12.5	13.3	11.9
Mongolia	50.0	36.6	9.4	7.6	11.6	6.3	0.9	5.1	7.9	12.1	4.3
Tajikistan	...	88.0	43.2	27.5	32.9	38.6	12.2	16.4	7.1	7.2	5.0
Turkmenistan	...	83.7	16.8	23.5	8.0	11.6	8.8	5.6	5.9	13.5	5.0
Ukraine	...	15.9	10.6	22.7	28.2	12.0	0.8	5.2	9.0	14.2	12.1
Uzbekistan	...	70.9	16.7	44.6	49.5	47.5	44.3	14.8	8.8	14.1	13.0

Table 11 *(continued)*

	Average 1987–96	1997	1998	1999	2000	2001	2002	2003	2004	2005	2006
Developing Asia	**11.0**	**4.9**	**7.8**	**2.5**	**1.9**	**2.7**	**2.1**	**2.6**	**4.2**	**4.2**	**4.7**
Afghanistan, I.S. of	...	...	...	...	...	...	5.0	23.9	14.3	12.0	7.5
Bangladesh	7.4	5.0	8.6	6.2	2.2	1.5	3.8	5.4	6.1	6.2	5.8
Bhutan	9.8	9.0	9.0	9.2	3.6	3.6	2.7	1.8	4.5	5.0	5.0
Brunei Darussalam	...	1.7	−0.4	—	1.2	0.6	−2.3	0.3	0.9	1.0	1.0
Cambodia	...	9.2	13.3	−0.5	−0.8	0.7	3.7	0.5	5.6	5.5	3.5
China	11.9	2.8	−0.8	−1.4	0.4	0.7	−0.8	1.2	3.9	3.0	3.8
Fiji	5.4	3.4	5.9	2.0	1.1	4.3	0.8	4.2	2.8	4.2	3.5
India	9.5	7.2	13.2	4.7	4.0	3.8	4.3	3.8	3.8	3.9	5.1
Indonesia	8.3	6.2	58.0	20.7	3.8	11.5	11.8	6.8	6.1	8.2	6.5
Kiribati	1.8	2.2	3.7	1.8	1.0	7.3	1.1	1.6	−0.6	0.5	2.5
Lao PDR	11.2	19.5	90.1	128.4	23.2	7.8	10.6	15.5	10.5	5.9	5.0
Malaysia	3.0	2.7	5.3	2.7	1.5	1.4	1.8	1.1	1.4	3.0	2.5
Maldives	10.1	7.6	−1.4	3.0	−1.2	0.7	0.9	−2.9	6.4	6.5	2.8
Myanmar	24.3	33.9	49.1	10.9	−1.7	34.5	58.1	24.9	10.0	21.0	32.5
Nepal	10.6	8.1	8.3	11.4	3.4	2.4	2.9	4.7	4.0	4.1	4.0
Pakistan	9.7	11.4	6.5	4.1	4.4	3.1	3.2	2.9	7.4	9.9	9.8
Papua New Guinea	6.7	3.9	13.6	14.9	15.6	9.3	11.8	14.7	2.1	2.4	2.5
Philippines	9.7	5.9	9.7	6.5	4.3	6.8	3.0	3.5	6.0	8.2	7.5
Samoa	5.7	6.9	2.2	0.3	1.0	3.8	8.1	4.2	2.4	2.4	2.2
Solomon Islands	12.1	8.0	12.3	8.0	6.9	7.6	9.4	10.1	6.9	6.2	8.1
Sri Lanka	12.1	9.6	9.4	4.7	6.2	14.2	9.6	6.3	7.6	14.0	9.5
Thailand	4.8	5.6	8.1	0.3	1.6	1.7	0.6	1.8	2.7	4.2	2.7
Timor-Leste, Dem. Rep. of	...	...	...	...	63.6	3.6	4.8	7.1	3.3	2.5	2.5
Tonga	5.7	1.8	2.9	3.9	4.9	7.3	10.0	10.7	11.8	11.2	9.0
Vanuatu	2.7	2.8	3.3	2.2	2.5	3.7	2.0	3.0	1.0	1.9	2.7
Vietnam	71.0	3.2	7.7	4.2	−1.6	−0.4	4.0	3.2	7.7	8.0	5.5
Middle East	**15.3**	**8.6**	**8.4**	**8.5**	**5.9**	**5.4**	**6.5**	**7.1**	**8.4**	**10.0**	**9.7**
Bahrain	0.6	4.6	−0.4	−1.3	−3.6	−1.2	−0.5	1.6	4.9	3.7	1.6
Egypt[5]	15.3	6.2	4.7	3.7	2.8	2.4	2.4	3.2	8.1	8.8	8.0
Iran, I.R. of[5]	25.5	17.3	18.1	20.1	12.6	11.4	15.8	15.6	15.6	18.5	18.5
Iraq	...	...	...	...	...	...	...	...	...	...	...
Jordan	5.4	3.0	3.1	0.6	0.7	1.8	1.8	1.6	3.4	3.7	8.4
Kuwait	3.1	0.8	0.6	3.1	1.6	1.4	0.8	1.0	1.8	1.8	1.8
Lebanon	72.8	7.7	4.5	0.2	−0.4	−0.4	1.8	1.3	3.0	2.0	2.0
Libya	7.2	3.6	3.7	2.6	−2.9	−8.8	−9.9	−2.1	−1.0	1.8	2.5
Oman	2.1	−0.4	0.4	0.5	−1.2	−0.8	−0.2	0.2	0.8	1.9	1.1
Qatar	3.5	1.1	2.9	2.2	1.7	1.4	1.0	2.3	6.8	3.0	2.7
Saudi Arabia	1.1	−0.4	−0.2	−1.3	−0.6	−0.8	0.2	0.6	0.3	1.0	1.0
Syrian Arab Republic	18.1	1.9	−1.0	−3.7	−3.9	3.0	0.6	5.0	4.6	10.0	5.0
United Arab Emirates	4.2	2.9	2.0	2.1	1.4	2.8	2.9	3.1	4.6	6.0	4.5
Yemen	38.1	4.6	11.5	8.0	10.9	11.9	12.2	10.8	12.5	10.3	11.4

Table 11 *(concluded)*

	Average 1987–96	1997	1998	1999	2000	2001	2002	2003	2004	2005	2006
Western Hemisphere	**181.9**	**11.9**	**9.0**	**8.2**	**7.6**	**6.1**	**8.9**	**10.6**	**6.5**	**6.3**	**5.4**
Antigua and Barbuda	4.4	0.2	3.4	1.1	−1.7	0.2	2.2	1.0	−1.3	—	—
Argentina	182.0	0.5	0.9	−1.2	−0.9	−1.1	25.9	13.4	4.4	9.5	10.4
Bahamas, The	4.0	0.5	1.3	1.3	1.6	2.0	2.2	3.0	0.9	1.8	2.0
Barbados	3.6	7.7	−1.3	1.6	2.4	2.8	0.2	1.6	1.4	3.2	2.0
Belize	2.8	1.0	−0.9	−1.2	0.6	1.2	2.2	2.6	3.1	3.5	1.9
Bolivia	13.5	4.7	7.7	2.2	4.6	1.6	0.9	3.3	4.4	5.5	3.2
Brazil	656.6	6.9	3.2	4.9	7.1	6.8	8.4	14.8	6.6	6.8	4.6
Chile	15.3	6.1	5.1	3.3	3.8	3.6	2.5	2.8	1.1	2.9	3.3
Colombia	25.0	18.5	18.7	10.9	9.2	8.0	6.3	7.1	5.9	5.2	4.8
Costa Rica	18.7	13.2	11.7	10.0	11.0	11.3	9.2	9.4	12.3	12.6	9.5
Dominica	3.3	2.4	1.0	1.2	0.9	1.6	0.1	1.6	2.4	1.3	1.5
Dominican Republic	21.8	8.3	4.8	6.5	7.7	8.9	5.2	27.4	51.5	3.7	7.8
Ecuador	42.4	30.6	36.1	52.2	96.1	37.7	12.6	7.9	2.7	2.0	2.0
El Salvador	16.0	4.5	2.5	−1.0	4.3	1.4	2.8	2.5	5.4	4.0	4.0
Grenada	2.8	1.3	1.4	0.5	2.2	1.7	1.1	2.2	2.3	3.0	2.0
Guatemala	16.1	9.2	6.6	5.2	6.0	7.3	8.1	5.6	7.6	7.6	5.3
Guyana	36.1	3.6	4.7	7.4	6.1	2.7	5.4	6.0	4.7	6.0	4.6
Haiti	17.2	16.2	12.7	8.1	11.5	16.8	8.7	32.5	27.1	16.6	9.6
Honduras	16.7	20.2	13.7	11.6	11.0	9.7	7.7	7.7	8.1	8.1	5.8
Jamaica	27.5	9.1	8.1	6.3	7.7	8.0	6.5	12.9	12.8	12.5	8.1
Mexico	36.7	20.6	15.9	16.6	9.5	6.4	5.0	4.5	4.7	4.3	3.6
Netherlands Antilles	2.8	3.2	1.3	0.8	5.0	1.7	0.4	1.9	1.5	2.7	2.4
Nicaragua	497.8	7.3	18.5	7.2	9.9	4.7	4.0	6.6	9.3	9.0	6.0
Panama	0.9	1.3	0.6	1.2	1.4	0.3	1.0	1.4	2.3	2.6	1.8
Paraguay	20.8	7.0	11.6	6.8	9.0	7.3	10.5	14.2	4.3	4.8	4.7
Peru	287.4	8.5	7.3	3.5	3.8	2.0	0.2	2.3	3.7	1.8	2.6
St. Kitts and Nevis	2.6	8.7	3.7	3.4	2.1	2.1	2.1	2.3	2.1	1.8	2.0
St. Lucia	3.7	—	2.8	3.5	3.6	2.1	−0.3	1.0	1.5	3.0	4.0
St. Vincent and the Grenadines	3.4	0.5	2.1	1.0	0.2	0.8	1.3	0.2	3.0	2.6	1.9
Suriname	63.8	7.3	19.1	98.7	58.6	39.8	15.5	23.1	9.0	8.6	6.6
Trinidad and Tobago	7.9	3.6	5.6	3.4	3.5	5.5	4.2	3.8	3.7	5.3	5.0
Uruguay	64.0	19.8	10.8	5.7	4.8	4.4	14.0	19.4	9.2	5.2	6.5
Venezuela	49.0	50.0	35.8	23.6	16.2	12.5	22.4	31.1	21.7	16.6	18.0

[1]In accordance with standard practice in the *World Economic Outlook*, movements in consumer prices are indicated as annual averages rather than as December/December changes, as is the practice in some countries. For many countries, figures for recent years are IMF staff estimates. Data for some countries are for fiscal years.

[2]The percent changes in 2002 are calculated over a period of 18 months, reflecting a change in the fiscal year cycle (from July–June to January–December).

[3]For many countries, inflation for the earlier years is measured on the basis of a retail price index. Consumer price indices with a broader and more up-to-date coverage are typically used for more recent years.

[4]Mongolia, which is not a member of the Commonwealth of Independent States, is included in this group for reasons of geography and similarities in economic structure.

[5]Data refer to fiscal years.

Table 12. Summary Financial Indicators
(Percent)

	1997	1998	1999	2000	2001	2002	2003	2004	2005	2006
Advanced economies										
Central government fiscal balance[1]										
Advanced economies	−1.6	−1.1	−1.1	0.2	−1.0	−2.4	−3.0	−2.8	−2.6	−2.6
United States	−0.6	0.5	1.2	2.0	0.5	−2.4	−3.4	−3.1	−2.6	−2.9
Euro area	−2.6	−2.4	−1.6	−0.4	−1.6	−2.1	−2.3	−2.3	−2.3	−2.3
Japan	−4.0	−3.8	−8.5	−6.9	−6.3	−6.9	−7.1	−7.0	−6.9	−6.7
Other advanced economies[2]	−0.4	−0.3	0.3	2.2	0.6	−0.2	−0.7	−0.3	−0.1	—
General government fiscal balance[1]										
Advanced economies	−1.9	−1.4	−1.1	—	−1.5	−3.4	−3.9	−3.4	−3.3	−3.4
United States	−1.1	0.1	0.6	1.3	−0.7	−4.0	−4.6	−4.0	−3.7	−3.9
Euro area	−2.6	−2.3	−1.3	−0.9	−1.8	−2.5	−2.8	−2.7	−3.0	−3.1
Japan	−3.8	−5.5	−7.2	−7.5	−6.1	−7.9	−7.8	−7.2	−6.7	−6.2
Other advanced economies[2]	−0.6	−0.2	0.6	2.6	0.3	−0.8	−1.1	−0.6	−0.5	−0.6
General government structural balance[3]										
Advanced economies	−2.0	−1.6	−1.4	−1.2	−1.8	−3.2	−3.4	−3.2	−3.1	−3.1
Growth of broad money[4]										
Advanced economies	5.0	6.7	5.9	4.9	8.7	5.8	5.5	5.1	...	...
United States	5.6	8.4	6.2	6.1	10.2	6.8	5.4	5.2	...	...
Euro area[5]	4.6	4.9	5.4	4.1	11.2	6.7	6.5	6.4	...	...
Japan	3.9	4.0	2.7	1.9	3.3	1.8	1.6	1.8	...	...
Other advanced economies[2]	6.1	9.3	9.1	6.9	7.4	6.2	8.0	5.6	...	...
Short-term interest rates[5]										
United States	5.2	4.9	4.8	6.0	3.5	1.6	1.0	1.4	3.1	4.2
Euro area	...	3.7	3.0	4.4	4.3	3.3	2.3	2.1	2.1	2.4
Japan	0.3	0.2	0.0	0.2	0.0	0.0	0.0	0.0	0.1	0.2
LIBOR	5.9	5.6	5.5	6.6	3.7	1.9	1.2	1.8	3.6	4.5
Other emerging market and developing countries										
Central government fiscal balance[1]										
Weighted average	−2.9	−3.8	−4.0	−3.0	−3.3	−3.5	−2.9	−1.7	−1.1	−0.7
Median	−2.5	−3.0	−3.1	−2.7	−3.6	−3.7	−3.1	−2.6	−2.5	−2.1
General government fiscal balance[1]										
Weighted average	−3.8	−4.9	−4.8	−3.5	−4.1	−4.4	−3.6	−2.2	−1.5	−1.1
Median	−2.4	−3.3	−3.3	−2.8	−3.4	−3.8	−2.9	−2.3	−2.4	−2.1
Growth of broad money										
Weighted average	19.3	18.0	17.7	13.1	14.5	17.5	16.7	16.8	15.2	13.4
Median	17.2	11.3	12.8	14.0	13.6	13.2	13.3	13.1	11.5	10.7

[1]Percent of GDP.

[2]In this table, "other advanced economies" means advanced economies excluding the United States, euro area countries, and Japan.

[3]Percent of potential GDP.

[4]M2, defined as M1 plus quasi-money, except for Japan, for which the data are based on M2 plus certificates of deposit (CDs). Quasi-money is essentially private term deposits and other notice deposits. The United States also includes money market mutual fund balances, money market deposit accounts, overnight repurchase agreements, and overnight Eurodollars issued to U.S. residents by foreign branches of U.S. banks. For the euro area, M3 is composed of M2 plus marketable instruments held by euro-area residents, which comprise repurchase agreements, money market fund shares/units, money market paper, and debt securities up to two years.

[5]Annual data are period average. For the United States, three-month treasury bills; for Japan, three-month certificates of deposit; for the euro area, the three-month EURIBOR; and for LIBOR, London interbank offered rate on six-month U.S. dollar deposits.

Table 13. Advanced Economies: General and Central Government Fiscal Balances and Balances Excluding Social Security Transactions[1]

(Percent of GDP)

	1997	1998	1999	2000	2001	2002	2003	2004	2005	2006
General government fiscal balance										
Advanced economies	**−1.9**	**−1.4**	**−1.1**	**—**	**−1.5**	**−3.4**	**−3.9**	**−3.4**	**−3.3**	**−3.4**
United States	−1.1	0.1	0.6	1.3	−0.7	−4.0	−4.6	−4.0	−3.7	−3.9
Euro area	−2.6	−2.3	−1.3	−0.9	−1.8	−2.5	−2.8	−2.7	−3.0	−3.1
Germany	−2.7	−2.2	−1.5	1.3	−2.8	−3.7	−4.0	−3.7	−3.9	−3.7
France[2]	−3.0	−2.6	−2.5	−1.5	−1.5	−3.1	−4.2	−3.7	−3.5	−3.9
Italy	−2.7	−2.8	−1.7	−0.8	−3.2	−2.7	−3.2	−3.2	−4.3	−5.1
Spain	−3.1	−2.9	−1.1	−0.9	−0.5	−0.3	0.3	−0.3	0.3	0.3
Netherlands	−1.1	−0.8	0.7	2.2	−0.3	−2.0	−3.2	−2.1	−2.3	−2.5
Belgium	−2.0	−0.7	−0.4	0.2	0.6	0.1	0.4	—	−0.8	−2.0
Austria[3]	−2.0	−2.5	−2.3	−1.6	0.1	−0.4	−1.3	−1.2	−2.0	−1.8
Finland	−1.2	1.6	2.2	7.1	5.2	4.2	2.3	1.9	1.5	1.5
Greece	−6.6	−4.3	−3.4	−4.1	−3.6	−4.2	−5.2	−6.1	−4.3	−4.1
Portugal	−3.0	−2.6	−2.8	−2.9	−4.4	−2.7	−2.8	−2.9	−6.2	−4.8
Ireland[4]	1.4	2.3	2.4	4.3	0.8	−0.4	0.2	1.4	−1.1	−0.6
Luxembourg	3.2	3.2	3.7	6.0	6.4	2.8	0.8	−1.3	−1.7	−2.1
Japan	−3.8	−5.5	−7.2	−7.5	−6.1	−7.9	−7.8	−7.2	−6.7	−6.2
United Kingdom	−2.2	—	1.1	3.9	0.8	−1.5	−3.2	−3.0	−3.2	−3.4
Canada	0.2	0.1	1.6	2.9	0.7	−0.1	—	0.7	0.5	0.3
Korea[5]	−1.5	−3.9	−3.0	1.1	0.6	2.3	2.7	2.3	2.2	2.8
Australia[6]	0.1	0.4	1.4	1.8	0.9	1.1	1.7	1.6	1.3	1.1
Taiwan Province of China	−3.8	−3.4	−6.0	−4.7	−6.7	−4.5	−2.9	−3.4	−3.0	−2.8
Sweden	−1.0	1.9	2.3	5.1	2.9	−0.3	0.5	0.7	0.6	0.4
Switzerland	−2.7	−1.5	−0.6	2.2	0.1	−1.2	−1.6	−1.0	−1.4	−1.2
Hong Kong SAR	6.5	−1.8	0.8	−0.6	−5.0	−4.9	−3.2	−0.8	−0.7	0.1
Denmark	0.4	1.1	3.2	2.5	2.8	1.6	1.2	1.4	1.6	1.7
Norway	7.7	3.6	6.2	15.6	13.6	9.3	7.6	11.4	16.7	18.3
Israel	−4.5	−3.7	−4.2	−2.0	−3.9	−4.2	−6.5	−5.1	−5.1	−4.7
Singapore	9.2	3.6	4.6	7.9	4.8	4.0	5.8	5.2	4.5	4.2
New Zealand[7]	2.2	2.1	1.5	1.3	1.6	1.7	3.5	4.6	4.1	3.7
Cyprus	−5.1	−4.2	−4.4	−2.4	−2.3	−4.5	−6.3	−4.2	−3.0	−2.8
Iceland	—	0.5	2.4	2.5	0.2	0.2	−1.0	0.4	1.0	0.8
Memorandum										
Major advanced economies	−2.0	−1.5	−1.2	−0.2	−1.8	−4.1	−4.6	−4.1	−4.0	−4.1
Newly industrialized Asian economies	0.3	−2.2	−3.2	−2.2	−4.8	−3.5	−1.9	−1.7	−1.5	−1.2
Fiscal balance excluding social security transactions										
United States	−1.5	−0.6	−0.4	0.2	−1.5	−4.4	−5.1	−4.3	−4.1	−4.4
Japan	−5.5	−6.9	−8.3	−8.0	−6.2	−7.7	−7.9	−6.9	−6.3	−5.8
Germany	−2.7	−2.3	−1.7	1.3	−2.6	−3.4	−3.6	−3.6	−3.2	−3.0
France	−2.6	−2.9	−3.1	−2.0	−1.7	−2.9	−3.5	−2.7	−2.9	−3.3
Italy	−0.7	1.3	2.7	3.3	0.8	1.5	1.1	1.2	0.2	−0.3
Canada	3.0	2.7	3.9	4.8	2.4	1.4	1.4	2.1	1.9	1.7

Table 13 (concluded)

	1997	1998	1999	2000	2001	2002	2003	2004	2005	2006
Central government fiscal balance										
Advanced economies	**−1.6**	**−1.1**	**−1.1**	**0.2**	**−1.0**	**−2.4**	**−3.0**	**−2.8**	**−2.6**	**−2.6**
United States[8]	−0.6	0.5	1.2	2.0	0.5	−2.4	−3.4	−3.1	−2.6	−2.9
Euro area	−2.6	−2.4	−1.6	−0.4	−1.6	−2.1	−2.3	−2.3	−2.3	−2.3
Germany[9]	−1.6	−1.8	−1.5	1.4	−1.3	−1.7	−1.8	−2.3	−2.1	−2.1
France	−3.6	−3.7	−2.5	−2.4	−2.2	−3.8	−3.9	−3.2	−3.1	−2.8
Italy	−2.9	−2.7	−1.5	−1.1	−3.0	−2.9	−2.7	−2.6	−3.2	−3.7
Spain	−2.6	−2.3	−1.0	−0.9	−0.6	−0.5	−0.3	−1.2	−0.5	−0.4
Japan[10]	−4.0	−3.8	−8.5	−6.9	−6.3	−6.9	−7.1	−7.0	−6.9	−6.7
United Kingdom	−2.2	—	1.2	3.9	0.9	−1.6	−3.5	−3.0	−3.2	−3.5
Canada	0.7	0.8	0.9	1.9	1.1	0.8	0.1	0.6	0.3	0.3
Other advanced economies	0.2	−0.8	−0.4	1.3	0.3	0.1	0.6	0.9	1.3	1.6
Memorandum										
Major advanced economies	−1.7	−1.0	−1.1	0.1	−1.2	−3.0	−3.6	−3.5	−3.2	−3.4
Newly industrialized Asian economies	0.7	−1.2	−1.1	0.8	−0.8	−0.3	0.2	0.4	0.5	0.9

[1]On a national income accounts basis except as indicated in footnotes. See Box A1 for a summary of the policy assumptions underlying the projections.
[2]Adjusted for valuation changes of the foreign exchange stabilization fund.
[3]Based on ESA95 methodology, according to which swap income is not included.
[4]Data include the impact of discharging future pension liabilities of the formerly state-owned telecommunications company at a cost of 1.8 percent of GDP in 1999.
[5]Data cover the consolidated central government including the social security funds but excluding privatization.
[6]Cash basis, underlying balance.
[7]Government balance is revenue minus expenditure plus balance of state-owned enterprises, excluding privatization receipts.
[8]Data are on a budget basis.
[9]Data are on an administrative basis and exclude social security transactions.
[10]Data are on a national income basis and exclude social security transactions.

Table 14. Advanced Economies: General Government Structural Balances[1]

(Percent of potential GDP)

	1997	1998	1999	2000	2001	2002	2003	2004	2005	2006
Structural balance										
Advanced economies	**−2.0**	**−1.6**	**−1.4**	**−1.2**	**−1.8**	**−3.2**	**−3.4**	**−3.2**	**−3.1**	**−3.1**
United States	−1.4	−0.5	−0.3	0.3	−0.8	−3.5	−3.8	−3.5	−3.2	−3.5
Euro area[2,3]	−1.9	−2.0	−1.6	−1.8	−2.4	−2.6	−2.5	−2.2	−2.3	−2.3
Germany[2]	−2.3	−1.9	−1.5	−1.7	−3.1	−3.5	−3.4	−3.2	−3.3	−2.9
France[2]	−1.1	−1.8	−2.2	−2.1	−2.1	−3.1	−3.4	−2.6	−2.6	−2.4
Italy[2]	−2.9	−3.1	−2.0	−2.7	−3.9	−3.5	−2.8	−2.9	−3.4	−4.0
Spain[2]	−1.2	−1.6	−0.4	−1.4	−1.3	−0.5	0.3	0.6	0.9	0.9
Netherlands[2]	−1.1	−1.4	−0.7	−0.2	−1.2	−2.3	−2.4	−1.2	−0.8	−0.9
Belgium[2]	−2.0	−0.7	−1.0	−1.6	−0.7	−0.1	−1.0	0.1	−0.2	−1.4
Austria[2]	−1.9	−2.7	−2.8	−3.4	−0.6	−0.2	−0.2	−0.7	−1.6	−1.7
Finland	−2.0	−0.2	−0.2	5.8	5.0	4.4	2.6	1.7	1.6	1.3
Greece	−3.9	−2.5	−2.0	−4.1	−3.8	−4.4	−5.9	−6.9	−5.0	−4.5
Portugal[2]	−2.6	−3.0	−3.8	−4.0	−4.7	−4.8	−4.8	−4.5	−5.2	−3.8
Ireland[2]	0.5	1.8	1.0	2.6	−0.5	−1.2	0.4	1.7	−1.0	−0.8
Japan	−4.3	−5.3	−6.6	−7.3	−5.5	−6.8	−6.9	−6.8	−6.6	−6.2
United Kingdom[2]	−2.2	−0.1	1.0	1.3	0.3	−1.7	−3.1	−3.0	−3.2	−3.2
Canada	0.7	0.5	1.3	2.0	0.4	−0.2	0.3	0.9	0.7	0.4
Other advanced economies	−1.1	−0.8	−0.1	0.8	0.7	—	0.3	0.6	0.5	0.3
Australia[4]	−1.8	−1.6	−0.7	−0.2	−0.2	0.1	0.6	0.7	0.8	0.7
Sweden	0.5	2.7	2.0	4.3	3.0	0.3	0.9	1.8	1.4	0.7
Denmark	—	0.8	2.2	2.2	2.5	2.0	2.3	2.0	1.7	1.7
Norway[5]	−3.2	−4.5	−3.7	−2.5	−1.2	−3.9	−5.5	−4.7	−5.0	−5.1
New Zealand[6]	1.7	1.8	0.9	1.2	2.1	3.3	4.4	4.5	4.3	3.7
Memorandum										
Major advanced economies	−2.1	−1.6	−1.5	−1.4	−2.0	−3.7	−3.9	−3.7	−3.6	−3.6

[1]On a national income accounts basis. The structural budget position is defined as the actual budget deficit (or surplus) less the effects of cyclical deviations of output from potential output. Because of the margin of uncertainty that attaches to estimates of cyclical gaps and to tax and expenditure elasticities with respect to national income, indicators of structural budget positions should be interpreted as broad orders of magnitude. Moreover, it is important to note that changes in structural budget balances are not necessarily attributable to policy changes but may reflect the built-in momentum of existing expenditure programs. In the period beyond that for which specific consolidation programs exist, it is assumed that the structural deficit remains unchanged.

[2]Excludes one-off receipts from the sale of mobile telephone licenses equivalent to 2.5 percent of GDP in 2000 for Germany, 0.1 percent of GDP in 2001 and 2002 for France, 1.2 percent of GDP in 2000 for Italy, 2.4 percent of GDP in 2000 for the United Kingdom, 0.1 percent of GDP in 2000 for Spain, 0.7 percent of GDP in 2000 for the Netherlands, 0.2 percent of GDP in 2001 for Belgium, 0.4 percent of GDP in 2000 for Austria, 0.3 percent of GDP in 2000 for Portugal, and 0.2 percent of GDP in 2002 for Ireland. Also excludes one-off receipts from sizable asset transactions, in particular 0.5 percent of GDP for France in 2005.

[3]Excludes Luxembourg.

[4]Excludes commonwealth government privatization receipts.

[5]Excludes oil.

[6]Government balance is revenue minus expenditure plus balance of state-owned enterprises, excluding privatization receipts.

Table 15. Advanced Economies: Monetary Aggregates[1]
(Annual percent change)

	1997	1998	1999	2000	2001	2002	2003	2004
Narrow money[2]								
Advanced economies	**4.5**	**5.8**	**8.2**	**2.6**	**9.8**	**9.1**	**7.9**	**6.3**
United States	−1.2	2.0	1.9	−1.7	6.9	3.3	7.1	5.4
Euro area[3]	7.3	10.7	11.0	5.4	9.7	10.0	9.6	8.7
Japan	8.6	5.0	11.7	3.5	13.7	23.5	4.5	4.0
United Kingdom	6.3	5.8	11.7	4.5	8.0	6.1	7.3	5.8
Canada[4]	10.6	8.7	8.9	14.4	15.3	4.6	11.1	11.5
Memorandum								
Newly industrialized Asian economies	−4.0	0.9	19.8	4.6	11.4	13.4	13.9	9.3
Broad money[5]								
Advanced economies	**5.0**	**6.7**	**5.9**	**4.9**	**8.7**	**5.8**	**5.5**	**5.1**
United States	5.6	8.4	6.2	6.1	10.2	6.8	5.4	5.2
Euro area[3]	4.6	4.9	5.4	4.1	11.2	6.7	6.5	6.4
Japan	3.9	4.0	2.7	1.9	3.3	1.8	1.6	1.8
United Kingdom	5.7	8.4	4.1	8.4	6.7	7.0	7.2	8.8
Canada[4]	−1.3	0.8	5.1	6.6	6.0	5.0	6.0	6.3
Memorandum								
Newly industrialized Asian economies	11.6	20.0	17.3	14.4	7.3	5.7	6.8	3.4

[1]End-of-period based on monthly data.

[2]M1 except for the United Kingdom, where M0 is used here as a measure of narrow money; it comprises notes in circulation plus bankers' operational deposits. M1 is generally currency in circulation plus private demand deposits. In addition, the United States includes traveler's checks of nonbank issues and other checkable deposits and excludes private sector float and demand deposits of banks. Canada excludes private sector float.

[3]Excludes Greece prior to 2001.

[4]Average of Wednesdays.

[5]M2, defined as M1 plus quasi-money, except for Japan, and the United Kingdom, for which the data are based on M2 plus certificates of deposit (CDs), and M4, respectively. Quasi-money is essentially private term deposits and other notice deposits. The United States also includes money market mutual fund balances, money market deposit accounts, overnight repurchase agreements, and overnight Eurodollars issued to U.S. residents by foreign branches of U.S. banks. For the United Kingdom, M4 is composed of non-interest-bearing M1, private sector interest-bearing sterling sight bank deposits, private sector sterling time bank deposits, private sector holdings of sterling bank CDs, private sector holdings of building society shares and deposits, and sterling CDs less building society of banks deposits and bank CDs and notes and coins. For the euro area, M3 is composed of M2 plus marketable instruments held by euro-area residents, which comprise repurchase agreements, money market fund shares/units, money market paper, and debt securities up to two years.

Table 16. Advanced Economies: Interest Rates
(Percent a year)

	1997	1998	1999	2000	2001	2002	2003	2004	August 2005
Policy-related interest rate[1]									
United States	5.5	4.7	5.3	6.4	1.8	1.2	1.0	2.2	3.3
Euro area[2]	...	...	3.0	4.8	3.3	2.8	2.0	2.0	2.0
Japan	0.4	0.3	0.0	0.2	0.0	0.0	0.0	0.0	0.0
United Kingdom	7.3	6.3	5.5	6.0	4.0	4.0	3.8	4.8	4.5
Canada	4.3	5.0	4.8	5.8	2.3	2.8	2.8	2.5	2.5
Short-term interest rate[2]									
Advanced economies	**4.1**	**4.0**	**3.4**	**4.4**	**3.2**	**2.0**	**1.6**	**1.8**	**2.5**
United States	5.2	4.9	4.8	6.0	3.5	1.6	1.0	1.4	2.9
Euro area	...	3.7	3.0	4.4	4.3	3.3	2.3	2.1	2.1
Japan	0.3	0.2	0.0	0.2	0.0	0.0	0.0	0.0	0.0
United Kingdom	6.9	7.4	5.5	6.1	5.0	4.0	3.7	4.6	4.8
Canada	3.2	4.7	4.7	5.5	3.9	2.6	2.9	2.2	2.7
Memorandum									
Newly industrialized Asian economies	9.3	10.6	4.6	4.6	3.7	0.7	3.0	3.7	3.4
Long-term interest rate[3]									
Advanced economies	**5.5**	**4.5**	**4.7**	**5.0**	**4.4**	**4.2**	**3.7**	**3.9**	**3.6**
United States	6.4	5.3	5.6	6.0	5.0	4.6	4.0	4.3	4.2
Euro area	6.1	4.8	4.7	5.5	5.0	4.9	4.2	4.3	3.5
Japan	2.1	1.3	1.7	1.7	1.3	1.3	1.0	1.5	1.3
United Kingdom	6.8	5.1	5.2	5.0	5.0	4.8	4.5	4.8	4.4
Canada	6.1	5.3	5.6	5.9	5.5	5.3	4.8	4.6	3.8
Memorandum									
Newly industrialized Asian economies	9.0	9.7	6.8	6.9	5.0	4.8	4.8	4.9	4.3

[1]Annual data are end of period. For the United States, federal funds rate; for Japan, overnight call rate; for the euro area, main refinancing rate; for the United Kingdom, base lending rate; and for Canada, target rate for overnight money market financing.

[2]Annual data are period average. For the United States, three-month treasury bill market bid yield at constant maturity; for Japan, three-month bond yield with repurchase agreement; for the euro area, three-month EURIBOR; for the United Kingdom, three-month interbank offered rate; for the Canada, three-month treasury bill yield.

[3]Annual data are period average. For the United States, 10-year treasury bond yield at constant maturity; for Japan, 10-year government bond yield; for the euro area, a weighted average of national 10-year government bond yields through 1998 and 10-year euro bond yield thereafter; for the United Kingdom, 10-year government bond yield; and for Canada, 10-year government bond yield.

Table 17. Advanced Economies: Exchange Rates

	1997	1998	1999	2000	2001	2002	2003	2004	Exchange Rate Assumption 2005
	U.S. dollars per national currency unit								
U.S. dollar nominal exchange rates									
Euro	...	...	1.067	0.924	0.896	0.944	1.131	1.243	1.249
Pound sterling	1.638	1.656	1.618	1.516	1.440	1.501	1.634	1.832	1.815
	National currency units per U.S. dollar								
Japanese yen	120.8	130.4	113.5	107.7	121.5	125.2	115.8	108.1	108.9
Canadian dollar	1.384	1.482	1.486	1.485	1.548	1.569	1.397	1.299	1.228
Swedish krona	7.628	7.948	8.257	9.132	10.314	9.707	8.068	7.338	7.436
Danish krone	6.597	6.691	6.967	8.060	8.317	7.870	6.577	5.985	5.977
Swiss franc	1.451	1.447	1.500	1.687	1.686	1.554	1.346	1.242	1.244
Norwegian krone	7.059	7.544	7.797	8.782	8.989	7.932	7.074	6.730	6.439
Israeli new sheqel	3.447	3.786	4.138	4.077	4.205	4.735	4.548	4.481	4.476
Icelandic krona	70.89	70.94	72.30	78.28	96.84	91.19	76.64	70.07	63.85
Cyprus pound	0.513	0.517	0.542	0.621	0.643	0.609	0.517	0.468	0.462
Korean won	931.5	1,389.2	1,188.4	1,130.3	1,290.8	1,249.0	1,191.2	1,144.1	1,014.8
Australian dollar	1.344	1.589	1.550	1.717	1.932	1.839	1.534	1.358	1.309
New Taiwan dollar	28.622	33.434	32.263	31.216	33.787	34.571	34.441	33.440	31.743
Hong Kong dollar	7.742	7.745	7.757	7.791	7.799	7.799	7.787	7.788	7.784
Singapore dollar	1.485	1.674	1.695	1.724	1.792	1.791	1.742	1.690	1.638
									Percent change from previous assumption[2]
				Index, 2000 = 100					
Real effective exchange rates[1]									
United States	87.0	92.4	92.1	100.0	108.8	107.3	94.3	86.7	2.2
Japan	87.1	81.5	92.8	100.0	88.7	80.6	78.2	78.6	−2.6
Euro[3]	123.8	120.4	113.4	100.0	99.2	102.2	112.8	115.5	−1.1
Germany	113.7	110.9	107.2	100.0	98.8	99.4	103.3	103.9	−0.5
France	107.3	106.8	105.3	100.0	98.7	99.8	103.5	104.4	−0.5
United Kingdom	88.4	93.6	95.4	100.0	99.6	101.7	98.0	103.3	−1.7
Italy	107.5	105.5	104.6	100.0	99.1	101.0	105.6	107.2	−0.5
Canada	107.0	100.4	99.5	100.0	96.2	95.6	106.6	114.0	3.9
Spain	99.6	101.6	101.6	100.0	102.1	104.9	109.8	112.0	−0.3
Netherlands	103.6	104.8	103.5	100.0	101.8	105.1	109.4	110.1	−0.4
Belgium	110.0	109.2	104.6	100.0	100.9	100.3	103.5	104.0	−0.4
Sweden	106.3	104.4	101.2	100.0	90.9	93.1	98.7	101.2	−3.0
Austria	107.5	105.6	103.2	100.0	99.3	100.2	103.3	104.6	−0.3
Denmark	103.3	104.9	104.4	100.0	101.1	103.1	108.4	110.8	−0.4
Finland	111.2	109.9	105.6	100.0	100.1	99.8	102.6	102.5	−0.3
Greece	107.6	103.8	104.3	100.0	100.1	103.2	108.4	111.2	−0.2
Portugal	99.2	100.7	101.1	100.0	102.3	105.1	109.9	112.3	−0.2
Ireland	132.7	120.4	112.0	100.0	98.7	99.5	105.6	106.3	−0.7
Switzerland	96.7	101.7	101.4	100.0	104.6	110.5	112.4	114.6	−1.5
Norway	93.8	94.7	99.0	100.0	105.5	118.5	119.0	118.0	1.7
Australia	114.8	101.8	105.2	100.0	93.2	97.8	107.6	114.9	2.2
New Zealand	129.7	112.6	111.3	100.0	96.2	105.0	120.5	129.7	−2.6

[1]Defined as the ratio, in common currency, of the normalized unit labor costs in the manufacturing sector to the weighted average of those of its industrial country trading partners, using 1999–2001 trade weights.

[2]In nominal effective terms. Average May 6, 2005–June 3, 2005 rates compared with July 8, 2005–August 5, 2005 rates.

[3]A synthetic euro for the period prior to January 1, 1999 is used in the calculation of real effective exchange rates for the euro. See Box 5.5 in the *World Economic Outlook*, October 1998.

Table 18. Other Emerging Market and Developing Countries: Central Government Fiscal Balances
(Percent of GDP)

	1997	1998	1999	2000	2001	2002	2003	2004	2005	2006
Other emerging market and developing countries	**−2.9**	**−3.8**	**−4.0**	**−3.0**	**−3.3**	**−3.5**	**−2.9**	**−1.7**	**−1.1**	**−0.7**
Regional groups										
Africa	−2.8	−3.8	−3.5	−1.3	−2.1	−2.5	−1.9	−0.2	0.6	2.4
Sub-Sahara	−3.5	−3.7	−3.8	−2.4	−2.5	−2.7	−2.5	−0.8	−0.3	1.2
Excluding Nigeria and South Africa	−3.7	−3.4	−4.9	−4.5	−2.8	−3.4	−3.1	−2.1	−1.5	−0.2
Central and eastern Europe	−3.9	−4.0	−6.0	−4.9	−7.1	−7.5	−5.7	−4.7	−4.1	−3.7
Commonwealth of Independent States[1]	−6.9	−5.3	−4.0	0.3	1.8	1.0	1.2	2.7	6.0	6.6
Russia	−7.7	−6.0	−4.2	0.8	2.7	1.3	1.6	4.4	8.6	9.6
Excluding Russia	−4.6	−3.1	−3.2	−1.4	−0.7	0.2	0.1	−1.7	−1.2	−1.6
Developing Asia	−2.6	−3.6	−4.5	−4.7	−4.2	−4.0	−3.5	−2.6	−2.7	−2.5
China	−1.9	−3.0	−4.0	−3.6	−3.1	−3.3	−2.8	−1.7	−1.7	−1.5
India	−4.7	−5.3	−6.6	−7.2	−6.6	−6.1	−5.3	−4.5	−4.5	−4.1
Excluding China and India	−2.0	−2.9	−3.1	−4.3	−4.1	−3.3	−3.2	−2.9	−3.0	−3.1
Middle East	−1.6	−5.2	−1.8	4.3	−0.5	−2.2	−0.1	1.6	6.8	7.8
Western Hemisphere	−1.9	−3.4	−2.9	−2.4	−2.6	−3.1	−3.1	−1.5	−2.1	−1.6
Brazil	−2.6	−5.4	−2.7	−2.3	−2.1	−0.8	−4.0	−1.5	−3.8	−2.6
Mexico	−1.9	−2.3	−2.2	−1.6	−1.3	−1.6	−1.6	−0.3	−0.7	−0.7
Analytical groups										
By source of export earnings										
Fuel	−1.0	−5.9	−2.3	6.3	0.2	−1.8	1.0	4.1	10.1	12.4
Nonfuel	−3.0	−3.7	−4.1	−3.8	−3.5	−3.6	−3.2	−2.1	−2.0	−1.6
of which, primary products	−2.1	−2.3	−3.8	−4.5	−2.9	−3.0	−3.0	−1.6	−1.0	−0.9
By external financing source										
Net debtor countries	−3.2	−3.9	−4.3	−4.2	−4.3	−4.3	−3.9	−2.9	−3.0	−2.6
of which, official financing	−2.9	−3.2	−3.6	−4.1	−4.0	−4.6	−3.0	−2.6	−2.5	−2.6
Net debtor countries by debt-servicing experience										
Countries with arrears and/or rescheduling during 1999–2003	−2.5	−2.9	−3.1	−3.1	−3.3	−3.9	−2.3	−1.3	−0.9	−0.3
Other groups										
Heavily indebted poor countries	−3.2	−3.5	−4.4	−5.3	−4.1	−4.4	−4.5	−3.6	−2.9	−2.6
Middle East and north Africa	−1.4	−4.7	−1.8	3.7	−0.5	−2.1	−0.1	1.6	5.9	7.3
Memorandum										
Median										
Other emerging market and developing countries	−2.5	−3.0	−3.1	−2.7	−3.6	−3.7	−3.1	−2.6	−2.5	−2.1
Africa	−2.4	−3.5	−3.2	−2.8	−3.4	−4.1	−3.1	−3.0	−2.4	−2.1
Central and eastern Europe	−2.0	−2.9	−3.2	−2.5	−3.5	−5.1	−3.5	−3.0	−3.5	−2.7
Commonwealth of Independent States[1]	−4.7	−4.4	−3.7	−1.0	−1.6	−0.6	−0.7	−0.9	−1.6	−1.9
Developing Asia	−3.0	−2.3	−3.3	−4.1	−4.4	−4.2	−3.2	−2.5	−3.5	−2.9
Middle East	−2.1	−5.7	−1.3	5.2	0.8	−0.8	−0.2	−0.2	3.4	3.6
Western Hemisphere	−2.5	−2.3	−2.9	−2.6	−4.1	−5.0	−3.9	−2.9	−2.8	−1.9

[1]Mongolia, which is not a member of the Commonwealth of Independent States, is included in this group for reasons of geography and similarities in economic structure.

Table 19. Other Emerging Market and Developing Countries: Broad Money Aggregates
(Annual percent change)

	1997	1998	1999	2000	2001	2002	2003	2004	2005	2006
Other emerging market and developing countries	**19.3**	**18.0**	**17.7**	**13.1**	**14.5**	**17.5**	**16.7**	**16.8**	**15.2**	**13.4**
Regional groups										
Africa	19.0	18.3	19.1	20.1	18.3	21.4	20.1	17.9	17.4	13.7
Sub-Sahara	20.5	16.8	21.2	22.9	18.5	24.8	23.1	20.6	19.3	14.0
Central and eastern Europe	51.8	37.1	37.1	24.0	30.6	12.2	11.6	13.2	12.5	11.2
Commonwealth of Independent States[1]	30.9	34.7	53.2	25.4	40.9	64.0	38.7	34.1	35.9	30.8
Russia	28.8	37.6	48.1	15.0	40.1	77.3	39.4	33.7	37.8	33.5
Excluding Russia	39.0	24.8	70.3	58.2	43.0	34.2	36.6	35.1	29.8	21.8
Developing Asia	18.1	18.4	14.4	12.3	13.1	15.5	16.2	14.6	13.5	13.0
China	19.6	14.8	14.7	12.3	14.8	19.7	19.6	14.5	13.0	12.0
India	17.6	20.2	18.6	16.2	13.9	15.1	15.9	18.0	16.2	16.6
Excluding China and India	16.8	21.5	11.5	9.6	9.5	8.5	10.3	12.1	12.5	12.3
Middle East	10.0	8.5	10.7	12.5	14.0	17.1	13.8	19.0	17.2	11.6
Western Hemisphere	12.1	11.0	10.1	7.1	6.5	13.6	15.0	15.9	11.2	9.7
Brazil	−7.3	5.5	7.8	3.3	13.3	23.6	3.7	19.3	12.0	9.4
Mexico	28.7	25.0	19.7	12.9	16.0	10.8	13.5	12.6	8.5	8.3
Analytical groups										
By source of export earnings										
Fuel	18.9	14.4	16.2	18.9	14.6	19.3	20.5	23.2	20.4	14.6
Nonfuel	19.3	18.4	17.9	12.5	14.5	17.3	16.3	16.0	14.5	13.3
of which, primary products	24.2	17.4	20.2	22.4	21.5	20.7	22.2	25.7	20.3	12.0
By external financing source										
Net debtor countries	18.1	18.1	16.8	12.8	13.0	14.0	13.9	15.1	12.8	11.9
of which, official financing	23.5	21.6	10.4	10.2	−1.0	10.3	20.7	13.3	13.4	12.7
Net debtor countries by debt-servicing experience										
Countries with arrears and/or rescheduling during 1999–2003	25.3	23.4	12.7	14.9	0.4	14.3	26.8	17.3	17.8	15.3
Other groups										
Heavily indebted poor countries	20.4	20.1	23.3	30.2	21.1	19.5	15.2	15.4	14.2	12.8
Middle East and north Africa	11.0	11.0	11.2	12.7	14.7	16.4	13.8	17.4	17.0	12.0
Memorandum										
Median										
Other emerging market and developing countries	17.2	11.3	12.8	14.0	13.6	13.2	13.3	13.1	11.5	10.7
Africa	14.0	8.6	12.1	14.1	14.4	17.7	14.3	13.4	12.4	11.8
Central and eastern Europe	34.1	13.0	14.2	16.5	21.4	10.4	10.9	13.5	11.3	11.9
Commonwealth of Independent States[1]	33.9	25.3	32.1	39.0	36.4	34.1	29.8	16.1	18.4	15.0
Developing Asia	17.6	11.7	14.7	12.3	11.7	13.4	14.6	14.1	12.8	11.9
Middle East	9.9	8.3	11.3	10.2	13.4	12.8	10.9	12.6	13.4	8.2
Western Hemisphere	14.0	11.7	10.8	8.5	8.9	7.5	9.7	11.3	8.1	8.7

[1]Mongolia, which is not a member of the Commonwealth of Independent States, is included in this group for reasons of geography and similarities in economic structure.

Table 20. Summary of World Trade Volumes and Prices
(Annual percent change)

	Ten-Year Averages		1997	1998	1999	2000	2001	2002	2003	2004	2005	2006
	1987–96	1997–2006										
Trade in goods and services												
World trade[1]												
Volume	6.6	6.6	10.5	4.6	5.8	12.4	0.1	3.4	5.4	10.3	7.0	7.4
Price deflator												
In U.S. dollars	3.1	0.8	−6.0	−5.7	−1.7	−0.6	−3.3	1.2	10.3	9.6	5.6	0.5
In SDRs	0.9	0.8	−0.8	−4.4	−2.4	3.0	0.2	−0.6	2.0	3.7	5.6	2.2
Volume of trade												
Exports												
Advanced economies	6.7	5.6	10.6	4.3	5.6	11.7	−0.9	2.2	3.1	8.3	5.0	6.3
Other emerging market and developing countries	6.9	9.4	12.8	6.0	4.3	14.9	3.6	6.7	10.8	14.5	10.4	10.3
Imports												
Advanced economies	6.6	6.0	9.3	5.9	8.0	11.7	−1.0	2.6	4.1	8.8	5.4	5.8
Other emerging market and developing countries	6.4	8.8	11.8	0.2	−0.1	15.4	3.3	6.5	11.1	16.4	13.5	11.9
Terms of trade												
Advanced economies	0.1	−0.2	−0.7	1.2	−0.3	−2.6	0.2	0.8	1.1	−0.2	−1.0	−0.5
Other emerging market and developing countries	−0.4	1.1	−0.5	−6.9	3.1	6.4	−3.2	1.2	0.9	2.9	6.2	1.7
Trade in goods												
World trade[1]												
Volume	6.7	6.9	11.1	4.9	5.6	13.2	−0.3	3.7	5.6	10.9	7.0	7.6
Price deflator												
In U.S. dollars	3.1	0.8	−6.5	−6.6	−1.4	—	−3.8	0.6	10.5	9.7	6.2	0.8
In SDRs	1.0	0.8	−1.4	−5.3	−2.1	3.6	−0.4	−1.1	2.2	3.8	6.3	2.5
World trade prices in U.S. dollars[2]												
Manufactures	4.0	0.6	−8.7	−4.1	−2.5	−5.9	−3.7	2.4	14.4	9.7	6.0	0.5
Oil	3.7	11.7	−5.4	−32.1	37.5	57.0	−13.8	2.5	15.8	30.7	43.6	13.9
Nonfuel primary commodities	2.7	0.5	−3.0	−14.3	−7.2	4.8	−4.9	1.7	6.9	18.5	8.6	−2.1
World trade prices in SDRs[2]												
Manufactures	1.8	0.5	−3.7	−2.7	−3.3	−2.4	−0.2	0.6	5.8	3.7	6.0	2.2
Oil	1.5	11.7	−0.2	−31.2	36.4	62.8	−10.7	0.8	7.1	23.6	43.7	15.8
Nonfuel primary commodities	0.6	0.5	2.3	−13.1	−7.9	8.6	−1.5	—	−1.2	12.1	8.6	−0.4
World trade prices in euros[2]												
Manufactures	1.3	1.0	2.2	−2.9	2.4	8.7	−0.7	−2.9	−4.4	−0.2	5.5	3.5
Oil	1.1	12.2	5.8	−31.3	44.4	81.3	−11.1	−2.8	−3.3	18.9	43.0	17.3
Nonfuel primary commodities	0.1	1.0	8.5	−13.3	−2.6	20.9	−1.9	−3.5	−10.8	7.8	8.1	0.8

Table 20 *(concluded)*

	Ten-Year Averages		1997	1998	1999	2000	2001	2002	2003	2004	2005	2006
	1987–96	1997–2006										
Trade in goods												
Volume of trade												
Exports												
Advanced economies	6.7	5.6	11.2	4.5	5.1	12.6	−1.4	2.3	3.2	8.6	4.5	6.4
Other emerging market and												
developing countries	6.7	9.3	13.1	6.2	3.5	15.9	3.2	7.0	10.0	14.4	10.2	10.4
Fuel exporters	6.0	4.7	7.2	2.6	−1.5	7.3	1.3	0.7	9.3	7.8	6.0	7.1
Nonfuel exporters	6.7	10.1	14.3	6.8	4.2	17.3	3.6	8.2	10.1	15.6	11.0	11.0
Imports												
Advanced economies	6.8	6.4	10.2	6.0	8.4	12.4	−1.5	2.9	4.8	9.6	5.6	6.0
Other emerging market and												
developing countries	6.2	9.2	11.8	1.4	−0.5	15.9	3.6	6.9	10.6	17.4	14.1	12.2
Fuel exporters	−0.6	9.8	16.0	2.9	1.4	10.6	12.5	11.0	3.1	14.8	17.9	9.3
Nonfuel exporters	7.3	9.1	11.4	1.3	−0.7	16.5	2.7	6.5	11.4	17.7	13.7	12.4
Price deflators in SDRs												
Exports												
Advanced economies	0.8	0.1	−2.2	−3.9	−3.3	0.4	−0.2	−0.9	3.0	3.2	4.3	1.5
Other emerging market and												
developing countries	1.7	3.1	0.4	−11.2	4.6	13.1	−1.7	0.1	2.8	6.9	13.6	5.1
Fuel exporters	0.7	9.2	−1.0	−30.2	40.0	50.0	−10.0	1.5	3.3	16.7	35.9	11.6
Nonfuel exporters	2.0	2.0	0.7	−8.0	0.1	7.0	0.1	−0.1	2.8	5.2	9.4	3.9
Imports												
Advanced economies	0.5	0.3	−1.7	−5.1	−3.2	3.6	−0.6	−1.8	1.4	3.2	5.2	2.1
Other emerging market and												
developing countries	2.3	1.5	0.9	−4.8	−1.0	5.4	1.3	−0.9	1.6	3.6	6.1	3.4
Fuel exporters	0.7	0.6	−1.6	−1.6	−1.8	1.1	2.3	−0.7	1.2	0.9	3.9	2.4
Nonfuel exporters	2.6	1.6	1.1	−5.2	−1.0	5.9	1.2	−0.9	1.6	3.8	6.3	3.5
Terms of trade												
Advanced economies	0.3	−0.1	−0.6	1.3	−0.1	−3.1	0.4	0.9	1.6	—	−0.8	−0.6
Other emerging market and												
developing countries	−0.6	1.6	−0.5	−6.7	5.7	7.2	−3.0	1.0	1.3	3.3	7.1	1.7
Fuel exporters	—	8.6	0.6	−29.1	42.6	48.4	−12.0	2.2	2.1	15.7	30.8	8.9
Nonfuel exporters	−0.5	0.4	−0.5	−3.0	1.1	1.0	−1.1	0.8	1.1	1.3	2.8	0.4
Memorandum												
World exports in billions of U.S. dollars												
Goods and services	4,655	9,065	6,897	6,787	7,038	7,827	7,565	7,938	9,235	11,150	12,589	13,627
Goods	3,721	7,262	5,518	5,386	5,583	6,295	6,031	6,306	7,365	8,939	10,153	11,045

[1]Average of annual percent change for world exports and imports.
[2]As represented, respectively, by the export unit value index for the manufactures of the advanced economies; the average of U.K. Brent, Dubai, and West Texas Intermediate crude oil spot prices; and the average of world market prices for nonfuel primary commodities weighted by their 1995–97 shares in world commodity exports.

Table 21. Nonfuel Commodity Prices[1]
(Annual percent change; U.S. dollar terms)

| | Ten-Year Averages | | 1997 | 1998 | 1999 | 2000 | 2001 | 2002 | 2003 | 2004 | 2005 | 2006 |
	1987–96	1997–2006										
Nonfuel primary commodities	**2.7**	**0.5**	**–3.0**	**–14.3**	**–7.2**	**4.8**	**–4.9**	**1.7**	**6.9**	**18.5**	**8.6**	**–2.1**
Food	2.3	–1.1	–8.6	–11.1	–12.6	2.5	0.2	3.4	5.2	14.3	–0.9	–0.7
Beverages	–4.0	–0.1	31.1	–13.2	–21.3	–15.1	–16.1	16.5	4.9	3.0	24.4	–0.8
Agricultural raw materials	5.9	–1.2	–4.7	–16.7	1.2	4.4	–4.9	1.8	3.7	5.5	0.3	–0.4
Metals	3.2	3.8	1.2	–17.7	–1.1	12.2	–9.8	–2.7	12.2	36.1	22.6	–4.3
Advanced economies	**3.2**	**0.8**	**–3.5**	**–15.8**	**–6.0**	**5.6**	**–6.1**	**1.9**	**8.1**	**20.6**	**10.1**	**–2.1**
Other emerging market and developing countries	**2.8**	**0.7**	**–1.5**	**–16.1**	**–7.3**	**4.5**	**–7.0**	**2.2**	**8.4**	**20.8**	**10.5**	**–2.3**
Regional groups												
Africa	2.5	0.4	–1.6	–14.7	–6.9	2.6	–6.9	4.4	8.1	14.7	9.3	–1.1
Sub-Sahara	2.5	0.5	–1.4	–14.8	–6.7	2.6	–7.2	4.5	8.3	14.7	9.7	–1.1
Central and eastern Europe	3.3	1.3	–2.5	–16.6	–4.6	6.5	–7.1	1.0	8.4	23.4	13.0	–2.6
Commonwealth of Independent States[2]	. . .	2.5	–1.7	–17.9	–2.6	9.9	–8.5	–0.7	10.6	29.8	17.4	–3.4
Developing Asia	3.0	—	–3.4	–13.6	–7.5	2.3	–6.3	2.8	6.7	16.6	7.7	–1.7
Middle East	3.1	1.1	–2.5	–15.4	–7.1	6.4	–7.2	0.9	9.8	21.8	11.4	–2.1
Western Hemisphere	2.3	0.6	1.0	–18.4	–10.0	4.6	–7.1	2.5	9.2	22.8	9.7	–2.8
Analytical groups												
By source of export earnings												
Fuel	3.2	2.0	–1.1	–17.0	–4.6	8.3	–8.4	–0.4	10.8	26.6	15.5	–2.9
Nonfuel	2.8	0.7	–1.5	–16.1	–7.4	4.4	–7.0	2.3	8.3	20.7	10.3	–2.3
of which, primary products	2.6	1.3	–1.2	–16.8	–7.7	4.6	–7.6	4.1	9.3	23.6	13.0	–2.6
By source of external financing												
Net debtor countries	2.7	0.6	–1.2	–16.1	–8.1	3.9	–6.9	2.6	8.3	20.1	9.9	–2.2
of which, official financing	2.0	0.2	–1.6	–12.9	–10.1	0.4	–7.1	4.5	8.1	15.7	9.5	–0.9
Net debtor countries by debt-servicing experience												
Countries with arrears and/or rescheduling during 1999–2003	2.1	0.5	—	–15.4	–9.6	2.6	–7.3	3.6	8.8	18.9	9.8	–2.0
Other groups												
Heavily indebted poor countries	0.7	0.1	0.8	–13.7	–12.4	–2.5	–7.6	9.7	9.5	12.3	9.6	–0.1
Middle East and north Africa	2.9	0.7	–3.0	–14.9	–7.7	5.5	–6.3	1.6	8.9	19.7	9.6	–1.8
Memorandum												
Average oil spot price[3]	3.7	11.7	–5.4	–32.1	37.5	57.0	–13.8	2.5	15.8	30.7	43.6	13.9
In U.S. dollars a barrel	18.26	31.05	19.27	13.08	17.98	28.24	24.33	24.95	28.89	37.76	54.23	61.75
Export unit value of manufactures[4]	4.0	0.6	–8.7	–4.1	–2.5	–5.9	–3.7	2.4	14.4	9.7	6.0	0.5

[1]Averages of world market prices for individual commodities weighted by 1995–97 exports as a share of world commodity exports and total commodity exports for the indicated country group, respectively.
[2]Mongolia, which is not a member of the Commonwealth of Independent States, is included in this group for reasons of geography and similarities in economic structure.
[3]Average of U.K. Brent, Dubai, and West Texas Intermediate crude oil spot prices.
[4]For the manufactures exported by the advanced economies.

Table 22. Advanced Economies: Export Volumes, Import Volumes, and Terms of Trade in Goods and Services
(Annual percent change)

| | Ten-Year Averages | | 1997 | 1998 | 1999 | 2000 | 2001 | 2002 | 2003 | 2004 | 2005 | 2006 |
	1987–96	1997–2006										
Export volume												
Advanced economies	**6.7**	**5.6**	**10.6**	**4.3**	**5.6**	**11.7**	**−0.9**	**2.2**	**3.1**	**8.3**	**5.0**	**6.3**
United States	9.1	4.5	11.9	2.4	4.3	8.7	−5.4	−2.3	1.8	8.4	8.2	8.8
Euro area	5.8	5.6	10.8	7.4	5.3	12.2	3.0	1.8	0.9	6.1	3.5	5.3
Germany	4.9	7.2	11.7	8.0	5.9	13.5	6.4	4.2	2.4	9.3	5.5	5.3
France	5.4	4.9	12.3	7.5	3.9	13.8	2.6	1.5	−1.7	2.0	2.1	6.2
Italy	6.2	2.1	6.4	3.4	0.1	9.7	1.6	−3.2	−1.9	3.2	−0.8	3.2
Spain	7.8	6.1	15.3	8.2	7.7	11.8	4.0	1.7	3.5	2.7	2.7	4.0
Japan	4.2	5.6	11.4	−2.3	1.5	12.2	−6.0	7.2	9.1	14.5	5.4	5.5
United Kingdom	5.2	4.3	8.3	3.1	4.3	9.1	2.9	0.2	1.2	3.4	5.8	5.5
Canada	6.4	4.5	8.3	9.1	10.7	8.9	−3.0	1.0	−2.1	5.0	2.8	5.7
Other advanced economies	8.7	7.2	10.3	2.4	8.4	14.7	−2.3	5.9	8.0	12.8	5.9	6.9
Memorandum												
Major advanced economies	6.1	4.9	10.6	4.0	4.3	10.8	−0.9	1.1	1.7	7.4	5.0	6.2
Newly industrialized Asian economies	12.1	8.8	10.8	1.4	9.2	17.1	−4.4	9.4	12.8	17.3	7.6	8.5
Import volume												
Advanced economies	**6.6**	**6.0**	**9.3**	**5.9**	**8.0**	**11.7**	**−1.0**	**2.6**	**4.1**	**8.8**	**5.4**	**5.8**
United States	6.1	7.7	13.6	11.6	11.5	13.1	−2.7	3.4	4.6	10.7	6.6	5.9
Euro area	5.6	5.7	8.9	9.8	7.5	11.2	1.2	0.4	2.9	6.2	4.1	5.3
Germany	5.2	5.7	8.2	9.4	8.6	10.2	1.2	−1.4	5.1	7.0	4.2	5.1
France	4.4	6.1	7.6	10.6	5.8	14.9	2.5	1.5	1.3	6.1	5.2	6.6
Italy	5.3	3.7	10.1	8.9	5.6	7.1	0.5	−0.5	1.3	2.5	0.6	1.3
Spain	9.9	8.8	13.3	13.2	12.6	13.4	4.2	3.8	6.2	8.0	7.0	7.0
Japan	8.5	3.2	0.7	−6.7	3.6	8.5	−0.7	1.2	3.8	8.9	6.7	6.6
United Kingdom	5.4	6.0	9.7	9.3	7.9	9.0	4.8	4.5	1.8	5.4	4.1	3.7
Canada	6.0	5.6	14.2	5.1	7.8	8.1	−5.1	1.5	4.1	8.1	6.9	6.1
Other advanced economies	9.3	6.2	8.7	−2.3	7.2	14.0	−4.1	5.7	7.0	13.5	6.3	7.1
Memorandum												
Major advanced economies	5.9	5.9	9.4	7.7	8.3	11.0	−0.5	1.9	3.6	7.9	5.3	5.3
Newly industrialized Asian economies	14.3	6.6	8.2	−8.2	8.2	17.4	−6.4	8.1	9.2	16.5	7.0	8.9
Terms of trade												
Advanced economies	**0.1**	**−0.2**	**−0.7**	**1.2**	**−0.3**	**−2.6**	**0.2**	**0.8**	**1.1**	**−0.2**	**−1.0**	**−0.5**
United States	−0.2	—	2.1	3.4	−1.2	−2.1	2.3	0.6	−0.9	−1.3	−1.6	−0.6
Euro area	−0.3	−0.2	−1.3	1.2	0.1	−3.9	0.7	1.2	1.2	−0.2	−0.7	−0.3
Germany	−1.2	−0.2	−2.3	1.7	0.1	−4.5	0.2	1.6	1.9	—	−0.3	−0.7
France	−0.6	−0.1	−0.5	1.4	0.3	−4.4	1.3	0.6	0.8	0.6	−0.9	—
Italy	0.5	−0.6	−1.5	2.0	0.3	−7.1	0.5	1.0	2.2	—	−2.4	−1.1
Spain	1.1	0.3	−1.1	0.9	−1.3	−1.8	2.4	3.0	1.7	−0.5	0.4	—
Japan	0.4	−2.1	−4.3	3.4	−0.2	−5.3	−2.4	0.1	−2.0	−3.7	−4.6	−1.5
United Kingdom	0.4	0.6	3.3	2.1	0.6	−0.8	−0.6	2.8	1.1	−0.2	−0.9	−1.3
Canada	0.4	0.8	−0.7	−3.9	1.4	4.0	−1.6	−2.4	5.9	3.9	1.6	0.1
Other advanced economies	0.4	−0.3	−1.0	−0.4	−0.9	−0.9	−0.4	0.2	—	−0.3	—	0.3
Memorandum												
Major advanced economies	—	−0.2	−0.5	2.0	−0.2	−3.3	0.2	0.9	1.6	−0.1	−1.6	−1.0
Newly industrialized Asian economies	0.3	−1.3	−1.3	0.2	−2.4	−3.3	−0.5	0.2	−1.6	−2.0	−2.4	−0.1
Memorandum												
Trade in goods												
Advanced economies												
Export volume	6.7	5.6	11.2	4.5	5.1	12.6	−1.4	2.3	3.2	8.6	4.5	6.4
Import volume	6.8	6.4	10.2	6.0	8.4	12.4	−1.5	2.9	4.8	9.6	5.6	6.0
Terms of trade	0.3	−0.1	−0.6	1.3	−0.1	−3.1	0.4	0.9	1.6	—	−0.8	−0.6

Table 23. Other Emerging Market and Developing Countries—by Region: Total Trade in Goods
(Annual percent change)

| | Ten-Year Averages | | 1997 | 1998 | 1999 | 2000 | 2001 | 2002 | 2003 | 2004 | 2005 | 2006 |
	1987–96	1997–2006										
Other emerging market and developing countries												
Value in U.S. dollars												
Exports	10.0	12.4	7.2	−7.1	7.9	25.5	−2.1	8.9	22.3	28.8	24.4	14.0
Imports	9.9	10.7	6.7	−4.7	−1.6	17.7	1.3	7.6	21.6	28.2	20.9	13.8
Volume												
Exports	6.7	9.3	13.1	6.2	3.5	15.9	3.2	7.0	10.0	14.4	10.2	10.4
Imports	6.2	9.2	11.8	1.4	−0.5	15.9	3.6	6.9	10.6	17.4	14.1	12.2
Unit value in U.S. dollars												
Exports	3.9	3.2	−4.8	−12.5	5.4	9.1	−5.1	1.9	11.2	13.1	13.6	3.3
Imports	4.5	1.5	−4.4	−6.2	−0.3	1.7	−2.2	0.9	9.8	9.5	6.1	1.6
Terms of trade	−0.6	1.6	−0.5	−6.7	5.7	7.2	−3.0	1.0	1.3	3.3	7.1	1.7
Memorandum												
Real GDP growth in developing country trading partners	3.5	3.2	4.0	1.8	3.5	4.7	1.6	2.2	2.9	4.5	3.4	3.4
Market prices of nonfuel commodities exported by other emerging market and developing countries	2.8	0.7	−1.5	−16.1	−7.3	4.5	−7.0	2.2	8.4	20.8	10.5	−2.3
Regional groups												
Africa												
Value in U.S. dollars												
Exports	6.3	11.0	3.0	−13.8	7.5	28.2	−6.4	2.6	25.5	28.8	26.5	18.0
Imports	5.8	9.0	4.9	−2.4	0.8	3.2	1.2	10.7	22.0	26.1	19.5	8.3
Volume												
Exports	3.8	4.9	5.6	2.3	1.4	10.7	1.5	1.7	6.4	7.1	4.5	8.6
Imports	3.1	6.6	9.2	4.1	1.9	1.7	6.6	9.7	6.1	8.8	11.4	7.1
Unit value in U.S. dollars												
Exports	2.6	5.9	−2.3	−15.8	6.5	15.6	−7.8	1.2	18.3	20.4	21.9	7.8
Imports	3.0	2.6	−3.9	−6.2	−0.9	1.7	−4.8	2.8	15.5	16.0	7.4	1.1
Terms of trade	−0.4	3.2	1.7	−10.3	7.6	13.7	−3.1	−1.6	2.5	3.8	13.5	6.7
Sub-Sahara												
Value in U.S. dollars												
Exports	5.9	10.7	3.0	−14.1	6.3	25.7	−6.6	3.0	26.2	29.9	25.0	18.0
Imports	5.8	9.3	7.8	−4.9	−0.2	2.8	1.0	10.4	24.6	26.1	21.8	8.2
Volume												
Exports	4.2	4.9	5.2	1.5	−0.7	12.2	1.4	0.6	7.1	7.6	5.2	10.2
Imports	3.4	6.6	10.8	2.1	1.3	0.4	5.5	10.4	7.1	9.0	12.8	6.9
Unit value in U.S. dollars												
Exports	1.9	5.5	−2.0	−15.5	7.6	11.8	−7.8	2.6	18.4	20.8	19.8	6.1
Imports	2.7	3.0	−2.6	−6.8	−1.4	2.6	−4.2	2.6	17.1	15.8	8.5	1.0
Terms of trade	−0.8	2.5	0.7	−9.4	9.1	9.0	−3.8	0.1	1.1	4.3	10.4	5.0

Table 23 *(continued)*

	Ten-Year Averages		1997	1998	1999	2000	2001	2002	2003	2004	2005	2006
	1987–96	1997–2006										
Central and eastern Europe												
Value in U.S. dollars												
Exports	7.4	13.0	6.6	6.4	−2.4	13.3	10.7	13.8	28.9	31.1	15.9	9.6
Imports	9.4	12.2	9.1	5.9	−4.2	16.0	−0.4	13.4	29.6	31.0	17.4	9.1
Volume												
Exports	3.2	11.1	16.3	11.7	2.6	16.1	10.1	8.6	14.3	15.3	8.2	9.0
Imports	7.1	9.8	16.8	11.7	−0.7	15.8	1.5	9.7	13.8	16.0	7.4	7.8
Unit value in U.S. dollars												
Exports	4.9	1.9	−8.1	−4.8	−4.7	−2.5	1.1	4.9	13.1	14.0	7.3	0.6
Imports	4.7	2.3	−6.2	−5.2	−3.5	0.2	−2.1	3.9	14.3	13.3	9.4	1.2
Terms of trade	0.2	−0.4	−2.0	0.4	−1.3	−2.6	3.3	0.9	−1.0	0.6	−2.0	−0.6
Commonwealth of Independent States[1]												
Value in U.S. dollars												
Exports	...	12.6	−1.4	−14.0	0.1	37.0	−0.9	6.3	26.8	37.0	34.6	15.0
Imports	...	8.3	4.0	−15.9	−25.8	14.6	15.0	8.4	26.6	28.5	28.4	14.7
Volume												
Exports	...	5.5	1.6	0.7	−1.2	9.3	4.2	7.2	8.1	12.1	7.0	6.7
Imports	...	7.2	12.7	−13.6	−22.2	15.5	17.4	8.3	13.9	16.7	20.4	12.9
Unit value in U.S. dollars												
Exports	...	7.0	−1.8	−14.0	1.0	24.6	−5.0	−0.9	17.5	22.3	26.6	7.8
Imports	...	1.3	−6.8	−3.0	−4.6	−0.6	−2.0	1.7	11.3	10.3	6.9	1.8
Terms of trade	...	5.6	5.4	−11.3	5.9	25.4	−3.1	−2.6	5.5	10.9	18.5	5.9
Developing Asia												
Value in U.S. dollars												
Exports	17.1	13.7	12.2	−2.4	8.5	22.3	−1.8	14.0	23.1	28.2	21.0	16.6
Imports	15.7	12.7	1.0	−13.8	9.2	26.9	−0.6	12.9	26.9	31.4	23.2	19.3
Volume												
Exports	12.5	13.1	18.6	7.9	5.9	23.7	1.3	12.6	12.7	19.4	15.6	15.5
Imports	11.6	11.4	6.1	−4.9	6.0	22.6	2.0	12.3	15.7	22.6	17.8	17.1
Unit value in U.S. dollars												
Exports	4.2	0.8	−5.1	−9.3	4.3	−0.9	−3.0	1.2	9.2	7.8	4.6	1.0
Imports	4.1	1.6	−4.6	−9.4	6.0	4.0	−2.4	0.5	9.4	7.6	4.6	2.1
Terms of trade	0.2	−0.8	−0.6	0.1	−1.5	−4.7	−0.6	0.7	−0.2	0.2	—	−1.1
Excluding China and India												
Value in U.S. dollars												
Exports	16.6	7.7	7.4	−4.2	10.3	18.9	−9.3	6.1	11.9	18.3	12.1	9.4
Imports	17.9	6.0	−1.0	−23.4	6.4	22.8	−6.8	6.3	13.4	23.4	18.2	10.1
Volume												
Exports	11.9	6.3	11.1	9.3	3.4	17.3	−6.7	5.9	4.9	7.9	5.5	6.5
Imports	14.1	4.3	1.8	−14.7	−0.6	20.3	−6.8	7.1	7.6	13.7	11.1	8.6
Unit value in U.S. dollars												
Exports	4.4	1.8	−3.1	−12.1	10.2	1.4	−2.8	0.3	6.9	9.9	6.3	2.7
Imports	3.7	2.2	−2.6	−10.3	12.4	2.2	—	−0.7	5.5	9.1	6.5	1.5
Terms of trade	0.7	−0.4	−0.6	−1.9	−1.9	−0.8	−2.9	1.0	1.3	0.7	−0.2	1.3

Table 23 *(concluded)*

	Ten-Year Averages		1997	1998	1999	2000	2001	2002	2003	2004	2005	2006
	1987–96	1997–2006										
Middle East												
Value in U.S. dollars												
Exports	9.5	13.5	1.6	−26.0	31.8	45.4	−8.0	6.2	22.5	27.8	40.4	14.3
Imports	5.0	9.0	5.2	−0.9	−1.5	9.2	8.8	9.0	14.9	19.8	18.1	9.9
Volume												
Exports	7.5	5.7	8.0	1.8	0.9	7.4	3.2	2.7	9.5	9.1	8.9	5.8
Imports	1.4	9.1	13.2	3.9	2.4	12.2	10.3	9.8	4.9	13.0	13.4	8.5
Unit value in U.S. dollars												
Exports	2.4	7.7	−5.9	−26.8	31.0	35.9	−10.9	3.9	11.8	17.9	29.9	8.2
Imports	3.9	—	−7.2	−4.5	−3.7	−2.6	−1.4	−0.7	9.5	6.1	4.2	1.4
Terms of trade	−1.5	7.7	1.3	−23.4	36.1	39.5	−9.6	4.6	2.1	11.1	24.6	6.7
Western Hemisphere												
Value in U.S. dollars												
Exports	10.9	8.4	9.9	−3.8	4.0	19.6	−3.8	1.1	11.1	24.4	18.0	7.2
Imports	13.1	7.0	19.1	4.7	−6.9	14.9	−1.5	−8.5	4.3	22.7	17.9	8.5
Volume												
Exports	8.7	6.4	15.2	7.5	4.1	11.2	3.5	−0.1	3.4	10.6	4.4	5.1
Imports	10.0	5.7	18.8	8.7	−4.0	12.6	—	−7.7	0.6	12.9	10.9	7.1
Unit value in U.S. dollars												
Exports	3.6	2.1	−4.3	−10.6	1.5	8.0	−7.1	1.4	7.6	12.2	13.5	2.2
Imports	4.1	1.2	0.1	−3.8	−3.1	2.0	−1.4	−1.0	3.7	8.8	6.1	1.2
Terms of trade	−0.5	0.9	−4.5	−7.1	4.7	5.9	−5.8	2.4	3.7	3.1	7.0	1.0

[1]Mongolia, which is not a member of the Commonwealth of Independent States, is included in this group for reasons of geography and similarities in economic structure.

Table 24. Other Emerging Market and Developing Countries—by Source of Export Earnings: Total Trade in Goods
(Annual percent change)

	Ten-Year Averages		1997	1998	1999	2000	2001	2002	2003	2004	2005	2006
	1987–96	1997–2006										
Fuel												
Value in U.S. dollars												
Exports	8.4	14.0	−0.1	−29.6	37.3	55.3	−11.9	3.6	22.2	32.7	42.2	17.3
Imports	2.0	10.4	8.3	0.2	0.5	8.0	11.3	9.9	13.3	22.0	22.6	10.1
Volume												
Exports	6.0	4.7	7.2	2.6	−1.5	7.3	1.3	0.7	9.3	7.8	6.0	7.1
Imports	−0.6	9.8	16.0	2.9	1.4	10.6	12.5	11.0	3.1	14.8	17.9	9.3
Unit value in U.S. dollars												
Exports	2.8	9.3	−6.2	−31.2	41.1	44.7	−13.1	3.3	11.7	23.4	35.8	9.7
Imports	2.9	0.6	−6.8	−3.0	−1.0	−2.5	−1.2	1.1	9.4	6.6	3.8	0.7
Terms of trade	—	8.6	0.6	−29.1	42.6	48.4	−12.0	2.2	2.1	15.7	30.8	8.9
Nonfuel												
Value in U.S. dollars												
Exports	10.4	12.0	8.6	−3.1	4.1	20.6	0.1	9.9	22.3	28.1	21.1	13.2
Imports	11.1	10.7	6.5	−5.2	−1.8	18.8	0.3	7.4	22.5	28.8	20.8	14.2
Volume												
Exports	6.7	10.1	14.3	6.8	4.2	17.3	3.6	8.2	10.1	15.6	11.0	11.0
Imports	7.3	9.1	11.4	1.3	−0.7	16.5	2.7	6.5	11.4	17.7	13.7	12.4
Unit value in U.S. dollars												
Exports	4.2	2.0	−4.6	−9.3	0.9	3.2	−3.4	1.6	11.1	11.2	9.3	2.1
Imports	4.8	1.6	−4.1	−6.5	−0.2	2.2	−2.3	0.8	9.9	9.8	6.3	1.7
Terms of trade	−0.5	0.4	−0.5	−3.0	1.1	1.0	−1.1	0.8	1.1	1.3	2.8	0.4
Primary products												
Value in U.S. dollars												
Exports	7.5	6.4	2.6	−9.7	2.1	4.7	−5.0	2.6	17.9	35.2	16.4	3.9
Imports	8.8	4.9	4.9	−6.7	−11.9	5.4	−0.7	0.3	15.7	25.7	16.1	6.0
Volume												
Exports	6.0	4.7	5.3	2.9	6.1	2.0	3.9	0.7	4.5	13.5	4.0	4.5
Imports	6.2	5.2	9.5	3.3	−8.4	3.6	4.3	1.5	7.0	12.4	13.1	6.9
Unit value in U.S. dollars												
Exports	2.7	1.7	−2.6	−11.9	−3.7	2.7	−8.3	2.1	13.1	18.5	12.0	−0.9
Imports	2.9	0.1	−4.1	−9.5	−3.8	2.3	−4.7	−1.2	8.8	12.3	3.1	−0.6
Terms of trade	−0.1	1.6	1.7	−2.6	0.1	0.3	−3.8	3.3	4.0	5.5	8.6	−0.3

Table 25. Summary of Payments Balances on Current Account
(Billions of U.S. dollars)

	1997	1998	1999	2000	2001	2002	2003	2004	2005	2006
Advanced economies	**71.0**	**25.5**	**−109.8**	**−262.0**	**−210.8**	**−222.5**	**−219.6**	**−314.0**	**−451.1**	**−499.0**
United States	−140.9	−214.1	−300.1	−416.0	−389.5	−475.2	−519.7	−668.1	−759.0	−805.2
Euro area[1]	95.5	57.7	31.7	−37.0	7.0	48.5	26.7	46.7	23.7	18.4
Japan	96.6	119.1	114.5	119.6	87.8	112.6	136.2	172.1	153.1	140.5
Other advanced economies[2]	19.9	62.8	44.1	71.4	83.9	91.6	137.2	135.3	131.1	147.3
Memorandum										
Newly industrialized Asian economies	5.9	64.6	58.0	40.1	50.6	59.3	84.4	90.2	78.0	75.7
Other emerging market and										
developing countries	**−84.7**	**−114.8**	**−17.5**	**88.4**	**42.5**	**85.8**	**143.9**	**227.7**	**410.1**	**493.6**
Excluding Asian countries in surplus[3]	−105.7	−171.8	−65.4	43.8	10.2	31.0	75.3	134.6	278.7	357.0
Regional groups										
Africa	−6.2	−19.4	−15.4	7.3	0.7	−8.2	−3.1	0.6	12.5	30.9
Central and eastern Europe	−21.1	−19.3	−26.6	−32.7	−16.6	−24.5	−37.3	−50.1	−56.4	−61.6
Commonwealth of Independent States[4]	−8.9	−9.7	20.7	46.1	32.6	32.1	35.9	63.1	105.3	122.0
Developing Asia	7.7	49.3	48.5	46.1	40.7	72.3	84.8	93.0	109.7	113.4
Middle East	10.7	−25.2	11.9	69.8	39.3	30.0	57.3	102.8	217.6	272.7
Western Hemisphere	−66.9	−90.6	−56.5	−48.2	−54.2	−16.0	6.3	18.3	21.5	16.3
Memorandum										
European Union	88.0	43.1	−15.6	−82.1	−26.0	22.1	7.5	13.3	−12.2	−23.3
Analytical groups										
By source of export earnings										
Fuel	16.0	−32.3	11.2	89.3	46.1	32.5	64.3	116.9	241.6	311.5
Nonfuel	−100.7	−82.5	−28.6	−1.0	−3.7	53.3	79.7	110.8	168.5	182.1
of which, primary products	−7.6	−7.5	−2.5	−2.7	−3.7	−2.8	−2.8	−1.3	−1.7	−2.2
By external financing source										
Net debtor countries	−131.9	−128.4	−85.5	−76.7	−65.7	−32.7	−28.2	−48.7	−86.3	−89.0
of which, official financing	−38.3	−32.4	−17.8	−11.7	−7.9	10.3	9.7	−5.3	−17.3	−19.1
Net debtor countries by debt-servicing experience										
Countries with arrears and/or rescheduling during 1999–2003	−31.3	−35.0	−22.7	−1.5	−6.3	1.8	4.8	−1.7	−5.2	6.8
Total[1]	**−13.7**	**−89.3**	**−127.3**	**−173.7**	**−168.3**	**−136.7**	**−75.6**	**−86.3**	**−41.0**	**−5.4**
Memorandum										
In percent of total world current account transactions	−0.1	−0.7	−0.9	−1.1	−1.1	−0.9	−0.4	−0.4	−0.2	—
In percent of world GDP	—	−0.3	−0.4	−0.6	−0.5	−0.4	−0.2	−0.2	−0.1	—

[1]Reflects errors, omissions, and asymmetries in balance of payments statistics on current account, as well as the exclusion of data for international organizations and a limited number of countries. Calculated as the sum of the balance of individual euro area countries. See "Classification of Countries" in the introduction to this Statistical Appendix.
[2]In this table, "other advanced economies" means advanced economies excluding the United States, euro area countries, and Japan.
[3]Excludes China, Malaysia, the Philippines, and Thailand.
[4]Mongolia, which is not a member of the Commonwealth of Independent States, is included in this group for reasons of geography and similarities in economic structure.

Table 26. Advanced Economies: Balance of Payments on Current Account

	1997	1998	1999	2000	2001	2002	2003	2004	2005	2006
	Billions of U.S. dollars									
Advanced economies	**71.0**	**25.5**	**−109.8**	**−262.0**	**−210.8**	**−222.5**	**−219.6**	**−314.0**	**−451.1**	**−499.0**
United States	−140.9	−214.1	−300.1	−416.0	−389.5	−475.2	−519.7	−668.1	−759.0	−805.2
Euro area[1]	95.5	57.7	31.7	−37.0	7.0	48.5	26.7	46.7	23.7	18.4
Germany	−9.5	−14.0	−25.6	−30.2	3.0	45.5	51.1	103.8	121.1	121.9
France	39.8	38.6	42.0	18.0	21.5	14.5	7.9	−8.4	−27.3	−31.0
Italy	32.4	20.0	8.2	−5.8	−0.7	−9.5	−19.6	−15.0	−29.9	−24.4
Spain	−0.8	−7.0	−18.1	−23.2	−23.6	−22.5	−31.6	−55.3	−69.4	−80.1
Netherlands	25.1	13.0	15.6	7.2	9.8	12.8	15.1	20.3	30.7	33.0
Belgium	13.8	13.3	20.1	9.0	8.9	14.1	13.7	12.0	15.2	14.5
Austria	−6.5	−5.2	−6.8	−4.9	−3.7	0.7	−1.3	1.7	−0.1	−1.0
Finland	6.9	7.3	7.8	9.2	8.6	8.9	6.4	7.4	6.5	8.5
Greece	−4.8	−3.6	−4.8	−7.8	−7.3	−8.1	−9.8	−8.0	−8.6	−9.1
Portugal	−6.0	−7.8	−9.7	−11.1	−11.1	−9.2	−7.9	−12.7	−14.5	−13.5
Ireland	2.5	0.7	0.2	−0.4	−0.7	−1.2	—	−1.5	−2.8	−3.7
Luxembourg	2.6	2.6	2.7	3.0	2.3	2.4	2.6	2.2	2.8	3.1
Japan	96.6	119.1	114.5	119.6	87.8	112.6	136.2	172.1	153.1	140.5
United Kingdom	−2.9	−6.6	−39.3	−37.0	−31.9	−24.8	−27.4	−42.1	−41.0	−40.1
Canada	−8.2	−7.7	1.7	19.7	16.2	13.5	13.2	22.2	16.7	19.5
Korea	−8.3	40.4	24.5	12.3	8.0	5.4	11.9	27.6	16.2	12.5
Australia	−12.7	−18.0	−22.2	−15.3	−8.2	−16.6	−30.2	−39.8	−38.8	−35.4
Taiwan Province of China	7.1	3.4	8.4	8.9	18.2	25.6	29.3	18.6	14.4	16.3
Sweden	10.3	9.7	10.7	9.9	9.7	12.4	23.0	28.5	26.3	23.6
Switzerland	25.5	26.1	29.4	30.7	20.0	23.3	42.4	43.0	39.3	40.5
Hong Kong SAR	−7.7	2.5	10.3	7.1	9.9	12.6	16.2	16.1	17.8	18.7
Denmark	0.7	−1.5	3.0	2.3	4.8	3.9	7.0	6.0	4.8	5.5
Norway	10.0	0.1	8.5	26.1	26.2	24.4	28.3	33.8	54.0	67.1
Israel	−3.8	−1.4	−1.6	−1.2	−1.6	−1.3	0.8	1.5	2.1	1.6
Singapore	14.9	18.3	14.8	11.9	14.4	15.7	27.0	27.9	29.6	28.2
New Zealand	−4.3	−2.2	−3.5	−2.5	−1.3	−2.2	−3.3	−6.1	−7.9	−8.3
Cyprus	−0.4	0.3	−0.2	−0.5	−0.3	−0.5	−0.5	−0.9	−0.7	−0.6
Iceland	−0.1	−0.6	−0.6	−0.9	−0.3	0.1	−0.5	−1.0	−1.7	−1.7
Memorandum										
Major advanced economies	7.2	−64.7	−198.4	−331.8	−293.6	−323.4	−358.3	−435.5	−566.3	−618.8
Euro area[2]	56.9	23.0	−32.5	−75.9	−3.0	61.0	23.1	58.1	38.4	28.2
Newly industrialized Asian economies	5.9	64.6	58.0	40.1	50.6	59.3	84.4	90.2	78.0	75.7

Table 26 *(concluded)*

	1997	1998	1999	2000	2001	2002	2003	2004	2005	2006
					Percent of GDP					
Advanced economies	**0.3**	**0.1**	**−0.4**	**−1.0**	**−0.8**	**−0.9**	**−0.8**	**−1.0**	**−1.3**	**−1.4**
United States	−1.7	−2.4	−3.2	−4.2	−3.8	−4.5	−4.7	−5.7	−6.1	−6.1
Euro area[1]	1.4	0.8	0.5	−0.6	0.1	0.7	0.3	0.5	0.2	0.2
Germany	−0.4	−0.6	−1.2	−1.6	0.2	2.2	2.1	3.8	4.3	4.4
France	2.8	2.6	2.9	1.3	1.6	1.0	0.4	−0.4	−1.3	−1.5
Italy	2.8	1.7	0.7	−0.5	−0.1	−0.8	−1.3	−0.9	−1.7	−1.4
Spain	−0.1	−1.2	−2.9	−4.0	−3.9	−3.3	−3.6	−5.3	−6.2	−6.9
Netherlands	6.6	3.3	3.9	2.0	2.4	2.9	2.8	3.3	4.9	5.3
Belgium	5.6	5.3	8.0	3.9	3.9	5.7	4.5	3.4	4.2	4.0
Austria	−3.1	−2.4	−3.2	−2.5	−1.9	0.3	−0.5	0.6	—	−0.3
Finland	5.5	5.6	6.0	7.6	7.0	6.7	4.0	4.0	3.4	4.4
Greece	−4.0	−3.0	−3.8	−6.9	−6.2	−6.1	−5.6	−3.9	−3.9	−4.0
Portugal	−5.7	−6.9	−8.5	−10.3	−10.1	−7.6	−5.4	−7.5	−8.4	−7.7
Ireland	3.1	0.8	0.2	−0.4	−0.6	−1.0	—	−0.8	−1.4	−1.8
Luxembourg	14.9	13.7	13.4	15.1	11.7	11.2	9.4	6.9	8.4	9.1
Japan	2.2	3.0	2.6	2.5	2.1	2.8	3.2	3.7	3.3	3.0
United Kingdom	−0.2	−0.5	−2.7	−2.6	−2.2	−1.6	−1.5	−2.0	−1.9	−1.8
Canada	−1.3	−1.2	0.3	2.7	2.3	1.8	1.5	2.2	1.5	1.7
Korea	−1.6	11.6	5.5	2.4	1.7	1.0	2.0	4.1	2.0	1.5
Australia	−3.1	−5.0	−5.7	−4.1	−2.3	−4.1	−5.9	−6.4	−5.7	−5.0
Taiwan Province of China	2.4	1.3	2.9	2.9	6.5	9.1	10.2	6.1	4.3	4.6
Sweden	4.2	3.9	4.3	4.1	4.4	5.1	7.6	8.2	7.4	6.7
Switzerland	9.7	9.7	11.1	12.4	8.0	8.4	13.2	12.0	10.8	11.3
Hong Kong SAR	−4.4	1.5	6.4	4.3	6.1	7.9	10.3	9.8	10.3	10.2
Denmark	0.4	−0.9	1.8	1.5	3.0	2.2	3.3	2.5	1.9	2.2
Norway	6.3	—	5.4	15.6	15.4	12.8	12.8	13.5	18.3	21.4
Israel	−3.7	−1.4	−1.5	−1.1	−1.4	−1.2	0.7	1.3	1.7	1.3
Singapore	15.6	22.3	17.9	12.9	16.8	17.8	29.2	26.1	25.7	22.7
New Zealand	−6.5	−4.0	−6.2	−4.8	−2.5	−3.7	−4.2	−6.4	−7.4	−7.7
Cyprus	−4.8	3.1	−1.8	−5.3	−3.3	−4.5	−3.4	−5.8	−4.0	−3.2
Iceland	−1.8	−7.0	−7.0	−10.5	−4.6	1.4	−5.1	−8.5	−12.0	−11.4
Memorandum										
Major advanced economies	—	−0.3	−1.0	−1.6	−1.4	−1.5	−1.5	−1.7	−2.1	−2.2
Euro area[2]	0.9	0.3	−0.5	−1.2	—	0.9	0.3	0.6	0.4	0.3
Newly industrialized Asian economies	0.5	7.5	5.9	3.7	5.0	5.5	7.4	7.2	5.5	5.0

[1]Calculated as the sum of the balances of individual euro area countries.
[2]Corrected for reporting discrepancies in intra-area transactions.

Table 27. Advanced Economies: Current Account Transactions
(Billions of U.S. dollars)

	1997	1998	1999	2000	2001	2002	2003	2004	2005	2006
Exports	4,232.0	4,191.1	4,293.7	4,676.3	4,445.8	4,580.6	5,255.0	6,220.0	6,771.7	7,191.8
Imports	4,156.1	4,132.8	4,371.1	4,906.2	4,639.2	4,765.8	5,474.0	6,533.8	7,248.0	7,707.9
Trade balance	75.9	58.3	−77.4	−229.9	−193.4	−185.1	−218.9	−313.8	−476.4	−516.0
Services, credits	1,103.1	1,133.6	1,197.4	1,251.0	1,246.6	1,323.7	1,518.2	1,765.2	1,920.5	2,011.5
Services, debits	1,020.3	1,057.4	1,121.7	1,179.3	1,186.4	1,247.3	1,423.4	1,652.4	1,783.6	1,863.7
Balance on services	82.8	76.2	75.7	71.7	60.2	76.4	94.9	112.8	137.0	147.7
Balance on goods and services	158.7	134.5	−1.7	−158.2	−133.2	−108.7	−124.1	−201.1	−339.4	−368.3
Income, net	30.1	23.4	22.3	35.2	50.4	32.2	83.5	88.7	85.9	59.0
Current transfers, net	−117.8	−132.3	−130.4	−139.0	−128.0	−146.0	−179.0	−201.7	−197.6	−189.6
Current account balance	**71.0**	**25.5**	**−109.8**	**−262.0**	**−210.8**	**−222.5**	**−219.6**	**−314.0**	**−451.1**	**−499.0**
Balance on goods and services										
Advanced economies	**158.7**	**134.5**	**−1.7**	**−158.2**	**−133.2**	**−108.7**	**−124.1**	**−201.1**	**−339.4**	**−368.3**
United States	−108.3	−165.0	−263.4	−378.3	−362.7	−421.2	−494.8	−617.6	−698.0	−728.1
Euro area[1]	157.1	141.1	100.7	37.4	90.6	155.6	166.4	187.2	155.7	151.1
Germany	23.3	26.6	12.6	2.7	36.0	85.9	99.1	139.0	156.6	156.8
France	44.9	42.3	36.3	16.5	21.4	24.7	19.1	4.9	−17.7	−20.4
Italy	47.6	39.8	24.6	10.7	15.5	10.4	8.6	12.9	−3.8	−0.4
Spain	4.0	−1.7	−11.5	−17.7	−14.0	−13.1	−18.7	−38.2	−53.2	−64.5
Japan	47.3	73.2	69.2	69.0	26.5	51.7	72.5	94.2	64.5	50.7
United Kingdom	1.4	−13.2	−24.9	−29.2	−38.8	−47.4	−50.6	−70.4	−72.0	−71.1
Canada	12.1	11.8	23.8	41.3	40.6	31.6	33.1	41.1	36.1	38.1
Other advanced economies	49.1	86.5	93.0	101.5	110.7	120.9	149.4	164.4	174.3	190.9
Memorandum										
Major advanced economies	68.4	15.5	−121.9	−267.2	−261.6	−264.2	−313.1	−395.8	−534.3	−574.3
Newly industrialized Asian economies	4.5	63.0	57.1	40.9	46.9	59.0	80.7	85.5	76.6	77.4
Income, net										
Advanced economies	**30.1**	**23.4**	**22.3**	**35.2**	**50.4**	**32.2**	**83.5**	**88.7**	**85.9**	**59.0**
United States	12.6	4.3	13.9	21.1	25.2	10.0	46.3	30.4	8.4	−17.8
Euro area[1]	−14.1	−31.4	−21.3	−27.1	−34.9	−56.3	−71.4	−64.2	−58.4	−57.6
Germany	−2.4	−10.3	−11.6	−6.7	−8.5	−13.9	−15.6	0.1	0.8	1.1
France	7.9	8.7	19.0	15.5	15.0	4.0	8.0	8.5	10.6	10.6
Italy	−11.2	−12.3	−11.1	−12.1	−10.3	−14.6	−20.1	−18.3	−16.0	−14.0
Spain	−7.4	−8.6	−9.6	−6.8	−11.2	−11.6	−13.1	−17.0	−18.0	−17.5
Japan	58.1	54.7	57.4	60.4	69.2	65.8	71.2	85.7	98.1	98.6
United Kingdom	5.4	20.4	−2.4	6.9	16.4	35.5	39.5	47.9	54.4	54.5
Canada	−20.9	−20.0	−22.6	−22.3	−25.4	−18.7	−20.0	−19.2	−19.1	−18.7
Other advanced economies	−11.0	−4.5	−2.8	−3.8	−0.1	−4.1	17.9	8.1	2.7	−0.1
Memorandum										
Major advanced economies	49.5	45.5	42.7	62.7	81.5	68.1	109.3	135.3	137.0	114.3
Newly industrialized Asian economies	5.8	2.5	3.9	4.1	9.8	7.5	12.3	14.2	12.1	9.8

[1]Calculated as the sum of the individual euro area countries.

Table 28. Other Emerging Market and Developing Countries: Payments Balances on Current Account

	1997	1998	1999	2000	2001	2002	2003	2004	2005	2006
	Billions of U.S. dollars									
Other emerging market and developing countries	**−84.7**	**−114.8**	**−17.5**	**88.4**	**42.5**	**85.8**	**143.9**	**227.7**	**410.1**	**493.6**
Regional groups										
Africa	−6.2	−19.4	−15.4	7.3	0.7	−8.2	−3.1	0.6	12.5	30.9
Sub-Sahara	−8.9	−17.7	−14.8	−0.6	−7.2	−13.3	−12.8	−11.0	−6.0	5.3
Excluding Nigeria and South Africa	−8.5	−12.4	−11.0	−5.8	−9.5	−8.6	−8.7	−7.5	−6.3	−0.2
Central and eastern Europe	−21.1	−19.3	−26.6	−32.7	−16.6	−24.5	−37.3	−50.1	−56.4	−61.6
Commonwealth of Independent States[1]	−8.9	−9.7	20.7	46.1	32.6	32.1	35.9	63.1	105.3	122.0
Russia	−2.6	−2.1	22.2	44.6	33.4	30.9	35.4	59.9	101.8	119.6
Excluding Russia	−6.3	−7.6	−1.5	1.5	−0.8	1.2	0.5	3.2	3.5	2.4
Developing Asia	7.7	49.3	48.5	46.1	40.7	72.3	84.8	93.0	109.7	113.4
China	34.4	31.6	15.7	20.5	17.4	35.4	45.9	68.7	115.6	121.3
India	−3.0	−6.9	−3.2	−4.6	1.4	7.1	6.9	−0.8	−13.5	−16.4
Excluding China and India	−23.8	24.6	36.0	30.2	21.8	29.8	32.1	25.1	7.7	8.4
Middle East	10.7	−25.2	11.9	69.8	39.3	30.0	57.3	102.8	217.6	272.7
Western Hemisphere	−66.9	−90.6	−56.5	−48.2	−54.2	−16.0	6.3	18.3	21.5	16.3
Brazil	−30.5	−33.4	−25.3	−24.2	−23.2	−7.6	4.2	11.7	13.1	6.0
Mexico	−7.7	−16.0	−13.9	−18.6	−17.6	−13.5	−8.6	−7.4	−8.3	−6.4
Analytical groups										
By source of export earnings										
Fuel	16.0	−32.3	11.2	89.3	46.1	32.5	64.3	116.9	241.6	311.5
Nonfuel	−100.7	−82.5	−28.6	−1.0	−3.7	53.3	79.7	110.8	168.5	182.1
of which, primary products	−7.6	−7.5	−2.5	−2.7	−3.7	−2.8	−2.8	−1.3	−1.7	−2.2
By external financing source										
Net debtor countries	−131.9	−128.4	−85.5	−76.7	−65.7	−32.7	−28.2	−48.7	−86.3	−89.0
of which, official financing	−38.3	−32.4	−17.8	−11.7	−7.9	10.3	9.7	−5.3	−17.3	−19.1
Net debtor countries by debt-servicing experience										
Countries with arrears and/or rescheduling during 1999–2003	−31.3	−35.0	−22.7	−1.5	−6.3	1.8	4.8	−1.7	−5.2	6.8
Other groups										
Heavily indebted poor countries	−6.6	−7.2	−8.6	−7.1	−7.0	−7.6	−7.0	−7.8	−9.0	−9.1
Middle East and north Africa	12.1	−28.7	9.6	75.7	45.0	33.7	65.6	112.8	234.0	298.5

Table 28 *(concluded)*

	Ten-Year Averages		1997	1998	1999	2000	2001	2002	2003	2004	2005	2006
	1987–96	1997–2006										
	Percent of exports of goods and services											
Other emerging market and developing countries	**−7.5**	**3.1**	**−5.4**	**−7.9**	**−1.1**	**4.7**	**2.3**	**4.2**	**5.8**	**7.2**	**10.5**	**11.2**
Regional groups												
Africa	−8.6	−2.2	−4.6	−16.2	−12.0	4.6	0.4	−5.3	−1.6	0.3	4.1	8.8
Sub-Sahara	−9.5	−7.8	−8.7	−19.6	−15.5	−0.5	−6.6	−11.8	−9.0	−6.1	−2.7	2.0
Excluding Nigeria and South Africa	−22.0	−13.9	−17.3	−27.6	−22.9	−10.7	−17.9	−15.0	−12.8	−8.6	−5.8	−0.2
Central and eastern Europe	−1.4	−10.1	−10.0	−8.5	−12.5	−13.6	−6.4	−8.5	−10.1	−10.6	−10.3	−10.3
Commonwealth of Independent States[1]	...	15.8	−6.0	−7.6	16.7	28.0	19.7	18.0	16.0	20.8	26.2	26.5
Russia	...	24.1	−2.5	−2.4	26.2	38.9	29.7	25.7	23.3	29.4	35.8	36.5
Excluding Russia	...	−2.4	−13.7	−18.7	−4.0	2.9	−1.5	2.1	0.7	3.2	3.0	1.8
Developing Asia	−8.1	7.1	1.4	9.2	8.4	6.6	5.9	9.2	8.9	7.5	7.3	6.5
China	3.1	10.8	16.6	15.2	7.1	7.3	5.8	9.7	9.5	10.5	14.0	12.1
India	−22.2	−3.4	−6.7	−15.1	−6.3	−7.7	2.3	10.0	8.3	−0.7	−8.8	−9.0
Excluding China and India	−11.1	5.3	−7.6	8.6	11.7	8.4	6.6	8.5	8.3	5.4	1.5	1.5
Middle East	−9.3	16.3	5.2	−15.9	5.9	24.7	14.9	10.7	16.8	23.8	36.6	40.3
Western Hemisphere	−13.5	−9.4	−22.5	−31.1	−18.8	−13.5	−15.8	−4.6	1.7	3.9	3.9	2.8
Brazil	−7.6	−20.6	−50.9	−56.6	−45.9	−37.5	−34.4	−10.9	5.0	10.8	10.0	4.3
Mexico	−24.2	−10.7	−9.0	−18.5	−14.2	−15.7	−15.5	−11.8	−7.3	−5.5	−5.4	−3.9
Analytical groups												
By source of export earnings												
Fuel	−9.4	17.5	7.8	−21.6	5.6	29.5	17.1	11.5	18.7	26.0	38.2	42.2
Nonfuel	−7.1	0.5	−7.4	−6.3	−2.1	−0.1	−0.2	3.0	3.8	4.1	5.2	4.9
of which, primary products	−12.6	−6.6	−14.8	−15.9	−5.2	−5.5	−7.8	−5.7	−4.9	−1.7	−2.0	−2.4
By external financing source												
Net debtor countries	−11.8	−6.8	−14.5	−14.4	−9.4	−7.2	−6.2	−2.9	−2.1	−3.0	−4.5	−4.2
of which, official financing	−17.6	−5.8	−19.2	−17.0	−9.5	−5.4	−3.8	4.8	4.0	−1.8	−5.2	−5.3
Net debtor countries by debt-servicing experience												
Countries with arrears and/or rescheduling during 1999–2003	−17.8	−4.5	−14.8	−17.8	−11.0	−0.6	−2.6	0.7	1.7	−0.5	−1.2	1.4
Other groups												
Heavily indebted poor countries	−32.4	−28.0	−29.9	−32.1	−39.8	−30.8	−29.3	−30.7	−24.0	−21.4	−21.9	−20.2
Middle East and north Africa	−9.7	15.4	5.0	−15.2	4.1	23.2	14.6	10.3	16.5	22.5	34.4	38.2
Memorandum												
Median												
Other emerging market and developing countries	−13.3	−10.0	−12.2	−16.2	−11.1	−9.7	−9.8	−9.3	−7.2	−6.7	−9.4	−8.2

[1]Mongolia, which is not a member of the Commonwealth of Independent States, is included in this group for reasons of geography and similarities in economic structure.

Table 29. Other Emerging Market and Developing Countries—by Region: Current Account Transactions
(Billions of U.S. dollars)

	1997	1998	1999	2000	2001	2002	2003	2004	2005	2006
Other emerging market and developing countries										
Exports	1,286.1	1,195.3	1,289.2	1,618.3	1,585.1	1,725.5	2,110.2	2,718.6	3,381.6	3,853.5
Imports	1,271.1	1,210.9	1,191.5	1,402.5	1,420.2	1,528.2	1,858.7	2,382.5	2,881.0	3,279.4
Trade balance	15.0	−15.6	97.7	215.8	164.8	197.3	251.5	336.2	500.6	574.1
Services, net	−54.8	−46.0	−47.9	−61.1	−63.1	−61.7	−69.6	−72.9	−81.8	−85.1
Balance on goods and services	−39.8	−61.6	49.8	154.7	101.7	135.6	181.9	263.3	418.8	489.0
Income, net	−97.1	−102.3	−120.2	−123.8	−125.3	−132.6	−154.9	−170.7	−166.2	−167.5
Current transfers, net	52.2	49.1	52.9	57.5	66.0	82.8	116.9	135.1	157.4	172.1
Current account balance	**−84.7**	**−114.8**	**−17.5**	**88.4**	**42.5**	**85.8**	**143.9**	**227.7**	**410.1**	**493.6**
Memorandum										
Exports of goods and services	1,561.8	1,462.5	1,547.4	1,899.6	1,872.9	2,034.0	2,461.6	3,164.5	3,896.4	4,424.1
Interest payments	126.3	137.8	134.6	131.7	127.6	118.9	120.7	128.3	140.4	156.1
Oil trade balance	159.2	102.3	157.5	253.3	210.0	220.2	276.7	363.1	536.1	632.1
Regional groups										
Africa										
Exports	113.9	98.2	105.6	135.3	126.6	130.0	163.2	210.2	265.8	313.6
Imports	103.3	100.9	101.7	104.9	106.2	117.6	143.5	181.0	216.2	234.2
Trade balance	10.6	−2.7	3.9	30.4	20.4	12.4	19.7	29.2	49.6	79.4
Services, net	−10.4	−11.7	−11.1	−11.3	−11.9	−12.0	−13.3	−16.5	−21.9	−28.0
Balance on goods and services	0.2	−14.4	−7.3	19.1	8.5	0.4	6.4	12.8	27.7	51.4
Income, net	−17.4	−16.2	−18.1	−23.3	−20.8	−22.6	−27.7	−34.6	−39.4	−44.7
Current transfers, net	11.0	11.2	10.0	11.5	13.0	14.0	18.2	22.4	24.1	24.2
Current account balance	**−6.2**	**−19.4**	**−15.4**	**7.3**	**0.7**	**−8.2**	**−3.1**	**0.6**	**12.5**	**30.9**
Memorandum										
Exports of goods and services	135.2	119.6	127.9	157.5	149.8	154.2	193.5	245.6	303.8	353.7
Interest payments	15.0	15.3	14.9	14.3	12.6	11.8	12.5	12.8	14.0	14.7
Oil trade balance	28.9	18.6	25.9	46.1	39.1	39.5	54.4	74.7	108.3	142.9
Central and eastern Europe										
Exports	151.8	161.5	157.6	178.6	197.7	225.0	290.0	380.2	440.7	483.2
Imports	197.3	208.9	200.2	232.2	231.2	262.2	339.8	445.0	522.2	569.9
Trade balance	−45.5	−47.4	−42.6	−53.6	−33.5	−37.2	−49.8	−64.7	−81.4	−86.6
Services, net	19.1	21.6	11.2	14.9	14.1	12.0	14.9	19.1	23.4	25.4
Balance on goods and services	−26.4	−25.8	−31.3	−38.7	−19.4	−25.2	−34.8	−45.7	−58.0	−61.3
Income, net	−5.2	−6.4	−6.6	−5.8	−8.4	−11.5	−15.4	−18.8	−18.9	−20.0
Current transfers, net	10.5	12.8	11.3	11.8	11.2	12.3	13.0	14.4	20.5	19.6
Current account balance	**−21.1**	**−19.3**	**−26.6**	**−32.7**	**−16.6**	**−24.5**	**−37.3**	**−50.1**	**−56.4**	**−61.6**
Memorandum										
Exports of goods and services	211.7	227.7	213.7	241.1	259.7	288.5	367.7	473.9	548.4	599.7
Interest payments	11.7	11.5	11.8	12.9	14.1	14.2	17.1	19.7	22.3	25.2
Oil trade balance	−17.5	−14.3	−14.1	−20.4	−19.4	−19.6	−24.0	−28.8	−34.1	−36.3

Table 29 *(concluded)*

	1997	1998	1999	2000	2001	2002	2003	2004	2005	2006
Commonwealth of Independent States[1]										
Exports	125.0	107.5	107.5	147.3	145.9	155.1	196.7	269.5	362.8	417.1
Imports	118.3	99.4	73.8	84.6	97.3	105.5	133.5	171.6	220.3	252.6
Trade balance	6.7	8.0	33.7	62.7	48.6	49.6	63.2	98.0	142.5	164.5
Services, net	−4.7	−3.7	−3.8	−6.9	−10.0	−10.8	−12.8	−17.5	−19.6	−23.8
Balance on goods and services	2.0	4.3	29.9	55.8	38.6	38.8	50.4	80.5	123.0	140.8
Income, net	−12.2	−15.3	−11.6	−12.0	−8.2	−9.7	−17.9	−20.7	−21.2	−22.5
Current transfers, net	1.3	1.4	2.4	2.4	2.2	3.1	3.4	3.3	3.5	3.8
Current account balance	**−8.9**	**−9.7**	**20.7**	**46.1**	**32.6**	**32.1**	**35.9**	**63.1**	**105.3**	**122.0**
Memorandum										
Exports of goods and services	147.1	127.2	123.6	164.7	165.2	178.0	224.2	302.9	402.2	459.6
Interest payments	13.9	17.0	12.7	12.9	10.5	9.3	9.6	11.7	13.7	15.7
Oil trade balance	20.0	13.2	19.6	38.4	36.3	42.3	56.4	83.6	131.1	160.8
Developing Asia										
Exports	466.5	455.4	493.9	604.2	593.6	676.7	833.3	1,068.5	1,292.7	1,507.6
Imports	449.6	387.8	423.4	537.4	534.0	602.7	764.7	1,005.0	1,238.2	1,476.8
Trade balance	16.8	67.6	70.5	66.8	59.6	74.0	68.6	63.5	54.6	30.8
Services, net	−11.1	−12.3	−8.0	−13.9	−13.6	−9.7	−16.5	−11.8	−3.0	9.5
Balance on goods and services	5.8	55.3	62.5	52.9	46.0	64.3	52.1	51.7	51.6	40.3
Income, net	−26.3	−27.9	−39.8	−36.4	−39.0	−34.4	−32.1	−29.1	−23.1	−22.5
Current transfers, net	28.2	21.9	25.7	29.7	33.7	42.4	64.8	70.4	81.3	95.5
Current account balance	**7.7**	**49.3**	**48.5**	**46.1**	**40.7**	**72.3**	**84.8**	**93.0**	**109.7**	**113.4**
Memorandum										
Exports of goods and services	564.8	538.3	579.0	697.1	690.1	786.6	953.0	1,241.8	1,499.8	1,747.6
Interest payments	28.0	33.2	33.2	25.1	25.6	23.6	23.7	23.8	29.7	36.3
Oil trade balance	−20.6	−12.4	−19.5	−39.1	−36.5	−41.0	−52.2	−83.4	−132.5	−165.2
Middle East										
Exports	178.9	132.4	174.5	253.7	233.5	247.9	303.8	388.3	545.1	623.3
Imports	134.1	132.9	130.9	142.9	155.4	169.3	194.6	233.2	275.3	302.4
Trade balance	44.8	−0.5	43.6	110.8	78.1	78.6	109.2	155.1	269.8	320.8
Services, net	−31.9	−23.8	−23.6	−30.5	−26.3	−30.9	−32.7	−36.9	−44.2	−47.7
Balance on goods and services	12.9	−24.3	20.0	80.3	51.8	47.7	76.6	118.2	225.6	273.2
Income, net	12.7	15.3	9.0	9.3	7.9	1.4	−0.3	2.8	10.5	19.7
Current transfers, net	−14.9	−16.2	−17.2	−19.9	−20.3	−19.1	−18.9	−18.2	−18.5	−20.2
Current account balance	**10.7**	**−25.2**	**11.9**	**69.8**	**39.3**	**30.0**	**57.3**	**102.8**	**217.6**	**272.7**
Memorandum										
Exports of goods and services	205.0	158.7	202.4	282.9	264.7	281.4	342.1	432.2	593.9	675.8
Interest payments	7.3	7.3	6.4	6.9	6.6	6.9	5.3	5.6	6.4	7.1
Oil trade balance	123.0	81.1	120.9	188.6	160.6	166.6	205.7	268.1	393.1	449.5
Western Hemisphere										
Exports	250.0	240.4	250.1	299.2	287.7	290.8	323.2	402.0	474.4	508.7
Imports	268.5	281.0	261.5	300.5	296.0	270.9	282.6	346.8	408.9	443.5
Trade balance	−18.5	−40.5	−11.4	−1.3	−8.3	19.9	40.5	55.2	65.5	65.1
Services, net	−15.8	−16.2	−12.6	−13.4	−15.4	−10.3	−9.3	−9.3	−16.5	−20.5
Balance on goods and services	−34.3	−56.7	−24.0	−14.7	−23.8	9.6	31.2	45.8	48.9	44.6
Income, net	−48.7	−51.9	−53.0	−55.5	−56.7	−55.7	−61.5	−70.3	−74.1	−77.4
Current transfers, net	16.1	18.0	20.6	22.1	26.3	30.1	36.5	42.7	46.6	49.1
Current account balance	**−66.9**	**−90.6**	**−56.5**	**−48.2**	**−54.2**	**−16.0**	**6.3**	**18.3**	**21.5**	**16.3**
Memorandum										
Exports of goods and services	298.0	290.9	300.7	356.2	343.3	345.3	381.1	468.0	548.3	587.7
Interest payments	50.4	53.5	55.6	59.5	58.3	53.1	52.5	54.7	54.3	57.2
Oil trade balance	25.4	16.1	24.8	39.6	29.9	32.5	36.5	48.9	70.2	80.4

[1]Mongolia, which is not a member of the Commonwealth of Independent States, is included in this group for reasons of geography and similarities in economic structure.

Table 30. Other Emerging Market and Developing Countries—by Analytical Criteria: Current Account Transactions
(Billions of U.S. dollars)

	1997	1998	1999	2000	2001	2002	2003	2004	2005	2006
By source of export earnings										
Fuel										
Exports	191.2	134.6	184.9	287.1	253.1	262.1	320.2	425.1	604.5	708.9
Imports	114.3	114.5	115.1	124.3	138.3	152.1	172.3	210.2	257.6	283.7
Trade balance	76.9	20.1	69.9	162.9	114.8	110.0	147.9	214.9	346.8	425.1
Services, net	−44.4	−35.6	−37.7	−44.0	−41.2	−44.5	−49.0	−59.7	−71.5	−80.8
Balance on goods and services	32.4	−15.5	32.2	118.8	73.5	65.5	98.9	155.2	275.3	344.3
Income, net	−1.6	−0.7	−3.5	−9.6	−7.7	−14.1	−17.4	−22.8	−19.5	−17.9
Current transfers, net	−14.8	−16.1	−17.6	−19.9	−19.8	−19.0	−17.2	−15.5	−14.3	−14.9
Current account balance	**16.0**	**−32.3**	**11.2**	**89.3**	**46.1**	**32.5**	**64.3**	**116.9**	**241.6**	**311.5**
Memorandum										
Exports of goods and services	205.1	149.5	199.7	302.8	270.4	281.5	342.8	449.8	631.7	738.5
Interest payments	14.5	15.1	12.8	13.4	13.6	13.2	11.7	13.7	12.9	12.5
Oil trade balance	162.0	107.0	156.1	250.0	213.5	219.3	268.9	357.2	516.6	604.6
Nonfuel exports										
Exports	1,094.9	1,060.7	1,104.3	1,331.2	1,332.0	1,463.4	1,789.9	2,293.5	2,777.1	3,144.6
Imports	1,156.7	1,096.4	1,076.4	1,278.3	1,281.9	1,376.2	1,686.3	2,172.3	2,623.3	2,995.7
Trade balance	−61.8	−35.7	27.9	52.9	50.1	87.3	103.6	121.2	153.8	148.9
Services, net	−10.4	−10.4	−10.3	−17.1	−21.9	−17.2	−20.6	−13.2	−10.3	−4.3
Balance on goods and services	−72.3	−46.1	17.6	35.9	28.2	70.0	83.0	108.0	143.5	144.7
Income, net	−95.5	−101.6	−116.7	−114.2	−117.6	−118.5	−137.4	−147.8	−146.7	−149.5
Current transfers, net	67.1	65.2	70.5	77.4	85.8	101.8	134.1	150.6	171.7	186.9
Current account balance	**−100.7**	**−82.5**	**−28.6**	**−1.0**	**−3.7**	**53.3**	**79.7**	**110.8**	**168.5**	**182.1**
Memorandum										
Exports of goods and services	1,356.7	1,313.0	1,347.7	1,596.7	1,602.5	1,752.5	2,118.7	2,714.6	3,264.7	3,685.6
Interest payments	111.8	122.6	121.8	118.3	114.0	105.7	109.0	114.6	127.5	143.6
Oil trade balance	−2.8	−4.6	1.4	3.3	−3.5	0.9	7.8	5.9	19.5	27.5
Nonfuel primary products										
Exports	43.5	39.3	40.1	42.0	39.9	40.9	48.2	65.2	75.9	78.8
Imports	43.8	40.9	36.0	37.9	37.7	37.8	43.7	55.0	63.8	67.6
Trade balance	−0.3	−1.6	4.1	4.1	2.2	3.2	4.5	10.2	12.1	11.2
Services, net	−3.9	−4.0	−4.0	−3.8	−3.8	−4.1	−4.1	−4.7	−5.8	−5.2
Balance on goods and services	−4.2	−5.6	0.1	0.3	−1.6	−0.9	0.4	5.6	6.3	6.0
Income, net	−6.2	−4.9	−5.5	−6.2	−5.8	−6.2	−8.5	−13.9	−16.1	−15.7
Current transfers, net	2.8	3.0	2.9	3.2	3.7	4.3	5.2	7.0	8.1	7.5
Current account balance	**−7.6**	**−7.5**	**−2.5**	**−2.7**	**−3.7**	**−2.8**	**−2.8**	**−1.3**	**−1.7**	**−2.2**
Memorandum										
Exports of goods and services	51.2	47.1	47.8	49.5	47.7	49.2	57.8	76.4	88.2	92.1
Interest payments	4.5	4.6	4.6	5.0	4.5	4.4	4.2	4.0	4.7	5.3
Oil trade balance	−1.8	−1.7	−2.0	−3.0	−3.0	−2.9	−3.6	−3.7	−4.7	−3.5

Table 30 *(continued)*

	1997	1998	1999	2000	2001	2002	2003	2004	2005	2006
By external financing source										
Net debtor countries										
Exports	709.3	694.9	724.7	859.9	853.3	907.2	1,068.5	1,337.2	1,563.6	1,731.6
Imports	831.1	806.4	786.8	907.9	892.6	925.9	1,091.6	1,382.4	1,660.3	1,828.4
Trade balance	−121.8	−111.5	−62.1	−48.0	−39.3	−18.7	−23.1	−45.1	−96.7	−96.8
Services, net	−2.0	−5.2	−1.4	−4.3	−8.8	−4.0	−2.7	5.1	7.0	10.1
Balance on goods and services	−123.9	−116.7	−63.4	−52.3	−48.1	−22.7	−25.7	−40.0	−89.8	−86.7
Income, net	−75.7	−78.3	−89.6	−97.5	−98.2	−103.0	−123.8	−143.9	−150.8	−162.6
Current transfers, net	67.7	66.6	67.6	73.1	80.7	93.0	121.4	135.2	154.3	160.3
Current account balance	**−131.9**	**−128.4**	**−85.5**	**−76.7**	**−65.7**	**−32.7**	**−28.2**	**−48.7**	**−86.3**	**−89.0**
Memorandum										
Exports of goods and services	908.3	891.9	914.1	1,064.5	1,057.7	1,119.5	1,309.9	1,645.3	1,919.1	2,121.9
Interest payments	94.5	98.9	102.2	98.4	95.5	87.5	90.2	93.0	100.4	108.9
Oil trade balance	−2.6	−1.8	10.2	20.4	14.8	17.3	22.3	24.3	32.4	56.3
Official financing										
Exports	163.0	156.7	154.8	182.0	172.0	177.9	201.2	237.3	272.8	294.6
Imports	181.7	169.3	155.9	173.1	163.6	155.4	179.7	226.3	274.6	298.1
Trade balance	−18.7	−12.6	−1.1	8.9	8.4	22.5	21.5	11.0	−1.8	−3.5
Services, net	−18.6	−21.1	−11.7	−16.6	−15.4	−12.4	−14.4	−16.1	−22.4	−24.1
Balance on goods and services	−37.3	−33.7	−12.9	−7.7	−7.0	10.1	7.0	−5.1	−24.1	−27.6
Income, net	−18.3	−16.9	−25.2	−26.8	−26.6	−29.6	−32.3	−39.0	−37.3	−36.8
Current transfers, net	17.3	18.2	20.2	22.8	25.7	29.8	35.0	38.9	44.1	45.3
Current account balance	**−38.3**	**−32.4**	**−17.8**	**−11.7**	**−7.9**	**10.3**	**9.7**	**−5.3**	**−17.3**	**−19.1**
Memorandum										
Exports of goods and services	199.9	190.4	188.4	217.5	209.3	215.8	241.9	295.2	333.8	359.3
Interest payments	26.1	29.5	30.4	23.8	23.4	20.8	20.4	20.7	19.8	20.3
Oil trade balance	3.1	3.2	4.2	5.1	2.0	1.9	1.7	−0.1	−2.7	−2.9
Net debtor countries by debt-servicing experience										
Countries with arrears and/or rescheduling during 1999–2003										
Exports	176.0	163.0	173.0	221.3	208.6	215.4	248.5	301.8	365.0	416.6
Imports	177.2	165.8	162.2	180.7	177.1	181.9	211.0	262.1	325.0	354.4
Trade balance	−1.2	−2.8	10.8	40.6	31.5	33.5	37.5	39.7	40.0	62.3
Services, net	−24.5	−26.5	−17.8	−23.0	−24.3	−21.5	−25.1	−28.9	−39.1	−46.2
Balance on goods and services	−25.6	−29.3	−7.0	17.7	7.2	12.0	12.4	10.8	0.9	16.1
Income, net	−22.4	−22.3	−31.4	−37.3	−34.0	−36.3	−40.2	−49.4	−47.2	−51.5
Current transfers, net	16.7	16.6	15.7	18.2	20.4	26.1	32.5	36.9	41.1	42.2
Current account balance	**−31.3**	**−35.0**	**−22.7**	**−1.5**	**−6.3**	**1.8**	**4.8**	**−1.7**	**−5.2**	**6.8**
Memorandum										
Exports of goods and services	211.8	196.6	205.7	256.6	244.3	253.1	288.7	359.4	426.6	482.4
Interest payments	28.3	32.7	33.9	27.5	26.2	22.9	22.8	23.2	22.9	23.5
Oil trade balance	26.2	20.5	32.3	53.0	47.9	47.9	58.4	74.4	94.9	120.9

Table 30 *(concluded)*

	1997	1998	1999	2000	2001	2002	2003	2004	2005	2006
Other groups										
Heavily indebted poor countries										
Exports	17.1	16.9	15.7	16.7	17.6	17.9	21.2	27.3	31.1	34.5
Imports	22.5	23.4	24.3	24.4	25.4	27.4	31.4	38.3	43.3	46.6
Trade balance	−5.3	−6.5	−8.6	−7.7	−7.8	−9.5	−10.2	−11.0	−12.2	−12.1
Services, net	−2.7	−3.0	−2.6	−2.3	−2.7	−2.5	−2.8	−3.0	−3.4	−3.8
Balance on goods and services	−8.1	−9.5	−11.2	−10.1	−10.5	−12.1	−13.0	−14.0	−15.7	−15.9
Income, net	−3.0	−2.6	−2.5	−2.8	−3.3	−2.8	−2.8	−4.2	−5.0	−4.6
Current transfers, net	4.4	4.9	5.0	5.8	6.7	7.3	8.9	10.4	11.7	11.4
Current account balance	**−6.6**	**−7.2**	**−8.6**	**−7.1**	**−7.0**	**−7.6**	**−7.0**	**−7.8**	**−9.0**	**−9.1**
Memorandum										
Exports of goods and services	22.1	22.4	21.7	22.9	24.0	24.7	29.0	36.2	41.0	45.1
Interest payments	3.0	3.3	2.8	2.7	2.6	2.5	2.4	2.4	2.3	2.4
Oil trade balance	−1.0	−1.1	−1.5	−2.0	−2.0	−2.2	−2.3	−1.5	−2.0	−2.0
Middle East and north Africa										
Exports	206.4	156.4	201.3	290.8	268.4	283.6	348.0	444.2	619.1	714.7
Imports	160.6	161.1	159.8	173.2	186.7	204.0	234.5	284.2	333.8	367.3
Trade balance	45.8	−4.7	41.5	117.7	81.7	79.6	113.5	160.1	285.3	347.4
Services, net	−30.8	−23.0	−22.8	−29.7	−25.1	−29.5	−30.9	−35.0	−42.7	−46.9
Balance on goods and services	15.0	−27.7	18.7	87.9	56.7	50.1	82.6	125.1	242.7	300.5
Income, net	7.2	10.2	3.6	3.0	2.8	−3.8	−6.3	−4.3	−0.5	7.2
Current transfers, net	−10.2	−11.2	−12.6	−15.3	−14.5	−12.6	−10.8	−7.9	−8.1	−9.2
Current account balance	**12.1**	**−28.7**	**9.6**	**75.7**	**45.0**	**33.7**	**65.6**	**112.8**	**234.0**	**298.5**
Memorandum										
Exports of goods and services	238.8	189.2	236.2	327.0	307.7	325.6	396.4	500.5	680.9	781.0
Interest payments	−12.3	−12.0	−11.0	−12.0	−10.9	−10.8	−9.1	−9.9	−11.1	−13.1
Oil trade balance	134.5	89.7	131.6	208.9	178.3	184.1	229.0	299.3	439.9	510.8

Table 31. Other Emerging Market and Developing Countries—by Country: Balance of Payments on Current Account
(Percent of GDP)

	1997	1998	1999	2000	2001	2002	2003	2004	2005	2006
Africa	**−1.4**	**−4.5**	**−3.6**	**1.6**	**0.1**	**−1.8**	**−0.5**	**0.1**	**1.6**	**3.5**
Algeria	7.2	−1.9	—	16.8	12.9	7.7	13.0	13.1	19.1	23.6
Angola	−11.5	−28.8	−27.5	8.7	−14.8	−2.9	−5.2	4.4	8.8	15.9
Benin	−7.0	−5.4	−7.3	−7.7	−6.4	−7.9	−8.3	−8.0	−8.4	−9.0
Botswana	13.9	4.1	12.3	10.4	11.5	2.2	6.5	9.5	9.3	7.9
Burkina Faso	−8.9	−8.4	−10.6	−12.2	−11.0	−10.0	−8.6	−7.8	−8.7	−6.8
Burundi	−1.0	−7.5	−6.1	−9.9	−5.8	−5.2	−4.8	−7.2	−7.1	−10.5
Cameroon	−2.5	−2.2	−3.8	−1.5	−3.7	−6.3	−2.1	−0.9	−0.7	−0.2
Cape Verde	−6.0	−11.0	−12.4	−11.2	−10.1	−11.4	−9.4	−6.2	−7.0	−8.7
Central African Republic	−3.0	−6.1	−1.6	−3.0	−2.5	−3.2	−4.9	−4.3	−4.1	−3.7
Chad	−9.0	−9.8	−15.9	−18.0	−35.1	−51.8	−40.1	−18.3	−9.4	−5.4
Comoros	−19.9	−8.4	−6.8	1.7	3.0	−0.7	−4.8	−2.4	−6.4	−8.2
Congo, Dem. Rep. of	−3.1	−9.0	−2.6	−4.6	−4.9	−2.8	−1.5	−5.5	−5.1	−7.9
Congo, Rep. of	−12.9	−20.6	−17.1	7.9	−3.2	−0.3	1.0	2.3	7.3	10.0
Côte d'Ivoire	−1.8	−2.7	−1.4	−2.8	−1.1	6.2	0.9	−1.4	2.1	2.6
Djibouti	0.8	−1.3	2.0	−3.4	3.8	5.5	6.6	−0.6	−0.7	−1.7
Equatorial Guinea	−38.6	−74.9	−83.4	−11.4	−36.2	−103.1	−61.7	−15.2	4.4	6.7
Eritrea	2.1	−23.8	−28.2	−11.7	—	0.3	−15.5	−12.3	−9.0	−7.7
Ethiopia	−3.0	−1.6	−7.9	−5.1	−3.6	−5.7	−2.7	−6.2	−5.7	−8.2
Gabon	10.0	−13.8	8.4	19.7	11.0	6.8	12.0	10.5	13.1	16.9
Gambia, The	−3.7	−2.4	−2.8	−3.1	−2.6	−2.8	−5.1	−11.8	−12.1	−8.4
Ghana	−14.4	−5.0	−11.6	−8.4	−5.3	0.5	1.7	−2.7	−4.0	−4.5
Guinea	−7.0	−8.5	−6.9	−6.4	−2.7	−4.3	−3.2	−3.7	−2.4	−1.9
Guinea-Bissau	−8.6	−14.3	−13.0	−6.1	−24.3	−11.5	−1.0	2.2	−10.5	−16.2
Kenya	−3.4	−4.0	−1.8	−2.3	−3.1	2.2	−0.2	−3.2	−5.6	−6.2
Lesotho	−30.9	−25.0	−22.8	−18.2	−13.2	−17.0	−11.9	−2.5	−7.9	−7.3
Madagascar	−5.5	−7.5	−5.6	−5.6	−1.3	−6.0	−4.9	−10.6	−11.2	−8.7
Malawi	−11.4	−0.4	−8.3	−5.3	−6.8	−11.2	−7.6	−8.0	−6.0	−3.2
Mali	−6.5	−6.8	−8.8	−10.0	−10.4	−3.1	−6.2	−4.8	−7.2	−7.9
Mauritania	1.5	−2.7	3.0	−2.4	−9.6	1.1	−7.7	−17.2	−18.8	14.9
Mauritius	0.4	−2.8	−1.6	−1.5	3.4	5.5	2.6	1.7	−0.5	−0.9
Morocco	−0.3	−0.4	−0.5	−1.4	4.8	4.1	3.6	2.2	−1.6	−2.8
Mozambique, Rep. of	−12.5	−14.4	−22.0	−18.2	−19.4	−19.3	−15.1	−8.5	−13.2	−13.6
Namibia	1.7	2.4	6.9	9.3	1.7	3.8	4.0	5.6	4.4	3.7
Niger	−7.2	−6.9	−6.5	−6.2	−4.8	−6.5	−6.0	−6.0	−6.7	−7.0
Nigeria	5.1	−8.9	−8.4	11.7	4.5	−11.7	−2.7	4.6	9.5	13.4
Rwanda	−9.5	−9.6	−7.7	−5.0	−5.9	−6.7	−7.8	−2.9	−9.0	−7.4
São Tomé and Príncipe	−30.9	−30.8	−52.4	−48.9	−54.3	−47.2	−46.0	−49.2	−48.2	−43.8
Senegal	−4.2	−4.1	−5.1	−6.8	−4.7	−6.0	−6.6	−6.7	−7.6	−6.9
Seychelles	−10.7	−16.5	−19.8	−7.2	−23.5	−16.3	−0.9	−3.0	−21.8	−15.1
Sierra Leone	−0.4	−2.6	−11.1	−15.2	−16.2	−4.8	−7.6	−4.8	−8.2	−7.4
South Africa	−1.5	−1.8	−0.5	−0.1	0.1	0.7	−1.5	−3.2	−3.7	−3.5
Sudan	−13.5	−15.9	−16.2	−15.1	−15.9	−9.8	−7.8	−6.2	−6.0	−0.8
Swaziland	−0.2	−6.9	−2.6	−5.4	−4.5	6.0	0.6	−0.6	−2.5	−2.6
Tanzania	−5.3	−11.0	−9.9	−5.3	−4.7	−3.8	−2.4	−5.5	−5.1	−6.6
Togo	−11.3	−8.8	−8.1	−10.5	−13.0	−9.7	−12.9	−12.3	−13.6	−13.5
Tunisia	−3.1	−3.4	−2.2	−4.2	−4.2	−3.5	−2.9	−2.0	−2.6	−2.5
Uganda	−4.0	−7.5	−9.4	−7.0	−3.8	−5.3	−6.3	−1.7	−3.2	−5.5
Zambia	−6.1	−16.7	−13.7	−18.2	−20.0	−15.4	−15.2	−11.5	−9.6	−9.0
Zimbabwe	−8.0	−4.7	2.5	0.2	−0.3	−0.6	−2.8	−6.9	−5.8	−1.5

Table 31 *(continued)*

	1997	1998	1999	2000	2001	2002	2003	2004	2005	2006
Central and eastern Europe	**−3.6**	**−3.1**	**−4.4**	**−5.4**	**−2.8**	**−3.6**	**−4.4**	**−4.9**	**−4.8**	**−5.0**
Albania	−8.7	−3.9	−3.9	−4.4	−3.4	−6.9	−5.6	−4.4	−5.6	−5.6
Bosnia and Herzegovina	...	−8.6	−9.2	−18.4	−20.8	−27.3	−23.3	−25.6	−24.1	−22.6
Bulgaria	10.1	−0.5	−5.0	−5.6	−7.3	−5.6	−9.2	−7.5	−9.0	−8.5
Croatia	−12.5	−6.7	−7.0	−2.6	−3.7	−8.4	−6.0	−4.8	−4.8	−4.1
Czech Republic	−6.2	−2.0	−2.5	−4.9	−5.4	−5.6	−6.1	−5.2	−3.5	−3.2
Estonia	−11.4	−8.7	−4.4	−5.5	−5.6	−10.2	−12.1	−12.7	−10.9	−9.9
Hungary	−4.5	−7.2	−7.9	−8.6	−6.2	−7.2	−8.8	−8.8	−8.5	−8.0
Latvia	−4.7	−9.0	−9.0	−4.6	−7.6	−6.7	−8.2	−12.3	−10.5	−9.4
Lithuania	−7.9	−11.7	−11.0	−5.9	−4.7	−5.2	−7.0	−7.1	−8.1	−7.9
Macedonia, FYR	−7.9	−7.5	−0.9	−2.1	−6.8	−8.5	−3.4	−8.2	−6.5	−5.2
Malta	−6.0	−6.2	−3.4	−12.6	−4.4	0.3	−5.8	−10.4	−10.5	−8.6
Poland	−3.7	−4.1	−7.6	−6.0	−2.9	−2.6	−2.2	−1.5	−1.0	−2.5
Romania	−5.4	−7.1	−4.1	−4.6	−6.5	−4.4	−6.8	−7.5	−7.9	−7.8
Serbia and Montenegro	...	−4.8	−7.5	−3.9	−4.6	−8.9	−7.3	−13.1	−9.5	−9.5
Slovak Republic	−9.2	−9.6	−4.8	−3.5	−8.4	−8.0	−0.9	−3.5	−6.3	−6.4
Slovenia	0.3	−0.5	−3.2	−2.8	0.2	1.4	−0.4	−0.9	−1.6	−0.8
Turkey	−1.1	1.0	−0.7	−5.0	2.4	−0.8	−3.3	−5.1	−5.6	−5.3
Commonwealth of Independent States[1]	**−1.7**	**−2.5**	**7.1**	**13.0**	**7.9**	**6.9**	**6.3**	**8.3**	**10.6**	**10.3**
Armenia	−18.7	−20.8	−16.6	−14.5	−9.5	−6.3	−6.8	−4.7	−5.1	−5.4
Azerbaijan	−23.1	−30.7	−13.1	−3.6	−0.9	−12.4	−27.8	−30.4	−12.8	9.0
Belarus	−6.1	−6.7	−1.6	−2.7	−3.2	−2.1	−2.4	−4.6	−3.7	−3.4
Georgia	−10.5	−10.2	−7.8	−4.3	−6.4	−5.8	−7.2	−7.6	−11.8	−7.2
Kazakhstan	−3.5	−5.5	−0.1	3.1	−5.3	−4.1	−0.9	1.3	3.9	2.8
Kyrgyz Republic	−8.3	−22.3	−14.8	−4.3	−1.5	−3.6	−3.0	−2.8	−4.9	−4.8
Moldova	−14.2	−19.7	−5.8	−8.9	−4.6	−3.1	−6.6	−4.4	−4.6	−3.2
Mongolia	7.3	−7.0	−5.9	−4.4	−4.6	−6.4	−4.8	1.2	−2.2	−4.6
Russia	−0.6	−0.8	11.3	17.2	10.9	9.0	8.2	10.3	13.2	13.0
Tajikistan	−5.0	−8.3	−3.4	−6.3	−4.9	−3.5	−1.3	−4.0	−4.9	−4.3
Turkmenistan	−21.6	−32.7	−14.8	8.2	1.7	6.7	2.7	1.2	3.2	2.2
Ukraine	−3.0	−3.1	2.6	4.7	3.7	7.5	5.8	10.5	5.0	0.2
Uzbekistan	−4.0	−0.8	−0.8	1.6	−1.0	1.2	8.9	0.8	4.5	3.9

Table 31 *(continued)*

	1997	1998	1999	2000	2001	2002	2003	2004	2005	2006
Developing Asia	**0.4**	**2.6**	**2.4**	**2.1**	**1.8**	**2.9**	**3.0**	**2.9**	**3.0**	**2.8**
Afghanistan, I.S. of	...	...	...	...	...	−3.5	3.1	—	−0.5	−1.2
Bangladesh	−1.5	−1.1	−0.9	−1.4	−0.8	0.3	0.2	−0.4	−1.5	−1.8
Bhutan	8.3	5.6	0.9	−1.6	1.5	−2.5	8.3	6.6	−1.0	3.5
Brunei Darussalam	35.7	44.7	34.9	68.2	69.7	59.3	68.0	68.2	72.8	67.0
Cambodia	−7.9	−5.9	−5.2	−3.0	−1.2	−1.0	−3.1	−3.4	−4.8	−3.8
China	3.8	3.3	1.6	1.9	1.5	2.8	3.2	4.2	6.1	5.6
Fiji	1.6	−0.3	−3.8	−5.8	−3.3	3.0	0.2	−1.2	1.7	−0.7
India	−0.7	−1.7	−0.7	−1.0	0.3	1.4	1.2	−0.1	−1.8	−2.0
Indonesia	−1.6	3.8	3.7	4.8	4.2	3.9	3.4	1.2	−0.4	0.7
Kiribati	22.0	35.2	12.4	13.1	2.0	−1.8	−19.3	−16.3	−9.4	−17.4
Lao PDR	−10.5	−4.6	−4.0	−10.5	−8.3	−7.2	−7.6	−13.2	−16.4	−15.6
Malaysia	−5.9	13.2	15.9	9.4	8.3	8.4	12.9	12.6	13.5	12.4
Maldives	−6.2	−4.1	−13.4	−8.2	−9.4	−5.6	−4.6	−12.0	−26.5	−22.6
Myanmar	−10.6	−10.9	−6.3	4.2	−3.7	1.7	0.2	−0.4	−0.7	−1.1
Nepal	−1.0	−1.0	4.3	3.2	4.9	4.5	2.1	2.5	0.9	0.6
Pakistan	−3.5	−2.6	−2.3	−1.6	0.3	3.7	3.4	0.2	−1.7	−2.3
Papua New Guinea	−5.4	0.6	2.8	8.7	6.8	−0.9	6.3	8.1	10.6	5.9
Philippines	−5.2	2.3	9.5	8.4	1.9	5.8	1.8	2.7	2.1	1.9
Samoa	−3.6	−3.4	−8.6	−6.1	−11.7	−8.1	−1.9	−1.1	−0.3	0.1
Solomon Islands	−5.6	−1.6	3.1	−10.6	−12.5	−7.2	1.3	12.5	−10.7	−13.2
Sri Lanka	−2.6	−1.4	−3.6	−6.4	−1.4	−1.4	−0.4	−3.2	−5.6	−5.4
Thailand	−2.1	12.8	10.2	7.6	5.4	5.5	5.6	4.5	−2.5	−2.5
Timor-Leste, Dem. Rep. of	...	...	2.1	11.8	12.5	7.6	5.0	35.0	42.6	24.4
Tonga	−0.9	−10.5	−0.6	−5.9	−9.2	4.9	−3.0	4.0	−2.2	−1.1
Vanuatu	−1.0	2.5	−4.9	2.0	2.0	−6.0	−8.5	−3.6	−4.6	−4.4
Vietnam	−6.2	−3.9	4.5	2.1	2.1	−1.2	−4.9	−3.8	−4.7	−4.7
Middle East	**2.0**	**−4.9**	**2.1**	**11.0**	**6.1**	**4.6**	**8.0**	**12.4**	**21.1**	**23.5**
Bahrain	−0.5	−12.5	−1.3	10.4	2.8	−0.6	2.1	3.8	9.2	11.8
Egypt	0.2	−2.9	−1.9	−1.2	—	0.7	2.4	4.4	4.6	3.4
Iran, I.R. of	2.1	−2.2	6.3	12.9	5.2	3.1	0.6	2.5	8.7	8.0
Iraq	...	...	...	...	...	...	...	...	...	...
Jordan	0.4	0.3	5.0	0.7	−0.1	5.6	11.3	−0.4	−12.3	−13.5
Kuwait	25.9	8.5	16.6	39.8	24.4	12.1	17.5	29.2	44.8	50.2
Lebanon	−25.2	−26.1	−19.1	−17.9	−21.9	−15.1	−12.5	−16.0	−16.9	−16.5
Libya	5.8	−1.2	7.0	22.5	12.3	0.6	15.5	23.6	39.4	41.8
Oman	−1.2	−22.3	−2.9	15.5	9.3	6.6	4.0	1.7	8.3	9.5
Qatar	−25.6	−21.5	6.8	18.0	19.9	16.5	29.0	41.0	50.3	55.6
Saudi Arabia	−0.1	−9.0	0.3	7.6	5.1	6.3	13.1	20.5	32.4	37.3
Syrian Arab Republic	1.9	−0.3	0.6	5.4	6.1	8.9	6.0	1.9	0.2	−1.1
United Arab Emirates	10.1	1.8	1.6	17.2	9.4	5.0	8.7	11.8	21.8	25.4
Yemen	1.6	−2.8	2.7	13.2	5.3	5.4	−0.1	2.0	7.6	4.5

Table 31 *(concluded)*

	1997	1998	1999	2000	2001	2002	2003	2004	2005	2006
Western Hemisphere	**−3.3**	**−4.5**	**−3.2**	**−2.4**	**−2.8**	**−0.9**	**0.4**	**0.9**	**0.9**	**0.6**
Antigua and Barbuda	−14.7	−10.8	−8.9	−9.7	−9.2	−15.2	−13.7	−13.2	−13.1	−13.8
Argentina	−4.2	−4.9	−4.2	−3.2	−1.4	8.5	5.8	2.0	1.3	0.1
Bahamas, The	−17.3	−23.2	−5.1	−10.4	−11.4	−6.3	−8.0	−5.3	−11.2	−11.5
Barbados	−2.2	−2.4	−6.0	−5.7	−3.7	−6.9	−6.9	−10.5	−10.4	−7.7
Belize	−3.5	−6.0	−10.4	−20.6	−22.6	−20.2	−19.5	−14.4	−11.1	−8.6
Bolivia	−7.0	−7.8	−5.9	−5.3	−3.4	−4.1	0.6	2.9	2.6	2.9
Brazil	−3.8	−4.2	−4.7	−4.0	−4.5	−1.7	0.8	1.9	1.7	0.7
Chile	−4.4	−5.0	0.1	−1.2	−1.6	−0.9	−1.5	1.5	0.3	−0.7
Colombia	−5.4	−4.9	0.8	0.9	−1.4	−1.7	−1.5	−1.0	−1.8	−1.5
Costa Rica	−4.8	−5.3	−5.2	−4.4	−4.5	−5.7	−5.3	−4.8	−6.8	−3.8
Dominica	−16.4	−9.0	−12.9	−19.7	−18.7	−14.8	−11.4	−15.4	−16.9	−14.7
Dominican Republic	−1.1	−2.1	−2.4	−5.1	−3.4	−3.7	6.3	7.6	1.6	0.4
Ecuador	−3.0	−9.3	4.6	5.3	−3.3	−4.9	−1.8	—	0.2	2.4
El Salvador	−0.8	−0.8	−1.6	−2.9	−0.9	−2.5	−4.3	−4.4	−4.7	−5.5
Grenada	−24.5	−23.5	−14.6	−21.5	−26.6	−32.0	−32.7	−17.4	−33.9	−41.0
Guatemala	−3.5	−5.3	−5.5	−5.4	−6.0	−5.3	−4.2	−4.6	−4.7	−4.5
Guyana	−14.2	−13.7	−11.4	−15.3	−18.8	−15.3	−11.9	−9.3	−24.8	−24.8
Haiti	−0.3	0.5	−1.0	−1.0	−2.0	−1.0	−0.1	0.4	1.7	−1.8
Honduras	−3.1	−2.4	−4.4	−3.8	−4.1	−3.1	−4.2	−5.3	−2.5	−2.5
Jamaica	−5.2	−2.0	−3.4	−4.9	−9.6	−15.2	−6.8	−8.5	−9.3	−12.0
Mexico	−1.9	−3.8	−2.9	−3.2	−2.8	−2.1	−1.4	−1.1	−1.1	−0.8
Netherlands Antilles	−3.0	−4.2	−5.5	−2.0	−8.1	−2.2	0.2	−4.1	−2.7	−2.5
Nicaragua	−24.9	−19.3	−24.9	−20.1	−19.4	−19.1	−18.1	−17.5	−16.7	−16.2
Panama	−5.0	−9.3	−10.1	−5.9	−1.5	−0.5	−3.4	−2.0	−1.5	−0.5
Paraguay	−7.4	−2.0	−2.3	−2.3	−4.1	1.8	2.2	0.4	−1.4	−0.8
Peru	−5.7	−5.8	−2.8	−2.9	−2.2	−2.0	−1.8	—	0.3	0.3
St. Kitts and Nevis	−23.2	−16.5	−22.5	−21.0	−32.7	−37.8	−34.1	−22.2	−20.5	−20.8
St. Lucia	−13.5	−9.5	−16.6	−14.1	−16.2	−15.2	−20.3	−13.2	−16.3	−21.6
St. Vincent and the Grenadines	−27.3	−29.1	−20.9	−6.8	−10.5	−11.3	−19.9	−25.5	−27.6	−25.4
Suriname	−6.4	−14.3	−19.0	−3.8	−15.2	−6.3	−13.8	−13.2	−12.3	−8.7
Trinidad and Tobago	−9.9	−10.6	0.5	6.6	5.0	0.9	9.3	13.5	16.4	17.4
Uruguay	−1.3	−2.1	−2.4	−2.8	−2.9	3.2	−0.3	−0.8	−2.8	−5.3
Venezuela	4.3	−4.9	2.2	10.1	1.6	8.2	13.6	12.7	15.9	14.9

[1]Mongolia, which is not a member of the Commonwealth of Independent States, is included in this group for reasons of geography and similarities in economic structure.

Table 32. Summary of Balance of Payments, Capital Flows, and External Financing
(Billions of U.S. dollars)

	1997	1998	1999	2000	2001	2002	2003	2004	2005	2006
Other emerging market and developing countries										
Balance of payments[1]										
Balance on current account	−84.7	−114.8	−17.5	88.4	42.5	85.8	143.9	227.7	410.1	493.6
Balance on goods and services	−39.8	−61.6	49.8	154.7	101.7	135.6	181.9	263.3	418.8	489.0
Income, net	−97.1	−102.3	−120.2	−123.8	−125.3	−132.6	−154.9	−170.7	−166.2	−167.5
Current transfers, net	52.2	49.1	52.9	57.5	66.0	82.8	116.9	135.1	157.4	172.1
Balance on capital and financial account	134.3	160.2	82.4	−28.8	11.5	−26.7	−168.1	−251.7	−397.0	−470.2
Balance on capital account[2]	20.0	7.0	10.0	8.7	9.0	8.3	5.1	8.3	11.7	13.8
Balance on financial account	114.3	153.2	72.4	−37.5	2.5	−35.0	−173.2	−260.0	−408.7	−483.9
Direct investment, net	148.9	158.3	158.1	148.8	171.1	151.7	143.0	174.4	191.0	187.2
Portfolio investment, net	47.3	28.6	23.4	−35.3	−55.4	−33.7	−34.8	12.1	−111.9	−120.7
Other investment, net	6.3	−32.7	−72.6	−81.8	−25.7	−11.1	11.3	−12.0	−23.6	−91.2
Reserve assets	−88.2	−1.0	−36.5	−69.2	−87.5	−141.9	−292.6	−434.4	−464.3	−459.2
Errors and omissions, net	−49.7	−45.4	−64.9	−59.6	−54.0	−59.0	24.1	24.0	−13.1	−23.4
Capital flows										
Total capital flows, net[3]	202.6	154.2	108.9	31.7	90.0	106.9	119.4	174.4	55.6	−24.7
Net official flows	8.6	58.8	38.4	−44.0	11.2	14.8	−47.4	−66.9	−125.1	−133.2
Net private flows[4]	205.8	98.9	55.8	60.3	80.4	79.2	162.8	224.7	155.0	73.0
Direct investment, net	148.9	158.3	158.1	148.8	171.1	151.7	143.0	174.4	191.0	187.2
Private portfolio investment, net	58.4	22.8	9.6	−8.3	−45.6	−35.6	13.8	81.1	3.9	11.8
Other private flows, net	−1.6	−82.1	−111.8	−80.1	−45.1	−36.9	6.0	−30.8	−40.0	−126.1
External financing[5]										
Net external financing[6]	423.7	296.4	250.3	242.9	178.0	202.5	269.3	453.6	394.5	393.2
Non-debt-creating flows	261.6	183.7	187.9	183.8	176.8	166.0	175.3	242.1	250.9	254.8
Capital transfers[7]	20.0	7.0	10.0	8.7	9.0	8.3	5.1	8.3	11.7	13.8
Foreign direct investment and equity security liabilities[8]	241.6	176.7	177.9	175.1	167.8	157.7	170.2	233.8	239.1	241.1
Net external borrowing[9]	162.1	112.7	62.4	59.0	1.2	36.5	94.0	211.5	143.6	138.4
Borrowing from official creditors[10]	13.7	51.2	31.9	−9.3	20.2	19.3	3.2	10.4	3.5	17.1
of which, credit and loans from IMF[11]	3.3	14.0	−2.4	−10.9	19.0	13.4	1.7	−14.7	. . .	. . .
Borrowing from banks[10]	10.2	6.9	−17.6	−4.2	−6.6	−3.7	29.9	54.5	65.1	71.1
Borrowing from other private creditors[10]	138.1	54.5	48.1	72.6	−12.3	20.9	60.9	146.6	75.0	50.2
Memorandum										
Balance on goods and services in percent of GDP[12]	−0.6	−1.1	0.9	2.5	1.6	2.1	2.5	3.1	4.2	4.4
Scheduled amortization of external debt	257.6	262.6	296.0	311.0	317.6	330.9	346.1	338.7	349.6	358.9
Gross external financing[13]	681.3	559.0	546.3	553.9	495.6	533.4	615.3	792.3	744.1	752.0
Gross external borrowing[14]	419.7	375.3	358.5	370.1	318.8	367.4	440.0	550.3	493.2	497.2
Exceptional external financing, net	−10.0	42.5	27.8	8.1	20.9	54.0	32.9	21.4	10.1	6.9
Of which,										
Arrears on debt service	−31.6	11.8	8.3	−17.8	1.9	13.6	15.5	10.3	. . .	. . .
Debt forgiveness	16.8	1.2	1.7	1.2	2.4	2.8	0.7	2.3	. . .	. . .
Rescheduling of debt service	10.6	8.4	14.3	2.7	8.9	13.2	6.6	8.6	. . .	. . .

[1]Standard presentation in accordance with the 5th edition of the International Monetary Fund's *Balance of Payments Manual* (1993).

[2]Comprises capital transfers—including debt forgiveness—and acquisition/disposal of nonproduced, nonfinancial assets.

[3]Comprise net direct investment, net portfolio investment, and other long- and short-term net investment flows, including official and private borrowing. In the standard balance of payments presentation above, total net capital flows are equal to the balance on financial account minus the change in reserve assets.

[4]Because of limitations on the data coverage for net official flows, the residually derived data for net private flows may include some official flows.

[5]As defined in the *World Economic Outlook* (see footnote 6). It should be noted that there is no generally accepted standard definition of external financing.

[6]Defined as the sum of—with opposite sign—the goods and services balance, net income and current transfers, direct investment abroad, the change in reserve assets, the net acquisition of other assets (such as recorded private portfolio assets, export credit, and the collateral for debt-reduction operations), and the net errors and omissions. Thus, net external financing, according to the definition adopted in the *World Economic Outlook*, measures the total amount required to finance the current account, direct investment outflows, net reserve transactions (often at the discretion of the monetary authorities), the net acquisition of nonreserve external assets, and the net transactions underlying the errors and omissions (not infrequently reflecting capital flight).

[7]Including other transactions on capital account.

[8]Debt-creating foreign direct investment liabilities are not included.

[9]Net disbursement of long- and short-term credits, including exceptional financing, by both official and private creditors.

[10]Changes in liabilities.

[11]Comprise use of IMF resources under the General Resources Account, Trust Fund, and Poverty Reduction and Growth Facility (PRGF). For further detail, see Table 36.

[12]This is often referred to as the "resource balance" and, with opposite sign, the "net resource transfer."

[13]Net external financing plus amortization due on external debt.

[14]Net external borrowing plus amortization due on external debt.

Table 33. Other Emerging Market and Developing Countries—by Region: Balance of Payments and External Financing[1]

(Billions of U.S. dollars)

	1997	1998	1999	2000	2001	2002	2003	2004	2005	2006
Africa										
Balance of payments										
Balance on current account	−6.2	−19.4	−15.4	7.3	0.7	−8.2	−3.1	0.6	12.5	30.9
Balance on capital account	8.2	4.5	5.1	3.9	4.4	5.6	5.2	7.0	6.3	6.4
Balance on financial account	−5.8	15.1	11.9	−10.0	−5.1	1.9	−2.9	−15.8	−18.9	−35.1
Change in reserves (− = increase)	−11.3	1.7	−2.8	−12.7	−12.4	−8.1	−19.4	−35.5	−38.6	−61.0
Other official flows, net	−4.4	2.6	1.8	0.2	−1.9	1.8	2.8	—	−8.7	1.7
Private flows, net	7.9	7.9	10.1	−1.0	7.4	3.4	10.7	14.2	22.7	18.3
External financing										
Net external financing	25.3	28.7	31.4	15.8	18.3	20.1	24.5	35.1	33.1	41.2
Non-debt-creating inflows	24.1	21.1	24.8	16.6	22.0	19.3	22.3	31.8	35.4	34.4
Net external borrowing	1.2	7.7	6.7	−0.8	−3.7	0.8	2.2	3.2	−2.3	6.7
From official creditors	−3.4	4.1	3.2	2.0	−1.0	4.3	4.3	2.7	−5.8	4.7
of which, credit and loans from IMF	−0.5	−0.4	−0.2	−0.2	−0.4	−0.1	−0.8	−0.5	...	...
From banks	1.3	−1.0	1.1	−1.2	—	0.5	1.0	1.1	—	—
From other private creditors	3.2	4.6	2.3	−1.6	−2.7	−3.9	−3.1	−0.6	3.5	2.0
Memorandum										
Exceptional financing	9.9	9.4	8.7	6.7	5.1	17.0	6.4	6.5	−0.5	4.4
Sub-Sahara										
Balance of payments										
Balance on current account	−8.9	−17.7	−14.8	−0.6	−7.2	−13.3	−12.8	−11.0	−6.0	5.3
Balance on capital account	8.1	4.4	4.8	3.9	4.2	5.4	5.1	6.9	6.2	6.3
Balance on financial account	−1.1	14.0	10.4	−2.3	3.4	7.6	6.8	−3.6	−0.2	−9.3
Change in reserves (− = increase)	−6.3	0.6	−3.2	−6.1	−2.2	−3.8	−10.1	−23.6	−20.9	−34.3
Other official flows, net	−2.6	4.0	3.2	2.5	0.3	4.3	4.9	2.6	−7.1	3.4
Private flows, net	7.3	8.3	9.2	0.7	5.7	4.6	10.9	14.8	24.5	18.6
External financing										
Net external financing	23.6	27.3	28.7	14.7	14.7	19.0	23.4	33.6	32.4	38.4
Non-debt-creating inflows	22.2	19.4	22.8	15.0	17.4	16.9	18.8	28.9	32.8	31.8
Net external borrowing	1.4	7.9	5.9	−0.3	−2.7	2.1	4.6	4.6	−0.3	6.6
From official creditors	−2.4	4.6	3.8	2.9	0.1	5.6	5.4	3.9	−5.4	4.9
of which, credit and loans from IMF	−0.5	−0.3	−0.1	—	−0.2	0.2	−0.4	−0.2	...	...
From banks	0.5	−1.1	−0.3	−1.5	−0.6	−0.4	0.2	0.8	0.1	−0.3
From other private creditors	3.2	4.3	2.4	−1.7	−2.3	−3.1	−1.0	—	4.9	2.0
Memorandum										
Exceptional financing	6.3	8.4	8.1	6.7	5.0	16.9	6.4	6.5	−0.5	4.4
Central and eastern Europe										
Balance of payments										
Balance on current account	−21.1	−19.3	−26.6	−32.7	−16.6	−24.5	−37.3	−50.1	−56.4	−61.6
Balance on capital account	10.2	0.4	0.3	0.6	0.8	0.7	0.5	1.8	4.3	6.0
Balance on financial account	6.3	18.5	23.0	38.3	25.4	36.2	30.8	36.3	48.9	53.2
Change in reserves (− = increase)	−10.7	−9.5	−11.3	−2.8	7.4	−11.6	−11.7	−14.8	−17.0	−2.3
Other official flows, net	−3.3	0.3	−2.6	1.6	5.6	−7.6	−5.4	−5.7	−5.7	−2.8
Private flows, net	20.2	27.3	36.7	39.0	11.8	55.8	48.1	58.0	72.3	58.6
External financing										
Net external financing	40.2	34.0	47.2	52.8	27.4	46.7	50.6	79.9	87.3	79.4
Non-debt-creating inflows	24.1	21.2	21.5	24.8	24.9	25.4	17.2	27.8	38.0	37.0
Net external borrowing	16.1	12.8	25.7	28.0	2.6	21.3	33.3	52.0	49.4	42.5
From official creditors	−3.3	0.5	−2.5	1.9	6.0	−7.6	−5.6	−6.3	−6.0	−3.0
of which, credit and loans from IMF	0.4	−0.5	0.5	3.3	9.9	6.1	—	−3.8	...	...
From banks	1.2	2.6	2.0	4.0	−7.5	2.7	8.5	9.1	11.0	9.9
From other private creditors	18.2	9.6	26.1	22.1	4.1	26.2	30.4	49.3	44.4	35.5
Memorandum										
Exceptional financing	0.2	0.4	0.6	0.3	0.1	0.1	0.3	0.1	—	—

Table 33 *(continued)*

	1997	1998	1999	2000	2001	2002	2003	2004	2005	2006
Commonwealth of Independent States[2]										
Balance of payments										
Balance on current account	−8.9	−9.7	20.7	46.1	32.6	32.1	35.9	63.1	105.3	122.0
Balance on capital account	−0.9	—	−0.2	−0.5	−0.7	−0.6	−1.0	−1.5	−1.3	−1.4
Balance on financial account	21.1	20.7	−10.8	−36.1	−21.2	−23.4	−27.4	−50.4	−95.0	−111.8
Change in reserves (− = increase)	−4.3	7.5	−2.7	−17.2	−11.3	−11.7	−33.8	−54.8	−80.7	−112.2
Other official flows, net	8.7	10.0	0.1	−4.3	−4.5	−1.7	−5.1	−4.6	−5.2	−2.9
Private flows, net	19.9	6.4	−6.4	−12.9	−1.9	−9.5	16.5	9.4	−10.3	0.4
External financing										
Net external financing	55.0	31.1	10.7	3.1	−5.2	11.5	35.5	56.1	36.9	54.9
Non-debt-creating inflows	6.8	5.7	4.6	2.7	3.1	3.3	10.1	13.8	13.4	15.7
Net external borrowing	48.2	25.4	6.1	0.4	−8.4	8.3	25.4	42.3	23.5	39.3
From official creditors	7.0	8.4	−0.8	−5.2	−5.0	−2.0	−2.1	—	−3.0	0.1
of which, credit and loans from IMF	2.1	5.8	−3.6	−4.1	−4.0	−1.8	−2.3	−2.1	. . .	. . .
From banks	15.7	0.1	−1.4	0.9	3.3	10.9	23.1	25.0	31.0	33.3
From other private creditors	25.4	16.9	8.2	4.6	−6.6	−0.7	4.5	17.4	−4.4	5.8
Memorandum										
Exceptional financing	−20.9	7.4	7.3	5.7	1.6	1.7	−1.8	−0.6	0.1	0.1
Developing Asia										
Balance of payments										
Balance on current account	7.7	49.3	48.5	46.1	40.7	72.3	84.8	93.0	109.7	113.4
Balance on capital account	0.8	0.6	0.5	0.4	0.5	0.4	0.4	0.4	0.4	0.5
Balance on financial account	34.7	−28.0	−26.1	−17.0	−32.2	−65.5	−94.0	−116.8	−116.0	−113.8
Change in reserves (− = increase)	−28.4	−21.0	−31.5	−9.4	−62.2	−105.5	−157.2	−260.0	−247.0	−189.0
Other official flows, net	11.4	19.0	19.7	−3.8	−0.5	9.6	−0.2	21.1	27.7	24.9
Private flows, net	51.6	−26.0	−14.3	−3.8	30.5	30.5	63.3	122.2	103.3	50.2
External financing										
Net external financing	171.3	55.7	67.3	70.7	51.6	75.5	101.2	196.2	192.7	184.4
Non-debt-creating inflows	127.9	67.8	66.0	70.2	57.0	69.4	82.9	106.8	106.4	108.5
Net external borrowing	43.4	−12.2	1.4	0.5	−5.4	6.0	18.3	89.4	86.2	75.8
From official creditors	11.4	19.0	19.7	−3.8	−0.5	9.6	−0.2	21.0	27.7	24.9
of which, credit and loans from IMF	5.0	6.6	1.7	0.9	−2.2	−2.7	−0.6	−1.9	. . .	. . .
From banks	13.5	−12.5	−11.8	−13.1	−5.3	−5.0	2.6	22.9	27.8	28.9
From other private creditors	18.4	−18.7	−6.6	17.5	0.4	1.4	15.9	45.5	30.8	22.0
Memorandum										
Exceptional financing	0.5	14.5	7.0	6.1	6.6	7.5	6.2	3.1	8.9	4.8
Excluding China and India										
Balance of payments										
Balance on current account	−23.8	24.6	36.0	30.2	21.8	29.8	32.1	25.1	7.7	8.4
Balance on capital account	0.8	0.7	0.5	0.5	0.6	0.5	0.5	0.5	0.5	0.5
Balance on financial account	33.6	−19.9	−28.9	−12.7	−19.0	−15.4	−22.8	−21.5	−15.1	−9.5
Change in reserves (− = increase)	12.1	−11.9	−17.0	7.2	−6.2	−11.1	−14.5	−30.1	−21.1	−20.5
Other official flows, net	9.9	13.4	12.7	−3.4	−1.5	8.3	4.4	1.5	2.6	2.4
Private flows, net	11.6	−21.4	−24.6	−16.5	−11.4	−12.6	−12.7	7.2	3.3	8.6
External financing										
Net external financing	92.3	13.2	13.2	1.9	0.7	11.8	13.7	40.2	31.1	37.6
Non-debt-creating inflows	76.3	24.9	25.0	14.4	6.5	16.8	21.3	36.3	26.1	26.2
Net external borrowing	16.0	−11.8	−11.8	−12.5	−5.8	−5.0	−7.6	3.9	5.0	11.4
From official creditors	9.9	13.4	12.7	−3.4	−1.5	8.3	4.4	1.5	2.6	2.4
of which, credit and loans from IMF	5.7	7.0	2.1	0.9	−2.2	−2.7	−0.6	−1.9	. . .	. . .
From banks	6.2	−15.4	−9.8	−6.7	−5.3	−7.1	−4.4	0.4	0.6	5.1
From other private creditors	−0.1	−9.7	−14.6	−2.4	1.0	−6.2	−7.6	2.0	1.8	3.9
Memorandum										
Exceptional financing	0.5	14.5	7.0	6.1	6.6	7.5	6.2	3.1	8.9	4.8

Table 33 *(concluded)*

	1997	1998	1999	2000	2001	2002	2003	2004	2005	2006
Middle East										
Balance of payments										
Balance on current account	10.7	−25.2	11.9	69.8	39.3	30.0	57.3	102.8	217.6	272.7
Balance on capital account	0.3	−0.3	0.9	1.4	1.5	1.7	−1.2	−0.8	0.9	1.9
Balance on financial account	−9.0	33.2	15.6	−54.1	−19.6	0.5	−65.2	−94.3	−206.6	−259.9
Change in reserves (− = increase)	−7.1	10.7	—	−28.7	−11.9	−4.0	−33.1	−45.6	−52.9	−75.0
Other official flows, net	−9.4	9.7	13.8	−30.5	−14.4	−7.9	−46.8	−72.2	−124.2	−144.6
Private flows, net	6.5	12.6	−8.8	−1.5	5.7	−1.3	5.7	11.0	−48.3	−63.2
External financing										
Net external financing	18.5	28.3	4.4	29.9	1.1	16.0	9.7	40.1	−6.6	−15.7
Non-debt-creating inflows	4.2	5.7	5.1	−0.9	3.3	3.6	3.1	8.2	15.4	15.5
Net external borrowing	14.3	22.6	−0.7	30.8	−2.2	12.4	6.6	31.9	−22.1	−31.2
From official creditors	0.4	3.8	4.3	0.1	−3.1	−1.2	0.2	−1.2	−0.1	−0.6
of which, credit and loans from IMF	0.2	0.1	0.1	−0.1	0.1	—	−0.1	−0.1	. . .	. . .
From banks	0.1	2.4	1.1	−0.1	−0.1	0.2	0.4	3.0	−0.2	0.9
From other private creditors	13.8	16.4	−6.1	30.8	1.0	13.4	5.9	30.1	−21.7	−31.5
Memorandum										
Exceptional financing	0.3	0.4	0.2	0.3	0.3	0.6	2.5	0.3	0.3	0.3
Western Hemisphere										
Balance of payments										
Balance on current account	−66.9	−90.6	−56.5	−48.2	−54.2	−16.0	6.3	18.3	21.5	16.3
Balance on capital account	1.5	1.8	3.4	2.9	2.5	0.4	1.2	1.4	1.1	0.3
Balance on financial account	67.1	93.7	58.8	41.5	55.3	15.3	−14.4	−18.9	−21.1	−16.5
Change in reserves (− = increase)	−26.5	9.6	11.9	1.5	2.9	−1.0	−37.5	−23.7	−28.1	−19.8
Other official flows, net	5.5	17.2	5.6	−7.2	27.0	20.6	7.3	−5.4	−9.1	−9.7
Private flows, net	99.7	70.8	38.5	40.5	27.0	0.4	18.5	9.9	15.2	8.5
External financing										
Net external financing	113.4	118.6	89.3	70.6	84.8	32.6	47.8	46.3	51.1	49.0
Non-debt-creating inflows	74.5	62.2	65.9	70.3	66.5	45.0	39.7	53.6	42.3	43.8
Net external borrowing	38.9	56.4	23.4	0.2	18.3	−12.3	8.1	−7.3	8.8	5.2
From official creditors	1.5	15.4	8.0	−4.3	23.8	16.3	6.6	−5.8	−9.2	−9.1
of which, credit and loans from IMF	−4.0	2.5	−0.9	−10.7	15.6	11.9	5.6	−6.3	. . .	. . .
From banks	−21.8	15.3	−8.8	5.3	3.1	−13.1	−5.7	−6.6	−4.4	−2.0
From other private creditors	59.1	25.7	24.2	−0.8	−8.6	−15.5	7.3	5.0	22.4	16.4
Memorandum										
Exceptional financing	−0.1	10.3	3.9	−11.0	7.2	27.0	19.5	12.1	1.3	−2.6

[1]For definitions, see footnotes to Table 32.
[2]Mongolia, which is not a member of the Commonwealth of Independent States, is included in this group for reasons of geography and similarities in economic structure.

Table 34. Other Emerging Market and Developing Countries—by Analytical Criteria: Balance of Payments and External Financing[1]
(Billions of U.S. dollars)

	1997	1998	1999	2000	2001	2002	2003	2004	2005	2006
By source of export earnings										
Fuel										
Balance of payments										
Balance on current account	16.0	−32.3	11.2	89.3	46.1	32.5	64.3	116.9	241.6	311.5
Balance on capital account	0.7	0.9	1.8	3.0	3.4	3.4	2.6	3.1	1.8	1.3
Balance on financial account	−20.7	35.7	9.1	−86.7	−34.0	−7.0	−69.6	−120.3	−240.3	−308.5
Change in reserves (− = increase)	−28.9	17.9	5.1	−42.4	−16.6	−2.0	−42.7	−65.7	−87.9	−128.9
Other official flows, net	−4.1	7.9	6.7	−29.3	−11.6	3.2	−30.7	−53.2	−99.8	−109.7
Private flows, net	11.7	12.0	−16.2	−32.0	−8.0	−14.9	—	−17.1	−77.1	−102.6
External financing										
Net external financing	25.4	16.2	10.1	4.7	6.3	10.9	12.7	19.9	−33.5	−34.1
Non-debt-creating inflows	12.3	14.1	10.0	10.1	13.4	13.8	18.1	20.4	23.3	23.4
Net external borrowing	13.1	2.1	0.1	−5.4	−7.1	−2.9	−5.4	−0.5	−56.8	−57.5
From official creditors	4.1	3.6	3.5	1.1	0.1	1.7	2.2	0.9	−5.9	1.0
of which, credit and loans from IMF	−0.1	−0.5	−0.4	−0.7	−0.3	−0.4	−0.5	−0.4	. . .	. . .
From banks	−2.2	0.3	−0.4	−1.6	−2.0	−1.1	−1.4	—	−1.2	−1.2
From other private creditors	11.3	−1.9	−2.9	−4.9	−5.2	−3.5	−6.3	−1.4	−49.7	−57.3
Memorandum										
Exceptional financing	7.9	6.1	4.5	2.8	2.2	2.6	2.1	1.8	−5.3	—
Nonfuel										
Balance of payments										
Balance on current account	−100.7	−82.5	−28.6	−1.0	−3.7	53.3	79.7	110.8	168.5	182.1
Balance on capital account	19.3	6.1	8.1	5.7	5.6	4.9	2.6	5.2	10.0	12.4
Balance on financial account	135.1	117.5	63.4	49.3	36.5	−28.0	−103.6	−139.7	−168.5	−175.5
Change in reserves (− = increase)	−59.4	−18.9	−41.6	−26.8	−70.9	−139.9	−249.9	−368.7	−376.4	−330.3
Other official flows, net	12.7	50.9	31.7	−14.6	22.7	11.6	−16.7	−13.7	−25.3	−23.6
Private flows, net	194.1	86.9	72.0	92.3	88.5	94.1	162.8	241.9	232.1	175.6
External financing										
Net external financing	398.3	280.2	240.2	238.2	171.8	191.6	256.5	433.7	428.0	427.3
Non-debt-creating inflows	249.3	169.6	177.9	173.7	163.5	152.2	157.2	221.6	227.6	231.4
Net external borrowing	149.0	110.6	62.3	64.5	8.3	39.4	99.4	212.1	200.4	195.8
From official creditors	9.7	47.6	28.4	−10.4	20.1	17.6	1.0	9.6	9.5	16.1
of which, credit and loans from IMF	3.4	14.5	−2.0	−10.2	19.3	13.8	2.3	−14.3	. . .	. . .
From banks	12.4	6.6	−17.2	−2.6	−4.6	−2.6	31.2	54.5	66.3	72.3
From other private creditors	126.9	56.4	51.0	77.5	−7.2	24.4	67.1	148.0	124.7	107.5
Memorandum										
Exceptional financing	−17.9	36.4	23.2	5.3	18.7	51.4	30.9	19.6	15.4	6.9
By external financing source										
Net debtor countries										
Balance of payments										
Balance on current account	−131.9	−128.4	−85.5	−76.7	−65.7	−32.7	−28.2	−48.7	−86.3	−89.0
Balance on capital account	21.0	7.3	9.6	6.6	6.5	7.4	4.9	9.9	12.9	15.0
Balance on financial account	116.6	124.8	89.7	91.5	75.4	50.1	18.4	29.0	63.2	73.2
Change in reserves (− = increase)	−26.3	−12.8	−23.6	−4.5	−13.9	−47.3	−92.4	−98.3	−79.7	−70.7
Other official flows, net	7.1	36.5	22.7	−3.2	25.6	15.7	0.7	−13.1	−22.5	−9.2
Private flows, net	144.3	99.9	86.5	97.4	64.8	72.1	104.4	133.9	159.6	145.6
External financing										
Net external financing	208.4	209.5	189.6	144.8	132.2	118.2	154.1	222.1	232.0	232.3
Non-debt-creating inflows	138.1	117.9	136.9	114.1	120.5	100.1	97.3	135.3	141.5	144.7
Net external borrowing	70.3	91.5	52.8	30.7	11.7	18.2	56.8	86.8	90.5	87.6
From official creditors	4.1	37.6	26.2	−3.2	24.2	18.0	5.5	−8.6	−18.5	−5.4
of which, credit and loans from IMF	1.3	8.8	1.4	−6.9	23.3	15.5	4.3	−12.3	. . .	. . .
From banks	−11.9	2.7	−14.5	3.3	−9.5	−14.9	1.6	8.4	9.6	15.4
From other private creditors	78.0	51.2	41.1	30.6	−3.0	15.1	49.8	87.0	99.3	77.6
Memorandum										
Exceptional financing	7.3	33.8	20.1	2.2	19.3	52.4	34.8	22.1	10.1	6.9

Table 34 *(continued)*

	1997	1998	1999	2000	2001	2002	2003	2004	2005	2006
Official financing										
Balance of payments										
Balance on current account	−38.3	−32.4	−17.8	−11.7	−7.9	10.3	9.7	−5.3	−17.3	−19.1
Balance on capital account	9.3	4.6	5.7	5.1	6.4	4.5	3.8	6.0	4.8	4.3
Balance on financial account	31.5	26.4	13.6	11.9	0.4	−4.1	1.4	4.5	5.7	13.9
Change in reserves (− = increase)	−12.4	−7.4	−6.1	6.3	6.7	2.0	−14.7	−14.1	−12.9	−15.3
Other official flows, net	−0.9	10.9	18.6	2.5	13.3	17.6	15.7	5.1	4.3	4.9
Private flows, net	44.2	22.5	0.6	2.4	−19.4	−23.6	0.6	13.9	14.3	24.5
External financing										
Net external financing	69.9	43.7	37.7	18.4	6.6	5.0	26.0	31.8	27.1	33.6
Non-debt-creating inflows	27.4	18.2	16.3	7.7	11.3	11.7	11.4	17.9	15.0	15.2
Net external borrowing	42.4	25.5	21.4	10.7	−4.7	−6.7	14.6	13.8	12.2	18.4
From official creditors	—	10.8	19.5	3.2	14.9	16.0	16.2	6.2	4.2	3.6
of which, credit and loans from IMF	2.6	5.4	0.8	1.7	8.2	—	0.5	−3.2	...	...
From banks	12.7	1.0	−0.5	−0.1	−4.1	−7.4	−0.9	−0.5	−2.0	4.2
From other private creditors	29.8	13.7	2.4	7.6	−15.5	−15.2	−0.7	8.1	9.9	10.6
Memorandum										
Exceptional financing	1.2	17.5	9.9	7.9	8.0	33.4	25.3	22.1	20.5	11.3
Net debtor countries by debt-servicing experience										
Countries with arrears and/or rescheduling during 1999–2003										
Balance of payments										
Balance on current account	−31.3	−35.0	−22.7	−1.5	−6.3	1.8	4.8	−1.7	−5.2	6.8
Balance on capital account	9.0	4.6	7.2	5.0	4.4	5.1	2.6	5.9	6.5	6.9
Balance on financial account	20.9	30.2	18.9	5.6	3.0	8.1	6.6	−1.7	−7.7	−11.1
Change in reserves (− = increase)	−15.6	−7.0	−5.0	−2.8	5.0	2.2	−9.4	−24.0	−28.8	−43.0
Other official flows, net	−2.8	11.9	18.8	2.9	12.3	9.2	12.0	4.1	−8.3	0.6
Private flows, net	38.2	25.9	4.7	5.4	−11.6	−9.6	1.6	15.7	27.8	29.9
External financing										
Net external financing	58.8	53.7	48.8	22.9	9.1	26.2	32.6	41.7	42.9	53.0
Non-debt-creating inflows	28.3	23.9	22.5	16.3	16.4	22.6	22.8	33.1	33.9	35.9
Net external borrowing	30.5	29.8	26.3	6.5	−7.4	3.7	9.8	8.6	9.0	17.1
From official creditors	−2.3	11.6	19.1	3.1	11.0	12.4	13.2	5.4	−7.4	1.3
of which, credit and loans from IMF	3.1	5.3	1.1	1.9	8.1	−1.5	−0.2	−3.8	...	...
From banks	11.8	−1.3	−1.5	−1.4	−4.5	−7.1	−1.6	−0.4	−1.9	3.4
From other private creditors	21.0	19.5	8.7	4.8	−13.9	−1.6	−1.7	3.6	18.3	12.4
Memorandum										
Exceptional financing	7.9	24.0	16.5	12.2	12.0	39.9	27.1	25.6	17.2	13.2
Other groups										
Heavily indebted poor countries										
Balance of payments										
Balance on current account	−6.6	−7.2	−8.6	−7.1	−7.0	−7.6	−7.0	−7.8	−9.0	−9.1
Balance on capital account	7.8	4.2	5.1	3.6	4.0	1.8	3.8	3.7	4.4	4.9
Balance on financial account	−5.4	3.2	2.4	2.6	2.6	6.0	3.1	3.7	4.9	5.8
Change in reserves (− = increase)	−1.1	−0.2	−0.9	−0.6	−0.9	−2.5	−2.0	−2.4	−1.8	−1.4
Other official flows, net	−4.3	1.5	1.2	1.3	−0.2	3.5	3.2	3.7	1.1	3.6
Private flows, net	−0.4	1.3	1.7	1.4	3.6	5.3	2.2	2.7	5.6	3.7
External financing										
Net external financing	3.9	8.3	8.6	6.9	7.4	10.1	9.4	10.0	11.5	12.0
Non-debt-creating inflows	9.9	6.4	8.0	6.0	6.7	5.8	7.7	7.5	8.4	8.9
Net external borrowing	−6.0	1.9	0.6	0.9	0.7	4.3	1.8	2.5	3.1	3.2
From official creditors	−4.1	1.8	1.4	1.6	−0.2	3.4	3.0	3.6	1.2	3.6
of which, credit and loans from IMF	—	0.2	0.3	0.1	—	0.2	−0.2	—	...	...
From banks	0.4	−0.1	0.1	−0.6	—	—	0.1	0.4	0.3	—
From other private creditors	−2.4	0.2	−0.8	−0.1	0.9	0.9	−1.3	−1.5	1.7	−0.5
Memorandum										
Exceptional financing	0.6	2.1	2.5	2.5	1.9	14.9	3.0	3.3	3.4	2.8

Table 34 *(concluded)*

	1997	1998	1999	2000	2001	2002	2003	2004	2005	2006
Middle East and north Africa										
Balance of payments										
Balance on current account	12.1	−28.7	9.6	75.7	45.0	33.7	65.6	112.8	234.0	298.5
Balance on capital account	0.4	−0.2	1.1	1.5	1.7	1.9	−1.1	−0.6	1.1	2.1
Balance on financial account	−12.3	36.1	18.7	−60.5	−26.6	−3.9	−73.2	−104.2	−222.6	−283.2
Change in reserves (− = increase)	−12.2	11.8	0.3	−35.4	−22.1	−8.6	−42.8	−58.2	−71.4	−103.5
Other official flows, net	−10.1	9.6	13.6	−31.6	−15.8	−9.6	−48.3	−74.3	−125.1	−145.5
Private flows, net	7.4	13.1	−7.4	−2.7	8.3	−1.3	7.3	12.9	−47.1	−59.9
External financing										
Net external financing	21.7	31.6	8.5	32.5	6.1	18.6	12.9	44.7	−2.3	−8.5
Non-debt-creating inflows	6.4	8.0	7.3	1.0	8.6	6.8	7.9	13.0	20.4	20.2
Net external borrowing	15.2	23.5	1.3	31.5	−2.5	11.8	4.9	31.7	−22.6	−28.6
From official creditors	0.5	4.4	4.9	0.3	−3.5	−2.0	−0.4	−1.8	0.1	−0.1
of which, credit and loans from IMF	0.3	−0.1	—	−0.3	−0.2	−0.3	−0.6	−0.6	. . .	. . .
From banks	0.8	2.4	2.5	0.2	0.4	0.9	1.2	3.4	−0.4	1.0
From other private creditors	13.9	16.7	−6.2	31.1	0.6	12.9	4.2	30.1	−22.3	−29.6
Memorandum										
Exceptional financing	5.3	2.9	2.3	1.8	1.3	1.5	3.2	1.0	0.9	0.9

[1]For definitions, see footnotes to Table 32.

Table 35. Other Emerging Market and Developing Countries: Reserves[1]

	1997	1998	1999	2000	2001	2002	2003	2004	2005	2006
					Billions of U.S. dollars					
Other emerging market and developing countries	**701.2**	**700.8**	**727.0**	**817.4**	**914.3**	**1,093.8**	**1,418.9**	**1,871.5**	**2,335.8**	**2,795.0**
Regional groups										
Africa	43.8	41.5	42.4	54.5	64.7	73.0	91.3	127.1	165.7	226.7
Sub-Sahara	29.5	28.1	29.6	35.5	35.9	37.0	41.0	63.3	84.1	118.4
Excluding Nigeria and South Africa	16.9	16.4	17.6	19.2	19.1	23.5	27.1	32.9	40.5	53.0
Central and eastern Europe	77.4	89.7	93.7	95.9	97.4	130.9	160.0	183.2	200.2	202.5
Commonwealth of Independent States[2]	22.3	15.1	16.5	33.2	44.2	58.2	92.6	148.4	229.1	341.3
Russia	13.7	8.5	9.1	24.8	33.1	44.6	73.8	121.5	195.6	304.1
Excluding Russia	8.6	6.6	7.4	8.4	11.0	13.5	18.8	26.9	33.5	37.2
Developing Asia	249.6	274.6	307.7	321.8	380.5	497.1	670.3	934.4	1,181.4	1,370.4
China	143.4	149.8	158.3	168.9	216.3	292.0	409.2	615.5	825.5	985.5
India	25.3	27.9	33.2	38.4	46.4	68.2	99.5	127.2	143.2	151.7
Excluding China and India	80.9	96.8	116.2	114.6	117.8	136.8	161.7	191.6	212.7	233.2
Middle East	137.6	126.5	123.2	155.9	168.3	173.3	208.7	256.9	309.8	384.7
Western Hemisphere	170.6	153.4	143.4	156.1	159.2	161.3	196.2	221.4	249.5	269.3
Brazil	51.0	34.4	23.9	31.5	35.8	37.7	49.1	52.8	57.7	58.0
Mexico	28.8	31.8	31.8	35.5	44.8	50.6	59.0	64.1	70.3	77.1
Analytical groups										
By source of export earnings										
Fuel	133.7	118.0	111.4	157.7	173.3	174.9	221.5	290.5	378.4	507.3
Nonfuel	567.5	582.8	615.6	659.8	741.0	918.9	1,197.4	1,581.0	1,957.4	2,287.7
of which, primary products	29.3	27.5	26.6	27.1	26.7	29.6	31.9	33.8	35.7	36.9
By external financing source										
Net debtor countries	395.6	404.5	421.1	444.7	469.3	549.5	667.3	777.9	857.6	928.3
of which, official financing	77.2	85.7	94.2	94.4	87.3	95.9	119.7	131.7	144.6	160.0
Net debtor countries by debt-servicing experience										
Countries with arrears and/or rescheduling during 1999–2003	78.1	84.8	92.8	100.7	93.9	99.8	116.6	138.3	167.1	210.1
Other groups										
Heavily indebted poor countries	8.8	8.5	9.4	9.9	10.8	13.8	15.6	18.9	20.6	22.1
Middle East and north Africa	152.2	140.3	136.5	175.4	197.7	210.2	260.3	322.9	394.3	497.8

Table 35 *(concluded)*

	1997	1998	1999	2000	2001	2002	2003	2004	2005	2006
				Ratio of reserves to imports of goods and services[3]						
Other emerging market and developing countries	**43.8**	**46.0**	**48.5**	**46.8**	**51.6**	**57.6**	**62.2**	**64.5**	**67.2**	**71.0**
Regional groups										
Africa	32.5	31.0	31.4	39.4	45.8	47.4	48.8	54.6	60.0	75.0
Sub-Sahara	28.0	27.3	28.9	33.8	33.6	32.0	28.6	35.6	39.3	50.4
Excluding Nigeria and South Africa	29.8	28.6	30.6	33.7	31.6	36.5	35.6	35.3	36.5	42.4
Central and eastern Europe	32.5	35.4	38.3	34.3	34.9	41.7	39.7	35.3	33.0	30.6
Commonwealth of Independent States[2]	15.4	12.3	17.6	30.5	34.9	41.8	53.3	66.7	82.1	107.1
Russia	14.9	11.5	17.2	40.6	45.4	53.7	71.5	93.4	115.7	155.1
Excluding Russia	16.2	13.6	18.2	17.6	20.6	24.1	26.6	29.1	30.4	30.3
Developing Asia	44.6	56.8	59.6	50.0	59.1	68.8	74.4	78.5	81.6	80.3
China	87.2	91.6	83.3	67.4	79.7	89.0	91.1	101.5	111.5	107.5
India	43.4	47.0	52.9	52.6	65.0	90.0	106.0	92.5	75.6	67.4
Excluding China and India	24.1	37.2	44.1	35.8	39.1	43.0	45.1	43.0	41.0	41.2
Middle East	71.6	69.1	67.6	76.9	79.1	74.2	78.6	81.8	84.1	95.5
Western Hemisphere	51.3	44.1	44.2	42.1	43.4	48.0	56.1	52.4	50.0	49.6
Brazil	66.0	45.4	37.6	43.5	49.2	61.1	77.2	65.9	58.3	51.6
Mexico	33.8	33.4	30.3	27.6	35.2	40.1	45.8	43.5	41.9	43.0
Analytical groups										
By source of export earnings										
Fuel	77.5	71.5	66.5	85.7	88.0	81.0	90.8	98.6	106.2	128.7
Nonfuel	39.7	42.9	46.3	42.3	47.1	54.6	58.8	60.7	62.7	64.6
of which, primary products	53.0	52.2	55.9	55.1	54.2	59.2	55.6	47.6	43.6	42.9
By external financing source										
Net debtor countries	38.3	40.1	43.1	39.8	42.4	48.1	50.0	46.2	42.7	42.0
of which, official financing	32.6	38.3	46.8	41.9	40.4	46.6	51.0	43.9	40.4	41.3
Net debtor countries by debt-servicing experience										
Countries with arrears and/or rescheduling during 1999–2003	32.9	37.5	43.7	42.1	39.6	41.4	42.2	39.7	39.3	45.1
Other groups										
Heavily indebted poor countries	29.0	26.5	28.7	30.0	31.2	37.4	37.2	37.6	36.4	36.2
Middle East and north Africa	68.0	64.7	62.7	73.4	78.8	76.3	82.9	86.0	90.0	103.6

[1]In this table, official holdings of gold are valued at SDR 35 an ounce. This convention results in a marked underestimate of reserves for countries that have substantial gold holdings.
[2]Mongolia, which is not a member of the Commonwealth of Independent States, is included in this group for reasons of geography and similarities in economic structure.
[3]Reserves at year-end in percent of imports of goods and services for the year indicated.

Table 36. Net Credit and Loans from IMF[1]
(Billions of U.S. dollars)

	1996	1997	1998	1999	2000	2001	2002	2003	2004
Advanced economies	**−0.1**	**11.3**	**5.2**	**−10.3**	**—**	**−5.7**	**—**	**—**	**—**
Newly industrialized Asian economies	—	11.3	5.2	−10.3	—	−5.7	—	—	—
Other emerging market and developing countries	**0.7**	**3.3**	**14.0**	**−2.4**	**−10.9**	**19.0**	**13.4**	**1.7**	**−14.5**
Regional groups									
Africa	0.6	−0.5	−0.4	−0.2	−0.2	−0.4	−0.1	−0.8	−0.7
Sub-Sahara	0.1	−0.5	−0.3	−0.1	—	−0.2	0.2	−0.4	−0.3
Excluding Nigeria and South Africa	0.1	−0.1	0.1	−0.1	—	−0.2	0.2	−0.4	−0.3
Central and eastern Europe	−0.8	0.4	−0.5	0.5	3.3	9.9	6.1	—	−3.8
Commonwealth of Independent States[2]	4.5	2.1	5.8	−3.6	−4.1	−4.0	−1.8	−2.3	−2.1
Russia	3.2	1.5	5.3	−3.6	−2.9	−3.8	−1.5	−1.9	−1.7
Excluding Russia	1.3	0.5	0.5	—	−1.2	−0.2	−0.3	−0.4	−0.5
Developing Asia	−1.7	5.0	6.6	1.7	0.9	−2.2	−2.7	−0.6	−1.9
China	—	—	—	—	—	—	—	—	—
India	−1.3	−0.7	−0.4	−0.3	−0.1	—	—	—	—
Excluding China and India	−0.4	5.7	7.0	2.1	0.9	−2.2	−2.7	−0.6	−1.9
Middle East	0.1	0.2	0.1	0.1	−0.1	0.1	—	−0.1	0.3
Western Hemisphere	−2.0	−4.0	2.5	−0.9	−10.7	15.6	11.9	5.6	−6.3
Brazil	−0.1	—	4.6	4.1	−6.7	6.7	11.2	5.2	−4.4
Mexico	−2.1	−3.4	−1.1	−3.7	−4.3	—	—	—	—
Analytical groups									
By source of export earnings									
Fuel	0.9	−0.1	−0.5	−0.4	−0.7	−0.3	−0.4	−0.5	—
Nonfuel	−0.1	3.4	14.5	−2.0	−10.2	19.3	13.8	2.3	−14.5
of which, primary products	0.1	−0.1	0.2	−0.1	−0.2	−0.2	0.1	−0.3	−0.3
By external financing source									
Net debtor countries	−3.9	1.3	8.8	1.4	−6.9	23.3	15.5	4.3	−12.0
of which, official financing	0.3	2.6	5.4	0.8	1.7	8.2	—	0.5	−3.3
Net debtor countries by debt-servicing experience									
Countries with arrears and/or rescheduling during 1999–2003	0.6	3.1	5.3	1.1	1.9	8.1	−1.5	−0.2	−3.4
Other groups									
Heavily indebted poor countries	—	—	0.2	0.3	0.1	—	0.2	−0.2	−0.1
Middle East and north Africa	0.6	0.3	−0.1	—	−0.3	−0.2	−0.3	−0.6	−0.1
Memorandum									
Total									
Net credit provided under:									
General Resources Account	0.291	14.355	18.811	−12.856	−10.741	13.213	12.832	1.741	−14.276
PRGF	0.325	0.179	0.374	0.194	−0.148	0.106	0.567	0.009	−0.175
Disbursements at year-end under:[3]									
General Resources Account	51.396	62.301	84.541	69.504	55.368	66.448	85.357	95.323	84.992
PRGF	8.379	8.037	8.775	8.749	8.159	7.974	9.222	10.108	10.426

[1]Includes net disbursements from programs under the General Resources Account and Poverty Reduction and Growth Facility (formerly ESAF—Enhanced Structural Adjustment Facility). The data are on a transactions basis, with conversion to U.S. dollar values at annual average exchange rates.
[2]Mongolia, which is not a member of the Commonwealth of Independent States, is included in this group for reasons of geography and similarities in economic structure.
[3]Data refer to disbursements at year-end correspond to the stock of outstanding credit, converted to U.S. dollar values at end-of-period exchange rates.

Table 37. Summary of External Debt and Debt Service

	1997	1998	1999	2000	2001	2002	2003	2004	2005	2006
					Billions of U.S. dollars					
External debt										
Other emerging market and developing countries	**2,343.1**	**2,549.4**	**2,590.6**	**2,511.8**	**2,536.2**	**2,605.2**	**2,836.3**	**3,035.2**	**3,181.0**	**3,321.1**
Regional groups										
Africa	284.4	283.2	280.8	269.9	258.5	263.3	283.8	293.2	285.8	260.6
Central and eastern Europe	235.9	269.7	286.6	309.5	315.0	368.8	459.3	544.3	580.9	613.4
Commonwealth of Independent States[1]	199.1	222.8	218.9	198.9	194.0	199.2	238.9	279.7	292.8	326.2
Developing Asia	659.6	695.9	693.0	656.7	663.8	665.1	696.7	746.0	834.0	917.6
Middle East	267.0	292.6	304.2	304.4	307.3	314.4	324.7	340.8	345.1	353.3
Western Hemisphere	697.1	785.1	807.0	772.3	797.6	794.4	832.9	831.3	842.4	850.0
Analytical groups										
By external financing source										
Net debtor countries	1,814.4	1,965.6	2,007.2	1,964.0	1,974.7	2,041.2	2,206.4	2,327.5	2,383.0	2,416.1
of which, official financing	539.9	583.3	587.9	575.4	598.9	592.8	640.2	666.4	674.5	684.1
Net debtor countries by debt-servicing experience										
Countries with arrears and/or rescheduling during 1999–2003	663.5	706.0	713.6	696.8	715.6	712.2	736.8	759.6	759.9	738.9
Debt-service payments[2]										
Other emerging market and developing countries	**363.2**	**388.3**	**409.7**	**428.7**	**438.9**	**413.1**	**449.9**	**443.3**	**488.5**	**504.8**
Regional groups										
Africa	32.8	27.6	27.2	27.8	27.8	23.1	26.8	29.4	31.8	27.4
Central and eastern Europe	40.9	55.0	58.0	64.7	74.5	77.0	96.0	102.4	116.6	132.4
Commonwealth of Independent States[1]	25.5	29.7	27.0	27.8	32.9	32.1	29.0	23.0	50.4	34.7
Developing Asia	84.7	99.3	93.9	98.3	106.4	115.7	114.4	98.6	105.0	118.4
Middle East	27.1	23.9	24.0	24.0	26.7	18.4	25.8	34.2	40.7	42.3
Western Hemisphere	152.3	152.8	179.6	186.0	170.5	146.8	157.9	155.6	144.0	149.6
Analytical groups										
By external financing source										
Net debtor countries	284.4	302.1	325.2	344.9	344.9	327.5	359.1	348.9	356.9	379.2
of which, official financing	80.2	83.9	79.0	89.9	95.8	81.3	80.6	66.4	61.8	63.0
Net debtor countries by debt-servicing experience										
Countries with arrears and/or rescheduling during 1999–2003	79.8	82.9	77.4	89.2	95.9	76.7	79.1	69.2	70.1	65.8

Table 37 *(concluded)*

	1997	1998	1999	2000	2001	2002	2003	2004	2005	2006
	Percent of exports of goods and services									
External debt[3]										
Other emerging market and developing countries	**150.0**	**174.3**	**167.4**	**132.2**	**135.4**	**128.1**	**115.2**	**95.9**	**81.6**	**75.1**
Regional groups										
Africa	210.4	236.7	219.5	171.4	172.6	170.8	146.7	119.4	94.0	73.7
Central and eastern Europe	111.4	118.4	134.1	128.4	121.3	127.8	124.9	114.9	105.9	102.3
Commonwealth of Independent States[1]	135.4	175.2	177.2	120.7	117.4	111.9	106.6	92.3	72.8	71.0
Developing Asia	116.8	129.3	119.7	94.2	96.2	84.6	73.1	60.1	55.6	52.5
Middle East	130.2	184.4	150.3	107.6	116.1	111.7	94.9	78.8	58.1	52.3
Western Hemisphere	233.9	269.9	268.3	216.8	232.3	230.1	218.5	177.6	153.6	144.6
Analytical groups										
By external financing source										
Net debtor countries	199.8	220.4	219.6	184.5	186.7	182.3	168.4	141.5	124.2	113.9
of which, official financing	270.1	306.4	312.1	264.6	286.1	274.7	264.7	225.7	202.0	190.4
Net debtor countries by debt-servicing experience										
Countries with arrears and/or rescheduling during 1999–2003	313.3	359.1	347.0	271.6	293.0	281.4	255.2	211.3	178.1	153.2
Debt-service payments										
Other emerging market and developing countries	**23.3**	**26.5**	**26.5**	**22.6**	**23.4**	**20.3**	**18.3**	**14.0**	**12.5**	**11.4**
Regional groups										
Africa	24.2	23.1	21.2	17.6	18.6	15.0	13.8	12.0	10.5	7.8
Central and eastern Europe	19.3	24.2	27.1	26.8	28.7	26.7	26.1	21.6	21.3	22.1
Commonwealth of Independent States[1]	17.3	23.3	21.9	16.9	19.9	18.0	12.9	7.6	12.5	7.6
Developing Asia	15.0	18.4	16.2	14.1	15.4	14.7	12.0	7.9	7.0	6.8
Middle East	13.2	15.0	11.9	8.5	10.1	6.5	7.5	7.9	6.9	6.3
Western Hemisphere	51.1	52.5	59.7	52.2	49.7	42.5	41.4	33.2	26.3	25.4
Analytical groups										
By external financing source										
Net debtor countries	31.3	33.9	35.6	32.4	32.6	29.3	27.4	21.2	18.6	17.9
of which, official financing	40.1	44.1	41.9	41.3	45.8	37.6	33.3	22.5	18.5	17.5
Net debtor countries by debt-servicing experience										
Countries with arrears and/or rescheduling during 1999–2003	37.7	42.2	37.6	34.8	39.3	30.3	27.4	19.3	16.4	13.6

[1]Mongolia, which is not a member of the Commonwealth of Independent States, is included in this group for reasons of geography and similarities in economic structure.
[2]Debt-service payments refer to actual payments of interest on total debt plus actual amortization payments on long-term debt. The projections incorporate the impact of exceptional financing items.
[3]Total debt at year-end in percent of exports of goods and services in year indicated.

Table 38. Other Emerging Market and Developing Countries—by Region: External Debt, by Maturity and Type of Creditor
(Billions of U.S. dollars)

	1997	1998	1999	2000	2001	2002	2003	2004	2005	2006
Other emerging market and developing countries										
Total debt	**2,343.1**	**2,549.4**	**2,590.6**	**2,511.8**	**2,536.2**	**2,605.2**	**2,836.3**	**3,035.2**	**3,181.0**	**3,321.1**
By maturity										
Short-term	347.4	339.3	333.0	314.7	330.1	319.3	392.6	468.6	534.8	583.5
Long-term	1,995.7	2,210.0	2,257.6	2,197.1	2,206.1	2,285.9	2,443.7	2,566.6	2,646.2	2,737.7
By type of creditor										
Official	962.7	1,026.1	1,029.6	994.1	1,006.4	1,038.9	1,082.4	1,088.1	1,082.6	1,053.6
Banks	699.0	717.8	717.0	673.8	649.4	656.4	703.7	796.2	845.4	923.0
Other private	681.4	805.4	844.0	843.9	880.4	909.8	1,050.2	1,150.9	1,253.0	1,344.6
Regional groups										
Africa										
Total debt	**284.4**	**283.2**	**280.8**	**269.9**	**258.5**	**263.3**	**283.8**	**293.2**	**285.8**	**260.6**
By maturity										
Short-term	30.1	35.0	36.4	15.9	14.0	17.4	18.1	18.9	17.0	15.2
Long-term	254.2	248.3	244.4	254.0	244.5	245.9	265.8	274.3	268.8	245.4
By type of creditor										
Official	204.0	206.9	204.4	201.5	199.0	203.7	219.9	224.0	213.6	185.7
Banks	50.9	48.0	46.7	41.7	38.7	37.6	41.5	43.4	43.4	44.2
Other private	29.4	28.3	29.6	26.8	20.9	22.0	22.5	25.8	28.7	30.8
Sub-Sahara										
Total debt	**222.6**	**220.6**	**220.9**	**215.2**	**208.3**	**211.2**	**227.4**	**238.5**	**234.1**	**210.1**
By maturity										
Short-term	28.1	33.1	34.5	14.0	12.1	15.1	15.7	16.1	13.5	11.9
Long-term	194.4	187.5	186.3	201.1	196.1	196.1	211.7	222.4	220.6	198.2
By type of creditor										
Official	158.7	160.4	160.5	160.9	161.4	163.4	175.8	181.1	173.3	146.4
Banks	40.6	37.0	34.6	30.3	27.7	26.6	29.1	31.5	32.0	32.9
Other private	23.2	23.2	25.8	24.0	19.1	21.2	22.5	25.8	28.7	30.8
Central and eastern Europe										
Total debt	**235.9**	**269.7**	**286.6**	**309.5**	**315.0**	**368.8**	**459.3**	**544.3**	**580.9**	**613.4**
By maturity										
Short-term	48.8	56.4	60.4	65.9	56.7	63.6	91.2	116.8	130.9	141.2
Long-term	187.1	213.3	226.3	243.6	258.3	305.2	368.0	427.5	450.0	472.2
By type of creditor										
Official	77.1	79.5	75.8	77.6	83.1	76.6	73.4	67.7	61.4	58.1
Banks	83.0	101.6	109.6	122.7	108.6	140.9	174.9	211.2	216.6	227.6
Other private	75.7	88.6	101.2	109.3	123.3	151.3	211.0	265.4	302.9	327.7
Commonwealth of Independent States[1]										
Total debt	**199.1**	**222.8**	**218.9**	**198.9**	**194.0**	**199.2**	**238.9**	**279.7**	**292.8**	**326.2**
By maturity										
Short-term	14.9	23.8	15.3	15.6	16.0	16.3	26.3	31.5	33.8	34.8
Long-term	184.2	199.0	203.7	183.3	178.0	182.8	212.6	248.2	259.0	291.4
By type of creditor										
Official	102.6	113.8	113.6	106.0	101.0	96.5	91.6	87.1	82.0	60.2
Banks	56.4	49.9	49.7	18.2	22.4	21.2	44.0	68.6	99.5	132.8
Other private	40.1	59.0	55.6	74.6	70.6	81.4	103.3	124.0	111.3	133.1

Table 38 *(concluded)*

	1997	1998	1999	2000	2001	2002	2003	2004	2005	2006
Developing Asia										
Total debt	**659.6**	**695.9**	**693.0**	**656.7**	**663.8**	**665.1**	**696.7**	**746.0**	**834.0**	**917.6**
By maturity										
Short-term	99.3	88.7	70.1	59.1	89.0	87.2	112.6	146.9	184.9	211.7
Long-term	560.3	607.2	623.0	597.6	574.8	577.9	584.1	599.1	649.1	705.9
By type of creditor										
Official	274.9	296.8	303.0	286.1	280.8	287.7	293.9	312.7	339.1	363.2
Banks	209.9	202.5	197.1	182.2	177.6	169.1	162.1	185.1	212.5	240.8
Other private	174.9	196.6	192.9	188.3	205.5	208.3	240.7	248.1	282.4	313.6
Middle East										
Total debt	**267.0**	**292.6**	**304.2**	**304.4**	**307.3**	**314.4**	**324.7**	**340.8**	**345.1**	**353.3**
By maturity										
Short-term	34.7	39.8	58.5	56.3	59.6	59.4	70.6	81.0	82.6	88.3
Long-term	232.3	252.8	245.7	248.2	247.7	255.0	254.1	259.7	262.5	265.0
By type of creditor										
Official	132.6	135.3	137.2	136.7	137.7	144.3	147.0	145.7	146.0	146.1
Banks	84.9	86.0	88.8	90.1	90.6	92.3	94.4	103.6	106.2	109.0
Other private	49.6	71.3	78.1	77.6	79.0	77.7	83.3	91.5	92.8	98.2
Western Hemisphere										
Total debt	**697.1**	**785.1**	**807.0**	**772.3**	**797.6**	**794.4**	**832.9**	**831.3**	**842.4**	**850.0**
By maturity										
Short-term	119.6	95.7	92.4	102.0	94.7	75.4	73.9	73.5	85.7	92.3
Long-term	577.5	689.4	714.6	670.4	702.8	719.1	759.0	757.8	756.7	757.7
By type of creditor										
Official	171.5	193.8	195.6	186.2	204.9	230.2	256.6	251.0	240.5	240.3
Banks	213.8	229.9	225.0	218.9	211.5	195.2	186.8	184.3	167.1	168.5
Other private	311.8	361.5	386.4	367.2	381.1	369.0	389.6	396.0	434.9	441.2

[1]Mongolia, which is not a member of the Commonwealth of Independent States, is included in this group for reasons of geography and similarities in economic structure.

Table 39. Other Emerging Market and Developing Countries—by Analytical Criteria: External Debt, by Maturity and Type of Creditor
(Billions of U.S. dollars)

	1997	1998	1999	2000	2001	2002	2003	2004	2005	2006
By source of export earnings										
Fuel										
Total debt	**315.5**	**338.1**	**346.2**	**342.9**	**340.7**	**345.8**	**353.6**	**363.3**	**359.0**	**339.0**
By maturity										
Short-term	47.3	55.1	55.4	32.3	33.9	34.0	43.2	52.6	50.0	53.3
Long-term	268.2	283.0	290.8	310.6	306.8	311.8	310.4	310.7	309.0	285.7
By type of creditor										
Official	164.6	168.5	172.8	172.8	173.9	183.1	191.3	192.7	183.4	159.2
Banks	77.7	83.1	83.9	83.9	82.5	82.1	82.1	87.9	89.1	89.6
Other private	73.1	86.5	89.5	86.2	84.4	80.6	80.1	82.7	86.5	90.2
Nonfuel										
Total debt	**2,027.6**	**2,211.2**	**2,244.4**	**2,168.9**	**2,195.5**	**2,259.4**	**2,482.7**	**2,671.9**	**2,822.0**	**2,982.2**
By maturity										
Short-term	300.1	284.2	277.6	282.5	296.2	285.3	349.4	416.0	484.8	530.2
Long-term	1,727.5	1,927.0	1,966.8	1,886.4	1,899.3	1,974.1	2,133.3	2,255.9	2,337.1	2,452.0
By type of creditor										
Official	798.1	857.6	856.8	821.4	832.5	855.8	891.1	895.4	899.2	894.4
Banks	621.3	634.7	633.1	589.9	566.9	574.3	621.5	708.3	756.3	833.4
Other private	608.3	718.9	754.5	757.6	796.0	829.3	970.1	1,068.3	1,166.5	1,254.3
Nonfuel primary products										
Total debt	**97.8**	**100.7**	**103.7**	**102.6**	**105.4**	**105.2**	**108.9**	**111.4**	**112.4**	**110.7**
By maturity										
Short-term	7.3	6.8	5.9	7.9	6.8	7.4	9.1	9.7	10.7	11.2
Long-term	90.5	93.9	97.8	94.7	98.6	97.8	99.7	101.7	101.7	99.5
By type of creditor										
Official	60.8	62.8	62.9	61.5	62.4	61.4	63.2	63.2	59.7	54.7
Banks	20.5	19.8	21.5	23.4	23.3	23.7	25.0	23.2	4.4	4.0
Other private	16.6	18.1	19.3	17.7	19.7	20.1	20.7	25.0	48.3	52.0
By external financing source										
Net debtor countries										
Total debt	**1,814.4**	**1,965.6**	**2,007.2**	**1,964.0**	**1,974.7**	**2,041.2**	**2,206.4**	**2,327.5**	**2,383.0**	**2,416.1**
By maturity										
Short-term	266.2	247.0	255.6	242.0	223.3	208.7	238.3	273.5	303.0	325.3
Long-term	1,548.2	1,718.7	1,751.6	1,722.0	1,751.3	1,832.5	1,968.1	2,054.0	2,080.0	2,090.9
By type of creditor										
Official	765.3	814.7	824.7	808.5	826.7	857.0	897.7	889.8	865.8	836.6
Banks	567.8	585.1	577.9	568.8	542.7	550.9	575.9	618.4	611.3	633.2
Other private	481.3	565.8	604.7	586.6	605.3	633.3	732.7	819.2	905.9	946.3
Official financing										
Total debt	**539.9**	**583.3**	**587.9**	**575.4**	**598.9**	**592.8**	**640.2**	**666.4**	**674.5**	**684.1**
By maturity										
Short-term	60.2	54.5	68.5	71.1	67.7	53.9	60.3	69.0	70.4	73.6
Long-term	479.6	528.8	519.5	504.3	531.2	538.9	579.9	597.4	604.1	610.4
By type of creditor										
Official	272.5	287.0	296.8	291.7	303.5	320.4	356.8	361.2	359.5	357.3
Banks	100.1	99.8	97.7	91.9	92.7	85.0	85.1	88.8	88.2	92.0
Other private	167.2	196.5	193.4	191.8	202.8	187.4	198.3	216.4	226.8	234.8
Net debtor countries by debt-servicing experience										
Countries with arrears and/or rescheduling during 1999–2003										
Total debt	**663.5**	**706.0**	**713.6**	**696.8**	**715.6**	**712.2**	**736.8**	**759.6**	**759.9**	**738.9**
By maturity										
Short-term	67.0	64.3	62.1	42.0	35.0	27.0	29.6	35.0	30.1	30.4
Long-term	596.4	641.6	651.5	654.8	680.6	685.2	707.2	724.6	729.7	708.4
By type of creditor										
Official	387.1	403.7	418.4	415.2	422.2	432.1	451.5	458.2	447.6	417.9
Banks	134.8	139.6	138.4	130.9	133.2	126.4	125.8	128.7	127.9	131.2
Other private	141.6	162.7	156.7	150.7	160.2	153.7	159.5	172.7	184.4	189.8

Table 39 *(concluded)*

	1997	1998	1999	2000	2001	2002	2003	2004	2005	2006
Other groups										
Heavily indebted poor countries										
Total debt	**97.9**	**99.9**	**99.0**	**98.0**	**97.2**	**90.7**	**92.5**	**95.0**	**96.4**	**92.7**
By maturity										
Short-term	1.3	2.8	2.9	3.0	2.9	3.0	2.6	2.8	2.9	2.9
Long-term	96.7	97.1	96.1	95.0	94.2	87.7	90.0	92.2	93.5	89.7
By type of creditor										
Official	93.2	95.1	93.5	93.1	93.0	88.4	90.7	93.2	94.6	90.8
Banks	4.2	3.6	3.6	2.6	2.6	1.2	0.9	0.6	0.5	0.5
Other private	0.6	1.2	1.8	2.3	1.6	1.2	0.9	1.2	1.3	1.4
Middle East and north Africa										
Total debt	**352.3**	**380.0**	**389.2**	**381.6**	**380.9**	**392.3**	**409.2**	**424.1**	**425.7**	**434.6**
By maturity										
Short-term	36.9	41.8	60.3	58.1	61.5	61.7	72.9	83.8	86.0	91.6
Long-term	315.4	338.2	328.9	323.5	319.4	330.6	336.3	340.3	339.7	343.0
By type of creditor										
Official	196.2	201.1	201.0	196.4	195.0	206.5	215.0	212.9	210.9	211.5
Banks	99.1	101.3	105.0	104.1	104.3	106.3	110.2	119.0	121.0	123.8
Other private	56.9	77.6	83.2	81.1	81.6	79.4	84.0	92.3	93.8	99.2

Table 40. Other Emerging Market and Developing Countries: Ratio of External Debt to GDP[1]

	1997	1998	1999	2000	2001	2002	2003	2004	2005	2006
Other emerging market and developing countries	**38.0**	**43.6**	**45.4**	**40.5**	**40.4**	**40.6**	**39.1**	**35.7**	**31.9**	**30.0**
Regional groups										
Africa	63.5	65.9	64.9	60.8	58.5	56.4	50.0	42.8	36.0	29.5
Sub-Sahara	64.1	67.7	67.4	63.9	62.6	59.8	52.7	45.7	38.6	31.1
Central and eastern Europe	40.7	43.0	47.9	50.7	53.1	53.7	54.5	53.4	49.7	49.3
Commonwealth of Independent States[2]	38.0	58.2	75.2	55.9	46.9	43.0	41.8	36.9	29.4	27.5
Developing Asia	32.0	36.7	33.8	30.0	29.2	26.9	25.0	23.3	23.2	22.9
Middle East	48.9	57.5	54.5	48.2	47.7	48.7	45.1	41.2	33.5	30.4
Western Hemisphere	34.8	39.2	45.3	39.2	41.6	47.1	47.4	41.4	35.5	32.7
Analytical groups										
By source of export earnings										
Fuel	54.2	62.8	58.9	50.7	48.6	51.0	46.2	39.3	30.8	25.3
Nonfuel	36.4	41.6	43.8	39.2	39.3	39.4	38.3	35.3	32.1	30.6
of which, primary products	56.3	60.9	65.4	66.8	69.8	62.0	65.1	57.1	52.6	47.4
By external financing source										
Net debtor countries	44.2	49.7	52.8	48.5	49.7	51.3	49.5	45.3	40.5	37.7
of which, official financing	54.2	67.6	66.3	64.0	67.9	77.7	74.3	68.4	62.6	58.8
Net debtor countries by debt-servicing experience										
Countries with arrears and/or rescheduling during 1999–2003	73.0	90.5	87.5	81.6	83.2	92.0	84.2	76.8	68.0	59.4
Other groups										
Heavily indebted poor countries	99.8	100.5	99.9	103.0	98.8	87.1	78.0	70.5	64.3	56.8
Middle East and north Africa	53.5	60.7	57.6	50.7	49.6	50.5	46.7	41.8	34.1	30.9

[1]Debt at year-end in percent of GDP in year indicated.
[2]Mongolia, which is not a member of the Commonwealth of Independent States, is included in this group for reasons of geography and similarities in economic structure.

Table 41. Other Emerging Market and Developing Countries: Debt-Service Ratios[1]
(Percent of exports of goods and services)

	1997	1998	1999	2000	2001	2002	2003	2004	2005	2006
Interest payments[2]										
Other emerging market and developing countries	**7.6**	**9.6**	**8.8**	**7.5**	**7.5**	**5.8**	**5.0**	**4.2**	**3.8**	**3.6**
Regional groups										
Africa	9.3	8.7	8.2	6.2	6.6	4.6	4.4	3.3	3.0	2.3
Sub-Sahara	8.4	7.6	7.4	5.7	6.4	4.1	4.2	3.0	2.9	2.1
Central and eastern Europe	5.7	10.1	10.2	9.8	9.9	8.8	8.4	7.3	6.9	6.7
Commonwealth of Independent States[3]	9.4	13.3	10.3	7.9	6.4	5.2	4.3	3.8	3.4	3.4
Developing Asia	5.0	6.2	5.4	4.7	4.6	3.6	3.0	2.4	2.4	2.4
Middle East	3.1	3.9	3.1	2.4	2.3	1.9	1.6	1.5	1.3	1.0
Western Hemisphere	15.6	17.3	17.9	15.9	16.2	12.3	10.6	9.0	8.4	8.3
Analytical groups										
By source of export earnings										
Fuel	5.0	6.5	5.1	3.5	4.0	2.8	2.6	2.1	2.0	1.4
Nonfuel	8.0	9.9	9.4	8.3	8.0	6.3	5.4	4.5	4.2	4.1
of which, primary products	6.0	6.9	7.0	8.0	7.4	5.7	4.9	3.4	2.2	1.8
By external financing source										
Net debtor countries	10.0	11.7	11.4	10.4	10.4	8.1	7.3	6.0	5.7	5.4
of which, official financing	13.3	14.5	14.1	13.6	13.5	9.4	7.6	6.0	5.8	5.4
Net debtor countries by debt-servicing experience										
Countries with arrears and/or rescheduling during 1999–2003	12.5	14.1	13.1	11.7	12.2	7.4	6.2	4.5	4.5	3.9
Other groups										
Heavily indebted poor countries	12.9	7.2	7.0	7.8	7.0	4.9	4.8	3.5	3.5	2.8
Middle East and north Africa	4.3	5.2	4.2	3.1	2.9	2.5	2.1	1.8	1.5	1.3
Amortization[2]										
Other emerging market and developing countries	**15.6**	**17.0**	**17.6**	**15.0**	**16.0**	**14.5**	**13.2**	**9.8**	**8.7**	**7.8**
Regional groups										
Africa	15.0	14.4	13.1	11.4	12.0	10.3	9.5	8.7	7.5	5.5
Sub-Sahara	14.5	12.3	10.8	9.8	11.1	8.5	7.8	7.0	7.1	4.3
Central and eastern Europe	13.7	14.0	17.0	17.0	18.8	17.9	17.7	14.3	14.4	15.3
Commonwealth of Independent States[3]	8.0	10.0	11.6	9.0	13.5	12.8	8.6	3.8	9.2	4.2
Developing Asia	10.0	12.3	10.8	9.4	10.8	11.1	9.0	5.6	4.6	4.4
Middle East	10.1	11.1	8.7	6.1	7.8	4.6	5.9	6.4	5.6	5.2
Western Hemisphere	35.5	35.2	41.8	36.3	33.5	30.2	30.8	24.3	17.9	17.2
Analytical groups										
By source of export earnings										
Fuel	15.6	18.0	13.7	9.1	9.3	7.8	9.3	9.2	7.6	5.7
Nonfuel	15.6	16.8	18.2	16.2	17.1	15.6	13.9	10.0	8.9	8.2
of which, primary products	11.9	12.5	14.0	16.2	16.6	18.9	15.8	14.0	7.3	7.3
By external financing source										
Net debtor countries	21.3	22.1	24.2	22.0	22.2	21.1	20.1	15.2	12.9	12.4
of which, official financing	26.8	29.5	27.9	27.7	32.2	28.2	25.7	16.5	12.7	12.1
Net debtor countries by debt-servicing experience										
Countries with arrears and/or rescheduling during 1999–2003	25.2	28.1	24.6	23.1	27.1	22.9	21.2	14.7	11.9	9.7
Other groups										
Heavily indebted poor countries	32.1	16.2	12.0	13.9	15.5	9.6	7.5	7.1	6.2	5.5
Middle East and north Africa	11.0	12.6	10.2	7.3	8.7	6.0	7.0	7.3	6.0	5.6

[1]Excludes service payments to the International Monetary Fund.
[2]Interest payments on total debt and amortization on long-term debt. Estimates through 2004 reflect debt-service payments actually made. The estimates for 2005 and 2006 take into account projected exceptional financing items, including accumulation of arrears and rescheduling agreements. In some cases, amortization on account of debt-reduction operations is included.
[3]Mongolia, which is not a member of the Commonwealth of Independent States, is included in this group for reasons of geography and similarities in economic structure.

Table 42. IMF Charges and Repurchases to the IMF[1]
(Percent of exports of goods and services)

	1997	1998	1999	2000	2001	2002	2003	2004
Other emerging market and developing countries	**0.6**	**0.6**	**1.2**	**1.2**	**0.7**	**1.1**	**1.2**	**0.7**
Regional groups								
Africa	0.9	1.1	0.5	0.2	0.3	0.4	0.3	0.2
Sub-Sahara	0.7	0.8	0.2	0.1	0.1	0.2	—	0.1
Excluding Nigeria and South Africa	0.4	0.5	0.4	0.3	0.3	0.4	0.1	0.1
Central and eastern Europe	0.3	0.4	0.4	0.3	0.8	2.7	0.8	1.3
Commonwealth of Independent States[2]	0.9	1.7	4.9	3.2	3.1	1.2	1.1	0.7
Russia	1.1	1.9	5.9	3.1	3.8	1.4	1.3	0.9
Excluding Russia	0.5	1.2	2.9	3.4	1.4	0.7	0.6	0.5
Developing Asia	0.2	0.2	0.2	0.2	0.6	0.6	0.3	0.2
Excluding China and India	0.2	0.2	0.3	0.4	1.2	1.4	0.8	0.5
Middle East	—	—	0.1	0.1	0.1	—	—	—
Western Hemisphere	1.9	1.1	3.2	4.2	0.6	2.0	5.3	2.6
Analytical groups								
By source of export earnings								
Fuel	0.5	0.8	0.5	0.3	0.2	0.2	0.2	0.1
Nonfuel	0.7	0.6	1.3	1.4	0.8	1.3	1.4	0.9
By external financing source								
Net debtor countries	0.8	0.6	1.3	1.6	0.8	1.8	2.0	1.3
of which, official financing	0.6	0.8	0.9	1.1	2.0	2.2	3.6	2.9
Net debtor countries by debt-servicing experience								
Countries with arrears and/or rescheduling during 1999–2003	0.7	0.9	1.0	1.0	1.8	1.9	3.1	2.3
Other groups								
Heavily indebted poor countries	0.5	0.5	0.2	0.2	0.3	1.0	0.1	—
Middle East and north Africa	0.3	0.4	0.3	0.1	0.1	0.1	0.2	0.1
Memorandum								
Total, billions of U.S. dollars								
General Resources Account	9.986	8.809	18.531	22.863	13.849	22.352	29.425	23.578
Charges	2.200	2.510	2.829	2.846	2.638	2.806	3.020	3.384
Repurchases	7.786	6.300	15.702	20.017	11.211	19.546	26.405	20.193
PRGF[3]	0.866	0.881	0.855	0.835	1.042	1.214	1.225	1.427
Interest	0.039	0.040	0.042	0.038	0.038	0.040	0.046	0.050
Repayments	0.827	0.842	0.813	0.798	1.005	1.174	1.179	1.377

[1]Excludes advanced economies. Charges on, and repurchases (or repayments of principal) for, use of IMF credit.
[2]Mongolia, which is not a member of the Commonwealth of Independent States, is included in this group for reasons of geography and similarities in economic structure.
[3]Poverty Reduction and Growth Facility (formerly ESAF—Enhanced Structural Adjustment Facility).

Table 43. Summary of Sources and Uses of World Saving
(Percent of GDP)

	Averages 1983–90	Averages 1991–98	1999	2000	2001	2002	2003	2004	2005	2006	Average 2007–10
World											
Saving	22.8	22.0	22.1	22.5	21.4	20.6	20.9	21.5	22.1	22.4	22.6
Investment	23.8	22.7	22.3	22.6	21.6	20.9	21.1	21.9	22.2	22.4	22.8
Advanced economies											
Saving	22.2	21.7	21.7	21.9	20.6	19.3	19.2	19.5	19.5	19.6	19.8
Investment	22.8	22.0	21.9	22.3	20.9	19.9	19.9	20.6	20.8	20.9	21.2
Net lending	−0.6	−0.3	−0.3	−0.4	−0.3	−0.6	−0.8	−1.1	−1.3	−1.3	−1.3
Current transfers	−0.4	−0.5	−0.5	−0.5	−0.5	−0.6	−0.6	−0.6	−0.6	−0.5	−0.5
Factor income	−0.2	−0.4	0.3	0.8	0.7	0.4	0.3	0.2	0.3	0.3	0.1
Resource balance	−0.1	0.5	—	−0.6	−0.5	−0.4	−0.4	−0.6	−1.0	−1.1	−0.8
United States											
Saving	17.5	16.1	18.1	18.0	16.4	14.2	13.4	13.4	13.7	13.7	14.1
Investment	20.2	18.5	20.6	20.8	19.1	18.4	18.5	19.6	19.8	19.8	20.2
Net lending	−2.8	−2.4	−2.6	−2.7	−2.8	−4.2	−5.0	−6.2	−6.1	−6.1	−6.1
Current transfers	−0.5	−0.5	−0.5	−0.6	−0.5	−0.6	−0.6	−0.7	−0.6	−0.5	−0.5
Factor income	0.1	−0.7	0.8	1.7	1.3	0.5	0.1	−0.3	—	−0.1	−0.7
Resource balance	−2.4	−1.2	−2.8	−3.9	−3.6	−4.0	−4.5	−5.3	−5.6	−5.5	−4.9
Euro area											
Saving	...	21.3	21.7	21.6	21.7	21.1	20.7	21.1	21.0	21.0	21.4
Investment	...	20.5	21.0	21.1	20.1	19.2	18.8	19.2	19.3	19.4	19.5
Net lending	...	0.8	0.7	0.5	1.6	1.9	2.0	2.0	1.7	1.6	2.0
Current transfers[1]	−0.5	−0.7	−0.7	−0.8	−0.8	−0.7	−0.8	−0.8	−0.7	−0.8	−0.8
Factor income[1]	−0.5	−0.5	−0.5	−0.2	−0.1	−0.4	−0.5	−0.5	−0.4	−0.4	−0.4
Resource balance[1]	1.3	1.4	1.5	0.6	1.5	2.3	2.0	2.0	1.6	1.5	1.8
Germany											
Saving	23.9	21.3	20.3	20.2	19.6	19.4	19.3	21.0	21.0	20.8	20.4
Investment	20.9	22.3	21.5	21.8	19.5	17.2	17.2	17.2	16.7	16.4	15.8
Net lending	3.1	−1.0	−1.2	−1.6	0.2	2.2	2.1	3.8	4.3	4.4	4.6
Current transfers	−1.5	−1.6	−1.2	−1.4	−1.3	−1.3	−1.3	−1.3	−1.3	−1.3	−1.3
Factor income	0.8	0.2	−0.5	−0.4	−0.4	−0.7	−0.6	—	—	—	0.1
Resource balance	3.8	0.4	0.6	0.1	1.9	4.2	4.1	5.0	5.6	5.7	5.9
France											
Saving	20.8	19.8	22.0	21.7	21.7	20.0	19.5	19.2	19.1	18.8	19.0
Investment	21.1	18.8	19.2	20.4	20.1	19.0	19.1	19.6	20.4	20.3	19.9
Net lending	−0.4	1.1	2.9	1.3	1.6	1.0	0.4	−0.4	−1.3	−1.5	−1.0
Current transfers	−0.6	−0.7	−0.9	−1.1	−1.1	−1.0	−1.1	−1.1	−1.0	−1.0	−1.0
Factor income	−0.2	−0.2	1.3	1.2	1.1	0.3	0.4	0.4	0.5	0.5	0.5
Resource balance	0.5	2.0	2.5	1.2	1.6	1.7	1.1	0.2	−0.8	−1.0	−0.5
Italy											
Saving	21.2	20.1	20.3	19.7	19.6	19.2	18.1	18.9	18.2	18.7	20.7
Investment	22.7	19.4	19.7	20.2	19.7	20.0	19.5	19.8	20.0	20.1	20.5
Net lending	−1.5	0.7	0.7	−0.5	−0.1	−0.8	−1.3	−0.9	−1.7	−1.4	0.1
Current transfers	−0.1	−0.6	−0.5	−0.4	−0.5	−0.4	−0.5	−0.6	−0.6	−0.6	−0.6
Factor income	−1.6	−1.7	−0.9	−1.1	−0.9	−1.2	−1.4	−1.1	−0.9	−0.8	−0.5
Resource balance	0.2	2.9	2.1	1.0	1.4	0.9	0.6	0.8	−0.2	—	1.2
Japan											
Saving	32.5	31.6	28.6	28.8	27.9	26.8	27.1	27.6	27.5	27.6	27.5
Investment	29.7	29.2	26.0	26.3	25.8	24.0	23.9	23.9	24.3	24.5	24.4
Net lending	2.7	2.4	2.6	2.6	2.1	2.8	3.2	3.7	3.2	3.1	3.1
Current transfers	−0.1	−0.2	−0.3	−0.2	−0.2	−0.1	−0.2	−0.2	−0.2	−0.2	−0.2
Factor income	0.5	1.0	1.3	1.3	1.6	1.6	1.7	1.8	2.0	2.2	2.4
Resource balance	2.3	1.6	1.5	1.5	0.6	1.3	1.7	2.0	1.4	1.1	0.9
United Kingdom											
Saving	17.4	15.6	15.2	15.0	15.0	15.2	14.8	14.8	14.8	15.1	15.8
Investment	19.4	16.8	17.8	17.5	17.2	16.7	16.3	16.7	16.7	16.9	17.6
Net lending	−2.0	−1.2	−2.7	−2.6	−2.2	−1.6	−1.5	−2.0	−1.9	−1.8	−1.8
Current transfers	−0.7	−0.8	−0.8	−1.0	−0.7	−0.8	−0.9	−0.9	−1.1	−1.1	−1.1
Factor income	—	0.3	−0.2	0.5	1.1	2.3	2.2	2.2	2.5	2.5	2.4
Resource balance	−1.4	−0.7	−1.7	−2.0	−2.7	−3.0	−2.8	−3.3	−3.3	−3.2	−3.1
Canada											
Saving	19.5	16.7	20.7	23.6	22.2	21.3	21.7	22.9	22.6	22.7	23.6
Investment	21.4	18.9	20.3	20.2	19.2	19.4	20.2	20.7	21.0	21.1	22.0
Net lending	−2.0	−2.3	0.4	3.4	3.0	1.8	1.5	2.2	1.5	1.7	1.6
Current transfers	−0.2	—	0.1	0.1	0.1	0.1	—	—	—	—	—
Factor income	−3.2	−3.6	−3.3	−2.4	−2.8	−2.5	−2.3	−1.9	−1.7	−1.6	−1.2
Resource balance	1.4	1.4	3.6	5.7	5.7	4.3	3.8	4.1	3.3	3.2	2.8

Table 43 *(continued)*

	Averages		1999	2000	2001	2002	2003	2004	2005	2006	Average 2007–10
	1983–90	1991–98									
Newly industrialized Asian economies											
Saving	34.6	34.2	32.7	32.0	29.9	30.0	31.6	33.0	32.3	32.4	32.3
Investment	28.3	32.0	27.1	28.3	25.3	24.5	24.4	26.0	26.4	26.9	27.1
Net lending	6.3	2.2	5.6	3.6	4.6	5.5	7.2	7.1	5.8	5.5	5.2
Current transfers	0.1	−0.1	−0.3	−0.5	−0.6	−0.7	−0.8	−0.8	−0.7	−0.8	−0.7
Factor income	0.7	0.8	0.1	0.3	0.6	0.7	0.9	1.0	1.2	1.1	1.0
Resource balance	5.5	1.6	5.9	3.8	4.6	5.5	7.1	6.8	5.4	5.1	4.8
Other emerging market and developing countries											
Saving	24.6	23.5	23.8	25.3	24.7	25.9	27.7	29.3	30.9	31.3	30.6
Investment	26.0	26.0	24.0	24.1	24.3	24.8	25.9	26.9	26.9	27.0	27.5
Net lending	−1.3	−2.5	−0.2	1.2	0.5	1.1	1.8	2.5	4.0	4.3	3.1
Current transfers	0.4	0.7	0.9	0.9	1.1	1.3	1.6	1.6	1.6	1.6	1.4
Factor income	−1.7	−2.1	−2.0	−2.2	−2.2	−2.3	−2.3	−2.2	−1.7	−1.7	−1.2
Resource balance	—	−1.1	0.9	2.5	1.6	2.1	2.5	3.1	4.2	4.4	2.9
Memorandum											
Acquisition of foreign assets	0.5	2.7	3.8	5.0	3.4	4.3	5.5	7.6	7.8	7.7	6.3
Change in reserves	−0.1	1.2	0.6	1.1	1.4	2.2	4.0	5.1	4.7	4.1	3.3
Regional groups											
Africa											
Saving	18.3	17.1	17.1	20.9	19.9	18.6	20.4	21.5	23.1	24.9	24.9
Investment	21.5	19.8	20.7	19.1	19.7	19.2	20.5	21.3	21.3	21.3	21.7
Net lending	−3.2	−2.7	−3.5	1.7	0.2	−0.6	−0.2	0.2	1.8	3.6	3.2
Current transfers	1.8	2.6	2.3	2.6	2.9	3.0	3.2	3.3	3.0	2.7	2.5
Factor income	−5.2	−4.3	−4.2	−5.1	−4.7	−3.7	−4.5	−5.0	−4.7	−4.9	−3.9
Resource balance	0.2	−1.1	−1.7	4.3	1.9	0.1	1.1	1.9	3.5	5.8	4.6
Memorandum											
Acquisition of foreign assets	0.4	0.9	3.3	5.0	5.0	2.5	3.3	4.5	5.2	7.6	6.6
Change in reserves	0.2	0.7	0.7	2.9	2.8	1.7	3.4	5.2	4.9	6.9	5.9
Central and eastern Europe											
Saving	28.1	20.7	19.4	19.1	19.0	18.8	18.6	19.6	20.0	20.3	21.3
Investment	28.0	23.3	24.3	25.0	22.0	22.8	23.2	24.5	24.3	24.7	25.4
Net lending	0.2	−2.5	−5.0	−5.9	−3.0	−4.0	−4.6	−4.9	−4.3	−4.4	−4.1
Current transfers	1.3	1.8	1.9	1.9	1.9	1.8	1.5	1.4	1.8	1.6	1.5
Factor income	−0.7	−1.9	−1.6	−1.5	−1.6	−2.1	−2.0	−1.8	−1.1	−1.1	−1.2
Resource balance	−0.5	−2.4	−5.2	−6.3	−3.3	−3.7	−4.1	−4.5	−5.0	−4.9	−4.4
Memorandum											
Acquisition of foreign assets	1.1	2.5	3.4	3.0	1.6	3.1	1.3	2.7	2.6	1.4	1.4
Change in reserves	−0.4	1.6	1.9	0.5	−1.2	1.7	1.4	1.4	1.5	0.2	0.2
Commonwealth of Independent States[2]											
Saving	...	...	23.1	31.3	29.3	26.8	26.8	29.3	30.5	30.1	25.7
Investment	...	...	14.9	17.9	21.2	19.7	20.6	20.9	19.9	19.8	20.6
Net lending	...	...	8.2	13.4	8.2	7.0	6.2	8.4	10.7	10.3	5.1
Current transfers	...	...	0.8	0.7	0.5	0.7	0.6	0.4	0.4	0.3	0.3
Factor income	...	...	−2.9	−3.0	−1.7	−2.0	−3.2	−2.6	−2.0	−1.9	−1.3
Resource balance	...	...	10.3	15.7	9.3	8.4	8.8	10.6	12.4	11.9	6.2
Memorandum											
Acquisition of foreign assets	...	...	9.9	12.9	5.9	8.5	10.5	14.2	13.1	13.8	8.2
Change in reserves	...	...	0.9	4.8	2.7	2.5	5.9	7.2	8.1	9.5	4.7

Table 43 *(continued)*

	Averages		1999	2000	2001	2002	2003	2004	2005	2006	Average 2007–10
	1983–90	1991–98									
Developing Asia											
Saving	25.7	31.4	32.1	31.9	32.5	34.7	37.0	38.3	39.8	39.8	39.4
Investment	28.9	33.7	29.5	29.9	30.8	31.8	33.7	35.4	36.6	37.1	36.9
Net lending	−3.2	−2.3	2.7	2.0	1.7	2.8	3.2	2.9	3.2	2.8	2.5
Current transfers	0.7	1.1	1.3	1.4	1.5	1.7	2.3	2.2	2.3	2.4	2.0
Factor income	−1.9	−2.6	−1.6	−1.7	−1.8	−1.5	−0.9	−0.9	−0.5	−0.6	−0.6
Resource balance	−2.0	−0.9	3.0	2.4	2.0	2.6	1.9	1.6	1.4	1.0	1.0
Memorandum											
Acquisition of foreign assets	0.8	4.6	5.4	5.1	3.6	5.7	6.6	8.9	8.2	7.1	5.9
Change in reserves	0.3	1.8	1.5	0.4	2.7	4.3	5.6	8.1	6.9	4.7	3.5
Middle East											
Saving	18.4	20.7	23.8	29.2	25.7	24.5	28.1	33.1	40.6	42.6	40.1
Investment	22.8	24.2	21.8	19.9	21.3	21.8	22.4	22.4	21.2	20.9	20.8
Net lending	−4.4	−3.6	2.0	9.3	4.4	2.6	5.7	10.7	19.4	21.7	19.2
Current transfers	−2.2	−4.1	−3.1	−3.1	−3.2	−3.0	−2.6	−2.2	−1.8	−1.7	−1.6
Factor income	0.1	2.5	1.4	−0.2	−0.5	−1.8	−2.3	−1.4	−0.7	—	1.8
Resource balance	−2.3	−1.9	3.6	12.7	8.0	7.4	10.6	14.3	21.9	23.5	19.0
Memorandum											
Acquisition of foreign assets	−0.4	−0.8	2.8	15.8	6.6	7.5	10.3	17.2	20.4	22.0	20.7
Change in reserves	−1.3	0.7	—	4.5	1.8	0.6	4.6	5.5	5.1	6.4	8.7
Western Hemisphere											
Saving	19.8	18.3	17.4	18.5	17.0	18.5	19.9	21.1	21.5	21.3	20.8
Investment	20.5	21.1	20.6	21.0	19.9	19.5	19.6	20.4	20.7	20.8	21.2
Net lending	−0.7	−2.8	−3.2	−2.5	−2.9	−1.0	0.3	0.7	0.8	0.5	−0.4
Current transfers	0.7	0.9	1.2	1.1	1.4	1.8	2.1	2.1	2.0	1.9	1.9
Factor income	−4.2	−2.5	−3.0	−2.8	−3.0	−3.4	−3.6	−3.7	−3.2	−3.1	−2.5
Resource balance	2.9	−1.2	−1.4	−0.7	−1.2	0.6	1.8	2.3	2.1	1.7	0.3
Memorandum											
Acquisition of foreign assets	0.4	1.9	1.4	0.7	1.6	0.7	2.8	2.7	2.9	2.4	1.9
Change in reserves	0.1	1.0	−0.7	−0.1	−0.2	0.1	2.1	1.2	1.2	0.8	0.4
Analytical groups											
By source of export earnings											
Fuel											
Saving	18.2	20.8	24.7	31.9	27.3	25.5	29.4	34.0	40.8	42.6	40.3
Investment	22.1	23.9	22.9	20.4	22.4	22.7	23.1	22.9	21.5	20.9	20.5
Net lending	−3.8	−3.1	1.8	11.5	4.8	2.8	6.3	11.1	19.3	21.8	19.8
Current transfers	−2.2	−3.9	−3.0	−2.9	−2.8	−2.8	−2.3	−1.7	−1.2	−1.1	−1.1
Factor income	−0.8	—	−0.7	−3.1	−2.8	−4.0	−4.4	−4.0	−3.1	−2.8	−1.1
Resource balance	−0.8	0.8	5.5	17.6	10.5	9.7	12.9	16.8	23.6	25.7	21.9
Memorandum											
Acquisition of foreign assets	−1.1	−1.7	3.2	13.7	7.6	6.2	10.4	14.2	17.4	20.2	19.8
Change in reserves	−1.0	0.4	−0.9	6.3	2.4	0.3	5.6	7.1	7.5	9.6	11.1
Nonfuel											
Saving	25.5	23.8	23.7	24.5	24.4	26.0	27.5	28.8	29.6	29.8	29.4
Investment	26.6	26.3	24.1	24.5	24.5	25.1	26.2	27.3	27.6	27.9	28.4
Net lending	−1.0	−2.4	−0.5	−0.1	−0.1	0.9	1.3	1.4	2.0	1.9	1.0
Current transfers	0.7	1.2	1.4	1.4	1.5	1.8	2.1	2.0	2.0	1.9	1.7
Factor income	−1.8	−2.4	−2.2	−2.1	−2.1	−2.1	−2.1	−2.0	−1.6	−1.5	−1.2
Resource balance	0.1	−1.3	0.3	0.6	0.5	1.2	1.3	1.4	1.6	1.5	0.5
Memorandum											
Acquisition of foreign assets	0.7	3.1	3.8	4.0	2.8	4.0	4.9	6.8	6.5	6.0	4.6
Change in reserves	0.1	1.3	0.8	0.5	1.3	2.4	3.9	4.9	4.3	3.4	2.3

Table 43 *(concluded)*

	Averages		1999	2000	2001	2002	2003	2004	2005	2006	Average 2007–10
	1983–90	1991–98									
By external financing source											
Net debtor countries											
Saving	20.0	19.7	19.1	19.6	18.7	19.9	20.7	21.5	21.4	21.7	21.9
Investment	23.0	23.3	21.2	21.7	20.5	20.8	21.3	22.5	22.7	23.0	23.3
Net lending	−2.8	−3.5	−2.2	−2.1	−1.8	−0.9	−0.6	−1.0	−1.3	−1.3	−1.4
Current transfers	1.2	1.7	1.8	1.8	2.0	2.3	2.7	2.6	2.6	2.5	2.4
Factor income	−3.4	−3.4	−2.3	−2.6	−2.6	−2.7	−2.7	−2.9	−2.4	−2.5	−2.1
Resource balance	−0.8	−2.4	−1.7	−1.3	−1.2	−0.6	−0.6	−0.8	−1.5	−1.4	−1.7
Memorandum											
Acquisition of foreign assets	0.2	1.8	2.5	1.4	1.7	2.0	2.6	3.0	2.3	2.1	1.8
Change in reserves	0.1	1.1	0.6	0.1	0.4	1.2	2.1	1.9	1.4	1.1	1.0
Official financing											
Saving	16.1	17.5	16.1	16.7	16.9	19.6	20.1	20.2	20.3	20.1	20.0
Investment	22.4	24.0	17.4	18.4	18.0	18.5	18.8	20.8	21.5	21.9	21.9
Net lending	−6.2	−6.4	−1.3	−1.7	−1.2	1.1	1.3	−0.6	−1.2	−1.8	−1.9
Current transfers	1.4	2.0	2.3	2.5	2.9	3.9	4.1	4.0	4.1	3.9	3.5
Factor income	−5.7	−5.7	−2.2	−3.4	−3.3	−4.1	−3.6	−4.1	−3.1	−3.3	−2.5
Resource balance	−1.9	−3.4	−1.5	−0.9	−0.8	1.3	0.8	−0.5	−2.2	−2.4	−2.9
Memorandum											
Acquisition of foreign assets	0.3	2.1	2.1	0.6	−0.2	2.1	4.5	3.0	1.1	1.5	0.9
Change in reserves	—	1.0	0.7	−0.7	−0.8	−0.3	1.7	1.4	1.2	1.3	0.8
Net debtor countries by debt-servicing experience											
Countries with arrears and/or rescheduling during 1999–2003											
Saving	15.0	17.1	16.2	17.8	17.1	18.9	19.6	20.6	21.1	21.6	21.6
Investment	21.5	24.0	18.2	18.8	18.4	18.6	18.7	20.7	21.1	21.2	21.2
Net lending	−6.6	−6.8	−2.1	−1.0	−1.3	0.4	0.8	−0.2	—	0.4	0.4
Current transfers	0.8	1.8	1.9	2.1	2.4	3.4	3.7	3.7	3.7	3.4	3.1
Factor income	−5.6	−5.6	−3.1	−5.2	−4.5	−4.6	−4.3	−5.0	−3.7	−4.3	−3.2
Resource balance	−1.9	−2.7	−0.9	2.1	0.8	1.6	1.4	1.1	0.1	1.3	0.5
Memorandum											
Acquisition of foreign assets	−0.8	1.7	2.7	2.2	0.1	3.5	4.3	3.8	3.2	4.6	3.6
Change in reserves	0.3	0.8	0.6	0.3	−0.6	−0.3	1.1	2.4	2.6	3.5	2.9

Note: The estimates in this table are based on individual countries' national accounts and balance of payments statistics. Country group composites are calculated as the sum of the U.S dollar values for the relevant individual countries. This differs from the calculations in the April 2005 and earlier *World Economic Outlooks,* where the composites were weighted by GDP valued at purchasing power parities (PPPs) as a share of total world GDP. For many countries, the estimates of national saving are built up from national accounts data on gross domestic investment and from balance-of-payments-based data on net foreign investment. The latter, which is equivalent to the current account balance, comprises three components: current transfers, net factor income, and the resource balance. The mixing of data source, which is dictated by availability, implies that the estimates for national saving that are derived incorporate the statistical discrepancies. Furthermore, error omissions and asymmetries in balance of payments statistics affect the estimates for net lending; at the global level, net lending, which in theory would be zero, equals the world current account discrepancy. Notwithstanding these statistical shortcomings, flow of funds estimates, such as those presented in this tables, provide a useful framework for analyzing development in saving and investment, both over time and across regions and countries.

[1]Calculated from the data of individual euro area countries.

[2]Mongolia, which is not a member of the Commonwealth of Independent States, is included in this group for reasons of geography and similarities in economic structure.

Table 44. Summary of World Medium-Term Baseline Scenario

	Eight-Year Averages		Four-Year Average					Four-Year Average
	1987–94	1995–2002	2003–06	2003	2004	2005	2006	2007–10
	Annual percent change unless otherwise noted							
World real GDP	**3.2**	**3.6**	**4.4**	**4.0**	**5.1**	**4.3**	**4.3**	**4.3**
Advanced economies	3.0	2.8	2.6	1.9	3.3	2.5	2.7	2.9
Other emerging market and developing countries	3.5	4.7	6.6	6.5	7.3	6.4	6.1	5.8
Memorandum								
Potential output								
Major advanced economies	2.7	2.6	2.5	2.5	2.5	2.5	2.5	2.6
World trade, volume[1]	**6.2**	**6.6**	**7.5**	**5.4**	**10.3**	**7.0**	**7.4**	**6.7**
Imports								
Advanced economies	6.3	6.5	6.0	4.1	8.8	5.4	5.8	5.5
Other emerging market and developing countries	5.3	7.2	13.2	11.1	16.4	13.5	11.9	9.9
Exports								
Advanced economies	6.4	6.0	5.7	3.1	8.3	5.0	6.3	5.7
Other emerging market and developing countries	6.3	8.3	11.5	10.8	14.5	10.4	10.3	9.2
Terms of trade								
Advanced economies	0.2	−0.2	−0.2	1.1	−0.2	−1.0	−0.5	0.2
Other emerging market and developing countries	−1.0	0.5	2.9	0.9	2.9	6.2	1.7	−0.5
World prices in U.S. dollars								
Manufactures	4.0	−2.0	7.5	14.4	9.7	6.0	0.5	1.3
Oil	1.5	5.8	25.4	15.8	30.7	43.6	13.9	−2.2
Nonfuel primary commodities	2.5	−2.2	7.7	6.9	18.5	8.6	−2.1	−2.9
Consumer prices								
Advanced economies	3.8	2.0	2.0	1.8	2.0	2.2	2.0	2.1
Other emerging market and developing countries	65.4	12.9	5.8	6.0	5.8	5.9	5.7	4.8
Interest rates (in percent)								
Real six-month LIBOR[2]	3.4	3.3	0.5	−0.8	−0.8	1.1	2.5	2.7
World real long-term interest rate[3]	4.3	3.3	2.1	1.9	1.9	1.8	2.6	3.0
	Percent of GDP							
Balances on current account								
Advanced economies	−0.2	−0.3	−1.1	−0.8	−1.0	−1.3	−1.4	−1.4
Other emerging market and developing countries	−1.5	−0.4	3.3	2.0	2.7	4.1	4.5	3.2
Total external debt								
Other emerging market and developing countries	33.0	40.7	34.2	39.1	35.7	31.9	30.0	27.6
Debt service								
Other emerging market and developing countries	4.3	6.3	5.2	6.2	5.2	4.9	4.6	4.2

[1]Data refer to trade in goods and services.
[2]London interbank offered rate on U.S. dollar deposits less percent change in U.S. GDP deflator.
[3]GDP-weighted average of 10-year (or nearest maturity) government bond rates for the United States, Japan, Germany, France, Italy, the United Kingdom, and Canada.

Table 45. Other Emerging Market and Developing Countries—Medium-Term Baseline Scenario: Selected Economic Indicators

	Eight-Year Averages		Four-Year Average					Four-Year Average
	1987–94	1995–2002	2003–06	2003	2004	2005	2006	2007–10
	Annual percent change							
Other emerging market and developing countries								
Real GDP	3.5	4.7	6.6	6.5	7.3	6.4	6.1	5.8
Export volume[1]	6.3	8.3	11.5	10.8	14.5	10.4	10.3	9.2
Terms of trade[1]	−1.0	0.5	2.9	0.9	2.9	6.2	1.7	−0.5
Import volume[1]	5.3	7.2	13.2	11.1	16.4	13.5	11.9	9.9
Regional groups								
Africa								
Real GDP	1.7	3.6	5.1	4.6	5.3	4.5	5.9	4.9
Export volume[1]	4.9	5.5	6.1	5.3	6.5	4.2	8.4	5.7
Terms of trade[1]	−2.4	1.4	5.7	2.7	3.6	11.6	5.2	−0.8
Import volume[1]	2.6	6.1	7.7	4.7	8.1	10.6	7.4	6.2
Central and eastern Europe								
Real GDP	−0.2	3.4	5.0	4.6	6.5	4.3	4.6	4.5
Export volume[1]	4.0	9.7	10.4	11.6	14.2	7.8	8.0	8.2
Terms of trade[1]	0.7	−0.1	−0.7	−0.8	—	−1.9	−0.3	0.4
Import volume[1]	5.4	10.6	10.1	12.3	14.3	6.6	7.2	8.2
Commonwealth of Independent States[2]								
Real GDP	...	1.6	7.0	7.9	8.4	6.0	5.7	5.2
Export volume[1]	...	4.8	8.1	7.7	11.3	7.0	6.4	6.0
Terms of trade[1]	...	1.7	10.2	6.3	9.4	18.9	6.5	−2.4
Import volume[1]	...	4.1	15.6	13.6	15.5	20.0	13.5	9.4
Developing Asia								
Real GDP	7.7	6.6	7.8	8.1	8.2	7.8	7.2	6.9
Export volume[1]	13.0	11.5	16.8	15.8	20.8	15.2	15.5	12.7
Terms of trade[1]	−0.1	−1.0	−0.4	−1.1	−0.3	0.4	−0.6	0.2
Import volume[1]	11.6	8.3	18.3	18.0	22.1	16.5	16.5	13.1
Middle East								
Real GDP	3.3	4.0	5.6	6.5	5.5	5.4	5.0	4.7
Export volume[1]	8.0	3.9	9.1	10.9	9.3	9.7	6.5	5.9
Terms of trade[1]	−3.2	5.7	10.6	1.4	10.3	25.0	6.9	−2.1
Import volume[1]	0.6	7.6	10.7	5.5	12.3	15.9	9.4	7.0
Western Hemisphere								
Real GDP	2.8	2.2	3.9	2.2	5.6	4.1	3.8	3.4
Export volume[1]	6.7	7.4	6.0	2.8	9.6	6.3	5.4	4.9
Terms of trade[1]	−0.2	−0.8	2.7	3.9	3.7	2.7	0.4	−1.3
Import volume[1]	9.9	4.5	7.5	0.9	12.1	10.0	7.2	5.7
Analytical groups								
Net debtor countries by debt-servicing experience								
Countries with arrears and/or rescheduling during 1999–2003								
Real GDP	3.6	3.2	6.1	5.8	6.6	6.0	5.9	5.6
Export volume[1]	6.3	7.7	6.3	4.7	7.1	5.8	7.8	6.0
Terms of trade[1]	−0.2	−1.0	2.7	0.6	2.4	5.3	2.5	−0.5
Import volume[1]	4.4	4.1	9.8	6.3	11.5	14.2	7.4	6.2

Table 45 *(concluded)*

	1994	1998	2002	2003	2004	2005	2006	2010
	\multicolumn{8}{c}{*Percent of exports of goods and services*}							
Other emerging market and developing countries								
Current account balance	−7.4	−7.9	4.2	5.8	7.2	10.5	11.2	6.6
Total external debt	179.2	174.3	128.1	115.2	95.9	81.6	75.1	64.7
Debt-service payments[3]	24.0	26.5	20.3	18.3	14.0	12.5	11.4	9.7
Interest payments	8.2	9.6	5.8	5.0	4.2	3.8	3.6	3.2
Amortization	15.9	17.0	14.5	13.2	9.8	8.7	7.8	6.5
Regional groups								
Africa								
Current account balance	−11.1	−16.2	−5.3	−1.6	0.3	4.1	8.8	7.4
Total external debt	276.8	236.7	170.8	146.7	119.4	94.0	73.7	64.0
Debt-service payments[3]	24.6	23.1	15.0	13.8	12.0	10.5	7.8	7.8
Interest payments	10.4	8.7	4.6	4.4	3.3	3.0	2.3	2.2
Amortization	14.2	14.4	10.3	9.5	8.7	7.5	5.5	5.6
Central and eastern Europe								
Current account balance	4.2	−8.5	−8.5	−10.1	−10.6	−10.3	−10.3	−8.1
Total external debt	135.2	118.4	127.8	124.9	114.9	105.9	102.3	88.0
Debt-service payments[3]	19.1	24.2	26.7	26.1	21.6	21.3	22.1	18.0
Interest payments	6.3	10.1	8.8	8.4	7.3	6.9	6.7	5.4
Amortization	12.8	14.0	17.9	17.7	14.3	14.4	15.3	12.7
Commonwealth of Independent States								
Current account balance	2.4	−7.6	18.0	16.0	20.8	26.2	26.5	9.7
Total external debt	132.8	175.2	111.9	106.6	92.3	72.8	71.0	91.0
Debt-service payments[3]	8.3	23.3	18.0	12.9	7.6	12.5	7.6	9.2
Interest payments	4.9	13.3	5.2	4.3	3.8	3.4	3.4	5.1
Amortization	3.4	10.0	12.8	8.6	3.8	9.2	4.2	4.1
Developing Asia								
Current account balance	−5.0	9.2	9.2	8.9	7.5	7.3	6.5	4.5
Total external debt	139.3	129.3	84.6	73.1	60.1	55.6	52.5	41.4
Debt-service payments[3]	17.4	18.4	14.7	12.0	7.9	7.0	6.8	5.6
Interest payments	6.5	6.2	3.6	3.0	2.4	2.4	2.4	2.1
Amortization	10.9	12.3	11.1	9.0	5.6	4.6	4.4	3.5
Middle East								
Current account balance	−3.6	−15.9	10.7	16.8	23.8	36.6	40.3	37.7
Total external debt	156.4	184.4	111.7	94.9	78.8	58.1	52.3	49.8
Debt-service payments[3]	10.1	15.0	6.5	7.5	7.9	6.9	6.3	6.8
Interest payments	3.0	3.9	1.9	1.6	1.5	1.3	1.0	1.2
Amortization	7.1	11.1	4.6	5.9	6.4	5.6	5.2	5.6
Western Hemisphere								
Current account balance	−25.3	−31.1	−4.6	1.7	3.9	3.9	2.8	−3.2
Total external debt	272.8	269.9	230.1	218.5	177.6	153.6	144.6	131.9
Debt-service payments[3]	57.3	52.5	42.5	41.4	33.2	26.3	25.4	21.9
Interest payments	16.8	17.3	12.3	10.6	9.0	8.4	8.3	7.0
Amortization	40.6	35.2	30.2	30.8	24.3	17.9	17.2	15.0
Analytical groups								
Net debtor countries by debt-servicing experience								
Countries with arrears and/or rescheduling during 1999–2003								
Current account balance	−19.6	−17.8	0.7	1.7	−0.5	−1.2	1.4	0.3
Total external debt	379.5	359.1	281.4	255.2	211.3	178.1	153.2	121.9
Debt-service payments[3]	31.8	42.2	30.3	27.4	19.3	16.4	13.6	12.5
Interest payments	12.9	14.1	7.4	6.2	4.5	4.5	3.9	3.2
Amortization	18.9	28.1	22.9	21.2	14.7	11.9	9.7	9.3

[1]Data refer to trade in goods and services.
[2]Mongolia, which is not a member of the Commonwealth of Independent States, is included in this group for reasons of geography and similarities in economic structure.
[3]Interest payments on total debt plus amortization payments on long-term debt only. Projections incorporate the impact of exceptional financing items. Excludes service payments to the International Monetary Fund.

WORLD ECONOMIC OUTLOOK AND *STAFF STUDIES FOR THE WORLD ECONOMIC OUTLOOK,* SELECTED TOPICS, 1995–2005

I. Methodology—Aggregation, Modeling, and Forecasting

II. Historical Surveys

IV. Inflation and Deflation; Commodity Markets

V. Fiscal Policy

VI. Monetary Policy; Financial Markets; Flow of Funds

VII. Labor Market Issues

VIII. Exchange Rate Issues

IX. External Payments, Trade, Capital Movements, and Foreign Debt

X. Regional Issues

XI. Country-Specific Analyses

***Staff Studies for the
World Economic Outlook***

World Economic and Financial Surveys

This series (ISSN 0258-7440) contains biannual, annual, and periodic studies covering monetary and financial issues of importance to the global economy. The core elements of the series are the *World Economic Outlook* report, usually published in April and September, and the semiannual *Global Financial Stability Report*. Other studies assess international trade policy, private market and official financing for developing countries, exchange and payments systems, export credit policies, and issues discussed in the *World Economic Outlook*. Please consult the IMF *Publications Catalog* for a complete listing of currently available World Economic and Financial Surveys.

World Economic Outlook: A Survey by the Staff of the International Monetary Fund

The *World Economic Outlook*, published twice a year in English, French, Spanish, and Arabic, presents IMF staff economists' analyses of global economic developments during the near and medium term. Chapters give an overview of the world economy; consider issues affecting industrial countries, developing countries, and economies in transition to the market; and address topics of pressing current interest.

ISSN 0256-6877.

$49.00 (academic rate: $46.00); paper.
April 2005 ISBN 1-58906-429-1. **Stock #WEOEA200501.**
September 2004 ISBN 1-58906-406-2. **Stock #WEOEA2004002.**
April 2004. April. ISBN 1-58906-337-6. **Stock #WEOEA200401.**
April 2003 ISBN 1-58906-212-4. **Stock #WEOEA0012003.**

Global Financial Stability Report: Market Developments and Issues

The *Global Financial Stability Report*, published twice a year, examines trends and issues that influence world financial markets. It replaces two IMF publications—the annual *International Capital Markets* report and the electronic quarterly *Emerging Market Financing* report. The report is designed to deepen understanding of international capital flows and explores developments that could pose a risk to international financial market stability.

$49.00 (academic rate: $46.00); paper.
September 2005 ISBN 1-58906-450-X. **Stock #GFSREA2005002.**
April 2005 ISBN-1-58906-418-6. **Stock #GFSREA2005001.**
September 2004 ISBN 1-58906-378-3. **Stock #GFSREA2004002.**
April 2004 ISBN 1-58906-328-7. **Stock #GFSREA0012004.**
September 2003 ISBN 1-58906-236-1. **Stock #GFSREA0022003.**

Emerging Local Securities and Derivatives Markets

by Donald Mathieson, Jorge E. Roldos, Ramana Ramaswamy, and Anna Ilyina

The volatility of capital flows since the mid-1990s has sparked an interest in the development of local securities and derivatives markets. This report examines the growth of these markets in emerging market countries and the key policy issues that have arisen as a result.

$42.00 (academic rate: $35.00); paper.
2004. ISBN 1-58906-291-4. **Stock #WEOEA0202004.**

Official Financing: Recent Developments and Selected Issues

by a staff team in the Policy Development and Review Department led by Martin G. Gilman and Jian-Ye Wang

This study provides information on official financing for developing countries, with the focus on low-income countries. It updates the 2001 edition and reviews developments in direct financing by official and multilateral sources.

$42.00 (academic rate: $35.00); paper.
2003. ISBN 1-58906-228-0. **Stock #WEOEA0132003.**
2001. ISBN 1-58906-038-5. **Stock #WEOEA0132001.**

Exchange Arrangements and Foreign Exchange Markets: Developments and Issues

by a staff team led by Shogo Ishii

This study updates developments in exchange arrangements during 1998–2001. It also discusses the evolution of exchange rate regimes based on de facto policies since 1990, reviews foreign exchange market organization and regulations in a number of countries, and examines factors affecting exchange rate volatility.

ISSN 0258-7440
$42.00 (academic rate $35.00)
2003 (March) ISBN 1-58906-177-2. **Stock #WEOEA0192003.**

World Economic Outlook Supporting Studies

by the IMF's Research Department

These studies, supporting analyses and scenarios of the *World Economic Outlook*, provide a detailed examination of theory and evidence on major issues currently affecting the global economy.

$25.00 (academic rate: $20.00); paper.
2000. ISBN 1-55775-893-X. **Stock #WEOEA0032000.**

Exchange Rate Arrangements and Currency Convertibility: Developments and Issues

by a staff team led by R. Barry Johnston

A principal force driving the growth in international trade and investment has been the liberalization of financial transactions, including the liberalization of trade and exchange controls. This study reviews the developments and issues in the exchange arrangements and currency convertibility of IMF members.

$20.00 (academic rate: $12.00); paper.
1999. ISBN 1-55775-795-X. **Stock #WEOEA0191999.**

Available by series subscription or single title (including back issues); academic rate available only to full-time university faculty and students. For earlier editions please inquire about prices.

The IMF *Catalog of Publications* is available on-line at the Internet address listed below.

Please send orders and inquiries to:
International Monetary Fund, Publication Services, 700 19th Street, N.W.
Washington, D.C. 20431, U.S.A.
Tel.: (202) 623-7430   Telefax: (202) 623-7201
E-mail: publications@imf.org
Internet: http://www.imf.org